D1241362

The Papers of
George Washington

The Papers of
George Washington

Dorothy Twohig, *Editor*

Philander D. Chase, *Senior Associate Editor*

Beverly H. Runge, *Associate Editor*

Frank E. Grizzard, Jr., Mark A. Mastromarino,
Elizabeth B. Mercer, and Jack D. Warren, Jr., *Assistant Editors*

Presidential Series
8

March–September 1791

Mark A. Mastromarino, *Editor*

Jack D. Warren, Jr., *Assistant Editor*

UNIVERSITY PRESS OF VIRGINIA

CHARLOTTESVILLE AND LONDON

This edition has been prepared by the staff of *The Papers of George Washington* sponsored by The Mount Vernon Ladies' Association of the Union and the University of Virginia with the support of the National Endowment for the Humanities and the National Historical Publications and Records Commission. The publication of this volume has been supported by a grant from the National Historical Publications and Records Commission.

THE UNIVERSITY PRESS OF VIRGINIA
Copyright © 1999 by the Rector and Visitors
of the University of Virginia
All rights reserved
Printed in the United States of America

First published 1999

∞ The paper used in this publication meets the minimum requirements of the American National Standard for Information Sciences—Permanence of Paper for Printed Library Materials, ANSI Z39.48-1984.

Library of Congress Cataloging-in-Publication Data
Washington, George, 1732–1799.
  The papers of George Washington, Dorothy Twohig, ed.

  Presidential series vol. 8 edited by Mark A. Mastromarino and Jack D. Warren, Jr.
  Includes indexes.
  Contents: 1. September 1788–March 1789—[etc.]—8. March–September 1791
    1. United States—Politics and government—1789–1797.
  2. Washington, George, 1732–1799—Correspondence.
  3. Presidents—United States—Correspondence.
  I. Twohig, Dorothy. II. Abbot, W. W. (William Wright), 1922– . III. Presidential series.
  E312.72   1987b   973.4'1'092   87-410017
  ISBN 0-8139-1103-6 (v.1)
  ISBN 0-8139-1810-3 (v. 8)

Frontispiece: George Washington, artist unknown but not from life, produced by Richard Champion and Company, not signed, not dated but before 1781. (Private collection, on loan to the Mount Vernon Ladies' Association of the Union, courtesy of anonymous owner.) Richard Champion (1743–1791) was born in Bristol, England, and formed there in 1773 Richard Champion and Company, a pottery that was dissolved in 1781. His letter to GW of 25 May 1791 presenting the plaque mentioned that it was made from "a beautiful native Porcelain, which is to be found in America." The clay probably was brought from Charleston to Bristol on his ship, the *Lloyd*, which traded between those two ports. The letter also mentioned that the image was taken when GW was young, but the artist of the likeness remains unknown despite various speculations. The relief with an accompanying one of Benjamin Franklin hung over the fireplace in Mount Vernon's "sitting parlor" and became Martha Washington's property after GW's death. It was acquired by her granddaughter Martha Parke Custis Peter and descended to W. G. Peter who lent it to the National Art Gallery in 1923. It was still owned by Peter descendants in 1982. See GW to Champion, 19 July 1791.

This volume is dedicated to the memory of
Eugene R. Sheridan, 1945–1996
Senior Associate Editor of
The Papers of Thomas Jefferson

Contents

Contents

Illustrations

Editorial Apparatus

Transcription of the documents in the volumes of *The Papers of George Washington* has remained as close to a literal reproduction of the manuscript as possible. Punctuation, capitalization, and spelling of all words are retained as they appear in the original document; only for documents printed in annotations has paragraphing been modified. Dashes used as punctuation have been retained except when a dash and another mark of punctuation appear together. The appropriate marks of punctuation have always been added at the end of a paragraph. When a tilde (~) is used in the manuscript to indicate a double letter, the letter has been doubled. Washington and some of his correspondents occasionally used a tilde above an incorrectly spelled word to indicate an error in orthography. When this device is used the editors have silently corrected the word. In cases where a tilde has been inserted above an abbreviation or contraction, usually in letter-book copies, the word has been expanded. Otherwise, contractions and abbreviations have been retained as written except that a period has been inserted after an abbreviation when needed. If the meaning of an abbreviation or contraction is not obvious, it has been expanded in square brackets: "H[is] M[ajest]y." Editorial insertions or corrections in the text also appear in square brackets. Angle brackets ⟨ ⟩ are used to indicate illegible or mutilated material. A space left blank in a manuscript by the writer is indicated by a square-bracketed gap in the text [   ]. Deletion of material by the author of a manuscript is ignored unless it contains substantive material, and then it appears in a footnote. If the intended location of marginal notations is clear from the text, they are inserted without comment; otherwise they are recorded in the notes. The ampersand has been retained and the thorn transcribed as "th." The symbol for per (℈) is used when it appears in the manuscript. The dateline has been placed at the head of a document regardless of where it occurred in the manuscript. All of the documents printed in this volume, as well as omitted routine Washington documents and various ancillary material cited in the notes, may be found in the CD-ROM edition of Washington's Papers (CD-ROM:GW). The reports of Washington's farm managers at Mount Vernon, some of which have been printed in previous volumes of the *Presidential Series,* from now on will appear only in CD-ROM:GW.

During both of Washington's administrations, but particularly in the period shortly before and after his first inauguration, he was besieged with applications for public office. Many of the applicants continued to seek appointment or promotion. The editors have usually printed only one of these letters in full and cited other letters both from the applicant and in support of his application in notes to the initial letter. When Washington replied to these requests at all, the replies were generally pro forma reiterations of his policy of noncommitment until the appointment to a post was made. In such cases his replies have been included only in the notes to the original application and do not appear in their chronological sequence. These and other letters to or from Washington that, in whole or in part, are printed out of their chronological sequence are listed in the table of contents with an indication of where they may be found in the volumes.

Since Washington read no language other than English, incoming letters written to him in foreign languages were generally translated for his information. Where this contemporary translation has survived, it has been used as the text of the document, and the original version has been included in CD-ROM:GW. If there is no contemporary translation, the document in its original language has been used as the text.

During the early years of the new government, the executive sent out a large number of circular letters, under either Washington's name or that of one of his secretaries. Circular letters covered copies of laws passed by Congress and sent to the governors of the states. They also covered commissions and announcements of appointment for public offices sent to individuals after their nominations had been approved by the Senate. In both instances, the circulars requested recipients to acknowledge receipt of the documents. The circulars and the routine acknowledgments of these circulars, usually addressed to Washington but sometimes to one of his secretaries, have been omitted unless they contain material of other interest or significance. In such cases the letters are either calendared or printed in full. The entire text of the documents is available in the CD-ROM edition.

Individuals mentioned in the text in each series are usually identified only at their first substantive mention in the series. The index to each volume indicates where an identification appears in an earlier volume of the Presidential Series.

During Washington's first administration, he depended upon the services of several secretaries: Tobias Lear and David Humphreys, who had been in his service at Mount Vernon, went with him to New York, and his nephew Robert Lewis of Fredericksburg joined the staff in May 1789. Thomas Nelson and William Jackson arrived later in the year; the former left Washington's service in November 1790, and the latter resigned in December 1791. Relatively few drafts in Washington's hand of letters from early 1791 have survived, and the sequence in which outgoing letters and documents were drafted and copied is often difficult to determine. In Record Group 59, State Department Miscellaneous Letters, in the National Archives, are numerous documents that appear to be the original retained copies of letters written by Washington shortly before he became president and in the first years of his first administration. Much of this correspondence is in the hand of Lear or Humphreys. In early 1791 letter-press copies of documents drafted by Lear in Philadelphia also began to appear. Occasionally the frequency with which the secretary's emendations and insertions appear suggests that the document was a draft prepared by him for Washington. More rarely Washington himself made changes and corrections to a document. On other occasions the documents appear to be simply retained copies either of his original draft or of the receiver's copy. For most of the letters found in Miscellaneous Letters, there are also letter-book copies in the Washington Papers at the Library of Congress. Some of the letters for this period probably were copied into the letter books close to the time they were written, but others obviously were entered much later. Occasionally Thomas Nelson's writing appears in the letter-book copies for the summer of 1789, as does Bartholomew Dandridge's, although Nelson did not join the staff until October and Dandridge was not employed until 1791. Finally, a few letter-book copies are in the handwriting of Howell Lewis, Washington's nephew, who did not assume his duties until the spring of 1792. When the receiver's copy of a letter has not been found, the editors have generally assumed that the copy in Miscellaneous Letters was made from the receiver's copy or the draft and have used it as the text, rather than the letter-book copy, and have described the document either as a copy or a draft, depending on the appearance of the manuscript.

Symbols Designating Documents

AD	Autograph Document
ADS	Autograph Document Signed
ADf	Autograph Draft
ADfS	Autograph Draft Signed
AL	Autograph Letter
ALS	Autograph Letter Signed
D	Document
DS	Document Signed
Df	Draft
DfS	Draft Signed
L	Letter

LS   Letter Signed
LB   Letter-Book Copy
[S]   Used with other symbols to indicate that the signature on the
            document has been cropped or clipped.

Repository Symbols and Abbreviations

Arch. Aff. Etr.	Archives du Ministère des Affaires Etrangères, Paris (photocopies at Library of Congress)
CD-ROM:GW	*See* "Editorial Apparatus"
CSfU	University of San Francisco
CSmH	Henry E. Huntington Library, San Marino, Calif.
CtHi	Connecticut Historical Society, Hartford
CtY	Yale University, New Haven
DLC	Library of Congress
DLC:GW	George Washington Papers, Library of Congress
DMS	Supreme Council, Ancient & Accept Scottish Rite, Washington, D.C.
DNA	National Archives
DNA:PCC	Papers of the Continental Congress, National Archives
MdAA	Maryland Hall of Records, Annapolis
MdHi	Maryland Historical Society, Baltimore
MeHi	Maine Historical Society, Portland
MH	Harvard University, Cambridge, Mass.
MHi	Massachusetts Historical Society, Boston
MHi-A	Adams Papers, Massachusetts Historical Society, Boston
MiU-C	William L. Clements Library, University of Michigan, Ann Arbor
NcSal	Rowan Public Library, Salisbury, North Carolina
NcU	University of North Carolina, Chapel Hill
NcWsM	Moravian Archives, Winston-Salem, North Carolina
NHi	New-York Historical Society, New York
NjWoG	Gloucester County Historical Society, Woodbury, New Jersey
NN	New York Public Library, New York
NNC	Columbia University, New York
NNGL	Gilder-Lehrman Collection at Pierpont Morgan Library, New York
NNPM	Pierpont Morgan Library, New York
OClWHi	Western Reserve Historical Library, Cleveland

PEL   Lafayette College, Easton, Pa.
PHi   Historical Society of Pennsylvania, Philadelphia
PPAmP   American Philosophical Society, Philadelphia
PPRF   Rosenbach Foundation, Philadelphia
P.R.O.   Public Record Office, London
PU   University of Pennsylvania, Philadelphia
PWacD   David Library of the American Revolution, Sol
                Feinstone Collection, on deposit at the American
                Philosophical Society
RG   Record Group (designating the location of docu-
                ments in the National Archives)
RPJCB   John Carter Brown Library, Providence
ScC   Charleston Library Society, Charleston, South Car-
                olina
ScU   University of South Carolina, Columbia
Vi   Library of Virginia, Richmond
ViFaCt   Fairfax County Courthouse, Fairfax, Virginia
ViMtV   Mount Vernon Ladies' Association of the Union
ViPC   Center Hill Museum, Petersburg, Virginia
WHi   State Historical Society of Wisconsin, Madison

Short Title List

Alvord, *Kaskaskia Records, 1778–90.*   Clarence Walworth Alvord, ed. *Kaskaskia Records, 1778–1790.* Springfield, Ill., 1909.

Archives parlementaires.   M. J. Mavidal, ed. *Archives parlementaires de 1787 à 1860.* Paris, 1877.

Arnebeck, *Through a Fiery Trial.*   Bob Arnebeck. *Through a Fiery Trial: Building Washington, 1790–1800.* Lanham, Md., and London, 1991.

ASP.   Walter Lowrie et al., eds. *American State Papers: Documents, Legislative and Executive, of the Congress of the United States.* 38 vols. Washington, D.C., 1832–61.

Bayley, *National Loans.*   Rafael A. Bayley. *The National Loans of the United States, from July 4, 1776, to June 30, 1880.* 1881. Reprint. New York, 1970.

Betts, *Jefferson's Garden Book.*   Edwin Morris Betts, ed. *Thomas Jefferson's Garden Book, 1766–1824.* Philadelphia, 1944.

Bowling, *Creation of Washington, D.C.*   Kenneth R. Bowling. *The Creation of Washington, D.C.: The Idea and Location of the American Capital.* Fairfax, Va., 1991.

Brighton, *Checkered Career of Tobias Lear.*   Ray Brighton. *The Checkered Career of Tobias Lear.* Portsmouth, N.H., 1985.

Brown, *George Washington, Freemason.* William Moseley Brown. *George Washington, Freemason.* Richmond, 1952.

Brumbaugh, *Maryland Records.* Gaius Marcus Brumbaugh. *Maryland Records, Colonial, Revolutionary, County, and Church, from Original Sources.* 2 vols. 1928. Reprint. Baltimore, 1975.

Brymner, *Report on Canadian Archives, 1890. Report on Canadian Archives by Douglas Brymner, Archivist, 1890 (Being an Appendix to Report of the Minister of Agriculture).* Ottawa, 1891.

Bullock, *Revolutionary Brotherhood.* Steven C. Bullock. *Revolutionary Brotherhood: Freemasonry and the Transformation of the American Social Order, 1730–1840.* Chapel Hill, N.C., and London, 1996.

Butterfield, *Rush Letters.* L. H. Butterfield, ed. *Letters of Benjamin Rush.* 2 vols. Princeton, N.J., 1951.

Calendar of Virginia State Papers. William P. Palmer et al., eds. *Calendar of Virginia State Papers and Other Manuscripts.* 11 vols. Richmond, 1875–93.

Carter, *Territorial Papers.* Clarence E. Carter et al., eds. *The Territorial Papers of the United States.* 27 vols. Washington, D.C., 1934–69.

Clark, "Origin of the Federal City." Allen C. Clark. "Origin of the Federal City." *Records of the Columbia Historical Society,* 35 (1935), 1–97.

Clarke, *Early and Historic Freemasonry of Georgia.* William Bordley Clarke. *Early and Historic Freemasonry of Georgia, 1733/4–1800.* Savannah, c.1924.

Cooke, *Coxe and the Early Republic.* Jacob E. Cooke. *Tench Coxe and the Early Republic.* Chapel Hill, N.C., 1978.

Crane, *Elizabeth Drinker Diary.* Elaine Forman Crane, ed. *The Diary of Elizabeth Drinker.* 3 vols. Boston, 1991.

Cruikshank, *Simcoe Papers.* E. A. Cruikshank, ed. *The Correspondence of Lieut. Governor John Graves Simcoe.* 5 vols. Toronto, 1923–31.

Custis, *Recollections.* George Washington Parke Custis. *Recollections and Private Memoirs of Washington.* New York, 1860.

Daves, *Proceedings of the Cincinnati.* John C. Daves, ed. *Proceedings of the General Society of the Cincinnati.* Vol. 1: 1784–1884. Baltimore, 1925.

Decatur, *Private Affairs of George Washington.* Stephen Decatur, Jr. *Private Affairs of George Washington, from the Records and Accounts of Tobias Lear, Esquire, His Secretary.* Boston, 1933.

Detweiler, *George Washington's Chinaware.* Susan Gray Detweiler. *George Washington's Chinaware.* New York, 1982.

DHFC. Linda G. De Pauw et al., eds. *Documentary History of the First Federal Congress of the United States of America.* 10 vols. to date. Baltimore, 1972—.

Diaries.   Donald Jackson and Dorothy Twohig, eds. *The Diaries of George Washington.* 6 vols. Charlottesville, Va., 1976–79.

Dove, *Proceedings of the Grand Lodge of Virginia.*   John Dove. *Proceedings of the M. W. Grand Lodge of Ancient York Masons of the State of Virginia, from Its Organization, in 1778, to 1822.* Richmond, 1874.

Dowd, *Records of the Office of Public Buildings.*   Mary-Jane M. Dowd, ed. *Records of the Office of Public Buildings and Public Parks of the National Capital.* Washington, D.C., 1992.

Eckhardt, *Pennsylvania Clocks and Clockmakers.*   George H. Eckhardt. *Pennsylvania Clocks and Clockmakers.* New York, 1955.

Elias and Finch, *Letters of Digges.*   Robert H. Elias and Eugene D. Finch, eds. *Letters of Thomas Attwood Digges (1742–1821).* Columbia, S.C., 1982.

Evans, *American Bibliography.*   Charles Evans. *American Bibliography.* Chicago, 1903–59.

Executive Journal.   *Journal of the Executive Proceedings of the Senate of the United States of America.* Vol. 1. Washington, D.C., 1828.

Fick, *Making of Haiti.*   Carolyn E. Fick. *The Making of Haiti: The Saint Domingue Revolution from Below.* Knoxville, Tenn., 1990.

Fields, *Papers of Martha Washington.*   Joseph E. Fields, comp. *"Worthy Partner": The Papers of Martha Washington.* Westport, Conn., and London, 1994.

Fitzpatrick, *Writings.*   John C. Fitzpatrick, ed. *The Writings of George Washington from the Original Manuscript Sources, 1745–1799.* 39 vols. Washington, D.C., 1931 44.

Franklin Papers.   William B. Willcox, Leonard W. Labaree, Whitfield J. Bell, Jr., et al., eds. *The Papers of Benjamin Franklin.* 33 vols. to date. New Haven and London, 1959—.

Fries, *Records of the Moravians in North Carolina.*   Adelaide L. Fries, ed. *Records of the Moravians in North Carolina.* 11 vols. Raleigh, N.C., 1922.

Geggus, *Slavery, War, and Revolution.*   David Patrick Geggus. *Slavery, War, and Revolution: The British Occupation of Saint Domingue, 1793–1798.* Oxford, 1982.

Greene Papers.   Richard K. Showman et al., eds. *The Papers of General Nathanael Greene.* 9 vols. to date. Chapel Hill, N.C., 1976—.

Griffin, *Boston Athenæum Washington Collection.*   Appleton P. C. Griffin, comp. *A Catalogue of the Washington Collection in the Boston Athenæum.* Cambridge, Mass., 1897.

Guthman, *March to Massacre.*   William H. Guthman. *March to Massacre: A History of the First Seven Years of the United States Army, 1784–1791.* New York, 1975.

Heads of Families (New York). *Heads of Families at the First Census of the United States Taken in the Year 1790* (New York). 1908. Reprint. Baltimore, 1966.

Heads of Families (Pennsylvania). *Heads of Families at the First Census of the United States Taken in the Year 1790* (Pennsylvania). 1908. Reprint. Baltimore, 1970.

Heads of Families (South Carolina). *Heads of Families at the First Census of the United States Taken in the Year 1790* (South Carolina). 1908. Reprint. Salt Lake City, 1978.

Henderson, *Washington's Southern Tour.* Archibald Henderson. *Washington's Southern Tour, 1791.* Boston and New York, 1923.

Hening. William Waller Hening, ed. *The Statutes at Large; Being a Collection of All the Laws of Virginia from the First Session of the Legislature, in the Year 1619.* 13 vols. 1819–23. Reprint. Charlottesville, Va., 1969.

Howell, *State Trials.* Thomas Jones Howell. *A Complete Collection of State Trials and Proceedings for High Treason and Other Crimes and Misdemeanors from the Earliest Period to the Year 1783, with Notes and Other Illustrations.* Vol. 23. *23–34 George III A.D. 1783–1794.* London, 1817.

Humphreys, *Life and Times of David Humphreys.* Francis Landon Humphreys. *Life and Times of David Humphreys, . . .* 2 vols. New York and London, 1917.

JCC. Worthington C. Ford et al., eds. *Journals of the Continental Congress.* 34 vols. Washington, D.C., 1904–37.

Jefferson Papers. Julian P. Boyd et al., eds. *The Papers of Thomas Jefferson.* 27 vols. to date. Princeton, N.J., 1950—.

Jones, *Dorchester County.* Elias Jones. *Revised History of Dorchester County, Maryland.* Baltimore, 1925.

"Journal of the S.C. House of Representatives." MS "Journal of the House of Representatives of South Carolina." (Microfilm Collection of Early State Records.)

"Journal of the S.C. Senate." MS "Journal of the Senate of South Carolina." (Microfilm Collection of Early State Records.)

Journals of the Council of State of Virginia. H. R. McIlwaine, Wilmer L. Hall, George H. Reese, and Sandra Gioia Treadway, eds. *Journals of the Council of the State of Virginia.* 5 vols. Richmond, 1931–82.

JPP. Dorothy Twohig, ed. *Journal of the Proceedings of the President, 1793–1797.* Charlottesville, Va., 1981.

Keane, *Paine.* John Keane. *Tom Paine: A Political Life.* Boston, 1995.

Kelsay, *Brant.* Isabel Thompson Kelsay. *Joseph Brant, 1743–1807: Man of Two Worlds.* Syracuse, N.Y., 1984.

Kilty, *Laws of Maryland.* William Kilty. *The Laws of Maryland. . . .* 2 vols. Annapolis, 1799–1800.

Kirkland and Kennedy, *Historic Camden.* Thomas J. Kirkland and

Robert M. Kennedy. *Historic Camden*. Pt. 1. *Colonial and Revolutionary*. Columbia, S.C., 1905.

Lafayette, *Mémoires.*   Marie-Joseph-Paul-Yves-Roch-Gilbert Du Motier, marquis de Lafayette. *Mémoires, correspondence et manuscrits du General Lafayette, publiés par sa famille*. 6 vols. Paris, 1838.

Lamb, "Unpublished Washington Portraits."   Martha J. Lamb, ed. "Unpublished Washington Portraits." *Magazine of American History*, 19 (April 1888), 272–85.

Ledger B.   Manuscript Ledger in George Washington Papers, Library of Congress.

Letters and Recollections of George Washington.   *Letters and Recollections of George Washington: Being Letters to Tobias Lear and Others between 1790 and 1799.* . . . New York, 1906.

Letters from Washington to Lear.   *Letters from George Washington to Tobias Lear with an Appendix*. Rochester, N.Y., 1905.

Lipscomb, *South Carolina in 1791.*   Terry W. Lipscomb. *South Carolina in 1791: George Washington's Southern Tour*. Columbia, S.C., 1993.

Mackey, *History of Freemasonry in South Carolina.*   Albert G. Mackey. *The History of Freemasonry in South Carolina*. 1861. Reprint. Charleston, S.C., 1936.

Madison Papers.   William T. Hutchinson, William M. E. Rachal, Robert A. Rutland, J. C. A. Stagg, et al., eds. *The Papers of James Madison*. [1st series]. 17 vols. Chicago and Charlottesville, Va., 1962–91.

Marshall Papers.   Charles T. Cullen, Herbert A. Johnson, et al., eds. *The Papers of John Marshall*. 8 vols. to date. Chapel Hill, N.C., 1974—.

Mattern, *Benjamin Lincoln.*   David B. Mattern. *Benjamin Lincoln and the American Revolution*. Columbia, S.C., 1995.

Matthews, *Journal of William L. Smith.*   Albert Matthews, ed. *Journal of William Loughton Smith, 1790–1791*. Reprint from Mass. Historical Society, *Proceedings,* 1917. Cambridge, Mass., 1917.

Mayo, *Instructions to British Ministers.*   Bernard Mayo, ed. *Instructions to the British Ministers to the United States, 1791–1812*. Annual Report of the American Historical Association for the Year 1936. Vol. 3. Washington, D.C., 1941.

Miller, *Treaties.*   Hunter Miller, ed. *Treaties and Other International Acts of the United States of America*. Vol. 2. Washington, D.C., 1931.

Morris, *Diary of the French Revolution.*   Beatrix Cary Davenport, ed. *A Diary of the French Revolution by Gouverneur Morris*. 2 vols. Boston, 1939.

Myers, *Liberty without Anarchy.*   Minor Myers, Jr. *Liberty without Anarchy: A History of the Society of Cincinnati*. Charlottesville, Va., 1983.

Nasatir and Monell, *French Consuls in the U.S.*   Abraham P. Nasatir and Gary Elwyn Monell. *French Consuls in the United States.* Washington, D.C., 1967.

Naval Documents Related to the Quasi-War. *Naval Documents Related to the Quasi-War between the United States and France.* 7 vols. Washington, D.C., 1935–38.

N.C. State Records. Walter Clark, ed. *The State Records of North Carolina.* 26 vols. Raleigh and various places, 1886–1907.

O'Neall, *Biographical Sketches of the Bench and Bar of South Carolina.* John Belton O'Neall. *Biographical Sketches of the Bench and Bar of South Carolina.* 2 vols. Charleston, S.C., 1859.

Pa. Archives. Samuel Hazard et al., eds. *Pennsylvania Archives.* 9 ser., 138 vols. Philadelphia and Harrisburg, 1852–1949.

Pa. Mag. *Pennsylvania Magazine of History and Biography.*

Parliamentary History of England. *The Parliamentary History of England from the Earliest Period to the Year 1803,* . . . 36 vols. London, 1806–20.

Parsons, "The Mysterious Mr. Digges." Lynn Hudson Parsons. "The Mysterious Mr. Digges." *William and Mary Quarterly.* 3d ser., 22 (1965), 486–92.

Philadelphia Directory, 1791. Clement Biddle. *The Philadelphia Directory.* Philadelphia, 1791.

Powell, *George Washington and the Jack Ass.* J. H. Powell. *General Washington and the Jack Ass and Other American Characters, in Portrait.* South Brunswick, N.J., etc., 1969.

Princetonians. *Princetonians:* . . . *A Biographical Dictionary, 1748–1794.* James McLachlan et al., eds. 5 vols. Princeton, N.J., 1976–91.

Prussing, *Estate of George Washington.* Eugene E. Prussing. *The Estate of George Washington, Deceased.* Boston, 1927.

Ramsey, *Annals of Tennessee.* J. G. M. Ramsey. *The Annals of Tennessee to the End of the Eighteenth Century.* 1853. Reprint. Kingsport, Tenn., 1926.

Reardon, *Edmund Randolph.* John J. Reardon. *Edmund Randolph: A Biography.* New York, 1974.

Robertson, *Letters and Papers of Andrew Robertson.* Emily Robertson, ed. *Letters and Papers of Andrew Robertson, A.M.* London, 1895.

Rogers, "Letters of William Loughton Smith." George C. Rogers, Jr., ed. "The Letters of William Loughton Smith to Edward Rutledge, June 6, 1789 to April 28, 1794." *South Carolina Historical Magazine,* 69 (1968), 1–25, 101–38, 225–42.

Sachse, *Washington's Masonic Correspondence.* Julius F. Sachse. *Washington's Masonic Correspondence.* Philadelphia, 1915.

Seilhamer, *American Theatre.* George O. Seilhamer. *History of the American Theatre.* 3 vols. Philadelphia, 1888–91.

Smith, *St. Clair Papers.* William Henry Smith. *The St. Clair Papers.* 2 vols. Cincinnati, 1882.

Spangler, "Memoir of Major John Clark." E. W. Spangler. "Memoir of Major John Clark, of York County, Pennsylvania." *Pa. Mag.,* 20 (1896), 77–86.

1 *Stat.* Richard Peters, ed. *The Public Statutes at Large of the United States of America.* Vol. 1. Boston, 1845.

6 *Stat.* Richard Peters, ed. *The Public Statutes at Large of the United States of America.* Vol. 6. Boston, 1848.

Stillwell, "Robertson." John E. Stillwell. "Archibald Robertson, Miniaturist, 1765–1835." *New-York Historical Society Quarterly Bulletin* 1929, 1–33.

Syrett, *Hamilton Papers.* Harold C. Syrett et al., eds. *The Papers of Alexander Hamilton.* 27 vols. New York, 1961–87.

Tatsch, *Freemasonry in the Thirteen Colonies.* J. Hugo Tatsch. *Freemasonry in the Thirteen Colonies.* New York, 1929.

Taylor, *William Cooper's Town.* Alan Taylor. *William Cooper's Town: Power and Persuasion on the Frontier of the Early American Republic.* New York, 1995.

Turner, *Correspondence of the French Ministers.* Frederick J. Turner. *Correspondence of the French Ministers to the United States, 1791–1797.* 2 vols. American Historical Association for the Year 1903. Washington, D.C., 1904.

Upham, *Pickering.* Charles W. Upham. *The Life of Timothy Pickering.* 4 vols. Boston, 1867–73.

Van Doren, *Franklin.* Carl Van Doren. *Benjamin Franklin.* New York, 1938.

Washington Papers Index. *Index to the George Washington Papers.* Washington, D.C., 1964.

Watson, *Annals of Philadelphia.* John F. Watson. *Annals of Philadelphia and Pennsylvania in the Olden Times. . . .* 2 vols. Philadelphia, 1857.

Wickwire, *Cornwallis.* Franklin and Mary Wickwire. *Cornwallis: The Imperial Years.* Chapel Hill, N.C., 1980.

Woolsey, *Memoir.* Melancthon Lloyd Woolsey. *Woolsey Papers. Melancthon Lloyd Woolsey . . . A Memoir.* Champlain, N.Y., 1929.

The Papers of George Washington
Presidential Series
Volume 8
March–September 1791

From Desbrosses

port au prince isle a cote
Mon general   St domingue 22. mars 1791

quoique je naye pas Lhonneur destre connu de vous permet-
tés moy de vous exposer ma Situation dans ce moment.

depuis vingt huits a trente ans jai lhonneur de servir mon roi
et ma patrie, depuis cette Epoque jai au moins mangé ⟨En⟩ service La moitié de mon patrimoine, et L'autre moitié mest aujourdhuy Enlevé par La revolution qui vient de Sopperer En
france.

il me restoit Encore mon general une resource a ma famille et
a moy, cetoit un ami, et il nous a eté Enlevé Le 4 de ce mois, Le
cher thomas de mauduit—colonel du regiment du port au
prince a perdu La vie a cette Epoque,[1] il me flattoit toujours que
par votre credit, il me feroit avoir des terres par concession,
meme En assez grande quantité pour y pouvoir placer toute ma
famille, et cela a peu de frais, et a vingt ou trente lieux de new
york, puis je Esperer mon general que sans aucunes recom-
mandations que vous voudrés Bien vous interesser au sort dun
militaire vraiment ⟨ma⟩lheureux, qui na aujourdhuy dautres de-
sirs, que de vivre sous Les Lois des Etats unis, et de faire nombre
parmi Les citoyens, mes moyens dans ce moment se reduisent a
peu de choses, mais je me Sens Encore assez de forces et d'ener-
gie pour m'acquitter Enver la patrie qui aura Bien voulu me
recevoir dans son Sein et je vous aurai monsieur toute ma vie
La plus vive reconnoissance de ce que vous voudrés Bien faire
pour a ce Sujet, je vous ai parlé particulièrement de new york
parceque Le che[valie]r massuroit quil y avoit Encore aux Envi-
rons Beaucoup de terres a conseder et a defricher, je me trouverai toujours Bien ou vous voudrés Bien avoir La Bonté de
me colloquer, et ferai honneur aux Engagemens que de toute
necessité il faudra contracter pour La Concession si toute fois
cela nexcede pas me facultés.

mr P. Penet avoit Envoyé icy quelques imprimé jai eu Lhonneur de luy Ecrire, je nai point Encore eu reponse de luy il par-
oit quil est Etabli a peupres dans La partie dont mr de mauduit
me parloit.[2]

je mets tout mon Espoir En vous persuadé que vous voudrés Bien m honnorer dune reponse.[3] je suis avec respect Mon general Votre tres humble et tres obeissant serviteur

Le ch[evali]er desbrosses

ALS, DNA: RG 59, Miscellaneous Letters (misfiled by archivists 22 Mar. 1790).

The Chevalier Desbrosses, a major in the French infantry who wrote GW from Gonave, off Port-au-Prince, Saint Domingue (now Haiti), was serving with British troops there under Lt. Col. George Hallam in 1797, when he was court-martialed for striking his superior officer and sentenced to death (Geggus, *Slavery, War, and Revolution,* 253–54).

1. Col. Thomas-Antoine, chevalier de Mauduit du Plessis, commander of the French garrison at Port-au-Prince since 1788, served under GW during the Revolutionary War and was a member of the French Society of the Cincinnati (see Gouverneur Morris to GW, 3 Mar. 1789, n.3). On 4 Mar. 1791 he was "executed by one of his own grenadiers," and "His clothes were torn from his body, his head fixed on a bayonet, and his naked body dragged through the streets," according to a letter extracted in the *Independent Chronicle* (Boston), 21 April 1791.

Mauduit's brother-in-law, Guyot de Villiers, wrote to GW from France on 27 June 1791: "ma Sœur en touchant au port se rejouissait de voir le meilleur des maris lors qu'elle apprit qu'il avait été assassiné le 4 mars, epoque fatale. on ne se contente de le lui avoir enlevé de la manière la plus affreuse, on le poursuit apres sa mort. on veut le noircir dans l'esprit de la malheureuse infortunée, mais chose impossible on lui prête divers ecrits qui rendraient sa Conduite Suspecte si l'on en doutait un instant: mais tout homme sensé quil L'a connu verra avec affliction les moyens que des Scélérats se servent pour faire voir a la nation qu'il aurait pu un jour lui faire un grand tort s'il eut vecu plus long tems. Jai appri avec sensibilité, Mon général, que vous portiés son deuil. je me plais a croire que vous estimiés et aimiés ce héros qui devait mourir autrement d'apres les qualités qu'il pratiquait et que vous lui aviés inspirées. Il ⟨av⟩ait projetté de vous aller rendre Ses devoirs, il devait etre accompagné de Sa famille, nous nous en faisions une fête" (DNA: RG 59, Miscellaneous Letters).

2. Trader Pierre Penet acquired from the Oneida Indians a 100-square-mile tract in New York near the St. Lawrence River two years before removing to Saint Domingue in 1790. See Penet to GW, c.1789, source note.

3. Desbrosses twice again wrote to GW, repeating that his family had lost everything in the French Revolution, that he desired to remove to New York, and that he hoped GW would advance him credit to buy land there on which to settle his family (Desbrosses to GW, 1 May, 17 July 1791, DNA: RG 59, Miscellaneous Letters).

From Tobias Lear

Sir,　　　　　　　　　　　Philadelphia March 23d 1791

　　I had the honor last evening to receive your commands, through Major Jackson, to deliver the letter for Colo. Clandenen to General St Clair, unless Genl Knox thought Genl Sevier a more direct conveyance or knew of a better, and in obedience thereto I made the inquiry of Genl Knox, who thought Genl St Clair would be most likely to give the letter a direct & speedy conveyance; I therefore delivered it to him—informing him of the purport, to impress the necessity of its being put into a safe and expeditious channel, which he assured me should be done. Genl St Clair leaves this City tomorrow morning. If any other opportunity should offer to send a letter from hence to Colo. Clandenen, I shall write to him by it.[1]

　　Mr Coxe, of whom I had made some inquiry respecting a certain person, sent me the enclosed letter today; but I cannot learn from whom the information comes.[2] Colo. Hamilton sent today for the Commissions for the Commissioners who are to receive subscriptions to the Bank. They are filled up with the names of Thomas Willing, David Rittenhouse, Samuel Howell of Pennsylvania—John Beale Bordley of Maryland & Lambert Cadwaladcr of New Jersey.[3]

　　We are very happy to hear that the roads will probably be better than you expected to find them. Mrs Lear, who continues in a fine way—unites with me in a respectful remembrance & best wishes for your health & happiness—and a pleasant Journey. I have the honor to be with the highest respect & most perfect Attachment Sir Your most Obedt Servt

　　　　　　　　　　　　　　　　　　　Tobias Lear.

ALS, DLC:GW; ALS (letterpress copy), MiU-C.

　　1. GW's instructions through Maj. William Jackson, his traveling secretary, to Tobias Lear, GW's chief secretary, who remained to head the president's household in Philadelphia, have not been found. The letter for "Colo. Clandenen" is probably GW to George Clendenin, 21 Mar. 1791. See also Clendenin to GW, 25 June 1791.

　　2. The enclosure was a letter from Tench Coxe to Lear, dated 23 Mar. 1791: "The gentleman with whom I conversed concerning the character and situation of one of the French emigrants has just called to inform me that letters have been since received from Europe containing information of a nature unfavorable to the persons integrity. He requested me to be guarded in the use

I might make of this hint. I think it my duty to give you, confidentially, immediate notice of it" (DLC:GW). For references to the French emigrant, John Joseph de Barth, to whom GW had sold his Kanawha lands, see GW to Clendenin, 21 Mar. 1791 and note 2, and Lear to GW, 5 June 1791.

3. Before leaving Philadelphia on 21 Mar., GW had signed commissions for the five commissioners for receiving subscriptions to the Bank of the United States (Df, DLC:GW). Among the commissioners, Samuel Howell (c.1748–1807) was a mariner and a founder of the First City Troop of Philadelphia who had been disowned by the Quakers, and John Beale Bordley (1727–1804), a founder of the Philadelphia Society for Promoting Agriculture in 1785, was a lawyer and agricultural innovator who resided near the mouth of the Wye River in Maryland.

From Tobias Lear

Philadelphia March 24th 1791
Sir,   11 O'Clock P.M.

The enclosed letters have been this moment brought to me by the Post Master, who informs thus they have just arrived at the Office in the Western Mail. As they may contain important intelligence I delay not a moment to forward them.[1]

Mrs Washington and the family are well. Nothing particular has transpired since your departure. I have the honor to be, with the highest respect & most sincere Attachment Sir, Your obliged & very humble Servt

Tobias Lear.

ALS, DLC:GW.
  1. The enclosed letters have not been identified.

From Henry Lee

My dear General   Alex[andri]a 24th March [17]91

Permit me to tell you that I have waited to the last moment in my power in the fond hope of seeing you.[1]

My necessitys force me away this day, or the satisfaction I covet, should not be lost. Deprived of what is so grateful to my feelings, I must use this mode of manifesting my happiness on your second return to our native state, on the confirmed health you enjoy, and on the lasting affection of your fellow citizens.

Let me hope you will not forget the pestilential effects of the southern sun in the hot season and that the month of may will not pass, before you revisit the potomac. I wish you an agreable journey & safe return & beg your acceptance of my most affectionate & respectful regards. I have the honor to be my dear general your most devoted h: servt

Henry Lee

ALS, DLC:GW.

1. Henry (Light-Horse Harry) Lee had been recommended for the command of the Virginia contingent of temporary levies to be raised for the planned expedition on the northwestern frontier. See Knox to GW, 14 Mar. 1791, first enclosure. Lee subsequently declined the appointment (see Knox to GW, 27 Mar. 1791). For the failure of Josiah Harmar's campaign against the Miami and Wabash Indians in the autumn of 1790 and Arthur St. Clair's subsequent expedition, see GW to Knox, 19 Nov. 1790, n.4, Knox to GW, 22 Feb., 18 Mar. 1791, Knox to Lear, 25 Feb. 1791 and note 1, and 19 Mar. 1791, GW to the U.S. Senate, 4 Mar. 1791 (second letter), and to the Miami Indians, 11 Mar. 1791 and source note.

Memorandum of Pierre-Charles L'Enfant

[Georgetown, Md., 26 March 1791]
Note relative to the Ground laying on the Eastern branch of the River Potowmack & being Intended to parallel the Severals position proposed within the Limits betwen that branch & George-town for the seat of the Federal City.

After coming upon the Hill From the Eastern Branch ferry the Country is level & on a Space of above tow mi[les] each way present a most elligible position for the First Setlement of a grand City & one which if not the only within the limits of the Federal territory is at least the More advantageous in that part laying betwen the Eastern branch & George-town.

the Soil is dry and notwithstanding well watered with abounding Springs it has an wholsome air and being of an easy ascent it is however so heigh that it Command on most of the surrounding Country and may be Effectually guarded from those Hill over looking it—these are on the oposite side of the Water and a branch from the Grand Western montain which Come Round and Extend down on that Eastern Shore in bordering on the River potowmack and they may rather be considered as a mean for protection as the securing of thier Subsoil with proper Establishment would render that situation most respectable.

with respect to navigation it lay at the head of an Extansive one & Cover & forme the bank of an harbor in Every respect to be prefered to that of the potowmack toward George town— Less impeded by ice & never so swelled with Fresh—the chanell is deeper & will admit any vessel as May pass over the shalow down below at the Mariland pt being moored to warfs while they most remain at half mile off from the bank of the potowmack owing to the Main chanel bearing from the Entrance into the eastern branch immediatly and all the way up on the Virginia Shore Until it Come to strik on Mason Island round which in turning it Come to wash for a Shorter Space on the Rock at hampsted pt, or Funk town, making its way to & from the warfs at george town were the grand navigation end.

This Spot made to derive Every possible advantages from water Conveyance Would in the same time be Free from the great Inconveniency attending the crossing of navigable River, the deep water in that branch not coming farther up than Evans pt about half mile Above the Ferry there the large bed of the river immediatly changes in to smal Run over the which bridges might easily be Erected to secure a Constant intercourse with the Eastern Continant in the mean while as it would facilitate seats being fixed on each border of a grand streem whose dept abound with fish and whose wild aspect would in affording a *delassement* from the great bustling rest the ayes from the grand sight below the City.

all the local of this ground is such as will favour Every Improvement as may render the City agreable Commodious & Capable of promoting all sort of util[itarian] establishement.

on its water side from the Mouth of the Eastern branch at Carroll bourough as far up as to Evans point A distance of above three Miles the Frequent winding of the Shore form—many natural wetdock which for not having Every were a great dept of water nevertheless would become very Convenient for the establishing of naval Store and for arsenals the which as well as ware house for marchant men might safly be rised on the water Edge without fear of impeding the prospect from on the Heigh flat behind. there were the level ground prevail on the water and all round were it decen'd but most particularly on that part termi-

nating in a ridge to Jenkins' Hill and runing in a parallel with
and at half mile off from the river potowmack separated by a
low ground intersected with three grand Streems—Many of the
Most desirable position offer for to Erect the publique Edifices
there on—from these height Every Grand building would rear
with a majistick aspect over the Country all round and might be
advantageously seen From twenty miles off—while Contigous to
the First Setlement of the City they would there Extand to ages
in a Central point to it, facing on the grandest prospect of both
of the branch of the potowmack—with the town of Allexandry
in front seen in its fullest Extant over many points of land pro-
jecting from the Mariland & Virginia shore in a Maner as add
much to the perspective at the end of which the cape of great
Hunting Creek appear directly were a Corner stone of the Federal district is to be placed and—in the room of which a majes-
tick Colum or a grand Pyramid being Erected would produce
the happyest effect and Compleatly finish the landscape.

thus in Every respect advantageously situated the federal City
would soon grew of itself & spread as the branches of a tree do
toward were they meet with most nourishment.

there the attractive local will lay all Round & at distance not
beyond those limits within the which a City [the] Capital of an
Extensive Empire may be deliniated.

having a bridge laid over the Eastern branch some were a
bove Evans pt there the natural limit of the eastern branch of
the City may be Extended while in its western Extrimity may be
Included george town itself which being situated at the head of
Grand Navigation of the potowmack Should be favoured with
the same advantage of a better Communication with the southern by having also a Bridge Erected over the potowmack at the
place of the tow sisters were nature would effectually Favour the
undertaking.

then betwen those tow points begining the setlement of the
Grand City on the bank at the eastern branch and promoting
the first improvement all along of the Heigh flat as far as were
it end on Jenkins Hill would place the City Central to the
ground left open to its agrandisement which most undoubtly
would be rapide toward both Extremity. provided never the less
that attention be paid immediatly on laying the first out Line of
the Establishment to open a direct & large Avenue from the

bridge on the potowmack to that on the Eastern branch the which should be well level passing a cross George town and over the Most advantageous ground For prospect trought the grand City, with a midle way paved for heavy Carriage and walks on eachside planted with double Rows of trees to the end that by making it A Communication as agreable as it will be Convenient it may the more induce the improvement of either place all along and prompt the Citizens in Both to Exertions to shorten the distance by building and insensibly affect the wished junction and Compleat a Street Laid out on a dimention proportioned to the Greatnes which a City the Capital of a powerfull Empire ought to manifest.

In viewing the Intended Establishment in this light & Considering how in progress of time a City so happily situated will Extend over a large surface of Ground, much deliberation is necessary For to determine on a plan for the local distribution and conceive that plan on a sisteem which in the mean while as it most render the place Commodious & agreable to the first settler in it may be Capable of being made a part of the whole when Enlarged by progressive Improvement, the which to be made agreable to what will first have been Erected and preserve the similar Correspondance with what may only be intended should be forseen in the first delination in a grand pland of the whol City Combined with the various ground it will Cover and with the particular Circumstances of the Country all round.

in Endeavouring to effect this it is not the regular assemblage of houses laid on in Squar & Forming Streets all parallel & uniform that is so necessary for such plan Could only do on a well level plain & were no surrounding object being interesting it become Indifferent which way the opening of a street may be directed.

but on any other Ground a plan of this sort most be deflective and it never would Answer for any of the Spots proposed for the federal City. and on that held here as the most eligible it would absolutly annulate Every of the advantage Enumerated and the securing of which will along Insure the success of the undertaking.

Such regular plan in deed however answerable as they may appear upon paper or seducing as they May be on the first aspect to the ayes of some people Most even when applayed upon that ground the best calculated to admit of it become at last tiresome and insipide & it never Could be in its orrigine but a Mear Contrivance of some Cool imagination wanting a sense of the real Grand & trewly beautifull only to be Met with were Nature Contribut with art and diversify the objects.

AD, DLC: Pierre-Charles L'Enfant Papers.

This and other documents relating to the establishment of the Federal City were to be stored temporarily in DLC by the Office of Public Buildings and Public Parks of the National Capital. Most of the other documents were transferred to DNA: RG 42 after construction of the National Archives, but the above document remained in DLC: L'Enfant Papers. Its date was supplied from a later cover sheet, which noted: "The above was personally handed to the executive on his arrival at Georgetown at that time." L'Enfant's memo was probably among the "works of Majr. L'Enfant" GW examined on 28 Mar. (*Diaries*, 6:103–4).

To St. John's College Faculty

Gentlemen,   [Annapolis, Md., 26 March 1791]

The satisfaction which I have derived from my visit to your infant Seminary is expressed with real pleasure, and my wishes for its progress to perfection are preferred with sincere regard.

The very promising appearance of its infancy must flatter all its friends, (among whom I entreat you to class me,) with the hope of an early, and at the same time a mature manhood.

You will do justice to the sentiments, which your kind regard towards myself inspires, by believing that I reciprocate the good wishes contained in your address—and I sincerely hope the excellence of your seminary will be manifested in the morals and science of the youth, who are favored with your care.[1]

G. Washington

LB, DLC:GW.

GW reached Annapolis on 25 Mar. 1791 after spending a wretched night in a boat stuck on a bar within a mile of the city. The president was greeted by Maryland governor John Eager Howard and visited the Maryland State House before proceeding to St. John's College, where he received a congratulatory address from the faculty of the school. GW remained in Annapolis on 26 Mar., "preparing papers &ca. against my arrival at George Town" for his meeting with the proprietors of land within the federal district. He attended a ball held that evening in his honor and departed the city the next morning, lodging for the night of 27 Mar. at Bladensburg, Md. (*Diaries*, 6:100–102).

1. The address, signed on behalf of the faculty by John McDowell (1751–1820), principal of St. John's College, who graduated from the College of Philadelphia before serving as a private in Capt. Samuel Patton's company during the Revolution, reads: "We the faculty of St John's College beg leave to express the sincere joy, which the honour of your presence in our infant seminary afforded us. In common with all those who superintend the education of youth, we must feel a lively gratitude to the defender of liberty, the guardian of his country's peace and consequently the great patron of literature. But as this Seminary was begun, since the united voice of free America called you to preside over its most important interests, and ensure to them the continuance of those blessings which your calm foresight and steady fortitude had been the happy means of procuring, it seems in a peculiar manner to look up to you with filial respect. That it dates its birth from this grand Era, which has placed you at the head of fifteen distinct sovereign states, united into one mighty republic, is regarded by its friends as an auspicious circumstance and flattering assurance of its future eminence and usefulness. To the friend of virtue and his country, the rise of Colleges, where the youth of generations yet unborn may be taught to admire and emulate the great and good, must give a heartfelt delight, as they promise perpetuity to the labours and renown of the Patriot and Hero. Our earnest prayer is, that a kind providence may continually watch over you and preserve a life, long indeed already, if measured by deeds of worth and fulness of honours, but too short as yet for your Country" (DLC:GW).

Letter not found: to Martha Washington, 26 Mar. 1791. On 27 Mar. 1791 GW referred Tobias Lear "to a letter I wrote to Mrs Washington from Annapolis yesterday."

Only four of GW's letters to his wife have survived to the present. Martha Washington's granddaughter Martha Parke Custis Peter wrote in 1828 that shortly after GW's death on 14 Dec. 1799 Martha had burned all but two of his letters to her, and only a handful more have since been found. See GW to Martha Washington, 18 June 1775, source note and note 5; Fields, *Papers of Martha Washington,* xxxi, xxxvii, n.39; and *Washington Papers Index,* viii.

From Alexander Hamilton

Sir   Sunday March 27, 1791.
     I have embraced the first moment of leisure to execute your wish, on the subject to which the enclosed Notes are applicable—They are neither so accurate nor so full, as I should have been glad to make them: but they are all that my situation has permitted.[1]
     Nothing new has occured in my Department worth men-

tioning—I thought that the following extract of a letter from Mr King might not be wholly uninteresting, and I there fore make it—"The Legislature of this State have incorporated the Bank, limiting its capital to a million of Dollars and its duration to twenty years. The Treasurer is authorised to subscribe to the Loan. proposed to Congress all the Continental paper in the Treasury and by a bill that passed the Legislature this morning, he is directed to take in behalf of the State, *one hundred and ninety shares* in the *National* Bank. I have seen a letter from Mr John Taylor of Albany which has created some uneasiness on account of our frontier settlements—He says—'there is great reason to apprehend danger from the Indians in this quarter;' but does not mention, nor have I been able to learn the grounds of this apprehension. You are sensible that almost every person here is interested in our Western lands; their value depends upon the settlement of the frontiers, these settlements depend on Peace with the Indians, and indeed the bare possibility of a war with the six Nations, would break up our whole frontier. It is from this state of things that the war with the Wabash Indians is so much disrelished here. The Legislature have authorised the Governor to draw Money from the Treasury and to take such measures as he may judge suitable to *preserve the good will* of the neighbouring Indians.[2] I have said, and I presume it will be the case, that all prudent steps will be pursued to keep the six Nations quiet; that we were embarked and that it had became necessary to go forward with the War if peace could be obtained by no other means; but I am more and more convinced that it behoves the government if practicable to finish this Indian business, in the course of the summer."

The clue to Mr Taylors apprehensions seems to be a late murder of some friendly indians within the limits of this State; the particulars of which I take it for granted will be made known to you by the Secretary at War.[3] With the most perfect respect and truest attachment I have the honor to be Sir Yr most Obedient & most hble servt

A. Hamilton

LB, DLC:GW.

1. The enclosed report, "Notes on the Advantages of a National Bank" (DLC:GW), summarizes the advantages of banks in general, particularizes the reasons to establish a new national bank, justifies its twenty-year duration, and

answers objections to its establishment, including a geographic inequality of its advantages and its interferences with extant state banks. See Syrett, *Hamilton Papers,* 8:218–23. For background to the establishment of the First Bank of the United States, see Edmund Randolph to GW, 12 Feb. 1791, Thomas Jefferson to GW, 15 Feb. 1791 and source note, GW to Alexander Hamilton, 16 Feb. 1791 and note 1, and 23 Feb. 1791 and note 2, James Madison to GW, 21 Feb. 1791 and source note, and Hamilton to GW, 23 Feb. 1791, and 24 Feb. 1791 and note 2.

2. On 24 Mar. 1791 the New York legislature authorized the governor to spend up to £1,000 to prevent the incursion of hostile Indians. See Rufus King to Hamilton, 24 Mar. 1791 and note 7, Syrett, *Hamilton Papers,* 8:212–13.

3. For the murder of four Senecas on Big Beaver Creek in western Pennsylvania on 9 Mar. 1791, see Seneca Chiefs to GW, 17 Mar. and note 1, and Knox to GW, 27 and 31 Mar. 1791.

From Thomas Jefferson

Sir   Philadelphia Mar. 27. 1791.

I have been again to see mister Barclay on the subject of his mission and to hasten him. I communicated to him the draught of his instructions, and he made an observation which may render a small change expedient. you know it had been concluded that he should go without any defined character in order to save expence. he observed that if his character was undefined they would consider him as an Ambassador, and expect proportional liberalities, and he thought it best to fix his character to that of Consul, which was the lowest that could be employed. thinking there is weight in his opinion I have the honour to inclose you a blank commission for him as Consul, and another letter to the emperor not otherwise different from that you signed, but as having a clause of credence in it. if you approve of this change you will be so good as to sign these papers & return them: otherwise the letter before you signed will still suffice.[1]

I inclose you a Massachusets paper whereby you will see that some acts of force have taken place on our Eastern boundery. probably that state will send us authentic information of them. the want of an accurate map of the bay of Passamaquaddy renders it difficult to form a satisfactory opinion on the point in contest. I write to-day to Rufus Putnam to send me his survey map referred to in his letter.[2] There is a report that some acts of force have taken place on the Northern boundery of New York, and are now under consideration of the government of that state.[3] the impossibility of bringing the court of London to an adjustment of any difference whatever, renders our situation perplexing. should any applications from the states or their citizens be so urgent as to require something to be said before your return, my opinion would be that they should be desired to make no new settlements on our part, nor suffer any to be made on the part of the British, within the disputed territory; and if any attempt should be made to remove them from the settlements already made, that they are to repel force by force, & ask aid of the neighboring militia to do this and no more. I see no other safe way of forcing the British government to come forward themselves & demand an amicable settlement. if this idea meets your approbation, it may prevent a misconstruction, by the British, of what may happen, should I have this idea suggested in a proper manner to Colo. Beckwith.

The experiments which have been tried of distilling seawater with Isaacs' mixture, & also without it, have been rather in favour of the distillation without any mixture.[4]

A bill was yesterday ordered to be brought into the H. of representatives here for granting a sum of money for building a federal hall, house for the President &c.[5]

You knew of mister R. Morris's purchase of Gorham and Phelps of 1,300,000. acres of land of the state of Massachusets, at 5d. an acre. it is said that he has sold 1,200,000. acres of these in Europe thro' the agency of W. Franklin, who it seems went on this business conjointly with that of printing his grandfather's works.[6] mister Morris, under the name of Ogden, & perhaps in partnership with him, has bought the residue of the lands held in the same country by Massachusets, for 1,000£. the Indian title of the former purchase has been extinguished by Gorham, but that of the latter is not. perhaps it cannot be. in that case a similarity of interest will produce an alliance with the Yazoo companies. perhaps a sale may be made in Europe to purchasers ignorant of the Indian right.

I shall be happy to hear that no accident has happened to you in the bad roads you have passed, & that you are better prepared for those to come by lowering the hang of your carriage, & exchanging the coachman for two postillions, circumstances which I confess to you appeared to me essential for your safety, for which no one on earth more sincerely prays both from public & private regard than he who has the honor to be with sentiments of the most profound respect, Sir, Your most obedient & most humble servant

Th: Jefferson

ALS, DNA: RG 59, Miscellaneous Letters; ALS (letterpress copy), DLC: Thomas Jefferson Papers; LB, DLC:GW.

1. In order to maintain friendly relations with Morocco, GW decided to send Thomas Barclay there after Yazid ibn-Muhammed became emperor upon the death of his father, Muhammed ibn-Abdallah (Sidi Muhammed), in March 1790. Barclay had negotiated a treaty with Morocco in 1786–87 that had cost the United States some $30,000 but did not call for annual tribute. Thomas Jefferson drafted new instructions for Barclay in early March 1791 as well as a letter from GW to the new emperor, which has not been found, and submitted both to GW for approval. GW returned them to Jefferson under a cover letter, dated 10 Mar., which has not been found. GW later signed Jefferson's revised letter to the emperor, dated 31 Mar., and returned it to Jefferson on 1 April with a signed consular commission for Barclay. See GW to the Emperor of Morocco, 31 Mar., and to Jefferson, 1 April 1791.

2. The enclosed newspaper has not been identified, nor has Jefferson's correspondence with Rufus Putnam been found. For the background to the American northeastern boundary dispute with Great Britain, see GW to the U.S. Senate, 9 Feb. 1790 (first letter) and source note and enclosure, and John Hancock to GW, 10 Feb. 1790 and note 1.

3. For the difficulties that New York and Vermont citizens had with the British garrisons in two posts on northern Lake Champlain, see Jefferson to GW, 5 June 1791 and note 2, George Clinton to GW, 7 Sept. 1791, and GW to Clinton, 14 Sept. 1791 and note 2.

4. For Jacob Isaacks's claim to have developed a process to desalinate seawater, see Isaacks to GW, 17 Aug. 1790, and editorial note and related documents in *Jefferson Papers*, 19:608–24.

5. The bill of 26 Mar. to provide funding for the construction of buildings for the accommodation of the federal government in Philadelphia was a thinly veiled effort to secure the permanent seat of government despite the determination of Congress, expressed in the 1790 Residence Act, to remove the government to the Potomac in 1800.

6. On the Phelps-Gorham purchase, see Seneca Chiefs to GW, 1 Dec. 1790, n.3, Tobias Lear to GW, 8 May 1791, n.4, and William Stephens Smith to GW, 6 June 1791, nn.2, 4.

From Henry Knox

Sir   War department 27 March 1791

I have the honor to enclose a representation received from the Cornplanter. The fact of murdering the friendly indians by

Capt. Samuel Brady, formerly of the Pensylvania Line, is mentioned in several letters from Fort Pitt, and that the people along the upper parts of the ohio are exceedingly alarmed on that account. The enclosed from Colo. Neville to General Butler, and from Major Craig to me, contain the most particulars.[1]

This event combined with others of a similar nature, will have most pernicious consequences. According to the statement received, it appears to have been an atrocious murder, and therefore merits a rigid inquiry, and if as represented, exemplary punishment.

As the crime was committed within Pensylvania I shall officially transmit the information to the Governor of this state and request him to demand the Governor of Virginia that the accused be given up for trial, by the laws of this state. This is the joint opinion of Mr Jefferson Colonel Hamilton and myself.

Although the accused will either not be apprehended, or if apprehended, will not be convicted, yet nothing farther on this point, can be attempted by the general government.

But I think it adviseable to write to Major General St Clair who sat out on the 23 instant, to inquire into the fact, and finding it as stated, to disavow and disapprove the murder in the strongest terms to the indians, and to assure them, that all possible means shall be taken to bring the accused to punishment; and in the mean time that he indemnify the relations of the deceased for the loss of the horses and other property.

Judge Rufus Putnam informs me of a letter dated at Marietta, the 16th instant, that from the intelligence he had received it would appear, that the Wyandots and Delawares will join in the war against us. and that appearances indicated a general indian War.

Arrangements are made and in operation for recruiting the two battalions of Levies to be raised in this State, and the prospects are good.

One company of the Levies is also recruiting in New Jersey. Lt Colonel Cummings declines taking the battalion and I have therefore offered it to Major Samuel Reading, who was a major, of reputation in the Jersey Line.[2]

Colonel Harry Lee has declined accepting any subordinate command. I humbly request therefore, that you would please to appoint the officers for the Virginia battalion, and to direct the Major to repair immediately to this office for instructions. I take the liberty of suggesting either Colo. Josias Carvel Hall, or Colonel Rawlings, in the place of Colonel Lee.[3]

Brigadier General Sevier has been detained from setting out by sickness, but he has recovered, and will set out tomorrow morning being entrusted with the means of raising a battalion of Levies, in the territory south of the Ohio, and with Instructions to Governor Blount—relative to the proposed treaty with the Cherokees.[4] I have the honor to be sir with the highest Respect Your obedient Servant[5]

H. Knox
secretary of War

ALS, DLC:GW; LB, DLC:GW.

1. For the representation from Cornplanter, see Seneca Chiefs to GW, 17 Mar. 1791. The enclosed letters from John Neville to Richard Butler and from Isaac Craig to Henry Knox have not been found. The murders of four Senecas at Beaver Creek in western Pennsylvania threatened to undo the administration's successful efforts to prevent the Seneca from joining the Miami and Wabash Indians and did not bode well for Col. Thomas Proctor's mission. See Knox to GW, 27 Dec. 1790 and note 4, and GW to Seneca Chiefs, 29 Dec. 1790 and note 5. Knox assured Cornplanter and the other Seneca chiefs on 28 Mar. 1791 that GW had not ordered the murders and "will be very angry indeed when he shall hear of it" and that Maj. Gen. Arthur St. Clair would be instructed to look into the matter and to compensate the victims' friends and relations. Knox also enjoined them to assist Proctor "in the good work of peace" (Knox to Seneca Chiefs, 28 Mar., *ASP, Indian Affairs*, 1:145).

2. Maj. Samuel Reading (1752–1838) served in the Revolutionary War as an officer with New Jersey troops in the Continental army.

3. The organization of the Maryland and Virginia battalions of temporary levies was of particular concern to Knox, who informed William Jackson on the day Jackson and GW left Philadelphia that GW had agreed to appoint the commissioned officers for the Maryland levies while GW was in that state. Knox asked Jackson to remind the president of this and to transmit a list of the appointments as soon as they were made (Knox to Jackson, 21 Mar., DLC:GW). While GW was at Annapolis, Gov. John Eager Howard gave him a list of potential subordinate officers and Benjamin Brooks's letter declining command of the battalion. GW then decided to offer the command to Moses Rawlings (1745–1809) of Frederick County, Maryland. Jackson informed Rawlings of his appointment on 29 Mar. (DLC:GW) and wrote to Knox on 30 Mar.: "The enclosed paper was delivered to the President by Governor Howard, and a letter has, in consequence been written to Colonel Rawlings informing him of his appointment to command the battalion of levies to be raised in Maryland, and requesting him to repair immediately to Philadelphia, or to signify his non-acceptance to you without delay. As you will recollect that no arrangements were taken between the President and yourself for appointing the Virginia Officers, in the event of Colo. Lee declining his appointment, the Presi-

dent finds himself at present unprepared for that contingency. He commands me to request you, if Colonel Lee has declined, to signify to Colonel Josiah Carval Hall that he appoints him to command the regiment, and desires that you will take measures with that Gentleman for officering and completing the battalions of levies directed to be raised in the States of Virginia and Maryland—observing in the choice of the Captains and subalterns to appoint such Gentlemen, who, in addition to other qualities, may be likely to recruit their men with the greatest dispatch—proximity of residence in the officers to the places of rendezvous the President likewise considers as an important object, as it may facilitate recruiting, and be a mean of procuring men most proper for the service. The President says he will, in the mean time make inquiries relative to the Officers, but that he will do nothing which may affect your arrangements until he has informed you thereof. The President will halt a few days at Mount Vernon where your letters will reach him, or overtake him at Fredericksburg" (DLC:GW). The next day Jackson instructed Governor Howard to notify the men he had recommended as subordinate officers of their appointments and transmitted to Knox GW's request that he communicate directly with the subordinate appointees (Jackson to Howard, 31 Mar., MdAA; Jackson to Knox, 31 Mar., DLC:GW). Knox replied to Jackson on 4 April that the Virginia regiment was offered to Hall, adding that "The recruiting service of the levies in this state is promising. According to present appearances, the levies will be completed both in this state and New Jersey by the time contemplated. The Clothing is preparing, and will be distributed as fast as the recruits shall be raised" (DLC:GW).

4. For Brig. Gen. John Sevier's militia expedition and Southwest Territory governor William Blount's proposed treaty with the Cherokees, see Knox to GW, 30 May 1791 and note 4.

5. GW replied on 1 April.

To Tobias Lear

Dear Sir   Bladensburgh [Md.] Mar. 27th 1791[1]
    My attention was so much occupied the days preceeding my departure from Philadelphia, with matters of a public nature, that I could scarcely think of those which more immediately related to my own.

    Who the Steward & House keeper shall be, must be left to Mrs Washington & yourself to determine from circumstances, & the offers that are made. Francis, unless Holkers man could be unexceptionably obtained, I should prefer, for reasons I have already mentioned to you; but be *him* or *them* who they may, it must be expressly understood that wine is not admissable at their Table—if it is so under any pretence whatever, it will terminate as the permission given Hyde has done.[2] It wd be well in all other respects to have a clear definition of the expectations, and obligations of the Parties, that mistakes may not happen. If Frauncis should be employed, it ought to be made known to him, that his services in the Kitchen as usual, will be expected; and that in case of the present Cooks leaving me, or attempting to raise his wages, that he is to do with Hercules, and such under aids as shall be found indispensably necessary; nay further, that if upon trial he finds, as I am *sure* is the case, that we can do without Vicars, he may be discharged. How far, under present circumstances the Dutch girl in the Kitchen is necessary, you must judge of, and act accordingly—As Jacobs wife is brought into the family, the new Landry woman will go out of course.[3]

I wish you would have all the packages moved out of the Garden & have it kept in compleat order, at *my expence* and the paved yard also. Rhemer & Jacob are, certainly competent to this business.[4] The top of one of the Urns in the Garden was broke off by its falling—I made John Mauld carry it to Mr Hyde—let it be cemented on again.[5]

Furnish Mrs Washington with what money she may want— and from time to time ask her if she does want, as she is not fond of applying. As I write in haste, I shall add no more at this time but my best wishes for Mrs Lear &ca—for the history of our travels & adventures *so far* I refer you to a letter I wrote to Mrs Washington from Annapolis yesterday.[6] I am your sincere and Affectionate friend

Go: Washington

ALS (photocopy), ViMtV.

1. GW reached Bladensburg, Md., on 27 Mar. 1791 and probably spent the night at the Indian Queen Tavern. See *Diaries,* 6:103.

2. Samuel "Black Sam" Fraunces served as steward to GW's New York household from May 1789 until February 1790. His replacement, John Hyde, removed to Philadelphia and served until late March 1791. See William Jackson to Clement Biddle, 7 Dec. 1789 and source note, Tobias Lear to GW, 27 Mar. 1791, and Decatur, *Private Affairs of George Washington,* 217. Lear made arrangements through Fraunces's son to rehire his father, who had quit earlier to tend his New York tavern. See GW to Lear, 5, 20 Sept. 1790, and Lear to GW, 12, 26 Sept. 1790, 27, 31 Mar., and 1, 3, 10, 15 April 1791.

3. Katy, the wife of GW's coachman Jacob Jacobus, joined the presidential household as washerwoman in April 1791 (Decatur, *Private Affairs of George Washington,* 215).

4. Henry Rhemur was a houseman at the presidential mansion.

5. John Mauld had replaced James Hurley as porter in the presidential household in December 1789.

6. No letter to Martha Washington dated 26 Mar. 1791 has been found.

From Tobias Lear

Sir, Philadelphia March 27th 1791

Since I had the honor to write to you on the 24th Inst. I have been informed that the Indians on the frontier of New York have lately given indications of a hostile disposition—and that the legislature of that State were about to take some measures of a temporary nature for conciliating the Indians—or, if that should prove ineffectual, to defend their frontiers. These measures, however, it was said, are not, by any means, intended to interfere with any arrangements of the General Government. They are only for the moment, and are to cease as soon as anything relative to the object can be carried into effect by the General Government. This Account I give as it was related to me on Friday evening by Mr Coxe—who informed me that it was received by Colo. Hamilton in a letter from Mr King.[1]

The Secretary of the Treasury has just now sent for a Commission to be filled up with the name of General Edwd Hand, who will accept the Appointment of Inspector of one of the Surveys of this district.[2]

I have heard nothing from Mr Fraunces since I informed his son of the terms upon which he would be admitted into the family. His son told me on Thursday last that he had written to his father as soon as he received my letter, which he had enclosed for his father's information; and as he had requested that he would let him know immediately if he should *not* incline to come, he presumes, from his having heard nothing from him, that he may be expected in a few days. Mr & Mrs Hyde have not yet gone out of the family. They denied that they might continue for a few days (unless some other person came in in their stead) until he could make some arrangements, for their support after leaving the family without going to the expense of boarding which he could illy bear.[3] This being but a reasonable request was granted—and they have continued to do such duties as they have heretofore done. Tomorrow or next day they expect to take their departure, but I do not know what plan they have fixed upon. They have delivered up the things which were committed to their charge, and with as little wear & tare as could be expected—so far they may have credit.

This letter will be directed to Mount Vernon, and Mr Jefferson suggested to me an idea to-day, of direct letters in future, which appears to be a good one—it is, to request the Post-Master of this place to make up a particular packet of such letters as may be sent to the Office for you, and direct them to the President of the United States, without enclosing them in the Mail for any particular place—and as the Mail is opened at every post-town on the Road, the Post-Masters will be able, either to deliver the letters to you if you should be at the place (of which they will certainly know) or forward or detain them as your progress may require. As it was your intention to return by a rout different from the common post road, you will then be better able to give directions for conveying letters to you than we are to calculate it.

Mrs Lear & the little boy are well.[4] We unite in best respects & most sincere affection for you, with—Sir, Your Obliged & very Hble Servt

Tobias Lear.

ALS, DLC:GW.

1. See Alexander Hamilton to GW, 27 Mar. 1791 and note 3.

2. Edward Hand accepted his appointment as an inspector of the excise for Pennsylvania on 18 April (Hand to GW, 18 April 1791, DNA: RG 59, Miscellaneous Letters). See also Executive Order, 15 Mar., and GW to Hamilton, 15 Mar. 1791.

3. For Mr. and Mrs. John Hyde, see William Jackson to Clement Biddle, 7 Dec. 1789, source note, and GW to Tobias Lear, 5 Sept. 1790, n.8, and 27 Mar. 1791. By July 1791 the Hydes were running a tavern that they rented on Tenth Street in Philadelphia (*General Advertiser and Political, Commercial and Literary Journal* [Philadelphia], 9 July 1791).

4. The "little boy" was sixteen-day-old Benjamin Lincoln Lear (1791–1832), only child of Lear and Mary (Polly) Long Lear. GW later referred to him as "our little favorite" (see Hamilton to GW, 15 Dec. 1790, n.1; Decatur, *Private Affairs of George Washington,* 129, 181; Fields, *Papers of Martha Washington,* 232, n.8), and Martha Washington wrote to his paternal grandmother that "The President sends his love to the child—he loves him dearly" (see Martha Washington to Mary Stillson Lear, 24 Aug. 1794, Decatur, *Private Affairs of George Washington,* 206).

From John Cooke

Tipperary, Ireland, 28 March 1791. "Understanding that the regulations of weights and measures is one of the objects of your Exellency's councils at present, and humbly expecting that the enclos'd invention may be instrumental in effecting that end," takes the liberty of laying it "at your Excellency's feet."[1]

ALS, DNA: RG 59, Miscellaneous Letters. Thomas Jefferson endorsed the address cover, "To the President. Delivered to Th:J. Aug. 18." 1791.

John Cooke has not been further identified.

1. The enclosed "Description of a new standard for Weights and Measures" has not been found. After its delivery to Jefferson, Cooke's essay was read at a meeting of the American Philosophical Society on 19 Aug. 1791 and published in the society's *Transactions*, 3 (Philadelphia, 1793), 328–31.

To Tobias Lear

Dear Sir,   George Town [Md.] March 28th 1791.

Late this afternoon your letters of the 23d & 24th instant came to hand, and as the Mail is about to be closed (leaving this before sun rise in the morning) I shall, as I must, be short.

I return some letters to be filed;—one from Colo Blaine to be given to Genl Knox, to be acted upon as he pleases;—he is as well acquainted with the man as I am, & knows the want of such a character better than I do;—another letter from Colo Cannon, which I may venture to say proves him to be, what I will not call him; and, that I need never look for any Rents from him.—I pray you to say to him, if he does not come to Philadelphia during my absence, that his *own* statement—given in at New York—does not justify his prest report—and that I am too well acquainted with the prices of grain and the demd for it last year in his own neighbourhood to be imposed upon by such a tale as his letter exhibits.—In a word, that I am by no means satisfied with his treatment of me;—for sure I am I shall get nothing from him but *assurances* of improvements, whilst he is either applying my rents to his own use—or suffering the tenants to go free from the payment of them.[1]

One of the Pads to the Waggon harness was left, it seems, at Mr Clark's—send it by the Stage to Alexandria;—if it comes too late the matter will not be great.[2]—I am not able to say yet, how long I shall be detained in this place—where I arrived before breakfast this morning. I am—Your affecte

Go: Washington.

P.S.—I send with my best remembrance a Sermon for Mrs W——n—I presume it is good, coming all the way from New Hampshire, but do not vouch for it not having read a word of it.—It was one of your enclosures.—[3]

Letters from Washington to Lear, 24.

The above letter is one of several from GW to Tobias Lear that survives only in print. The original receiver's copies were bequeathed by Lear's widow, Frances Dandridge Henley Lear, to distant relatives, and many of them were subsequently acquired by manuscript collector William K. Bixby, who had them transcribed by William H. Samson and published in a limited edition in 1905. The editors will henceforth use the printed Bixby-Samson transcripts as source texts for those letters for which neither receiver's copies nor contemporary letter-book copies have been found, having previously relied on Jared Sparks's early nineteenth-century transcripts as published by Lear's granddaughter Louisa Lear Eyre in 1906. See GW to Lear, 9 Sept. 1790, source note, and *Letters and Recollections of George Washington,* v, vii, xi.

1. The enclosed letters from Ephraim Blaine (1741–1804) of Carlisle, Pa., and John Cannon, GW's western Pennsylvania land agent, have not been found. Blaine, who had served in the Revolutionary War as deputy commissary general of purchases from 1777 until he became commissary general in 1780, apparently wrote to GW seeking a role in supplying Maj. Gen. Arthur St. Clair's expedition. See GW to Cannon, 26 Dec. 1788, source note, and Lear to GW, 1, 3 April 1791.

2. Philadelphia carriage maker David Clark apparently had been engaged to work on GW's baggage wagon.

3. For the enclosed pamphlet, see John C. Ogden to GW, 9 Jan. 1791 and note 1.

To Charles Pinckney

Dear Sir,　　　　　George Town, Maryland, March 29th 1791.

I had the pleasure to receive your Excellency's obliging letter of the 8th instant last evening.

I am thus far on my tour through the southern States—but, as I travel with only one sett of horses, and must make occasional halts, the progress of my journey is exposed to such uncertainty as admits not of fixing a day for my arrival at Charleston.[1]

While I express the grateful sense which I entertain of your

Excellency's polite offer to accommodate me at your house during my stay in Charleston, your goodness will permit me to deny myself that pleasure.

Having, with a view to avoid giving inconvenience to private families, early prescribed to myself the rule of declining all invitations to quarters on my journies, I have been repeatedly under a similar necessity with the present of refusing those offers of hospitality, which would otherwise have been both pleasing and acceptable.[2]

I beg your Excellency to be persuaded of the sincere esteem and regard with which I am, dear Sir, Your affectionate and obedient Servant

G. Washington

LB, DLC:GW.

For GW's decision to undertake a tour of Virginia, the Carolinas, and Georgia in the spring of 1791 to complement his earlier presidential visits to the New England states, see GW to William Washington, 8 Jan. 1791, source note, and Itinerary for the Southern Tour, February 1791, editorial note. The Southern Tour gave GW an opportunity to observe firsthand political, socioeconomic, demographic, and agricultural conditions of the southern states, to judge the mood of the citizenry toward the federal government and his administration's measures, and to lend his prestige to Federalist politicians, particularly in North Carolina, which had ratified the federal Constitution in November 1789. On a more personal level, GW probably welcomed the two-month-long trip as an extended period of physical exercise, as he earlier had sought such escape from a sedentary lifestyle that he felt was contributing to a decline in his health. See William Jackson to Clement Biddle, 12 May, editorial note, GW to Biddle, 20 July, and to the Clergy of Newport, R.I., 18 Aug. 1790, source note. The Southern Tour also enabled GW to renew his acquaintance with old comrades, meet other former Revolutionary War officers, and tour southern battlefields.

1. GW left Philadelphia on 20 Mar. 1791 with eleven horses: four for his coach, four for his outriders, two to pull the baggage wagon, and one mount for himself. During the Southern Tour, GW rode Prescott, his parade horse, one of two white horses of his Philadelphia stable, chiefly when the presidential party was greeted ceremoniously by mounted dignitaries. GW's usual practice upon approaching a town seems to have been to alight from his carriage and mount his steed before being welcomed by any official escorts. The president bought three new horses before his departure from Philadelphia: two bays purchased from William Davidson's stables on 7 Mar. 1791 for $213.34 and a bay mare for which he paid $93.34 to Isaac Clark on 18 Mar., and which remained in Philadelphia. See GW to Tobias Lear, 21 April, and Lear to GW, 15 May 1791, Lipscomb, *South Carolina in 1791*, 3, and Decatur, *Private Affairs of George Washington*, 207, 209. GW left Mount Vernon on 7 April "with Horses

apparently well refreshed and in good spirits" but almost lost his four carriage horses the same day when they fell off the Colchester ferry (*Diaries,* 6:107). He engaged two more horses after leaving Petersburg, Va., to rest those pulling the wagon, as they were "rather too light for the draught; and, (one of them especially) losing his flesh fast" (ibid., 112).

2. GW had intended to observe the same policy of utilizing only public accommodations on his Southern Tour as he had during his presidential visits to the New England states. Travel conditions in the South, however, occasionally forced the president to accept the overnight hospitality of private Carolinian families. See GW to William Washington, 8 Jan. 1791 and source note, to Edward Rutledge, 16 Jan. 1791, and *Diaries,* 6:115, 116, 121–22, 122–23.

Agreement of the Proprietors of the Federal District

[Georgetown, Md., 30 March 1791]

We the subscribers, in consideration of the great benefits we expect to derive from having the Federal City laid off upon our Lands, do hereby agree and bind ourselves, heirs, executors & administrators, to convey in Trust, to the President of the United States, or Commissioners, or such person or persons as he shall appoint, by good and sufficient deeds in fee simple, the whole of our respective Lands, which he may think proper to include within the lines of the federal City for the purposes and on the Conditions following—

The President shall have the sole power of directing the Federal City to be laid off in what manner he pleases. He may retain any number of squares he may think proper for public Improvements, or other public uses, and the Lots only which shall be laid off shall be a joint property between the Trustees on behalf of the Public and each present Proprietor, and the same shall be fairly and equally divided between the Public and the Individuals, as soon as may be, after the City shall be laid off.

For the streets, the Proprietors shall receive no compensation, but for the squares, or Lands in any form which shall be taken for Public buildings or any kind of Public Improvements, or uses, the Proprietors, whose Lands shall be so taken shall receive at the rate of twenty five pounds ℔ Acre, to be paid by the Public.

The whole wood on the Lands shall be the Property of the Proprietors: But should any be desired by the President to be reserved or left standing, the same shall be paid for by the Public at a just and reasonable valuation, exclusive of the Twenty five pounds ℔ Acre, to be paid for the Land, on which the same shall remain.

Each Proprietor shall retain the full possession and use of his Land, untill the same shall be sold and occupied by the purchasers of the Lotts lain out thereupon, and in all cases where the public arrangements, as the streets, lotts &c. will admit of it, each Proprietor shall possess his buildings and other Improvements and grave yards, paying to the public only one half the present estimated value of the Lands, on which the same shall be, or twelve pounds ten shillings ℔ Acre—But in cases where the Arrangements of the Streets, lotts, Squares &c. will not admit of this, and it shall become necessary to remove such buildings Improvements &c. the Proprietors of the same shall be paid the reasonable value thereof, by the Public.

Nothing herein contained, shall affect the Lotts which any of the Parties to this Agreement many hold in the Towns of Carrollsburgh or Hamburgh.

In Witness whereof we have hereunto set our hands and Seals, this thirtieth day of March 1791.

LB, DNA: RG 42, Proceedings of the Commissioners of Public Buildings and Grounds; copy, DNA: RG 42, General Records, Deeds, and Other Records Relating to Property of the Original Proprietors; copy, DNA: RG 233, Sixth Congress, 1799–1801, Records of Legislative Proceedings, Committee Reports, and Papers—Select Committee.

For GW's arrival at Georgetown, Md., early on 28 Mar. and his negotiations with the owners of land in the federal district the following two days, see *Diaries*, 6:103–6.

The signatures on the finished agreement—which apparently was retained in Georgetown by William Deakins, Jr.—of Robert Peter, David Burnes, James M. Lingan, Uriah Forrest, Benjamin Stoddert, Notley Young, Daniel Carroll of Duddington, Overton Carr, Thomas Beall of George, Charles Beatty, Anthony Holmead, and James Peerce [Pierce] were witnessed by William Bayly, William Robertson, and John Suter. The signatures of other proprietors were added after the meeting with GW: Abraham Young (witnessed by Samuel Davidson), Edward Peerce (witnessed by Benjamin Stoddert), Benjamin Stoddert, signing on behalf of John Waring, from whom he had a power of attorney (witnessed by Joseph E. Rowles), William Prout (witnessed by Deakins), and William King (witnessed by Deakins). Robert Peter signed the agreement a second time as "attorney in fact for Eliphas Douglass [Eliphaz Douglas]." GW and his agents thus obtained the signatures of eighteen proprietors of land within the federal district, constituting most of the landowners within the proposed Federal City exclusive of Hamburgh and Carrollsburgh. Landowners Joseph Coombs, Jr., and Enoch and Thomas Jenkins did not subscribe to the agreement. At the time of their signings, Prout had only a bond for a conveyance, and Carr had not received a conveyance. The title to the land claimed by Douglas was most clouded of all. His fifty-acre tract on the east side of the proposed city had belonged to his father, a Glasgow merchant named Robert Douglas, but was confiscated by Maryland during the Revolution. See Robert Douglas to GW, 15 April 1791. The completed agreement with all of the signatures apparently was deposited with the commissioners.

According to the terms of the separate agreement GW completed on 30 Mar., the proprietors of Carrollsburgh lots would be compensated for permitting the Federal City to be laid out on their lands. Each would receive half as many Federal City lots as they had claimed in Carrollsburgh, and their new lots would be located as close to their existing lots as consistent with the city plan. Those who owned only one Carrollsburgh lot would receive half the proceeds from the sale of a comparable lot in the new city. This separate agreement was signed by Thomas Johnson, Daniel Carroll of Duddington, William Bayly, Deakins, and Young. Young also signed on behalf of Mary Young and Charles Carroll, and Daniel Carroll of Duddington signed on behalf of Thomas Morton (DNA: RG 42, General Records, Letters Received, 1791–1867). Both of these agreements were ratified by an act of the Maryland general assembly passed on 19 Dec. 1791 (Kilty, *Laws of Maryland*, chap. 45).

From François de Bruyeres

Crest, France, 30 March 1791. Recommends "M. Le Chevr Vaumane de Fonclaire, who after having served in the German War as an Officer of Dragoons in the french Service was disbanded at the peace. He is yet young, without estate or fortune, he goes to America to endeavour to obtain them by some honest means" and "has fixed his residence in the City of Johnstown."[1]

Translation, DNA: RG 59, Miscellaneous Letters; ALS, in French, DNA: RG 59, Miscellaneous Letters. Text is taken from translation prepared for GW; receiver's copy appears in CD-ROM:GW.

François-Pons-Laurent-Louis, baron de Bruyeres de St. Michel (b. 1729), was maréchal of the French army in 1784 and commander at Crest, in Dauphiné, in 1790. He later joined the counterrevolutionary army of the emigré princes and died abroad.

1. The 1790 federal census listed a John Vonde Fonclair as living in Caughnawaga Town, Montgomery County, N.Y., with four other free white males and two white females (*Heads of Families* [New York], 103).

Proclamation

[Georgetown, Md.] Mar. 30. 1791.

Whereas by a proclamation bearing date the 24th day of January of this present year, & in pursuance of certain acts of the States of Maryland & Virginia, & of the Congress of the U.S. therein mentioned, certain lines of experiment were directed to be run in the neighbourhood of George town in Maryland for the purpose of determining the location of a part of the territory of 10. miles square for the permanent seat of the government of the U.S. & a certain part was directed to be located within the said lines of experiment on both sides of the Potomac & above the limit of the Eastern branch prescribed by the sd act of Congress:

And Congress by an amendatory act, passed on the 3d day of the present month of March, have given further authority to the President of the U.S. "to make any part of the territory below the said limit & above the mouth of Hunting creek, a part of the said district, so as to include a convenient part of the Eastern branch, & of the lands lying of the lower side thereof, & also the town of Alexandria."

Now therefore for the purpose of amending & completing the location of the whole of the said territory of the ten miles square in conformity with the said amendatory act of Congress, I do hereby declare & make known that the whole of the said territory shall be located & included within the four lines following, that is to say:

Beginning at Jones's point, being the upper cape of Hunting creek in Virginia, & at an angle in the outset of 45. degrees West of North: & running in a direct line ten miles for the first line: then beginning again at the same Jones's point, and running another direct line at a right angle with the first across the Potomack, ten miles for the second line: then from the terminations of the said first & second lines, running two other direct lines of ten miles each, the one crossing the Eastern branch aforesaid, & the other the Potomac, & meeting each other in a point.

And I do accordingly direct the Commissioners named under the authority of the said first mentioned act of Congress, to proceed forthwith to have the said four lines run, & by proper metes and bounds defined & limited, & thereof to make due report under their hands & seals: and the territory so to be located, defined & limited, shall be the whole territory accepted by the said acts of Congress as the district for the permanent seat of the government of the U.S.[1]

In testimony whereof I have caused the seal of the U.S. to be affixed to these presents, & signed the same with my hand. Done at Georgetown aforesaid the 30th day of March in the year of our Lord 1791. and of the Independence of the U.S. the fifteenth.

LB, DLC:GW; Df, in Thomas Jefferson's hand, DNA: RG 59, Miscellaneous Letters.

For background to this document, see GW to Jefferson, 2 Jan. 1791, editorial note. GW forwarded the proclamation to Jefferson on 31 Mar. for publication.

1 At this point in his draft, Jefferson included the following paragraph, which was struck through: "And Whereas the sd first mentioned act of Congress did further enact that the said Commissioners should, under the direction of the President of the U.S. provide suitable buildings for the accomodation of Congress & of the President & for the public offices of the government of the United States; I do hereby further declare & make known, that [the highest summit of lands in the town heretofore called Hamburg, within the said territory, with a convenient extent of grounds circumjacent, shall be appropriated for a Capitol for the accomodation of Congress, and such other lands between George town and the stream heretofore called the Tyber, as shall on due examination be found convenient and sufficient, shall be appropriated for the accomodation of the President of the United States for the time being, and for the public offices of the government of the U.S.] And I do hereby direct the sd commissioners accordingly." At the bottom of the page, Jefferson added the note: "The part within [   ] being conjectural, will be to be rendered conformable to the ground when more accurately examined."

To Thomas Jefferson

Dear Sir,   Mount-Vernon March 31st 1791.

Having been so fortunate as to reconcile the contending interests of Georgetown and Carrollsburg, and to unite them in such an agreement as permits the public purposes to be carried into effect on an extensive and proper scale, I have the pleasure to transmit to you the enclosed proclamation, which after annexing your counter signature and the seal of the United States, you will cause to be published.[1]

The terms agreed on between me, on the part of the United

States, with the Landholders of George town and Carrollsburg are. That all the land from Rock creek along the river to the eastern-branch and so upwards to or above the Ferry including a breadth of about a mile and a half, the whole containing from three to five thousand acres is ceded to the public, on condition That, when the whole shall be surveyed and laid off as a city, (which Major L'Enfant is now directed to do) the present Proprietors shall retain every other lot—and, for such part of the land as may be taken for public use, for squares, walks, &ca—they shall be allowed at the rate of Twenty five pounds per acre— The Public having the right to reserve such parts of the wood on the land as may be thought necessary to be preserved for ornament &ca. The Landholders to have the use and profits of all their ground until the city is laid off into lots, and sale is made of those lots which, by this agreement, become public property. No compensation is to be made for the ground that may be occupied as streets or alleys.

To these conditions all the principal Landholders except the purchaser of Slater's property who did not attend have subscribed, and it is not doubted that the few, who were not present, will readily assent thereto: even the obstinate Mr Burns has come into the measure.[2] The enlarged plan of this agreement having done away the necessity and indeed postponed the propriety, of designating the particular spot, on which the public buildings should be placed, until an accurate survey and subdivision of the whole ground is made, I have left out that paragraph of the proclamation.

It was found, on running the lines that the comprehension of Bladensburg within the district, must have occasioned the exclusion of more important objects—and of this I am convinced as well by my own observation as Mr Ellicott's opinion.[3] With great regard and esteem I am dear Sir Your most Obedient Servant

Go: Washington

LS, DLC: Thomas Jefferson Papers; Df, DNA: RG 59, Miscellaneous Letters; LB, DLC:GW.

1. The enclosed final version of the proclamation, presumably based on the draft prepared by Jefferson that GW probably took with him from Philadelphia, has not been found.

2. Jonathan Slater had recently sold his 500-acre plantation, which ran along the east side of Jenkins Hill to the Eastern Branch, for £20 an acre to William Prout, an Englishman who had established himself as a merchant in

Baltimore. GW sent an express rider for Prout, who probably assumed that his new property would not be included in the city itself and apparently met with GW at Mount Vernon before 7 April 1791, when the president resumed his Southern Tour and recommenced making entries in his diary. Prout wrote to his brother in England that "the President treated me with the greatest politeness," and he did add his name to the agreement (quoted in Arnebeck, *Through a Fiery Trial*, 45, 47). On negotiations with David Burnes, see GW's letter to William Deakins, Jr., and Benjamin Stoddert, 28 Feb. 1791.

3. Jefferson's proposed shift would have excluded a portion of the land west and northwest of Alexandria that GW specifically wished to include in the district. See GW to Jefferson, 2 Jan., editorial note, and Jefferson's memorandum to GW, 11 Mar. 1791.

From Henry Knox

Sir,   War Department [Philadelphia], 31st March 1791

I had the honor to inform you on the 27th of the murder of certain friendly Indians at the Big beaver Creek, on the 9th instant.

I enclose a Proclamation of the Governor of this State, relative to that affair. I assured him of the readiness of the General Government, to pay the reward offered upon the conviction of the Offenders. The Governor has directed the Magistrates to make inquisition into the transaction; and to transmit Affidavits thereon—Upon the receipt of proper Affidavits and finding the affair as has been stated, he will demand the Offenders.[1]

I have written to Major Genl St Clair to take every step to avert the evil consequences of this murder of the Indians, by sending for the Relations of the deceased, and the Chiefs of the tribes to which they belonged, and making ample satisfaction for the loss of property sustained.[2]

But it is to be exceedingly apprehended, that the wound will not be easily healed. For on the 18th instant, the Indians killed one Man and took three Prisoners besides horses, within two miles of Fort-Pitt, on the west side of the Allegheny River.

The Cornplanter writes me from Fort-Pitt on the 20th instant, and thinks the indians who committed this mischief, were those who escaped from Big beaver on the 9th instant, and that they belonged to the Delawares.

The Cornplanter's assurances are highly friendly—He had sent Big-tree off on that day to the Miami Indians—and was to set off the next day, accompanied by Lieutt Jeffers for his own

Country. I am glad Mr Jeffers accompanies him; as it will serve to strengthen his friendship, and may prevent his being injured by any of our parties.

The Governor of this State has this day requested the loan of Two hundred Arms and a proportional quantity of Ammunition, at Fort Pitt for the Militia, with which I readily complied in your behalf.[3]

I shall not be able to give any account of the success of recruiting either the Levies or Regulars until next week, but the Reports are good.

Arrangements are made for the supply of the Levies, both at Winchester, and Hagers Town, with Rations; and as soon as I shall receive the information of the Officers, the recruiting service in Virginia, and Maryland shall commence. I have the honor to be Sir, With the highest respect, Your Obedit Servt

H. Knox
Secy of War

LS, DLC:GW; LB, DLC:GW.

For the background to this letter, see Seneca Chiefs to GW, 17 Mar., and Henry Knox to GW, 27 Mar. 1791.

1. Thomas Mifflin's proclamation of 29 Mar. 1791, issued upon Knox's request, reads: "Whereas I have received authentic information, that on the ninth Instant, a body of armed men entered the territory of this Commonwealth, and, in a Lawless and unprovoked manner attacked a party of Friendly Indians who were peaceably Assembled for the purposes of Trade, at a Block House on the West side of Beaver Creek, in the County of Allegany and then and there murdered three Men and one woman belonging to the said party of Indians, and Committed divers other Acts of violence and Plunder. And whereas The Honor and reputation of the Government, the Peace and security of its Citizens, and the obligations of Justice and Humanity require, that the perpetrators of an Offence so atrocious should be speedily discovered and severely punished, I have therefore thought it proper to issue this Proclamation, hereby offering a Reward of one thousand dollars to any person or persons who shall cover apprehend and secure the Men, or any of them, who were guilty of the murders aforesaid to be paid upon conviction of the said Murders, or any of them. Hereby Further requiring and Commanding all Judges Justices, Sheriffs, Coroners, Constables and other officers, according to the duties of their respective Offices and Stations to be vigilent in enquiring after and bringing the said murderers, and every of them to Justice" (*Pa. Archives*, 9th ser., 1 [pt. 1], 57).

2. See Knox to Maj. Gen. Arthur St. Clair, 28 Mar. 1791 (*ASP, Indian Affairs*, 1:174).

3. For Knox's compliance with Mifflin's request, see *Pa. Archives*, 9th ser., 1 (pt. 1), 59.

From Tobias Lear

Sir,   Philadelphia March 31st 1791

Since I had the honor to write to you on the 27th Instant, nothing of a public nature, worthy notice, has come to my knowledge.

I have heard nothing yet from Mr Fraunces, and his son can give me no information relative to his coming. However, no inconvenience is felt at this time from the want of him; for as no large entertainments are now made, such arrangements are taken as render the keeping and delivery of such things as are consumed in the family—very convenient and infinitely more œconomical than has hitherto been the case. Mr & Mrs Hyde have left the family. They talk of taking a house a small distance from the City, and keeping a tavern. I think they now see very fully their folly in quitting the family. But as it regards your interest I am pursuaded it is best that they have done it.

We have not had the pleasure to hear from you since your crossing the Bay, but are in hopes that the Post of this evening will give us accounts of your safe arrival either at Annapolis or George-Town. Mrs Lear unites in sentiments of respect veneration & affection for you, with, Sir, Your Obliged & very humb. Sert

                                                    Tobias Lear.

ALS, DLC:GW; ALS (letterpress copy), PWacD.

To the Emperor of Morocco

Great and magnanimous Friend.   [31 March 1791]

Separated by an immense Ocean from the more ancient Nations of the Earth, and little connected with their Politics or Proceedings, we are late in learning the Events which take place among them, and later in conveying to them our Sentiments thereon.

The Death of the late Emperor, your Father and our Friend, of glorious Memory, is one of those Events which, though distant, attracts our Notice and Concern. Receive, great and good Friend, my sincere Sympathy with you on that Loss; and permit me at the same Time to express the Satisfaction with which I learn the Accession of so worthy a Successor to the Imperial Throne of Morocco, and to offer you the Homage of my sincere Congratulations. May the Days of your Majesty's Life be many and glorious, and may they ever mark the Aera during which a great People shall have been most prosperous and happy under the best and happiest of Sovereigns.

The late Emperor, very soon after the Establishment of our Infant Nation, manifested his royal Regard and Amity to us by many friendly and generous Acts, and particularly by the Protection of our Citizens in their Commerce with his Subjects. And as a further Instance of his Desire to promote our Prosperity and Intercourse with his Realms, he entered into a Treaty of Amity and Commerce with us, for himself and his Successors, to continue Fifty Years. The Justice and Magnanimity of your Majesty leave us full of Confidence, that the Treaty will meet your royal Patronage also; and it will give me great Satisfaction to be assured, that the Citizens of the United States of America may expect from your Imperial Majesty the same Protection and Kindness, which the Example of your Illustrious Father has taught them to expect from those who occupy the Throne of Morocco, and to have your Royal Word, that they may count on a due Observance of the Treaty which connects the two Nations in Friendship.

This will be delivered to your Majesty by our faithful Citizen Thomas Barclay, whom I name Consul for these United States in the Dominions of your Majesty, and who to the Integrity and Knowledge qualifying him for that Office, unites the peculiar Advantage of having been the Agent through whom our Treaty with the late Emperor was received. I pray your Majesty to protect him in the Exercise of his Functions for the patronage of the Commerce between our two Countries, and of those who carry it on. May that God, whom we both adore, bless your Imperial Majesty with long life, Health, and Success, and have you always, great and magnanimous Friend, under his holy keeping. Written at Philadelphia the Thirty first Day of March, in the Fifteenth Year of our Sovereignty and Independence, from Your good and faithful Friend

> Go: Washington
> By the President
> Th: Jefferson.

DS, anonymous donor; letterpress copy, DLC: Thomas Jefferson Papers; copy, DNA: RG 59, Credences.

For background to this letter, see Jefferson to GW, 27 Mar. 1791 and note 1.

To William Deakins, Jr., and Benjamin Stoddert

Gentn,   Mount Vernon April 1st 1791.

Being accustomed to write to you respecting the grounds for the fedl City, I continue the practice.

It may be tuesday or wednesday next before I shall leave this place, by which (say by mondays Post) I should be glad to hear what progress has been made, and what still remains to be done, in the business which so happily commenced on tuesday last under the accommodating spirit which then prevailed.

The subscription paper has been, I presume, deposited in the hands of the Commissioners, for the purpose of drawing conveyances—I should be glad nevertheless to receive a copy of it with the names of the subscribers annexed thereto for my own satisfaction—The general tenor of the agreement was I well remember pleasing to me, and, in my opinion reciprocally beneficial to *all* the parties, but I do not now recollect with precision whether it is fully expressed that the lots left to the disposal of the several proprietors by the conditions of their grants are subject to *all* the rules and regulations (with respect to the buildings &ca &ca) as the public ones are. This unquestionably ought to be the case—it was evidently my meaning that they *should* be so—and unless it is so, one of the great objects—to wit—uniformity and beauty—may be defeated.[1]

The Mail of Wednesday brought me a letter from Mr Jefferson dated the 27th ulto in which is the following paragraph "A bill was yesterday ordered to be brought into the house of representatives here for granting a sum of money for building a federal-hall, house for the President &c." This (though I do not wish that it should be expressed as my sentiment) unfolds most evidently the views of P——, at the same time that it proves in a striking manner the propriety of the measure adopted by the Georgetown and Carrollsburgh proprietors on wednesday last— as also the necessity of their *compleating* the good work they have begun in a speedy, and in an effectual manner that the con-

sequent arrangements may take place without delay. with esteem & regard I am—Gentn Yr obedt Hble Servt

Go: Washington

ADfS, DLC:GW; LB, DLC:GW.
   1. See Agreement of the Proprietors of the Federal District, 30 Mar. 1791.

Letter not found: from Fenwick, Mason, & Co., 1 April 1791. On 7 July
Tobias Lear referred Fenwick, Mason, & Co. to the firm's letters to
GW "of the 9th of July and 10th of August 1790, and of the 1st of
April 1791."

To Thomas Jefferson

Dear Sir,   Mount Vernon, April 1st 1791
   I have had the pleasure to receive your letter of the 27th ult.
with the papers which accompanied it.
   Referring to your Judgment whether a commission, similar to
that intended for Mr Barclay, may be given without the agency
of the Senate, I return both papers to you signed, in order that
the one you deem most proper may be used.
   Your opinions respecting the acts of force which have already
taken place, or may yet take place on our boundaries, meet my
concurrence, as the safest mode of compelling propositions to
an amicable settlement and it may answer a good purpose to
have them suggested in the way you mention. Should this matter assume a serious aspect during my absence I beg you to communicate particulars with all possible dispatch.[1]
   The most superb edifices may be erected, and I shall wish
their inhabitants much happiness, and that too very disinterest-
edly, as I shall never be of the number myself.[2]
   It will be fortunate for the American public if private Speculations in the lands, still claimed by the Aborigines, do not aggre-
vate those differences, which policy, humanity, and justice concur to deprecate.
   I am much indebted to your kind concern for my safety in
travelling—no accident has yet happened either from the high
hanging of the carriage, or the mode of driving—The latter I
must continue as my Postilion (Giles) is still too much indisposed
to ride the journey.

It occurs to me that you may not have adverted to Judge Putman's being in the Western Country at present. Perhaps General Knox can furnish you with the Maps you want, or they may be found among those that are in my study in Philadelphia.

I expect to leave Mount Vernon, in prosecution of my Southern tour, on tuesday or wednesday next—I shall halt one day at Fredericksburgh and two at Richmond—thence I shall proceed to Charlestown by the way of Petersburg, Halifax, Tarborough, Newbern, Wilmington, & George Town, without making any halts between Richmond & Charleston but such as may be necessary to accommodate my journey.[3] I am sincerely and affectionately Yours

Go: Washington

ALS, DLC: Thomas Jefferson Papers; DfS, DNA: RG 59, Miscellaneous Letters; LB, DLC:GW.

1. For Jefferson's report on difficulties with British troops on the Lake Champlain border, see Jefferson to GW, 5 June 1791.

2. GW is alluding to buildings the state of Pennsylvania intended to erect in Philadelphia for the use of the federal government. See Jefferson to GW, 27 Mar. 1791, n.5, and GW to the Commissioners for the Federal District, 3 April 1791.

3. For GW's route, see Itinerary for the Southern Tour, February 1791, editorial note.

To Henry Knox

Sir,   Mount-Vernon April 1st 1791

Your letter of the 27th Ultimo was received last evening. Your proceeding upon the intelligence therein contained (which I think truly alarming) meets my entire approbation, and appears to promise as good effects as the limited sphere of action, allotted to the general government, in cases so deeply effecting its dignity and the happiness of the citizens will allow.

Should you suppose that additional instructions to General St Clair or any other measures within the reach of propriety may have a tendency to appease the friends of the murdered Indians, I wish you to confer with the Heads of departments and to carry into immediate effect the result of your deliberation.

The letters which have already been written to you, on the subject of officering the Maryland and Virginia battalions of levies will shew the difficulties produced by Colonel Lee's declining; and the necessity of exertion to repair the delay which it must occasion.[1]

I shall endeavour to obtain information of some officers for the Virginia battalion—but it will not be possible for me to act upon it until I learn what may be determined between you and Colonel Hall—indeed it is my wish as it regards dispatch, that your determination, may render any future interference on my part unnecessary.

To prevent clashing in the measures we may adopt to officer the battalion of this State, if any thing satisfactory results from my enquiry, I will give immediate information of it. I am Sir Your obedt Servt

G.W.

Df, in William Jackson's hand, DLC:GW; LB, DLC:GW.

1. For Henry Lee's declination of the command of the Virginia regiment of temporary levies, see Henry Knox to GW, 27 Mar. 1791.

From Tobias Lear

Sir,   Philadelphia April 1st 1791.

I was, by the post of last evening, honored with your letters of the 27th & 28th Ultimo and the enclosures contained in the latter.

We have not yet received any account of Fraunces. As measures were taken before your departure, to give him an opportunity of coming again into the family if he chose to accede to the terms & conditions upon which he might return, nothing has since been done towards engaging any particular person until we learn somthing further from Fraunces. But I have not failed to pursue my inquiries in a general way whenever opportunities have offered. Nothing has transpired respecting Holker's man; and no applications have lately been made that have the least prospect of answering the purpose. Should Fraunces not incline to comply with the stipulations which will be made for his coming, I shall then pursue the object without relaxation until a proper person & one in whom Mrs Washington fully concurs and can confide, is obtained. As much in the way of œconomy and regularity in the family will depend upon a *good Housekeeper,* no pains will be spared to get such an one. Mrs Washington being better acquainted with the qualifications requisite in such a person than I am, her judgment must be my guide in whatever I may do towards obtaining this Character. We need not be in haste to fix upon persons unless such should offer as may appear to be in every respect properly qualified: for in the present state of the family we feel no particular want of such persons. To obtain them before your return will be the only wish, in point of time that we have.

The Boxes &c. which were in the Garden were all removed the day after your departure, and from that time to this there has been a man employed in the Garden (sent by Mr Morris, and Mrs Washington tells me by your desire, you having informed Mr Morris that it would be at *your expense*) in trimming the trees—putting in order the Borders—grass plats—walks &c. He says he shall complete everything tomorrow; and from that time I think it will be very hard if it cannot be kept in the nicest order by our own people. The top of the Urn which fell off (it was not broken, being annexed to the Urn by an iron spindle) is put on as before.[1]

I shall be particularly attentive to your directions relative to furnishing Mrs Washington with money; and I should be extremely unhappy, if she should have cause to apply to me through an inattention on my part in asking if it is wanted.

The Washer woman who was employed before Jacob's wife came into the House has been discharged[2]—and the woman in the Kitchen may be discharged also, there will be no want of one there at least before your return. But nothing can be expected from Richmond—he is an idle ignorant boy, and they tell me (I believe with truth) that he is of no manner of service there.

The Pad belonging to the Waggon harness is sent by the Stage of this morning—*The carriage of it is paid.* But as it will not reach Alexa. 'till monday evening, I presume you will hardly get it before you leave that part of the Country.[3]

I enclosed Colo. Blaine's letter to Genl Knox immediately upon receiving it, with the extract from your letter relating to it.

If Colo. Cannon comes to this place I shall say to him what you request—and what he appears richly to deserve.

Mrs Washington gave us a gloomy history from your letter, of your crossing the Bay.[4] Its termination without material damage brightened the scene which commenced in a pretty dark manner. We had a very severe thunder-gust here on Thursday evening, and were not without our apprehensions that you might be crossing the Bay at that time, which proved too true. The failure of your horses or a part of them will be a serious inconvenience. The high flesh & want of exercise previous to your depa⟨rture⟩ must have been a great disadvantage to them.

Mrs Washington has been pretty well since you left us—Nelly has been as usual—and Washington for several days past has been confined with a very severe cold, but is now recovering. Mrs Lear & our little boy are in fine health. She begs that her best respects may be presented to you. My friends at Mount Vernon and in its vicinity are remembered by me with affection and have my best wishes. I have the honor to be with the highest respect & most sincere attachment—Sir Your Obliged & very hble Sert

Tobias Lear.

ALS, DLC:GW.

1. Robert Morris owned GW's residence in Philadelphia. See GW to Tobias Lear, 5 Sept. 1790, n.4. His garden worker has not been identified.

2. Mary Helm, who became washerwoman after Mary Wilson was made a housemaid, was replaced by Mrs. Jacob Jacobus.

3. Lear paid fifty cents on 31 Mar. to Kerlin & Co. for shipping the pad to Alexandria (Decatur, *Private Affairs of George Washington*, 216).

4. GW's letter of 26 Mar. 1791 to Martha Washington has not been found.

To Hannah Fairfax Washington

My dear Madam,   Mount Vernon, April 1st 1791.

The letters with which you were pleased to honor me dated the 24th of February and 12th of March came duly to hand—The last at George-Town, the other at Philadelphia—but neither before arrangements had been taken (by letter) with the Supervisor of the Virginia District respecting the appointment of proper characters for collecting the duty on ardent Spirits and Stills.[1]

At all times it would give me pleasure, as far as is consistent with my public duty, to comply with any request or wish of yours—To fill offices with characters best qualified to discharge the duties thereof (as far as I am able to judge of them) must

always be the primary motive to every appointment with me—
When, happily, such considerations as you have urged in favor
of Mr Norton can be combined therewith it would be highly
pleasing to my mind to give them their due weight—but, as I
have just observed, measures had been taken previous to the
receipt of either of your letters for fixing on proper persons as
receivers of the above duties—how far the choice of them is
made I am unable to inform you.[2]

Mrs Washington, I can answer for it, will be much pleased by
your friendly recollection of her—and if we should once more
enjoy in retirement this peaceful mansion, it would add to the
pleasures of it to see you under its roof. I will not conclude without offering my condolence on the occasion of your late loss—
and the strongest assurances of the affecte regard, with which I
am &ca

G.W.

LB, DLC:GW.

Hannah Fairfax Washington (1742–1804) of Fairfield, Clarke County, Va.,
was the daughter of William Fairfax of Belvoir and sister to GW's friend
George William Fairfax. In 1764 she married GW's first cousin Warner Washington (b. 1722), who died on 23 June 1790.

1. Hannah Washington's letters of 24 Feb. and 12 Mar. 1791 to GW recommended George Flowerdew Norton (b. 1751) of Winchester, Va., for a position
in the excise service (DLC:GW). Edmund Pendleton also recommended Norton to GW, on 9 April: "the mercantile Assistance of the House [John Norton &
Sons] (of which this Gentn was a member) to the State, has been signal &
beneficial. The first Instance was before the dispute with Britain, when,
through their Agency, Mr Nicholas defeated a combination of the Merchants
here to depreciate our old paper on the death of Mr Robinson. In the Fall of
1774, their Ship (instead of being loaded with tobacco, which would have been
a proffitable remittance & considerable diminution of their debts here that
have been ever since a dead stock & may be finally lost) narrowly escaped
being burnt, & was compelled to sail empty, or what was nearly equal, because
some tea had made part of a Cargoe imported in her for a Native Merchant,
ordered before, & not countermanded after the Association. Notwithstanding
this stroke from the intemperance of the times, the very next year in Our
necessity & anxiety for powder, that House, Advanced £5600. Sterling to procure us that Article, wch money being repaid here in depreciated paper when
there was no mean of remittance, was in a manner ⟨j⟩unk to them." Pendleton
added that after his father's death, Norton "resolved to remove wth the Family
to this his native Countrey, but being obliged to accomplish it through the
British West Indies, the death of his worthy mother, & loss of considerable
property there were added to the other misfortunes of the Family, so that on
his Arrival he was reduced to depend for Subsistance principally on a list of

outstanding debts, the stability of which, even if their payment could have been legally inforced, your excellency is too well acquainted with to need information, and will I am sure commend him (who had been accustomed to & had reason to expect a State of ease & plenty if not of Opulence) for wishing by some honest emploiment, to place himself in a less precarious situation" (DLC:GW). GW replied to Pendleton on 14 April.

2. Norton himself wrote GW on 19 Feb.: "You must well remember Sir, that my Father, Brother & Self at the commencement of the late war with Great Britain advanced to this State a loan of £5,600 Sterling at the peril of our lives and fortunes which Sum I actually accepted the bills drawn for by Mr Ro: C. Nicholas, and paid the amount—Since which I returned to this Country with the relicks of my family, in very reduced Circumstances indeed, totally out of the line of business I have been bred to, & owing to some unfortunate Circumstances that have attended me, I am renderd incapable of resuming my former station in life" and referred GW to Edmund Randolph for his "moral and political Character" (DLC:GW).

From John Baptista Ashe

Halifax, N.C., 2 April 1791. Introduces Benjamin Easley, a cadet in Captain Montfort's company, who "flatters himself with filling" an ensigncy in the U.S. Army, and recommends his "Merit, and Abilities, equal to doing honor to the profession."[1]

ALS, DNA: RG 59, Miscellaneous Letters.

1. Joseph Montfort wrote GW, from Chesterfield Court House, N.C., on 11 April: "the Company under my Command has a long March before them that there is but one Officer beside Myself & that to our usual duty the secretary has enjoined that of supplying ourselves with provision & forrage on the March" and requested GW to appoint Benjamin Easley "to do the duty of Ensign until the further pleasure of Congress is known," or at least to permit him to employ Easley in purchasing their supplies on the march (DNA: RG 59, Miscellaneous Letters). William Jackson replied to Montfort on 13 April that GW "commands me to inform you that he is not now here for the purpose of making appointments—and to observe to you that your orders from the Secretary of war must be obeyed with promptitude and punctuality" (DLC:GW). Easley received no commission from GW but was appointed a captain in the U.S. Army in 1800 (*Executive Journal*, 1:343, 355).

From Thomas Jefferson

Sir   Philadelphia Apr. 2. 1791.
I had the honor of addressing you on the 27th Ult. since which letters are received of Jan. 26. from mister Carmichael,

and of Jan. 3. & 15. Madrid, and Feb. 6. and 12. Lisbon from
Colo. Humphreys. as these are interesting and may tend to settle
suspense of mind to a certain degree I shall trouble you with
quotations from some parts & the substance of others.[1]

Colo. H. says "I learn from other good authority, as well as
from mister Carmichael, that all the representations of Gardoqui (when minister in America) tended to excite a belief that the
most respectable & influential people throughout the U.S. did
not wish to have the navigation of the Missisipi opened for years
to come, from an apprehension such event would weaken the
government & impoverish the Atlantic states by emigrations. it
was even pretended that none but a handful of settlers on the
Western waters & a few inhabitants of the Southern states would
acquiesce in the measure." this is the state of mind to which they
have reverted since the crisis with England is passed, for during
that the Count de Florida Blanca threw out general assertions
that we should have no reason to complain of their conduct with
respect to the Missisipi; which gave rise to the report it's navigation was opened.[2] the following passages will be astonishing to
you who recollect that there was not a syllable in your letters to
mister G.M. which looked in the most distant manner to Spain.
Mr Carmichael says "something however might have been done
in a moment of projects & apprehension had not a certain negociation carried on on our part at London, transpired, & which
I think was known here rather from British policy than from the
vigilance of the Marquis del Campo. entirely unacquainted with
this manoeuvre, although in correspondence with the person
employed I was suspected to be in the secret. this suspicion banished confidence, which returns by slow degrees. this circumstance induced me to drop entirely my correspondence with
G.M. to continue it would have done harm, & certainly could do
no good. I have seen extracts of the President's letter communicated to the Duke of Leeds, perhaps mutilated or forged to serve
here the views of the British cabinet. I do not yet despair of
obtaining copies of those letters through the same channel that
I procured the first account of the demands of G.B. & the signature of the late convention." Colo. Humphreys says "the minister
had intimations from del Campo of the conferences between
mister Morris & the Duke of Leeds, which occasioned him to
say with warmth to mister Carmichael now is your time to make
a treaty with England. Fitzherbert availed himself of these con-

ferences to create apprehensions that the Americans would aid
his nation in case of war." your genuine letter could have made
no impression. the British court then must have forged one, to
suit their purpose, & I think it will not be amiss to send a genuine copy to Carmichael, to place our faith on it's just ground.
the principal hope of doing any thing now, is founded, either on
an expected removal of the count de F.B. from the ministry, in
which case persons will be employed who are more friendly to
America, or to the bursting out of that fire which both gentlemen think but superficially covered. Mr Carmichael justifies
himself by the interception of his letters. he has shewn the originals to Colo. H. he concludes his present letter with these words.
"relying on the good opinion of me that you have been pleased
to express on many occasions, I intreat you to engage the President to permit me to return to my native country." Colo. Humphreys on the subjects of his justification & return says (after
speaking of the persons likely to come into power) "mister Carmichael being on terms of intimacy with the characters here, is
certainly capable of effecting more at this court than any other
American. he is heartily desirous of accomplishing the object in
view at all events, & fully determined to return to America in
12. or 18. months at farthest. he has expressed that intention
repeatedly. to be invested with full powers, perhaps he would be
able to do something before his departure from the continent"
in his letter of Jan. 15. he says "mister Carmichael's ideas are
just: his exertions will be powerful & unremitting to obtain the
accomplishment of our desires before his departure from this
country. the task will now be difficult if not impracticable." in
that of Feb. 6. he says. "Mr Carmichael is much mortified that
so many of his dispatches have miscarried. by the original documents, which I have seen in his hands I am convinced he has
been extremely assiduous & successful in procuring early & authentic intelligence. it is difficult for a person at a distance to
form an adequate judgement of the embarrasments to which a
public man, situated as he was, is subjected, in making written
communications, from such an inland place, & under such a
jealous government. he appears disgusted with the country &
the mode of life he is compelled to lead. he desires ardently to
return to his native land; but he wishes to distinguish himself
first by rendering some essential service to it if possible."
   I propose to write to mister Carmichael that your absence pre-

vents my asking the permission he desires, that as it is natural he should wish to do something which may make favorable impressions here before his return & an opportunity is now offered him, I will suspend asking his recall till I hear further from him.

Governour Quesada, by order of his court, is inviting foreigners to go & settle in Florida.[3] this is meant for our people. debtors take advantage of it & go off with their property. our citizens have a right to go where they please. it is the business of the states to take measures to stop them till their debts are paid. this done, I wish a hundred thousand of our inhabitants would accept the invitation. it will be the means of delivering to us peaceably, what may otherwise cost us a war. in the mean time we may complain of this seduction of our inhabitants just enough to make them believe we think it very wise policy for them, & confirm them in it. this is my idea of it. I have the honour to be with sentiments of the most perfect respect & attachment, Sir, your most obedt & most humble sert

Th: Jefferson

ALS, DNA: RG 59, Miscellaneous Letters; ALS (letterpress copy), DLC: Thomas Jefferson Papers; LB, DLC:GW.

1. Jefferson is probably referring to William Carmichael's letter of 24 Jan. (*Jefferson Papers*, 18:597–600). See also ibid., 472–75, 497–98, 19:254–56, 270–71, for David Humphreys to Jefferson, 3, 15 Jan., and 6, 12 Feb. 1791.

2. For the administration's attempt during the Nootka Sound crisis to negotiate with Spain its recognition of America's right to the free navigation of the Mississippi River, see Jefferson to GW, 8 Aug. 1790, source note and note 1.

3. For American protests against the Spanish policy of allowing debtors, criminals, and runaway slaves to take refuge in Florida, see GW to James Seagrove, 20 May 1791 and notes 1 and 2.

From Thomas Ustick

Philadelphia, 2 April 1791. Has left a package at the presidential residence that Isaac Backus requested him to deliver to GW.[1]

ALS, DLC:GW.

Thomas Ustick (1753–1803) of New York City graduated from the College of Rhode Island (Brown University) in 1771 and studied theology in New York. He served as pastor of the First Baptist Church of Philadelphia from 1782 until shortly before his death.

1. For the enclosures from Isaac Backus, see Backus to GW, 15 Nov. 1790 and note 5.

From Robert Ballard

Sir   Balt[imore] April 3d 1791.

I discover by the Act of Congress for laying an Additional duty on Forriegn Spirits and Spirits Distilled in the U.S.—and that your Excellency & the Supervisor are to make appointments for carrying into effect the Services the Act requires to be performed. and furthermore that your Exellency may appoint such Officers of the Custom's as may seem Proper to you. I am therefore humbly to sollicit your Exellency's favor in granting and giving me the appointment of superintending and performing the duties for the Port of Baltimore agreeable to Law.[1]

I have not had time to peruse the Law with strict attention, but I observe that the duties to be performed, will come more immediately under the Observation of the surveyor in Sea Port Town's, than any other Person; he, being constantly employed on the Water & Wharfs. If Sir, I have read the Law right, the Supervisor makes appointments for the home made Spirits. In this Town at present there are only two both immediately on the Water; by each I pass in my Barge four times a day—the Duty to be performed there like wise come natural and easy for the Surveyor, and at the same time, save the Additional expence of another Boat and hands. Your kindness in giving me the Surveyors Place for this District will make a lasting impression on my mind, and I hope to merit by my works the good opinion of your Excellency. I beg to observe that altho⟨'⟩ I am pleased with the Office your Excellency has intrusted to my care, yet the Emoluments fall short of maintaining my family. My only wish *now* is to live to maintain my house full of Boys, give them an Education and make them usefull Citizens. I have the Honor to be with the greatest respect Your Excellency's Most Obedt hum. Servt

Robert Ballard

ALS, DLC:GW.

1. Robert Ballard, whom GW had previously named surveyor for the port of Baltimore, was appointed excise inspector during the recess of Congress. His appointment was confirmed by the Senate on 8 Mar. 1792 (*Executive Journal*, 104, 111). For Ballard's later complaints about the inadequacy of his compensation, see his letter to GW, 4 Sept. 1791.

To the Commissioners for the Federal District

Gentlemen,   Mount Vernon April 3d 1791

As the Instrument which was subscribed at George Town, by the Land holders in the vicinity of that place & Carrollsburg, was not given to me, I presume it has been deposited with you. It is of the greatest moment to close this business with the Proprietors of the lands on which the federal City is to be, that consequent arrangements may be made without more delay than can be avoided.[1]

The form of the conveyances as drawn by the Attorney General will, I presume, require alteration, or a counterpart, as the present agreement essentially differs from the former—If Mr Johnson could, conveniently undertake to prepare such a deed as he thinks would answer all the purposes, of the public and the Grantees, I am sure it would be effectually done. If this cannot be, then it might be well to furnish the Attorney-General of the United States with a copy of the agreement—with the papers I left with you—and such other information as will enable him to do it.[2]

To accomplish this matter so as that the Sales of the lots—the public buildings—&ca may commence with as much facility as the nature of the case will admit, would be, I conceive, advisable under any circumstances; perhaps the friends of the measure may think it materially so from the following extract of a letter from Mr Jefferson to me, dated the 27th Ult. "A Bill was yesterday ordered to be brought into the House of Representatives here for granting a sum of money for building a federal-hall, house of the President, &ca." This (though I do not want any sentiment of mine promulgated with respect to it) marks unequivocally in my mind, the designs of that state; and the necessity of exertion to carry the Residence Law into effect agreeably thereto. With great and sincere esteem & regards I am—Gentlemen Yr most Obedt Hble Servt

Go: Washington

ALS, DLC: Presidential MSS; ADf, DLC:GW; LB, DLC:GW; copy, DNA: RG 42, Records of the Commissioners for the District of Columbia, Letters Sent, 1791–1802. The draft and letter-book copy have "efficiently" for "effectually."

1. Shortly after signing the Agreement of the Proprietors of the Federal District of 30 Mar. 1791, Edward Peerce sold 150 acres of the Port Royal tract

northwest of the site of the White House to Georgetown merchant Samuel Davidson for $6,000 and a 500-acre farm north of Baltimore, and GW probably feared that other signatories would soon dispose of their lands to speculators. The sale was completed 2 May 1791 (Clark, "Origin of the Federal City," 90–91).

2. The former agreement to which GW refers was that made with Georgetown area landowners the previous fall. Edmund Randolph had prepared a form of conveyance for the lands given up by the Agreement of the Georgetown, Md., Property Owners of 13 Oct. 1790, but this form apparently did not suit the terms of the Agreement of the Proprietors of the Federal District of 30 Mar. 1791.

From Augustus Christian George Elholm

Sir. Natchez Aprl 3d 1791

As it is not to a singular Aptness nor the peculiar zeal! of a Suitor to wish I am indebted for the Progress in the Mathematics but to an indulged indefatigable Desire of finding or assertaining the Natural Opporation of the Causes from their Visible Effects! and sensible of Your Extensive Knowledge in this Science! and also from Experience that a Powerfull Share of an innate Sanguinity may lead us imperceptibly astray; and that the strenght of Our Reason can not be esteemed perfect, nor it's Decree inseparable from irror unless with Success it has Stood the Tryal by an infalible Judge! It is now first that the approved Axioms of Eucid's Elements Could Concquor My diffidence to render the Efforts of My Study known to You! and declare that I have discovered the Quadrature of the Circle heretofore Sought in Vain![1] and Solicit a Public Examination under the wings of Your influensive Patronage! and presence to give Lusture to So long hidden a Solution: a Discovery that will enable Skillfull Mathematicians to explain the Physicle Cause of the Obliguity of the Ecliptic with the Equator: the annual Revolution and Rotation of Our Globe! with other Phenomina—and as it is with greater endeavor if Greater can be than what acquired me the Sense of the honoble Congress Recorded on it's journal the 11th of May 1785 that I now address Your influence to give Sanction to a Public Utility;[2] Your Magnanimity Affords me the pleasing assurance that my Philosophic Toil Shall benefit from Your Love of Arts!

I here beg leave to refere You to the following Extract of a

Letter written to the honble Brigdr Genl Charles C. Pinckney viz:

"In the Cours of my above mentioned Study; I have happily discovered the true proportion between the Diametter, and it's Pheriphery: a Resolution that has ever been desired by the greatest Mathematicians but not expected to be found: Who therefore have Contented themselves with an approximation.

"I wish that a premium may be offered to him who Can solve this Problem! to Effect which I [k]now none redier in Your Government; nor supperiour in Intrest than Yourselve and Your Freinds; By doing this You will propose no useless Expence to Your fellow Citizens but on one hand give a Singular Proof: that the Western Spirit Conscious of it's Own Ability thinks no Problem within the Bounds of Human imagination unresolvable by Man! Whilst on the other You will advance an infalible Step to promode a usefull System to the World."

The Method Geomettrically, as well as by Calculation with exactness to give the Length of the imaginary Line that divides the Area; of a Circle from the Compliment of the Contents of it's Circumscribed Sqare promises a perfection in Astronomy, Gonery; Mechanism, and Navigation; and consequently Can no less Claim the attention of Yourselve, the Honble Senate, and Representitives than What it will Sooth the united Spirit in Your System.

To conclude I beg leave to repeat my incessent wish for a public Examination "that both the Learned And unlearned may See I do not avoit the judgment of any" by Submitting My discovery to the investigation of a Collected body of able Mathematicians, and the most popular Personage to preside.

It was thus Nicolas Copernicus Successfully dedicated his Astronomical knowledge to the Popular Pontiff Leo Xth Similar to Myself from a Remote Corner of the Earth.

I wish You health and peace and that you may live to the highest period of a Most desirable Age; at the head of a Wise Senate, a Spiritid and equally Patriotic House, of Representitives, and a powrfull united People! under the peculiar Care of heavn.[3]

Augstus Christn Geo: Elholm

ALS, DNA: RG 59, Miscellaneous Letters.

Augustus Christian George Elholm, a native of Schleswig-Holstein, served as a lieutenant in Pulaski's Legion from 1778 to 1781 and as a captain in the service of South Carolina from 1781 to the end of the Revolutionary War.

1. A solution to the problem of "squaring of the circle," which consists of constructing a square of the same area as a given circle using only a straight edge and compass, is impossible since it involves the square root of pi, a transcendental number.

2. The Confederation Congress on 11 May 1785 adopted, on the motion of Charles Pinckney, a resolution acknowledging and certifying Elholm's wartime services (*JCC*, 28:347).

3. Elholm added a postscript, dated 25 Oct. 1791: "Being informed by Your Secetary that he believes You have not Recieved neither the original nor the Duplicate I do myself the honor to send this (: from the Red Lion Brewer's alley [Philadelphia] :) which is Verbatim with the Original as near as My Memory permits. for I lost the Copy with my Bagage the 23d of june last, in consequence of Shipwrek. I have now nearly refinished the problems of the above Stated Solution."

To Tobias Lear

Dear Sir,   Mount Vernon April 3d 1791.

Since my last to you—from George Town—I have, I believe, received your letters of the 23d, 24th, & 27th ult.

Whether a certain Gentleman is the man I conceived him to be, or such a one as is hinted at in the letter you enclosed me, is not yet certain; but, admitting the latter, it is too late to look back.[1]—I cannot be in a less productive situation by the engagement than I was;—the principal disadvantage resulting from it will be, that I can never count upon the payments until they are actually made;—consequently, can never speculate upon the money which I wished to have done. —If I recollect rightly, there is something in Colo. Cannons letter (transmitted to you) concerning the Kanhaway lands—if it is indicative of an intention to let them, or, that he conceives himself empowered to do it, I desire you will inform him of the Sale of them.—[2]

You did well in forwarding the letters from the Western territory, although they were, upon opening of them, found to be laws only.—

Until we can restrain the turbulance and disorderly conduct of our own borderers it will be in vain I fear to expect peace with the Indians,—or that they will govern their own people better than we do our's.

Mr Jefferson's ideas with respect to the dispatches for me, is a very good one, & I desire it may be put into execution.[3]— I send you some letters to file, not finding it convenient to be encumbered with them on my journey.[4]—My best wishes attend Mrs Lear and I am Yr sincere friend and Affectionate Servant,

GO: WASHINGTON.

Letters from Washington to Lear, 24–25.

1. For Tobias Lear's letter and its enclosure concerning John Joseph de Barth, see Lear to GW, 23 Mar. 1791 and note 2. See also GW to George Clendenin, 21 March.

2. For John Cannon's letter to GW, see GW to Lear, 28 Mar. and note 1. See also Lear to GW, 10 April and note 1.

3. For Thomas Jefferson's ideas on reaching GW during the Southern Tour, see Lear to GW, 27 Mar. 1791.

4. The enclosures have not been identified.

From Tobias Lear

Sir,   Philadelphia April 3d 1791.

General Knox informed me that in consequence of Colo. Blaine's letter he had recommended it to Colo. Duer, the Contractor, to employ him in that Country in the way that he wishes, if Blaine will accept of a secondary part in the business of supplying the troops. But whether it will be done or not, was uncertain at the time of General Knox's mentioning the matter to me.[1]

As we have not yet heard anything from Fraunces, I informed his Son, last evening, that, unless he either came on, or it was ascertained that he would come by next thursday, there would be no obligation on your part to with-hold any longer engaging a suitable Character for Steward if any could be found who might be unexceptionable. After that time, if Fraunces does not come, I will endeavour to take such measures as will determine the point with respect to Holker's man. If he cannot be *unexceptionably* obtained, the best means that can be devised shall be used to get some other person qualified for the place.

I am sorry to say that the progress which Washington makes at his School by no means justifies the high Character given of that Seminary, nor in any degree answers the expectation which was formed of its excellence. I have lately taken several occasions to examine him, and have been surprized to find that he seems to have made no advances in the Latin since he left his instructor in New York. In reading & writing it is evident he has lost much, and as it was mentioned at the time of his entering that he would not be put to arithmetic, it is not to be wondered at now that he cannot tell 100 from 1000. From the accounts which I have heard for some time part of the dignity wanting in the immediate government of the College—and the little subordination among the boys, particularly in the School where Washington attends, I have been led to doubt whether all that advantage would result from placing him there which the flattering account gave reason to expect. So fully are Colo. Hamilton and the Attorney General impressed with the circumstance of their Sons making no progress there that they are determined to remove them. The former sends his son, tomorrow, to Mr [Joseph] Bend who has opened a private School, in which the number of Scholars is limited to 25. Whether the latter has determined to send his son there or elsewhere I do not know; but he says that he finds his son has lost rather than otherwise since his being at the College—and he is therefore determined upon removing him. My having understood that these Gentlemen intended to remove their sons, all due to the unfavourable accounts which I had heard from other quarters, put me upon making more particular inquiries into the State of things there—which inquiries have terminated in convincing me that there are just grounds for censure in the conduct of that Seminary. If dignity be wanting in the head it is absurd to expect that there will be a due respect paid to the subordinate parts—Dr S. has so little of it that he makes himself rediculous to the lowest boys in the Schools who do not hesitate to speak of him in the most disrespectful terms—there has been more than one instance lately of the subordinate masters being hissed by the boys—and one of them pelted with dirt and Stones as he came out of School. The number of boys in each School is likewise a great Objection. In that where Washington goes there are upwards of one hundred boys, to attend whom there are but two masters, besides the principal. This circumstance is in itself a strong objection to the boys making any great progress, for I do not beleive that any man, let his talents & industry be what they may, can do justice to more than twenty five scholars at a time.

I have thought it a duty incumbent on me, Sir, to be thus explicit on this subject with you; because as I consider this Child to be in some measure under my inspection in this respect in your absence, I should be justly liable to censure if I neglected to inform you of these circumstances which have come to my knowledge. I shall take an opportunity to inform Doctor Smith that the boy makes no progress, and must leave it to him to learn the cause of it until I have the honor to hear from you on the subject. Perhaps when it is found that members are leaving the School (which I am informed will be the case to the amount of 12 or 15 at least) new arrangements may be made and such measures taken as m[a]y ensure better management in future. Should this be the case, I am of opinion, as I ever have been, that it will be best for him to lay the foundation of his education in that Seminary where he may finish it. But if the present lax system is pursued I have no doubt but that he should be removed.[2]

As Dunlap's paper did not come yesterday I shall enclose the others of that date—and as there was an arrival in a short passage from Bristol yesterday after noon, I shall not close this letter 'till the last moment of the Mail in order that I may put in the papers of tomorrow morning if they come in in time.

Mrs Lear presents her best respects to you and unites with me in best wishes for all my friends at Mt Vernon &c.—if this letter should reach you before you leave that place. I shall direct this letter to Mt Vernon, Fredericksburg or Richmond—as you mentioned in your letter to Mrs Washington that you did not know when you should be able to leave George Town we cannot calculate upon your pursuing your journy on Monday as you expected when you left this place. With sentiments of the highest respect & purest affection I have the honor to be Sir, Your obliged & very humble Servt

Tobias Lear.

ALS, DLC:GW.

1. For Ephraim Blaine's letter, see GW to Lear, 28 Mar. 1791 and note 1.

2. For Tobias Lear's superintendence of the education at the academy of the College of Philadelphia of George Washington Parke Custis, Martha Washington's nine-year-old grandson, see GW to Lear, 3 Oct., 7 Nov. 1790, and 12 April, 29 May 1791, and Lear to GW, 24 Oct., 14 Nov. 1790. Lear wrote to David Humphreys on 12 April 1791: "Nelly & Washington have every advantage in point of instructors &c. that this Country can give them, and they certainly make good progress in those things which are taught them: But I apprehend the worst consequences, particularly to the boy, from the unbounded indulgence of his grandmama—& the impressions which he daily receives from that quarter of his being born to such noble prospects both in

estate & otherways—It has already tainted his manners, and I fear has too deeply insinuated itself into his mind to be easily driven out. I saw it with regret in the early stages—and avowed my opinion of the consequences in the most explicit manner. The fact was acknowledged; but an unconq(uo)rable fondness was urged in its defence. I offered to take the boy under my immediate charge at all times when he was out of School—and considering myself as accountable for him—I proposed that he should know that to me only he was to look for indulgence or expect reprehension. The offer was accepted with gratitude—and for a few weeks pretty well adhered to: but the old habit at length overcame everything, & he has now returned to his former manners. I must give him up—I regret it; because I clearly see that he is in the high road to ruin. . . . The President sees it with pain; but as he considers that Mrs W.'s happiness is bound up in the boy—he is unwilling to take such measures as might reclaim him, knowing that any rigidity used towards him would perhaps be productive of serious effects on her" (PPRF).

To Battaile Muse

Sir,   Mount Vernon April 3d 1791
Your letter of the 20th of Jany came duly to hand, but at a time when public business pressed so heavily upon me that I could give no attention to private concerns.

I am sorry to hear of Mr Hickman's loss & in consequence of it, remit his last years Rent. Buying & selling of leases with as much facility as one would do a horse or an Oxe, does not comport with my ideas of the improvement of the land; and for that reason it was, that the practice is guarded against. However, in the case of Mr Hickman, if the purchaser is a person of good character, and in appearance likely to answer my purposes as well as the prest occupier, I shall not object to the transfer.

Mr Hickman in his application to me, does not ask to be released from the transfer Rent—nor do I see upon what ground he could, as it will fall more upon the purchaser than seller; yet, if there is any thing in the case to make it necessary, I will not object to it. I am Yr Very Hble Servt

Go: Washington

ALS, CtY: Benjamin Franklin Papers.

To William Tilghman

Sir,   Mount Vernon April 3d 1791.

The enclosed letters contain all the information I can give respecting the proceedings of Colvils Executors against Mr Sydney George. It will appear from these (as I think I mentioned to you) that the bond had been considered as lost, and that, the only resort, in case of non-payment was supposed to be to a Court of Chancery. Whether such a suit was instituted by Mr Chalmers is more than I am able to inform you, or whether any farther correspondence took place between Mr West & him does not appear from any papers I possess, or have access to.[1]

It will be recollected that our dispute with G. Britain commenced soon after the interchange of the enclosed letters, and that the Courts of Justice were long shut up. During this period Mr John West, the acting Exr, died; Mrs Francina Colvil Executrix of the Will having done so before him. By these events I became the *only* surviving Exr and it must be noticed that from the year 1774 until the close of the War I was from home, and unable to give attention to this, or any other private concern—that previous thereto the Execution of the Will rested nearly, if not wholly, upon Mr John West—and that it is but lately that the bond has been recovered.

Under these circumstances I pray you to apply to the Representative of Mr Sydney George for payment of it—and in case of refusal to bring suit thereon, that in any event my administration in this particular may stand Justified. Through any channel you may direct, your fee & the cost of Suit shall be paid.[2] I am Sir Your Most Obedient Servt

Go: Washington

ALS, RPJCB.

William Tilghman (1756–1827) belonged to a prominent family on the Eastern Shore of Maryland. After graduating from the College of Philadelphia in 1772, he studied law with Benjamin Chew, Sr., and was admitted to the bar in Maryland in 1783. Tilghman served in both houses of the Maryland legislature in the late 1780s and early 1790s, until his resignation in 1794, when he returned to Philadelphia and was admitted to the Pennsylvania bar. He was appointed a judge of the Pennsylvania circuit court in 1801 and served as chief justice of the state supreme court from 1806 until his death.

For the background to GW's role as an executor of the estate of Thomas Colvill, see GW to John West, Jr., December 1767, and Thomas Montgomerie to GW, 24 Oct. 1788, source note.

1. The enclosures have not been found but apparently dealt with the pre-Revolutionary War proceedings of the Colvill estate against lawyer Sidney George (d. 1774) of Cecil County, Md., who died indebted to the estate. See GW to West, 4 July 1773.

2. Tilghman replied from Chestertown, Md., on 14 July 1791 that application to the younger Sydney George had produced an 8 Sept. 1774 receipt from George Chalmers, attorney for West and the Colville estate, acknowledging the younger George's £100 payment made as executor of his father's estate. Tilghman enclosed a copy of the receipt, which also acknowledged a bond, dated 13 Aug. 1774, for £180, stipulating the payment of £90 with interest to West on 10 June 1775 and added: "Mr George informs me, that the bond passed by him, and mentioned in this receipt, has never been discharged. If this bond is not to be found amongst the papers of Mr West, perhaps some intelligence concerning it may be got from Mr Chalmers, who it is said, is in London. If it cannot be found, I make no doubt but I can prevail on Mr George to pay the Debt, without a suit, on your giving him such a discharge, as will be sufficient to protect him, in case the bond should be hereafter discovered" (DLC:GW). GW replied on 18 August.

To William Darke

Dear Sir,   Mount-Vernon, April 4th 1791.

The purport of this letter is to request your service in a matter of immediate importance to the United States—my knowledge of your public dispositions assures me that it will receive your ready attention.

I shall premise its object by informing you that in pursuance of an act of the last session of Congress an additional military force consisting of one regular regiment, two regiments of levies for six months, and such a proportion of militia as may be thought necessary is ordered to be raised for the service of the United States, to be employed, unless the measures now taking to restore peace should make it unnecessary, in an expedition against certain tribes of western Indians.[1]

The command in chief is given to General St Clair—that of the levies to General Butler—and that of the militia to General Scott—The command of one regiment of levies, to consist of three battalions, to be raised in Pennsylvania, Maryland, and Virginia, was given to Colonel H. Lee, and, on his declining, before I adverted to the idea of appointing you, Colonel Hall was, on the suggestion of the Secretary of war, named to succeed him—should Colonel Hall decline it is my wish that you would accept the command of the regiment—and that, in the mean-time whether you enter into the service or not yourself, you would be so good as, immediately on the receipt of this letter, which will be your authority for so doing, to appoint from among the Gentlemen that are known to you, and who you would recommend as proper characters, and think likely to re-cruit their men, three persons as Captains, three as Lieutenants, and three as Ensigns in the Battalion of levies to be raised in the State of Virginia, for the service of the United States, for the term of six months, after arriving at their place of rendezvous—That you would instruct the said officers immediately to set about engaging recruits who may be ready, on the order of the Secretary of war, or the Commandant of the battalion, to em-body and march to the place of rendezvous—Enclosed is a state-ment of the pay, clothing, forage, and rations to be allowed to the Levies.

My confidence in your ability and disposition to render that service to the public which I now request of you, persuades me that you will immediately appoint three Captains, three Lieuten-ants, and three Ensigns, so well qualified for their several trusts that these companies of the Virginia battalion of levies will be recruited without delay, and ready to repair to their rendezvous by the time that the order for so doing is received either from the Secretary of war or the Commandant of the battalion.

You will be pleased to make a return of the Officers, whom you appoint, to General Knox at Philadelphia, and signify at the same time your own determination with respect to accepting the command if Colonel Hall should have declined.

I am thus far on a tour through the southern States, and a press of business only allows me time to repeat my belief that you will complete this matter in a manner highly honorable to yourself, and beneficial to the public.[2] I am, with great regard, Dear Sir, Your most obedient servant

G. Washington.

P.S. Should there be any officers of the late army, who you think in all other respects equal to the appointments I wish them to be preferred—but the substantial requisites of being proper for the service, and likely to recruit their men, must ever be held in view and they must be raised on your side of the river.

G.W.

LB, DLC:GW, misaddressed to "Colonel John Darke."

1. For "An Act for raising and adding another Regiment to the Military Establishment of the United States, and for making further provision for the protection of the frontiers" of 3 Mar. 1791, see 1 *Stat.* 222–24.

2. William Darke apparently replied c.9 April to either this letter or GW's letter of 7 April. On 14 April William Jackson sent Henry Knox a "letter from Colonel Darcke to the President" (DLC:GW).

From Boissieu de Gibert

au Cap français isle St Domingue
Maison de Mr Bouger negt Rue des religieuses
Monseigneur   Le 4 avril 1791

Le Mois De juin Dernier, jai Eû L'honneur de vous Ecrire une Premiere pour vous Supplier vous interesser a Mon Sort, a L'effet D'avoir une Plaçe auprès de vous ou Dans votre Dépendence.[1] Mes talents se Bornent aux affaires Contentieuses a suivre une Correspondance française dresse des Memoires &c., mon âge Meur D'Environ quarante ans donne une asseurance d'assiduité a remplir mon Devoir, Et jose Le Dire a La Probité La plus intacte, Ce qui est Libre a Prendre information. Mon Cher fils agé de 16 an qui a une très Belle Pleume ne Demanderait pas moins D'avoir Conjointement avec moy Une Plaçe, soit Le Climat Pezant de cette Colonie, derengement de notre Santé, soit Le Changement tout nous Permet de nous En Retirer.

Veuillés Monsieur nous trouver en azile affin de nous Soutenir avec Agréement Chès vous a un Employ, j'ose Esperer que votre humanité Connûe vous y Portera, Je Suis avec Réspect Et Soumission Monseigneur Votre Soumis serviteur

Boissieu de Gibert

ALS, DLC:GW.

1. No previous letter from Boissieu de Gibert to GW has been found.

To Alexander Hamilton

Dear Sir,   Mount Vernon April 4th 1791

Your letter of the 27th Ult. came duly to hand. For the information contained in it—and for the notes which accompanied the same, I thank you.

Every expedient, as I believe you know, is in operation to avert a War with the hostile Indian tribes—and to keep those who are in treaty with us in good temper; but I am nearly thoroughly convinced that neither will be effected, or, if effected, will be of short duration while land jobbing and the disorderly conduct of our borderers is suffered with impunity; and whilst the States individually are omitting no occasion to interfere in matters which belong to the general Government.

It is not more than four or five months since the Six Nations or part of them were assured (through the medium of Colo. Pickering) that thence forward they would be spoken to by the Government of the United States *only* and the same thing was repeated in strong terms to the Cornplanter at Philadelphia afterwards. Now, as appears by the extract from Mr King, the Legislature of New York are going into some negotiations with these very people. What must this evince to them? Why, that we pursue no system, and that our declarations are not to be regard. To sum the whole up in a few words—the interferences of States, and the speculations of Individuals will be the bane of all our public measures.[1] Sincerely & Affectionately I am Yrs

Go: Washington

ALS, DLC:GW; LB, DLC:GW. There are minor variations between the two texts.

1. For the frontier defensive measures of the Pennsylvania and New York legislatures, see Samuel Powel to GW, 19 Mar., Alexander Hamilton to GW, 27 Mar. and note 2, and Henry Knox to GW, 31 Mar. 1791 and notes 1 and 3.

Hamilton replied from Philadelphia on 10 April: "It is to be lamented that our system is such as still to leave the public peace of the Union at the mercy of each state Government. This is not only the case as it regards direct interferences, but as it regards the *inability* of the National Government in many particulars to take those direct measures for carrying into execution its views and engagements which exigencies require. For example—a party comes from a County of Virginia into Pennsylvania and wantonly murders some friendly Indians—The National Government instead of having power to apprehend the murderers and bring them to justice, is obliged to make a representation to *that* of Pennsylvania: That of Pennsylvania again is to make a requisition of that of Virginia. And whether the murderers shall be brought to Justice at all must depend upon the particular policy and energy and good disposition of two state Governments, and the efficacy of the provisions of their respective laws—And the security of other States and the money of all is at the discretion of one. Those things require a remedy but when it will come—God knows. From present appearances a pretty general Indian war is not a little to be apprehended—But there is now nothing for it, but to encounter it with vigour—and thus far in my Department the provisions are adequate" (DLC:GW).

To Alexander Hamilton, Thomas Jefferson, and Henry Knox

Gentlemen,   Mount Vernon, April 4. 1791.

As the public service may require that communications should be made to me, during my absence from the seat of government, by the most direct conveyances—and as, in the event of any very extraordinary occurrence, it will be necessary to know at what time I may be found in any particular place, I have to inform you that unless the progress of my journey to Savannah is retarded by unforeseen interruptions it will be regulated (including days of halt) in the following manner.

I shall be on the 8th of April at Fredericksburg

11th	Richmond
14th	Petersburg
16th	Halifax
18th	Tarborough
20th	Newbern
24th	Wilmington
29th	Georgetown, south-Carolina
2nd of May	Charleston, halting five days.
11th	Savannah, halting two days.

Thence, leaving the line of the mail, I shall proceed to Augusta, and, according to the information which I may receive there, my return, by an upper road will be regulated.

The route of my return is at present uncertain, but in all probability, it will be through Columbia, Camden, Charlotte, Salisbury, Salem, Guilford, Hillsborough, Harrisburg, Williamsburg to Taylor's ferry on the Roanoke, and thence to Fredericksburg by the nearest and best road.

After thus explaining to you, as far as I am able at present, the direction and probable progress of my journey, I have to express my wish, if any serious and important cases should arise during my absence, (of which the probability is but too strong) that the Secretaries for the Departments of State, Treasury, and War may hold consultations thereon, to determine whether they are of such a nature as to require my personal attendance at the seat of government—and, if they should be so considered, I will return immediately from any place at which the information may reach me—Or should they determine that measures, relevant to the case, may be legally and properly pursued without the immediate agency of the President, I will approve and ratify the measures, which may be conformed to such determination.

Presuming that the Vice-President will have left the seat of government for Boston, I have not requested his opinion to be taken on the supposed emergency—should it be otherwise I wish him also to be consulted.[1] I am, Gentlemen, your most obedient Servant

Go: Washington

LS, in Tobias Lear's hand, DLC: Thomas Jefferson Papers; LS (letterpress copy), DLC:GW; Df, DNA: RG 59, Miscellaneous Letters; LB, DLC:GW; copy, NNGL: Henry Knox Papers; copy, MHi-A; copy, DNA: RG 59, Domestic Letters.

For the background to this document, see Itinerary for the Southern Tour, February 1791, editorial note.

1. John Adams went home with his family to Braintree on 2 May and did not return to Philadelphia until 21 Oct. (Tobias Lear to GW, 8 May; *General Advertiser and Political, Commercial and Literary Journal* [Philadelphia], 6 May; *Gazette of the United States* [Philadelphia], 26 Oct. 1791). Before his departure he discussed policy with the department heads. See GW to Jefferson, 4 April and note 1, and Knox to GW, 10 April, 30 May 1791.

To Thomas Jefferson

Dear Sir,   Mount-Vernon April 4 1791.

You will readily agree with me that the best interests of the United States require such an intimation to be made to the Governor of Canada, either directly or indirectly, as may produce instructions to prevent the Indians receiving military aid or supplies from the british posts or garrisons—The notoriety of this assistance has already been such as renders enquiry into particulars unnecessary.

Colonel Beckwith seems peculiarly designated to be the channel of an indirect intimation. Referring the mode and extent of communicating with him to your own discretion, I wish it may be suggested in such manner as to reach Lord Dorchester, or the Officer commanding in Canada, that certain information has been received of large supplies of ammunition being delivered to the hostile Indians, from british posts, about the commencement of last campaign[1]—And, as the United States have no other view in prosecuting the present war against the Indians, than, in the failure of negociation, to procure, by arms, peace and safety to the inhabitants of their frontier, they are equally surprised and disappointed at such an interference by the servants or subjects of a foreign State, as seems intended to protract the attainment of so just and reasonable an object.[2]

These are my sentiments on this subject at the present moment—yet so unsettled do some circumstances appear that it is possible you may see a necessity either to treat it very delicately, or to decline acting on it altogether. The option is therefore left to your judgment as events may make the one or the other the part of propriety.[3] The enclosed paper is transmitted and referred to you in the state I received it.[4] I am dear Sir, Your most obedient Servant

Go: Washington

ALS, DLC: Thomas Jefferson Papers; Df, in William Jackson's hand, dated 3 April, DNA: RG 59, Miscellaneous Letters; LB, DLC:GW. Significant variations between the draft and the source text are noted below.

1. In the draft Jackson originally wrote: "I wish it may be suggested in such manner as to reach Lord Dorchester, or the Officer commanding in Canada, that the United States cannot any longer regard with indifference the aid which is afforded to the hostile tribes of indians by the british garrisons."

2. In the draft Jackson originally wrote: "as the United States have no other view in prosecuting the present war against the indians than to procure peace and safety to the inhabitants of their frontier, they must find the happiness of their citizens and the dignity of their government deeply interested in preventing such interference, by the servants or subjects of a foreign state, as may have a tendency to protract the attainment of so just and reasonable an object." After "to the inhabitants of their frontier," Jackson at some point wrote and then crossed out "they cannot but necessarily regard with astonishment such."

3. In accordance with GW's circular letter to the department heads of 4 April, Jefferson chose to consult the vice-president and the secretaries of war and treasury about using George Beckwith to convey a message to Quebec. Adams, Jefferson, Hamilton, and Knox met at Jefferson's house on 11

April and determined to approach Dorchester through Beckwith (see Jefferson to GW, 17 April 1791). For other matters discussed on 11 April, see Hamilton to GW, 11, 14 April.

4. The enclosure has not been identified.

To Henry Knox

Sir,   Mount Vernon April 4th 1791

To avoid the inconvenience of future delay in officering the Virginia battalion of levies, and to remove the uncertainty which your want of information might occasion, I have determined to attempt its completion, with the assistance of Colonel Darck, whom I have authorized by a letter of this date, to appoint three Captains, three lieutenants, and three Ensigns from among the Gentlemen of his part of the State, Berkley County—I shall take immediate measures for appointing a Major and the officers of the other Company[1]—The Major will be directed to call on Colonel Darck, on his way to the War Office, and he will then carry a report to you of what has been done. I am Sir, Your most obedt Servt

G.W.

Df, DLC:GW; LB, DLC:GW.

1. For GW's appointment of Robert Powell as major of the Virginia levies, see GW to Powell, 4 April 1791 and note 1.

To Pierre-Charles L'Enfant

Sir,   Mount Vernon April 4th 1791

Although I do not conceive that you will derive any material advantage from an examination of the enclosed papers, yet, as they have been drawn by different persons, and under different circumstances, they may be compared with your own ideas of a proper plan for the Federal City (under the prospect which now presents itself to us.)—For this purpose I commit them to your *private* inspection until my return from the tour I am abt to make. The rough sketch by Mr Jefferson, was done under an idea that *no* offer, worthy of consideration, would come from the Land holders in the vicinity of Carrollsburg (from the backwardness which appeared in them); and therefore, was accommodated to the grounds about George Town.[1] The *other,* is taken up upon a larger scale, without reference to any described spot.[2]

It will be of great importance to the public interest to comprehend as much ground (to be ceded by individuals) as there is any tolerable prospect of obtaining. Although it may not be *immediately* wanting, it will nevertheless encrease the Revenue; and of course be benificial hereafter, not only to the public, but to the individual proprietors; in as much, as the plan will be enlarged, and thereby freed from those blotches, which otherwise might result from not comprehending *all* the lands that appear well adapted to the general design; and which, in my opinion, are those between Rock Creek, Potowmac river and the Eastern branch, as far up the latter as the turn of the channel above Evans' point; thence including the flat back of Jenkin's height; thence to the Road leading from George Town to Bladensburgh, as far Easterly along the same as to include the branch which runs across it, somewhere near the exterior of the George Town cession; thence in a proper direction to Rock Creek at, or above the ford, according to the situation of the ground.

Within these limits there may be lands belonging to persons *incapacitated,* though *willing* to convey on the terms proposed; but such had better be included, than others excluded, the proprietors of which are not only willing, but in circumstances to subscribe.[3] I am Sir Your Most Obedt Servt

Go: Washington

ALS, DLC: Digges-L'Enfant-Morgan Papers; ADfS, DLC:GW; LB, DLC:GW.

For the background to this letter, see the Agreement of the Proprietors of the Federal District, 30 Mar. 1791, source note.

1. Thomas Jefferson probably presented his rough plan of the Federal City to GW in March 1791. See Memorandum from Jefferson, 11 March.

2. GW's second enclosure was probably the plan of the Federal City presented to him on 5 Dec. 1790 by Joseph Clark.

3. These boundaries correspond generally to those that Pierre-Charles L'Enfant proposed in his plan presented to GW on 22 June 1791.

To Robert Powell

Sir,   Mount-Vernon, April 4th 1791.

Being induced by the fair representation which is made to me of your character I do hereby notify to you your appointment to be Major Commandant of a battalion of Levies, directed by an act of Congress to be raised for the service of the United States in the State of Virginia—and I enclose to you a statement of the pay, clothing, and rations, and forage allowed to the said battalion.

It will be necessary, if you accept the appointment, that you should come immediately to Mount-Vernon, as I shall leave it within a day or two—and I wish to give you some directions before you repair to the Secretary of war, from whom you will receive your commission and instructions.[1] I am Sir, Your most obedient Servant

G. Washington.

LB, DLC:GW.

Capt. Robert Powell of Fairfax County (1753–1815) was commissioned a lieutenant in the Continental army in February 1776 and promoted the same year. He resigned in 1779 and became a major in the Virginia militia in 1781.

1. As Powell neither immediately replied nor appeared at Mount Vernon, William Jackson asked James Craik of Alexandria, on 7 April 1791, if a letter from Powell had been received by the postmaster there and, if not, requested him to transmit another letter to Powell by express. Jackson informed Craik that if GW did not hear from Powell before he left Mount Vernon on 8 April, he would refer the appointments of major, captain, and subalterns to William Darke (DLC:GW). Powell, who was not at home when GW's letter arrived, wrote to GW from Culpeper, Va., on 7 April that he had just received it and would accept the appointment but could not reach Mount Vernon before 9 or 10 April (DNA: RG 59, Miscellaneous Letters).

To Beverley Randolph

Sir, Mount-Vernon, April 4th 1791.

The enclosed letter to Colonel Carrington, requesting him to meet me at Richmond on the 11th of the present month, is transmitted to your Excellency's care to ensure the certainty of it's conveyance, and I beg leave to request, if there is no other immediate and direct opportunity, that you may cause it to be forwarded to him by express.[1] I have the honor to be, with great regard and esteem, Your Excellency's most obedient Servant

G. Washington.

LB, DLC:GW.

1. The enclosed letter to Edward Carrington of 4 April 1791 reads: "I shall be at Richmond on the 11th instant, where I desire to have the pleasure of

meeting you on that day, to take measures for arranging the Inspectorates of the district of Virginia of which you have been appointed Supervisor. To ensure certainty to the transmission of this letter it is enclosed to Governor Randolph, who is requested to forward it by express, if no direct conveyance offers immediately" (LB, DLC:GW). GW reached Richmond on 11 April and met with Carrington the next day. For their conversation, see *Diaries*, 6:109–10. On 13 April William Jackson wrote to the secretary of the treasury transmitting the arrangements that GW and Carrington had agreed upon and instructing Alexander Hamilton not to issue commissions to appointees until informed by Carrington of their willingness to accept (DLC:GW). He also sent to Hamilton that day a memorandum, probably on the Virginia federal revenue cutter, by Capt. Richard Taylor (DLC:GW).

From John Bowman

Peachtree, S.C., 5 April 1791. Invites GW to accept the accommodations of his house near the Charleston road fourteen miles from Georgetown, S.C., where he "will do my self the honour of meeting your Excellency."[1]

ALS, DLC:GW.

John Bowman (1746–1807), a native of Scotland, settled in Georgia in 1769. He had moved to St. James Santee Parish in South Carolina by the mid-1780s, where he married Sabina Lynch, daughter of Thomas Lynch. Bowman between 1788 and 1799 served in both houses of the South Carolina general assembly and represented his parish in the 1788 convention that ratified the federal Constitution, which he opposed, and in the state constitutional convention of 1790.

1. Bowman wrote to GW on 16 April that indisposition would prevent him from meeting GW at Georgetown: "I apprehend my Indispositon to be the Measles—But as your Excellency & the Gentlemen attending you have probably had that disorder, I hope my illness, which is not severe, will be no impediment to your coming here" (DLC:GW).

From Benjamin Hawkins

Sir   Petersburg [Va.] 5th of April 1791

I came here from North Carolina the 31st of March under the expectation of the pleasure of meeting you. It being necessary that I should attend to some business interesting to an Orphan of a friend and it being probable that the season is too far advanced for your journey I shall this day return.

I found on my arrival in North Carolina the people pretty generally disposed to think favourably of the federal government although considerable pains had been taken to misrepresent them. Some of the Antifederal gentlemen are as violent or more so than ever. Mr Willie Jones reveres very much the character of General Washington but he will not invite the President of the United States to dine with him.[1]

I saw two gentlemen from Georgia who informed me that there was an acquiescence in that State with the measures of government, That the Yazou company have it in contemplation to obtain the assent of the Indians to the terms of their purchase from Georgia and then to apply to the government for their assent. Under an Idea that this is practicable and being informed that the Creeks are not satisfied with their treaty they have ceased to misrepresent public measures. I have been twice applied to for my Opinion on this plan and in conversation with Mr Willis one of the company the member of the house of Representatives in the Room of Genl Matthews I observed that I was well assured that the assent of the Indians can be not be fairly and freely obtained and without it a war would be the inevitable consequance.[2]

The Creeks have a very high Idea of our strength those of them who traveled through the Country have induced the nations to believe that it is indespensably necessary for them to be at peace with us. I have the honor to be with perfect respect sir your most obedient Sert

Benjamin Hawkins

ALS, DNA: RG 59, Miscellaneous Letters.

1. Planter Willie Jones (1741–1801) served as a North Carolina legislator during the Revolution and as a member of the Continental Congress in 1780–81. A leading Antifederalist, he declined serving as a delegate to the Federal Convention and actively opposed ratification of the federal Constitution in the state convention of 1788.

2. For GW's discussion of the Yazoo companies, on 9 April in Fredericksburg, Va., with his nephew John Lewis, see *Diaries*, 6:107–8. Francis Willis (1745–1829) of Wilkes County, Ga., served in Congress from 1791 to 1793.

From Tobias Lear

Sir,   Philadelphia April 5th 1791.

The enclosed letter from Mr G. Morris, was yesterday put into my hands by Mr R. Morris, having come under cover to him.[1]

I was yesterday asked by the Vice-Presidt if it was true that information had been received of Count Andriani's having written things to Europe unfavourable to and disrespectful of this Country.[2] I told him that such information had been received—repeating the purport of that contained in Colo. H.'s Letter. He appeared extremely vexed at the Count, and spoke of him in very harsh terms. He said that the Count had brot a letter to him from Dr Price recommending him to his notice, but not having formed a very good opinion of him, he had paid him but little Attention. In future he should make it a point to deny himself if the Count should call upon him, and should he meet him elsewhere he should treat him with a marked contempt. He further added that he should let Dr Price know what an unworthy Character he had introduced to him—and beg in future that he would be more cautious in his recommendations. I relate this conversation, because it struck me as being pointedly introduced.

The Attorney General called upon Mrs Washington today, and informed her that three of his Negroes had given him notice that they should tomorrow take advantage of a law of this State, and claim their freedom—and that he had mentioned it to her from an idea that those who were of age in this family might follow the example, after a residence of six months should put it in their power. I have therefore communicated it to you that you might, if you thought best, give directions in the matter respecting the blacks in this family.[3]

Mrs Washington has just now received your letter from Mount Vernon, where we are happy to hear that you arrived well.[4] She does not write at this time, but desires to be remembered. The family continue in good health. Mrs Lear unites with me in best respects. I have the honor to be with the highest respect & warmest attachment—Sir—Your most Obedt Servt

                                        Tobias Lear.

ALS, PHi: Gratz Collection.

1. The enclosure was probably the letter of Gouverneur Morris to GW dated

19 Nov. 1790, which was transmitted under cover to Robert Morris (see Gouverneur Morris to GW, 22 Nov. 1790, n.1).

2. For Count Paolo Andreani's disparaging comments on the United States, see David Humphreys to GW, 31 Oct. 1790 and note 6, and GW to Humphreys, 16 Mar. 1791. Tobias Lear wrote to Humphreys on 12 April 1791: "The Account which you gave the President of certain things which Count Andriani had written to Europe respecting this Country—has been handed abroad (with the President's permission) in order that he might be treated in the way that he ought. It has operated much against him in general. He does not shew himself in this house—and whenever he is met by the family a pointed contempt is shewn him: He is, however, still carressed by some—particularly by Mr & Mrs Bingham & others who are fond of everything that does not belong to their own Country" (PPRF).

3. The Pennsylvania act of 1780 providing for the gradual abolition of slavery automatically freed any slaves brought into the state after an uninterrupted residence of six months. GW sent Lear directions concerning the Philadelphia household slaves on 12 April.

4. The letter to Martha Washington has not been found.

To Tobias Lear

Dear Sir,   Mount Vernon April 6th 1791.

Your letters of the 31st Ult. and 1st instant have been received—Tomorrow I continue my journey. A request of General Knox's (consequent of Colo. Lee's declining his appointment) to name Officers for the Battn of Levies to be raised in Berkeley &ca has prevented its being done sooner.

I am perfectly satisfied that every necessary & proper step will be taken to procure a good Steward, and a good House keeper; and therefore shall add nothing further on this head—Let the man who is at work in the Garden, or has been there, be paid— I mean to be under no obligation to anyone.

The pad arrived in good time, and I expect my horses (as they seem well recruited) will go on better than they have come. I send more letters to be filed[1]—my best wishes attend Mrs Lear and the Child, and I am sincerely & Affecty Yrs

Go: Washington

ALS, ViMtV: Storer-Decatur Collection.
1. The enclosed letters have not been identified.

To Richard Butler

Sir,   Mount Vernon, April 7th 1791.

The necessity of placing the organization of the Virginia battalion of levies upon a certain footing before I leave Mount Vernon, which I shall do this morning, has induced me to authorise Colonel Darke, who lives near Shepherd's town in Berkley-county to appoint all the Officers to the battalion, and when they are appointed to direct the Major to repair to Philadelphia to receive the orders of the Secretary of war, and the other officers to commence the recruiting service.

Should Colonel Hall decline, and Colonel Darke chuses to accept, he will be appointed to command the regiment.

I have given this information to you to prevent any clashing in the measures which might be adopted to officer the battalion, and as it may be best that you should see Colonel Darke as soon as you have finished what remains to be done in Maryland—I have informed him that you are on the way through Maryland to Virginia for the purpose of completing the arrangements of both battalions, informing him that he is in the meantime to continue the service which I have requested him to perform.[1] I am Sir, your most obedient Servant

                                                        G. Washington.

LB, DLC:GW.

Richard Butler (1743–1791), a native of Ireland, settled with his father near Lancaster, Pa., and served in the French and Indian War, afterwards establishing himself as a trader on the Pennsylvania frontier. Brevetted a brigadier general during the Revolutionary War, he concluded several important treaties with the western Indian nations and was appointed superintendent of Indian affairs for the northern district in 1786. GW appointed Butler major general and second-in-command of Arthur St. Clair's campaign, and he was given command of the temporary levies. Disputes between Butler and St. Clair undoubtedly contributed to the failure of the expedition. Butler led the right wing of the army during the battle of 4 Nov. 1791 and was mortally wounded.

1. For GW's correspondence with William Darke concerning command of the Virginia battalion, see GW to Darke, 4, 7 April. On 7 April GW asked Otho H. Williams to deliver the above letter to Butler, noting that "It is of importance to the public service that the enclosed letter should be received by General Butler as soon as possible" (LS, MdHi: Otho Holland Williams Papers).

To William Darke

Dear Sir,   Mount-Vernon April 7th 1791.

A second necessity having arisen for my troubling you on the subject of officering the Virginia battalion of levies, I again beg leave to request your assistance therein.[1]

I had written to Major Powell, who lives about six miles from Alexandria, informing him of his appointment to the majority of the battalion, and requesting to see him at Mount-Vernon immediately—but he has not appeared nor have I heard from him, which leads me to conclude he cannot be found.[2]

The necessity of placing this business upon a certainty before I proceed on my journey to Savannah which I shall do to-day, induces me to refer it entirely to you.

You will therefore, in addition to the appointments, which, in consequence of my first letter, you may have already made, be pleased to appoint a proper person to be Major Commandant of the battalion—another Captain, one lieutenant, and one Ensign.

The enclosed gazette contains the law for raising the troops, which shews that a bounty of three dollars a man is allowed to the levies—This encouragement in aid of the pay, rations, and clothing, of which I enclosed to you an abstract, induces me to hope that the recruiting service will go on briskly.[3]

The Virginia-battalion will be ordered to rendezvous at Winchester, where supplies of arms, ammunition, clothing, and rations will be provided for them. On this subject further instructions will be given by the Secretary of war, to whom I have communicated the authority which I have devolved on you to appoint all the officers of the battalion, and to instruct them, when appointed, to enter on the recruiting service.

Should Colonel Hall decline his appointment, and you agree to accept the command of the regiment, the repayment of expence, which you may incur in this business, will be in a regular train. But, should you not enter into the service yourself, you will, in that case, transmit your account to the Secretary of war, who will be instructed to discharge it.

As a battalion is recruiting in Maryland, it will be necessary, to prevent interference, that the Virginia levies should be raised on your side of the river—and, to effect this facility, you may find it necessary to appoint the officers from different districts—but, of this, being on the spot, you will be the best judge. And to your care and zeal I refer, with confidence, the whole arrangement—not doubting that your report of it to the Secretary of War will be perfectly satisfactory.

Major Bedinger's name presents itself to my mind, and therefore I just mention it to you.[4]

As without men the Officers will not be wanted, you will be pleased to inform them that the confirmation of their appointments must necessarily depend on them being able to raise the men. You will instruct the Gentleman, who is appointed Major-Commandant of the battalion, to repair immediately to Philadelphia to receive the orders of the Secretary of war.

Major General Butler, who, in my former letter, I informed you is appointed to command all the levies, is now on his way, through Maryland, to Virginia to close all the arrangements respecting them—he will of course see you—but I request that this circumstance may in no degree delay the measures I have requested you to take for organising the battalion. The only change necessary is that you should direct the Major to see General Butler before he goes to Philadelphia, as that may make his going unnecessary.

Should Captain Hannah be the Bearer of this letter, you will please to appoint him to one of the companies, allowing him to appoint his own subalterns, and they will recruit the company perhaps in the neighbourhood of Alexandria.[5]

Should the letter be delivered to you by an Express you will then proceed to make all the appointments as you think proper. With great regard and esteem, I am dear Sir, Your most obedient Servant

G. Washington.

LB, DLC:GW.

1. GW last wrote to William Darke on 4 April.

2. See GW to Robert Powell, 4 April.

3. The enclosure has not been found. For the terms of enlistment for the temporary levies, see 1 *Stat.* 222–24.

4. GW had met with Darke and Henry Bedinger the previous fall at Shepherdstown, Va. (now W. Va.). See Bedinger and William Good to GW, 1 Dec. 1790.

5. After Arthur St. Clair's campaign, GW gave Capt. Nicholas Hannah (d. 1794) a commission in the regular army (see GW to the U.S. Senate, 14 Mar. 1792).

To Henry Knox

Dear Sir   Mount Vernon April 7 1791.

Judging it necessary, before I left Mount Vernon, which I shall do this morning, to place the organization of the Virginia battalion of Levies on a certainty, I have devolved on Colonel Darck, who lives near Shepperds town in Berkley County, an authority to appoint all the officers, and, when appointed, to direct the Major to repair immediately to Philadelphia, to receive your instructions—and the Captains and Subalterns to commence the recruiting service.[1]

Your further instructions, on this subject, you will either communicate to Colonel Darck by letter or forward to him by the Major when he waits on you.

If Colonel Hall declines, and Colonel Darck agrees to accept the command of the regiment, every thing will be in a regular train of settlement with Colonel Darck—but, if he should not enter into the service himself, I have directed him to report his expences in this business to you, and I have to request that his accounts may be examined and paid.

Should neither of these Gentn agree to command the regiment, I wish you to appoint some other person, the best qualified, who will accept. Your letter of the 1st instt to Major Jackson is received—a summary of what has been written to Colonel Darck will be communicated to Genl Butler for his government, in a letter, this morning. I am Dear sir &ca

G.W.

Df, DLC:GW; LB, DLC:GW.
1. See GW's letter to William Darke of this date.

To the Officials of Fredericksburg, Virginia

Gentlemen,   [Fredericksburg, Va., 9 April 1791]

At all times flattered by the esteem, and grateful for the good wishes of my fellow citizens I am particularly so when to my respect for their public worth is united the endearment of private acquaintance—in this regard I have the pleasure to receive your congratulatory address on my arrival in Fredericksburg, and, thanking you with sincerity for the sentiments it expresses, I desire to assure you of the affectionate gratitude which they inspire.[1]

G. Washington

LB, DLC:GW.

After leaving Mount Vernon early on 7 April, GW had an accident crossing Occoquan Creek at Colchester, Virginia. Fifty yards from shore one of his four coach horses bolted off the ferry, leading the rest of the team into the water, where they were saved only "with the utmost difficulty" (*Diaries*, 6:107). For GW's trip to Fredericksburg, his first visit there since the death of his mother, Mary Ball Washington, see ibid., 107–8.

1. After a dinner in GW's honor on 9 April, town officials presented him an address signed by Fredericksburg mayor William Harvey (d. 1798): "We the Mayor, Aldermen and common council of the Corporation of Fredericksburg are happy in this opportunity of tendering you the sincere and unanimous congratulations of the Citizens on your arrival in this Town, The Inhabitants of Fredericksburg Sir! as they can boast the first acquaintance with your Virtues claim a peculiar pleasure in testifying to the world your exalted Merit and in Joining with the rest of America to express their entire Approbation of your conduct thro life which has been so productive of blessings to its citizens. The long and fatiguing Journey you have undertaken will further manifest your Unremitted Attachment to that Country whose obligations to you can be better felt than described and we trust will not only influence the present generation to admire public and private Virtues from your example, but teach your Successors how to watch over the welfare of this extensive Union. We have the fullest confidence in divine Benevolence that the disposer of all good will be graciously pleased long to continue you in health and reward you both here and hereafter with blessings adequate to your Merit which he alone can give" (DLC:GW).

The protocol of the Southern Tour addresses to GW, of which this was the first, seems to have been the prior delivery of a written address to William Jackson, who usually made a copy and drafted a reply, which the president would verbally approve (none of the extant drafts in DLC:GW have any emendations in GW's hand). Jackson would then make a fair copy of the president's reply, which GW would sign, and then return the original address to the local officials. At a mutually agreed time the officers would read aloud their original address and present it to the president with due ceremony, and then GW would read his official reply and likewise deliver it to the officials. Editor Benjamin Franklin Bache wrote disapprovingly in the *General Advertiser and Political, Commercial and Literary Journal* (Philadelphia) on 23 April: "We find by the southern papers that the President, on his journey, is still perfumed with the incense of *addresses*. However highly we may consider the character of the Chief

Magistrate of the Union, yet we cannot but think the fashionable mode of expressing our attachment to the defender of the Liberty of his country, favors too much of Monarchy to be used by Republicans, or to be received with pleasure by a President of a Commonwealth."

From Giuseppe Chiappe

Excellence   Mogador [Morocco] 10 Avrîl 1791
    Ja'i eû L'honneaur d'ecrire a V.E. voie de Londres & sous couverte du Consul General des Venerables Etats, Le 18me Janvier añe courent, informente V.E. de Tout ce que êtoit passè dans Le noveau Regnè de Sid Mulai Liezid jousque a cette Epoque, & comme je crois mon devoir de continuer Les de plus novelles passêes après je me fais L'honeaur de les humilier à V.E.
    S.M.I. à dejá recûes avec beaucoup de distinction Trois ambassades; La primiere celle de Raguza, La 2de de Portogal & La 3me d'Englaterre qui est arrivè a Salè (ū Se Trouve encore S.M.) Le 22me du passè Mars. Toutes Les Trois ils se sont faites hoñeaier mais en particulier Les deux de Portogal & Englaterre qu'ils ont portes des beaux riches presents, un accompagnement d'Officiers, Musiciens & soldats, outre L'avoir dispenchè une bonne parti d'Argent aux Ministres & Officiers de La Court; Ce que je previen avec respect a V.E. pour gouvernement, êtant que aujourdhuy Les Presents & Les despenches de La Court sont alterèes & differentes considerablement de les passèes.
    On attend en peu de Temps Toutes Les autres Ambassades, & ceux que nous voions plus proches sont. De Françe, d'Ollande, de Venize & de Genes des quelles nous en avôns quellques Noveles. Je souaite que celle des Etats-Unis Tres respectables, puisse Les devençer pour prouver a S.M.I. l'empressément qu'ils Anime a Se procurer son amitiè & correspondence.
    S.M. en peu de jour passerà sanz doute a la Court de Maroc selon Toutes Les dernieres Noveles de Salè & il faudra que je haitte me presenter comme Les de plus Charges des Nations, & a mon retour J'aurai l'honneaur de faire part de Tout a V.E.
    Le 1⟨3⟩ me Fevrier êst arrivè a cet Port venant de Londres avec des Merchandisses La Sloop Ameriquene Le Dolphin sous Capn William Sharpe, son Equipage de six persones & je me prend La Libertè de rapresenter a V.E. Les procedures du susdit

Capn pour qu'ils me Soient de justification dans L'activitè & Zele avec Le quelle je procure d'assister L'Illre Nation.

Le jour apree son arrivé il se me presenta en acte de Compliment avec son Racomendataire, je L'ai informè del encharge que j'avoit pour l'asistençe de la Nation, je lui ai offert La même & mes particulieres Services, & depuis se jour La je n'ai eû plus Le plaisir de Le voir, & il est parti pour Londres Le 15me mars Sanz prendere, ne Manifest, ne Patent de Santè, de mon office.

Mes hautes desires sont Toujour d'être utile aux respectables Etats, & de pouvoir demontrer a V.E. Le grand respect & consideration avec le quelle j'ai L'hoñeaur d'être Tres profondement De Votre Excellence Le Tres Humble & Tres Obbt Serviteu⟨r⟩

Giuseppe Chiappe

ALS, DNA:PCC, item 98.

For the background to this letter, see Giuseppe Chiappe to GW, 18 July 1789, 13 May 1790, and 18 Jan. 1791. Despite Chiappe's efforts to ingratiate himself with the U.S. government, American envoy Thomas Barclay's instructions directed him to deal exclusively with Chiappe's brother Francisco, who the secretary of state thought "has merited well of the United States by his care of their peace and interests. . . . The place he holds near the Emperor renders his friendship peculiarly important. Let us have nothing further to do with his brothers or any other person." Jefferson added that "the money which would make one good friend, divided among several will produce no attachment" (Official Instructions for Barclay, 13 May 1791, *Jefferson Papers*, 20:397–400). See also Jefferson to GW, 27 Mar. 1791 and note 1.

From Alexander Hamilton

Sir   Treasury Department [Philadelphia] April 10th 1791.

I have the honor of your letter of the 4th instant addressed to the Secretary of State the Secretary at War and myself; to which due obedience shall be paid on my part.

A letter from Mr Short dated at Amsterdam the 2d of December has just come to hand giving me an account of his proceedings to that period; a copy of which will be forwarded by the tuesday's post. He informs me, among other things, that he had concluded with the Bankers of the United States to open a loan in February for two millions and a half of Guilders, at five per Cent interest and four per Cent charges, which is a half per Cent less than the last. The term of reimbursment fifteen years, begining at the end of ten, with liberty to the United States to reimburse at any time sooner.[1]

You will recollect that by a particular instruction from you to me, no succeeding *Loan* is to be opened, until *that* preceding has been submitted to you, and received your approbation.[2] As it is very desireable that no delay may attend the progress of the business, both as it regards payments to France and the domestic operations, to which the loans may be applied; I have concluded to submit Mr Shorts letter tomorrow to the Vice President, and the heads of Departments, that they may consider how far the case is within the purview of your letter; and whether it will not be expedient to authorise Mr Short to proceed upon a further loan to the amount of three millions of guilders, which is the sum to which the money lenders have been accustomed, and *that* recommended by our Bankers as the most proper to consitute each Loan.[3]

I request nevertheless to receive your instruction as soon as possible upon the subject—And I submit whether it will not be adviseable to change the restriction above mentioned so as to leave Mr Short at liberty to open his loans successively for three millions of Dollars each; no new one to commence till after the preceding one has been filled; but without waiting for a ratification from this Country; provided the terms be not in any case less advantageous than those now announced. There is always danger of considerable delay in waiting for approbation from hence, before a new loan can be undertaken; and favourable *moments* may be lost; for there are periods more or less favourable.

I think there is no probability for sometime to come that loans can be obtained on better terms. And I may add that as far as I can judge, Mr Short has conducted himself in the affair with judgment and discretion; and there will be safety in allowing him the latitude proposed. I believe also it will be adviseable to apply the present loan in the same manner as the former, that is to say one half, or perhaps 1,500,000 guilders to the use of France, and the residue to the purchase of the Debt here; on this point also I request your direction. I have the honor to be with the most perfect respect Sir Your most Obedient & humble servant

Alex: Hamilton

LB, DLC:GW; copy, DNA: RG 233, Third Congress, 1793–1795, Records of Legislative Proceedings, Committee Reports, and Papers.

1. Alexander Hamilton is referring to the Holland loan of March 1791, negotiated by the firm of Willink, Van Staphorst, and Hubbard, the bankers of the United States in Amsterdam. Hamilton authorized William Short, the American chargé d'affaires in Paris, on 1 Sept. 1790 to open a new loan for the United States in Amsterdam, instructing him to borrow "*on the best terms which shall be found practicable*" the sums needed to pay the principal and interest due on the foreign debt to the end of 1791. Short was not to engage for additional sums unless it could be done on terms more advantageous to the United States than the terms upon which the debt now stood. See Hamilton to GW, 3 Sept. 1790, n.2; Syrett, *Hamilton Papers*, 7:6–14. Short's letter to Hamilton of 2 Dec. 1790 announcing the new loan described in detail the Amsterdam money market, the terms upon which foreign loans were negotiated, and the bankers who negotiated them in the city. Since it was an inauspicious time for opening loans there, Short warned that filling the new loan of 2,500,000 guilders, or one million dollars, would proceed slowly and suggested that it might be best to postpone opening the loan until February 1791, which would create no inconvenience, as payments on the American debt to France could continue as planned (ibid., 175–87).

2. Hamilton is probably referring to the injunction GW suggested incorporating in instructions to the United States bankers in Amsterdam: "That the Agent shall never . . . open a new loan 'till the old one has been expressly approved of by the President of the United States" (Tobias Lear to Hamilton, 26 Aug. 1790, DLC:GW).

3. The cabinet, in what was probably its first formal meeting, met at Jefferson's residence on 11 April. See Thomas Jefferson to GW, 10 April, n.1, and Hamilton to GW, 14 April. See also GW to Hamilton, Jefferson, and Henry Knox, 4 April; Hamilton to John Adams, and Adams to Hamilton, both 9 April, in Syrett, *Hamilton Papers*, 8:258.

From Thomas Jefferson

Sir   Philadelphia Apr. 10. 1791.

I had the honor of addressing you on the 2d inst. which I presume would overtake you at Richmond. the present I imagine will not overtake you till you get to Wilmington. since my last I have been honoured with your two letters of March 31. and two others of Apr. 4. one of which was circular. a copy of this I sent to the Vice president, and as Colo. Hamilton has asked a consultation on a letter of mister Short's we shall have a meeting with the Vice-president tomorrow. I will then ask their advice also on the communication to Colo. Beckwith relative to the supplies to the Indians.[1] finding, within a day or two after my letter to you of Mar. 27. that Putnam was gone to the Westward, I detained my letter to him, and applied to Genl Knox from whom I obtained some information on the Eastern boundary. no official information of the affair of Moose island is received here.[2] perhaps it is on the road to you. nor do we hear anything more of the disturbance said to have arisen on the borders of New York.[3] I have asked the favour of my friend mister Madison to think on the subject of the Consular commission to mister Barclay. so far as we have done so & conferred together as yet, we are both of opinion it may be used; but we shall think & confer further. I presume your only doubt arose on the constitutional powers to 'supply vacancies' during the recess of Congress. there was an omission also (which might strike your mind) of the limitation of the commission 'till the end of the next session of Congress.' as the constitution limits them, this clause is always useless; however as it does no harm it has been usually inserted in the commissions. but in the case of mister Barclay such a clause would require a very awkward explanation to the Emperor of Marocco: and as mister Barclay is apprised of the constitutional determination of his commission it was thought better to omit the useless expression of it. the acquisition of ground at George town is really noble. considering that only £25. an acre is to be paid for any grounds taken for the public, and the streets not to be counted, which will in fact reduce it to about £19. an acre, I think very liberal reserves should be made for the public. your proclamation came to hand the night of the 5th. Dunlap's & Bache's papers for the morning of the 6th being already filled, I could only get it into Brown's evening paper of the 6th or the 7th.[4] the bill for the federal buildings passed the representatives here by 42. to 10. but it was rejected yesterday by 9. to 6. in the Senate, or, to speak more exactly, it was postponed till the next session. in the meantime spirited proceedings at George-town will probably, under the continuance of your patronage, prevent the revival of the bill.[5] I received last night from Majr L'Enfant a request to furnish him any plans of towns I could, for his examination. I accordingly send him, by this post, plans of Frankfort on the Mayne, Carlsruhe, Amsterdam, Strasburg, Paris, Orleans, Bordeaux, Lyons, Montpelier, Marseilles, Turin and Milan, on large & accurate scales, which I procured while in those towns respectively. they are none of them however comparable to the old Babylon, revived in Philadelphia, & exemplified. while in Europe I selected about a dozen or two of the handsomest fronts of private buildings of which I have the plates. perhaps it might decide the taste of the new town, were these to be engraved here, and distributed gratis among the inhabitants of Georgetown. the expence would be trifling.[6]

I inclose you extracts from a letter of mister Short's of Jan. 24. one of Jan. 28. has since come to hand, containing nothing but a translation of the Letter said to have been written by the emperor to the king of France, but which he suspects to be a forgery, a forged bull of the pope having lately appeared in the same way. he says very serious differences have arisen between the minister of Prussia at Liege, and the Imperial commanding officer there.[7]

I also inclose the debates of the Pennsylvania assembly on the bill for the federal buildings, and the bill itself;[8] and have the honor to be with sentiments of the most perfect respect & attachment Sir Your most obedient & most humble servt

Th: Jefferson

ALS, DNA: RG 59, Miscellaneous Letters; ALS (letterpress copy), DLC: Thomas Jefferson Papers; LB, DLC:GW.

1. For GW's suggestion to use George Beckwith to convey to Quebec a demand that the British cease arming and supplying hostile Indians, see GW to Jefferson, 4 April. On 11 April John Adams and the department heads met to discuss a letter Alexander Hamilton had received from William Short, and then they considered Henry Knox's concern that the Six Nations might join the northwestern tribes in a more general Indian war. Finally they turned to the matter of Beckwith's communication. Hamilton informed the others that Beckwith had assured him that the British had given the Indians only customary annual presents. The group agreed that Knox should approach Beckwith informally and impress upon him the administration's dissatisfaction with Lord Dorchester's policies. That evening Knox personally informed Beckwith that the American government had received credible reports that the British posts were supplying the Indians with arms in quantities sufficient to carry on the war, which Beckwith denied. Knox made no formal report of this conversation, but see his draft "Memorandum of a conversation which passed between the subscriber and Lt Colonel Beckwith . . . ⟨Evening⟩ of the 11th of April 1791" (NNGL: Knox Papers). Regarding Knox's efforts a failure, Jefferson turned to James Madison to convey the American position more forcefully. See Jefferson to GW, 17, 24 April.

2. On 1 April Jefferson wrote to Benjamin Hawkins: "There has been also a small fracas on our disputed territory to the Eastward, by our sheriff's levy-

ing taxes on the inhabitants of Moose island, who as to that article, wished to be neutrals" (*Jefferson Papers*, 20:89–90). Possession of Moose Island, which separates Passamaquoddy Bay from Cobscook Bay, was not settled until 1817 when a British-American commission awarded the island to the United States.

3. For the disturbances on Lake Champlain, see Jefferson to GW, 5 June 1791 and note 2.

4. Andrew Brown published GW's proclamation of 30 Mar. in the *Federal Gazette* [Philadelphia], 6 April.

5. For the bill in the Pennsylvania legislature to provide buildings for the federal government in Philadelphia, see Jefferson to GW, 27 Mar. and note 5.

6. For Jefferson's letter of 10 April to Pierre-Charles L'Enfant, see *Jefferson Papers*, 20:86–87. His suggestion that his collection of plates be reproduced and distributed in Georgetown was not acted upon.

7. For William Short's letters to Jefferson of 24, 28 Jan., see ibid., 18:603–10, 19:117–18.

8. These enclosures have not been found.

From Henry Knox

Sir,   War Department [Philadelphia], 10th April, 1791.

I have the honor to acknowledge the receipt of your separate letter of the 4th instant, and also of your joint letter of the same date, to the heads of the departments.

By the information from Fort Harmar of the 17th, and Pittsburg of the 31st, it would appear that the Delawares and Wyandots are committing depredations, and that they will be joined in the War against us.

But what is still more disagreeable, it is to be apprehended that the Senekas mainly may be in the same predicament.

For a party of Munsey or Delaware Indians, who reside upon the waters of the Allegany, towards lake Erie, on the 21st ultimo, murdered Nine Men, Women and Children, within twenty miles of Fort Pitt, on the west side of the Allegany.

This was on the day the Cornplanter set out from Fort Pitt. The inhabitants were so blindly enraged, as to suspect the Cornplanter and his party, and agitated plans to cut him off—had they proceeded and succeeded, it would have completed the business, and the War would indisputably have become general—Lieutenant Jeffers, of the federal troops, accompanied the Cornplanter, and would probably have shared his fate.[1]

Every exertion must be made to prevent the six Nations from

joining the Western Indians—The Post at french Creek must be strengthened, and perhaps a party sent to protect the Cornplanter's settlements from the fang of the Whites.

Affairs being so critical with the six Nations, I have judged it adviseable to assemble them as soon as possible, in order to brighten the Chain of friendship and to prevent all jealousies. I have accordingly desired Colonel Pickering, who may be depended upon to invite them to a Meeting, at some convenient place at an early day—and that in the mean time, that he should repair to this City for particular Orders.[2] I shall lay this subject before the Vice-President, and the other heads of departments tomorrow, for their approbation.

The recruiting service proceeds well. I judge we have about three hundred Regulars and levies inlisted at different places, to Connecticut inclusively.

One Company of levies well clothed, will march from Carlisle about the 25th and the rest as fast as recruited.

The marching of the Regulars will commence by Companies. I hope by the first of May, and follow in succession, as fast as recruited.

Present appearances indicate, that the main force will be collected by the 15th of July, as originally designed.

Brigadier General Butler, was directed to have set off for Maryland on the 6th but he has delayed it until this day. But as the Virginia and Maryland Levies, will not have far to march, I hope they will be on the frontiers, by the 15th or 20th of June. I have the honor to be With the highest Respect Your Obedient humble servant

H. Knox
secy of War

LS, DLC:GW; LB, DLC:GW.

1. Lt. John Jeffers served as a private in the Continental army during the Revolution. He was appointed an ensign in the U.S. Army in 1789 and was promoted in October 1790. Jeffers was accompanying Cornplanter and his party home when residents of western Pennsylvania set out to attack them in retaliation for the murder of nine white settlers twenty miles from Pittsburgh by Delaware, Wyandot, and Seneca warriors. The enraged frontiersmen plundered the boat carrying the gifts that were presented to the Seneca chiefs during their visit to Philadelphia in December 1790. See Henry Knox to GW, 31 Mar. 1791.

2. After returning to Philadelphia from his mission to the Seneca in the fall

of 1790, Timothy Pickering reported to GW before going home to Luzerne County, Pennsylvania. Hoping to be made postmaster general, he declined the superintendency of Indian affairs for the Northern Department. On 10 April Knox asked Samuel Hodgdon if Pickering might be persuaded to undertake another mission to the Indians, and Hodgdon recommended to Pickering that he accept the assignment (Upham, *Pickering*, 2:485–86). Pickering met with Knox in Philadelphia and agreed to undertake a mission to the Six Nations (see Pickering to GW, 2 May and notes 1 and 2).

From Tobias Lear

Sir,   Philadelphia April 10th 1791.

Since my letter of the 5th I have been honored with your favors of the 3d & 6th of the present month, with their enclosures.

In Colo. Cannon's letter to you there appear'd (as you apprehended) an idea that he conceived himself authorized to let your lands on the Ohio and Kanawa; but he does not express an intention of doing anything respecting them until he shall have seen you, which he expected would have been the case this spring. I have, however, written to him (by the post) giving information of your having disposed of those lands—and shall send a duplicate of my letter to him by one of the Representatives from that County when the Assembly rises, which it is expected to do this week.[1]

As there have been no further accounts from Fraunces, either through his son or from himself, it is presumable that he does not intend to come; I have, therefore, taken such measures to ascertain the point with respect to Holker's man, that if he inclines, and has it in his power to come, he may do it without any impropriety on either part.[2]

The man who has been employed in the Garden shall be paid agreeable to your directions; and every attention shall be given to have it kept in complete order by our own people. Rhemur and Jacob have little else to do at present.

Mrs Washington has, for some days past, been very much afflicted with a violent cold—which confined her to her Chamber and swelled her face very much; but she is now, thank God, recovering very fast, and today appears tolerably well.[3] The Children and the rest of the family enjoy good health—Mrs Lear begs you to accept her grateful respects & best wishes for a con-

tinuance of your health—With the most sincere Attachment
& highest respect, I have the honor to be—Sir, Your obliged &
very humble svt

Tobias Lear.

ALS, DLC:GW.

1. Tobias Lear wrote to John Cannon on 9 April 1791: "In a letter which
you wrote to the President of the United States on the 17 of last month, you
mention that many people had applied to you to go upon his lands lying on
the Ohio and Kanawa rivers From this circumstance the President is apprehensive that you might give some encouragement to those who have applied
as above, and induce them to remove thither—He has therefore directed me
to inform you that he has disposed of all those lands which he possessed on
those rivers, and requests that no steps may be taken to engage settlers to go
there on his account" (DLC:GW). Cannon's letter to GW of 17 Mar. 1791 has
not been found.

2. Samuel Fraunces finally returned to the president's household on 12 May
(Decatur, *Private Affairs of Washington*, 233).

3. Martha Washington was sufficiently recovered to visit Peale's Museum on
16 April (ibid., 222).

From Alexander Hamilton

Sir   Philada April 11th 1791.

I have just received a letter from Mr King in these words[1]—
"Mr Elliot, who it has been said was appointed will not come to
America, owing say his friends here to a disinclination on his
part which has arisen from the death of his eldest or only son.[2]
Mr Seaton yesterday read me an abstract of a letter from London dated February 2. & written, as he observed, by a man of
information, which says—'Mr Frazer is appointed Plenipotentiary to the United States of America and will go out as soon
as it is ascertained here that a correspondent character is appointed in America'—Although Mr Elliott might not have been
altogether adequate to the appointment, yet he would not have
been a bad choice; it is questionable whether we can say even as
much as that for Mr Frazer, who is probably the Gentleman
lately resident with the Hans towns, and formerly consul at Algiers, and who is said to be a wrong headed impetuous man.
Should this information be correct, the appointment is not only
unpromising but is also a pretty strong proof of the misguided
opinions of the British administration concerning this Coun-

try."[3] Nothing except the foregoing letter occurs worth communication more than is contained in my official dispatch herewith.[4] With the truest and most respectful attachment I have the honor to be Sir Your Obedt. Servant

A. Hamilton

LB, DLC:GW.

1. The editors of the *Hamilton Papers* found no such letter from Rufus King to Alexander Hamilton.

2. For Andrew Elliot's declination of the appointment of British minister to the United States, see John Graves Simcoe to Evan Nepean, 16 Mar., in Cruikshank, *Simcoe Papers*, 1:21. See also Simcoe to Henry Dundas, 12 Aug., ibid., 48.

3. "Mr Seaton" is William Seton. "Mr Frazer" is probably Charles Henry Fraser, who served as secretary of the British legation in Russia in 1787–88 and later served in Madrid as minister plenipotentiary until his recall in November 1790, when he became minister resident of the Hanse towns. Archibald C. Fraser served as British consul in Algiers from 1766 to 1774.

4. For Hamilton's enclosed "official dispatch," see Hamilton to GW, 10 April 1791 (first letter).

To Tobias Lear

Dear Sir,   RICHMOND [Va.], April 12th. 1791.

Since my last to you from Mount Vernon, your letters of the 3d. and 5th. Instant have been recd., the last at this place where I arrived yesterday to dinner.[1]

If the case is as you suspect, it is expedient and proper to remove Washington to a School in which he will make some progress in his learning; and that it is so, I have had some suspicions for some time, principally on account of his fondness of going to the College. Boys of his age are better pleased with relaxed discipline—and the inattention of their tutors, than with conduct that brings them forward. It would have been highly pleasing to me (for the reasons, which I have often expressed) to have continued Washington at the College, but, if after the enquiries you have made, it should appear, that there is either incompetency in the masters from the number of boys in the School, or from other causes, I will not waste his time in compliment to that Seminary,—but before you finally decide on this matter, it is my wish as Colo. Hamilton, Genl. Knox and the Attorney-General have sons in the same predicament (if they are not removed) that you would consult and act in Concert with them; & I shall be satisfied in whatever is done in consequence of it. And should like to have him at the same School that Hamilton's son goes to.

The Attorney-General's case and mine I conceive, from a conversation I had with him respecting our Slaves, is some what different. He in order to qualify himself for practice in the Courts of Pennsylvania, was obliged to take the Oaths of Citizenship to that State; whilst my residence is incidental as an Officer of Government only, but whether among people who are in the practice of *enticing* slaves *even* where there is *no* colour of law for it, this distinction will avail, I know not, and therefore beg you will take the best advise you can on the subject, and in case it shall be found that any of my Slaves may, or any for them shall attempt their freedom at the expiration of six months, it is my wish and desire that you would send the whole, or such part of them as Mrs. Washington may not chuse to keep, home—for although I do not think they would be benefitted by the change, yet the idea of freedom might be too great a temptation for them to resist. At any rate it might, if they conceived they had a right to it, make them insolent in a State of Slavery. As all except Hercules and Paris are dower negroes, it behoves me to prevent the emancipation of them, otherwise I *shall* not only loose the use of them, but may have them to pay for. If upon taking good advise it is found expedient to send them back to Virginia, I wish to have it accomplished under pretext that may deceive both them and the Public;—and none I think would so effectually do this, as Mrs. Washington coming to Virginia next month (towards the middle or latter end of it, as she seemed to have a wish to do) if she can accomplish it by any convenient and agreeable means, with the assistance of the Stage Horses &c. This would naturally bring her maid and Austin—and Hercules under the idea of coming home to *Cook* whilst we remained there, might be sent on in the Stage. Whether there is occasion for this or not according to the result of your enquiries, or issue the thing as it may, I request that these Sentiments and this advise may be known to none but *yourself* & *Mrs. Washington.* From the following expression in your letter "that those who were of *age* might follow the example of his (the Attorney's people) after a residence of six months"—it would seem that *none* could apply before the end of May—& that the non age of Christopher, Richmond & Oney is a bar to them.[2]

I offer Mrs. Lear the child and yourself my best wishes—and with Sincere Esteem I am Your Affecte. friend

Letters and Recollections of George Washington, 37–39.

1. GW left Fredericksburg, Va., early on 10 April and arrived at Richmond the next afternoon (*Diaries,* 6:108).

2. For the background to the status on GW's slaves in Philadelphia, see Lear to GW, 5 April and note 3. Tobias Lear corrected GW's mistaken assessment of the legal standing of his slaves in Philadelphia in a letter to GW of 24 April.

To the Officials and Citizens of Richmond

Gentlemen,   [Richmond, Va., 12 April 1791]

The very distinguished manner in which you are pleased to notice my public services, and to express your regard towards me, demands and receives a grateful and affectionate return.[1]

If to my agency in the affairs of our common-country may be ascribed any of the great advantages, which it now enjoys, I am amply and most agreeably rewarded in contemplating the happiness, and receiving the approbation of my fellow-citizens, whose freedom and felicity are fixed, I trust for ever, on an undecaying basis of wisdom and virtue.

Among the blessings which a gracious Providence may be pleased to bestow on the people of America, I shall behold with peculiar pleasure the prosperity of your city, and the individual happiness of its inhabitants.

G. Washington.

LB, DLC:GW.

1. At three o'clock on 12 April, GW received an address from Richmond mayor George Nicholson and the city aldermen and common council members: "If in you the Mayor Aldermen and Commonality of Richmond beheld only the chief Magistrate of the United States of America, they would indeed feel all that Respect which is due to the ruler of a free people; but when they contemplate those virtues which have excited the universal approbation of your own Country, and the admiration of all mankind, they cannot approach you without emotions of veneration too big for utterances too pleasing to be suppressed. If the voice of the people be the trumpet of the Almighty, the universality of that gratitude which pervades every bosom in America, will ever remain an incontestible proof of the plaudit of heaven on the fortitude and wisdom which secured to our Country independence and Empire, and

which now leads her to wealth & glory. We well know that to a mind like yours which is fraught with benevolence and affection for all mankind, the gratitude and love of the nation which you have saved must be the best reward; yet we are aware that to such a mind, nothing could be more painful than that servility which would convert the sentiment of Love into the Language of Adulation; we shun therefore the expression of the one least we should incur the imputation of the other; and while we beg leave to congratulate you on the astonishing Success which has heretofore attended all your indeavours for promoting the public welfare, we look forward with confidence and joy to the continuance of the administration, which, thro the blessing of the Supreme Being, hath already been productive of so much general happiness to the American Empire; and we implore that being, propitiously to Smile on all your future designs, to guard and protect you in your intended tour, to grant you every earthly good, and, that, when his providence shall see fit to summon you hence, you may be wafted to the regions of eternal happiness Lamented by Men and welcomed by Angels" (DLC:GW). For GW's arrival and stay at Richmond, see *Diaries*, 6:108–11.

From Thomas Sumter, Sr.

Dear Sir   Stateburgh [S.C.] 12th April 1791.
Being informed by my son that he will wait on you in Cha[rle]ston at your arrival, I am happy in having an Occasion of offering you the sincerest welcome to our State, together with my best wishes for your health & happiness, not only at present but in perpetuity.[1]

In your travels you may yet remark the traces of British devastation, & I am afraid, the pernicious effects of impolitic counsels, and lax principles—But you will also discern a happy contrast to this representation, in the prospects of vigor & prosperity, that are now budding from the unity of Our American Governments, & which, have been so strongly Assured to us by the happy management which has charactered the first & most trying period of your Presidency—I hope Sir, this freedom will be excused as I have been moved to it from considerations of the highest esteem & the evermost regard—And likewise to declare how happy the People of this quarter & myself should be made, by having an opportunity of receiving *one* amongst us, who, is always thought & spoken of with most affectionate emotion.

We have been led to suggest our desire from a report of your having it in your intention to visit Collumbia & Camden, the first, lies opposite to State b⟨*mutilated*⟩ 30 miles distance & the

latter at not m⟨*mutilated*⟩ 20—So that the deviation will be perhaps, more trifling than the pleasure which the view of those
Highlands, may afford, which have been doubtless described to
you[2]—Allow me Dear Sir, to subscribe myself with the truest
sentiments of respect & regard yr most Obdt Hbe Sert

Thos Sumter senr

ALS, PHi: Gratz Collection; copy, WHi: Draper Collection, Sumter MSS.

    Congressman Thomas Sumter, Sr. (1734–1832), a native of Hanover
County, Va., served in the French and Indian War before he was arrested for
debt in the early 1760s. He escaped from jail and fled to the backcountry of
South Carolina. During the American Revolution, Sumter distinguished himself as the commander of a band of partisan militia that successfully harassed
the British in 1780–81. He served in the state legislature until 1790 and voted
against the federal Constitution in the state ratifying convention of 1788.

    1. Thomas Sumter, Jr. (1768–1840), was his father's only surviving child.

    2. GW did not make the suggested detour to Stateburg.

From Samuel Coleman

Sir,   Council Office Richmond [Va.] April 13th 1791.

    Having declined the Appropriation to your *own private Emolu-
ment* of certain shares in the Potowmack and James river Companies, which it was the intention of the Legislature of this State
to have vested in you; and having given the preference to such
public Appropriation of them *as to you may appear most subservient
to the enlightened and patriotic Views of the Legislature* in that particular Instance:[1] Can you, sir, pardon an individual of little consequence to the community, but as he may be the instrument of
Service to it, for presuming to suggest, that the encouragement
of a Free School in the neighbourhood of this place, might be
attended with much public benefit; and that an Appropriation
of one or more share or shares in the James river Company as
to you may seem proper may with the encouragement of the
Citizens of Richmond, effectually answer so salutary a purpose.

    I inclose a temporary subscription, which will in some mea-
sure serve to show the sense of the Citizens of this place on the
subject.[2] And have the Honour to be Sir, your very obedt
Servant

Samuel Coleman.

The nature of the inclosed paper will plead its excuse for coming
before you in so defaced a garb.

ALS, DLC:GW.

1. For GW's decision to dedicate to a public purpose the shares in the Potomac and James River companies granted to him by the state of Virginia, see Benjamin Harrison to GW, 6 Jan. 1785 and note 1.

2. Tobias Lear docketed the letter's cover: "The Paper mentioned to be enclosd was not recd by T.L. with this letter."

To the Commissioners for the Federal District

Gentlemen,   Richmond [Va.], April 13, 1791.

Agreeably to the assurance given to Mr Carroll, I applied, immediately upon my arrival in this city, to Governor Randolph for two thousand dollars for federal purposes under your direction. Although by the law of this State, the payments of the one hundred and twenty thousand dollars are to be made by installments, the Governor is well disposed to advance the money at earlier periods—but alas! the treasury is empty—He has promised me however that, so soon as he can obtain the above sum, it shall be remitted or made subject to your draught.[1]

My anxiety to have the agreement which was entered into at Georgetown on the 30th ult. carried into full and complete effect, by legal conveyances, is such (thereby leaving nothing to chance) that I cannot forbear repeating my wish that it may be done without delay, notwithstanding the persuasion I am under that the propriety of the measure will prompt you to the execution of the business in a manner best calculated to answer the public purposes.[2]

It having been intimated to me that the Proprietors of Georgetown are desirous of being comprehended within the limits of the federal city, I see no objection to the measure provided the Land holders, adjoining to it, included within the red lines of Messrs Beatty and Orme's survey, referred to in the first offer from Georgetown, agreed to cede to the public on the same terms with those under the last (or combined) agreement—and if those within the blue lines are likewise desirous of being comprehended, on the same terms, it may be done—The doing of which would only place them on the same footing with the rest of the Subscribers, at the same time that it would render the plan more comprehensive, beneficial, and promising—drawing the centre of the federal city nearer to the present town.[3]

If this measure is seriously contemplated the present is the fit moment for carrying it into effect; because, in that case it will become part of the original plan, and the old and new towns would be blended and assimilated as nearly as circumstances will admit—and Major L'Enfant might be instructed to lay out the whole accordingly. I have the honor to be, Gentlemen, Your most obedient Servant

Go: Washington

P.S. Since writing the foregoing I have again conversed with Governor Randolph, and have drawn upon him, payable to your order, for forty thousand dollars, being the first installment—one thousand of which he hopes to have ready within a few days—the remainder to be subject to your draughts. He will endeavor to transmit the money so as to prevent trouble or inconvenience—but, on this head he will write to you himself more at large.[4]

G.W.

LS, DLC: Presidential MSS; LB, DLC:GW; copy, DNA: RG 42, Records of the Commissioners for the District of Columbia, Letters Sent, 1791–1802.

For the background to this letter, see Agreement of the Proprietors of the Federal City, 30 Mar. and source note, and GW to the Commissioners for the Federal District, 3 April and note 1.

1. According to the terms of "An act concerning an advance of money to the government of the United States for public buildings," passed by the Virginia general assembly on 27 Dec. 1790, $120,000 was to be disbursed to the federal government in three annual payments of $40,000 (13 Hening 125).

2. Richard Bland Lee wrote James Madison on 17 April that GW had informed him in Fredericksburg on 8 or 9 April "that all the preparatory steps for the selection of the scite for the federal city would be completed by his return to Mt. Vernon in the beginning of June" (*Madison Papers*, 14:6–7).

3. For the prior agreement with the Georgetown proprietors, see Agreement of the Georgetown, Md., Property Owners, 13 Oct. 1790. For the Beatty and Orme plat (not found), see William Deakins, Jr., to GW, 3 Nov. and note 1, and 18 Nov. 1790 and note 2.

4. GW wrote to John Pendleton (1719–1799), auditor of Virginia, on 13 April 1791: "In conformity to an Act of the General Assembly of Virginia intituled 'An Act concerning an advance of money to the Government of the United States for public Buildings,['] please to issue a Warrant to the amount of forty thousand dollars, in favour of Messrs Johnson, Stuart, and Carrol; Commissioners, appointed agreeably to an Act of Congress for establishing the temporary and permanent seat of the Government of the United States" (LS, Vi).

From Robert Gamble

Sir.   Richmond [Va.] April 13. 1791

I cannot suppress the impulse I feel at this oportunity to acquaint you, that I have honored one of my Children (now Six
years old) with the name of *Washington*. Notwithstanding so
many distinguished Characters have done *themselves & family that
honor;* I flatter myself none were influenced with more respect
for your person & character.

Having intruded thus far, I trust the goodness of your heart
will over-look any impropriety there may *appear* in the communication—You will ascribe it to the irresistible influence of affection, at this happy moment of seeing a person so beloved;
and not to any improper motive Permit me to add my sincerest
wishes for your happiness. And am With due respect Your mo.
Obt and mo. Hum. Svt

Ro. Gamble

LS, DLC:GW. GW mistakenly docketed this letter "Rich Gamble Esq." The
handwriting is clearly that of Robert Gamble, who wrote to GW on 3 Jan.
1796 (DLC:GW).

Robert Gamble (1754–1810) served as a first lieutenant of Virginia troops
in the Continental army from 1776 until his promotion to captain in 1778. He
was captured at Camden, S.C., in 1780 and retired from the army in January
1783.

To Thomas Jefferson

Dear Sir,   Richmond [Va.] April 13th 1791

Your letter of the 2d came to my hands at this place. Part of
it did as you supposed, & might well suppose, astonished me exceedingly.

I think it not only right that Mr Carmichael should be furnished with a copy of the genuine letters to Mr G. Morris, but
that Mr [Morris][1] should also know the result of his conferences
with the Duke of Leeds at the Court of Madrid. The contents of
my official letters to him you are acquainted with—my private
ones were few, and nothing in either of them relative to England
or Spain; how it comes to pass therefore that such interpretations as the extracts recite, should be given, he best can account for.

Being hurried, I shall only add that I shall proceed on my journey to morrow, & from good information have a dreary one before me in some parts thereof.[2] Yrs sincerely

Go: Washington

P.S. The footing upon which you have placed Mr Carmichael is good.

G.W.

ALS, DLC: Thomas Jefferson Papers; LB, DLC:GW.
  1. "Morris" is supplied from the letter-book copy.
  2. For GW's departure from Richmond early on 14 April, see *Diaries,* 6:111–12.

From John K. Read

Sir,   [Richmond, Va., 13 April 1791][1]

I have taken the freedom, to enclose for your perusal, a Copy of the preface to a work intitled, "the new *Ahiman Rezon,*["] assigned to me for publication, by the *Grand Lodge* of *Virginia,* which work being now ready for the press (so soon as a competent number of subscribers are procured to defray the expence) I have adventured to sollicit the honour, of dedicating it to you.[2]

If you should find on perusal of the preface, (which will give you the outlines of the work) that there is utility in the production, I flatter myself the obscurity of my name will not militate against the success of my application—I beg leave to refer you to my friend the honble Mr Lyons, for my caracter as a *Man*—as an *Author* my claim to your attention, can only be, in proportion to the merits of the work.[3]

The Grand secretary, who will deliver you this, will do me the favour, of conveying your Answer,[4] I have the honour to be, with the most perfect respect and Esteem Sir yr Most Obdet & devoted Servt

J. K. Read

L, probably in the handwriting of Basil Wood, DLC:GW.
  John K. Read (1746–1805) was the son of Benjamin Franklin's brother-in-law. He became a physician and moved to The Grove in Hanover County, Va., before relocating to Goochland County. During the Revolution Read served as a surgeon with the Virginia militia and afterwards settled in Richmond. An active Mason, he was appointed deputy grand master of Virginia on 28 Oct. 1790.

1. GW endorsed the undated letter as "received 13th April 1791." The Grand Lodge of Virginia held its annual meeting on 13–14 April 1791 at Mason's Hall in Richmond, but there is no evidence that GW attended it.

2. The enclosed three pages was a manuscript copy, apparently in Read's handwriting, of the draft of a preface to *The New Ahiman Rezon: Containing the Laws and Constitutions of the Grand Lodge of Virginia . . .* (Richmond, 1791), which Read undertook at the direction of the Grand Lodge of Virginia in consequence of a resolution adopted 29 April 1790. Published at the author's considerable expense by John Dixon, it received the formal sanction of the Grand Lodge in May 1792. Read petitioned the Grand Lodge in November 1794 that it purchase 250 copies for distribution to Virginia lodges across the state (Dove, *Proceedings of the Grand Lodge of Virginia,* 58, 59, 93–94, 130, 142–43).

3. Mr. Lyons was probably Peter Lyons (d. 1801) of Hanover County, Va., who was appointed to the Virginia Court of Appeals in 1789. His second wife, Judith Bassett, was a sister of Burwell Bassett, Sr., who was married to Martha Washington's sister.

4. Basil Wood was the grand secretary of the Grand Lodge of Virginia. Read noted to William Jackson on the letter's cover that "The grand secretary will wait on the president in the morning for an answer to this letter." No reply from GW has been found, nor do the published minutes of the Grand Lodge indicate that he made any.

From James Simpson

Sir　　　　　　　　　　　　　　　Gibraltar 13th April 1791.

I had the honor of addressing Your Excellency 21st September last year by the American Brig Ann—John Martin Master bound for Philadelphia, accompanying a dispatch from Francis Chiappe Esqr.[1]

By this opportunity of the English Ship Roman Eagle—Samuel Glover Master for New York, I now send another packet for Your Excelly received a few days ago from Mr Chiappe.[2] I have the honor to be with great respect Your Excellencys Most Obedient and Most Humble Servant

James Simpson

ALS, DNA: RG 59, Despatches from Consular Officers: Gibraltar. A duplicate of the letter sent by Simpson, minus the first paragraph, is also in the dispatches from Gibraltar.

1. For James Simpson's letter of 21 Sept. 1790 and the dispatch from Francisco (Francesco) Chiappe it covered, see Simpson to GW, 25 Aug. 1790, n.3.

2. The enclosed letter from Chiappe to GW, dated Rabat, Morocco, 22 Mar. 1791 (DNA:PCC, item 98), covered a duplicate of his dispatch to John Jay of 3 Dec. 1790 and described the diplomatic corps at the Moroccan court. When

Chiappe on 8 Nov. sent GW a duplicate of his dispatch of 22 Mar., he also enclosed two lists of the gifts that the Danish and Swedish ambassadors had presented as tribute to the emperor of Morocco. Tobias Lear transmitted Simpson's letter with its enclosures to the secretary of state, with the president's request that he take Chiappe's letter under consideration (Lear to Thomas Jefferson, 9 July 1791, DNA: RG 59, Miscellaneous Letters).

From Samuel Waldo

Portland [District of Maine] 13 April 1791. Applies for the post of excise inspector for the District of Maine and reminds GW of the prior recommendation of the late James Bowdoin.[1]

ALS, DLC:GW.
   1. Samuel Waldo had applied to GW for an excise post on 25 Oct. 1790. Leonard Jarvis recommended Waldo to GW on 11 June, noting that Waldo had been "educated in my Counting house" and was a young man of "Modesty & Sence of Honor as well as of Abilities & Integrity" (DLC:GW). Both apparently were unaware that GW had specified that the duties of excise inspector for Maine, the first survey of Massachusetts, were to be performed by the state supervisor, Nathaniel Gorham (see Executive Order, 15 Mar. 1791).

From Martha Dangerfield Bland

Sir,   Cawson [Va.], April 14th 1791
   When I did myself the honour to write to you upon the Subject of My Slave withheld by the Quakers of Phyladelphia it was by the advice of a lawer Eminent in the Country—that it was necessary to apply to a power Superior to the Executive of that State, I meant not Sir, *to intrude* my request upon you, as Mr Randolph seems to hint, but I have the pleasure to find, that however dignified you are in your public character, your Mind, is infinitely Superior to the fancied greatness which accident has made so important in others.
   I beg pardon for all the trouble I have given you on two occasions, & be assured that I will never plague you again.
   I woud ask you to Visit Cawson but apprehend it woud be a useless invitation, & perhaps it may be deem'd presumtuous.[1] Adieu Sir! May you injoy Every blessing this world Can Give You.

                                              M. Bland

ALS, DLC:GW.
1. GW replied to Martha Dangerfield Bland's letter of 23 Feb. on 18 Mar. 1791, enclosing a copy of Edmund Randolph's opinion on her case.

To John Brown

Sir,   Richmond [Va.], April 14. 1791.
Although the deed of bargain and sale from Muse, dated in 1774, conveys all the right he had to lands in the patent for 7276 acres—yet as there must have been some inducement to take the subsequent deeds in 1784 I am inclined, though unable to account for them, to have them fully recorded—especially as the quantity of land thereby conveyed differs pretty considerably⟨.⟩[1] I am Sir, your most obedient Servant

G. Washington.

LB, DLC:GW.
"Mr Brown," the addressee, was probably John Brown (1750–1810), clerk to the general court of Virginia.
1. Under the terms of Gov. Robert Dinwiddie's Proclamation of 1754, GW and other officers of the Virginia Regiment were entitled to 200,000 acres in the Ohio country. Among these officers was Lt. Col. George Muse (1720–1790) who resigned after the Battle of Fort Necessity in 1754 under accusations of cowardice. Uncertain if he would receive his grant, Muse agreed to give GW one-third of it if GW would bear the cost of surveying it and pay related expenses (see Agreement with George Muse, 3 Aug. 1770). In 1770 the Virginia council did grant the land to Muse, who agreed to exchange his remaining two-thirds of the 7,276-acre tract for 2,000 acres on the Kanawha that GW had purchased from William Bronaugh (see Muse to GW, 30 Nov. 1774). See also Edmund Pendleton to GW, 9 April 1784.

From the Commissioners for the Federal District

Sir   George Town—14th April 1791
We take the Liberty to inclose you a rough Plat of the lands between the Eastern Branch and Rock Creek with several different back lines, and a copy of an Entry of this Day in our proceedings, which will perhaps Sufficiently explain our present Circumstances—But as the inclosed Letter was addressed to us with a view of its being laid before you, we also send that and a Copy of the Written agreement.[1]

It is much to be regretted that your endeavours, and our Attendance here since Tuesday should produce no happier Effect; yet our anxiety to forward this Business could not prevail on us to accept of Limits which might narrow your Views and add to your Embarrasment—Any instruction you may be pleased to give shall have instant attention. but our difficulties follow you rather from our desire that you should have time to consider them, than any expectation that your time and situation will permit you to come to a final resolution and communicate it to us.

Majr LEnfant and Majr Ellicot are to proceed according to their Ideas of your Instructions as if the Conveyances had been made in the utmost Extent. We are Sir with the highest Respect Your Most obedt Servts

Thos Johnson
Dd Stuart
Danl Carroll

P.S. Since writing the above we have recd another Letter for the extention of the limits which we also inclose.

Copy, DNA: RG 42, Records of the Commissioners for the District of Columbia, Letters Sent, 1791–1802.

For background to this letter, see Agreement of the Proprietors of the Federal City, 30 Mar. 1791 and source note, and GW to the Commissioners for the Federal District, 3 April 1791 and notes 1 and 2.

1. The enclosed plat has not been found; nor has the enclosed extract from the commissioners' proceedings for 14 April, in which they recorded that, instead of receiving conveyances from the proprietors, they were met with protests from landowners who contended that the commissioners had exceeded the spirit of the agreement of 30 Mar. (DNA: RG 42, Records of the Commissioners for the District of Columbia, Proceedings, 1791–1802). Also enclosed were a copy of that agreement and copies of two letters (see postscript). The enclosed letters have not been located, but the copy of the first one among the records of the commissioners reads: "When the President communicated his Ideas to the Proprieters of land within both the offers, of the insufficiency of either, and the necessity of an union of Interests(:) He was requested to explain his views with respect to the form & extent of Territory he would wish, for the Federal City—and his reply was, to the best of our recollection—'that he would desire to begin at Evans's point on the Eastern Branch, & run from thence over Goose Creek some distance above the Fording place, to intersect the road leading from Geo. Town to Bladensburg about half a mile from Rock Creek—thence to Rock Creek, & with the Creek River & Branch, to the begining—supposing that about 3500 Acres was to be comprehended—but

upon some explanations by some of the Proprietors, it seemed to be understood, that more would be included, & probably 4000 Acres or upwards.['] In compliance with the views of the President, an agreement was prepared, in which the lines as mentioned by him, were omitted to be inserted, in the fullest confidence that though not mentioned in the agreement, they would be adhered to—or at least, if they were varied, it would not be include any considerably greater quantity of land, which we conceive, besides taking land, we never had it in contemplation would be required, would only tend to lessen the value of the rest, without any real benefit to the Public—As the price of lots would diminish in proportion as the number for sale increased. The Deed which you now present for signing goes far beyond our Idea of what was the Spirit of the Agreement—we would therefore wish to decline signing it—and hope it will answer every purpose of the President, to confine the lines of the City, agreeably to his explanation on the right of the Union of Interests, when there will be no difficulty on our part to making the proper conveyances" (Robert Peter, Notley Young, James M. Lingan, and Forrest & Stoddert to the Commissioners for the Federal District, 14 April, DNA: RG 42, Records of the Commissioners for the District of Columbia, Letters Sent, 1791–1802). The copy of the second letter, in the same record group, reads: "We are extremely Sorry to find, you are at this time prevented, from taking Deeds and Conveyances, of the lands granted to the President of the United States, by the respective proprietors, who Signed and Sealed the Agreement made with him on the 30th day of March last; owing to Some of these gentlemen, now alledging that, they had conceived, the President Should be confined to certain bounds and limits, as well as extent of territory, in laying out the Federal City. We however conceiving that, according to the beforementioned Agreement, the President has a right to lay out the City upon our lands, where and in what manner he pleases, are ready and willing on our part, fully to confirm by Deed and Conveyance, what we have already ratified by our hands and Seals: And we confide that, you will not Accede to any System, that may mutilate, disfigure, or render inconvenient the great Metropolis of America. Whatever might drop from the President in course of conversation, concerning the lands to be Occupied by the City, we do not consider conclusive; as it could not then be expected, he could with precision determine, what might be proper to include within its limits; the great object in view, being the founding an elegant, convenient, and agreeable Capital for the Union—Indeed it was our expectation, that after the different interests of Georgetown and Carrolsburgh were happily reconcilled, that no future cause of discontent would arise; neither did we expect, that it was ever imagined, the President Should be excluded from Accepting of Such grants as Should be made him, for the purposes of erecting the public buildings. We hope therefore, that nothing will be done to frustrate the views of the President, in Accomplishing the important Object of establishing the residence of Congress upon the Patowmack" (Charles Beatty, George Walker, Thomas Beall of George, and Samuel Davidson to the Commissioners for the Federal District, 14 April).

From Alexander Hamilton

Sir   Treasury Department [Philadelphia] April 14th 1791

I have the honor to send herewith a copy of my letter of the 10th inst: and of that from Mr Short of the 2d of December to which it refers; and also the copy of another letter from Mr Short of the 25th of January.[1]

The result of my submission to the Vice President and the heads of Departments has been, that they have unanimously advised me to instruct Mr Short to proceed to open a second loan as soon as the first shall be filled, and to extend the sum from two and a half to three millions of Guilders. I nevertheless request your direction concerning the alteration in his instruction, generally which is proposed in my letter.

Finding on recurring to it, your instruction to me competent to the disposition of the sum borrowed; I have directed Mr Short to apply one million and a half of the loan which was to commence in February, as a payment to France. The exchange between France & Holland afforded a benefit of more than ten ℔ Cent to the United States on the last payment.

I thought it adviseable to dispose of a principal part of the loan to this object, not only from the general considerations which operate in the case, but from a desire to counteract the success of some Negotiations with the French Court for the purchase of the Debt due from us, which are not for the interests of the United States.[2] I have the honor to be with the most perfect respect Sir Your most Obedt & most hble servant

Alexander Hamilton

LB, DLC:GW; copy, DNA: RG 233, Third Congress, 1793–1795, Records of Legislative Proceedings, Committee Reports and Papers.

1. William Short's letter to Alexander Hamilton of 25 Jan. 1791 announced that the terms of the new loan opened by Willink, Van Staphorst, and Hubbard, were substantially the same as those of the bankers' previous loan, except for their commission, which was ½ percent lower. The loan was to be opened in mid- or late February (Syrett, *Hamilton Papers,* 7:454–56). The contract for the loan—usually referred to as the Holland Loan of March 1791—stipulated that the loan was to run for eleven years at 5 percent interest. Redemption was to begin on 1 Mar. 1802 at the rate of 500,000 guilders per annum due on 1 Mar. of each year until the loan was repaid. The commission and brokerage fees amounted to 4 percent (Bayley, *National Loans,* 23).

2. For attempts in Paris to purchase the American debt to France, see Gouv-

erneur Morris to GW, 27 May 1791 (first letter). Before receiving GW's letter of 7 May acknowledging Hamilton's of this day, Hamilton wrote to Short on 13 April, authorizing him to open another loan for three million guilders as soon as the current loan was filled and noting that one and a half million of the March 1791 loan "is destined as a payment to France, and you will please to take as early measures as possible to have the million remitted to Paris, the half million will wait for a further direction" (Syrett, *Hamilton Papers,* 8:280–83).

From Harriott Pinckney Horry

Hampton, Santee [S.C.] 14 April 1791. Requests that her house may serve as a stage on GW's route to Charleston.

ALS, DNA: RG 59, Miscellaneous Letters.
    Harriott Pinckney Horry was the sister of Charles Cotesworth Pinckney and the widow of Col. Daniel Horry (d. 1785). She lived at Hampton, her rice plantation in St. James Santee Parish, Charleston District. GW arrived there in time for breakfast on 1 May and was greeted by Mrs. Horry, her mother and daughter, and several nieces, all of them "arrayed in sashes and bandeaux painted with the general's portrait and mottoes of welcome." See *Diaries,* 6:125–26.

From Louis Paronneau

                Penobscot [District of Maine] April 14th 1791
    Oh! Glorious Deliverer of your Country; I most Humbly beg you to excuse my temerity in Daring to expose before your Highness a Picture of woes to which your mild Heart will be very sensible:
    I have left my Country, at that prayer of a beloved uncle: The most Horrid murder has Deprived me of this Dear father, and (Could your Excellency believe the sad tale) black injustice with all its most Criminal Jury accuses me of being his murderer: I am Dragged in a Narrow Gaol where innocence ought Never to go: Nor my tears, nor my prayers, nor my innocence Can move the flinted Heart of inhumans who perhaps (oh Horror) are guilty of the Crime of which they accuses me.
    be your Greatness Judge of my griefs in thinking of the Sorrow of a father and of a Mother that tenderly Cherish their son who pay's em with the same Love. I weep bitterly: not for myself,

I weep, since I am innocent: but for a whole family of which I have always been the Delight.

In the name of your shining glory, in the name of Humanity, Deign to interest yourself in the behalf of an unjustly accused youth; in the name of the love your greatness bear to the French Nation may your remedy the Dangerous sickness of one of her Limbs. with the most profound respect I implore all the succour, all the pity, all the tears that Justly Deserves of your Highness, the most unfortunate, the most thankful to the part you will take to his misfortunes, & most Humble Servt,

Louis Paronneau

ALS, DNA: RG 59, Miscellaneous Letters.

Louis Paronneau (born c.1775) of La Rochelle, France, attended the College de Soregu-Languedoc before joining his uncle Junin in the fur trade at Penobscot Bay between 1789 and 1790. Shortly thereafter his uncle was murdered, according to a jury of inquest, and young Paronneau was imprisoned for the crime. The French consul at Boston, Philippe-André-Joseph de Létombe, hired a lawyer for the boy and attended his trial in Maine in July 1791. After the jury found Paronneau not guilty, Létombe sent him home to his parents (see Nasatir and Monell, *French Consuls in the U.S.*, 56). Before leaving Boston Paronneau again wrote to GW on 3 Aug.: "My Lord, Pardon my Freedom if I dare flatter my Self that your generous Heart (if Nevertheless great objects interest themselves to small ones) hath heard with pleasure & joy the News of my Delivrance. yes: Justice hath taken place, & them who Seeked my Death have been Disappointed. your Highness hath, without Doubt, received the Letter I took the liberty of writing at the time of My Detention. Knowing your greatness was the father of Humanity, I have take the Leave of expounding my misfortunes; Misfortunes which I had not merited. the Love I bear to my parents too Strongly engages me to return to them; to make any Delay: therefore, I go: to Consolate a Desperate family, Mourning Brothers, & Sorrowful friends. if ever fortune favours me as much as to bring me to this Country again; please your excellency to give me the Leave of presenting my Self before" (DNA: RG 59, Miscellaneous Letters).

To Edmund Pendleton

My dear Sir,   Petersburgh [Va.] April 14th 1791

The letter with which you were pleased to favor me—dated the 9th instt—overtook me at Littlepages bridge the 11th.[1]

The hurry into which I was thrown by a variety of occurrances at Richmond, prevented my acknowledging the receipt of it before I left that City. I now do it, with assurances that it gave me sincere pleasure to find by it that you were well.

The *general* arrangement of the Surveys of Inspection for this District—and the characters designated for the collection of the duties—had, in a great measure, been previously made before I came into this State. I have, however, desired the Supervisor to make the best provision he can for Mr Norton in the subordinate distribution of the Offices, if an appointment of this sort should meet his approbation.[2] With sincere esteem, and affectionate regard I am—my dear Sir Your most Obedient

Go: Washington

ALS, MHi: Washburn Papers; LB, DLC:GW.

1. For Edmund Pendleton's letter of 9 April, see Hannah F. Washington to GW, 1 April, n.1. Littlepage's bridge spanned the Pamunkey River on the road from Bowling Green to Richmond.

2. For GW's discussions with Edward Carrington, excise supervisor for Virginia, see GW to Beverley Randolph, 4 April, n.1.

To the Officials of Petersburg, Virginia

Gentlemen,   [Petersburg, Va., 14 April 1791]

Receiving with pleasure, I reply with sincerity to your flattering and affectionate address.[1] I render justice to your regard and to my own feelings, when I express the gratitude which the sentiments it contains have inspired—and you will allow me to say, that gratitude, so impressed, must be lasting.

The government of the United States, originating in the wisdom, supported by the virtue, and having no other object than the happiness, of the people, reposes not on the exertions of an individual yet, as far as integrity of intention may justify the belief, my agency in the administration will be consonant to your favorable opinions—and my private wishes will always be preferred for the prosperity of Petersburg and the particular welfare of its inhabitants.

Go: Washington

DS, ViPC; LB, DLC:GW.

1. The address of the mayor, recorder, alderman, and common council of Petersburg, signed by Mayor Joseph Westmore, reads: "We avail ourselves of the earliest oppertunity that your Presence has afforded us, to offer you our Sincere and Affectionate respects—to welcome you, most Cordially, to this

place, and to Assure you, which we do with Confidence, of the high regard
and great Affection the Inhabitants of this Town entertain for your Person and
your many virtues. We look upon you, Sir, as the Father of your Country and
the friend of mankind &, when we Contemplate your Charecter in that light,
we feel ourselves impressed with the purest Sentiments of gratitude respect
and veneration. May you long continue at the head of our Government honour'd, respected and beloved as you are at Present, and we pray, most ardently,
that the all wise director of human Events, may Prolong your life to a far
distant period of time and bless you, to your latest breath with Health, uninterrupted, and with that happy Tranquility of mind which ever flows from
conscious rectitude and from a Heart always anxious to promote the happiness
of the human race. We Sincerely wish that the Tour which you are about to
make may be an Agreable one and that it may afford you every imaginable
Satisfaction" (DLC:GW). For GW's arrival at Petersburg on 14 April and his
activities there before his departure early the next morning, see *Diaries*, 6:111–
12, and Edward Carrington to James Madison, 20 April, *Madison Papers*,
14:10–11.

To Beverley Randolph

Sir   Richmond, April 14, 1791.
   The Secretary of War having transmitted to me a copy of your
Excellency's letter to him, relative to the protection of the frontier counties of Virginia, with his answer thereto—I have now
to observe that the Counties of Russell and Wythe, not having
been considered as equally exposed with the others, were not
included in the arrangements taken for defending the frontier[1]—But, as the protection to be afforded was intended to embrace every county that might be exposed to inroad or invasion,
if it shall appear to your Excellency a necessary measure, I request that you will be pleased to direct such an extension of the
defense as will cover these counties, and place them in equal
security with the others.
   Should it comport with the state of your Treasury to make an
advance of Two thousand dollars, of the sum appropriated by
the State of Virginia for federal purposes on the Potowmac, I
beg that an intimation thereof may be given to Mr Johnson,
Doctor Stuart, and Mr Daniel Carroll, who are the Commissioners, and who will take measures, in consequence, for drawing
the money. This supply is very essential, and requires that the
earliest intimation, which the state of your funds will allow,

should be given to the Commissioners.[2] I have the honor to be, with respectful consideration, Your Excellency's most obedient Servant

Go: Washington

LS, PHi: Dreer Collection.

1. For background to Gov. Beverley Randolph's communications regarding the defense of the Virginia frontier, see Randolph to GW, 4 Jan. 1791 and note 1. Henry Knox wrote GW on 4 April: "I have the honor to enclose you a copy of letter of the 25th Ulto from the Governor of Virginia relative to the protection of the frontier counties and my answer there to. I conceived that it would have been improper for me to have written decissively to him respecting Wythe and Russell as you would probably be at Richmond. It appears that the danger of Russell and Wythe a rises from the Cherokees. If Governor Blounts proposed treaty should be effectual, this evil would be cured. But in the mean time, it would be good policy, to extend to Russell and Wythe, the same sort of protection as has been afforded to the other counties of the Ohio" (DLC:GW).

2. For the money pledged by Virginia for the construction of buildings in the Federal City, see GW to the Commissioners for the Federal District, 13 April and notes 1 and 3.

To William Tatham

Sir,　　　　　　　　　　Richmond [Va.], April 14th 1791.

I have received your letters numbered 1, 2, 3, and 4. thanking you for your attention in presenting to me a copy of your map, and wishing you the best success in completing that in which you are now engaged, I return the subscription papers, with my name affixed for a copy of each map, on which, the money to be advanced, will now be paid—and I have to observe that there appears to me greater propriety in your pursuing the plan, on which it was originally undertaken, than in adopting any other.[1]

My tour through the southern States, being in the nature of a short visit, will not require the assistance, which you are so obliging as to offer—my public situation forbids any interference in questions of individual claims otherwise than as they may come before me officially in the form of an act of Congress—This will be satisfactory to you for my declining to direct any investigation of the vouchers which you mention. I am Sir, Your most obedient Servant

G. Washington.

LB, DLC:GW.

William Tatham (1752–1819) immigrated to Virginia from England in 1769 and moved in 1775 to what became east Tennessee, where he served as a militia adjutant in campaigns against the Creeks and Cherokees. Returning to Virginia in 1778, he served as a volunteer under Gen. Charles Scott. After the Revolutionary War he was clerk to the Virginia council of state and studied law, being admitted to the bar in 1784. Two years later Tatham moved to North Carolina and later served in the state legislature before returning to Virginia to organize its geographical department. In September 1790 Tatham proposed publishing a comprehensive map of the southern United States and solicited aid from the house of delegates two months later. He published *A Topographical Analysis of the Commonwealth of Virginia: Compiled for the Years 1790–1* (Richmond, 1791), but he never completed his map of the South, even though in 1791 the Virginia general assembly authorized a lottery to support his work. GW dispatched him to Spain in 1795 to settle a boundary dispute with Florida, after which Tatham became superintendent of the London Docks at Wapping from 1801 until his return to Virginia in 1805, when he became employed as military storekeeper at the Richmond arsenal. He apparently committed suicide when he walked in front of a cannon fired in celebration of GW's birthday. See Map Subscription, 29 Sept. 1790, n.1, *Marshall Papers,* 2:62.

1. Tatham wrote four letters to GW on 24 Mar. 1791. The first, seeking his aid in recovering losses incurred during the Revolution, described Tatham's service as a volunteer and referred to testimonials in his possession written by Thomas Jefferson, Edmund Randolph, Peter Muhlenberg, James Monroe, Benjamin Hawkins, Baron von Steuben, and a Major Walker, among others. He also mentioned that Continental army veterans Solomon Bush and Richard Clairborne could testify to his sacrifices (DLC:GW). Tatham's second letter of 24 Mar. sought GW's patronage for his map of the southern states, presented his reasons for undertaking it, and suggested a plan to further its publication, by having state legislatures authorize a subscription for a copy for each county and governmental department (DLC:GW). Tatham's third letter covered a copy of his *Topographical Analysis of the Commonwealth of Virginia* and noted: "His Excellency Governor Randolph was requested last year to furnish the Secretary at War with a delineation of the western Counties of this State, on some of the former Maps. I was applied to in the execution of this business: but found it impracticable on any I could procure. I have since collected information which flatters me with a prospect of greater accuracy, than I expected to have met with; and I hope the large Map I am now engagd on, will contain every thing wanted for public or private use. I have in the interim endeavour'd to annalize the state of this Commonwealth, in such a manner as may offer the best substitute for this defect: adding such military, and political matter, as I thought the plan capable of containing. I beg leave to present You herewith a copy for your own use; and will chearfull furnish any others you may direct, for the public Offices" (DLC:GW). In his fourth letter of 24 Mar., Tatham applied for public office, stressing his willingness to accept any appointment for which he might be thought qualified (DLC:GW).

From Robert Douglas

Honbl. Sir,   Scotland, Port Glasgow 15th April 1791
On the 26th Septr last I had a letter form Mr Robt Peter, Mercht in Georgetown, Potomack River Maryland who Acquaints me that a small Plantation that belonged to me on the Eastern Branch said River was confiscated by order of the State of Maryland, it consists of Fifty Acres of Land & upon it, there is a dwelling & some outhouses built[.]¹ by a letter from Mr Peter to me of the 26th Novr 1788 he says it remaind unsold & that he was afraid to move in it and did not know how the State of Maryland might Act in regard to my property, I have another letter from him dated 9th Novr 1789 wherein he does not mention the Land being confiscated I got it by my Wife Mary Riley, now deceased and Daughter to Mr Eliphaz Riley & by a Deed from him dated the 9th Novr 1760 it was convey'd to me, it rented at £18—Maryd Curry pr Annum & all that I have received from Mr Peter, is £29.19.9 Sterling, remitted me by a Bill in June 1769—by my Marriage I have five Children Alive born me in this Country, by my Will lying by me I had left the Plantation to my Oldest Son, Eliphaz, who was in Maryd—the time of the War & who took the Oath of Citizinship to the State, little did I think my Plantation was to be confiscated, I was no way concernd in the War between Britain and America, when I Married I Commanded a Ship, and left off going to Sea about 26 years ago & since that period I have resided in my Native Country, my thus presumeing to write you the Honble President of the United States of America I know is Novel and taking too much upon me, at same time from your Amiable Character & well knowen humanity I am emboldined to lay my Complaint before you and I flatter myself that you will cause enquirey to be made if Justice has been done me, a Gentleman in your Exalted Station must have little time to Attend about such triffles as now mentioned, at same time it would give me vast pleasure if you Vouchsafe to order this letter to be answer'd—from your love of Justice I presume you will agree with me, that it is very hard my Children should be deprieved of their Mothers Inheritance, had the Land been confiscated soon after the War ended, I would have been paid value by the British Government, it is now too late & no Claims are Admitted, by the VI Article of the treaty

between Britain & America, sign'd at Paris the 3d day of Sepr 1783, it is Stipulated that there shall be no more confiscations made in future from that date, I left the rights of my Plantation with Mr Peter & by a letter he writes me in Decr last, he sends me a Certificate of the confiscation a Copy of which I beg herewith to send you for your perusal, also a paragraph from his letter of 26th Sepr 1789[2]—James White Junr who bought the Plantn was 2d Cousine to my Wife & Grandson to James White, Senr who is greatly in Arrears to Mr Peter, James White Junr is Heir to the Old Man & I suppose my Plantn will go to pay part of the Debt owing to Mr Peter—who is my 1st Cousine I am suspicious of his Conduct, tho I have not told him so, to conclude, my sincere wish is for good health to you & Happiness to preside over a free & independent People & I am very Respectfully Honourable Sir your Most Humble & Obedt Servt

Robt Douglas

ALS, DNA: RG 42, General Records, Letters Received, 1791–1867; copy, DNA: RG 42, Records of the Commissioners for the District of Columbia, Letters Sent, 1791–1802.

Robert Douglas emigrated from Scotland to America in his youth and worked as a clerk in a store kept by Robert Shadden on the plantation of Anthony Strother on the Rappahannock River opposite Fredericksburg, Virginia. Strother's plantation bordered Augustine Washington's Ferry Farm, where GW spent much of his youth. Douglas was acquainted with the Washingtons and was working for Shadden in December 1740 when a fire consumed the Washingtons' first house on the site. See Douglas to GW, 25 May 1795. He married Mary Riley, the daughter of Eliphaz Riley of Maryland, who bore him a son, Eliphaz. Douglas returned permanently to Scotland about 1765. He remarried after the death of his first wife and began a second family.

1. The property was part of the Hop Yard tract patented in 1686–87 by Walter Houp. It extended along the Eastern Branch from present Fourth Street, S.E., to Kentucky Avenue, S.E., and extended inland to present H Street, N.E., forming a narrow quadrilateral bordered on the west by the property of Daniel Carroll of Duddington. Eliphaz Riley conveyed his fifty-acre portion to his son-in-law Robert Douglas in May 1760. Maryland confiscated the land following the Revolution on the grounds that Douglas was a Loyalist, and James White, Jr., purchased it from the state and conveyed it to Overton Carr in January 1791. Five months later Carr conveyed it to Georgetown merchant George Walker (Clark, "Origin of the Federal City," 94–95). Article VI of the Treaty of Paris provided "that there shall be no future Confiscations made, . . . by reason of the Part which he or they may have taken in the present War, and that no person shall on that account suffer any future Loss or Damage either in his Person, Liberty or Property" (Miller, *Treaties*, 99).

2. Douglas enclosed a certificate attesting to the confiscation, an appraisal, dated 6 Dec. 1790, stating the property was worth £90 sterling, and an extract of a letter from Peter to Douglas, dated 26 Sept. 1789: "Your land is now sold by the State of Maryland to James White" who had indicated that he would sell the land to Douglas at his own cost and expenses, if Douglas was interested in recovering it; "this was the very design of his Application to the State for it . . . for to be plain I set him upon it, that it should not be a total [loss] to the Family, as one of your Family I might have reserved it for my self on paying the State, but as it came by your Wife I would not Meddle" (DNA: RG 42, General Records, Letters Received, 1791–1867). Douglas again wrote to GW on 5, 12 Aug. 1794 (letters not found), and 25 May 1795.

From Tobias Lear

Sir,   Philadelphia April 15th 1791.

Since I had the honor to write to you on the 10th Inst. we have had the pleasure of learning that you reached Fredericksburg on the 8th.

Mr Jefferson has been so good as to furnish me with a copy of the Stages which you intended to make on your journey southward, and the times at which you expected to be in the principal towns, together with a list of the places through which you would pass on your return.[1] By which I find that this letter will not reach you until your arrival at Charleston, and that which I shall send by the post of monday will probably find you at Savannah.[2] After which, letters will be directed to those places through which you intend passing on your return, and to which there may be cross posts leading from the town on the main post-road to which it is most convenient, calculating the time as nearly as we can (from your departure from Savannah) at which you will be in the different places, and so timing the letter that they may meet you at those places to which they may be directed. There will likewise be one or more opportunities in the course of a week to write to Charlestown by water, which shall be improved, and may possibly convey letters to you before this gets to hand. Mr Smith sails for So. Carolina in a few days, to whose care a letter will be committed. Mrs Smith has presented him with a daughter within a few days.[3]

I am today to receive a decided answer with respect to Mr Holker's man; but I confess I have not much expectation of his coming. Fraunces has undoubtedly given up the matter for there has not been a syllable heard from him. Should we not be able to get a person who understands perfectly the arrangement of a table, and is properly qualified in other respects; I would beg leave to suggest the following idea. There is a Confectioner in town who advertises to furnish a desert for entertainments in the handsomest style, and to receive back such parts of them as may not be consumed, at the same rate which he charges; this, I conceive, will be attended with a saving in this family—where we have a large quantity of those things carried untouched from the table, and which I very much doubt whether they ever made their appearance there the second time. The Man also arranges the desert or second course before it is brought in & attends himself to take it away as soon as the company have risen from table to prevent any purloining by the Servants. I mentioned his advertisement to Mrs Washington, who wished to have an experiment made of him with a small company which she had invited on Tuesday consisting of the Vice Presidt & family & Mr Morris & family. This was done & the desert & arrangement pronounced very genteel & tastey. He is to bring his bill today, by which I shall see the expence of that day & from thence form an estimate of the expense attending this mode with any company.[4] Should this be found an elegible thing in all respects, I conceive we shall have no occasion to engage a person in the capacity of Steward. If a good, steady, & respectable woman (in her place) can be obtained to act as Housekeeper, William could do many things which were done by Hyde, as the Marketing will not come in his hands, that being done by the Cook, who has certainly furnished us with better things & at a less rate than Hyde did. The liquors are in bottles and I find it no manner of trouble to give out now to Fidus before dinner what may serve for the day—and the same meathod, if thought good, might be pursued hereafter. I have just suggested that as it has occurred to me, and Mrs Washington that if a person cannot be obtained for a Steward who is perfectly qualified & quite unexceptionable, that this would be a much better mode than to be at the expence & trouble of an ignorant or bad man.

I have the happiness to inform you that Mrs Washington has recovered from her indisposition occasioned by a violent cold, and with the Children the rest of the family is now in good health. Mrs Lear unites with me in a most respectful remem⟨brance⟩ & warmest wishes for the preservation of your health. I have the honor to be with the highest respect & most sincere attachment Sir Your obliged & very hum⟨e Servt⟩

Tobias Lear.

ALS, DLC:GW.

1. For the itinerary Thomas Jefferson gave to Tobias Lear, see GW to Alexander Hamilton, Jefferson, and Henry Knox, 4 April, a copy of which, in Lear's hand, is in DLC:GW.

2. Lear probably posted his letter of 17 April to GW the following day.

3. South Carolina congressman William Loughton Smith's wife, Charlotte Izard Smith (c.1769–1792), a daughter of U.S. Senator Ralph Izard, had recently given birth to Anne (Ann) Caroline Smith.

4. The confectioner was Joseph Delacroix to whom Lear paid $17.44 on 25 May "for furnish'g a desert 3 days" (Decatur, *Private Affairs of Washington*, 238).

From John Rutledge, Sr.

Dr Sir   Charleston [S.C.] April 15. 1791.

I am extremely sorry, that official Duty prevents (which nothing but indispensable necessity should,) my going, with my Son, to meet you, at the Boundary-Line of North-Carolina:[1] He will do himself the Honour of waiting on you, from thence but I flatter myself, that I shall have an opportunity of paying my Respects, to you, in Person, on your Tour thro' the upper Country, (where I must be for several Weeks, on the Circuit,) & of joining my Fellow Citizens there, in expressing, & testifying those Sentiments of Affection for your Person, & Veneration for your Character, which prevail in every part of this State, as much as in any part of the United States. I have the Honour to be, with the greatest Esteem & Respect, Dr Sir yr obliged & most obedt Sert

J. Rutledge

ALS, DLC:GW.

1. John Rutledge, Sr., resigned as senior associate justice of the U.S. Supreme Court in February 1791 to become chief justice of South Carolina. See Jacob Read to GW, 16 Feb. 1791 and note 1. On 3 May GW breakfasted privately with Rutledge's wife, Elizabeth Grimké Rutledge (1741–1792), in Charleston. See *Diaries*, 6:129.

From Alexander Hamilton

Treasury Department [Philadelphia] 17 April 1791. Informs GW of the death of the comptroller of the Treasury, whose "loss is sincerely to be regretted as that of a good officer and an honorable & amiable man."[1]

ADf, CtHi: Oliver Wolcott, Jr., Papers; LB, DLC:GW.

1. Nicholas Eveleigh, whom GW had named comptroller on 11 Sept. 1789, had been in poor health since he took office, and Eveleigh's chief clerk, Joseph Hardy, was performing the comptroller's functions since at least March 1791 (see Hamilton to Commissioners of Loans, 9 Mar., in Syrett, *Hamilton Papers*, 8:169). Even before Eveleigh's death on 16 April, applicants began presenting themselves for the impending vacancy. See Christopher Richmond to GW, 7 Mar. 1791.

From Alexander Hamilton

Sir   Philadelphia April 17 1791

You will probably recollect that previous to your departure from this place, anticipating the event which has taken place with regard to the death of Mr Eveleigh, I took the liberty to mention to you that Mr Woolcott the present Auditor would be in every respect worthy of your consideration as his successor in office.

Now that the event has happened, a concern as anxious as it is natural, for the success of the Department united with a sentiment of Justice towards Mr Woolcott leads me to a repetition of that Idea—This Gentleman's conduct in the station he now fills, has been that of an excellent officer. It has not only been good but distinguished. It has combined all the requisites which could be desired; moderation with firmness, liberality with exactness, indefatigable industry with an accurate & sound discernment, a thorough knowlege of business & a remarkable spirit of order and arrangement. Indeed I ought to say, that I owe very much of whatever success may have attented the merely executive operations of the department to Mr Woolcott. And I do not fear to commit myself, when I add, that he possesses in an eminent degree all the qualifications desireable in a Comptroller of the Treasury—that it is scarcely possible to find a man in the United States more competent to the duties of that station than himself, *few* who would be equally so. It may truly be said of him that he is a man of *rare* merit. And I have good evidence that he has been viewed in this light by the members of Congress extensively from different quarters of the Union, & is so considered by all that part of the public who have had opportunities of witnessing his conduct.

The immediate relation too, which his present situation bears to that of Comptroller is a strong argument in his favour. Though a regular gradation of office is not admissible in a strict sense in regard to offices of a civil nature and is wholly inapplicable to those of the first rank (such as the heads of the great executive departments) yet a certain regard to the relation, which one situation bears to another is consonant with the natural ideas of Justice and is recommended by powerful considerations of policy. The expectation of promotion in civil as in military life is a great stimulous to virtuous exertion: while examples of unrewarded exertion, supported by talent & qualification, are proportionable discouragements. Where they do not produce resignations they leave men dissatisfied & a dissatisfied man seldom does his duty well.

In a government like ours, where pecuniary compensations are moderate, the principle of gradual advancement, as a reward for good conduct is perhaps more necessary to be attended to than in others where offices are more lucrative. By due attention to it, it will operate as a mean to secure respectable men for offices of inferior emolument and consequence.

In addition to the rest, Mr Woolcotts experience, in this particular line, pleads powerfully in his favour. This experience may be dated back to his office of Comptroller of the State of Connecticut and has been perfected by practice in his present place.

A question may perhaps Sir arise in your mind whether some inconvenience may not attend his removal from his present office. I am of opinion that no sensible inconvenience will be felt on this score; since it will be easy for him as Comptroller, who is the immediate superior of the auditor to form any man of business for the office he will leave in a short period of time. More inconvenience would be felt by the introduction of a Comptroller, not in the immediate train of the business. Besides this it may be observed that a degree of inconvenience on this score cannot be deemed an obstacle, but upon a principle, which would bar the progress of merit from one station to another.

On this point of inconvenience a reflection occurs which I think I ought to suppress. Mr Woolcott is a man of sensibility, not unconscious of his own value; and he doubtless must believe that he has pretentions from situation to the Office. Should another be appointed & he resign, the derangement of the department would truly be distressing to the public service.

In suggesting thus particularly the reasons which in my mind operate in favour of Mr Woolcott, I am influenced by information that other characters will be brought to your view by weighty advocates, and as I think it more than possible that Mr Woolcott may not be mentioned to you by any other person than myself, I feel it a duty, arising out of my situation in the department to bear my full & explicit testimony to his worth; confident that he will justify by every kind of *substantial* merit any mark of your approbation, which he may receive.

In contemplating the appointment of the Auditor as Comptroller, a question naturally arises concerning a substitute for the former. In making up your Judgment on this point you would probably desire to know what may be the pretentions of the next officer in the department below the Auditor namely the Register. I say nothing of the Assistant Secretary or the Treasurer, because neither of them I presume would think the place of Auditor an eligible exchange for that which he now has and because I regard them both as distinct and irrelative branches of the department.[1] The Register is a most excellent officer in his place. He has had a great deal of experience in the department is a perfect accountant and a very upright man. But I cannot say that I am convinced he would make as good an Auditor as he does a Register. I fear he would fail on the score of firmness & I am not sure that his mind is formed for a systematic adherence to principle. I believe at the same time that he is perfectly content to remain where he is.

There will therefore be no difficulty in adjusting this matter to any collateral calculation which may be deemed requisite. A number of persons well qualified occur in this Quarter; but you probably will prefer directing your enquiries to the South on the principle of distribution. There is a circumstance which on this point I ought to mention. If I am rightly informed Mr Nourse is originally from Virginia.

There is another circumstance which I ought not to conclude

without mentioning to you. Mr Coxe has signified to me his wish to be considered for the Office of Comptroller. On this point I have answered him & very sincerely to this effect "I am well convinced that the office under your direction would be in perfectly good hands. On the score of qualification my preference would not incline to any other man, and you have every reason to believe that on personal accounts none would be more agreeable to me. But I am equally well satisfied on the other hand that no man ought to be preferred to Mr Woolcott on the score of qualification for the office; and this being the case, I am of opinion that the relation which his present station bears to that in question gives him pretentions superior to any other person." He then asked me whether it would be disagreeable to me that he should make his wish known to you. To this my answer was in substance, that I could have no possible objection to his doing it and that I would even do it myself but that I apprised him it should be done in such a manner as would make it clearly understood to you that all circumstances considered, I thought that Mr Woolcott had a decidedly preferable claim.[2]

I trust sir that in thus freely disclosing my sentiments to you you will be persuaded that I only yield to the suggestions of an honest zeal for the public good, and of a firm conviction that the prosperity of the department under my particular care (one so interesting to the aggregate movements of the government) will be best promoted by transferring the present Auditor to the office of Comptroller of the Treasury. I have the honor to remain with the most respectfull Attachment Sir Your Most Obedient & humble servant

Alexander Hamilton

P.S. If you should be of opinion to Appoint the Auditor as Comptroller and the Register as Auditor—There would be a choice of valuable characters in the department well qualified to take the station of the register should you think it adviseable to persue that Course. That I may not be misapprehended, I beg leave to observe that though I do not think the Register well qualified for an Auditor in all respects—I do not think him so defective as to be a bad appointment.

ADf, CtHi: Oliver Wolcott, Jr., Papers; LB, DLC:GW; copy, CtHi: Oliver Wolcott, Jr., Papers.

1. The register was Joseph Nourse, who remained in office until removed by Andrew Jackson in 1829. The assistant secretary was Tench Coxe, and the treasurer of the United States was Samuel Meredith.

2. For Coxe's application of 16 April, see Thomas Jefferson to GW, 17 April and note 4.

From Thomas Jefferson

Sir   Philadelphia Apr. 17. 1791.

I had the honor of addressing you on the 2d which I supposed would find you at Richmond, and again on the 10th which I thought would overtake you at Wilmington. the present will probably find you at Charleston.[1]

According to what I mentioned in my letter of the 10th the Vice-president, Secretaries of the Treasury & war & myself met on the 11th. Colo. Hamilton presented a letter from mister Short in which he mentioned that the month of February being one of the periodical months in Amsterdam, when from the receipt of interest and refunding of capitals, there is much money coming in there, & free to be disposed of, he had put off the opening his loan till then, that it might fill the more rapidly, a circumstance which would excite the presumption of our credit. that he had every reason to hope it would be filled before it would be possible for him, after his then communication of the conditions to recieve your approbation of them, & orders to open a second; which however should be awaited, according to his instructions; but he pressed the expediting the order, that the stoppage of the current in our favor might be as short as possible. we saw that if, under present circumstances, your orders should be awaited, it would add a month to the delay, and we were satisfied, were you present, you would approve the conditions & order a second loan to be opened. we unanimously therefore advised an immediate order, on condition the terms of the 2d loan should not be worse than those of the 1st—Genl Knox expressed an apprehension that the 6. nations might be induced to join our enemies; there being some suspicious circumstances; and he wished to send Colo. Pickering to confirm them in their neutrality. this he observed would occasion an expence of about 2000 dollars, as the Indians were never to be met empty-handed. we thought the mission adviseable. as to myself,

I hope we shall give the Indians a thorough drubbing this summer, and I should think it better afterwards to take up the plan of liberal & repeated presents to them. this would be much the cheapest in the end, & would save all the blood which is now spilt: in time too it would produce a spirit of peace & friendship between us. the expence of a single expedition would last very long for presents. I mentioned to the gentlemen the idea of suggesting thro' Colo. Beckwith, our knowlege of the conduct of the British officers in furnishing the Indians with arms & ammunition, & our dissatisfaction. Colo. Hamilton said that Beckwith had been with him on the subject, and had assured him they had given the Indians nothing more than the annual present, & at the annual period. it was thought proper however that he should be made sensible that this had attracted the notice of government. I thought it the more material, lest, having been himself the first to speak of it, he might suppose his excuses satisfactory, & that therefore they might repeat the annual present this year. as Beckwith lodges in the same house with mister Madison, I have desired the latter to find some occasion of representing to Beckwith that tho an annual present of arms & ammunition be an innocent act in time of peace, it is not so in time of war: that it is contrary to the laws of neutrality for a neutral power to furnish military implements to either party at war, & that if their subjects should do it on private account, such furnitures might be seised as contraband: to reason with him on the subject, as from himself, but so as to let him see that government thought as himself did.[2]

You know, I think, before you left us, that the British parliament had a bill before them, for allowing wheat, imported in *British* bottoms, to be warehoused rent-free. in order further to circumscribe the carrying business of the U.S. they now refuse to consider as an American bottom, any vessel not built here. by this construction they take from us the right of defining by our own laws what vessels shall be deemed ours & naturalized here; and in the event of a war, in which we should be neutral, they put it out of our power to benefit ourselves of our neutrality, by increasing suddenly by purchase & naturalization our means of carriage. if we are permitted to do this by building only, the war will be over before we can be prepared to take advantage of it. this has been decided by the Lords Commissioners of the treasury in the case of one Green, a merchant of New York, from whom I have recieved a regular complaint on the subject. I inclose you the copy of a note from mister King to Colo. Hamilton, on the subject of the appointment of a British minister to come here. I suspect it however to be without foundation.[3]

Colo. Eveleigh died yesterday. supposing it possible you might desire to appoint his successor as soon as you could decide on one, I inclose you a blank commission, which when you shall be pleased to fill up & sign, can be returned for the seal & countersignature. I inclose you a letter from mister Coxe to yourself on the subject of this appointment, and so much of one to me as related to the same, having torn off a leaf of compliment to lighten & lessen my inclosures to you.[4] should distributive justice give preference to a successor of the same state with the deceased, I take the liberty of suggesting to you mister Hayward, of S.C. whom I think you told me you did not know, and of whom you are now on the spot of enquiry.[5] I inclose you also a continuation of the Pennsylvania debates on the bill for federal buildings. after the postponement by the Senate, it was intended to bring on the reconsideration of that vote. but the hurry at winding up their session prevented it. they have not chosen a federal Senator.[6] I have the honour to be with the most profound respect & sincere attachment, Sir, your most obedient & most humble servt

Th: Jefferson

ALS, DNA: RG 59, Miscellaneous Letters; ALS (fragment, letterpress copy), DLC: Thomas Jefferson Papers; ALS (fragment, letterpress copy), MHi: Thomas Jefferson Papers; copy, in Jefferson's hand, DNA: RG 59, Miscellaneous Letters; LB, DLC:GW.

1. GW did not receive and acknowledge this letter until after his return to Virginia. See GW to Jefferson, 17 June.

2. For the meeting between John Adams, Alexander Hamilton, Jefferson, and Henry Knox on 11 April, see Jefferson to GW, 10 April and note 1.

3. William Green, a New York merchant, complained to Jefferson on 21 Jan. that his brig *Rachel,* built in France, had been denied access to British ports on the grounds that it was not an American vessel. It was detained from 22 Oct. to 24 Dec. 1790 while a final decision was pending in the case (see Thomas Paine to GW, 21 July 1791 and note 5). The enclosed extract of Rufus King's note on prospective British ministers to the United States was similar to that forwarded to GW by Hamilton on 11 April.

4. The enclosed letter of 16 April 1791 from Tench Coxe to GW reads: "It is with the greatest hesitation that I contribute to the unpleasing circumstances, that are obtruded on your mind by too numerous applications for

public office. The decease of the Comptroller of the Treasury having created the necessity of an appointment, I most humbly beg leave to present myself to your consideration. The relation which exists between the offices of the Treasury and the respectful solicitude for the honor of your countenance, which is felt by every good citizen, and which is anxiously desired by every faithful Servant of the public will be received, I hope Sir, in apology for this step. Honor and Emolument may be generally deemed the inducements to these applications, but I trust I do not deceive myself in the belief that these considerations do not influence me more decidedly than a sincere desire to evince the highest respect for the government of the United States and for the peculiar character of their Chief Magistrate" (DLC:GW). Jefferson also enclosed a leaf from a letter Coxe had addressed to him in the evening of 16 April: "The vacancy produced in the Treasury department by the death of the Comptroller has occasioned me to take the liberty of making this communication to you. It will not appear unnatural, that a person in my situation should be led, by the relation the offices of the Treasury bear to each other, to entertain a wish for the appointment, and I should, at as early a moment as decorum permitted, have done myself the honor to make that desire known to you. But Mr Hamilton having led me this afternoon into a free conversation on the subject I find it proper to be more early in this communication than it was my intention to have been. There appear to be circumstances, which originated at the time of Mr Wolcotts appointment to his present office, that operate to restrain the Secretary of the Treasury from moving in favor of any other person, & this information he gave me unasked. he entertains an opinion, also, that the relation between the office of the Comptroller and Auditor creates a kind of pretension in the latter to succeed the former. He however added in a very kind and flattering way his opinion, that he should see as many public advantages resulting from the appointment of myself as any other person, and that he would by no means advise my declining to apply to the President. The station you fill in the Government together with the impressions I feel concerning" (DNA: RG 59, Miscellaneous Letters). Jefferson retained the remaining two leaves of the letter, in which Coxe asked him either to transmit his application to GW "with your opinion on the subject" or to "commit it to the fire." Jefferson did neither but simply passed Coxe's application on to GW without comment.

5. Thomas Heyward (1746–1809), former South Carolina legislator who had supported ratification of the federal Constitution in the state ratifying convention of 1788, received no appointment from GW.

6. The enclosed printed report on the Pennsylvania debates over the construction of buildings to house the federal government has not been found. Sen. William Maclay's term ended with the close of the First Congress, and Pennsylvania Federalists in the upper house of the legislature under the new state constitution of 1790 insisted that U.S. senators should be elected by concurrent vote of the two houses; the lower house favored a joint vote. The impasse was not resolved until February 1793 when the state senate finally agreed to a joint vote, which resulted in the election of Albert Gallatin who sat from December 1793 until 28 Feb. 1794 when his election was declared void on the grounds that he had not been an American citizen for a sufficient period.

From Henry Knox

Sir   War department [Philadelphia] April 17th 1791

The last letter which I had the honor to write to you was dated on the 10th instant. Since which I have received your favor of the 7th instant. Colonel Hall having declined Colonel Darck agreably to your orders, will have the offer of the 1st regiment of Levies, and if he should decline, it is probable that Colonel Rawlings would accept it.

We shall march between the 25th instant, and the 1st of May two full companies of regulars, amounting to 152 non commissioned and privates. One company from this City, and the other from Delaware. And within the same period, two companies of Levies will commence their march, one from Trenton and the other from Carlile, These several companies together with the levies who may be expected to have assembled at Fort Pitt of the upper battalion of this state will nearly amount to four hundred men.

The clothing complete for General Seviers battalion sailed from hence for Richmond on the 15th. Waggons are waiting there to transport the clothing to Holstein, at which it will arrive by the 20th of May, by which time the battalion I hope will be raised and in readiness; to march—the Goods for Governor Blounts treaty are involved in this arrangement, all being under the charge of General Seviers Son.[1]

About one half the clothing for the Maryland and Virginia battalions will be sent from hence tomorrow, by Land, to Hagers Town and Winchester. B. General Butler did not set out until the 13th but he has promised great exertions.

The Clothing for Roberts's company will sail from New York for charlestown in a few days. The money for recruiting his company and the arms and accoutrements have already been forwarded. But flattering expectations ought not to be formed of its being of any service during the present campaign.

The prospects of recruiting at the eastward are satisfactory, and the companies of that quarter will begin to move forward early in May.

I have written to Governor Clinton to endevor to engage Brandt in the business of conciliating the western Indians, provided it could be effected without disgusting the Cornplanter. I expect Colonel Pickering every hour, on the business mentioned in my letter of the 10th.[2]

I have not heard of Colonel Proctor since his departure. Nor have I heard of Genl St Clair, but the next post which will arrive on the 20th will probably bring some information from him. Neither have I received any information from Fort Pitt, since the 10th instant. I have the honor sir to be with the highest respect Your obedient Servant

H. Knox

ALS, DLC:GW; LB, DLC:GW.

1. For the background to Southwest Territory governor William Blount's negotiations, which would lead to the Treaty of Holston, see Henry Knox to GW, 10, 27 Mar., and GW to Knox, 14 Mar., Enclosure II. "General Sevier's son" was probably John Sevier, Jr.

2. Knox informed Gov. George Clinton of New York on 12 April of Timothy Pickering's mission to the Six Nations and solicited his assistance in persuading Joseph Brant to intervene with the western tribes. Clinton responded on 27 April that Pickering's negotiations only would lead to a potentially dangerous revival of unity among the Six Nations but promised to use his influence with Brant (*ASP, Indian Affairs,* 1:167–68). See also Knox to GW, 8 June 1791, n.2.

From Henry Knox

Private
Sir   Philadelphia 17th April 1791

Mr Eveleigh the Comptroller of the Treasury died yesterday. There will be a number of candidates for his office, who will urge their several pretensions with some specious, and perhaps some weighty arguments.

Having been taught by your goodness to address myself to you unreservedly, and knowing your desire to learn through different mediums, existing opinions relative to candidates, I take the liberty of transmitting you mine, on this occasion.

From the view I have taken of ⟨*mutilated*⟩ subject, it appears to me, that more personal political and official considerations unite in favor of Mr Wolcott the present auditor of the treasury as a proper character to succeed Mr Eveleigh than in any other person within my knowledge.

He is in the exercise of habits necessary to the investigations of public accounts, and eminently possesses the talents to form proper judgements of the cases which may be in his department.

Should he not be appointed the State of Connecticut may think itself neglected, as some of its citizens are of opinion that it has not its proportion of the great offices of government.

And there appears to be a propriety and fitness, in advancing persons of integrity and highly approved conduct from a lower to an higher grade. And I beg leave to observe that this appointment would be most acceptable to the secretary of the treasury. A circumstance of great importance in the harmonious conducting of the business of the treasury.

The general principle which you have been pleased justly to adopt of distributing offices according to the divisions of eastern middle and southern states may have its operation in this case, as a character from a southern state may be found for the auditors office.

Mr Kean of South Carolina has been mentiond for the auditor. But he informs me, that he is of opinion, the duties would require too intense an application, for the infirm state of his health.

Being upon the subject of offices I beg leave further to state that Judge Pendleton district Judge of Georgia has requested me to mention his name to you as a candidate for the vacancy in the circuit Court occasioned by Mr Rutledges resignation.[1] In your tour you will be able to obtain all necessary information relative to him. I have the honor to be sir with perfect respect Your Obedient Servant

H. Knox

ALS, DLC:GW.

1. For Nathaniel Pendleton's application to succeed John Rutledge, Sr., as associate justice of the U.S. Supreme Court, see Pendleton to GW, 5 Mar. 1791.

From Tobias Lear

Sir,   Philadelphia April 17th 1791.

Since I had the honor of writing to you on the 15th Inst. Young Fraunces has informed me that he has received a letter from his father, in which he mentions his intention of coming on here to take the place of Steward in this family, agreeably to the answer given to his application for that purpose. The reason which he assigns for not having made known his determination on this subject sooner, is, that it was necessary for him to effect certain measures relative to the support &c. of his family in his absence, before he could finally decide upon his coming. This he has, at length, done; and speaks of coming on in the course of 10 or 12 days after he shall have settled certain matters in New York which he must do previous to his quitting that place, or be under the necessity of returning thither for that purpose in a short time. He likewise requested the advance of half a year's Salary to enable him to discharge some debts which he owed in New York.

To this last request I told Fraunces I could give him an immediate answer, which was that it could not be complied with. And further, that it was doubtful whether his father could *now* come into the family at any rate; for it has been so long before he made known his determination, that some steps had been taken towards engaging another person (meaning Holker's man) from a pursuason that his father did not intend to come; and especially as I had given him (young Fraunces) notice that if I heard nothing from his father by a certain day (which has elapsed some time ago) I should not consider that there was any obligation to wait longer for him—and measures would accordingly be taken to obtain some other person. Young Fraunces acknowledged the justness of these observations, but still appeared anxious that his father might come, and observed that altho' he had requested a half year's salary advanced, yet he did not think a non-compliance with that would be an obstacle to his coming, if he was not precluded by the foregoing causes which I had mentioned. I told him I must consult Mrs Washington on the Subject, and would give him a final answer in time for him to write to his father by the post of Monday.

Upon conferring with Mrs Washington on the matter it was thought best to know with certainty what reliance there might be on Holker's man before an answer was given to Fraunces. This was soon after determined, by information that Mr Holker's man had no intention of quitting his present place. Fraunces was therefore informed that his father might come on.

Was it not for the aid which is expected from Fraunces in the Cookery, I should rather have objected to his coming than otherwise, for the reasons which I had the honor to mention in my last letter. If the marketing is put in the hands of the Cook & a good house keeper provided, I can see nothing (with the number of Servants in this family) that a Steward can employ himself about. However, I shall take care to oblige Fraunces, in his Articles, to attend particularly to the Cooking—and if the present Cook quits, that he shall do with Hercules. I mentioned in a former letter that the woman in the Kitchen would be discharged, but upon submitting the matter to Mrs Washington, by whose superior knowledge in these things I shall always be pleased to be governed, she thought the woman might as well be continued, especially as she intended to send Richmond home by the first opportunity which will be about next wednesday. Hercules is perfectly willing that he should go.

Mr Eveleigh died yesterday morning. This event has been expected for some time past: And within a few weeks every prospect of his recovery has vanished and for himself, his dissolution has been rather wished for than otherwise, as a relief from the pain which he suffered & which it was impossible to remove.

I am informed that the Post Master General intends to resign his office upon your return to this place. The information is said to have come from his Assistant who speaks of it as a matter upon which Mr Osgood has determined & makes no secret.

Mrs Lear begs your acceptance of her best respects & fervent prayers for the preservation of your health in which she is most sincerely joined by Sir, Your Obliged & grateful Servt

Tobias Lear.

ALS, DLC:GW.

To the Inhabitants of New Bern, North Carolina

Gentlemen,   [New Bern, N.C., c.20–21 April 1791]

I express with real pleasure the grateful sentiments, which your address inspires.[1]

I am much indebted, in every personal regard, to the polite attentions of the citizens[2] of Newbern, nor am I less gratified by their patriotic declarations on the situation of our common country—pleasing indeed is the comparison which a retrospect of past scenes affords with our present happy condition, and equally so is the anticipation of what we may still attain, and long continue to enjoy. A bountiful providence has bless'd us with all the means of national and domestic happiness—To our own virtue and wisdom are referred their improvement and realization.

That the Town of Newbern may eminently participate the general prosperity and its inhabitants be individually happy is my sincere wish.

G. Washington

Df (incomplete), in the hand of William Jackson, DLC:GW; LB, DLC:GW.

1. When GW was met by New Bern citizens at West's ferry on the Neuse River on 20 April, he probably was presented with an address signed by James Coor, Mayor Joseph Leech, Federal District Court judge John Sitgreaves, Benjamin Williams, Daniel Carthy, William McClure, Samuel Chapman, and Isaac Guion: "Sir, With hearts impressed with the most lively emotions of Love, Esteem and Veneration, We meet you at this time to express the joy We feel in your visit to the State of North Carolina. We Sympathize with You in those delightful sensations, which you now so fully experience when We reflect with you on our past difficulties and dangers during a long and arduous War—and contrast these with the bright, the glorious prospects which present themselves—of our beloved Country's enjoying in perfect peace, the inestimable blessings of Civil and Religious Liberty. Our Souls overflow with gratitude to the bountiful Dispenser of all good Gifts, that He has committed to your hands the reins of Government in that Country during peace, of which you have been so lately the defence against the Arm of Despotism and Arbitrary Sway. May Almighty God prolong that Life, which has been so eminently useful to the Human Race, for it is not America Alone—but the World shall learn from your example to what a stupendous heigth of Glory, a Nation may be elevated—whose free born souls are fired with a sincere love of Liberty. It is our most earnest Prayer to the throne of Heavenly Grace that the divine Benediction may accompany you here and hereafter" (DLC:GW). For GW's trip from Petersburg, Va., to New Bern, and his activities at the latter, see *Diaries*, 6:112–17.

2. The text from the middle of this word on is taken from the letter-book copy.

From James McHenry

Baltimore, 20 April 1791. Mr. Purviance has requested that his name be suggested for consideration for the vacancy occasioned by the death of the comptroller. "His chief reason for begging to be again brought to your mind is the small income of his present office, which last year produced only he tells me 801 dollars, and this year it is not expected to exceed 600. You who do not disdain to think of the distressed will readily comprehend the relief which a grade higher in rank and salary would be to one who has nothing besides the mere income of office to support a wife and nine children, more especially at his time of life."[1]

ALS, DLC:GW.

1. Robert Purviance, naval officer at Baltimore, was not named comptroller of the U.S. Treasury upon the death of Nicholas Eveleigh, but GW appointed him collector at Baltimore in 1794 (see Purviance to GW, 19 May 1789, source note and n.2).

Letter not found: from Thomas Smith, 20 April 1791. On 8 July GW wrote to Thomas Smith that he received his "letter of the 20th of April."

To Tobias Lear

Dear Sir, NEWBURN, NO. CARA Aprl. 21st. 1791.

Not having heard from you since I wrote to you from Richmond, the purpose of this is only to let you know where we are, and to cover the enclosed for Mrs. Washington.[1]

We have, all things considered, come on tolerably well, yet, some of the horses, especially the two last bought—are not a little worsted by their journey, & the whole if brought back, will not cut Capers as they did at setting out.[2]

I came to this place yesterday and shall proceed on tomorrow.[3] Wilmington 100 Miles from hence will be my next halting place, from whence if the Post of this evening brings letters to me, they will be answered, for there will be no time to do it here, as not more than an hour is allowed him to stay. My best wishes to Mrs. Lear.[4] I am Yr Sincere & Affecte. friend P. S. The Post is just arrived without any letters for me.

Letters and Recollections of George Washington, 39. What is presumably the original receiver's copy was privately owned in 1939 by Mr. Henry Eyre of New York City (Fitzpatrick, *Writings of Washington,* 31:285, n.65).

1. The enclosure has not been identified.

2. The "two last bought" horses were probably the bays GW purchased from William Davidson's stables in Philadelphia on 7 March. See GW to Charles Pinckney, 29 Mar. 1791, n.1.

3. GW left New Bern early on 22 April and dined the same day at Trenton, N.C., where he was greeted by members of King Solomon's Masonic Lodge, who presented an address drafted and signed by William Gardner: "Sir, Impressed with the purest Sentiments of Gratitude & Brotherly love, Permit us the Members of King Solomons Lodge at Trenton North Carolina (now in

Lodge Assembled) to Hail You Welcome to this State, & Salute you as a Brother. We should feel ourselves remiss in our Duty were we not to Congratulate you on your Appointment to the Head of the Executive Department of the United States—That the great Architect of the Universe may long preserve your invaluable life to preside over a great & free People & to the Advancement of the United States in Opulence, order & Felicity, is the sincere wish of the Members of this Lodge" (DLC:GW). No reply of GW's to this address has been found. See *Diaries*, 6:118.

4. Tobias Lear replied on 15 May.

Letter not found: from Robert Morris, 21 April 1791. On 16 June GW acknowledged Morris's "letter of the 21th of April."

To the Masons of New Bern, North Carolina

Gentlemen,   [New Bern, N.C., 21 April 1791]

I receive the cordial welcome which you are pleased to give me with sincere gratitude.[1]

My best ambition having ever aimed at the unbiassed approbation of my fellow-citizens, it is peculiarly pleasing to find my conduct so affectionately approved by a fraternity whose association is founded in justice and benevolence.

In reciprocating the wishes contained in your address, be persuaded that I offer a sincere prayer for your present and future happiness.

G. Washington.

LB, DLC:GW.

1. The members of St. John's Lodge of New Bern, chartered in January 1772, resolved on 1 April to present an address "to Brother GEORGE WASHINGTON, in behalf of this Lodge, on his arriving in this town" (Sachse, *Washington's Masonic Correspondence*, 44–45). The address, which was dated 20 April and signed by Lodge Master Isaac Guion, Senior Warden Samuel Chapman, Junior Warden William Johnston, Solomon Halling, Edward Pasteur, James Carney, and F. Lowthrop, was probably presented before a public dinner on 21 April: "Right Worshipful Sir, We the Master, Officers and Members of St John's Lodge No. 2 of Newbern, Beg leave to hail You welcome with three times three. We approach You, not with the language of adulation, but sincere fraternal affection—your works having proved You to be 'the true and faithful Brother, the skilful and expert Craftsman, the just and upright Man.' But the powers of eloquence are too feeble to express with sufficient energy the cordial warmth with which our bosoms glow towards You. We therefore most ardently wish, most fervently and devoutly pray—That the Providence of the Most High, May streng[t]hen, establish and protect You, in your walk through this

life; and when You shall be called off from your terrestrial labors by command of our Divine Grand Master, and your operations sealed with the Mark of his approbation, May your soul be eternally refreshed with the streams of living water which flow at the right hand of God. And when the Supreme Architect of all Worlds shall collect his most precious Jewels, as Ornaments of the Celestial Jerusalem, May You everlastingly shine among those of the brightest Lustre" (DLC:GW). The address and GW's reply were read into the lodge minutes at its next meeting, on 29 April, and GW's original answer was lost, probably during the Civil War when the lodge's property was pillaged.

From Thomas Jefferson

Sir   Philadelphia Apr. 24. 1791.

I had the honour of addressing you on the 17th since which I have recieved yours of the 13th. I inclose you extracts from letters received from mister Short in one of the 7th of Feb. mister Short informs me that he has received a letter from mister de Montmorin, announcing to him that the King has named Ternant his minister here.[1] the questions on our tobacco & oil have taken unfavorable turns. the former will pay 50. livres the thousand weight less when carried in French than foreign bottoms. Oil is to pay twelve livres a kental which amounts to a prohibition of the common oils, the only kind carried there.[2] tobacco will not feel the effect of these measures till time will be given to bring it to rights. they had only 20,000 hogsheads in the Kingdom in Novemb. last, & they consume 2000 hogsheads a month; so that they must immediately come forward & make great purchases, & not having, as yet, vessels of their own to carry it, they must pay the extra duties on ours.[3] I have been puzzled about the delays required by mister Barclay's affairs he gives me reason to be tolerably assured, that he will go in the first vessel which shall sail after the last day of May.[4] there is no vessel at present whose destination would suit. believing that even with this, we shall get the business done sooner than thro' any other channel, I have thought it best not to change the plan. the last Leyden gazettes give us what would have been the first object of the British arms had the rupture with Spain taken place. you know that Admiral Cornish had sailed on an unknown destination before the Convention was recieved in London. immediately on it's reciept, they sent an express after him to Madiera, in hopes of finding him there. he was gone, & had so short a passage that in 23 days he had arrived in Barbadoes, the general rendezvous. all the troops of the islands were collecting there, and Genl Matthews was on his way from Antigua to take command of the land operations, when he met with the packet-boat which carried the counter orders. Trinidad was the object of the expedition. Matthews returned to Antigua, & Cornish is arrived in England. this island, at the mouth of the Oronoko, is admirably situated for a lodgment from which all the country up that river, & all the Northern coast of South America, Spanish, French, Dutch, & Portuguese, may be suddenly assailed.[5]

Colo. Pickering is now here, & will set out in two or three days to meet the Indians, as mentioned in my last. The intimation to Colo. Beckwith has been given by mister Madison. he met it on very different ground from that on which he had placed it with Colo. Hamilton. he pretended ignorance & even disbelief of the fact: when told that it was out of doubt, he said he was positively sure the distribution of arms had been without the knowlege and against the orders of Ld Dorchester, & of the government. he endeavored to induce a formal communication from me. when he found that could not be effected, he let mister Madison percieve that he thought however informal his character, he had not been sufficiently noticed: said he was in N. York before I came into office, and that tho' he had not been regularly turned over to me, yet I knew his character. in fine he promised to write to Ld Dorchester the general information we had recieved & our sense of it; and he saw that his former apologies to Colo. Hamilton had not been satisfactory to the government.[6] nothing further from Moose island nor the posts on the Northern border of New-York, nor any thing of the last week from the Western country.

Arthur Campbell has been here. he is the enemy of P. Henry. he says the Yazoo bargain is like to drop with the consent of the purchasers. he explains it thus. they expected to pay for the lands in public paper at par, which they had bought at half a crown the pound. since the rise in the value of the public paper they have gained as much on that, as they would have done by investing it in the Yazoo lands: perhaps more, as it puts a large sum of specie at their command which they can turn to better account. they are therefore likely to acquiesce under the determination of the government of Georgia to consider the contract as forfeited by non-payment. I direct this letter to be forwarded from Charleston to Cambden. the next will be from Petersburg to Taylor's ferry; and after that I shall direct to you at Mount Vernon. I have the honor to be with sentiments of the most affectionate respect and attachment Sir Your most obedient & most humble sert

Th: Jefferson

ALS, DNA: RG 59, Miscellaneous Letters; ALS (letterpress copy), DLC: Thomas Jefferson Papers; LB, DLC:GW, copy, DNA: RG 59, Miscellaneous Letters.

1. Jefferson enclosed three extracts from William Short's letter of 16 Jan. 1791. The first extract concerned political developments in France. The second noted if Spain still contemplated a conflict with Britain, "she would be well disposed still to favor the wishes of the U.S." The third discussed ship timber, the proposed contracts of a Boston merchant with the French and Spanish governments to provide salt provisions to their West Indian ships and garrisons, general Dutch dissatisfaction with the quality of American shipbuilding, and Dutch mercantile interest in New York maple sugar samples. For Short's letter with Jefferson's extracts bracketed, see *Jefferson Papers,* 18:500–507.

2. Jefferson was not yet aware that the National Assembly of France had reduced the duty on American oil from twelve livres per quintal to six on 2 March. See *Archives parlementaires,* 22:470–71, 23:602, 611.

3. For the National Assembly's decree of 1 Mar. concerning the importation of tobacco, see ibid., 23:595.

4. For Thomas Barclay's mission to Morocco, see Jefferson to GW, 27 Mar. and note 1.

5. "Admiral Cornish" was probably Capt. Samuel Pitchford (d. 1816) who took the name Cornish when he inherited the estate of his uncle Vice Admiral Sir Samuel Cornish (d. 1770). Edward Mathew (1729–1805) was appointed commander in chief of British army troops in the West Indies in 1782 and served as governor of Grenada in 1784–85, immediately after the island was wrested from France.

6. For the background to James Madison's conversations with George Beckwith, see Jefferson to GW, 17 April. Madison reported in an undated memorandum to Jefferson, probably written on or shortly after 18 April, that the previous evening Beckwith answered "that it was impossible" that any arming of the hostile Indians "could have proceeded directly or indirectly from the British Government," as Lord Dorchester was opposed to Indian hostilities. Beckwith offered, informally, to transmit any statement or official complaint the U.S. government might wish to make regarding the matter, and he inquired whether GW had any "particulars of time place or persons" involved or "any evidence that the articles supplied were in greater quantities than were

usual for other purposes than war." Madison replied that "the information received by the President" probably would not "be made known to him [Beckwith] in any way more authentic," but that Madison was certain that "If the dispositions of Lord Dorchester were such as were described," he would certainly act to prevent arms from reaching the Indians. Madison told Beckwith that he could not say what particular information GW had at his disposal but commented that "As the Indians at war traded with British subjects only, their being able to carry on hostilities was of itself sufficient evidence in the case." Beckwith promised to inform Lord Dorchester of the substance of the conversation at the earliest opportunity (*Madison Papers*, 14:7–10).

Letter not found: to Tobias Lear, c.24–26 April 1791. On 15 May Lear wrote GW that he received a letter from GW that covered one to Mrs. Washington, "which she informed me was dated at Wilmington." GW was in Wilmington, N.C., from 24 to 26 April.

From Tobias Lear

Sir,   Philadelphia April 24th 1791

On thursday last I had the honor to receive your letter of the 12th Instant with its enclosures. As no vessel has sailed for So. Carolina or Georgia, from this place, since the date of my last letter (the 17th) (altho' several are up for Charleston, and according to their advertisements shou'd have sailed before this time), I intend this letter to go by the mail to Charleston, with a request to the Post-master there, to forward it by a private conveyance either to Augusta or Columbia as the first opportunity may Offer. Should it go on by the Post to Savannah, it would not reach that place before you leave it, provided you meet with nothing to interrupt your intended movements.

As I mentioned in a former letter that I should, I accordingly have spoken to Dr Smith respecting Washington. The Doctor observed that after the Easter Holy-days (which terminate on Tuesday next) he should make some new regulations in the Schools which he hoped would be productive of good effects: and that Washington should be put to Cyphering immediately and particular attention paid to his writing, reading & as well as to Latin. I have conversed with the Several Gentlemen mentioned in your letter upon the subject. They are decidedly of opinion that the boys have gained nothing, but rather lost, since their entrance into that seminary, and nothing prevents their taking them from thence but the want of a suitable master to place them under, and this want they conceive may be applied whe[ne]ver a sufficient number unite to employ one. Colo. Hamilton observes that so fully is he impressed with the fact, that there are such radical defects in the present mode of government & instruction at the College as can only be removed by an almost total change of the system now prevailing, that he would not, upon any consideration, continue his son there. He according[ly] removed him some weeks ago, and placed him under the care of Mr Bend, who I mentioned in a former letter has opened a private school. This Gentleman was spoken of as eminently qualified to discharge the duties of an instructor to Boys. But it is said that he has very lately received an invitation from Baltimore to fill the place which has become vacant by the death of the Revd Mr West, and that so flattering & advantageous is the offer there is no doubt of his accepting it.[1]

As there are assurances that an advantageous alteration will immediately take place in the School where Washington goes, I conceive it would be highly proper to continue him there 'till the effects of a change can be known. If it should be favourable it will be highly pleasing that he should remain where he is. If otherwise—there will be a proper & convenient season to remove him after the August vacation (as it is called) which commences the latter part of July, and gives a recess of six weeks, in which time Mrs Washington says she intends to carry the Children to Mount Vernon. Should it be found necessary to remove Washington, the recess will afford a good opportunity for taking the proper steps to enable him to commence a new care⟨:⟩ And the time between this & the beginning of the Vacation will shew the effects of such regulations as may take place in the school this week.

I have had a very full conversation with the Attorney General respecting your slaves, without however, letting him know that I had heard from you on the subject; but entered upon it with this introduction that as you were absent, and could not return before the expiration of the term which the law of this State specifies for the residence of a Slave, I thought it my duty to take such advice & such measures in the business, with the concurrence of Mrs Washington, as might be proper in the occasion, having a due regard to your public station.[2]

The Attorney General made the following observations on the subject. That he found it was a received construction of the law, and one which he thought the words of the law fully warranted, that if a Slave is brought into the State and continues therein for the space of six months, he may claim his freedom, let the cause of his being brought be what it may; and that this extends, in its full force, to those slaves who may be brought here by the Officers of the General Government or by members of Congress. If a man becomes a *Citizen* of the State, six months residence of the slave is not necessary for his liberation; he is free from the moment his master is a citizen; the term of six months being only intended for the slaves of such as might travel through or sojourn in the State. That those Slaves who were under the age of 18, might, after a residence of six months, apply to the Overseers of the Poor, who had authority to bind them to a master until they should attain the age of 18, when they would become free. That the overseers made it a point to bind the young Slaves to their original masters, unless there should be some special reason against it; but after they are so bound they cannot be carried out of the State without their own consent. That the Society in this city for the abolition of slavery, had determined to give no advice and take no measures for liberating those Slaves which belonged to the Officers of the general Government or members of Congress.[3] But notwithstanding this, there were not wanting persons who would not only give them (the Slaves) advise; but would use all means to entice them from their masters. This being the case, the Attorney General conceived, that after six months residence, your slaves would be upon no better footing than his. But he observed, that if, before the expiration of six months, they could, upon any pretence whatever, be carried or sent out of the State, but for a single day, a new era would commence on their return, from whence the six months must be dated for it requires an *entire* six months for them to claim that right. As the matter stands upon this footing I think that there will be but little difficulty in it; for Austin is now at home on a visit to his wife, by Mrs Washington's permission. This will oblige him to commence a new date for six month from his return—which will be next week.[4] Richmond goes in a Vessel that sails tomorrow for Alexandria—and I shall propose to Hercules, as he will be wanted at home in June when you return there, to take an early opportunity of going thither, as his services here can now be very well dispenced with, and by being at home before your arrival he will have it in his power to see his friends— make every necessary preparation in his Kitchen & as he must return when you do to this place.[5] Mrs Washington proposes in a short time to make an excursion as far as Trenton, and of course, she will take with her Oney & Christopher, which will carry them out of the State; so that in this way I think the matter may be managed very well.[6] If Hercules should decline the offer which will be made him of going home, it will be a pretty strong proof of his intention to take the advantage of the law at the expiration of six months. As Mrs Washington does not incline to go to Virginia until you return to this place, the foregoing arrangement is the best I can think of to accomplish this business.

You will permit me now, Sir, (and I am sure you will pardon me for doing it) to declare, that no consideration should induce me to take these steps to prolong the slavery of a human being, had I not the fullest confidence that they will at some future period be liberated, and the strongest conviction that their situation with you is far preferable to what they would probably obtain in a state of freedom.[7]

Mr Ellicott has returned to this City from surveying the federal territory, and the flattering account which he gives of the spot and the prospect of things in that quarter, added to other information of the same kind which has been received, have created a serious, and to many an alarming expectation, that the law for establishing the permanent seat of Government will be carried fully into effect.[8] This idea has heretofore been treated very lightly by people in general here. They now begin to view it in another shape, and the opposition given in the Assembly of this State to appropriating money for the purpose of erecting suitable buildings for the accommodation of the President & Congress, carried along with it (in the course of the debates) this aspect, that the western parts of Pennsylvania will be more pleased with having the seat of the general Government on the Potomack than in Philadelphia. The consideration of the question was postponed to the next session; but it is very doubtful whether it will then be determined in favor of building or not.

Fraunces has not yet come on; but it is probable he will in the course of this week. Mrs Washington thinks that if Fraunces comes into the family, there will be little or no occasion for a HouseKeeper. At any rate that it would be best to make an experiment without one. In this opinion I agree so far as this, that one Person to superintend the household affairs is enough; but I cannot help thinking that an honest, managing woman, with the ⟨hosper⟩ we now have belonging to the family, would do better.

I am happy to say that Mrs Washington has entirely recovered for her severe cold &, with the rest of the family, enjoys good health. Mrs Lear & our little boy are well, she begs your acceptance of her best thanks for your kind remembrance of them, and presents her sincere wishes for your health & happiness— in which she is most heartily joined by, Sir, Your grateful & most Obliged Humble Servant

Tobias Lear.

P.S. A letter from Major Jackson, enclosed in yours of the 12th, requests that I would "inform you whether orders have been transmitted to the Collectors at Savannah & Charleston, by the Secretary of the Treasury, to supply you with money should you have occasion for it." This has been done—But I could give no information of it that would have reached you before you left those places (unless one had offered by water). I therefore mention it here only to shew that I have not been inattentive to the direction.[9]

T.L.

ALS, DLC:GW; ALS (letterpress copy), PWacD.

1. The Rev. Thomas West, rector of St. Paul's Episcopal Church in Baltimore, had died on 30 March. For the problems with George Washington Parke Custis's schooling at the academy of the College of Philadelphia, see Tobias Lear to GW, 3 April, and GW to Lear, 12 April.

2. For previous correspondence concerning the status of GW's slaves under the provisions of the Pennsylvania statute of 1780 providing for the gradual abolition of slavery, see Lear to GW, 5 April, and GW to Lear, 12 April.

3. As U.S. attorney for Pennsylvania and GW's appointee for federal district judge in July 1791, William Lewis, chief legal counsel of the Pennsylvania Society for Promoting the Abolition of Slavery, was as anxious as other leaders of the society to avoid a clash with federal officials.

4. Austin departed for Mount Vernon on 19 or 20 April, carrying with him stays for the young women at the estate, seeds for the plantation's gardens, and a letter dated 19 April from Martha Washington to Fanny Bassett Washington, explaining that Austin was coming home "to see his friends" and that "his stay will be short indeed I could but illy spare him at this time but to fulfill my

promise to his wife." Mrs. Washington also wrote that she had not heard from GW since he left Mount Vernon (ViMtV).

5. Herculas was sent to Mount Vernon in early June. See Lear to GW, 5 June 1791 and note 2.

6. For Martha's excursion to Trenton on 17–19 May to visit Philemon Dickinson and his wife Mary Cadwallader Dickinson, see Lear to GW, 15, 22 May 1791 and note 4.

7. This first expression of antislavery sentiment in Lear's surviving letters to GW suggests that GW had earlier revealed to Lear an intention to free his slaves.

8. For Andrew Ellicott's private disparagement of the site of the federal district, see GW to Thomas Jefferson, 1 Feb. 1791, n.1.

9. No such letters from Alexander Hamilton to George Abbott Hall, collector at Charleston, or to John Habersham, collector at Savannah, were found by the editors of the *Hamilton Papers*. On 20 May 1791 Habersham wrote to Hamilton acknowledging receipt of Hamilton's letter of 31 Mar. (not found), which might have included instructions to supply GW with money as needed. No evidence has been found that GW availed himself of either of these sources of funds. If he kept expense records of his Southern Tour, they have not been found.

Letter not found: to Martha Washington, c.24–26 April 1791. On 15 May Tobias Lear wrote to GW: "a letter for Mrs Washington came under cover to me, which she informed me was dated Wilmington." GW was at Wilmington, N.C., from 24 to 26 April.

To William Cooke

Sir,   Wilmington [N.C.] April 25th 1791.

In consequence of the fair representation which has been made to me of your character, I do hereby appoint you to the command of the Cutter, directed by an act of Congress, to be stationed for the protection of the revenue of the United States on the coast of the State of North Carolina.[1]

On application to the Secretary of the Treasury, which you will make immediately, you will be furnished with particular instructions and your commission.[2] I am Sir, your most obedient Servant

G. Washington.

LB, DLC:GW.

William Cooke of Wilmington commanded a privateer during the Revolutionary War. GW appointed him to command the revenue cutter *Diligence*, being fitted out for service in North Carolina waters. When subordinate officers were being selected for the cutter in 1792, Cooke recommended his own son, William Harrison Cooke, as third mate (John Daves to Alexander Hamilton, 17 July 1792, in Syrett, *Hamilton Papers*, 12:42).

1. When GW's party arrived at Wilmington, William Jackson asked North Carolina federal district attorney William Henry Hill (1767–1808) to make inquiries regarding appropriate men to command the revenue cutter for North Carolina. Hill replied to Jackson on 25 April that "Capt. Amaziah Jocelin or Capt. William Cook are both consider'd as proper men" (DLC:GW). Unaware that GW had already decided to appoint him to the command, Cooke petitioned Washington for the office on 27 April, noting that he had suffered financial reverses and had a "family of Small Children" to provide for and enclosing a certificate of his moral character and abilities as a seaman signed by nineteen men (DLC:GW). GW received at least two other applications for the cutter command. Lt. William Rickard (d. 1813), a native of Massachusetts, who served as an officer in the Continental army from 1777 until 1784, wrote him on 15 June from Washington, N.C., referring GW to William Blount, John Sitgreaves, and Richard Dobbs Spaight for recommendations (DLC:GW). Rickard later applied to GW for appointment as militia inspector and referred GW to Henry Knox and Henry Jackson for his "Military Character" (Rickard to GW, 8 Nov. 1791, DLC:GW). Rickard did not receive that appointment but was tendered an appointment as an infantry lieutenant in 1792 and was promoted to captain in 1794 (see GW to the U.S. Senate, 3 May 1792, 9 May 1794). Another application for the cutter command, dated 15 July, was submitted by Stephen Tinker, New Bern merchant captain, whose brief note referred GW for recommendations to former North Carolina governor Samuel Johnston, Spaight, James Iredell, and to the members of the North Carolina delegation to Congress (DLC:GW). Tinker received no appointment from GW.

2. On 25 April Jackson wrote to Hamilton that upon inquiry of Thomas Kelly's character, "it has been suggested that he is an intemperate man," and that, "in consequence of the fair reputation" of Cooke, GW had determined to appoint Cooke captain of the North Carolina cutter; "he is directed to apply to you for his instructions, and his commission" (DLC:GW). For Thomas Kelly's application, see GW to Hamilton, 8 Nov. 1790 and note 3. Hamilton later instructed Tobias Lear to fill in Cooke's name on one of the blank commissions in the secretary's possession (see Lear to GW, 29 May 1791, n.3).

To the Inhabitants of Wilmington, North Carolina

Gentlemen,   [Wilmington, N.C., 25 April 1791]

Appreciating with due value the sentiments you are pleased to express for my station and character, I should fail in candor and respect not to avow the grateful sensations excited by your address, for which I thank you with unfeigned sincerity.[1]

Reasoning from the rapid progress of improvement throughout the United States, and adverting to the facility which every undertaking must derive from a settled system of government, the obviation of those disadvantages imposed by situation on your town, may, I think, be calculated upon within no very distant period.

The sanction which experience has already given to the salutary influence of the general government on the affairs of the United States, authorises a well founded expectation that every aid which wise and virtuous legislation can render to indivudual industry will be afforded, and creates a pleasing hope that the happiness of her citizens will be commensurate with the growing dignity and importance of our country.

I express a heartfelt sentiment in wishing to your town and its inhabitants a full proportion of general and particular prosperity.

G. Washington.

LB, DLC:GW.

1. The address of the Wilmington inhabitants, signed by James Read, William Campbell, John Bradley, Dr. James Fergus, George Hooper, William Henry Hill, and Edward Jones, probably was presented to the GW before noon on 25 April (Henderson, *Washington's Southern Tour,* 108, 113): "We wait on you to offer the tribute of respect, gratitude and esteem, so justly due to your exalted Station, your eminent public services, and the extraordinary virtues that adorn your Character. We thank you for the high honor conferred on us by your visit to this place in your tour through the Southern States, and salute you with the most cordial welcome, to the chief Sea port Town of the extensive State of North Carolina. It may be proper to observe, Sir, that if the progress of Agricultural and Commercial improvement, in the State of which we are a part, has any proportion to the great natural resources it contains, the Town would probably have surmounted some of the obvious disadvantages of its Situation, and become more worthy of the honor it now enjoys by your presence. Truly sensible, that a system of Government at once benign and efficient, is the sure source of safety and prosperity to any Country where it obtains, We Anticipate with great pleasure the effectual Operation of the New Constitution, persuading ourselves that the same wisdom, liberality and genuine Patriotism, of which there is so illustrious an example in the conduct of our beloved Chief Magistrate, have hitherto influenced and will continue to temper the council of the Nation. We ardently hope, that *that* admirable political Fabric, reared upon the basis of Public Virtue, may prove a strong Pillar of support to the Union of the States: Improved and strengthened by revolving years, may it be as durable as your Fame, and extend the blessing of civil liberty to the latest Ages. Accept Sir, our humble testimony, in Addition to the innumerable

instances you have experienced—in proof that the same sentiment pervades the breasts of the Citizens of the United States universally, that to you principally, under providence, our common Country is indebted for Liberty & Independence. That those invaluable acquisitions are become the means of permanent happiness, is equally an occasion of gratitude to you. May you long continue on Earth your Country's Glory and human nature's great ornament, and finally in an immortal State receive from the great protector of Nature the rich reward that awaits the distinguished benefactor of Mankind" (DLC:GW). For GW's journey from New Bern to Wilmington and his activities at the latter from 24 to 26 April, see *Diaries*, 6:118–21. GW's baggage handler, Paris, remained in Wilmington an additional week because of illness, according to Read's letter of 1 May to William Jackson (DLC:GW).

To the Citizens of Fayetteville, North Carolina

Gentlemen,   [Brunswick County, N.C., c.26 April 1791]

It is due to your goodness, and to my own feelings, that I should express the sensibility excited by your address, and that I should acknowledge the grateful pleasure with which I receive it.[1]

My best services are more than compensated by the affectionate partiality of my fellow-citizens—and my most anxious wishes are gratified in observing the happiness which pervades our country.

The very favorable change already manifested in our political system, justifies the prediction that the future operations of the general government will be alike conducive to individual prosperity and national honor.

Should it consist with the necessary arrangements of my journey I shall be happy in a personal opportunity of confessing my obligations to the regard of the citizens of Fayetteville. In any event I entreat them to be persuaded of my sincere wishes for their welfare.

                                        G. Washington.

LB, DLC:GW.

1. After Congressman William Barry Grove returned to Fayetteville with the news that GW would shortly visit North Carolina, Grove's brother-in-law John Hay presided over a town meeting on 15 April that voted to have Grove deliver an address to GW. Hay notified GW on 16 April that Grove would present the address whenever and wherever the president appointed (DNA: RG 59, Miscellaneous Letters). Grove met GW's party on 26 April at Russ's Tavern in

Brunswick County, where he presented GW the "address of the Merchants, Traders and Principal Inhabitants, of the Town of Fayetteville," signed by Hay: "Altho' our voice can add little to the general acclamation which attends you, and to your Excellency must be of small moment, yet amidst the warm congratulations on the appearance in this State of their beloved chief Magistrate, our silence would indicate a want of respect, a silence which would be the more reprehensible in a community so largely interested in Trade & Navigation more peculiarly under the directing hand of that Government in which you preside. Could any incident improve the admiration we feel for your illustrious character, heretofore so fully established as the Soldier, the Statesman, and the Patriot; it is your present expedition, in undertaking at an advanced period of life, a long and laborious journey, for the purpose of advising yourself by personal observation, and inquiry, of the true interests of the several States which compose our confederation. From this tour we presage the happy consequence, that those who are not yet satisfied with the tendency, operation, and effects of the present constitution of the Union will be convinced of its superior excellency to all former systems of Government. Throughout your journey we wish you as much satisfaction as can attend it, and if in its progress we are to be honoured by your visitation, the Citizens of Fayetteville will be happy in every attention which may contribute to your pleasure, and conveniency. Under the impression of the importance of a life so valuable to our Country, we commit it to God with our most fervent prayer that it may long be preserved as full of happiness, as it hath been already full of Glory" (DLC:GW).

From Charles Pinckney

Dear Sir   April 26—179⟨1⟩ Meeting Street [Charleston, S.C.]

Hearing that Colonel Washington will set out in a few days to meet you at Waccamaw, I take the Liberty of acquainting You that I have requested General Moultrie to ask the favour of yourself & the gentlemen of your family to dine with me on the day of your arrival in Charleston—the arrangements for the other days, the General will shew you & I trust they will prove acceptable—You may be assured that the people of this country feel themselves on this occasion so strongly bound by every principle of Gratitude and affection that no exertion will be wanting on their part to render your stay among us as agreeable as possible.[1]

In Your way down General Moultrie will request you to make a stage at a little farm of mine in Christ Church a few miles distant from hence. I must apologize for asking you to call at a Place so indifferently furnished, & where Your fare will be entirely that of a farm. it is a place I seldom go to, or things perhaps would be in better order—but such as they are, they are very much at your service & I hope You will consider yourself when there as at home—As soon as I know the day you are to be there I shall request a gentleman to go over and meet You.[2] I am dear Sir, with Esteem, & Respect, much Obliged Your's Truly

Charles Pinckney

ALS, without address cover, NNPM; original address cover, in Charles Pinckney's hand, with note: "honoured by Col. W. Washington," DLC:GW.

1. GW accepted Pinckney's dinner invitation, noting on 2 May: "I dined at the Governors (in what I called a private way) with 15 or 18 Gentlemen" (*Diaries*, 6:127).

2. GW did in fact stop at Snee Farm, one of Pinckney's plantations, in Christ Church Parish (see ibid., 126).

From Uriah Forrest

Sir   George town [Md.] 27 April 1791.

Having for the last two or three Years done very little business other than the Winding up of that, which had been too extensive in former Years—Having effected this so far as to enable my Partner to compleat it—Having been obliged to make such Sacrafices in collecting from my debtors in order to satisfy my Creditors, as will leave me little or no part of the Profits which ought to and otherwise would have attended my business, and Having determined to avoid meddling again with Commerce; togethcr with a great desire of being employed by You, and of rendering myself useful to the Public, has induced me to present myself for any appointment You may think proper.

It was not my intention to have made this application until Your return from the South—But the unfortunate Event of the Comptrollers death Occasions a Vacancy in that Line where perhaps I am most fit to act, and where I cannot but confess I should be highly gratified in being placed by you, Sir.

Permit me to remark that it is not in your Power by any Favors you may bestow or by any Honors You can confer, to add to the Affectionate Consideration and Respect with which I am Sir Your most Obedt humle Servt

Uriah Forrest

ALS, DLC:GW.

Letter not found: from Thomas Attwood Digges, c.28 April 1791. On 28 April Digges introduced William Pearce to Thomas Jefferson and wrote: "I have so little time before the Vessel sails to address The President and yourself . . . , that I hope You will escuse haste & inaccuracys" (*Jefferson Papers*, 20:313–15).[1]

1. William Pearce arrived at Philadelphia and presented to GW Digges's letter of introduction on 12 July (see GW to Thomas Jefferson, 12 July and note 2).

Letter not found: from Anthony Whitting, 29 April 1791.

What is presumably the receiver's copy of this letter was offered for sale in the catalog of George Smith, "Autograph Letters," 1960, item 199.

To the Inhabitants of Georgetown, South Carolina

Gentlemen,   [Georgetown, S.C., 30 April 1791][1]

I receive your congratulations on my arrival in South Carolina with real pleasure, and I confess my obligation to your affectionate regard with sincere gratitude.[2]

While the calamities, to which you were exposed during the war, excited all my sympathy, the gallantry and firmness, with which they were encountered, obtained my entire esteem.[3] To your fortitude in those trying scenes our country is much indebted for the happy and honorable issue of the contest—From the milder virtues, that characterise your conduct in peace our equal government will derive those aids, which may render its operations extensively beneficial.

That your participation of every national advantage, and your prosperity in private life, may be amply proportioned to your past services and sufferings is my sincere and fervent wish.

Go: Washington

DS (facsimile), in Henderson, *Washington's Southern Tour*, facing 134 (from original owned [1923] by Winyah Indigo Society, Georgetown, S.C.); LB, DLC:GW.

1. GW entered South Carolina on 27 April and was met at Capt. William Alston's Clifton plantation on 29 April by William Moultrie, William Washington, and John Rutledge, Jr., who served as GW's official escort to Charleston. For GW's journey from Wilmington, N.C., and his arrival and activities at Georgetown, see *Diaries*, 6:121–25.

2. The undated address, signed by Hugh Horry, George Heriot, Robert

Brownfield, Joseph Blyth, Erasmus Rothmahler, Matthew Irvine, and Samuel Smith, was presented to GW at two o'clock: "We, the Inhabitants of George Town and of it's vicinity, beg leave to congratulate you upon your safe arrival in South Carolina, and to assure you that having ever entertained a high sense of the obligations which you have conferred upon your Fellow Citizens in general, We are happy to embrace this opportunity of testifying to you, our particular sentiments of Gratitude, and of affection: We are no less happy, Sir, at being called upon by the Laws to obey and to respect as first Magistrate of the Fœderal Republic, that person whom of all men we were most disposed to revere as our Benefactor and to love as the Father of his Country. Having shared in the distresses of the War and been exposed to those calamities, and to that loss of property which were the consequences of it, we have been taught to set a proper value upon the exertions which were made in our behalf; we have experienced the happy influence of your counsels Sir, and have distinguished you as the Guardian of our laws, and of our liberties; as an instrument in the hands of Providence, to protect our dearest rights & to save us from oppression. The breath of popular applause is fleeting, but the merit of such illustrious actions, can never be effaced: they carry with them their best reward, & we trust Sir, that in pursuing your progress through this State, you will have the satisfaction to perceive a Spirit of Freedom, which your Services during the War enabled us to maintain, a degree of order and tranquillity which your administration has diffused, and a growing prosperity, than which no better proof could exist of the goodness and efficacy of that government over which you preside. Such Sir are the sentiments with which we approach you upon this occasion, and such the sentiments, which we shall in honour and in gratitude transmit to our latest posterity" (DLC:GW).

3. Georgetown was occupied by the British army from July 1780 to May 1781, and many of its buildings were burned in August 1781 by a Loyalist privateer.

To the Masons of Georgetown, South Carolina

Gentlemen, [Georgetown, S.C., 30 April 1791]

The cordial welcome which you give me to George Town, and the congratulations you are pleased to offer on my election to the chief Magistracy receive my grateful thanks.[1]

I am much obliged by your good wishes and reciprocate them with sincerity—assuring the fraternity of my esteem, I request them to believe that I shall always be ambitious of being considered a deserving Brother.

G. Washington.

LB, DLC:GW.

Prince George's Lodge, No. 16, of Georgetown, apparently the only "Modern" Lodge of Freemasons to address GW, was one of the six original lodges warranted in the colony by the Grand Lodge of England before 1756, having received its charter in 1743. In the 1730s dissenting Freemasons in Britain split from the English Grand Lodge, believing that its 1723 *Book of Constitutions* had introduced too many innovations, and styled themselves "Ancient" in opposition to the label "Modern" they pinned to their brethren. In 1756 Boston's St. Andrew's Lodge, founded in 1752, was the first "Ancient" lodge to be warranted in America, receiving its charter not from the "Modern" Grand Lodge of England, but from the Grand Lodge of Scotland, which was sympathetic to the "Ancient" movement. See Sachse, *Washington's Masonic Correspondence,* 51; Tatsch, *Freemasonry in the Thirteen Colonies,* 33–38, 89, 90; Bullock, *Revolutionary Brotherhood,* 85–133.

1. Addressed "To Our Illustrious Brother George Washington—President of the United States," the address, signed by Isaac White, Robert Grant, Abraham Cohen, Joseph Blyth, and James Carson, was presented to GW before a public dinner on 30 April: "At a time when all men are Emulous to Approach you to Express the lively Sensations you inspire as the father of our Country—Permit us the Bretheren of Prince George's Lodge No. 16. to have our Share in the general Happiness in Welcoming you to Georgetown—& the pleasure of reflecting that we behold in you the Liberator of Our Country—The distributor of its equal Laws & a brother of our Antient & most honourable institution. At the same time indulge us in Congratulating you on the truly honourable and happy Situation in which you now Stand as the Grand Conductor of the Public Interest of these United States. Having by your Manly Efforts caused the beautious Light of Liberty to beam on this Western Hemisphere—and by the Wisdom Heaven has Graciously endowed you with Established the Liberties of America on the justest and firmest Basis that was ever yet Recorded on the Annals of History—you now enjoy the Supremest of all Earthly Happiness—that of Diffusing Peace liberty and Safety to Millions of your fellow Citizens. As a due reward for your Patriotic Noble and Exalted Services We fervently Pray the Grand Architect of the Universe long to bless you with Health, Stability and Power to Continue you the Grand Pillar of the Arch of Liberty in this Vast Empire which you have been so eminently Distinguished in Raising to this pitch of Perfection at which we now behold it. May the Residue of your life be Spent in ease Content & happiness and as the Great Parent of these United States may you long live to See your Children flourish under your happy Auspices and may you be finally Rewarded with Eternal Happiness. We Conclude our present Address with a fervent wish that you will continue as you have hitherto been, the friend of our Antient and Honourable Order and of all Worthy Masons" (DLC:GW).

From Thomas Jefferson

Sir   Philadelphia May. 1. 1791.
I had the honour of addressing you on the 24th Ult. which I presume you will have recieved at Cambden. the present is or-

dered to go from Petersburg to Taylor's ferry. I think it better my letters should be even some days ahead of you, knowing that if they ever get into your rear they will never overtake you. I write to day indeed merely as the watchman cries, to prove himself awake, & that all is well, for the last week has scarcely furnished any thing foreign or domestic worthy your notice. Truxton is arrived from the E. Indies and confirms the check by Tippoo-Saib on the detachment of Colo. Floyd, which consisted of between 3. & 4000 men. the latter lost most of his baggage & artillery, and retreated under the pursuit of the enemy. the loss of men is pretended by their own papers to have been 2, or 300 only. but the loss and character of the officers killed, makes one suspect that the situation has been such as to force the best officers to expose themselves the most, & consequently that more men must have fallen. The main body with General Meadows at their head are pretended to be going on boldly.[1] yet Ld Cornwallis is going to take the field in person. this shews that affairs are in such a situation as to give anxiety. upon the whole the account recieved thro' Paris proves true notwithstanding the minister had declared to the house of Commons, in his place, that the public accounts were without foundation, & that nothing amiss had happened.[2]

Our loan in Amsterdam for 2½ million of florins filled in two hours & a half after it was opened.

The Vice-president leaves us tomorrow. we are told that mister Morris gets £70,000. sterl. for the lands he has sold.[3]

A mister Noble has been here, from the country where they are busied with the Sugar-maple tree. he thinks mister Cooper will bring 3000 £'s worth to market this season, and gives the most flattering calculations of what may be done in that way. he informs me of another very satisfactory fact, that less profit is made by converting the juice into spirit than into sugar. he gave me specimens of the spirit, which is exactly whiskey.[4]

I have arrived at Baltimore from Marseilles 40. olive trees of the best kind from Marseilles, & a box of the seed. the latter to raise stocks, & the former cuttings to engraft on the stocks. I am ordering them on instantly to Charleston, where if they arrive in the course of this month they will be in time. another cargo is on it's way from Bordeaux, so that I hope to secure the commencement of this culture and from the best species.[5] sugar &

oil will be no mean addition to the articles of our culture. I have the honour to be with the greatest respect and esteem, Sir, your most obedt & most humble sert

Th: Jefferson

ALS, DNA: RG 59, Miscellaneous Letters; ALS (letterpress copy), DLC: Thomas Jefferson Papers; LB, DLC:GW; copy, DNA: RG 59, Miscellaneous Letters. Jefferson addressed the letter to: "The President of the United States. to be lodged at Taylor's ferry on the Roanoke. to which place the post-master at Petersburg is desired to forward it by the first private conveyance. for the Petersburg mail." Taylor's ferry on the Roanoke River in Mecklenburg County, Va., was on a more westerly route than GW's original itinerary.

1. Long Island, N.Y., native and Revolutionary War privateer Thomas Truxtun (Truxton; 1755–1822) commanded the 310-ton *Canton*, Philadelphia's first China trader, which had returned to the city from Calcutta and the East Indies on 29 April with papers containing intelligence directly from India, extracts of which editor Benjamin Franklin Bache printed in the *General Advertiser and Political, Commercial and Literary Journal* (Philadelphia), 30 April, 2, 10 May, 1791. See also *Gazette of the United States* (Philadelphia), 4 May 1791.

2. Charles Cornwallis, Earl Cornwallis (1738–1805), arrived in India in 1786 as governor general. In a campaign against Tippoo Saib, sultan of Mysore, Cornwallis in January 1791 assumed command of Gen. William Medows's forces and marched against Tippoo's stronghold at Seringapatam, but he was forced to abandon his campaign against the sultan in mid-May 1791 (see Wickwire, *Cornwallis*, 136–53). Cornwallis and the Mysore war featured prominently in parliamentary debates on 28 Feb. and 2 Mar. 1791 (see *Parliamentary History of England*, 28:1271–1364, esp. 1318–22, 1362, 1363).

3. For the departure of John Adams, see GW to Alexander Hamilton, Jefferson, and Henry Knox, 4 April 1791 and note 1. For Robert Morris's Genesee land speculations in New York, see Lear to GW, 8 May 1791 and note 4.

4. On 7 Aug. 1791 Arthur Noble delivered to the president on behalf of himself and William Cooper "Some Samples of Maple Sugar Manufactured at Cooperstown in the State of New york," claiming "that a Suffi⟨cie⟩nt quantity of this Sugar may be made in A few years to Suply the whole United States" (DLC:GW). GW's reply of 8 Aug., "The President of the United States is much obliged by the polite attention of Messiur's Cooper and Noble—he thanks them for the present of Maple Sugar, and learns, with great pleasure, the progress of that promising manufacture," was reprinted in the *Albany Register* on 29 Aug. 1791 (Taylor, *William Cooper's Town*, 125, 468 n.30). Jefferson became an avid proponent of American maple sugar and gave GW some sugar maple seeds in 1792 that GW instructed his farm manager to plant at Mount Vernon (see Jefferson to GW, 16 Oct. 1792, Anthony Whitting to GW, 31 Oct. 1792, and GW to Whitting, 4 Nov. 1792; Betts, *Jefferson's Garden Book*, 157 n.1, 159, 166–69, 179, 210, 375, 417).

5. Before leaving France Jefferson commissioned Stephen Cathalan, Jr., at Marseilles to send a number of olive trees to the Agricultural Society of South Carolina in Charleston (William Drayton to Jefferson, 25 Nov. 1787, Jefferson

to Cathalan, 7 Sept. 1790, *Jefferson Papers,* 12:380–82, 17:497–98). Jefferson on 30 April 1791 received Cathalan's letter of 22 Jan. informing him of the shipment to Baltimore of forty trees and a chest of olives for planting. On 1 May Jefferson requested Robert Gilmor & Co. to forward the plants from Baltimore to Charleston (Jefferson to Drayton, 1 May, to Robert Gilmor & Co., 1 May, ibid., 20:332–33).

From Tobias Lear

Sir,   Philadelphia May 1st 1791.

We have not had the pleasure of hearing from you, since I had the honor to write on the 24 of last month; which letter was sent by the mail to Charleston, with a request to the Post Master to convey it by a private opportunity to Augusta or Columbia. As it would reach Charleston by the 12th of may there is no doubt but an opportunity will offer of sending it to either one or the other of those places before your arrival there, especially to the latter, between which and Charleston I am informed a Stage plys weekly. This letter goes by the mail to Petersburg, the Post Master at which place will be requested to send it by a private conveyance to Taylor's ferry, where it will undoubtedly get some time before your arrival; but from every information I can obtain, this seems to be the most certain mode of conveying letters so as to meet you; for there is said to be but little communication between the Post Road in North Carolina and that by which you will return through the same State. For three weeks past I have written but once a week, as nothing has transpired of sufficient importance to render it necessary to write oftener, and I thought it better to direct one letter in such a manner as to be upon a moral certainty of reaching your hands, than to send two within the week with a probability of the miscarriage of one.

In my last letter I mentioned the intention of not engaging a House-keeper, unless experience should, after Fraunces' arrival & the family being collected together, point out the necessity of such a character. But since that time there has been an application in behalf of a person for that place with such strong and favorable recommendations that Mrs Washington and myself have thought best to engage her, lest if this opportunity of engaging such a person should be neglected—we might not have it in our power to obtain so suitable a one, if one should be found necessary hereafter. And upon a further consideration of the matter Mrs Washington thinks a House-keeper will be necessary at any rate. The History of the woman is this. She was brought up by Mrs Hill, wife of H. Hill Esqr. and lived with her many years as a House-keeper. About 6 or 8 years ago she married, and then left Mrs Hill. She married a Captain Emerson and has lived in a reputable & respectable manner with him till his death, which happened about 6 months since. As she was not left in circumstances to support herself & 3 Children without some employment, she has, through Mr Hill, made application for the place of House keeper in this family. Mr Hill recommends her in the warmest terms for *honesty, industry & excellent management* in a family. He says that Mrs Hill committed everything to her relative to family affairs, and had never, in any instance, cause to be dissatisfied with her doings. He likewise speaks highly of the goodness of her disposition, and the address with which she governs the Servants. Her prudence & œconomy, he says, will not be found among the least of her qualifications. The Known manner in which Mr Hill's household affairs are conducted leave no room to doubt of his judgement in these matters; and there can be as little reason to doubt his veracity in respect to this woman, especially as he pledges himself for everything in which he recommends her. He further adds, that he would not have ventured to say so much in her behalf had he not known that she has conducted herself with as much propriety since she left Mrs Hill as she did while living with her. I took occasion to ask him why he did not take her into *his* family, as he must undoubtedly have occasion for a good house keeper. He observed that no consideration would induce him to pass by this opportunity of engaging her in that capacity, if he could, with any shadow of decency, discharge the woman who now holds that place in his family; but that she having lived with him for several years and conducted herself in a very blameless manner, he could not think of putting her off, althô he was sensible that this woman was possessed of qualifications much superior. The account given by Mr Hill is corroberated by Mr & Mrs Meredith & Clymer who had the best opportunity of knowing the woman while she lived at Mr Hill's. She is about 45 years old. Her terms are £50 per year, with the privilege of having one of her children, a girl about 7 years old, with her. This girl has, she says, been for some time past at Mr Wigden's School—(where Nelly goes) and that she shall continue her there. Her other two Children she says she shall put out. To the sum of £50 objections were made as being much too high; but she did not incline to make any abatement. with respect to her Child, Mrs Washington told her that she did not beleive, upon experience, that she herself would be fond of its being in the family where it would be liable to receive so many bad impressions from the Servants— and, if that should be no objection, that she (Mrs Washington) had rather it should not be brought into the family. However, as the woman appeared very anxious on this head, it was granted on this condition, that, if, on your return, it should not be perfectly agreeable to you & to Mrs Washington she should then be removed from the family; and the woman's engagement, Mrs Washington thought proper, should be only for six months, at the expiration of which, she is to engage to continue on the same terms, if her services are approved of.[1]

Fraunces has not yet come on, and since this woman is engaged, I cannot say that I am anxious he should; his son, however, says there is no doubt but he will.

Captain Truxton, in a Ship of Mr Morris', arrived here a few days ago from the East Indias. He says he frequently saw Lord Cornwallis, by whom he was treated with very great civility, and from whom he had a message to deliver to you to this effect: His Lordship congratulates General Washington on the establishment of a happy government in his Country—and the country on the accession of General Washington to the Office of Chief Magistrate—His Lordship wishes Genl Washington a long enjoyment of tranquility & happiness: for himself—his Lordship still continues to be in troubled waters, but for once he *hopes* he is in the *right*. Lord Cornwallis was about to take the field in person agains Tippo when Captain Truxton sailed. Truxton is said to have made one of the most lucrative voyages that has been made from this Country to the Indies.[2]

The family is in good health. Mrs Lear unites with me in sentiments of the highest respect for you & in sincere prayers for your health. I have the honor to be with the truest attachment & most grateful affection Sir, Your Obliged & Very Hble Sert

Tobias Lear.

ALS, DLC:GW.

1. A widow by the name of Ann Emerson was listed in the 1790 federal census as living alone on Pruen Street, Philadelphia (*Heads of Families* [Pennsylvania], 244). The wine merchant Henry Hill (1732–1798) and his wife Ann, daughter of Reese and Martha Carpenter Meredith, lived on South Fourth Street with their only daughter, who died young. Mrs. Hill was sister of U.S. Treasurer Samuel Meredith and of Elizabeth Meredith, who married George Clymer in 1765 (Crane, *Elizabeth Drinker Diary*, 3:2162; *Philadelphia Directory*, 1791, 58).

2. See Richard Rush, *Washington in Domestic Life: From Original Letters and Manuscripts* (Philadelphia, 1857), 57–58.

From Benjamin Smith

Sir   Belvidere [Brunswick County, N.C.] 1st May 1791

The inclosed letters were handed to me this day[1]—I very much regret that they did not arrive in time—They are however forwarded, to shew you, that, the common Anxiety, which I believe pervades the Continent, to make your path smooth & your Journey light, was not wanting between this part of the Country & Santee; also in justice to the Parties, who perhaps would be mortified that their very proper Intentions were not made known. At the same time I cannot omit the opportunity of returning You, Sir, the warmest thanks for softening in my favour, the rigour of a Rule, which although adopted upon the soundest principles of propriety & with the very best meaning, must punish all the first Characters of the Country where you travel with great Chagrin.

Had Circumstances permitted; a longer visit would have afforded me the most heartfelt Gratification. An assurance of this however cannot be felt in its full force; without a belief in that Attachment with which I was inspired at New York & Long Island in 1776. An Attachment, which has followed You not less to the peaceful tranquil Shades of Mount Vernon, than your Memorable Entry of New York as first Magistrate of the Union—An Attachment however, that has been attended with a keen regret that will end but with my life, in having been forced from partaking of your Fortunes, amongst the variety of which, I am most pained at my absence in the Retreat through New Jersey & when you changed the Fate of America at Trenton— But whither will my recollection hurry me? Excuse me illustrious Sir, for this Intrusion—I hope it will find you perfectly at leisure, & that your goodness will pardon a fault not likely to be repeated.

Tomorrow, you will probably enter my Native City amidst the applauding Shouts of a grateful People & the welcoming Acclamations of some personal friends—Believe me there is not amongst the whole, one heart more sensibly expanded with offerings to Heaven for the happy prolongation of a life essential to the tranquillity of our Country than that of Virtuous & Great Sir Your sincerely attachd & most devoted

Benja: Smith.

ALS, DNA: RG 59, Miscellaneous Letters.

North Carolina state legislator and Brunswick County militia colonel Benjamin Smith (1756–1826) lived at Belvidere plantation on the Brunswick River, where GW breakfasted on 26 April (see *Diaries*, 6:121). Smith, who studied law in London before the Revolution, supported adoption of the federal Constitution as a member of the North Carolina ratifying conventions of 1788 and 1789.

1. The enclosures were probably letters to Smith from Charles Cotesworth Pinckney and Francis Allston (Alston; b. 1753), a Brunswick County planter. Pinckney's letter, dated "Hampton—Santee—April 15. 1791," covered an unidentified letter to be delivered to GW "as soon as you see him" (Pinckney to Smith, 15 April 1791, DNA: RG 59, Miscellaneous Letters). The unidentified letter may have been that of John Rutledge, Jr., to GW, 15 April 1791. The letter from Allston to Smith was dated Caulkin's Neck, N.C., 21 April 1791, and reads in part: "Upon a Reconsideration, with regard to the purpose I last intimetated to you of Entertaining His Excellency General Washington, at the Boundary House . . . from the Letter you will Receive inclosed from Major Mitchell on the subject, I judge it more proper to entertain him at my own House. . . . I shall expect the favor of your introducing the General with his private suit to my House, and should also (in such cace) thank you to give me some previous Notice of his coming" (DNA: RG 59, Miscellaneous Letters). The enclosed letter from Ephraim Mitchell to Allston, dated Boundary House, N.C. and S.C., 18 April 1791, reads in part: "I find by the information of Coll B. Smith that it is most probible the President of the United States, will do us the Honour of Calling at the Boundary (where perhaps he may Spend ⟨A⟩ Day or Two). . . . any thing you may have in your power to Assist us in makeing provision to Entertain him will be Greatfully accepted—we have no Other Liquer but Rum we have no wheet flower" (DNA: RG 59, Miscellaneous Letters). GW's route did not take in the Boundary House, built before 1754 squarely on the border of the Carolinas.

From Timothy Pickering

(Duplicate)

Sir,   Philadelphia May 2d 1791.

Of the measures pursuing by general Knox, relative to Indian affairs, he doubtless makes to you the necessary communications. In those communications, he may, perhaps, have mentioned my being here, preparatory to my undertaking another mission to the Indians of the Six Nations, for the purpose of confirming the peace and friendship subsisting between them and the United States, and as a mean of preventing their being seduced to engage with the Western Indians, in the war against us.[1]

Upon my arrival, I heard of the vacancy of the office of Comptroller of the Treasury; & also learned that there were divers applicants who wished to succeed to it. For my own part, as I had already made known to you my desire of obtaining a permanent office in the general government, I had concluded not to trouble you with a fresh application at this time. But upon farther reflection, it seemed proper to address you. Because among many applications pointing to the particular office of comptroller, a former general application might not come into view; because if there be any office in the treasury department to which I am competent, I conceive it to be this; and because, being now at the seat of government, not to apply might be construed as a relinquishment of all pretensions to it.

A general knowledge of public business—a reasonable share of discernment—industry—cool deliberation—integrity & strict impartiality, are the great requisites of the office. Whether, Sir, I have or have not, just pretensions to any or all of those qualities, you, who have long known me, can accurately determine: to you alone, therefore, I make my suit; without asking the patronage ⟨or⟩ recommendation of any man. Such aid cannot be necessary, nor proper, nor decent: for no patronage, no recommendation, could make you *better acquainted with my character;* and that is the only ground on which a recommendation could pertinently be offered. For mere patronage will never determine appointments to office, while you preside in the government of the United States.[2] I have the honour to be, with the truest respect, Sir, your most obedient servant,

                                           Timothy Pickering.

(P.S. I hope the deep interest I cannot but feel in the object of this letter, will apologize for my solicitude that my request may come before you prior to your decision on the question to which it relates; and considering the uncertainty of the route by which you may return from the southward, excuse my sending forward a duplicate & triplicate.)

ALS (duplicate and triplicate), DLC:GW (location of original unknown); ADf, MHi: Timothy Pickering Papers; ALS (copy), MHi: Timothy Pickering Papers. The duplicate is the source text; the word in angle brackets and the postscript, which do not appear in the duplicate, are both taken from the triplicate.

1. For Pickering's mission to the Seneca Indians in 1790, see GW to Pickering, 4 Sept., 31 Dec. 1790, Pickering to GW, 5 Sept., 4, 23 Dec. 1790, and Henry Knox to GW, 27 Dec. 1790. For his 1791 mission, see Knox to GW, 10 April, 30 May, 6 Aug. 1791, and Pickering to GW, 27 Aug. 1791.

2. For Pickering's ongoing desire for an appropriate federal position, see Pickering to GW, 3 Sept. 1790 and notes 1 and 2, 8 Jan. 1791, n.1, GW to Pickering, 20 Jan. 1791, and Knox to Tobias Lear, 25 Feb. 1791 and note 1. GW gave Pickering the post of postmaster general after Samuel Osgood resigned in July 1791 (Osgood to GW, 11 July, and Pickering to GW, 27 Aug. 1791).

From Charles Pinckney

Dear Sir   [Charleston, S.C.] 2d May 1791.

I beg leave to remind you that I shall expect the honour of your company *at dinner* on Thursday at four O Clock[1]—and to *a Ball on friday* Evening at seven O Clock.[2] I am with respectful Regard Dear Sir Your's Truly

Charles Pinckney

ALS, PHi: Gratz Collection.

GW landed at two o'clock in Charleston at Prioleau's wharf to an artillery salute, pealing bells, and "reiterated shouts of joy" from "an uncommonly large concourse of citizens" (*Gazette of the United States* [Philadelphia], 21 May 1791).

1. According to GW the dinner at the governor's residence on Meeting Street was attended by "the principal gentlemen of the civil, clerical, and military professions" (*Diaries,* 6:131).

2. GW recorded in his diary that on 6 May he "Dined at Majr. [Pierce] Butlers, and went to a Ball in the evening at the Governors where there was a select company of ladies" (ibid.).

Letters not found: to Martha Washington, c.2–9 May 1791. Tobias Lear informed GW on 22 May 1791 that "Mrs Washington had the pleasure to receive two letters from you" by the brig *Philadelphia*, which had just arrived from Charleston.

To the Charleston Merchants

Gentlemen,   [Charleston, 3 May 1791]

   Your congratulations on my arrival in South Carolina, enhanced by the affectionate manner in which they are offered, are received with the most grateful sensibility.[1]

   Flattered by the favorable sentiments you express of my endeavors to be useful to our country, I desire to assure you of my constant solicitude for its welfare, and of my particular satisfaction in observing the advantages which accrue to the highly deserving citizens of this State from the operations of the [federal][2] government.

   I am not less indebted to your expressions of personal attachment and respect—they receive my best thanks and induce my most sincere wishes for your professional prosperity, and your individual happiness.

                                                G. Washington

LB, DLC:GW.

   1. At 3:30 on 3 May a delegation of Charleston merchants presented an address to the president, following which GW "dined with the Citizens at a public dinr. given by them at the Exchange" (*Diaries*, 6:129–30; Henderson, *Washington's Southern Tour*, 170–71). The address, signed by Edward Darrell, reads: "The Merchants of Charleston, entertaining a just Sense of the high Honor conferred on this City by your Presence, take the earliest Opportunity of congratulating you on your Arrival. The Obligations which are due to you from every Member of the Republic, are acknowledged by all; to enter into a Detail of them, would be to produce the History of your Life, and, to repeat what is re-echoed from one end of the Continent to the other. Were it possible, Sir, for your Fellow-Citizens to omit doing Justice to your Merits, the Testimony of other Nations would evince their Neglect, or Ingratitude; the whole World concurring in the same Opinion of you. Convinced as we are of your constant Solicitude for the general Welfare, it must afford you particular Satisfaction to find the progressive Effects of the Federal-Government in this State; and, that the Inhabitants are fast emerging from the heavy Calamities, to which they were subjected by the late War. Sensible of the numerous Blessings our Country has derived from your Wise and judicious Administration, we feel animated with the most lively Sentiments of Gratitude towards you: Suffer

us then, on the present Occasion, to represent to you the affectionate Sensibility with which we are impressed, by assuring you that we yield to *none* in sincere Respect and Attachment to your Person; and, we earnestly implore the Almighty Father of the Universe, long to preserve a Life, so valuable and dear to the People over whom you preside" (DLC:GW).

2. The copyist mistakenly wrote "several."

To the Officials of Charleston

Gentlemen,   [Charleston, 3 May 1791]

The gratification you are pleased to express, at my arrival in your metropolis, is replied to with sincerity, in a grateful acknowledgement of the pleasing sensations which your affectionate urbanity has excited—Highly sensible of your attachment and favorable opinions, I entreat you to be persuaded of the lasting gratitude which they impress, and of the cordial regard with which they are returned.[1]

It is the peculiar boast of our country that her happiness is alone dependent on the collective wisdom and virtue of her citizens, and rests not on the exertions of any individual. While a just sense is entertained of our natural and political advantages we cannot fail to improve them; and with the progress of our national importance to combine the freedom and felicity of individuals.

I shall be particularly gratified in observing the happy influence of public measures on the prosperity of your city, which is so entitled to the regard and esteem of the american Union.

G. Washington

LB, DLC:GW; Df, DLC:GW. The letter-book copy, in William Jackson's hand, is used as the source text, as it was apparently made on the scene.

1. On the day of GW's arrival, 2 May 1791, the Charleston city council ordered the city recorder to ask GW when he could receive an official welcoming address; GW specified 3:00 P.M. the following day. The address of the intendant and wardens of the city of Charleston, signed by Arnoldus Vanderhorst, was presented to the president at that time: "The Intendant and Wardens, representatives of the Citizens of Charleston, find themselves particularly gratified by your arrival in the metropolis of this State. It is an event, the expectation of which, they have for some time, with great pleasure indulged. When, in the person of the Supreme Magistrate of the United States, they recognise the Father of the People, and the Defender of the liberties of America, they feel a peculiar satisfaction in declaring their firm persuasion that they speak the language of their constituents, in asserting that no body of

men throughout this extensive Continent, can exceed them in attachment to his Public Character, or in revering his private Virtues: And they do not hesitate in anticipating those blessings which must ultimately be diffused amongst the inhabitants of these States, from his exertions for their general welfare, aided by those in whom they have also rested a share of their confidence. Go on, Sir, as you have done. Continue to possess, as well as To deserve, the love and esteem of all your fellow citizens; while millions in other parts of the Globe, though strangers to your person, shall venerate your name. May you long be spared to receive those marks of respect, which you so entirely merit from a grateful people; and may all who live under your auspices, continue to experience that freedom and happiness which is so universally acknowledged to have proceeded from your wise, judicious and prudent administration" (DLC:GW).

The city council also presented to GW a copy of its unanimous resolution requesting him to sit for a portrait by John Trumbull for the city hall (DLC:GW). See GW to William Moultrie, 5 May 1792.

From David Humphreys

Private.

My dear Sir,   Mafra [Portugal] May 3d 1791.

I write this short letter for the sole purpose of thanking you for nominating & appointing me Minister Resident at this Court.[1] The language of affection & gratitude is brief. It is with a sensibility not expressed in words, that all the instances of your friendship & particularly the kind expressions in the close of your letter of March 16th,[2] are indelibly impressed on the heart of Your sincerest & most grateful friend

                                                    D. Humphreys.

P.S. I pray you to remember me to Mrs Washington & the family with those tender sentiments of attachment, which you know I entertain for them.

                                                    D.H.

ALS, DLC:GW.

1. For GW's nomination of his former secretary David Humphreys to become U.S. minister to Portugal, see GW to the U.S. Senate, 18 Feb. 1791. Humphreys arrived in Lisbon from Madrid on 6 Feb. 1791 but did not have his first audience with Queen Maria until 22 May (Humphreys, *Life and Times of David Humphreys*, 2:76, 91–92, 106, 109).

2. On the eve of his departure on the Southern Tour, GW wrote a private letter to Humphreys acknowledging his two previous letters. See Humphreys to GW, 31 Oct., 30 Nov. 1790, and GW to Humphreys, 16 Mar. 1791.

From St. Philip's Church Officials

[Charleston, 3 May 1791]
At a Meeting of the Vestry & Church Wardens of St Philips Church
Resolved—   3d May 1791
   That the President of the United States, be invited to Service in St Philips Church, & the Church Wardens do inform him, that a Pew is ready for his Accommodation on Sunday next, or on any other day that he may think proper.[1]

D, DLC:GW.
   1. On Sunday, 8 May 1791, his last full day in Charleston, GW "Went to Crouded Churches in the Morning & afternoon" (*Diaries*, 6:132). The city wardens escorted him from his lodgings to morning services at St. Philip's Church held by its rector Dr. Robert Smith (1732–1801). In the afternoon GW was escorted to Dr. Henry Purcell's services at St. Michael's Episcopal Church. See Lipscomb, *South Carolina in 1791*, 41–42.

To the South Carolina Masons

Gentlemen,   [Charleston, c.4 May 1791]
   I am much obliged by the respect which you are so good as to declare for my public and private character—I recognise with pleasure my relation to the Brethren of your Society—and I accept with gratitude your congratulations on my arrival in South Carolina.
   Your sentiments on the establishment and exercise of our equal government are worthy of an Association, whose principles lead to purity of morals, and beneficence of action—The fabric of our freedom is placed on the enduring basis of public virtue, and will long continue to protect the Posterity of the Architects who raised it.
   I shall be happy on every occasion to evince my regard for the Fraternity, for whose happiness individually I offer my best wishes.[1]

Df, in the hand of William Jackson, DLC:GW.
   A convention of the masters, past masters, and wardens of the five lodges of Ancient York Masons in South Carolina instituted a Grand Lodge in March 1787, which became the rival of the Grand Lodge of the Most Ancient and Honorable Society of Free and Accepted Masons ("Modern"), the regular suc-

cessor to the Provincial Grand Lodge instituted in 1736. The two Grand Lodges, both of which were incorporated by the state in 1791, did not unite until the nineteenth century, and only the "Ancient" Grand Lodge addressed GW during his tour (Mackey, *History of Freemasonry in South Carolina*, 68–69, 73).

1. An address, signed in Charleston on 2 May 1791 by Grand Master Mordecai Gist, was presented to GW by the Grand Lodge officers after a levee on 4 May at GW's lodgings in Thomas Heyward's mansion and before GW's dinner at four o'clock with the Society of the Cincinnati. See *Diaries*, 6:130n; Sachse, *Washington's Masonic Correspondence*, 57–58 and note 41; Lipscomb, *South Carolina in 1791*, 31. The address reads: "Induced by respect for your public and private character, as well as the relation in which you stand with the brethren of this Society, we, the Grand Lodge of the State of South Carolina, Ancient York Masons, beg leave to offer our sincere congratulations on your arrival in this State. We felicitate you on the establishment and exercise of a permanent Government, whose foundation was laid, under your auspices, by military achievements, upon which have been progressively reared the pillars of the Free Republic over which you preside, supported by wisdom, strength and beauty, unrivalled among the nations of the world. The fabric thus raised and committed to your superintendence we earnestly wish may continue to produce order and harmony, to succeeding ages, and be the asylum of virtue to the oppressed of all parts of the universe. When we contemplate the distresses of war, the instances of humanity displayed by the Craft afford some relief to the feeling mind; and it gives us the most pleasing sensation to recollect that, amidst the difficulties attendant on your late military stations, you still associated with and patronized the Ancient Fraternity. Distinguished always by your virtues more than the exalted stations in which you have moved, we exult in the opportunity you now give us of hailing you, brother of our Order, and trust from your knowledge of our institution, to merit your countenance and support. With fervent zeal for your happiness, we pray that a life so dear to the bosom of this Society, and to society in general, may be long, very long preserved; and, when you leave the temporal symbolic Lodges of this world, may you be received in the Celestial Lodge of light and perfection, where the Grand Master Architect of the universe presides" (Mackey, *History of Freemasonry in South Carolina*, 84).

From Hugh George Campbell

Charleston, S.C., 6 May 1791. Offers himself as a candidate for the command of the United States revenue cutter for South Carolina and refers to the accompanying certificate for information respecting his character.[1]

ALS, DNA: RG 59, Applications and Recommendations for Public Office, 1797–1901. Archivists filed the letter under 1798.

1. The enclosure, dated 6 May 1791 and written in Hugh George Camp-

bell's hand, was signed by Daniel DeSaussure, Arnoldus Vanderhorst, and fourteen other men who certified that Campbell (1760–1820) was a "Gentleman of respectable Character and of proffessionall abillities, that he Served last war in the Navy of the United States, and we do think him a very proper person to Command the Revenue Cutter of this State" (DNA: RG 59, Applications and Recommendations for Public Office, 1797–1901). Campbell accepted the position of first mate of the South Carolina cutter after GW named Robert Cochran its captain (see GW to Hamilton, 8 May 1791 and note 2, and 20 May 1791). For Campbell's subsequent naval career, see *Naval Documents Related to the Quasi-War,* 7:134–35, 321, 367.

From Wakelin Welch & Son

London 6th May 1791

Inclosed we trouble your Excellency with copy of our last of 5th March which we forwarded by the New York Packet since then nothing has transpired from Mr Morris from which we may suppose he is still in France.[1]

Mr Young about ten days ago sent us a case containing a Bag of Seeds, Books & some Yarn manufactured from your own Fleece of Wool which he sends ⟨*mutilated*⟩ a curiosity. This last article being prohibited he was ⟨*mutilated*⟩y anxious about its going & therefore requested our particular attention We have luckily succeeded & hope it will come safe[2] The Bill of Lading for its being on board the Peter Capt. Brooks is inclosed[3] The charges of its coming from Bury & putting on board the Ship 16/6 which we have placed to your Excellency's account. We Remain Your Excellency's Much Hond Servts[4]

Wake' Welch & Son

LS, DLC:GW. The address cover bears the notation "℘ the Peter Capt. Brooks Q: D: C," as well as the postmark "N. YORK july. 12 [1791] FREE."

1. For background to GW's transactions with the London mercantile firm of Wakelin Welch & Son, see Wakelin Welch & Son to GW, 29 Nov. 1790 and note 2, 5 Mar. 1791, and GW to Gouverneur Morris, 17 Dec. 1790 and note 2. See also note 4.

2. For English agricultural journalist Arthur Young's parcel of succory seeds, yarn samples, and volumes of his *Annals of Agriculture,* which GW received at the beginning of August 1791, see Young to GW, 25 Jan. 1791 and notes 1 and 2, and GW to Young, 15 Aug. 1791.

3. The enclosed bill of lading has not been found. GW's entry of 6 May 1791 in his account with Wakelin Welch & Son reads: "By Sundy Charges Shipping a case for N. Yk 0.16.6" (Ledger B, 302).

4. No further communications between GW and Wakelin Welch & Son have been found, and GW wrote to Young on 15 Aug. 1791 that he had closed his correspondence with the firm. According to his ledger GW balanced his account with Wakelin Welch & Son on 7 June 1791, "By Mr G. Morris pd him on my Acct 42.9.6" (ibid.). On 8 June 1791 Morris wrote to GW from London enclosing "an Account settled Yesterday with Wakelyn Welch and Son who as you will see have paid me £42.9.6 Sterling. I shall announce this to Messieurs William Constable and Company from whose Letters I am led to suppose that they beleive the Amount received here to have been more considerable or else that the Sum I first received from Messrs Welch & Son was on Account of the Articles shipped from hence for you whereas it was the Amount of what I had sent long before from france. Mr Welch offered to pay me £60 but I preferred receiving the Ballance only because you seem desirous to close with him and I think it will be best . . ." (DLC:GW). Constable wrote Tobias Lear on 25 Aug. that he had that day received a letter from Morris informing him of that news. Constable requested Lear "to have this matter adjusted" (NN: Constable-Pierrepont Papers) and on 31 Aug. acknowledged Lear's response of 29 Aug. (not found) covering M. Lewis & Co.'s draft upon Strachan & McKenzie of London for £17.10.6 sterling, "which when paid will be in full for the Balance of the President's account. I regret that through Mr G. Morris's Management you have had so much Trouble in this affair" (DLC:GW).

To the Commissioners for the Federal District

Duplicate
Gentlemen,   Charleston, May 7th 1791.
   I have received your letter of the 14th of last month.
   It is an unfortunate circumstance in the present stage of the business, relative to the federal city, that difficulties unforeseen and unexpected should arise to darken, perhaps to destroy, the fair prospect which it presented when I left Georgetown—and which the instrument, then signed by the combined interest (as it was termed) of Georgetown and Carrollsburg, so plainly describes—The pain which this occurrence occasions me is the more sensibly felt, as I had taken pleasure, during my journey through the several States, to relate the agreement, and to speak of it, on every proper occasion, in terms, which applauded the conduct of the Parties, as being alike conducive to the public welfare, and to the interest of individuals, which last it was generally thought would be most benefitted by the amazing encrease of the property reserved to the Land holders.
   The words cited by Messrs Young, Peters, ⟨Lingan⟩, and For-

rest and Stoddert may be nearly what I expressed—but will these Gentlemen say this was given as the precise boundary, or will they, by detaching these words, take them in a sense unconnected with the general explanation of my ideas and views upon that occasion, or without the qualifications, which, unless I am much mistaken, were added, of running *about* so and so—for I had no map before me for direction—Will they not recollect my observation that Philadelphia stood upon an area of three by two miles, and that, if the metropolis of *one State* occupied so much ground, what ought that of the United States to occupy? Did I not moreover observe that before the city could be laid out, and the spot for the public buildings be precisely fixed on, the water courses were to be levelled, the heights taken &ca &ca?[1]

Let the whole of my declaration be taken together, and not a part only, and being compared with the instrument then subscribed, together with some other circumstances which might be alluded to, let any impartial man judge whether I had reason to expect that difficulties would arise in the conveyances.

When the instrument was presented I found no occasion to add a word with respect to boundary, because the whole was surrendered upon the conditions which were expressed—Had I discovered a disposition, in the subscribers to contract my views I should then have pointed out the inconveniences and the impolicy of the measure.

Upon the whole I shall hope and expect that the business will be suffered to proceed—and the more so as they cannot be ignorant that the further consideration of a certain measure in a neighbouring State stands postponed—for what reason is left to their own information or conjectures.

I expect to be with you at the time appointed, and should be exceedingly pleased to find all difficulties removed.[2] I am, with great esteem, Gentlemen, Your most obedient Servant

Go: Washington

LS (duplicate), DLC: D.C. Miscellany, Letters of the Presidents; LB, DLC:GW; LB, DNA: RG 42, Records of the Commissioners for the District of Columbia, 1791–1925, Letters Sent, 1791–1802.

For background to this letter, which William Jackson forwarded to Tobias Lear by the brig *Philadelphia* and which Lear had received and transmitted to the recipients by 22 May, see Agreement of the Proprietors of the Federal District, 30 Mar. 1791, and Commissioners for the Federal District to GW, 14 April 1791.

1. For GW's account of his meeting with proprietors of the federal district, see *Diaries*, 6:104–6.

2. At his meeting with the commissioners and the proprietors of the federal district on 29–30 Mar., GW had agreed to meet with the commissioners in Georgetown on 27 June 1791. For this meeting, see ibid., 164–66, and Commissioners for the Federal District to GW, 30 June 1791.

From Miss Elliott

Charleston [S.C.] May. 7. 1791.

Miss Elliott presents her compliments to The President of the United States, and as a small tribute of her grateful respect, begs that he will Honor her by the acceptance of a Sword Knot.

L, DLC:GW.

This correspondent has not been positively identified but might have been one of the in-laws of GW's cousin William Washington, who had married Jane Reiley Elliott, daughter of Charles Elliott of Charleston.

To Alexander Hamilton

Sir   Charleston [S.C.] May 7th 1791.

I have received your Letters of the 11th & 14th of last month—Concluding from ⟨Mr⟩ Shorts statement of his negotiation in Amsterdam, and from the opinions offered in your letter of the 11th, that the loan has been obtained on the best terms practicable, and that its application in the manner you propose will be the most advantageous to the United States, I do hereby signify my approbation of what has been already done, as communicated in your letters of the 11th[1] and 14th of April. Assenting to the further progress of the loans as recommended by you in these letters, I request that instructions may be given for completing them agreeably thereto. I am sir, Your most Obedt servt

Geo: Washington

LB, DLC:GW; LB, DNA: RG 233, Third Congress, 1793–1795, Records of Legislative Proceedings, Committee Reports, and Papers. The abbreviation in angle brackets is taken from the letter-book copy in DNA.

1. GW probably was referring to Alexander Hamilton's letter of 10 April concerning the new loans that William Short had been authorized to open in Holland. No letter of 11 April from Hamilton has been found.

Letter not found: to Henry Knox, c.7–8 May 1791. Tobias Lear wrote to GW on 22 May: "I had the pleasure to receive a letter from Major Jackson—enclosing one for each of the heads of the Departments."[1]

1. GW's letters to the secretaries of state and treasury bear Charleston, 7 and 8 May, datelines.

To Alexander Hamilton

Sir   Charleston [S.C.] May 8th 1791.

Mr Cogdell, the Collector of Georgetown appearing on enquiry a proper Person to be appointed Inspector of Excise for that Survey—You will signify his appointment to that Office & transmit to him his instructions.[1]

Capt. Robert Cochran seems in all respects best qualified to command the revenue Cutter on this station, and I have in consequence appointed him to that Office. He is desired to apply to you for his commission and instructions which you will transmit & communicate to him.[2] I am, Sir Your most Obt servt

G. Washington

LB, DLC:GW.

1. On 2 Aug. 1791 John Cogdell, collector for the port of Georgetown, S.C., wrote to GW: "Honour'd Sir Sometime past I gave notice of my intention of resigng the Collectors Office, Since that I have had a Commission hand'd me for the Inspectors Office, the business I do not wish to enter On as it clashes with my Own Domestic concerns, not this Only but my time of life being upwards of Sixty, I may drop of and the Affairs may fall into Such hands that may not understand the Settleing the business—I have also Acquaid the Secretary & Comptroler of the Treasury, my Intentions—I therefore take the Liberty of Incloseing you my Commissions, you have been pleased to Honour me with—I am ready to Settle every farther when Call'd On, please direct my bond to be returnd me that I may Satisfy my Sureties (give me leave to recommend Mr Jacob William Harvey to your Notice in those Offices as he is a man well Acquainted with business, has been regularly brought up to it &c.[)]" (DNA: RG 59, Miscellaneous Letters). Cogdell, however, withdrew his recommendation of Harvey, on 16 Aug., "as I am told he is too fond of Liquor" (DNA: RG 59, Miscellaneous Letters). For earlier references to Cogdell's appointment to the excise inspectorship of South Carolina Survey No. 2, see GW to Alexander Hamilton, 15 Mar. 1791 (second letter).

2. Early in GW's presidency Robert Cochran (1735–1824), a Boston native, requested the president's assistance in retaining his post as harbor master of Charleston, S.C., referring to his Revolutionary War services, which included "the expedition to Augustine for Gun powder—which I effected and which your Excellency, may recollect was Sent from This State to Cambridge—that to the northward to recruit Seamen for the defence of this State And the voyage I undertook to France prior to any Alliance with that Kingdom for military Stores, which terminated happily for the State and Army" (undated, DLC:GW). On 22 June 1791 Cochran wrote to GW from Charleston: "The appointment you was pleased to confer on me while in Charleston gave me room to have Some conversation with Mr [George Abbott] Hall the Collector on the busyness and from him I obtain'd the information, that it was intended to have the cutter built in Virginia as it was thought the carpenters here could not do it on the Same terms that they could there—upon this I made it my busyness to make Some enquiry among them and found that Mr [Paul] Pritchard would agree to take the Eleven hundred dollars allowed by Congress and trust to Subscriptions to make up the Sum Mr [Thomas] Penrose got for building the Philadelphia Cutter—taking into consideration the Superior advantages which would accrue from the materials being of live oak & Cedar And the best yellow pine plank—Stuff calculated to Stand the heat of the climate— also the only and first opportunity of finding employ for the Seamen of this place, I apprehend are inducements Sufficiently Strong to have her constructed here particularly as I imagine She will be obliged to be copper'd—we having no fresh water ports or inlets to run into to Stop the ruinous effects of the worms in the Summer months an advantage all the other States have. I will likewise beg leave to inform you that Captain Campbell recommended by the Merchants here, has accepted of the first Mate's berth—the Vacances of the other Officers allowed I shall endeavor to fill up with such persons as are well acquainted with every part of the coast—waiting for the arrival of the respective commissions and my particular instructions" (DNA: RG 59, Miscellaneous Letters). Tobias Lear transmitted Cochran's letter to Alexander Hamilton with the president's request that he give it "such consideration as it may merit" (Lear to Hamilton, 7 July 1791, DLC:GW).

To Thomas Jefferson

Sir,   Charleston [S.C.] May 8th 1791.

The round of business and of ceremony, which now engages my attention, only allows me leisure to acknowledge the receipt of your letter of the 10th of last month, which will receive a more particular consideration.[1] I am, with great esteem Sir, Your most obedient Servant

Go: Washington

LS, DLC: Thomas Jefferson Papers.

1. Jefferson sent his letter to GW at Wilmington, N.C., which the president reached on 24 April and left two days later. It was the last communication GW received from the secretary of state before returning to Virginia (see Jefferson to GW, 10 April, 20 June, GW to Jefferson, 15, 17, 26 June 1791, and *Diaries*, 6:118–21).

From Thomas Jefferson

Sir   Philadelphia May 8. 1791.

The last week does not furnish one single public event worthy communicating to you: so that I have only to say 'all is well.' Paine's answer to Burke's pamphlet begins to produce some squibs in our public papers. in Fenno's paper they are Burkites, in the other Painites. one of Fenno's was evidently from the author of the discourses on Davila.[1] I am afraid the indiscretion of a printer has committed me with my friend mister Adams, for whom, as one of the most honest & disinterested men alive, I have a cordial esteem, increased by long habits of concurrence in opinion in the days of his republicanism: and even since his apostacy to hereditary monarchy & nobility, tho' we differ, we differ as friends should do. Beckley had the only copy of Paine's pamphlet, & lent it to me, desiring when I should have read it, that I would send it to a mister J. B. Smith, who had asked it for his brother to reprint it. being an utter stranger to J. B. Smith, both by sight & character, I wrote a note to explain to him why I (a stranger to him) sent him a pamphlet, to wit, that mister Beckley had desired it; & to take off a little of the dryness of the note, I added that I was glad to find it was to be reprinted, that something would at length be publicly said against the political heresies which had lately sprung up among us, & that I did not doubt our citizens would rally again round the standard of Common sense. that I had in my view the Discourses of Davila, which have filled Fenno's papers for a twelvemonth, without contradiction, is certain. but nothing was ever further from my thoughts than to become myself the contradictor before the public. to my great astonishment however, when the pamphlet came out, the printer had prefixed my note to it, without having given me the most distant hint of it.[2] mister Adams will unquestionably take to himself the charge of political heresy, as conscious of his own views of drawing the present government to the form of the English constitution, and I fear will consider me as meaning to injure him in the public eye. I learn that some Anglomen have censured it in another point of view, as a sanction of Paine's principles tends to give offence to the British government.[3] their real fear however is that this popular & republican pamphlet, taking wonderfully, is likely at a single stroke to wipe out all the unconstitutional doctrines which their bell-weather Davila has been preaching for a twelvemonth. I certainly never made a secret of my being anti-monarchical, & anti-aristocratical: but I am sincerely mortified to be thus brought forward on the public stage, where to remain, to advance or to retire, will be equally against my love of silence & quiet, & my abhorrence of dispute. I do not know whether you recollect that the records of Virginia were destroyed by the British in the year 1781. particularly the transactions of the revolution before that time. I am collecting here all the letters I wrote to Congress while I was in the administration there, and this being done I shall then extend my views to the transactions of my predecessors, in order to replace the whole in the public offices in Virginia. I think that during my administration, say between June 1. 1779. & June 1. 1781. I had the honour of writing frequent letters to you on public affairs, which perhaps may be among your papers at Mount Vernon.[4] would it be consistent with any general resolution you have formed as to your papers, to let my letters of the above period come here to be copied, in order to make them a part of the records I am endeavoring to restore for the state? or would their selection be too troublesome? if not, I would beg the loan of them, under an assurance that they shall be taken the utmost care of, & safely returned to their present deposit.

The quiet & regular movement of our political affairs leaves nothing to add but constant prayers for your health & welfare and assurances of the sincere respect & attachment of Sir Your most obedient & most humble servt

Th: Jefferson

ALS, DNA: RG 59, Miscellaneous Letters; ALS (letterpress copy), DLC: Thomas Jefferson Papers; LB, DLC:GW. The letter was addressed to "The President of the United States to be put into the mail for Petersburg the postmaster at which place is desired to forward it by the first safe conveyance to

Taylor's ferry on the Roanoke, there to await the arrival of the President." Its cover is postmarked 9 May and bears a note stating that it arrived at Petersburg on 14 May and was forwarded. GW did not receive the letter until after his return to Virginia.

1. The "squibs" to which Jefferson refers, were written in reaction to Thomas Paine's *Rights of Man: Being an Answer to Mr. Burke's Attack on the French Revolution* (Philadelphia, 1791). Paine's work, which was dedicated to the president in its first complete American edition, was published in the United States on 3 May. The enclosures were probably: the essays by "A FRENCH CITIZEN," and "A FRENCH TRAVELLER," in *General Advertiser and Political, Commercial and Literary Journal* (Philadelphia), 3 May; a reprint in John Fenno's *Gazette of the United States* (Philadelphia), 7 May, of the anonymous "THE BEAUTIFUL AND SUBLIME OF BLACKGUARDISM," which originally appeared in a Boston newspaper and was attributed to John Adams, anonymous author of "Discourses on Davila," published in the *Gazette*, 28 April 1790–27 April 1791; and "Proposed species of obituary," *Federal Gazette and Philadelphia Daily Advertiser*, 7 May 1791. See editorial note, "*Rights of Man:* The 'Contest of Burke and Paine . . . in America,'" *Jefferson Papers*, 20:268–90.

2. John Beckley obtained one of the first copies of the *Rights of Man* to have reached Philadelphia, around 16 April, and arranged for its publication with Jonathan Bayard Smith (1742–1812), a Philadelphia merchant and justice of the Philadelphia court of common pleas, before lending it to James Madison, who was about to leave for New York. After Madison left the pamphlet with Jefferson, Beckley probably asked him to forward the pamphlet to Smith, which Jefferson did on 26 April (Jefferson to Smith, 26 April 1791, *Jefferson Papers*, 20:271). Samuel Harrison Smith (1772–1845), the son of Jonathan Bayard Smith, announced in the *General Advertiser and Political, Commercial and Literary Journal*, 3 May, that the *Rights of Man* was published that day (*Jefferson Papers*, 20:271, n.10, 272). In his note to Jonathan B. Smith, Jefferson wrote that he was "extremely pleased to find it will be re-printed here, and that something is at length to be publicly said against the political heresies which have sprung up among us. He has no doubt our citizens will rally a second time round the standard of Common sense" (Jefferson to Smith, 26 April 1791, ibid., 290). Samuel B. Smith quoted Jefferson in his edition of the *Rights of Man* with "hopes the distinguished writer will excuse its present appearance."

3. For British reaction to Jefferson's recognition of the *Rights of Man*, see Lear to GW, 8, 22 May.

4. British troops under Benedict Arnold invaded Virginia and entered Richmond on 5 June 1781, after Governor Jefferson and other state authorities had fled the capital, and captured and destroyed government stores and records. Included in the captured archives were eighteen retained copies of Jefferson's reports to the American commander-in-chief. GW complied with Jefferson's request after his arrival at Mount Vernon (see GW to Jefferson, 26 June 1791), and eleven contemporary transcripts of the missing letters are in DLC: Jefferson Papers, probably made by Jefferson's nephew John Wayles Eppes before 1793 (see *Jefferson Papers*, 19:549).

From Tobias Lear

Sir,   Philadelphia May 8th 1791

Since I had the honor of writing to you on the first of this month, nothing of a public nature, sufficiently important to trouble you with a communication, has come to my knowledge. Our domestic Affairs are in the same state they were when I had the honor to write last. The family is in good health. Fraunces has not yet come on; but his son called yesterday to tell me that he would certainly be here the first of the week.

Together with the papers I enclose an American Edition of Mr Paine's answer to Mr Burke's Attack on the French Revolution. You will observe that the printer of this Edition has prefaced the work with an extract from a note sent to him by Mr Jefferson, who furnished him with the pamphlet for publication.[1] As the following sketch of a conversation which took place last friday evening, at Mrs Washington's Room, between Colo. Beckworth & myself on this subject may afford you a moment's amusement you will pardon me for repeating it—which I do as nearly in the same words as I can recollect.

B. Have you seen Mr Paine's pamphlet in Answer to Mr Burke?

L. I have not yet been favored with a perusal of the work; but have read some extracts from it which have been published in the papers.

B. I observe Mr Paine has dedicated it to the President.[2]

L. So I understand.

B. I am very much surprized at it; for it is always thought that the person to whom a book is dedicated approves the sentiments therein contained, as well as their tendency, and I should hope that *everything* in that Book did not meet the President's approbation.

L. Why?

B. Because there are many things in it which reflect highly on the British Government & administration, and as it is dedicated to the President, it may lead to a conclusion that he approves of those things, & that the Author has his sanction for publishing them. Had Mr Paine dedicated this pamphlet to General Washington, it would then have been considered as addressed to him in his personal capacity—and would not have excited the same ideas that are produced by its being dedicated to *the President of the United States;* for I beleive it will appear somewhat singular, that a Citizen of the United States should write & publish & book in a foreign Country, containing many things highly disrespectful to the Government & administration of the Country where he writes, & dedicate that book to the Chief magistrate of his own Country. It will naturally appear to the world that, from the dedication, it meets the approbation of the Chief magistrate of the Country whereof the writer is a citizen, and I therefore conceive that Mr Paine has not, in this instance, treated the President with that delicacy which he ought.

L. As I have not read Mr Paine's book I can say nothing with respect to the sentiments or tendency of it relative to the Government & administration of Great Britain. But it is well known that the President could not have seen it, or have had any knowledge of its contents before it was published, it would therefore be absurd to suppose, *merely from the circumstance of its being dedicated to him,* that he approves of every sentiment contained in it. Upon this ground, a book containing the most wicked or absurd things might be published & dedicated to the President &c. without his Knowledge, and this dedication would be considered as his having given his sanction to them. Or, a book might be written under the circumstances which you have observed that Mr Paine's is—and contain many unjust & unjustifiable strictures upon the government & governors of the Country where the writer resides, and a dedication of it to the Chief Magistrate of his own Country would, according to your idea, cause such chief Magistrate to be considered as the patron of its author, and the abettor of its sentiments. If Mr Paine has, in this instance, not acted with that delicacy & propriety which he ought, he must answer for it himself to those who are authorized to call him to an Account.

B. True! But, I observe, in the American Edition, that the *Secretary of State* has given a most unequivocal sanction to the book, as Secretary of State—it is not said as Mr Jefferson.

L. I have not seen the American, nor any other edition of this pamphlet. But I will venture to say that the Secretary of State has not done a thing which he would not justify.

B. On this subject you will consider that I have only spoken as an individual & as a private person.

L. I do not know you, Sir, in any other Character.

B. I was apprehensive that you might conceive that, on this occasion, I ment to enter the lists, in more than a private Character.

At this moment the Gentlemen of the Cincinnati who are here at the general meeting, entered the Room, in form, to pay their respects to Mrs Washington.[3] This broke off the conversation, and as Colo. Beckworth did not afterwards seek an occasion to renew it, there was nothing more passed on the subject. Yesterday the Attorney General & Mrs Randolph dined, in a family way, with Mrs Washington; and after dinner, the subject of Mr Paine's pamphlet coming on the Carpet, I related to the Attorney General the substance of my conversation with Colo. Beckworth.

Soon after I had finished my relation to the Attorney General a person called for him at the door, with whom he went out upon business. In the evening I saw him again, when he informed me, that upon being called upon after dinner, he went to Mrs House's with the person who called him.[4] While he was there Colo. Beckworth came in, and in the course of conversation the subject of Mr Paine's pamphlet was introduced, when Colo. B. made the same observations, which I had before related. Upon leaving Mrs House's the attorney Genl said he went to Mr Jefferson's, to know from him if he had authorized the publication of the extract from his note which appeared prefixed to the American Edition of Mr Paine's Pamphlet. Mr Jefferson said that so far from having authorized it, he was exceedingly sorry to see it there; not from a desavowal of the approbation which it gave the work; but because it had been sent to the Printer, with the pamphlet for re-publication, without the most distant idea that he would think of publishing any part of it. And Mr Jefferson further added, that he wished it might be understood that he did not authorize the publication of any part of his note.

This publication of Mr Jefferson's sentiments respecting Mr Paine's pamphlet will set him in direct opposition to Mr Adams's political tenets, for Mr Adams has, in the most pointed manner, expressed his detestation of the Book, & its tendency. I had, myself, an opportunity of hearing Mr Adams' sentiments on it one day soon after the first copies of it arrived in this place. I was at the Vice-President's house, & while there Dr & Mrs Rush came in. The conversation turned upon this Book, & Dr Rush asked the Vice-President what he thought of it. After a little hesitation he laid his hand upon his breast, & said in a very solemn manner, I detest that book & its tendency from the bottom of my heart.

The Vice President & family was off for massachusetts last monday—and on Thursday Mr Morris set out for Boston, it is said on some business relative to his late purchase of the Genesee Lands.[5]

Mrs Lear unites with me in sentiments of the highest respect & in best wishes for your health and an agreeable Journey. I have the honor to be, with the utmost sincerity, Sir, Your affectionate & grateful Servt

Tobias Lear.

ALS, DLC:GW.

1. See Thomas Jefferson to GW, this date, n.2.

2. For Paine's dedication to GW, see Paine to GW, 21 July 1791 and note 2.

3. Representatives of the state societies of the Cincinnati attended an extra general meeting of the society in Philadelphia on 2–5 May 1791. "In form" meant appearing in full dress uniform. See Daves, *Proceedings of the Cincinnati*, 44, 46–50, and Myers, *Liberty without Anarchy*, 180.

4. The boardinghouse of Mrs. Mary House on the corner of Fifth and Market streets not far from the presidential mansion had been the traditional lodgings of Virginia officials visiting Philadelphia since the 1780s. See *Diaries*, 5:156, and Reardon, *Edmund Randolph*, 96.

5. In August 1790 Robert Morris agreed to purchase one million acres in western New York from Oliver Phelps and Nathaniel Gorham, and he handsomely profited from the sale of the tract to the Pulteney Associates, a British partnership. Unable to meet their obligations, Phelps and Gorham reconveyed to Massachusetts in June 1790 two-thirds of their original purchase, and Morris proposed a partnership with them in December 1790 for repurchasing this remaining land. When they backed out Morris instructed Samuel Ogden to buy the land from the state, which he did on 12 Mar. 1791. Morris apparently traveled to Boston in early May to oversee conveyance of the tract in five parcels (see Barbara A. Chernow, "Robert Morris: Genesee Land Speculator," *New York History*, 58 [1977], 198–201, 207 and note 26).

To Charleston Officials

SIR, [Charleston, S.C., 9 May 1791]

I beg you will accept and offer my best thanks to the corporation and the citizens of Charleston, for their very polite attention to me.

Should it ever be in my power, be assured, it will give me pleasure to visit again this very respectable city.[1]

City Gazette, or the Daily Advertiser [Charleston, S.C.], 14 May 1791.

1. GW's party left Charleston at 6:00 A.M. on 9 May 1791 accompanied to the Ashley River by Gov. Charles Pinckney, U.S. senators Ralph Izard and Pierce Butler, members of the Society of the Cincinnati, and local militia officers. Charleston intendant Arnoldus Vanderhorst addressed the president at the city limits at Boundary Street: "SIR, The Intendant and Wardens, in behalf of themselves and their constituents, beg leave to offer you their unfeigned thanks for the visit with which you have honored this city; and they are hopeful it will not be the last. They sincerely wish you a pleasant tour and happy return to your mansion: and may health, that greatest of all temporal blessings, attend you" (*City Gazette, or the Daily Advertiser* [Charleston, S.C.], 14 May 1791. For GW's trip from Charleston to Savannah, see *Diaries*, 6:133–34.

From Thomas FitzSimons

sir　　　　　　　　　　　　　　　　　　Philada 10 May 1791.

I have no better Apology to Offer for Giving you the trouble of this letter than that it is written at the desire of some of Mr Peter's friends who wish him to be honored with the Appointment held by the late Judge Hopkinson.

of his fitness for the Station I presume not to say any thing but as delicacy, on his part will prevent his offering himself it has been thot that a doubt might arise: as to his exchanging his present situation: Upon that point I am authorised to say that the Appointment Would be very Acceptable to him and a Great gratification to many of his fellow Citizens.[1]

I hope I shall be pardoned for haveing taken the liberty of giving this information. And have the honor to be with the Greatest respect sir Your Most Obdt & Most hble servt

Thomas FitzSimons

ALS, DLC:GW.

Thomas FitzSimons (Fitzsimons, Fitzsimmons; 1741–1811), a native of Ireland, in 1761 married Catharine Meade, daughter of the Philadelphia merchant Robert Meade, and shortly thereafter formed with her brother the firm George Meade & Co., which traded extensively with the West Indies. He helped found the Bank of North America in 1781 and was elected to the Continental Congress in 1782. FitzSimons was an active member of the Federal Convention and supported the administration's measures in the House of Representatives in the First through Third Congresses.

1. Francis Hopkinson, whom GW appointed federal district judge for Pennsylvania in September 1789, died suddenly on 9 May 1791. On 16 May, six days after FitzSimons recommended Richard Peters to succeed Hopkinson, the Rev. William Smith, provost of the College of Philadelphia, wrote to GW to urge the appointment of his half brother, Thomas Smith, "a Man of the most unquestionable Integrity and Abilities." After describing Thomas's Revolutionary War service and noting the public offices he afterwards held, Smith continued: "His Practice in the Law has been large & sufficiently lucrative; but, extending over Seven or Eight Counties, even to the Extremities of the State, has become too laborious for his advanced Years. The *Governor* of this State has been pleased to designate Him for a Seat on the Bench in our new Judiciary Arrangement, with a Salary of £500 and travelling Charges, sufficient to gratify his Wishes in Point of Emolument—But by the Constitution of this Commonwealth, Residence where he now lives, viz. at Carlisle, is required; being 120 Miles from Philadelphia, where he wishes to educate his Children" (DLC:GW). GW chose neither Peters nor Smith as district judge at this time but offered the position to William Lewis, U.S. district attorney for Pennsylvania, who reluctantly accepted it in July 1791 but resigned five or six months later. The president then in January 1792 appointed Peters, who served until his death in 1828. See Edmund Randolph to GW, 13 July 1791, n.1, GW to the U.S. Senate, 12 Jan. 1792, and Lewis to Lear, 12 Jan. 1792, DNA: RG 59, Miscellaneous Letters.

From Moses Robinson

Sir   Bennington [Vt.] May 10th 1791

I beg leave to Recommend to your notice Mr Tolman a Citizen of Vermont who is on a tour for his health; and, Consisting with that, wishes for an Employment at the Seat of the Goverment of the union if an office of which he is Capable, and in which the public Service might be promoted, might be Conferrd.[1] Mr Tolman has the merit of long & Satisfactory Services in Sundry public Employments for his request, perticularly, in this State those of paymaster, & Secretary to the Governor & Council; and I Can freely Recommend him as a man of Good moral Character—of faithfulness in Business, and, I believe, Ingenious in the good branches of Clerkship. If an office of this kind Could be Conferrd, in which the public might be benifited by his service (his health permitting) and he Receive a Compensation, it would lay him and his Family under perticular Obligations—be Considered as a token of your favour towards this newly Confederated Republic, and Could not fail of being duly acknowledged. With the most Ardent wish for your happiness, and the prosperity of the Government of the union, I have the honor to be, with Sentiments of the highest Respect, Sir, your very obedient & humble servant

Moses Robinson

ALS, DLC:GW.

Moses Robinson (c.1742–1813) was born in Hardwick, Mass., the son of Samuel Robinson, a founder of Bennington, Vermont. During the Revolutionary War he served as a colonel in the militia and sat on the Vermont governor's council and the council of censors. In 1778 he was elected first chief justice of Vermont's supreme court and sat on the bench until he was elected governor of the state in October 1789. In January 1791 Robinson was elected one of the new state's first U.S. senators.

1. A docket on the letter's cover reads: "Mr Tolman respectfully informs that he has put up, at Dr [Benjamin] Vanleer's, in South Eighth Street, between Market & Chesnut. July 4th." Thomas Tolman (1757–1842) of Cornwall, Vt., who had served as a lieutenant and paymaster during the Revolutionary War, also presented to GW a recommendation, dated 30 April 1791, from Vermont governor Thomas Chittenden (DLC:GW). No evidence has been found that Tolman was offered a federal appointment.

To the Citizens of Prince William Parish, South Carolina

Gentlemen,   [Prince William Parish, S.C., c.11 May 1791]

My best thanks for your cordial welcome and affectionate address are not more justly due than sincerely offered.[1]

I am much indebted to your good wishes, which I reciprocate with grateful regard.

G. Washington.

LB, DLC:GW.

1. GW and his party on 10 May lodged at O'Brian Smith's plantation in St. Bartholomew's Parish and the next afternoon reached Pocotaligo, S.C., "where a dinner was provided by the Parishoners of Prince William for my reception; and an Address from them was presented and answered" (*Diaries*, 6:134). The address, signed by John McPherson, Felix Warley, James Maine, John A. Cuthbert, and John and William Heyward, reads: "Permit us Great Sir to Welcome you most cordially into this Parish in your progress thro' the State. We are sensibly affected with the Honour you do us, by this kind condescending Visit—And cannot but embrace the Opportunity of declaring that our Hearts are Penetrated with the Warmest Sense of our Obligations to you, Who under God have been the deliverer of the Country and its eminent Benefactor in War & in Peace—May you continue to Enjoy the Exquisite satisfaction that

Arises from the Veneration and gratitude of a great People that has been signally benefitted by you as an Anticipation of your heavenly Reward" (DLC:GW).

From George Eimbeck

May it Please Yr Excellency
Sir   Savannah. May 12th 1791

Having for some years had the Command of Fort Wayne Am Inform'd by his Honr the Governor the Appointment and Salary must be made by the Union likewise that my Salary Ceases from the 31st July 1789.[1]

Therefore Humbly Request your Excellency to Give such Orders Concerning the Business as your Excellencies Wisdom may Dictate.[2] Am with the Greatest Respect Yr Excellencies Most Obet Humble Sert

Geoe Eimbeck

ALS, DNA: RG 59, Miscellaneous Letters. George Eimbeck addressed the letter's cover to the president, "Now in Savannah." William Jackson noted on the cover that on 14 May Eimbeck was "informed that the President cannot interfere—the paper returned." The enclosed paper has not been identified.

George Eimbeck (Embrick) served during the Revolutionary War as barrack master of the Georgia Continental establishment. For GW's trip from South Carolina to Savannah, which included a brief visit to Mrs. Nathanael Greene's plantation on the Savannah River, see *Diaries*, 6:134–37.

1. Fort Wayne was erected on the Savannah River to protect Savannah from naval attack during the Revolutionary War and was manned by a battery of artillery consisting of various brass and iron cannons.

2. Eimbeck on 13 Aug. 1791 again wrote to GW about his "Disagreeable Situation," enclosing a petition to Congress and noting: "I have Serv'd in the war Seven years, and Since Peace have been Station'd at fort Wayne with A Captains Commission Keeper of Military Stores and Powder Receiver for which the State was to Allow me £30. Per Annum and Certain fees On all Vessels Leaving this Harbour—these fees have been Stopt—from the Commencement of the Present Constitution which Alltogether was Supposd to be One Hundred pound Sterg" (DNA: RG 59, Miscellaneous Letters). GW apparently replied to neither of Eimbeck's letters, and there is no evidence that Eimbeck's petition was presented to Congress. Eimbeck sent GW another petition for Congress sometime in 1793 (undated, DNA: RG 59, Miscellaneous Letters).

From David Humphreys

(Secret)

My dear Sir   Lisbon May 12th 1791

Lest my letters to the Secretary of State on the subject of the Persons executing the Duties of the Consulate here, should have been so inexplicit as to leave your mind in doubt respecting the merits or pretensions of those persons, I take the liberty to add a few facts; not because I feel myself interested in the decision, but because I wish to remove embarrassments from your mind.[1]

The family of the Dohrmans ought certainly to be considered by the Americans as having great merit for their conduct in time of the war & since; Mr Jacob Dohrman does not seem much to expect an appointment, but earnestly wishes that Mr Harrison, may be appointed, as Vice-Consul, untill some native of America shall be named. Mr Dohrman is very desirous to obtain a share in the consignment business if possible.[2]

Mr Samuel Harrison has for some years past, done all the business of the American Consulate in this Port; and, I believe, to very good acceptance. I have had occasion lately to employ him in one way or another a good deal myself; and I have found him, so far as I am able to form a judgment, active, faithful & intelligent in business. I should conceive him very competent to act as *Vice Consul* until & even after some American shall be established as Consul here. Indeed this will now, of course, be the case until Orders may be received to the contrary.

Mr John Bulkeley is my very good friend.[3] He has taken uncommon pains to shew civilities to me, & continues to do the same. On every occasion evincing his politeness, hospitality & disposition to to serve me. He is one of the wealthiest Merchants of the Factory & a man well versed in business. I understand he has applied for the American Consulship. Indeed he has intimated the same to me, & produced to my view a letter from Mr Thomas Russel of Boston in answer to one from himself on the subject. Mr Bulkeley has made a principal part of his fortune in the American Trade; and from a desire of extending his connections in it, has doubtless been useful to othe[r] Americans as well as to me. I conceive him to be a good Englishman & a true Merchant, in heart. In the time of the war, he conducted in general prudently: not, however (as I have understood) without being concerned in an English Privateer.

Truth, & the interest of the Republic are my only objects. I write at the desire of no Person—nor with the knowledge of any one. For I can have no possible interest in the matter, nor the remotest byas to an option, distinct from what may comport with the public weal. With sentiments of the purest esteem & respect I have the honor to be My dear Sir Your devoted Servant

D. Humphreys

P.S. At St Ubis, Bellem &c. it will be necessary for somebody or another to act in behalf of our Citizens. At the former is a Mr Bush, a Hambourgoise, now acting—at the latter, a Portuguese by the name of Bonventura Joze Morera, who is Vice Consul for, at least, half a Dozen nations.

ALS, DLC:GW.

1. For David Humphreys's earlier letters to the secretary of state concerning consular appointments, see Humphreys to Thomas Jefferson, 31 Mar., 3 May 1791, *Jefferson Papers*, 19:643–44, 20:361–62.

2. The Dutch merchant Henry Arnold Dohrman (Arnold Henry; 1749–1813) resided in Lisbon at the commencement of the American Revolution. During the war he provided relief and the means of repatriation to American sailors captured by the British, for which he was rewarded by the Continental Congress in June 1780 with the position of agent for the United States in the kingdom of Portugal (*JCC*, 17:541–42; *Madison Papers*, 2:34, n.4). In 1786 he left his brother Jacob in charge of his office and embarked for America, where he petitioned Congress for reimbursement of his expenses and reasonable compensation for his services (DNA: PCC, item 178). Henry eventually settled in Steubenville, Ohio, on the land Congress granted him on 1 Oct. 1787. Jacob Dohrman continued to act as his brother's agent until at least 1792 (*JCC*, 30:415, 32:119–21, 216, 291–92, 33:586–88; 6 *Stat.* 43–44, 193, 573; Humphreys, *Life and Times of David Humphreys*, 2:91, 143).

3. John Bulkeley of the successful Lisbon firm of John Bulkeley & Son came from a prominent family of New England Loyalists and established himself at Lisbon during the Revolutionary War. Although Massachusetts congressmen also recommended Bulkeley for the Lisbon consulate, the post was instead offered to Stephen Moylan and then to Edward Church. In early 1797 Humphreys married Bulkeley's daughter Anne Frances.

Letters not found: to Martha Washington, c.12–15 May 1791. On 5 June Martha Washington wrote Frances Bassett Washington from Philadelphia: "I have had letters from the President from savanna" (Fields, *Papers of Martha Washington*, 231–32).

To the Georgia Society of the Cincinnati

Gentlemen,   [Savannah, c.13 May 1791]

Your congratulations on my arrival in this State are received with grateful sensibility—your esteem and attachment are replied to with truth and affection.[1]

Could the praise of an individual confer distinction on men whose merits are recorded in the independence and sovereignty of their country, I would add, with grateful pride, the tribute of my testimony to the public acknowledgement—I would say how much you had atchieved, how much you had endured in the cause of freedom—Nor should my applause be confined to the military virtues of your character—With the endearing epithet of gallant brother soldiers, your civic worth has connected the respectable title of deserving fellow-citizens—Your conduct in war commanded my esteem, your behaviour in peace exacts my approbation.

My opinions will ever do justice to your merits, my heart will reciprocate your affection, and my best wishes implore your happiness.

G. Washington

LB, DLC:GW.

1. On 13 May 1791, the day after GW arrived at Savannah, he "Dined with the Members of the Cincinnati at a public dinner given" at Brown's Coffeehouse, where he had dined the previous evening (*Diaries*, 6:137). It was probably at the dinner that the Georgia Society of the Cincinnati presented to the president its address, signed by Anthony Wayne: "We, the members of the society of Cincinnati, of the State of Georgia, beg leave to offer our most cordial congratulations on your safe arrival in this State. It is more easy for you to imagine, than for us to describe the mingled emotions of gratitude, of respect, and affection your presence inspires. Whether we look back to the interesting scenes of the late War, when three millions of people committed their dearest treasure—their Liberties to your protection—or to the present time, when the same people, become an Independent Empire, have called you with one voice to be the guardian of their Government, and Laws—in either view, we shall find equal motives of admiration for the wisdom of your conduct, and of reverence for your virtues. In these sentiments we are conscious we do but express the feelings of every American Citizen—yet, we flatter ourselves we may justly be supposed to have a more lively degree of sensibility in our Affection for you, from the relation in which we stand, as officers who had the honor to serve under you during the late War, and as president General of our Society—a relation in which it is our highest pride to be considered. This is

perhaps the last opportunity we may have of tendering to you in person, the sincere professions of our attachment: be pleased to accept them, Sir, as the genuine effusions of our hearts; and suffer us at the same time to assure you, that it shall be our constant endeavor to pursue the same conduct towards our Country, that formerly procured us the honor of your Esteem, and regard. That you may long—very long live to enjoy the grateful applause of mankind; the noblest reward of virtue—and make your fellow citizens happy, is our ardent wish, and shall be our constant prayer" (DLC:GW).

To the Congregational Church of Midway, Georgia

Gentlemen,   [Savannah, c.13 May 1791]

I learn with gratitude proportioned to the occasion your attachment to my person, and the pleasure you express on my election to the Presidency of the United States.[1]

Your sentiments on the happy influence of our equal government impress me with the most sensible satisfaction—they vindicate the great interests of humanity—they reflect honor on the liberal minds that entertain them—and they promise the continuance and improvement of that tranquillity, which is essential to the welfare of nations, and the happiness of men.

You over-rate my best exertions when you ascribe to them the blessings which our country so eminently enjoys. "From the gallantry and fortitude of her citizens, under the auspices of heaven, America has derived her independence—To their industry and the natural advantages of the country she is indebted for her prosperous situation—From their virtue she may expect long to share the protection of a free and equal government, which their wisdom has established, and which experience justifies, as admirably adapted to our social wants and individual felicity."

Continue, my fellow-citizens, to cultivate the peace and harmony which now subsist between you, and your indian-neighbours—the happy consequence is immediate, the reflection, which arises on justice and benevolence, will be lastingly grateful. A knowledge of your happiness will lighten the cares of my station, and be among the most pleasing of ther rewards.

G. Washington.

LB, DLC:GW; Df, DLC:GW.

1. The "Address Of the Congregational Church and Society of Midway, (formerly St John's Parish)" to the president was dated Midway, Liberty County, Ga., 12 May 1791. The church is thirty miles below Savannah, and it is unlikely that the address was presented to GW on that day since he was traveling all day, with only a brief stop at a private plantation, and the evening of his arrival at Savannah was completely occupied. The address, signed by James Maxwell, Daniel Stewart, Abiel Holmes, Henry Wood, and John P. Mann "in behalf of the Church and Society," reads: "Sir, We feel ourselves happy in an opportunity of expressing our attachment to your person, and our peculiar pleasure in your election, by the unanimous voice of your country, to the Presidency of the United States. Though situated in the extreme part of the Union, we have gratefully to acknowledge that we already experience the propitious influence of your wise and parental administration. To the troops stationed on our frontiers by your order, and to the Treaty lately concluded with the Creek Nation under your auspices, are we indebted, under Providence, for our present tranquillity. The hatchet is now buried, and we smoke with our Indian neighbours the calumet of peace. This, while it affords us a happy pressage of our future protection, gives, at the same time, a recent proof how justly you have earned, in your civil, as well as military, capacity, the glorious title of FATHER OF YOUR COUNTRY. With the Laurel, then, be pleased to accept the Civic Wreath from a grateful people. We readily conceive how arduous must be the duties, how weighty and complicated the cares, of office, in the government of so extensive a Republic as that over which you are called to preside. Impressed with a deep sense of this, we will not fail to implore the divine blessing in your behalf—May you continue to be directed by that 'wisdom from above,' which is necessary to the successful discharge of the duties of your high and important station; and may you long be preserved the favoured Instrument of Heaven, to secure to a Free People those invaluable rights, which you so eminently contributed to secure from the hand of Oppression! Distant as our situation is from the seat of Government, permit us to assure you that our influence, however inconsiderable in the national scale, shall not be wanting in encouraging submission to the laws of the United States, and thus, under GOD, perpetuating the blessings of an efficient, federal government, now so happily established" (DLC:GW).

To the Savannah Citizens

Gentlemen,   [Savannah, c.13 May 1791]

I am extremely happy in the occasion now afforded me to express my sense of your goodness, and to declare the sincere and affectionate gratitude, which it inspires.[1]

The retrospect of past scenes, as it exhibits the virtuous character of our country, enhances the happiness of the present hour, and gives the most pleasing anticipation of progressive prosperity—The individual satisfaction, to be derived from this grateful reflection, must be enjoyed in a peculiar degree by the deserving citizens of Georgia—a State no less distinguished by its services, than by its sufferings in the cause of freedom.

That the city of Savannah may largely partake of every public benefit, which our free and equal government can dispense, and that the happiness of its vicinity may reply to the best wishes of its inhabitants is my sincere prayer.

Go: Washington

DS, PWacD; LB, DLC:GW.

1. An undated address, signed by Noble Wimberly Jones, Lachlan McIntosh, Joseph Clay, John Houstoun, and Joseph Habersham "In the Name and Behalf of a number of Citizens of Savannah and it's Vicinity convened for the reception of the President," was presented to GW on 13 May 1791: "Sir, When having accomplished the great objects of a War, marked in it's progress with events that astonished while they instructed the World, you had again returned to the domestic enjoyments of life, to which you were known to be so strongly attached, there was little probability, in the common order of things, that the People of Georgia, however ardently they might desire, should ever be indulged, the happiness of a personal interview with you—but summoned again, as you were, from your retirement, by the united voice and the obvious welfare of your Country, you did not hesitate to furnish one more proof that, in comparison to the great duties of social life, all objects of a private nature are with you but secondary considerations—And to this your ruling passion of love for your Country it is that we owe the opportunity now afforded of congratulating you on your safe arrival in the City of Savannah—An office we the Committee, under the warmest impressions of sensibility and attachment, execute in the name and behalf of a respectable and grateful number of Citizens. History furnishes instances of some eminently qualified for the field, and of others endued with Talents adequate to the intricate affairs of State, but you, Sir, have enriched the annals of America with a proof to be sent abroad to all mankind that, however rare the association, the virtues and talents of Soldier and republican Statesman will sometimes dwell together, and both characters derive additional lustre from a subserviency to the precepts of Religion. Roused by oppression at home, and inspired by example from America, the People of enlightened Nations in Europe are now beginning to assert their rights—And it is observable that those brave Men, the subjects of foreign Powers, who were Votaries to our Cause and Companions in your Victories, are always found foremost in the struggle for just and equal Government. You have now, sir, an opportunity of viewing a State which from it's exposed situation has been peculiarly affected by the calamities of War, but which, under the influence of a happy Government, will rise fast to that rank of prosperity and importance to which her natural advantages so justly entitle her, and which will enable her to reflect back upon the Union all the benefits derived

from it. We shall always take a deep concern, in common with the other Citizens of the United States, in whatever regards your personal welfare and happiness—We make it our prayer to Almighty God that you may be long continued to your Country, her Ornament and Father—And that it may be more and more exemplified in you, sir, that to know how to conquer, and to improve the advantages of Conquest into blessings to a community, are faculties sometimes bestowed on the same Mortal" (DLC:GW).

To Savannah Officials

Gentlemen,   [Savannah, c.13–14 May 1791]
Your affectionate congratulations on my arrival in this city, and the very favorable sentiments you express towards me, are received with gratitude and thanked with sincerity.[1]

Estimating favors by the cordiality with which they are bestowed, I confess, with real pleasure, my obligations to the Corporation of Savannah, and I can never cease to entertain a grateful sense of their goodness.

While the virtuous conduct of your citizens, whose patriotism braved all the hardships of the late war, engaged my esteem, the distresses peculiar to the State of Georgia, after the peace, excited my deepest regret.

It was with singular satisfaction I perceived that the efficacy of the general government could interpose effectual relief, and restore tranquillity to so deserving a member of the Union—Your sentiments on this event are worthy of citizens, who placing a due value on the blessings of peace, desire to maintain it on the immutable principles of justice and good faith.

May the harmony of your city be consequent on your administration, and may you individually be happy.

G. Washington

LB, DLC:GW.
1. An address signed by Savannah mayor Thomas Gibbons and dated 13 May 1791 at the city council chamber apparently was presented to the president the same day, probably before the Society of the Cincinnati dinner. A copy drafted and signed by Gibbons (DLC:GW) most likely was given earlier to William Jackson, from which he was able to draft GW's reply. See *Diaries*, 6:137–39, Henderson, *Washington's Southern Tour*, 221. The address reads: "The Mayor and Aldermen of the City of Savannah, do unanimously concur, in presenting their most affectionate congratulations to you, on your arrival in this City. Impressed with a just sense of your great, and eminent services to

America, permit us, the Representatives of the City, to assure you of the high opinion the Citizens entertain of your elevated virtues. We respect you as one of the richest and most valuable blessings, divine goodness has bestowed on the People of these United States, your presence is an evidence of the watchful care you have for every part of the extended empire over which you preside. If we cannot by external shew, demonstrate that respect for you, which is in the power of the more wealthy of our sister States to display, yet none estimate your merits higher than the People of Georgia. The historic page bears record of our sufferings in the late revolution, and the vestiges of War remain within view of our Capital; and although peace was in 1783 restored to America, yet Georgia continued to suffer under the destructive ravages of an Indian war, and it has been reserved for the efficacy of the present government to give Peace to our State. May the blessings of the government long continue under your administration, and may it please the great ruler of events, to grant you long residence on Earth, and, to length of days, add the Blessings of uninterrupted health, that the advantages of the present government, may be permanently established" (DLC:GW).

From the Ebenezer, Ga., German Congregation

Savannah. d. 14. May 1791.
Permittas, quaeso, Illustrissime Washington! ut devoti piique animi sensa TIBI declarem, cui contigerit insignis illa felicitas, TE Savannae adeundi, virum, tot tantisque factis illustrem. Profecto admiratus sum TUAM humanitatem et indulgentiam, qua me hominem ignotum excepisti, qui non ausus essem ad TE accedere nisi ab amico optimo certior factus essem, tristem abs TE discedere neminem. Georgia laetatur de TUA Splendidissima praesentia, qua eam exhilarare dignatus es. Diu vivas o Washington! deliciae americani populi, tuumque nomen, et facta illustria Sera posteritas celebrabit. Semper precabor Deum Optimum Maximum, qui TE Praesidem harum civitatum constituit, ut omnibus rebus conatibusque Tuis propitius adsit. Accipe hanc tenuiorem epistolam, nullo ornatu commendabilem, eadem indulgentia, qua me excipere dignatus es. Anglia quidem scripturus eram si facultate pollerem eleganter scribendi, et ut dignum esse posset insignibus virtutibus et illustrissimis factis TUIS. Peregrinus, in hanc provinciam missus sum benignissimam doctrinam Redemtoris nostri profitendi inter posteros colonorum Salisburgensium, quos inprimis quia curae meae concrediti sunt, cum omni gente germanica Georgiae Americanae Tuo potentissimo patrocinio magnopere commendo. Ego vero

nunquam desinam ardentissimas preces mittere ad Deum be-
nignissimum, pro totius populi Americani salute.[1]

John Earnst Bergman,
Minister of the German Congregation of Ebenezer.

ADS, DLC:GW.

Ebenezer, Ga., was founded twenty-five miles northwest of Savannah in
1734 by German Lutherans. Johann Ernst Bergmann (John Earnest Bergman; c.1755–1824), from a poor family of Peretz, Saxony, studied at the University of Leipzig before being ordained at Augsburg. He immigrated to
America in 1786 and succeeded the Loyalist minister, who was not permitted
to return to Ebenezer. The scholarly Bergmann, who spoke only broken English, served as pastor of Jerusalem Church at Ebenezer until his death.

1. No reply to the Latin address, which was probably presented to the president the same day it was written, has been found.

To the Georgia Masons

Gentlemen,   [Savannah, c.14 May 1791]

I am much obliged by your congratulations on my arrival in
this city—and I am highly indebted to your favorable opinions.

Every circumstance concurs to render my stay in Savannah
agreeable, and it is cause of regret to me that it must be so short.

My best wishes are offered for the welfare of the fraternity,
and for your particular happiness.[1]

Go: Washington

DS, DMS; LB, DLC:GW.

1. The Grand Lodge of Georgia ("Ancients"), formed in December 1786,
most likely presented its address, dated Savannah, 14 May, and signed by
Grand Master George Houstoun, to the president the same day it was written,
and GW probably replied shortly thereafter on his last full day in Savannah.
See *Diaries*, 6:138–40. Savannah merchant George Houstoun (1744–1795), son
of Sir Patrick Houstoun, became grand master of the Grand Lodge in December 1789 (Clarke, *Early and Historic Freemasonry of Georgia*, 31). A delegation of
the Grand Lodge gathered at Brown's Coffeehouse on 14 May and proceeded
in Masonic order to GW's lodgings where Houstoun delivered the address to
the president: "Sir and Brother. The Grand Master, Officers and Members of
the Grand Lodge of Georgia, beg leave to Congratulate you, on your arrival
in this City. Whilst your exalted Character, claims the respect and deference
of all Men, They, from the benevolence of Masonic principles approach you
with the familiar declaration of Fraternal affection. Happy indeed That Society, renowned for its Antiquity, and pervading influence over the enlightened
World, which having ranked a Frederick at its head, can now Boast of a Wash-

ington as a Brother, A Brother who is justly hailed the Redeemer of his Country, raised it to Glory, and by his conduct in Public and private life has evinced to Monarchs, that true Majesty, consists not in splendid Royalty, but in intrinsic Worth. With these sentiments they rejoice at your presence in this State, and in common with their Fellow Citizens, Greet you Thrice Welcome, flattering themselves, that your Stay will be made agreeable. May the Great Architect of the Universe preserve you, whilst engaged in the Work allotted you on Earth, and long continue you the Brightest Pillar of our Temple, and when the Supreme Fiat Shall Summon you hence, They pray the Mighty I am, may take you into his holy keeping" (DLC:GW).

To Tobias Lear

Dear Sir,   Savannah May 1[4]th 1791[1]
I have not, I believe, written to you since I left Richmond.[2] At Charleston, towards the last of my stay there, I received your letters of the 10th & 15th of Apl but the continual hurry into which I was thrown by entertainments—visits—and ceremonies of one kind or another, scarcely allowed me a moment that I could call my own—nor is the case much otherwise here.

No letters North of Virginia will now reach me until I arrive at Fredericksburg in that State, which is the first place at which I shall strike the line of the Post. There are no cross-posts on this side Alexandria, and the chances of letters getting to me by private hands, as my rout back will be very wide of the Post-Road is so unfavourable that I have ordered all letters to be stopped at Charleston and sent back to the Post Office in Fredericksburg to await my arrival there.

The silence of Frauncis is evidence sufficient that nothing is to be expected from him; and if your prospects with the other person (mentioned in your letters) are no better, the plan suggested in your letter of the 15th may be tried as the best expedient that offers. A little experience (and there is time for it before the next meeting of Congress) will prove the utility or inutility of the measure.

I came to this place on Thursday afternoon, and shall leave it tomorrow, after attending the first Church.[3] The Roads are abominably sandy & heavy—my horses (especially the two I bought just before I left Philadelphia, & my old white horse) are much worn down—and I have yet 150 or 200 miles of heavy sand to pass before I fairly get into the upper, & firmer roads.[4]

Offer my best wishes to Mrs Lear I hope she the child & yourself are in good health. I remain your sincere and Affectionate friend

Go: Washington

ALS, MeHi. Besides the docket in Tobias Lear's hand and the notation "No. 23" in another hand, the following signed note in a third hand appears on the letter's cover: "This letter was obtained from Mrs [Frances Dandridge Henley] Lear, relict of the Col. Lear to whom it was addressed, by Rev. Professor [Joseph] Packard of the Theological Seminary, Fairfax Co. Va, & by him given to A[lpheus] S[pring] Packard, & by him placed in the archives of Me Hist. Society, A. S. Packard." For the background to the numerical notation and the dispersal of Tobias Lear's papers, see GW to Lear, 9 Sept. 1790, source note.

1. GW wrote "May 13th 1791" but more likely meant 14 May, as it can be inferred from the statement in the letter's fourth paragraph, "I came to this place Thursday afternoon, and shall leave it tomorrow, after attending the first Church," that he was writing on his only Saturday in Savannah, 14 May. According to his diary, GW arrived there on Thursday, 12 May, and left after church on Sunday, 15 May (*Diaries*, 6:135–40). He seems to have made a similar slip of the pen in his 15 May diary entry: "After morning Service, . . . I set out for Savanna" (ibid., 139). GW set out from Savannah for Augusta (see n.3 below). To add to the confusion of this letter's dateline, Lear wrote to Alexander Hamilton on 29 May: "In a letter which I received from the President yesterday dated at Savannah May 13th the enclosed from John H. Mitchell respecting a mint was transmitted with directions to hand the same to the Secretary of the Treasury—which I have now the honor of doing" (DLC:GW). The enclosed letter has not been found, and no directions about its transmittal appear in the above letter to Lear (although GW might have written them on the cover of Mitchell's letter). Finally, Lear also wrote to David Humphreys on 3 June: "I had a letter a few days ago from the President dated Savannah May 14th" (PPRF). This, however, must have been in reference to a second letter, now lost, actually bearing a 14 May dateline, that GW apparently wrote to Lear from Savannah on that day.

2. GW wrote Lear from Richmond on 12 April but apparently forgot that he wrote him a brief note on 21 April from New Bern, North Carolina.

3. GW attended morning service at Christ Church on Johnson Square in Savannah on Sunday, 15 May 1791, after which he received "a number of visits from the most respectable ladies of the place (as was the case yesterday)" and was escorted beyond the city limits. He then visited Mulberry Grove plantation a final time (*Diaries*, 6:139–40).

4. The "old white horse" was probably GW's parade horse Prescott, one of two white horses of the president's Philadelphia stable (Lipscomb, *South Carolina in 1791*, 3).

Letter not found: to Tobias Lear, 14 May 1791. On 3 June 1791 Lear wrote to David Humphreys: "I had a letter a few days ago from the President dated Savannah May 14th" (PPRF).

From Thomas Jefferson

Sir   Philadelphia May 15. 1791.

We are still without any occurrence foreign or domestic worth mentioning to you. it is somtime since any news has been recieved from Europe of the political kind, and I have been longer than common without any letters from mister Short.[1]

Colo. Hamilton has taken a trip to Bethlehem.[2] I think to avail myself also of the present interval of quiet to get rid of a headach which is very troublesome, by giving more exercise to the body & less to the mind. I shall set out tomorrow for New York, where mister Madison is waiting for me, to go up the North river, & return down Connecticut river and through Long-island. my progress up the North river will be limited by the time I allot for my whole journey, which is a month. so that I shall turn about whenever that renders it necessary.[3] I leave orders, in case a letter should come from you covering the commission for Colo. Eveleigh's successor, that it should be opened, the great seal put to it, and then given out. my countersign may be added on my return. I presume I shall be back here about the time of your arrival at Mount-Vernon, where you will recieve this letter.[4] the death of Judge Hopkinson has made a vacancy for you to fill. should I pick up any thing in my journey, I will write it to you from time to time. I have the honor to be with sincere respect & attachment, Sir, your most obedient and most humble servt

Th: Jefferson

ALS, DNA: RG 59, Miscellaneous Letters; ALS (letterpress copy), DLC: Thomas Jefferson Papers; LB, DLC:GW.

1. For William Short's dispatches, which Jefferson received on 23 April 1791, see Short to Jefferson, 7, 18, 22 Feb. 1791, *Jefferson Papers*, 19:257–59, 289–90, 323–25, 361–63.

2. Alexander Hamilton left Philadelphia with his wife sometime after 9 May and apparently lodged alone at the Sun Inn in Bethlehem, Pa., before returning to Philadelphia by 24 May ("Excerpts from the Waste Books of the Sun Inn," *Pa. Mag.*, 39:473; Hamilton to Short, 24 May 1791, Syrett, *Hamilton Papers*, 8:356–57).

3. The joint tour of Jefferson and James Madison to New York and New England in May and June 1791 was seen by contemporary supporters of Hamilton and many historians since primarily as a political expedition. Both Jefferson and Madison, however, were also interested in exploring the natural history of the region, and Jefferson the enlightened agriculturalist also hoped to

study the depredations of the Hessian fly, the larvae of which had been destroying mid-Atlantic wheat crops since at least the late 1770s. He also took the opportunity provided by the trip to obtain information about maple sugar production and acquire saplings to transplant at Monticello (see Jefferson to GW, 1 May 1791, n.4).

4. Jefferson addressed the letter to Mount Vernon. GW arrived home on 12 June, and Jefferson returned to the capital on 19 June.

From La Luzerne

Sir,　　　　　　　　　　　　　　　　　　　　　London May 15th 1791

Although for a long time I have not had the honor to recall me to Your Excellency's goodness, I pray you to be well persuaded that I have not been the less occupied in your glory and successes—and that it is with great pleasure I see the confidence in, and the consideration of, the United States daily rising in every country of Europe. Those Persons who, like me, have had the happiness to know Your Excellency ought assuredly to have expected that, when you accepted the first place in the government, your personal eclat would be reflected on your country—but it was impossible to foresee to what point, and with what rapidity the United States would inspire confidence, and how much their new government would be revered by all the nations of the world—I have been witness of the patience, the courage and the energy which your fellow-citizens have displayed to obtain their liberty—but there has arisen among them a great man, who united all suffrages, to make them sensible of all the advantages of that precious liberty, which is a great good when well directed—but which is only a horrible bandage when a wrong road is taken. Our nation in its intimate connection with yours has perceived the good which it had obtained, and desired to share in such an advantage.

The many and enormous abuses of our ancient government required great reforms, and a change in the State was absolutely necessary—but, with some causes of disease, the body of the monarchy was full of force and vigor—The Sovereign was good, just, œconomical, devoted to the greatest sacrifices for the good of his people—From the principle of convoking the States-General the Sovereign had proposed all the concessions which could have been desired to assure the individual liberty of the subject, and to secure every species of property. With these concessions, with the inestimable advantage of a representative body, the happiness and the credit of France was established for ever. Time, and a knowledge of affairs would have enabled the national assembly to reform all the abuses in the detail of the administration—and we should have been perhaps already one of the happiest nations in the world—but the Mania to be creators, the desire to go beyond all other people, the ignorance of political principles, united with abstracted ideas of philosophy, have plunged us into an abyss from which it is perhaps impossible we should ever recover, at least for a long time.

Our legislative Body has passed some wise decrees, which may one day or other lead to a good constitution, but it has not perceived that in order to the people being free they should always be obedient to the law, that there should also exist an Executive power, who, himself submitting to the laws, should possess the necessary force to execute them.

It has been thought necessary to demolish the royal power the better to establish the legislative, which is clothed with authority to perform the functions of the Executive. The people no longer sensible of an immediate restraint have revolted on all sides, and against all authority—The Soldiers have no longer regarded their Officers as their Superiors—all authority has vanished, and to a very strong government, an absolute anarchy has succeeded. Our friend The Marquis de la fayette has been placed at the head of the national militia of Paris, and to a certain point has maintained order, and notwithstanding what Detractors say, who are very numerous, he has done much good, and prevented still more harm—His courage, his personal virtues always assure him a great number of suffrages but his popularity is lost—he has already several times desired to resign—it is only his patriotism which continues him in a place impossible to fill. If, like the Americans we had possessed a Man sufficiently elevated by his reputation and his virtues to command all the nation, and to know exactly the length we ought to have gone, we should have been, like the Americans, one of the happiest of the nations of the world, having the best laws, and I may say at present without fear of being thought to flatter, we should have been governed by a prince the best qualified by the dispositions of his heart to make subjects happy. Pardon, Sir, this long discussion of the misfortunes of my country—but I am so much affected by them, and I am so sensible of the interest which you take in them that I could not avoid pouring them out into your breast. I am not however without some hope that the affairs of my country will be re-established—I will serve to the end my King and my country, whom I passionately love because I think I may love them and liberty too—but if we are to continue in anarchy, if all the laws are overturned, if monarchy, the only government fitted for us is destroyed, I will retire into a strange land with all my family, and in that event you can judge which country my inclination and my taste will lead me to chuse. I will demand goodness and assistance for me and mine from your Excellency, and I shall be happy to live under a government, where your influence prevails so much.[1] In the meanwhile, and independent of all events I pray you to be persuaded of the sincere attachment and respect with which I am your Excellency's &a

La Luzerne

I recommend to your Excellency's goodness the Chevr Ternant, who goes to succeed Mr de Moustier.

Translation, DLC:GW. ALS in French, listed as item 212 in Thomas Birch's Sons, Auctioneers, *Catalogue #663* (Philadelphia, 1891), has not been found.

1. GW replied to this letter from Anne-César, marquis de La Luzerne, on 10 September.

From Tobias Lear

Sir,   Philadelphia May 15th 1791.

On thursday last I had the honor to receive your letter of the 21st of April from New burn; and at the same time a letter for Mrs Washington came under cover to me, which she informed me was dated at Wilmington. Yesterday we had the pleasure to see your arrival at Charleston announced in the papers.[1]

My letters must certainly have met with some interruption or you would have found at least one at Wilmington. Between Richmond & that place I did not calculate upon any reaching you; for the one dated the 5th of April reached you at Richmond, which place you left on the 13th. The next letter which I wrote was dated the 10th—left this place on the 11th—and ought, by the common progress of the mail, to have reached Wilmington on the 22d or 23d, which would have been a day or two before your arrival there. The dates of my letters since that time are April 15th—17th—24th—May 1st & 8th—all of which I flatter my self you will receive.

I am not surprized to learn that the horses are somewhat worn down. I rather wonder at their holding out so well—it is contrary to the opinion of almost every one who knows the nature of the travelling in that Country. Should you be so fortunate as to bring them all back it will be more than is expected. The mare which was bought of the Quaker a few days before you left this place—turns out to be a very good creature—She is high in flesh & spirits—and makes a very tolerable figure—she will be large—she is now higher than the largest of the Colts, and appears to grow every day.

On tuesday Mrs Washington proposes going over to Jersey for a few days—she makes her visit to Mrs Dickinson. It was thought best & cheapest, by Mrs Washington & myself, that she should hire a Coach, 4 horses & a driver for the trip—the whole of which is engaged of Mr Page for *twenty four dollars* the trip, he bearing all expences of horses & driver—(Daniel is to be the driver). This is cheaper than Mrs Washington could have gone in her own Coach, without taking into consideration any damage which it or the horses might sustain by the jaunt; for two horses must have been hired in addition to her own—and the expense of the whole & Jacob must have been borne for 4 or 5 days. Mrs Washington takes the children with her & Christopher & Oney. I shall have the honor to attend her on horse back.

Fraunces arrived here on Wednesday, and after signing his Articles of Agreement—going over the things in the house & signing an inventory thereof, entered upon the duties of his station. I think I have made the agreement as full, explicit & binding as any thing of the kind can be. In the Articles prohibiting the use of wine at his table—and obliging him to be particular in the discharge of his duty in the Kitchen & to perform the Cooking with Hercules—I have been peculiarly pointed. He readily assented to them all (except that respecting Hercules, upon which he made the following observation—"I must first learn Hercules' abilities & readiness to do things, which if good, (*as good as Mrs Read's*) will enable me to do the Cooking without any other *professional* assistance in the Kitchen; but this experiment cannot be made until the return of the President when there may be occasion for him to exert his talents"—)—and made the strongest professions of attachment to the family, & his full determination to conduct in such a manner as to leave no room for impeachment either on the score of extravagence or integrity. All these things I hope he will perform.[2]

The House-keeper who, I mentioned in a former letter, was engaged, came into the family on the same day. She has taken her stand also—and received into her charge those things which belong particularly to her department. Her proceedings thus far speak much in her favour, and I confess that I have formed a very excellent opinion of her abilities in this line.[3] The greatest difficulty which she has to apprehend, is in bringing the Servants to bear that particular inspection into their conduct which is proper & which she says she is determined to do. The Servants in the family have been impressed with an idea that they are the best Servants that can be obtained—and in pursuing this idea they are likely to become the worst; for they conceive it an insult offered them to have their doings examined into or superintended; and another idea which they have taken up—and which I have laboured hard to do away, is, that the President's should be considered rather as a public than a private family, and therefore that it would be lessening the dignity of it to observe those rules & that subordination which may be necessary in a private family. From whence this idea originated I cannot pretend to say. But certain I am that it is not consonant to your way of thinking on the subject.

Since your departure I have necessarily had a more immediate inspection of the Servants than I ever had before, and I have less cause to doubt the justness of those complaints which have heretofore been made of them, than I ever thought I should have. Nothing but the establishment of certain rules & a strict adherence to them, with the peremptory discharge of such as refused or neglected to attend to them, will reduce the family to that state of regularity & pleasantness as will make it a desireable one to live in. These ideas which I mention to have obtained are not confined to the men—the women are likewise infected with them. I shall not fail, with the assistance of Mrs Washington, to take such steps upon this new arrangement of the family as appear best calculated to produce order—and a proper understanding among them.

Vicar, the Cook, takes his discharge tomorrow. He requested it himself, from a determination, as he says, not to be under the immediate direction of Fraunces in the Kitchen as he understands will be the case if he was to continue.[4]

The enclosed papers will give a more particular account of the events of the week past—such as the death of Judge Hopkinson—the fires which took place on Sunday & on Monday night &c. The death of the District Judge is said to occasion much inconvenience to individuals who had suits depending & which must now be delayed until a new appointment takes place.[5]

I received the enclosed letter last week from Colo. Wadsworth, containing a proposal to purchase your young Jack. I have acknowledged the receipt of it and informed him that it should be transmitted to you.[6]

Mrs Lear begs her best respects may be made acceptable to you—and we are happy to say that our little boy has been inoculated & is now fast recovering from the Smallpox—he has had it pretty severely & at one period we had almost given him up— He has been baptized by the name of Benjamin Lincoln, in memory of the deceased son of General Lincoln, and as a testimony of the grateful remembrance in which I hold that friend who took me by the hand at a moment when I needed a friend, and through whose means I had the happiness of being made known to you.[7] And as a proof of the high estimation in which I hold that happiness, I trust I shall never neglect an opportunity of shewing the sincere attachment & high respect with which I have the honor to be Sir, Your grateful, affectionate & very humble Servant

Tobias Lear.

ALS, DLC:GW.

1. Neither GW's letter to his wife nor the letter to Tobias Lear covering it has been found. Lear probably was referring to the account printed in the *Federal Gazette and Philadelphia Daily Advertiser,* 14 May 1791.

2. For Herculas (Hercules), a Mount Vernon slave GW took with him to Philadelphia in November 1790 to serve as cook, see GW to Lear, 17 Sept. 1790, n.2, and 12 April 1791.

3. For the new housekeeper, Ann Emerson, see Lear to GW, 1 May 1791 and note 2.

4. John Vicar had served as cook to the presidential household since May 1790. See Lear to Daniel Grant, 28 Feb. 1790, n.3.

5. On Sunday afternoon, 8 May 1791, a fire in David Kennedy's house at 329 High Street was extinguished after causing considerable property damage. Ten to twenty houses and shops were destroyed the night of 9 May by a fire that spread from a livery stable on Dock Street. See *General Advertiser and Political, Commercial and Literary Journal* (Philadelphia), 10, 11 May, and *Gazette of the United States* (Philadelphia), 10, 11 May. For references to Francis Hopkinson's death, see *General Advertiser and Political, Commercial and Literary Journal*, 10 May, and *Gazette of the United States*, 11 May.

6. The enclosed letter and proposal have not been found, but on 15 May Lear wrote Jeremiah Wadsworth: "I have the pleasure to acknowledge the receipt of your letter of the 1st instant, communicating a proposal from Messrs Whetman & Perkins to purchase the President's young Jack, and to inform you that I have transmitted the same to the President" (CtHi: Jeremiah Wadsworth Papers). On 13 July Lear wrote to Wadsworth: "the President now directs me to inform you, that it is not his intention to part with his young Jack, the offspring of the Spanish Jack and the Maltese Jenny; but that, in case *a very handsome offer* should be made, he would (tho previous to your Application the matter had not been contemplated) dispose of his large Spanish Jack. The President has bred almost entirely from this Jack, and the Mules which have descended from him are large-boned, stout, and perfectly well tempered. He means, however, to breed next season from the Maltese Jacks—after which the young Jack (now three years old) which promises to be very large, will be old enough to take up, or assist in the business, as shall be judged best—and this is the reason of his inclining to part with the Spanish Jack in preference to the young one. But it must be understood that it is not *a small price* which will induce the President to dispose of this Animal. The manner in which he came to the President, proving him to be of the first quality—his size (upwards of fifteen hands high, and his form indicating strength and firmness almost beyond conception)—his age, being now about nine years old, which is said to be far short of their prime for the business for which they are wanted—and the vast advantage which must accrue to the owner of such a creature, especially in a Country where mules are raised for exportation, and Jacks of all kinds much in demand, are circumstances which will have their weight with the President in his expectation for him; and the same things will undoubtedly be well considerd by the Purchaser. You will be so good, my dear Sir, as to communicate this to the persons who proposed purchasing the young Jack; and if they incline to come forward with such an Offer in *Cash* as may be thought adequate to such an Animal, they must do it *immediately;* for when the President was to the Southward he was much pressed to send this Jack there for a Season, and so strong was the importunity on this head that he engaged to send him to Colo. Washington of South Carolina the ensuing fall, unless prevented by some circumstance which he did not know of at that time. If, therefore, such a proposition should not come forward in the course of two months as will induce the President to dispose of him, he will be sent to Carolina agreeable to promise. It is but right it should be known that this Jack is slow in covering, and must

have a she-Ass to stimulate him to the performance of the duty expected from him" (CtHi: Jeremiah Wadsworth Papers; the editors wish to thank Reference Librarian Kelly Nolin for her assistance with this document). Whetman and Perkins in August made an offer of £500 Virginia currency for "the young Jack" (Lear to Perkins, 18 Aug. 1791, DLC:GW), but GW never closed the deal with Perkins. For reference to Royal Gift, Knight of Malta, and GW's other Mount Vernon jacks, jennies, and mules, see George Augustine Washington to GW, 16 July 1790, n.4, and J. H. Powell, *General Washington and the Jack Ass* . . . (Cranbury, N.J., 1969), 176–90.

7. Martha reported on 5 June to Fanny Bassett Washington that Benjamin Lincoln Lear "has got quite well, and grows finely" (Fields, *Papers of Martha Washington,* 232). His father wrote to Benjamin Lincoln on 8 April 1791 that "The formalities of Christening have not yet taken place; but will in a few days when my son shall have the name of Benjamin Lincoln given to him, as well to express, in some degree, the grateful remembrance in which I hold that name—as to impress it upon the mind of the boy that he must imitate the virtues of him who has borne and of him who bears the name" (MHi: Benjamin Lincoln Papers). Benjamin Lincoln's son Benjamin had died on 18 Jan. 1788 at the age of thirty-one (see Lincoln to GW, 20 Jan. 1788; *Massachusetts Centinel* [Boston], 23 Jan. 1788; Mattern, *Benjamin Lincoln,* 179). For the introduction of Lear to GW by Benjamin Lincoln, Sr., and Jr., see Lincoln to GW, 4 Jan. 1786 and note 1.

Indenture with John Cowper

[Gates County, N.C., 17 May 1791]. John Lewis as GW's attorney conveys to John Cowper four tracts (approximately 1,093½ acres) of land at White Oaks Spring, Gates County, N.C., originally purchased by GW and Fielding Lewis from Marmaduke Norfleet on 26 April 1766. Signed and sealed by Lewis and witnessed by Dempsey Copeland, Riddick Hunter, Thomas Mann, and Arthur Jones.[1]

Typescript, NcU: Southern Historical Collection (Richard Green Cowper Papers).

1. For the background to this land transaction, see particularly Deed from Marmaduke Norfleet, 26 April 1766, John Lewis to GW, 15 Dec. 1787, 7 Dec. 1788, and George Augustine Washington to GW, 7 Dec. 1790 and note 7. On 18 May 1791 Lewis and Cowper signed another indenture before the same witnesses, by which Cowper paid Lewis five shillings and promised to remit at least £600 Virginia currency in the following manner: £200 interest free to be paid on or before 1 Sept. 1791, £200 and one year's interest to be paid on or before 18 May 1792, and the balance of £200 plus interest due by 18 May 1793. If Cowper did not meet the terms, Lewis would be at liberty to sell the land at public auction (Richard Green Cowper Papers, NcU). For correspondence concerning Cowper's difficulty in meeting the terms of the sale, see GW

to Cowper, 3 Oct. 1792, 26 Oct. 1793, and 27 Jan., 9 Mar., 30 July, and 4 Sept. 1794.

To the Citizens of Augusta, Georgia

Gentlemen,   [Augusta, Ga., c.19 May 1791]

I receive your congratulations on my arrival in Augusta with great pleasure—I am much obliged by your assurances of regard, and thank you, with unfeigned sincerity, for the favorable sentiments you are pleased to express towards me.[1]

Entreating you to be persuaded of my gratitude, I desire to assure you that it will afford me the most sensible satisfaction to learn the progression of your prosperity—My best wishes for your happiness collectively and individually are sincerely offered.

G. Washington

LB, DLC:GW.

1. GW left Savannah on 15 May 1791 and arrived at Augusta, Ga., three days later. For his reception at the state capital, see *Diaries,* 6:141, and Henderson, *Washington's Southern Tour,* 234–37. The next day, 19 May, GW noted: "Received & answered an Address from the Citizens of Augusta; dined with a large Company of them at their Court Ho.; and went to an Assembly in the evening at the Acadamy" (*Diaries,* 6:141–42). The address, signed "In the name of all the Citizens" by George Walton, John Meals, Thomas Cumming, Peter Johnston Carnes, and Seaborn Jones, reads: "Sir, Your journey to the Southward being extended to the Frontier of the Union, affords a fresh proof of your indefatigable zeal in the service of your Country, and an equal attention and regard to all the people of the United States. With these impressions, the Citizens of Augusta present their congratulations upon Your arrival here in health; with the assurance, that it will be their greatest pleasure, during your stay with them, to testify the Sincere affection they have for your Person, their sense of obligations for your merits and services, and their entire confidence in you as the Chief Magistrate of their Country. On Your return, and at all times, their best wishes will accompany you, while they retain the hope that a life of virtue, benevolence and Patriotism may be long preserved, for the benefit of the Age, and the Example of Posterity" (DLC:GW).

From Robert Hawes

Queen Street, Moorfields, London, 19 May 1791. Presents with sincere respects the enclosed "effort of a solitary Individual to avenge america's and his injur'd Country's wrongs. May the God of Liberty preserve you continually—is The Prayer of Sir Your Excellency's most affectionate Friend, and admiring Servant, with a *Bible* open, and presenting 1. Maccabees Xth Chapter 15 & 16 Verses to my View."[1]

ALS, DLC:GW.

A London printer by the name of Robert Hawes published in 1786 a memorial against a tax on windows and in 1793 several political squibs, acrostical addresses, and prophetic pamphlets. His 1791 enclosure has not been identified, and no acknowledgment to this letter has been found.

1. "Now when king Alexander had heard what promises Demetrius had sent unto Jonathan: when also it was told him of the battels and noble acts which he & his brethren had done, and of the paines that they had indured, He said, Shall we find such another man? Now therefore we will make him our friend, and confederate."

From Edmund Bacon

[Augusta, Ga., 20 May 1791]

In ages past, we see a splendid train
Of heroes shine, in panegyric's strain.
Historic pens have varnish'd o'er their crimes,
And prais'd, in them, the vices of the times:
To conquer nations; millions to devour;
To reign in all the wantonness of power;
To follow glory; to acquire a name;
Their cause ambition, and their object fame.
'Tis ours to boast a hero great and good;
With courage and *benevolence* endued.

Superior genius! you, whose breast can feel
No other motive but your country's weal.
Superior firmness! with such virtues arm'd;
By power, untainted,—by no flattery charm'd.
Superior chief! by selfish views unmov'd;
Your people loving, by your people lov'd.
Let not th'expressions of our love offend
Our saviour, father, citizen and friend.
Deny us not the pleasure thus t'impart,
Without disguise, the feelings of the heart.

Thou friend of science, liberty, and laws,
Forever active in thy country's cause;

We are thy children—let thy fancy trace,
In us, the congregated, rising race—
Adopted, ere we drew the vital air,
And snatch'd from slavery by thy watchful care.
Heirs of that freedom, by that valor won;
May we ne'er mar the work by thee begun!
As we've been taught to glow at thy renown,
So we'll transmit by bright example down.
Each future babe shall learn to lisp thy name;
To love thy worth and emulate thy fame.
Whene'er the powers of infant reason dawn,
Full in his view thy portrait shall be drawn:
Hence on his mind these truths will be impress'd;
That virtue only can be truly blest.
Though power may glare in all the pomp of state;
That virtue only can be truly great.
Though vanity may bask in flattery's rays;
That virtue only meets with honest praise:
That virtue only claims our whole esteem;
That virtue only reigns with power supreme.

In our full hearts, what grateful raptures rise!
When, o'er past scenes, our active fancy flies:
We hail the day, you took the glorious field,
And made the haughty British Lion yield!
Then, though a scepter waited on your word,
For calm retirement, you resign'd the sword.
You scorn'd the glory power usurp'd imparts;
You scorn'd to reign but in a people's hearts.
Again we see you bless Potomack's shore,
Resolv'd to leave sweet Vernon's shades no more.
Delightful seat! by your fond choice design'd,
T'enjoy, in peace, your self-approving mind.
Again your country call'd you to her aid;
And you again your country's call obey'd.
With fond regret, you left your fav'rite shore,
To feel the weight of public cares once more.

Hail joyous day! what acclamations rung!
Joy fil'd each eye, and rapture mov'd each tongue,
At your instalment!—never Monarch wore

So bright, so rich a diadem before.
No more let sparkling dross ambitions move;
Your diadem, is—*universal love.*

But hold—this theme is painful to your ear;
Though lightly touch'd, by gratitude sincere—
Indulge our joys, forgive our forward zeal;
Let your own heart imagine what we feel!
What various transports in our bosoms glow,
Swell the full heart, and at the eyes o'er flow!!—

Almighty God! Since virtue is thy care;—
O hear a nation's universal prayer!
May all the joys, this transient scene can know,
Full on his heart, in gentle currents, flow!—
May all the joys, benevolence inspires,
Pursue him still when he from time retires!—
May this one joy, forever crown the whole;
And with immortal rapture fill his soul!
May he, from heaven's sublime, eternal scenes,
See future millions happy through his means!!!—

And let mankind this serious truth confess;
None e'er was prais'd so much,—none ever flatter'd less.

Augusta Chronicle (Georgia), 4 June 1791 supplement.

Edmund Bacon (1776–1826) was a student in the coeducational Academy of Richmond County, established in Augusta in 1783. At the time of GW's visit, 20 May 1791, about fifty students were enrolled. Rector and senior tutor Augustus Baldwin apparently selected Bacon as the occasion's principal speaker on the basis of his outstanding scholarship, as demonstrated by the gold medal he won at the academy's 1789 examinations and another prize he was awarded for the best translations from Aristotle's *Ars Poetica* (Cordle, "Academy of Richmond County," 79–80). After GW returned to Philadelphia, he sent the young man a set of lawbooks, and Bacon subsequently studied law at Tapping Reeve's law school in Litchfield, Conn., before settling at Savannah, where he became the chief attorney for Nathanael Greene's estate. He was later a popular member of the Edgefield, S.C., bar and a renowned classicist and belletrist (O'Neall, *Biographical Sketches of the Bench and Bar of South Carolina*, 2:222–30). The *Augusta Chronicle* reported that Bacon delivered his address to GW "with such distinctness of articulation; such propriety of pauses and emphasies; and in a manner so truly pathetic, as to keep that illustrious hero and a numerous collection of gentlemen in tears almost the whole time the little orator was speaking" (4 June 1791 supplement).

To Alexander Hamilton

Sir   Augusta [Ga.] May 20th 1791.

While at Charleston I appointed Robert Cochran of that place to command the revenue Cutter for the station of South Carolina, & empowered him, with the approbation of the Governor & general Moultrie, to appoint his mates.[1]

I have appointed John Howell Commander—Hendricks Fisher, first Mate, and John Wood second mate of the revenue Cutter to be stationed on the coast of Georgia.[2] You will transmit the Commissions and your instructions to these Gentlemen. I am, sir, Your most Obedt servt

G: Washington

LB, DLC:GW.

1. See GW to Alexander Hamilton, 8 May 1791, n.2.

2. William Jackson wrote from Augusta on this day to John Habersham, federal customs collector at Savannah, informing him of the president's appointment of the officers of the Georgia revenue cutter and requesting him to inform the secretary of the treasury if the two mates should decline their appointments (DLC:GW). Native Georgian John Wood was recommended to GW on 6 May by George Houstoun, John Wallace, Leonard Cecil, and Robert Bolton, the commissioners of pilotage of Savannah (DLC:GW).

To James Seagrove

Sir,   Augusta [Ga.] May 20th 1791.

The confidence, which your character inclines me to place in you, has induced me to commit the enclosed letter, from the Secretary of State to Governor Quesada, and the negotiation which will be consequent thereon to your care and management. The letter which is under a flying seal, to be closed before it is delivered, will inform you of the import, and serve to instruct you in the mode of conducting the object of your mission—delicate in its nature, it will require the greatest address and temper in its treatment—nor must any proposition or declaration be made, which in its consequence might commit the government of the United States.[1]

The enclosed copy of a letter, written by my direction, from the Secretary of State to the Governor of Georgia, which is now confidentially communicated to you, is another source, whence some information may be drawn[2]—but, as my ideas of your personal acquaintance with this business combined with my opinion of your character and talents to transact it, have determined me to appoint you, it is from your own knowledge, and the circumstances, which may arise, that you must decide on the best means to accomplish the negotiation—Your first care will be to arrest the farther reception of fugitive slaves, your next to obtain restitution of those slaves, who have fled to Florida, since the date of Governor Quesada's letter to Mr Jefferson, notifying the orders of his catholic Majesty[3]—and your last object, which may demand the greatest address, will be to give a retrospective force to the orders of the Court of Spain, beyond the date of that letter, and to procure the Governor's order for a general relinquishment of all fugitive slaves, who were the property of citizens of the United States. This last instruction will require peculiar delicacy, and must be entered on with caution and circumspection, or not be taken up at all, as appearances of compliance may justify the one or the other.

If your collectorate cannot furnish money to defray your expenses, in which you will observe due oeconomy, and of which you will transmit an account to the Secretary of State, you will supply yourself from the Collector of Savannah.[4] I am Sir, Your most obedient Servant

G. Washington.

LB, DLC:GW.

1. On 20 May 1791 GW "Dined at a private dinner with Govr. Telfair to day; and gave him dispatches for the Spanish Govr. of East Florida, respecting the Countenance given by that Governt. to the fugitive Slaves of the Union—wch. dispatches were to be forwarded to Mr. Seagrove, . . . who was requested to be the bearer of them, and instructed to make arrangements for the prevention of these evils and, if possible, for the restoration of the property—especially of those Slaves wch. had gone off since the orders of the Spanish Court to discountenance this practice of recg. them" (*Diaries*, 6:142–43, 144). Since the end of the Revolutionary War, Spanish East and West Florida had been a haven for Georgia and Carolina runaway slaves, criminals, and debtors fleeing their creditors. Georgia slaveowners had frequently entered Spanish territory to recover their slaves, prompting an official Spanish protest to the Confederation Congress in 1785. Thomas Jefferson wrote on the subject to American chargé at Madrid, William Carmichael, in August 1790, the same month that the newly installed Spanish governor of Florida, Juan Nepomuceno de Quesada, informed Jefferson that his instructions forbade him to permit the entry of fugitive slaves into the province. After Jefferson notified the governor of

Georgia of the new Spanish policy, Edward Telfair wrote him on 12 Jan. 1791 requesting federal assistance in recovering the refugees, which resulted in James Seagrove's mission (see Jefferson to Quesada, 12 Aug. 1790, source note, to Carmichael, 29 Aug. 1790, and Telfair to Jefferson, 12 Jan. 1791, *Jefferson Papers*, 17:341, 472–73, 18:491–92).

The enclosed letter from Jefferson to Quesada of 10 Mar. 1791 informed Quesada that GW's administration appreciated the Spanish sovereign's orders prohibiting the protection of fugitive American slaves in Florida and expressed confidence that Quesada would also assist the American slaveowners to recover their refugee slaves, noting: "The Bearer hereof *James Seagrove Esqr.* is authorized to wait on your Excellency to confer on this Subject, and to concur in such Arrangements as you shall approve for the Recovery of such Fugitives. I beg you to be assured that no Occasion shall be neglected of proving our Dispositions to reciprocate these Principles of Justice and Friendship, with the Subjects of his Catholic Majesty" (*Jefferson Papers*, 19:518–19). In a note Jefferson appended to his letter to Telfair (see note 2 below), he wrote to GW: "This letter leaves it to Govr. Telfair to explain to the President, (if he chuses) the number of negroes fled from Georgia into Florida, and which may probably be there now. If the value be so considerable, and the recovery so probable, as to induce the President to make the demand from the Governor of Florida, he will only have to fill up the blank in the letter . . . to Don Quesada, with the name of the person he may think proper to send" (ibid., 432). GW filled in Seagrove's name in the blank.

2. The enclosed letter from Jefferson to Gov. Edward Telfair, dated 26 Mar., originally was dated 16 Mar. and probably was submitted for approval to the president at Philadelphia. Jefferson observed that the Spanish orders referred to a future prohibition and questioned how far Quesada might think himself authorized to give up slaves who had already taken refuge in Florida: "an application from us to give them retrospective effect, may require his asking new orders from his court. The delay which will necessarily attend the answer, the doubts what that answer may be, and, if what we wish, the facility of evading the execution if there be a disposition to evade it, are circumstances to be weighed beforehand, as well as the probable amount of the interest which it would be possible to recover. If this last be small, it may be questionable how far the government ought in prudence to commit itself by a demand of such dilatory and doubtful effect." Jefferson suggested that Governor Telfair personally explain the details of the problem to the president when he reached Augusta (ibid., 519).

3. GW was probably referring to Quesada's letter to Jefferson of 28 Aug. 1790 (DNA: RG 59, Miscellaneous Letters).

4. William Jackson on 20 May 1791 informed John Habersham, collector of customs at Savannah, that Seagrove was going to St. Augustine on public business and was authorized to draw from Habersham money to defray his expenses (DLC:GW). Seagrove wrote at least five letters to GW in July and on 16 and 25 Aug. 1791, none of which has been found. See GW to Seagrove, 14 Sept. 1791.

To Edward Telfair

Sir,   [Augusta, Ga., c.20 May 1791]

Obeying the impulse of a heartfelt gratitude I express with particular pleasure my sense of the obligations which your Excellency's goodness, and the kind regards of your citizens have conferred upon me.[1]

I shall always retain a most pleasing remembrance of the polite and hospitable attentions which I have received in my tour thro' the State of Georgia, and during my stay at the residence of your government.

The manner in which you are pleased to recognise my public services and to regard my private felicity, excites my sensibility, and claims my grateful acnowledgement.

Your Excellency will do justice to the sentiments which influence my wishes by believing that they are sincerely offered for your personal happiness and the prosperity of the State in which you preside.

G. Washington

LB, DLC:GW.

1. GW most likely received and replied on the same day to an address of 20 May from Gov. Edward Telfair, which reads: "My warm congratulations on your arrival at the residence of Government in this State are presented with a peculiar pleasure, as well as a feeling sensibility, and I am persuaded that these emotions are perfectly congenial with those of my fellow citizens. After the gratification felt from your presence among them, they will naturally contemplate the many unavoidable inconvencies arising in so arduous and extensive a tour with the most solicitous anxiety; not less impressed, my cordial wishes shall accompany you through every stage, on your return to the seat of the Government of the United States. Long may you remain to fill the exalted station of Chief Magistrate of the American republics, as the just reward of that patriotism which marked every act of your life, whilst engaged in the arduous struggles of a long and complicated war, gave tone to the liberties of your Country, immortalized your name throughout the nations of the world, and created an unbounded confidence in your virtue with the strongest attachment to your person and family in the minds of American citizens" (DLC:GW). When GW took his final leave of Augusta gentlemen and state officials at about 6:00 A.M., 21 May, at the Savannah River bridge, he supposedly left behind the corpse of a greyhound named Cornwallis, whose 1798 marble tombstone and brick burial vault were allegedly unearthed by workmen a century later. See *Augusta Chronicle* (Georgia), 1 April 1892.

From Tobias Lear

Sir,   Philadelphia May 22nd 1791

Since I had the honor of writing to you on the 15 instant, the Brigantine Philadelphia has arrived from Charleston, by which Mrs Washington had the pleasure to receive two letters from you, and we were all made very happy by hearing that you had got that far on your tour without any interruption in your health, and without meeting with any material accident.[1] By the same Vessel I had the pleasure to receive a letter from Major Jackson—enclosing one for each of the heads of the Departments—and one for Messrs Johnson, Carroll & Stuart—all of which were sent to their respective addresses.[2]

The Articles shipped from Charleston came in good order and agreeable to the list enclosed by Major Jackson. The Horse-Covers have been exposed to the air & appear to be in perfect order.[3]

I had the honor, last week to attend Mrs Washington on a visit to General Dickinson's—we left this city on tuesday morning & returned on thursday—The weather was pleasant & the ride charming—Our reception & entertainment at Genl Dickinson's was replete with candour, openness & hospitality. The prospect of Crops in that part of the Country, as well as about this city, is pleasing; we have lately been favoured with seasonable rains.[4]

Our House-keeper seems to answer the high character given of her. She has hitherto conducted with prudence & judgement. Mrs Washington expresses herself much pleased with her.[5] Fraunces appears to have every disposition to please, and I trust he will succeed. I have no apprehension for him but on the score of expense—his ideas of which still appear to be extravagant. I have repeated to him that everything, with him, depends on this point; and I am not without hopes that the constant checks which he will meet with will at length reform him on this head. Hercules has been told that it is necessary for him to be at Mount Vernon on your return there, as his presence at that time will be indispensable there & he can be very well spared here; and as you may be there very soon, I have recommended it to him to go home this week in the Stage, as there is no vessel now up, which he has promised to do, and I shall accordingly make arrangements for his departure.[6]

Mr Jefferson left town last monday on a tour through the upper parts of New York—into Vermont—about the Lakes &ca—He meets Mr Madison in New York (where he has been for 3 or 4 weeks past) who accompanies him. He informed me that he expected to return in 3 or 4 weeks from the time of his departure. The letter for him I delivered to Mr Remsen who had directions where to forward letters to him. Colo. & Mrs Hamilton have been out of town on a visit to Bethlehem about 10 or 12 days, and are expected home this week. The letter for him I delivered to Mr Coxe to forward. General Knox has removed, for the summer, to Bush Hill which place he occupies during the absence of the Vice-President to Massachusetts.

In my letter of the 8th instant I gave a sketch of a conversation between Colo. Beckworth & myself respecting Mr Paine's pamphlet in answer to Mr Burke. Last friday evening the Colo. again made his appearance at Mrs Washington's room, and took an opportunity to request me to go with him into the yellow drawing room; and when there, he observed that he was apprehensive he might have appeared to have been uncommonly interested in the conversation which took place between us some time before on the subject of Mr Paine's book, and that he had been ever since wishing for an opportunity to assure me that he had only spoken of the subject as a private individual, and that he had only given his opinion on the book with that freedom which he should have done respecting any book that might have happened to have been the subject of conversation. In reply, I told him I could only repeat what I had observed on the former occasion, that I knew him only as a private man—and that every person had an undoubted right to form such an opinion of Mr Paine's book, as best suited them; But that it contained a great deal of good sense, and some serious truths which were perhaps, not pleasing to *every one*. Yes, says the Colo. it is certainly a well written book—and I will venture to say a very bold one to be written in England. True, I replied, and more especially since it has been determined there that *truth* may be a Libel.[7]

The conversation on this subject then dropped, & the Colo. told me he intended to take a ride as far as Connecticut to waste a few weeks & should return to this place in the latter part of June as he understood you were expected here at that time. He took occasion to speak of the New Government of Canada, &

observed that there was every reason to beleive that it would be pleasing to the Inhabitants of that Country—and added, that he thought it probable Lord Dorchester would return to England early next fall, and that it was possible he might come into the United States—visit this place & New York—and embark at one or the other. But this, he requested me to observe, was only a matter of opinion with him, he could not say that it would take place.[8]

The Marshall of Delaware District yesterday delivered to me the return of the enumeration of that District, a copy of which is enclosed—90,000 had been held out as the probable number in that State by some of its inhabitants—but it falls much short of that—and will not give them another Representative.[9]

Governor Patterson dined at General Dickinson's the day that Mrs Washington & myself were there, and the conversation turning upon the Census, he observed that the Marshall of New Jersey had informed him that according to the Census taken by him & his deputies there would be but 75 wanting to give them six representatives—and that there was no doubt but several thousands were unenumerated in the State, owing to a backwardness in many persons to give in the real numbers from an apprehension of a direct tax being the consequence.[10]

Mrs Lear unites with me in grateful respects & best wishes for your health & happiness. I have the honor to be with the most sincere attachment & highest respect Sir, Your Obliged & Affectionate Hble Servt

Tobias Lear.

ALS, DLC:GW; ALS (letterpress copy), PWacD.

1. GW's letters to Mrs. Washington have not been found. The brig *Philadelphia,* Captain Foster, arrived at Philadelphia on 18 May.

2. William Jackson's letter of c.7–8 May 1791 from Charleston to Lear, covering letters from GW to Thomas Johnson, Daniel Carroll, and David Stuart of 7 May, to Alexander Hamilton of 7, 8 May, and to Thomas Jefferson of 8 May, has not been found. No letter from GW to Henry Knox of that time has been found.

3. Jackson's list has not been found, nor have the articles shipped from Charleston been identified. The "Horse-Covers" would have been made of cloth.

4. U.S. Senator Philemon Dickinson lived with his wife, Mary Cadwallader Dickinson, at the Hermitage, his estate near Trenton, New Jersey. See Lear to GW, 15 May 1791.

5. For the housekeeper Ann Emerson, see Lear to GW, 1 May 1791 and note 2.

6. For Herculas and the reason for his return to Virginia, see GW to Lear, 12 April 1791 and note 3.

7. Lear enclosed a copy of the first American edition of Thomas Paine's *Rights of Man*. It was either this copy or a second one forwarded by Lear the following month that was in GW's library at his death. See Jefferson to GW, 8 May 1791, and Lear to GW, 23 June 1791; Griffin, *Boston Athenæum Washington Collection*, 560.

8. Sir Guy Carleton, Lord Dorchester, the governor of Quebec, sailed directly for Britain in August 1791 without visiting an American port. See Hamilton to GW, 8 July 1790 and note 2.

9. The enclosed copy of the Delaware census returns delivered by federal marshal Allan McLane has not been found, but Lear transmitted a copy to Jefferson on 12 July 1791 (DNA: RG 59, Miscellaneous). McLane's official enumeration of 4 May 1791 totaled 59,094 people—906 free persons short of the 30,000 required for an additional representative to Congress.

10. Federal marshal Thomas Lowrey completed his returns in early April 1791 and officially forwarded them to the president before 20 Aug., when Lear transmitted them to Jefferson (DNA: RG 59, Miscellaneous Letters). New Jersey's total enumeration was 184,139 persons.

To Charles Cotesworth Pinckney and Edward Rutledge

Private

Gentlemen—   Columbia [S.C.] May 24th 1791.

An address to you jointly on a subject of the following nature may have a singular appearance; but that singularity will not exceed the evidence which is thereby given of my opinion of, and confidence in you; and of the opinion I entertain of your confidence in, and friendship for each other.

The Office lately resigned by the Honble Mr J. Rutledge in the Supreme Judiciary of the Union remains to be filled. Will either of you two Gentlemen accept it? and in that case, which of you? It will occur to you that appointments to Offices in the recess of the Senate are temporary, but of their confirmation on such a case there can be *no* doubt.

It may be asked why a proposition similar to this has never been made to you before; this is my answer—your friends whom I have often conversed with on like occasions, have always given it as their decided opinion that no place in the disposal of the

genl Government could be a compensation for the relinquishment of your private pursuits; or, in their belief, would
withdraw you from them. In making the attempt, however, in
the present instance, I discharge my duty, and shall await your
answer (which I wish to receive soon) for the issue.[1] Of my sincere esteem & regard for you both I wish you to be assured and
that I Am—Gentlemen—Your Most Obedt & Affecte Humble
Servant

Go: Washington

ALS, ScC; LB, DLC:GW.

1. Charles Cotesworth Pinckney and Edward Rutledge wrote this joint reply
from Charleston on 12 June: "We embrace the earliest opportunity which has
presented itself to acknowledge the Receipt of your very friendly Letter of
the 24th May, and return you our best Thanks for the Confidence with which
you have treated us. Living as we do, and as we long have done, in the uninterrupted Habits of Friendship we feel a mutual Delight in every Measure
which tends to the Happiness of either; and every Honor which may be confer'd on one, will unquestionably reflect Pleasure on the other. Altho' our
Minds had been long made up, with respect to the acceptance of Offices, yet
the arrival of your Letter, very naturally called for a reconsideration of the
Subject—The Sincerity, with which the offer was marked—the great Esteem
which we entertain for you—and an anxious desire to yield, to what appeared
to be your wish, led us to review the Reasons which had formerly occasioned
our Determination: and having done that, we feel a deep Regret indeed, in
being obliged to decline the acceptance of a Seat on the Federal Bench. Private
Considerations have had their weight: but others of a general & more powerful
nature have influenced our hesatation. We think we can be of more real Advantage to the General Government, & to our own State Government⟨,⟩ by
remaining in the Legislature than we could possibly be, by accepting of any
Office under either, which fills the Public Eye with the appearance of being
lucrative. Under this Opinion, you will be in Sentiment with us, that it is our
indispensible Duty to continue in the ⟨*illegible*⟩ we are, so long as we possess
the Confidence of the Public. But as we devoted a large portion of our early
Years to the Service of our Country, so, whenever her Honor, or her Interest,
shall seem to require our Aid, we shall chearfully lay aside all private or partial
Considerations, & imitate as far as may be in our Power, the best, & brightest
of Examples" (DLC:GW). For the resignation of U.S. Supreme Court associate
justice John Rutledge, Sr., see Rutledge to GW, 5 Mar. 1791 and note 1.

To the Citizens of Camden, South Carolina

Gentlemen, [Camden, S.C., c.25 May 1791]
The acknowledgements which your respectful and affectionate address demands I offer to you with unfeigned sincerity—I

receive your congratulations with pleasure, and, estimating your welcome of me to Camden by a conviction of its cordiality, I render those thanks to your politeness and hospitality, to which they are so justly entitled.[1]

Your grateful remembrance of that excellent friend and gallant Officer, the Baron de Kalb, does honor to the goodness of your hearts—With your regrets I mingle mine for his loss, and to your praise I join the tribute of my esteem for his memory.[2]

May you largely participate the national advantages, and may your past sufferings, and dangers, endured and braved in the cause of freedom, be long contrasted with future safety and happiness.

G. Washington

LB, DLC:GW.

1. After GW was welcomed to Camden, S.C., by local officials in the afternoon of 25 May 1791, he was given a public reception and dinner, at which an address, "Signed by order of the inhabitants of Camden and its Vicinity" by William Lang, Joseph and James Kershaw, John Chesnut, Adam Fowler Brisbane, Joseph Brevard, Samuel Boykin, Douglas Starke, Dr. Isaac Alexander, and Isaac Dubose, was most likely presented: "Impress'd with every sentiment of Friendship, esteem and Gratitude which can actuate the human Heart, and Amid the Congratulations and Voluntary homage of *Freemen* and fellow *Citizens* that Accompany your Progress in the Southern States, the Citizens of Camden—and its Vicinity in whose County the ravages & Distresses of War were *once* as Severely and Painfully felt, as the blessings of Peace and good government are now gratefully cherished. Yielding to the Universal sentiment, but more to the impulse of our own hearts, beg leave to express the satisfaction and happiness, we feel at seeing among us our great deliverer. The venerated Chief, who heretofore under the Standard of Liberty, defended the invaded rights of America, and led her Troops with success thro' all the doubtfull changes of a Perilous War—Now our first Civil Magistrate, under whose administration we forget our dangers and sufferings past, and rest in the Perfect enjoyment of those invaluable rights, secured to us by his Labors. We Congratulate you Sir, on your return thus far; and we hail your arrival in this Town, with a Welcome, tho' less splendid, yet not less sincere than what you have any where received. And now Sir Permit us to bring to your recollection that Noble foreigner the Baron de *kalb* whose dust with that of many other brave Officers is intombed on the Plains of Camden, to him we owe this grateful mention, who despising ease & inaction, when the liberties of his fellow creatures (however distant) were threatened, entered the lists in our late Contest & fell bravely fighting for the rights of Mankind. May Almighty God, long Preserve a life so Beloved, and make the future as happy, as the Past has been illustrious, and at the close of a life rendered thus illustrious, may you greet on the happy shores of blissful immortality the kindred spirits of those Heroes & Patriots, who have in all past ages been distinguished as the Guardians of Liberty, and

the Fathers of their Country" (DLC:GW). For GW's arrival and activities at Camden, see *Diaries*, 6:147–48.

2. Bavarian native Johann Kalb (baron de Kalb; 1721–1780) received a commission as a major general in the Continental army in 1777 and was mortally wounded on 16 Aug. 1780 at the Battle of Camden. GW visited his grave in the southwestern part of the city on 26 May (ibid., 148; Lipscomb, *South Carolina in 1791*, 72, 73).

To the Citizens of Columbia and Granby, South Carolina

Gentlemen, [Columbia, S.C., c.25 May 1791]

I am much obliged by your professions of respect and affection, and I am truly grateful for your kind regards and good wishes. Replying to them with sincere acknowledgement, I desire to assure you that I shall always remember with pleasure your polite attentions.[1]

G. Washington.

LB, DLC:GW.

1. GW arrived late on 22 May 1791 at Columbia, S.C., and was forced to remain there until 4:00 A.M. on 25 May because of a foundered horse (see *Diaries*, 6:145–47). Before dawn on 25 May, GW was presented with an address signed by state legislator and city commissioner Alexander Gillon (1741–1794): "The Citizens of Columbia, Granby, & the Vicinity; offer their professions of respect, & affection for your attentive Visit. Could the expression of our Sentiments add Lustre to the justly merited Eulogy of an admiring World, we would account with pleasing recollection, the Eventfull Scenes of Glory, in which you have borne so Conspicuous a part: But, as no Idea of Gratitude or praise, can transcend your Merit, so has no term of approbation been omitted to Express it. It is then but left for us, to declare, that our Hearts chearfully adopt those Plaudits of Praise, which have resounded, from every quarter of our Gratefull Continent. And since the Duties of your important Station, call you from us, Go, America's best Friend: leaving us to implore our Eternal Guardian, to bestow on you, Every Felicity he admits on Earth. And that when it shall please him to summon you from us, that he Enfold you as that, which, in Perfection, nearest approached these, selected to Waft you to his Cælestial Abode" (DLC:GW).

From Gouverneur Morris

Dear Sir Paris 27 May 1791

I have the Honor to enclose a Letter and sundry Papers from Messieurs Schweizer Jeanneret and Company. I have referred these Gentlemen to Mr Short telling them that it is most fitting in many Respects that they should apply to him.[1]

As it is possible however that this Business may come before you, I think it a Duty to convey Some Observations which occur to me and which may not perhaps strike you because Matters of that Sort have not I beleive much occupied your Attention. Previous thereto I beg Leave however to give you a History of my Acquaintance with it. In a Letter to Colonel Hamilton of the 31st of January 1790 I mentioned what had passed between Mr Necker and me respecting the Debt due by the United States to France, and I hinted at the Means of turning to useful Account a very precipitate step of the public Agents in Holland.[2] About this time I received your Orders to communicate with the british Ministers and altho' I did by no means consider that in the Light of an Appointment to Office, yet from Motives of Delicacy I determined to extricate myself from the Affair of the Debt as speedily as I could with Propriety.[3] Various Applications were made to me from different Quarters to which I replied evasively but on my Arrival in this City last November I informed the Parties that I had Reasons of a private Nature which deterred me from holding any Share in their Speculation. I conversed with Mr Short on the same Subject and communicated to him confidentially my Reason for declining an Interest as well as my Opinion respecting the Use which might be derived from such Negotiation.[4] A few Days after the President of the Committee of finance happening to meet me at the Count de Montmorins mentioned some Proposals then before them which to the best of my Remembrance were extravagant. I declined giving an Opinion without previously seeing and considering the Terms; upon which he and Mr de Montmorin agreed together that before any thing was concluded the various Propositions which might be made should be submitted to my Examination.[5] There the Thing dropt and the enclosed Papers shew the Reason why; for it appears from them that a Bargain was made shortly after by the Controleur general with a different Company. Mr Short mentioned this to me on his Return hither in the End of March telling me that the Parties concerned were (as he was informed in Amsterdam) Men of no Credit nor Capital. I of Course agreed with him in Opinion that if so it was not worth while to listen to them.[6] A few Days after one of them called on me and after giving a History of the Affair begged me to make Use of my good

Offices. I told him at once that it was ridiculous to ask a Commission of 5 ⅌% on changing the Nature of our Debt. That it was quite as convenient to owe France as to owe the Subjects of France, and further that before any Treaty was offered Persons of Credit and Capital should appear. As soon as I had made this last Observation he drew out the Letters of the Comptroller general and shewing me the second Clause of it replied that after what was there contained no Man had a Right to question the Solidity of the Society: he then added that for my private Satisfaction he would prove that People of the first Fortune were connected therein and indeed he gave me such Proof. I told him upon this that they must apply to Mr Short or to their own Ministry whose Support would be much more efficacious than the Sentiments of any private Individual. I ment⟨ioned⟩ nevertheless to Mr Short the Substance of this Conversation. While h⟨e⟩ was in the Country the enclosed Letter was received. He returned to Town Yesterday and called on me in the Evening when I communicated to him the Purport of it.[7]

I have ever been of Opinion that as we are not in Condition to pay our Debt to France a Bargain by which the Period can be prolonged without Loss to either Party is desirable. I say with⟨out⟩ Loss because the Conduct of this Nation has been so generous to us tha⟨t⟩ it would be very ungrateful indeed to take Advantage of those Necessities which the Succor afforded to America has occasioned. Suc⟨h⟩ a Bargain must be either with the Government or with Individuals⟨.⟩ But after the repeated Delays on our Part to ask longer Time now would not look well. Indeed no such Treaty could be made withou⟨t⟩ the Consent of the Assembly and their Observations would not be pleasant. A Bargain with Individuals has the Advantage of bringing in the Aid of private Interest to the Support of our Credit, and what is of very great Consequence it would leave us at Liberty to make Use of that Credit for the Arrangement of our domestic Affairs. And on this Head I must mention that it has been my good fortune to prevent some Publications which would have been particularly injurious to us. Their Object was to complain of the United States for speculating in their own Effects with the Funds of France. Urging that while we owe heavy Installments already due here all the Loans we obtain in Holland ought to be applied to the Discharge of them and therefore that the Speculations in our domestic Debt were a double Violation of good faith &ca &ca &ca—The present State of Things here has occasioned so great a Fall in the Exchange that Money borrowed in Holland is remitted with great Gain; consequently Loans made there just now answer well and it is evident that the Parties who are endeavoring to contract count on a considerable Profit from that Circumstance. Much however is to be said on this Part of the Subject. First it is questionable whether our Reputation may not be a little affected for you will recollect that about one third of our Debt to France arose from a Loan made on our Account in Holland of five Million of florins for which the King paid us here ten Million of Livres without any Deduction for Charges of any Sort.[8] The Nation is now obliged to pay those five Millions in Holland, and for us to borrow that Amount there and then squeeze them in an Exchange which distresses both their Commerce and Finances looks hard. There was a good Deal of Murmuring about it when the last Operation of 1500000 Guilders took Place and I should not be at all surprized if some *Patriot* by Way of shewing his Zeal should make a violent Attack in the Assembly when the next Payment is made. There are many of these patriots who if they can inculpate Ministers and distress those of different Sentiments don't care a Jot for Consequences. But supposing this not to happen it is not possible for a Nation to make the Advantages which Individuals do in such things because they must employ Individuals each of whom will be too apt to look a little to his own Advantage. There is a Difference also between the Gain made upon Parts and that which would arise on the whole for even if we could borrow all at once so large a Sum there can be no Doubt that the Remittance of it hither would greatly alter the Exchange. But it is not possible to borrow it speedily, and the present unnatural State of Things will in all Probability be changed. In fact the leading Characters are very seriously alarmed at it. If their Paper Currency should be either redeemed or annihilated or abolished Tomorrow the Exchange would immediately turn in Favor of France and then we should loose on Remittances. So much for this Affair in its little Details but there is a great View of it which forcibly strike my Mind. If we were at Liberty to turn all our Efforts towards our domestic Debt we should by raising its Value prevent Speculations which are very injurious to the Country if not to the Government. Millions have already been bought at low Price and afterwards negotiated in Europe; neither is that all for if we can borrow at five per Cent and buy up our six per Cent Debt at Par we gain at once by that Operation one fifth of the Interest or twenty per Cent which besides all the other good Consequences is much more than ever we shall get by any Management of our Debts on this Side of the Water.

I have given you my dear Sir these Hints in Abridgement because my Time will not permit of dilating them attribute them I pray you to the true Cause and beleive me always very sincerely yours[9]

Gouvr Morris

ALS, DNA: RG 59, Miscellaneous Letters; LB, DLC: Gouverneur Morris Papers. Material in angle brackets is taken from the letter-book copy.

1. For background to William Short's agency in negotiating new American loans in Holland, see Alexander Hamilton to GW, 26 Aug. 1790 (second letter) and 3 Sept. 1790. For Gouverneur Morris's involvement in attempts to purchase the American debt to France and the schemes of the Paris banking firm of Jean Gaspar Schweitzer, François Jeanneret, et Compagnie, see editorial note in *Jefferson Papers*, 20:175–97.

The enclosed letter from Schweitzer, Jeanneret, & Cie to Gouverneur Morris, dated Paris, 15 May 1791, reviewed the firm's contacts with Short and the French government, stated that their investors agreed to renounce their commission on their proposed loan of 40 million livres to the United States, and requested the sanction of the deal by the American government (in French, DNA: RG 59, Miscellaneous Letters). The letter covered copies of: Schweitzer, Jeanneret, & Cie's proposal of 22 Nov. 1790; Schweitzer, Jeanneret, & Cie to Charles-Guillaume Lambert, 22 Nov. 1790; Lambert to Armand-Marc, comte de Montmorin Saint-Hérem, 26 Nov. 1790; Montmorin to Lambert, 29 Nov. 1790; Lambert to Schweitzer, Jeanneret, & Cie, 30 Nov. 1790; Schweitzer, Jeanneret, & Cie to Short, 14 Dec. 1790; Short to Schweitzer, Jeanneret, & Cie, 17 Dec. 1790; Schweitzer, Jeanneret, & Cie to Short, 27 Dec. 1790; Schweitzer, Jeanneret, & Cie to Montmorin, 10 Jan. 1791; Montmorin to Schweitzer, Jeanneret, & Cie, 20 Jan. 1791; and Montmorin to Louis-Guillaume Otto, January 1791 (all in DNA: RG 59, Miscellaneous Letters). Short sent different copies of Schweitzer, Jeanneret, & Cie to Lambert, 22 Nov., Lambert to Montmorin, 26 Nov., and Short to Schweitzer, Jeanneret, & Cie, 17 Dec., to Hamilton on 18 Dec. 1790. See Syrett, *Hamilton Papers*, 7:357–61, 367–68.

2. For Morris to Hamilton, 31 Jan. 1790, see ibid., 6:234–39.

3. Morris received on about 21 Jan. 1790 GW's letter of 13 Oct. 1789 enclosing authorization of his private mission to London to discover the disposition of the British ministry toward the United States (see GW to Morris, 13 Oct. 1789 [second letter] and note 1, and Morris to GW, 22 Jan. 1790 [first letter]).

4. Morris recorded on 9 Nov. 1790: "Converse with Short on general Mat-

ters. He is going to see Montmorin and I tell him that I have declined an Interest and assign in Confidence the Reason. I find that his Mission is for the Purpose of borrowing the two Million of Dollars only. He agrees with me in Opinion that it will be useful to the United States that Individuals should contract for the French Debt, but thinks the french Government ought to be apprized of the true Situation of Things. I fully accord in this Sentiment and add that they should know also as nearly as possible what they have to depend on in Regard to the future" (Morris, *Diary of the French Revolution*, 2:53–54).

5. Morris noted on 21 Nov. 1790: "After Dinner I converse a little with Montmorin about his own Situation. He feels himself very aukward, not knowing whether to stay or go, or staying what to do. [Anne-Pierre, marquis de] Montesquiou[-Fézénsac] comes up and asks Information from me respecting the Debt from America to France. In the Result of his Enquiries it is agreed between him and Montmorin that no Proposition shall be accepted without taking first my Opinion on it" (ibid., 67).

6. In forwarding to Hamilton Montmorin's letter of 24 Jan. 1791 to Short, the chargé wrote on 11 Mar. 1791: "I have learned lately what I had before reason to suspect that Jeanneret & Co. are entirely without capital or credit & further of a character which shews it would be unsafe to treat with them their offers being supported by the minister is the only circumstance which entitles them to any kind of attention" and concluded that it showed the French ministry was "in the disposition you would desire with respect to this affair" (Short to Hamilton, 11 Mar. 1791, Syrett, *Hamilton Papers*, 8:170–76). During "a long Conversation on American Finance" on 9 April 1791, Morris endeavored to convince Short "that the Proposition made in Name of Schweitzer Jeanneret and Co: is a good one for the United States, provided they abate the Commission. This is my sincere Belief. I tell him also that from what the Parties have said to, and shewn to, me I am convinced that they have great Strength both with the Court and in the Assembly. That an Operation of this Sort would be so much the more useful as the United States might make Use of all their Credit to support their Domestic Operations. The Conversation is long, and he is a little changed in his Opinions" (Morris, *Diary of the French Revolution*, 2:157–58).

7. Morris recorded in his diary entry of 26 May 1791 that Short "does not come till near ten and stays with me till one. We converse a good Deal about various Affairs but particularly Loans for the United States, and the Offers made for the french Debt. I give him my sincere Opinion that a Bargain in the Lump would be the best Mode of treating that Affair" (ibid., 192).

8. For Louis XVI's guarantee of a five-million-florin American loan in Holland in 1782, see Hamilton to GW, 26 Aug. 1790 (second letter), n.1. See also Board of Treasury to GW, 15 June 1789, n.13.

9. GW had Tobias Lear on 15 Aug. 1791 "transmit to the Secretary of the Treasury a letter from Mr Governr Morris to the President respecting the Debt of the United States in France; which the President requests the Secretary to take into consideration, and to draft such an answer as will be proper for the President to give to Mr Morris on this subject" (Lear to Hamilton, 15 Aug. 1791 [first letter], DLC:GW). For GW's reply, see GW to Morris, 12 Sept. 1791.

From Gouverneur Morris

Dear Sir   Paris 27 May 1791
I did intend to give you a pretty full detail of various Matters and Things by Colonel Ternant who will have the Honor to deliver this Letter but I am just about setting off to London which prevents me.[1] Colo. Ternant however will give you every Information respecting the Decrees of the Assembly affecting our Commerce and the like[2]—This he will do confidentially as a man of Honor at least so I beleive because in the first Place there is no Secret in them and because secondly he is very much disposed to do what we would wish to have done, and no man is better informed Very few so well. Accept I pray you the Assurances of my sincere Regard and beleive me truly yours[3]
                                              Gouvr Morris

ALS, DLC:GW.
    1. Gouverneur Morris noted in his diary that on 28 May he met with the new French minister to the United States, Jean-Baptiste, chevalier de Ternant, and entrusted him with letters to be delivered in America. Morris left Paris the following morning (Morris, *Diary of the French Revolution*, 2:194–95).
    2. For the acts of the French National Assembly of March 1791 limiting the American tobacco and whale oil trades, see Lafayette to GW, 28 July 1791.
    3. GW acknowledged the letter on 12 Sept. 1791.

From Barbé-Marbois

Sir,   Metz [France] mai the 28th 1791.
I have So many times experienced the friendly disposition of your Excellency that I rejoice in the opportunity which is offered to me of introducing to you one of my nephews, Mr de Kellerman.[1] he accompanies M. de Ternant with Some hope of replacing by interim my brother the Vice Consul & it would be happy for him in a Station either public or private to deserve the Same Kindness which I was so happy as to obtain. Mrs Marbois joins her recommendation to mine & as she is an american I hope it will make it easier for her nephew to obtain the friendship of her countrymen.[2]
We could not be Strangers to hispaniola to the commotion by which the Kingdom has been agitated: we have returned to my native country which for being on the boundaries has not been less exposed to a confusion almost general. the result is as yet

quite unknown. the prevailing opinion is that of an impending war. & many prognosticate it for next Summer. I cannot think it So near & though our frontiers beginn to Swarm with troops within & without I consider these last as having no other destination but to give more weight to the negotiation. The country to whose government your Excellency so hapily presides appears to me to be the only one in the world where peace & hapiness are to be found. I have the honour to be with great respect Sir, Your Excellencys the humble obedient servant

De marbois

ALS, DLC:GW.

François Barbé-Marbois (Barbé de Marbois; 1745–1837) was the eldest son of the director of the royal mint at Metz. He came to Philadelphia in 1779 as secretary to the French legation, became consul general in 1781, and acted as chargé until 1785, when he was appointed intendant of Saint Domingue. Revolutionary ferment in Haiti and his unpopularity with the planters led to his recall in October 1789.

1. François-Etienne Kellermann (de Kellerman; 1770–1835) was the son of Barbé-Marbois's sister Anne-Marie Barbé (1742–1812) and her husband, François-Christophe, duc de Valmy (1735–1820), maréchal de France. He served under Jean-Baptiste, chevalier de Ternant, in the French embassy in Philadelphia until 1793, when he returned to France to serve as his father's aide-de-camp. Barbé-Marbois's younger brother, Pierre-François, served as French vice-consul for Pennsylvania and Delaware from April 1785 until his appointment as interim vice consul at New York in November 1791.

2. Barbé-Marbois married in 1784 Elizabeth Moore (c.1765–1834), only daughter of wealthy Philadelphia merchant William Moore.

From Louis XVI

Tres chers grands amis et alliés   [Paris, 28 May 1791]

nous avons choisi le sieur de Ternant Colonel Commandant du Régiment royal Liegiois pour aller résider auprès de vous en qualité de notre Ministre Plenipotentiaire.[1] Il est parfaitement instruit des sentiments et des principes qui font la baze de nos liaisons avec vous, et nous ne doutons pas qu'il ne nous donne une nouvelle preuve de son zêle pour tout ce qui peut intéresser notre service, en se conduisant de la maniere la plus propre à vous convaincre du desir que nous avons de les perpetuer et de les resserrer de plus en plus.[2] Nous vous prions d'ajouter une foi entiére à tout ce qu'il vous dira de notre part. Il ne peut trop vous assurer, et vous ne sauriez etre trop persuadés de l'affection constante et de l'amitié sincére que nous portons aux Etats unis en général et à chacun d'Eux en particulier. Sur ce nous prions Dieu qu'il vous ait Tres chers grands amis et Alliés en sa sainte et digne garde. Ecrit à Paris le 28 mai 1791. Votre bon Ami et Allié

Louis Montmorin

DS, DNA: RG 59, Communications from Heads of Foreign States.

1. Jean-Baptiste, chevalier de Ternant, served as a lieutenant colonel in the Continental army from 1778 until his capture at the surrender of Charleston, S.C., after which he was exchanged in May 1780 and later promoted to brevet colonel. Returning to France in 1783, he served in the French army as a colonel. The unpopular Eléanor-François-Elie, comte de Moustier, was recalled in 1789, and on 17 Jan. 1791 Ternant was chosen to replace him as minister to the United States. Ternant left France on 25 or 26 June and arrived at Philadelphia on 10 Aug., when he met privately with GW. Ternant presented his credentials on 12 Aug. and reported to his superior the following day. See Ternant to Montmorin, 13 Aug. 1791, Turner, *Correspondence of the French Ministers*, 2:43–45.

2. Although France and the United States stood at the brink of a trade war in the spring of 1791, Ternant carried no instructions to negotiate a new commercial treaty based on full reciprocity to replace the disputed Treaty of Amity and Commerce of 1778 (see Thomas Jefferson to GW, 18 Jan. 1791, and GW to the U.S. Senate, 19 Jan. 1791 and source note; Miller, *Treaties*, 2:7; 1 *Stat*. 27–28, 135–36). Despite William Short's lobbying efforts against the measure, the National Assembly in early March 1791 issued decrees repealing American trade privileges, and GW approved Jefferson's policy of having Short privately consult with Lafayette before protesting officially (Lafayette to GW, 7 Mar. 1791, GW to Lafayette, 28 July 1791, and Jefferson to GW, 30 July 1791). Almost two months before Jefferson wrote to Short, however, the French legislature seemed to have acted more favorably to the United States but in actuality offered only a palliative. On 2 June the National Assembly decreed "that the King be prayed to cause to be negociated with the United States, a New Treaty of Commerce that may tend to strengthen those mutual relations of friendship and good understanding, so highly beneficial to them both." The president of the National Assembly himself sent a copy of the decree to Jefferson, which was received on 9 Aug. (Jean-Xavier Bureau de Pusy to Jefferson, 6 June 1791, in *Jefferson Papers*, 20:524–28). Short informed Jefferson of the decree, and Lafayette wrote Jefferson on 7 June that Ternant carried a letter from the National Assembly "Expressing sentiments Most sincerely felt. He will Explain How it Happened the Assembly Blunderd in the duties on oil and tobacco, and I Hope You will Be satisfied with His Accounts on these Matters" (Short to Jefferson, 6, 10 June, Lafayette to Jefferson, 7 June 1791, ibid., 528–36, 539–41, 548–50). But three months after Ternant's arrival, Jefferson wrote to Short: "M. de Ternant tells me he has no instructions to propose to us the negociation of a commercial treaty, and that he does not expect any" (Jefferson to Short, 24 Nov. 1791, ibid., 22:328–32).

Tobias Lear to Alexander Hamilton

[Philadelphia] 29 May 1791. Transmits under the president's direction the enclosed from John H. Mitchell, which came in a letter from GW, dated Savannah, 13 May, received yesterday.[1]

LB, DLC:GW.

1. The enclosure has not been found but was probably drafted c.2–14 May 1791 and concerned the ambitions of John Hinckley Mitchell, a city warden of Charleston, S.C., to provide the U.S. Mint with coinage. Mitchell most likely discussed his plans with GW during the Southern Tour. See John Bailey to GW, 17 April 1790, n.1, and Charles Pinckney to GW, 2 May 1791, source note.

From Tobias Lear

Sir,   Philadelphia May 29th 1791.

I had the honor, yesterday, to receive your letter of the 13th Instant, with its enclosures, from Savannah.[1] It gives every body great pleasure to hear that you have reached the southern extremity of your journey without any interruption to your health, and their united prayers are offered up for as happy a return.

Since the time that I knew you must have reached Charleston, I have directed my letters to Petersburg, with a request to the Postmaster there to forward them, by a safe conveyance, to Taylor's ferry, which Mr Jefferson informed me you would cross on your return, and between which place & Petersburg there was a constant communication. To this place my three last letters have been directed.[2]

At the request of the Secretary of the Treasury, I have filled up & delivered to him two of the blank Commissions which you left with me—One with the name of John Whitaker as Inspector of the Revenue for Survey No. 4 in the District of North Carolina—and one with the name of Joseph McDowell, the elder, as Inspector of the Revenue for Survey No. 5 in the same District.[3] The Secretary at the same time wished to be furnished with a Commission for William Cooke, as Master of a Revenue Cutter in the service of the United States; but as you had not signed any of that description before your departure it was not in my power to comply with his request. He observed that no inconvenience could arise from not having this Commission before your return—as it was not probable that the Cutter which Captn

Cooke is to Command will be in readiness till some time after that period.

In consequence of Representations made by the Attorney General & myself, the Trustees of the College have undertaken to investigate thoroughly the`mode in which the boys are instructed in the Schools & every circumstance attending them. A Committee of that body have, for several days past, been employed in the examination of the Schools &ca. They have expressed themselves, as I understand, obliged to us for making those representations, and they trust that such a reformation will take place as to render any future complaints unnecessary. Altho I have been informed through one Channel that the Trustees say they are thankful for our representations; yet I have been told by others that they are not pleased with my meddling with the business, and consider it as an unjustifiable liberty which I have taken. However, I feel perfectly easy about the matter, knowing that I had just cause & sufficient authority for my complaints—and being certain that many things will be found in that system which require correction.[4]

Our family affairs seem to go on pretty smoothly under the administration of Fraunces & Mrs Emerson. I flatter myself they will both conduct well & meet approbation. Some attempts have been made to overthrow their authority; but a steady & resolute conduct, particularly on the part of Mrs Emerson, rendered these attempts abortive. She has, however, been told by them, upon expressing her disapprobation of some parts of their Conduct, that if she found cause to disapprove now, she must expect much greater cause on your return, when all the Servants would be together, for that they were not accustomed to have a person to preach to them or inspect their conduct in the house.[5]

Mrs Lear thanks you very gratefully for your kind remembrance of herself & our little boy—I am happy to inform you that they are both in good health. She joins with mine, sentiments of respectful attachment and sincere prayers for your health & happiness. I have the honor to be, with the highest respect, Sir, Your Obliged & grateful Servt

Tobias Lear.

ALS, DLC:GW; ALS (letterpress copy), PWacD.
   1. See GW to Tobias Lear, 14 May 1791 and note 1.
   2. Lear's last three letters were dated 8, 15, and 22 May 1791.

3. GW on 15 Mar. wrote Alexander Hamilton that he intended to appoint John Whitaker and Joseph McDowell, Sr., as North Carolina excise inspectors and would leave blank commissions to be filled with their names if GW reported nothing contrary before 10 June (GW to Hamilton, 15 Mar. 1791 [first letter]). On 25 April he had William Jackson write to Hamilton from Wilmington, N.C., that the president's inquiries revealed that Whitaker appeared "unexceptionable" and that McDowell was perhaps in all regards "the most proper person" for the inspectorship of Survey No. 5 (CSmH). John Whitaker (1747–1816) represented Halifax County in the North Carolina general assembly in 1778, 1780, and 1783 and sat in the state ratification convention of 1789. Joseph McDowell, Sr.'s younger kinsman, physician Joseph McDowell, Jr. (1758–1795), who fought in the Revolutionary War as a militia major and represented Burke County, N.C., in the general assembly from 1787 to 1792 and the ratifying conventions of 1788 and 1789, was the man being considered. After receiving Jackson's letter the secretary of the treasury wrote to Lear requesting him to fill up some of the blank commissions in his possession with the names of Whitaker and McDowell, and William Cooke, which Lear did two days later (Hamilton to Lear, 25 May, Lear to Hamilton, 27 May 1791, DLC:GW). For the background to the creation of the federal excise service, see Executive Order, 15 Mar. 1791 and source note.

4. For George Washington Parke Custis's education at the academy of the College of Philadelphia, see Lear to GW, 3 April, and GW to Lear, 12 April 1791.

5. For housekeeper Ann Emerson and steward Samuel Fraunces, see GW to Lear, 27 Mar., n.1, and Lear to GW, 1 May 1791 and note 2.

From d'Estaing

Sir,   Paris 30th May 1791

The devottees love to importune heaven—and every good Citizen seizes, with a delight mingled with the most respectful veneration, every opportunity of recalling himself to your memory. For this purpose no time can be more favorable, I will not say for myself; but for the whole nation, than the moment when a Minister of France, such as M. de Ternant goes to reside with you.

The President of the United States will find in the heart—in the principles—and in the talents of M. Ternant that which he loves, and that which he esteems. Our Revolution, which can be but imperfectly viewed at a distance, goes in this manner to announce its approach to General Washington. The Representative of France has communicative virtues; and it is permitted me to wish, as an individual who neither interferes with, nor is instructed in anything, that they may extend themselves even so far as to have an influence upon the Ancient french Americans, for whom they are framing a Constitution at London. You are not ignorant that to see them even creating one, was one of my most ardent wishes when I was a public man. I am, with respect, Sir, Your very humble & Obedt servt[1]

Estaing

Translation, DLC: GW; ALS, in French, PHi: Gratz Collection. Receiver's copy transcribed for CD-ROM:GW.

1. GW replied to the letter on 7 September.

From Henry Knox

Sir,   War Department [Philadelphia], 30th May, 1791.

The last Letter which I had the honor to address you was dated on the 17th ultimo. Since which your progressive distance rendered it improper for me to write, as it was almost certain that my Letters could not overtake you.[1]

I now have the honor to address with the expectation of the Letters reaching you at Taylor's ferry, and a Duplicate to be left at Mount Vernon.

Without entering into details, I shall have the honor at present to submit a general view of the most interesting affairs, relative to the proposed campaign.[2]

The raising of the Levies, in New Jersey, this State, Maryland and Virginia has in general succeeded so well, that I conceived it unnecessary to have recourse to drafting the Militia, which not only seems entangled in some States with embarrassments, but the measure would occasion Substitutes at a much higher rate of compensation, than is allowed by the United States. This inequality in its best state would occasion uneasiness among the troops, and under certain circumstances might cause great evils.

The upper battalion, or that raised on the frontiers of this State has not succeeded, owing to the Militia being drafted, and Substitutes at high compensations being established; but as the Militia have been, or will be shortly dismissed, it is expected the battalion will soon be filled.

The recruiting of the regulars in New Hampshire, Massachusetts and Rhode Island, contrary to all expectations has not succeeded, owing as it is said, to the lowness of the pay. The Clothing being now distributed at the respective rendezvouss and the working season arrived, there are better prospects of success.

In Connecticut the service has succeeded better. One full company marched ten days past, and another is completing fast.

By the enclosed Schedule it will appear, that Thirteen hundred and two Regulars and Levies, have marched forward, and will march, on or before the first of June.[3]

The advanced Guard consisting of One hundred and sixty Levies, reached Fort Pitt on the 18th instant, and they would be followed in close succession by other Companies and detachments.

The raising the battalion of rifle men, being part of the Levies in the territory of the United States, south of the Ohio, will have been retarded by the sickness of Brigadier General Sevier, who was dangerously ill at Richmond. But he had recovered, and on the 28th ultimo set out from thence, and assured me he had no doubt of the battalion being completed before the first of June. General Sevier had charge of the money for the battalion, and the Clothing moved from Richmond on the 25th ultimo—together with all the Goods necessary for Governor Blount's treaty with the Cherokees, to be held on the last day of the present month.[4]

From the train in which the business is in, I think it may be relied upon that about One thousand Regulars and Levies, will be on their march before the 20th of June—this opinion includes Sevier's battalion—and the further number of Five hundred: before the first of July. This would make the number Two thousand eight hundred regulars and Levies, to which the number of Two hundred and fifty of the old troops who may be collected, may be added.

All the troops which shall march in the course of June, may be expected at the farthest to be at Fort Washington by the 15th of August. Hence it would appear that reliance may be had upon about Three thousand being assembled at Fort Washington, at the latest by the month of September. That period will be considerably later than was at first contemplated, but by good information, it will be the proper time.

I shall in due season communicate these prospects to Major General St Clair, and if he should judge the force inadequate to the appearances, he must be empowered to call forth the additional number he shall think necessary from the Kentucky Militia, to act either conjointly or collaterally with the Army as he shall think proper.

The frontiers, as far as I have been informed, although much alarmed, have not been greatly injured. The mischiefs and depredations on the frontiers of this State, and Ohio county in Virginia, would appear to have been committed by the Delawares and Wyandots, and flowing directly from the murder of the friendly indians of those tribes by the party headed by Captain Brady on the 10th of March last.[5]

The Cornplanter continues firmly attached to the United States, although some of his party was plundered and abused by the people of Westmoreland county of this State. Notwithstanding this circumstance, he with a large number of his people assembled in and about Fort Franklin on french creek, on a report of a large body of Western indians being in the vicinity with hostile intentions.[6]

Colonel Procter made all possible expedition, but could not meet the Cornplanter, until the 8th of April, which was effected at Fort Franklin. Although it was Procter's earnest desire to have gone forward to the western indians from Fort Franklin, yet the indians conceived that they should not be justified by their tribes, without making a previous communication. They dispatched their Runners to call a Council at Buffaloe creek, and Colonel Procter accompanied them to that place.[7]

If the business be approved, the Cornplanter proposes himself to accompany Colonel Procter, with Two hundred Warriors.

This detention will retard General Scott's desultory expedition, as it would not have a good appearance, to strike the Wabash indians first and invite them to peace afterwards.[8]

Major General St Clair left Fort Harmar on the Muskingum, on the 2d of this month, intending to go to Lexington to concert measures with General Scott.

Major General Butler is at Fort Pitt—He will at present employ part of the Levies, so as to dismiss the Militia who were called out in consequence of the orders of the 10th of March last. Although it may be supposed by some people that the County Lieutenants have called out a greater number of men than actual circumstances rendered necessary, yet I am convinced as the measure respects the reputation and dignity of the General government that it was right.

The Ordnance, Military stores, Medicines and Quarter Masters Stores, necessary for the Campaign, have been forwarded to Fort Pitt.

The force and the preparations, of all kinds, are in as much forwardness as the circumstances of the case would possibly admit, and I flatter myself as much as the public interests require.

The Vice President, the Secretary of State, and the Secretary of the Treasury, concurring with me in the propriety of assembling the Senekas, and others of the six Nations at this crisis, not only to prevent their joining the hostile indians—but, if necessary to induce them to join the troops of the United States: I have instructed Colonel Pickering accordingly—The 17th of June is the time, and the painted Post the place, at which the Council is to be held.

The goods necessary for the treaty have been forwarded to Colonel Pickering, and all the other necessary arrangements made.[9]

I beg you to accept this general information until I shall have the honor to submit to you all the particular details which you may require.

Anxious that your journey may have been productive of health and satisfaction, I have the honor to be, With the most perfect Respect, Your Obedient humble servt

H. Knox
secy of War

LS, DLC:GW; LS (duplicate), DNA: RG 59, Miscellaneous Letters; LB, DLC:GW.

1. Henry Knox actually wrote two letters to GW on 17 April 1791, neither of which apparently reached him during his tour, as GW answered one of them only after his return to Mount Vernon on 12 June. See also GW to Knox, 19 June.

2. Knox is referring to the preparations for the campaign commanded by Arthur St. Clair in the fall of 1791.

3. The enclosed schedules of troops, signed and dated at the War Department by Knox on 28 May 1791, consist of a "Schedule of the Troops actually marched from the respective rendezvous for Fort Pitt 1791," totaling 643; "Troops which will march on or before the first of June," totaling 659; and an "Estimate of Regulars and Levies (Brigadier Genl Sevier's battalion included)

which will march from their respective rendezvous for the frontiers during the course of the month of June," totaling 1,500. The total troop strength listed was 2,802 regulars and levies (DLC:GW). Knox sent similar schedules to St. Clair on 9 June (*ASP, Indian Affairs,* 1:177).

4. For the appointment of John Sevier as brigadier general of militia and his intended expedition, see Knox to GW, 22 Feb. 1791 and note 9 and 17 April 1791, and GW to the U.S. Senate, 22 Feb. 1791. Sevier had recovered from his illness and set out from Richmond on 28 Mar., not 28 April (see Knox to GW, 27 Mar. 1791). As governor of the Southwest Territory, William Blount was also superintendent of its Indian affairs. For the background to his treaty with the Cherokee, completed at Holston on 2 July 1791, see GW to Thomas Jefferson, 10 Mar. 1791 and note 2, and Knox to GW, 14 Mar. (second enclosure) and 17 April 1791.

5. For references to the murder of four friendly Indians trading on Big Beaver Creek in Allegheny County, Pa., on 9 Mar. 1791 by an armed party under Samuel Brady and Francis McGuire, see the Seneca Chiefs to GW, 17 Mar. 1791 and note 1 (*ASP, Indian Affairs,* 1:174–75). On 29 Mar. 1791 Pennsylvania governor Thomas Mifflin offered a thousand-dollar reward for the capture of the perpetrators, and on 23 April, after discovering that Brady and McGuire had fled to Virginia, applied to Gov. Beverley Randolph for their extradition (*Pa. Archives,* 9 ser., 1 [pt. 1], 57, 89).

6. For the administration's attempts to attach Cornplanter and his Seneca to the interest of the United States, see Knox to GW, 27 Dec. 1790, and GW to the Seneca Chiefs, 29 Dec. 1790 and note 5. For Cornplanter's difficulties with the western Indians, see Knox to GW, 10 April 1791.

7. For background to Col. Thomas Proctor's (Procter's) mission, see Knox to GW, 27 Dec. 1790, n.4, 13 Mar. 1791, and GW to the Miami Indians, 11 Mar. 1791, source note. Copies of Knox's instructions, which required Proctor to return to Fort Washington on the Ohio River by 5 May 1791, and of Proctor's reports are in *ASP, Indian Affairs,* 1:145–46, 148–65. Proctor left Philadelphia with an aide, Capt. Michael Gabriel Houdin, on 12 Mar. 1791 and in late April reached the village of the Seneca chiefs, Farmer's Brother and Red Jacket, at Buffalo Creek, six miles from Fort Erie and thirty-five miles from Fort Niagara, both at that time still occupied by British troops. The council at Buffalo Creek lasted from 27 April to 21 May. When the British commandant at Niagara refused Proctor permission to hire a trading vessel to transport him and accompanying headmen to Sandusky and Fort Washington for a council with the Miami and Wabash, he abandoned his mission, sent dispatches to Knox on 21 May, and left for Fort Franklin. He reached Pittsburgh soon after, set out from there on 29 May, and reached Philadelphia in the afternoon of 7 June (see Knox to GW, 8 June 1791 and note 1; ibid., 156–62).

8. For reference to Brig. Gen. Charles Scott's expedition of the Kentucky militia against the Ouiatanon (Wea) villages on the Wabash River, authorized by GW in Knox's instructions of 9 Mar. 1791 to Scott, see Knox to GW, 22 Feb. 1791 and note 8. Scheduled to commence its march on 10 May 1791, Scott's force did not cross the Ohio until 23 May, but this was before Proctor's dispatches could have reached St. Clair and long before Knox's 9 June orders

giving Scott and his men "free scope" could have arrived at Fort Washington (Knox to St. Clair, 9 June 1791, *ASP, Indian Affairs*, 1:177; Guthman, *March to Massacre*, 202–3).

9. For background to Timothy Pickering's second mission to the Seneca, see Knox to GW, 10 April 1791. Knox's instructions of 2 May 1791 to Pickering are in *ASP, Indian Affairs*, 1:165–66.

To the Inhabitants of Salisbury, North Carolina

Gentlemen,   [Salisbury, N.C., c.30 May 1791]
Your expressions of satisfaction on my arrival in Salisbury are received with pleasure, and thanked with sincerity.

The interest, which you are pleased to take in my personal welfare, excites a sensibility proportioned to your goodness— While I make the most grateful acknowledgement for that goodness, allow me to observe that your own determination, co-operating with that of your fellow-citizens throughout the Union, to maintain and to perpetuate the federal-government, affords a better assurance of order and effective government, with their concomitants, private and public prosperity, than the best meant endeavors of any individual could give.

Our national glory, and our domestic tranquillity, can never be tarnished or disturbed, while they are guarded by wise laws, founded-in public virtue among the measures which an enlightened and patriotic Legislature will pursue to preserve them. I doubt not the means of diffusing useful information will be duly considered.[1]

My best wishes for the prosperity of your Village, and for your individual happiness are sincerely offered.

Go: Washington

DS, NcSal; LB, DLC:GW. The editors are grateful to Kevin Cherry at the Rowan Public Library, Salisbury, N.C., for sharing his research on this document.

1. For GW's arrival at Salisbury, N.C., in the morning of 30 May 1791, see *Diaries*, 6:150–51. Before noon he met with John Steele, Spruce Macay (McCay, McCoy, McKay, McKoy), Maxwell Chambers, and other Salisbury gentlemen, who presented GW with this address, signed by Macay, Chambers, Steele, Montfort Stokes, Charles Harris, and Lewis Beard: "We have the honour to signify to you, the joy, which your presence, after a tedious journey undertaken at an advanced period of life, affords to the inhabitants of this place: Words are wanting to express our gratitude to heaven for continuing

your life, on which our national glory, and domestic tranquility, are even at this day, depending. Situated at a remote distance from the seat of government; deriving no advantage from the establishment of post-roads, and destitute of regular information, we are sometimes at a loss to form proper opinions of national measures: But we, nevertheless, boast, that we have been and still are zealously attached to order and effective government. And having been ranked with those who have suffered in the late war we pledge ourselves to be among the foremost to maintain and perpetuate the Foederal Government. That your life, justly dear to the people of this Country, a life precious to freedom, an ornament to human nature, and a blessing to the United States of America, may long be preserved, is the fervent and unanimous prayer of the people of this village" (DLC:GW).

To the United Brethren of Wachovia, North Carolina

Gentlemen,   [Salem, N.C., 1 June 1791]

I am greatly indebted to your respectful and affectionate expressions of personal regard, and I am not less obliged by the patriotic sentiments contained in your address.[1]

From a Society, whose governing principles are industry and the love of order, much may be expected towards the improvement and prosperity of the country, in which their settlements are formed—and experience authorises the belief that much will be obtained.

Thanking you with grateful sincerity for your prayers in my behalf, I desire to assure you of my best wishes for your social and individual happiness.

Go: Washington

LS, NcWsM; LB, DLC:GW.

In August 1753 the Unitas Fratrum (Unity of the Brethren), or Moravians, purchased 98,000 acres on Muddy Creek in Rowan County, N.C., and named the tract Wachovia. Moravians from Pennsylvania founded the towns of Bethania and Salem there a few years later. GW on 31 May described the latter as "a small but neat Village; & like all the rest of the Moravian settlements, is governed by an excellent police—having within itself all kinds of artizans. The number of Souls does not exceed 200" (*Diaries*, 6:152). See also Johanna Miller Lewis, *Artisans in the North Carolina Backcountry* [Lexington, Ky., 1995], 35, 88–89). For GW's arrival and activities at Salem, see *Diaries*, 6:152–54, and Fries, *Records of the Moravians in North Carolina*, 2324–25. Samuel Gottlieb Kramsch, a schoolteacher at Salem, wrote Abraham Steiner of Bethabara, N.C., on 1 June: "our illustrious President . . . will go from here to the Battle Ground of Guilford to morrow morning. . . . This forenoon he visited the publik build-dings and came also in my school. We had just english reading School out of Noah Websters' American Spelling book and as one boy was called up for reading it happened that he read the following words: 'A cat may look on a King,['] whereupon he said to me, that, they think it now also. This day abt 2 o clok he received our humble Adress and gave an excellent answer" (NcWsM).

1. "The humble Address of the United Brethren in Wachovia" was dated Salem, 31 May, and signed by Wachovia *oeconomus* (chief administrator) Frederic William Marshall (1721–1802), Salem minister John Daniel Koehler, and Marshall's assistant, Christian Ludwig Benzien (1753–1811): "Happy in sharing the Honour of a Visit from the Illustrious President of the Union to the Southern States, the United Brethren in Wachovia humbly beg Leave upon this joyfull Occasion to express their highest Esteem Duty and Affection for the great Patriot of this Country. Deeply impressed as we are with Gratitude to the great Author of our Being for his unbounded Mercies, we cannot but particularly acknowledge his gracious Providence over the temporal & political Prosperity of the Country, in the Peace whereof we do find Peace, and wherein none can take a warmer Interest than ourselves, in particular when we consider that the same Lord who preserved Your precious Person in so many imminent Dangers, has made you in a conspicuous Manner an Instrument in his Hands to forward that happy Constitution, together with those Improvements, whereby our United States begin to flourish, over which you preside with the Applause of a thankfull Nation. Whenever therefore we sollicit the Protection of the Father of all Mercies over this favoured Country, we can not but fervently implore his Kindness for Your Preservation, which is so intimately connected therewith. May this gracious LORD vouchsafe to prolong your valuable Life as a further Blessing and an Ornament of the Constitution, that by your worthy Example the Regard for Religion be encreased, and the Improvements of Civil Society encouraged. The Settlements of the United Brethren though small, will allways make it their Study to contribute as much as in them layeth, to the Peace and Improvement of the United States and all the particular Parts, they live in; joining their ardent Prayers to the best Wishes of this whole Continent, that Your Personal as well as Domestic Happiness may abound, and a Series of Success may crown Your Labours for the Prosperity of our Times and an Example to future Ages, untill the glorious Reward of a faithfull Servant shall be your Portion" (DLC:GW). Marshall entered one copy of the address into the official church records (NcWsM) and sent another, with GW's reply, to Gov. Alexander Martin, who forwarded it to state printers Abraham Hodge and Henry Wills at Edenton for publication in the *State Gazette of North-Carolina* (Fries, *Records of the Moravians in North Carolina*, 2340, 2342, 2404).

From Henry Emanuel Lutterloh

Sir! Fayetteville [N.C.] June 3th 1791
On the 8th of Aprill 1787, You honoured me, with an Answer, upon my Proposition, to bring several German family's, into the

State of Virginia—You was pleased to Mention the Dismal Swamp Company; and that you would convene them together to make my Proposalls &c. I took the Liberty to state My Reasons in My Answer of the 15th of May following why I could not come there.[1]

Since that time, I have Obtained from this assembly the inclosed Grand—and a Lottery for five Succeding Years—to Support, and to carry My Importation Plan into Effect.[2]

I feel myself exceedingly happy, to be able Thro' this Grand, to offer my Service again, to Supply You, those few Mechanicks, which you were pleased to order: I wish to Know what Sort of Workman, You wante; and in which Ports, they should be delivered in Virginia.

The dismal Swamp Canal Company—is to finish The Canal, in which this state has joined—Therefore I wish to offer my Service to Them—and most humbly beg to honour me with, a recomendation That I may make my Proposalls, of my present plans. I Know by information from Europe; That I can procure any Number, of good Manufactoring, and Labouring Germans.

My Plan at present is not to receive any Cash in advance. but when the people arrived, to be paid in Produce.

if it was necessary and I received the order, I would come to Meet the Gentlemen of the Company—My being at Hilsborough with the Governor and Counsell to receive the inclosed Grand, prevented me, to show my respectfull attandance at Wilmington to assure in person, my profoundest respects in which, I have the honour to be. Sir, Your Most obedient and Most humble Servant

Henry, Emanuel Lutterloh.

ALS, DNA: RG 59, Miscellaneous Letters.

For background to this letter, see Henry Emanuel Lutterloh to GW, 3 Jan. 1787, John Page to GW, 9 Mar. 1787, and GW to Lutterloh, 8 April 1787 and 1 Jan. 1789 and source note.

1. No 15 May 1787 or 1788 letter to GW has been found, but Lutterloh might have been referring to his letter of 13 June 1787.

2. In November and December 1790 the North Carolina legislature passed "An Act to authorize Henry Emanuel Lutterloh to raise by way of Lottery a sum sufficient to enable him to bring into this State foreigners who are Artisans in various Branches of Business," which authorized him to raise by lottery up to $6,000 a year for five years, provided he lay before the governor and council within a year "the plan and scheme of the said lottery upon which the Gover-

nor is required to issue unto . . . Lutterloh a license under the Great Seal of the State authorizing him to carry into effect the plan and scheme of the lottery aforesaid." As soon as Lutterloh complied with that requirement the governor was to issue to him under the state seal another grant or patent "in which shall be comprehended the meaning of this Act" (*N.C. State Records*, 21:802, 826, 831–32, 899, 969, 970, 994, 997, 1000, 25:94–95). The enclosed copy of this c.24–26 April 1791 grant has not been found.

From Thomas Jefferson

Sir   Bennington [Vt.] June 5. 1791.

In my last letter from Philadelphia, I mentioned that mister Madison & myself were about to take a trip up the North river as far as circumstances should permit. the levelness of the roads led us quite on to Lake George, where taking boat we went through that, and about 25 miles into Lake Champlain. returning then to Saratoga, we concluded to cross over thro' Vermont to Connecticut river and go down that instead of the North river which we had already seen, and we are so far on that rout. in the course of our journey we have had opportunities of visiting Still water, Saratoga, Forts Wm Henry & George, Ticonderoga, Crown point, & the scene of Genl Starke's victory.[1]

I have availed myself of such opportunities as occurred to enquire into the grounds of the report that something disagreeable had taken place in the vicinities of the British posts. it seems to have been the following incident. they had held a small post at a blockhouse on the North Hero, an island on the Vermont side of Lake Champlain, & something further South than their principal post at the Point au fer. the Maria, hitherto stationed at the latter, for Custom-house purposes, was sent to the Block-house, & there exercised her usual visits on boats passing to & from Canada. this being an exercise of power further within our jurisdiction became the subject of notice & clamour with our citizens in that quarter. the vessel has been since recalled to the Point au fer, & being unfit for service, a new one is to be built to perform her functions. this she has usually done at the Point au fer with a good deal of rigour, bringing all vessels to at that place, & sometimes under such circumstances of wind & weather as to have occasioned the loss of two vessels & cargoes. these circumstances produce strong sensations in that quarter, &

not friendly to the character of our government. the establishment of a custom-house at Alburg, nearly opposite to Point au fer, has given the British considerable alarm. a groundless story of 200 Americans seen in arms near Point au fer, has been the cause, or the pretext, of their reinforcing that place a few days ago with a company of men from St John's. it is said here they have called in their guard from the Block-house, but the information is not direct enough to command entire belief.[2]

On enquiring into the dispositions in Canada on the subject of the projected form of government there, we learn, that they are divided into two parties; the English who desire something like an English constitution but so modelled as to oblige the French to chuse a certain proportion of English representatives, & the French who wish a continuance of the French laws, moderated by some engraftments from the English code. the judge of their Common pleas heads the former party, & Smith the chief justice secretly guides the latter.[3]

We encounter the Green mountains tomorrow, with cavalry in part disabled, so as to render our progress a little incertain. I presume however I shall be in Philadelphia in a fortnight. I have the honour to be with sentiments of the most perfect respect & attachment, Sir, your most obedient & most humble servant

Th: Jefferson

ALS, DNA: RG 59, Miscellaneous Letters; ALS (letterpress copy), DLC: Thomas Jefferson Papers; LB, DLC: Jefferson Papers; LB, DLC:GW.

1. Jefferson wrote a more descriptive travel account to his son-in-law from Bennington on this day (see Jefferson to Thomas Mann Randolph, Jr., 5 June, *Jefferson Papers*, 20:464–66). His "last letter" to GW was dated 15 May.

2. Two posts retained by the British after the Revolutionary War were located on northern Lake Champlain below the Canadian border of 45° latitude: at Point au Fer, five miles south of the border on New York territory, and at Dutchman's Point on North Hero Island, twelve miles within Vermont territory. Dealing with complaints about the activities of their garrisons, of which Gov. George Clinton of New York informed GW on 21 May 1790, became a federal responsibility after Vermont joined the Union on 18 Feb. 1791. The "Act giving effect to the laws of the United States within the state of Vermont" of 2 Mar. 1791 designated Alburg, an unincorporated settlement of 446 people on disputed territory one-half mile north of Dutchman's Point, as the only port of entry for the new federal customs district of Vermont (see GW to the U.S. Senate and House of Representatives, 9 Feb. 1791, source note, and 1 *Stat.* 191, 197–98). See also George Beckwith's report of 14 June enclosed in Lord Dorchester's letter of 27 July to Lord Grenville, Brymner, *Report on Canadian*

Archives, 1890, 171. GW appointed Stephen Keyes collector for the port of Alburg on 4 Mar. (GW to the U.S. Senate, 4 Mar. 1791 [first letter] and note 3), and Keyes immediately informed the British commander at Point au Fer of his appointment (Dorchester to Lieutenant Colonel Buckeridge, 16 May, Brymner, *Report on Canadian Archives, 1890,* Q. 50–1, pp. 288–89). Alexander Hamilton told Beckwith on 15 June that Keyes was "one of those busy characters, who are anxious to shew their own consequence; I have written to him in such terms, as will I trust obviate any sort of inconvenience in the discharge of his duty," adding: "I understand that the place fixed upon by law for the Custom house is at least thirty miles from Pointe au fer" (Syrett, *Hamilton Papers,* 8:475–77). He delayed implementing the provisions of the act of 2 Mar. 1791, and the customshouse was still unbuilt on 22 Aug., when Hamilton requested Keyes to procure a map of northwest Vermont and send a larger-scale sketch of the Alburg area along with his advice on where "the office may be established with the greatest degree of propriety and utility free from the inconveniences of the situation which has been fixed upon" (ibid., 9:91). Keyes two months later forwarded a map to Hamilton by John Doughty, whom Henry Knox had sent to the Champlain border as a secret observer (see Doughty to Knox, 26 Oct., in GW to Clinton, 14 Sept., n.2).

3. On 25 Feb. 1791 the king announced to Parliament that he intended to divide Quebec into the two provinces of Upper and Lower Canada, and on 4 Mar. Prime Minister William Pitt introduced a bill in the House of Commons that created local legislatures in both provinces. For an American newspaper's reports of the news, see *General Advertiser and Political, Commercial and Literary Journal* (Philadelphia), 16, 19 April. The Commons passed the Constitutional Bill on 18 May; it was considered in the House of Lords on 30 May and received the royal assent on 10 June (*Parliamentary History of England,* 28:1271, 1376–79, 29:104–13, 359–430, 655–60). Jefferson had reversed the names and roles of the Canadian party leaders. Scotsman Adam Mabane (c.1734–1792), a judge of the Court of Common Pleas, member of the Council of Quebec, and adviser to Gov. Frederick Haldimand, was recognized as the leader of those who wished to protect the rights of the French majority. Chief Justice William Smith (1728–1793), a Yale College graduate and the Loyalist chief justice of New York who left New York City with Sir Guy Carleton in 1783 and went with him to Canada, became the chief opponent of Mabane and the French party.

From Tobias Lear

Sir, Philadelphia June 5th 1791

Since I had the honor of writing to you on the 29 of last month, the two Platteaux, which Mr G. Morris sent from France, have arrived. One of them has received a slight fracture in the corner; but it has injured it very little.[1]

In my letter of the 22d of may I mentioned that Hercules was to go on to Mount Vernon a few days after that. When he was about to go, somebody, I presume, insinuated to him that the motive for sending him home so long before you was expected there, was to prevent his taking the advantage of a six month's residence in this place. When he was possessed of this idea he appeared to be extremely unhappy—and altho' he made not the least objection to going; yet, he said he was mortified to the last degree to think that a suspicion could be entertained of his fidelity or attachment to you. and so much did the poor fellow's feelings appear to be touched that it left no doubt of his sincerity—and to shew him that there were no apprehensions of that kind entertained of him, Mrs Washington told him he should not go at that time; but might remain 'till the expiration of six months and then go home—to prepare for your arrival there. He has accordingly continued here 'till this time, and tomorrow takes his departure for Virginia.[2]

The Gentleman to whom you sold your Kanawa Lands is now in this place, and told me yesterday that he had purchased a Seat called Springsbury situated between Bush Hill & Mr Morris' farm—and from another quarter I was informed he was to give eight thousand pounds for it with about 65 acres of land. This looks as if there was some confidence placed in him, and is a virtual contradiction of some accounts which I had the honor to transmit to you. He tells me it is his intention to build pretty extensively upon that place, in order to receive & accommodate such French Gentlemen as may come over here with their families to settle in the Western County (of whom he says he expects a considerable number this summer) until the Gentlemen can go out into that Country with their settlers & make such accommodations for their Ladies & children as will prevent those severe inconveniencies which have already been felt by some who have carried their families into the wilderness without having any previous accommodations made for them. He further says that for several years hence he shall find it necessary for him to be nearly half the time in this part of the Country in order to fecilitate the arrangements which he shall make for his settlements, and that this is another cause for becoming a purchaser here. I hope too many plans may not prove injurious to him.[3]

In a vessel which arrived from Havre de Grace last week was

a quantity of wine which Mr Jefferson had ordered for your use & his own. But as he is still out of town it cannot be divided till his return which is expected the latter part of this week.[4]

We have lately experienced a spell of excessive hot weather for the season. The Thermomiter stood for 5 days between 87 & 90 degrees. Since that time we have been favored with abundant & refreshing showers which have cheered the heart of the farmer and braced up the relaxed frame of the citizen. The prospect of Crops is very pleasing hereabouts. In Jersey the Hessian fly is said again to have made its ravages in the wheat.

On the 1st Instant, at the request of the Secretary of the Treasury, I delivered to him Commissions filled up with the following persons—viz.

Drury Ragsdale, as Inspector of the Revenue for Survey No. 1 in the district of Virginia.

Edward Stevans, as ditto for Survey No. 2. in do.

Mayo Carrington, as ditto for Survey No. 3. in do.

Thomas Newton, as ditto for Survey No. 4. in do.

Edward Smith, as ditto for Survey No. 5. in do.

James Brackenridge, as Inspector for Survey No. 6 in ditto.[5]

As the Secretary of State was absent when the seal of the United States was affixed to these Commissions they were not countersigned by him as is customary. This, however, does not make them less valid.

Mrs Lear Joins me in sentiments of respect & gratitude for you & sincere prayers for the preservation of your health—and a continuation of your happiness.

Mr Dandridge arrived here yesterday and is this day to be inoculated for the small pox, as a person who has not had it would be unsafe in this City for a single day.[6] With the highest respect & most sincere attachment I have the honor to be Sir, Your obliged & grateful servt

Tobias Lear.

ALS, DLC:GW; ALS (letterpress copy), PWacD.

1. Gouverneur Morris purchased the two plated table furnishings for GW in Paris and sent them to Robert Morris on 19 Nov. 1790 for delivery (see GW to Gouverneur Morris, 1 Mar., 15 April 1790, and Gouverneur Morris to GW, 22 Nov. 1790, n.1). Tobias Lear paid the duty of $2.66 on them on 30 May 1791 (Decatur, *Private Affairs of George Washington*, 238).

2. Lear purchased two new shirts for Herculas on 3 June and gave him at

least $7.20 the next day to cover the costs of his stage ride from Philadelphia to Baltimore, his passage from Baltimore to Alexandria, and any other expenses he might incur before reaching Mount Vernon (ibid., 239).

3. John Joseph de Barth, to whom GW sold his Kanawha lands (see GW to George Clendenin, 21 Mar. 1791), also purchased Springsbury (Springettsbury) near the Schuylkill River just northwest of Philadelphia to house temporarily French settlers for the Scioto company (see Louis Le Bègue de Presle Duportail to GW, 10 Feb., source note). One of the Penn family's original manors, it was subdivided and sold in the early 1700s, except for the main portion retained by Thomas Penn until the mid-eighteenth century, when he sold off most of it. After the manor house, which was the temporary country home of Robert Morris in 1779 and 1780, burned in 1784, its overgrown gardens and ruins were a popular setting for pastoral outings of the elite, including GW (see *Diaries*, 5:172, and Watson, *Annals of Philadelphia*, 2:478–80). De Barth and GW agreed to void their Kanawha deal in 1793, and GW later leased the land to James Welch of Greenbrier County (see GW to de Barth, 30 April 1793, Welch to GW, 24, 29 Nov., 9 Dec. 1797, GW to Welch, 1, 7 Dec. 1797, and to James Keith, 10 Dec. 1797).

4. In mid-1790, after GW discussed with Thomas Jefferson the possibility of acquiring French wines for the presidential household, that noted connoisseur arranged through William Short to purchase the wine from the best French vineyards (see Jefferson to Short, 12 Aug., 6 Sept., and to Joseph Fenwick, 6 Sept. 1790, *Jefferson Papers*, 17:342, 493–94, 496–97) and have it transported and safely stored before the heat of summer. On 16 June Jefferson's secretary informed him that four unopened baskets and four boxes had arrived from France, and, presuming that they contained the wine, he placed them in Jefferson's cellar. Henry Remsen, Jr., also wrote in the same letter that Lear had taken charge of the president's wine and that fourteen more cases had arrived from Charleston (ibid., 20:555–56). For further correspondence about GW's wine, see Lear to GW, 12, 23 June.

5. After receiving instructions from GW and information from Virginia district supervisor Edward Carrington, Alexander Hamilton requested Lear on 1 June to fill out these commissions and send them to the Treasury Department "as speedily as may be." Lear complied the same day (Hamilton to Lear, 1 June, and Lear to Hamilton, 1 June, DLC:GW).

6. Bartholomew Dandridge, Jr. (c.1772–1802), was the son of Martha Washington's brother, who had died in 1785. Upon his arrival at Philadelphia, probably from his mother's in New Kent County, Va., his aunt commented, "Batt Dandridge arrived hear yesterday he is as yellow as a mulato,—he is inoculated this day for the small pox" (Martha Washington to Fanny Bassett Washington, 5 June, Fields, *Papers of Martha Washington*, 231–32). The following autumn his older brother wrote Martha: "Bart is very well pleased with his situation I find by his letters, & I hope he will endeavor to please every body he acts for—I trust you will exercise your authority as a relation as well as your advisor to inforce on him a proper sense of his Duty, & to guard him from being led astray by the temptation to idleness & extravagance which surround him" (John Dandridge to Martha Washington, 6 Sept., ibid., 234–35).

It is unknown exactly when Dandridge joined GW's household. Lear wrote David Humphreys on 8 April 1793: "Major Jackson left the family about 11 months ago—since which a Nephew of Mrs Washington's (Mr Bartholomew Dandridge) . . . joined us . . . [he] is a young Gentleman of an excellent mind—strong natural parts, tho' but little acquainted with the world—his education has been very limited, but his talent for improvement is great and his industry equal to it—he will make a valuable & useful man—he is about 21 years of age" (PPRF). Dandridge did much of the Philadelphia household's shopping, acted as GW's traveling secretary during his return to Mount Vernon in September and October 1791, apparently replaced William Jackson, and eventually filled Lear's shoes after Lear left the president's service in 1793 (Decatur, *Private Affairs of George Washington,* 241, 253). After GW's retirement Dandridge became secretary to William Vans Murray, American minister to the Hague, served as secretary to the legation at the Court of St. James under Rufus King, and ended his life and career as an American consul in Saint Domingue (see ibid., 326–27, and *Diaries,* 6:236n).

From Pierce Butler

Dear Sir   Charleston [S.C.] June the 6th 1791

soon after Your departure I received the inclosed letter from Genoa[1]—it came under Cover of one to me that I send with it—If You shall at any time hereafter think proper to Nominate a Consul at Genoa I believe the person in question as elligible as any foreigner to be got. He is very strongly recommended to me by the first Banker in that City; and by other respectable persons.

I beg leave to mention to You, that I had early in the second Session of Congress wrote to Itally and Holland for information on the subject of public Loans to the United States; to those letters I have only now received explicit answers; from these I have the fullest Conviction that Loans may be obtained for the United States on more Advantageous terms than are proposed by the Commissners in Holland to Mr Short; and which they by letter inform me that He has agreed to. I mention this for Your own information only—not wishing to have my Name spoken of in this business, because it woud in future prevent the Commissioners in Holland from Communicating to me as freely as they do at present, the State of Money transactions there—When I have the honor of seeing You I will shew You the proposals made to me from a Quarter that admits of no doubt.

I hope Sir You get well Home and feel no inconvenience from

Your Journey.[2] I have the honor to be, with great respect and sincere Attachment—Dear sir Yr Most Obedt humble servant

P. Butler.

ALS, DNA: RG 59, Miscellaneous Letters; LB, ScU.

1. GW dined at the Charleston residence of U.S. Senator Pierce Butler three days before leaving the city on 9 May 1791. The enclosure was Genoese merchant Gaetano Drago de Domenico's letter of 24 Dec. 1790 to GW. Domenico's cover letter of 24 Dec. 1790 to "the Honorable Peter Buttler Philadelphia" notes that he has renounced for the present his hopes of being appointed American consul at Genoa after hearing from a friend in Amsterdam that "Congress reserves itself to think on this point" and concludes: "Inclosed I take the liberty to remit you a few Lines for the Venerable President Washington: I leave the thought to your Wisdom to make use of them Should you think it proper, & not forsee too much boldness in this step of mine: to you I hold myself reccommended, & I dare say if you will allow me your benevolence, it will be at every time Justify'd & acknowledged by my proceedings (DNA: RG 59, Miscellaneous Letters).

2. GW gave this letter and its enclosures to Thomas Jefferson, who docketed the former: "not answered."

From Henry Knox

Sir,   War Department [Philadelphia], June 6th 1791.

On the 30th of the last month I had the honor to submit to you, a general view of the Affairs in my department—Nothing material has occurred since.

The frontiers seem to be quiet—Major General Butler in a letter dated at Fort Pitt, on the 22d ultimo says "that a boat has this day arrived up the river in 22 days from Fort Washington without seeing one Savage or meeting the least molestation on the passage."[1]

Mr Brown in a letter dated at Danville on the 26th of April says, "the plan of the expedition meets with universal approbation throughout the district, and the proposed number of Volunteers are already engaged. The board will again meet at this place on the 2d of May, to appoint and commission Officers, and to make final arrangements for putting the army in motion— General Scott will take the command, and unless countermanded will be in readiness to march upon the 12th or 15th of May—Doctor O'Fallon's schemes have all blown up, not *one* man will join him from this Country."[2]

I have heard nothing from or of Colonel Procter since the 8th of April, as mentioned in my former letter.

I am apprehensive that his delay may interfere with, and retard General Scott's expedition. But I hope that General St Clair will not permit it to be suspended too long.

The recruiting service still continues to languish in the eastern States—But in the States from Connecticut westward, recruits are obtained in greater numbers—from this State eastward, about Two hundred and fifty regulars are recruited, and additions are daily making to the number. Those in this City, will march in day or two, and those in New Jersey, about one hundred, will march next week—Those more east are ordered to move forward as fast as a company shall be collected at any rendezvous.

The upper battalion of the Levies of this State are nearly completed according to General Butler's account—The number of Fifteen hundred at least, which I mentioned in my last will in all probability be marched in the course of the present month—This number is exclusively of those recruits who marched during the months of April and May—I have the honor to be Sir With perfect Respect Your most Obedt hume servt

H. Knox
secy of War

LS, DLC:GW; LB, DLC:GW.

1. Richard Butler's letter of 22 May, which arrived at the War Department while Henry Knox was absent for several days, was acknowledged on 2 June by chief clerk John Stagg, Jr. (*ASP, Indian Affairs*, 1:187). A copy of it probably was forwarded to Congress and examined with other correspondence by the House committee on the causes of the failure of Arthur St. Clair's expedition (see Thomas FitzSimon's report, 8 May 1792, *ASP, Military Affairs*, 1:36).

2. The letter, probably from John Brown, a member of the Kentucky District's board of war who accompanied Brig. Gen. Charles Scott's militia expedition against the Ouiatanon (Wea) Indians on the Wabash River, has not been further identified. For background to the schemes of Dr. James O'Fallon, see Knox to GW, 22 Jan., n.4, Thomas Jefferson and Edmund Randolph to GW, 14 Feb. and source note, and GW's Proclamation of 19 Mar. 1791. Knox's instructions of 21 Mar. to St. Clair noted: "The conduct of the said Doctor O'Fallon is considered of such a nature as that the attorney of the district of Kentucky has been directed to commence a prosecution against him, . . . and, in order that all concerned under him should be warned of their situation, the President of the United States has issued another proclamation, which is hereunto annexed. . . . It is presumed that the arrest of Doctor O'Fallon, and

the issuing of the proclamation, will operate to prevent the execution thereof; but, if they should not, and the party proceed in the execution of their plan, it becomes an important consideration whether the military shall interfere to prevent them. This point is now under consideration of the legal department, and you shall be informed of the result" (*ASP, Indian Affairs,* 1:172–73). On 15 Aug. Tobias Lear returned to Jefferson a letter concerning O'Fallon that the federal district attorney for Kentucky had written to Jefferson on 12 May (DNA: RG 59, Miscellaneous Letters). See also William Murray to Jefferson, 12 May, *Jefferson Papers,* 20:395–97.

From Lafayette

My dear General   Paris june the 6th 1791
    I Most Heartly thank You for Your letter dated March the 19th, the more welcome to me, as I Had long lamented Your Silence, and was panting for News from You, My dear General, wherein I Could Be informed of every thing Respecting Your public and private Concerns—I Rejoice and Glory in the Happy Situation of American Affairs—I Bless the Restoration of Your Health, and wish I Could Congratulate You on Your Side of the Atlantick—But we are not in that State of tranquillity which may Admit of My absence—the Refugees Hovering about the fronteers—intrigues in most of the despotic and Aristocratic Cabinets—our Regular Army divided into tory officers, and Undisciplined Soldiers—licentiousness Among the people Not easily Repressed—the Capital that Gives the tone to the Empire tossed about By AntiRevolutionary or factious parties—the Assembly fatigued By Hard labour, and very unmanageable—the priests that Have taken the Oath, and those who Have not playing the devil. However, According to our popular Motto, *Cà ira,* it will do—we are introducing as fast as we can Relligious liberty— The Assembly Has put an end to Her existence By a New Convocation, Has Unfitted Her own Members for Immediate Rëelection, or placed in the Executive—and is Now Reducing the Constitution to a few Principal Articles, leaving to the legislative Assemblies to Examine and mend the others, and Preparing Every thing for a Convention, as soon as our Machine will Have Had a fair trial[1]—I stand the Continual Check to all interior factions, and plots—By the Enclosed speech of mine, and the Giving up my Commission I Gave a spring to the power of law

over licentiousness, and was I equally supported in Repressing it, as I would be Against Aristocratic exertions the people would soon Be Brought to a proper sense of liberty[2]—as to the Surrounding Governements they Hate our Revolution, But don't know How to Meddle with it, so Affraïd they are to *Catch the plague*—we are Going to take Measures to discipline the Army, Both officers and soldiers—They will prepare to encamp and leave the Cities—Their Generals will Have the same power as in time of war—M. de Condé and His party will be summoned to explain themselves, and if they Continue Cabaling and enlisting declared traitors—to M. de ternant I defer for more particulars.[3]

M. jefferson and Myself Had long thought that ternant was a very proper man to act as french Minister in America—He In a Great measure Belongs to Both Countries—He is Sensible, Honest, well informed, and Has a plain and decisive way of doing Bussiness which will be very Convenient—He Has long Been an officer Under Your Commands—feeling and acting in an American Capacity—He is personnally Much At'ached to you, and I Had in this Revolution many instances to Experience His friendship to me—He might Have Been a Minister in the Council, But was Rather Backward on the occasion, and Beháved like a prudent, not an Ambitious Man—so that I take Him to be fit to Answer Your purpose.

He will let you know what Has Past in the Assembly Respecting American affairs—the last transactions are an Undoubted proof of their Sentiments, and Show that their faux pas in the Regulation of duties are to Be Attributed to want of knowledge Or Sense, not of friendship—they Have Considered me as an American, who did only mind American profit, and did not know matters so well as a few mercantile men, Most of them on the Aristocratic Side of the House, who Presented foolish Calculations—and you know the difficulty to unmake our decrees But You May depend on this point, that Brotherly Measures to Unite the two Nations with the ties of Most intimate affection, of Common principles, and Common interest will Be Most Heartly Received in france, and on that Ground You may work Your plan, and Send it to france, with a private Copy for me. The United States and france Must Be one people, and so Begin the Confederation of all Nations who will assert their own Rights.

I Have, in the affair of the Black free men, Voted according to my Conscience, not to policy—Should the British take Advantage of My Honesty, I Hope You will influence the Colonies to Submit to a decre so Conformant to justice.[4]

M. Short who does the Business of the United States with all the zeal and ingenuity of a most patriotic and most Sensible man—who is Respected and loved in france in a manner equally useful to the public and Honourable to Himself Has writen to M. jefferson Respecting New orleans—france will do every thing in Her power to Bring Spain to Reason. But will Have a difficult, and probably Unsuccessful task—upon the whole that Navigation we must Have, and in Case the people of louïsiana wish to make a fifteenth State, who devil Can Help it, and who ought, Spaniards excepted, not Rejoice at it—Certainly I should'nt Be a Mourner.[5]

My Best Respects to Mrs Washington—My Compliments to the family—to my dear aid George and His family—Most Respectfully and Affectionately My Beloved General, Your filial friend[6]

Lafayette

ALS, PEL; ADf (in French), Lafayette Papers, La Grange, France, microfilm on deposit at DLC:GW.

1. The National Constituent Assembly reorganized the Catholic church in France with the civil constitution of the clergy of 12 July 1790 and on 27 Nov. 1790 decreed that all priests swear an oath of fidelity to the nation, the law, the king, and the constitution; "refractory" or "non-juring" clergy who refused to take the oath were removed from public office the following spring. The assembly also passed a decree on 16 May 1791 prohibiting reelection of any of its current members to the Legislative Assembly to be created by the new national constitution that had been under consideration since 1789 (*Archives parlementaires,* 26:111). On 8 April 1791 William Short informed Thomas Jefferson that he did not think the assembly would end soon or voluntarily: "first because I am persuaded that a large majority wish to remain as long as possible, and secondly because I think that movements abroad or disorders at home, the one arising from the imprudence and folly of the Refugees and the other from an habitual state of anarchy, will furnish the pretext of their remaining" (*Jefferson Papers,* 20:170–74). The Constituent Assembly did not complete work on the first French constitution until 3 September.

2. On 25 April Short also sent Jefferson a copy of Lafayette's speech of 22 April and described the events that precipitated it (*Jefferson Papers,* 20:256–62). The speech is printed in Lafayette, *Mémoires,* 3:67–69.

3. Louis-Joseph de Bourbon, prince de Condé (1736–1818), immigrated to Turin in 1789 after having served in the Assembly of Notables and by February

1791 had assumed leadership of the émigrés. He established himself at Worms and organized an army that he led against French Revolutionary forces from 1792 to 1796. The National Assembly passed a decree on 11 June 1791 ordering him to return to France (*Archives parlementaires,* 27:130–31), and Short reported to Jefferson on 29 June that "the person sent by the King to the Prince de Condé with the decree of the assembly injoining his return, writes that he was at Worms the 22d., that he had been well recieved, and was to follow the Prince to Coblentz where he is to have his answer" (*Jefferson Papers,* 20:584–88).

4. Lafayette had earlier written to GW about his purchase of a plantation in the French colony of Cayenne on which he intended to free the slaves and have them work the land as tenant farmers. See Lafayette to GW, 14 July 1785 and note 3, and 6 Feb. 1786). On 11 May he spoke in the National Assembly in support of extending civil rights to free black men in the French colonies. The motion of 15 May, for which Lafayette voted, however, named only the sons of free blacks as *citoyens actifs* (*Gazette Nationale ou le Moniteur Universel* [Paris], 13 May, and *Archives parlementaires,* 25:753).

5. For background to Lafayette's involvement in the administration's attempts to enlist French assistance in achieving American foreign policy objectives with Spain, see Jefferson to GW, 8 Aug. 1790, source note and note 6, 18 Mar. 1791, and Jefferson to Short, 12 Mar. 1791, *Jefferson Papers,* 19:527–28. Short's dispatch to Jefferson regarding New Orleans was written this day (ibid., 20:528–37).

6. GW replied on 10 September.

From William Stephens Smith

Sir   New York June 6 1791

It becomes my duty to state to the President, that when I visited England the last winter, I noticed a very great change in the Public opinion, relative to the situation of affairs of my country, since I had the honor of residing their in a Public capacity, and in every company found the subject dwelt on in a flattering manner, except in one or two cases—when Merchants who had experienced injury from & obliquely reflecting on the subject of Legislative interference between the creditor and debtor—but even on this point I found them attentive, while not unsucsesfully I endeavoured to palliate the circumstances, and relieve the general government of my Country from the operation of opinions too hastily formed as to *their* countenancing such arrangements, or having any agency in their existance or operation. Without entering too minutely into a detail of those conversations, I shall take the Liberty of presenting Copies of such

Letters and notes as passed between me and several respectable Gentlemen, on subjects which may not be uninteresting; I shall take the Liberty of accompanying them with such observations only, as may tend to elucidate the objects they had in view and the circumstances which produced them.

It may not be improper here to remark, that I have received more Polite attention as an American, from some of the first characters in England during the Last Winter, than for the whole 3 years of my former public residence—this in some degree tended to lead me into a greater expence than I had Calculated on, considering the real object of my excursion, and greater than I should have wished to have been exposed to as a private gentleman. But having long been in the habits of sacrificing my private fortune to the service of my country, I could not restrain the disposition of carrying it still a little further, particularly as by submitting to it in the Present case, such information might be obtained, as might be serviceable to the President in his public station, and tend to relieve his mind from some uncertainty on those unexplained and apparantly rather jarring points, between America and Great Britain.

In the course of a few weeks after my arrival in London I was very earnestly solicited to wait on the Minister Mr Pitt or Lord Grenville, But this I pointedly declined, upon the principle of my appearing in London, in no other capacity than that of a private Gentleman, pursuing his private affairs, I was told, they had expressed a great desire to see me, and that my visit would be acceptable; I acknowledged myself complimented by this communication, and said, "that neither for my country nor myself, having any objects in view, that would Justify the apparent advance, I considered the step, as being a greater commitment on the part of my country than any private individual had a right to make, and as it related to myself; I wished rather to avoid the observations that such a visit might expose me to, both on the one & the other side of the atlantic; But however I observed, if any of the Gentlemen in the administration of England wished to see me, and they thought proper to communicate in writing that wish, and had been led to suppose that a private individual of that country merited such a mark of their attention—The great respect I entertained of the present administration would not permit me to pass by the communication unnoticed," some considerable time passed, without being marked with any other circumstance than numberless visits and invitations, tending to interrupt my private pursuits in such a manner as to deprive me of the ability of returning in the March packett as I wished. But having perfectly embraced the objects of my visit, I made arrangements to sail in the april packet, agreeably to my communication to the President, in December Last.[1] After I had taken leave of my friends accordingly, Mr Colquhoun a Gentleman at the Head of the manufacturing interests of England,[2] and from whom I had received many marks of friendship and civility, called on me, and said "since I had been in London he had had several interviews with Mr Dundas, and other Gentlemen in administration, who he knew would be disappointed if I left London without their seeing me, that the present convulsed state of European affairs so fully engrossed their attention, that they had frequently lamented that it had not been in their power to pay me those civilities which (they were pleased to say) from various circumstances they thought me entitled to" He then read me a copy of a note which he had sent to Mr Dundas; and haveing requested he would favour me with a copy of it, I have the honor of submitting the perusal of it to the President marked No. 1.[3] I passed that evening being the 5th of April with the Honourable Mr Pultney of Bath House Picadilly, intending it as my last visit previous to my departure, which I had arranged for the next day, that I might be in time for the Packet at falmouth which was to sail on Saturday the 9th our conversation was chiefly political and without entering into a detail of It I shall only say, that I flatter myself that I had constantly in view the honor & dignity of my Country Her attachment to peaceble systems and the reluctance that she would feel at being obliged (from the injustice and cross-grained Politicks of Britain) to take any steps in the vindication of her own honor or the security of her frontiers, which at the present juncture might tend further to embarrass England and perhaps finally force America to throw herself into a Political scale decidedly inimical to the interests of Great Britain, he also, expressed great anxiety on the prospect of my leaveing England previous to the ministers having seen me, and was solicitous that I should postpone my voyge untill the May Packett, and was *so pointedly pressing on the subject, that* I was obliged to say, I would consider of it, and let him know my determination in the morning and took my leave, The enclosed No. 2 is a Copy of what I addressed to him the next morning,[4] and at 3 OClock in the afternoon Mr Pultney paid me a visit, informing me that he had just received a Letter from Lord Grenville one of the Principal Secretaries of state, which he gave me, upon my requesting permission to take a copy of it, he said the original was at my service it is marked No. 3.[5] He then asked me if I could make it convenient to wait on his Lordship at the time mentioned, I told him I most certainly would, As I should think myself unpardonable in not makeing every return in my power to his polite communications at the same time requesting, that his Lordship might perfectly understand that by waiting untill saturday, I should risk the Loss of my passage, unless he should think proper to guard me from this inconvenience by an order to the Post office that the Packet should not leave me, about 5 OClock, I received a note from Mr Pultney containing one from Lord Grenville, marked No. 4[6] I consequently postponed my departure untill saturday, when agreeably to the wish of Lord Grenville, I waited on him at his house at St James.s—Upon being introduced he was pleased to express himself obliged by my attention to his request, made thro' Mr Pultney & said "that he had, had several conversations with that gentleman & others Lately, on the subject of affairs between Great Britain and The United states of America, and that it was his wish not only in his private capacity, but as one of the Ministers of England; and He could assure me, a similar wish pervaded the cabinet that some amicable arrangements might take place between the 2 Countries, if their Mutual interests be examined with a frindly eye, and every point between them, explained and adjusted upon principles equally advantageous—he did not doubt that during the time I had been in England, I had noticed that the national wish fully corresponded with what he then declared to be the disposition of the present Administration, that they viewed with pleasure the rising dignity of America, and was happy to find the foundation so well Laid in a firm, wise, and Liberal Constitution, one that appeared to him, wisely calculated, to promote the happiness of America, and furnish its government with the ability of carrying into effect, any Arrangement that under it, they might consider themselves, authorised to make—that from the communications that had been made to him, since my arrival in England, by some Gentleman who were in habits of intimacy with me, he had early expressed a wish to see me, and was extreamly sorry, that my departure was to be so sudden, and that it had not been in his power to see me sooner, owing to the pressure of the Present Political affairs of Europe, which so engrossed the attention of Ministers that they had scarcely time to think on other subjects, he hoped however, that America nourished equally friendly dispositions towards England, and that some means might be fallen upon at Least to unite them again in the bonds of frindship"— I answered that "his Lordship communication thro' Mr Pultney to a private Citizen of America was so extreamly polite and complimentaray, that it became incumbent on me as a Gentleman, to make the return I then did, by attending his Lordships appointment and acknowledged myself much obliged by the care he was pleased to take in the detention of the Packet—that I should not in consequence of this interview be obliged to wait the sailing of the next—that I could scar[c]ely harbour a thought, that the Ministers of Great Britain had any room to doubt of the friendly dispositions of the United States of America, particularly when they took a retrospective view of the conduct of America at the conclusion of the war, when she came forward by her Ministers, expressing her dispositions to examine and arrange upon liberal Principles all disagreeable points between the two Nations, that her Minister remained at the court of St James.s for 3 years and finally was obliged to return without having fulfilled the objects of his mission and not very favourably impressed with Ideas of the friendly intentions of England, towards the United States—That his Lordship must doubtless recollect, that the ostensible reason on the part of the ministers of England, why the friendly advances on the part of America were not at that time attended to, was, and it was publickly given, 'that they did not conceive the then Government of America sufficiently coercive to carry into effect their engagements,['] this answer at the time did not appear overcharged with delicacy particularly, when other Nations of Europe with Whom America had made engagements did not complain, but found her Government fully competent to carry into effect every arrangement they had made, that under these circumstances America had no other alternative consistant with that dignity of

Character, which it was her intention to support, but to wait untill England by her Minister, inform'd her, that she was satisfied with the Ability, and Honourable intentions of the government & rulers in America to fulfill their engagements, and that she was disposed to enter into an investigation of the affairs of the respective nations, and to make such establishments as might appear consistant with the real interests of each—That I felt no diffidence in declaring as a private Gentleman, somewhat acquainted with the dispositions of my countrymen, that as soon as England should think proper to take this step she would meet with every return of civility from the Government of the United states of America, that could be wished, but that the Ministers of England might not deceive themselves, I seriously thought that no other step could Lead to it, for they could not expect a second advance on the part of America, when the circumstances under which the first was made, and the causes that put a period to it, were fairly considered—" His Lordship Said "they had already determined to send a minister to America that Mr Elliot had been called to proceed to the United States in that Capacity, but a Letter had been received from him within a few days, declining the appointment, from some private reasons, and that ministry, were then in quest of some proper character, one that would be agreeable to the President & Legislature of America, and that as soon as they had fixed upon the Gentleman, no time would be lost in his makeing arrangements for an immediate departure, that he was sorry it was not from this Circumstance in his power to inform me, at what time he might be decidedly expected in America, but that he thought he might with safety say, it would not exceed 2 or 3 months, and observed, that it would be very agreeable if ⟨I⟩ would be so oblidging as to say what kind of Character would be most acceptable in America, and by what means a good understanding might be spedily produced, supposing it probable, that opposition was to be expected from those attached to a french party, who he had been informed were very strong in America"—I answerd, that "his Lordship appearing disposed to enter with great freedom, and with a very flattering degree of Confidence into this Conversation I should without reserve communicate to him my Ideas on the subjects he mentioned, in full Confidence, that they would be received with the same Liberallity and candour, with which they were given, that it was a truth strongly impressed upon my mind, that most of the disagreeable points which had been raised and still existed between the United States of America and Great Britain, proceeded from a total want of Just information, relative to the real situation of affairs of that country, and of the principles that governed its people, or perhaps in some cases too great a disposition, in the former administrations of England, to believe, that nothing honourable, great, or dignified, could possibly issue from thence as a Source, the particular Class of Character in England who advocated this opinion, and the information of those on the other side the Atlantic upon which it was founded, could not be unknown to his Lordship—that it was a Circumstance Americans were at this present moment Lamented yet also excited their Astonishment that notwithstanding the freedom of intercourse between the 2 Countries, the affairs of America were even at present, by no means understood in England—that with respect to his first question, In my opinion the Minister sent from England to America to be agreeable to the Latter, should be a man of a fair mind and unblemished reputation, one whose character had never been committed in the late Contests between us & who from thence might at least be supposed capable, of makeing honourable and Just statements to the British court of what he notices in America worthy of Communication, that as I could not suppose England had any objects in view, relative to America at which a perfectly honourable and fair Character would hesitate in negotiating I supposed such a Character would be equally as agreeable to England as to America, and as america was in pursuit of no systems either foreign or domestic but such as Justice would warrant, She would not hesitate at haveing those pursuits examined by a Liberal and candid eye, neither with such a Character would she object at entering into a friendly Examination of the points to be discussed between the respective nations and in short, that a purely British Character, appeared to me the only one in a diplomatic point of view, which the one could promise themselves any advantage in employing, or the other feel its itself perfectly at ease in negotiating with, that with respect to the means by which a good understanding might be spedily produced, and the hint his Lordship was pleased to throw out, on the subject of a french Party in America & which I had before heard spoken of, it might not be improper, in explaining the only means which in my mind could produce the good understanding wished for, a Little to contrast the conduct of England, and france relative to America, the opposition alluded to, was doubtless a matter clearly to be calculated on, that there were parties in America, might be readily allowed without the shadow of reflection, and that they consistd of the Principal Leading men in the country, one set very numerous, powerful and respectable in favour of France & another not so numerous or powerful, but Perhaps individually equally ⟨res⟩pectable in favour of England, and the 3rd was composed of that Class ⟨of⟩ americans who had attached themselves singly to the American Character unbiased by french or english Systems, excepting that which honor Justifies, and the strictest adherence to engagements require, that they could look with a friendly eye both on the one & the other but thier attachments were to there Country independent of Party, they reguarded measures and not men. That the french party (the term being made use of simply in contrast) was of course solicitous to strengthen itself by the Assistance and Countenance of France in order if possible to acquire the ascendency, while the english party is equally solicitous to acquire a preeminence through the medium of the same Countenance and attention from England—That the national Assembly of france notwithstanding the present supposed Confusion of their affairs, aware of this circumstance and the growing consequence of America as a source for the Consumption of Manufactures had already manifested a desire to Cultivate (in addition to their past acts of friendship) a Closer friendship and connection with America, by the Late appointment of Colo. Ternant as their Minister Plenipotentiary to the United States, a Gentleman of Abilities and popular in America, from the circumstance of his having served with the reputation of A Gentleman and a Soldier thro' the whole of the war in the American army—That while France was thus strengthening her friends in America by acts of friendship and Attention to the United States, England was decidedly loosing ground by that species (perhaps) of unintentional neglect, which in the present state of political contention, if not soon remedied, might be productive of much injury, if not annihilation to the British interest in America, That the friends to this interest wished [(]& the third party men-

tioned, Join them decidedly here) to see England come forward
by her minister and manifest a desire (now the American Government was fully organized) to discuss all points of difference
relative to a compliance with the late treaty of peace as a primary
essential, that all matters of varience on either side, might be
finally adjusted agreeably to the principles of Good Faith an National Justice, which doubtless was the intention of the parties
at the time it was concluded; That after these points relative to
the Late Treaty of Peace should be thus amicable adjusted and
settled, The Friends of Great Britain and America would wish
that a more friendly intercourse might take place, by means of
a Treaty of Commerce, by which those disagreeable fluctuations
in the duties upon British ships and British Manufactures might
be done away, and the subjects of Great Britain treated in
America in all respects as a most favoured nation, which was not
the case at present, and would not be the case, untill there was
a commercial Treaty between the two Countries—That by this
means only, the duties on British Goods and British Shipping,
would be fixed, never to exceed a certain rate—Greater facilities
would be given to the collection of debts and to the transactions
of merchants—The Power of consuls would be defined and the
office rendered useful on both sides, which also could not be
effected but by an explicit treaty—Many other regulations useful to both countries might be established; when the various
objects which must compose a Treaty between two Countries
so Circumstanced as Great Britain and The United States of
America, come into full discussion, the result of which would
probably be, to secure to Great Britain a preeminence in the
American trade, over every other Country in Europe and to render those advantages permanent—That many Circumstances in
the affairs of the United states of America pressed exceedingly at
present for an almost immediate decission on the part of Great
Britain before new difficulties arose, from some Loose operating
causes or from the intrigues of rival nations—That it would be
doubtless of advantage to the British interests in America, if All
Public Characters, sent to that Country as was before Observed
on the particular subject of Ministers, were men of whose characters had not been committed in the Late war, but above all,
that, the office of Minister and Consul General, should be filled
with pure British Characters—That as the connection between

Great Britain and America must be principally commercial, a Character should be fixed on for Consul General, who had not only some Local knowledge of the commerce of America but also Local & if possible practical knowledge of the trade of Great Britain and the other countries in Europe, so far as related to their commerce and intercourse with the United Stat⟨es⟩—Such Characters would acquire a preeminence over most foreign Consuls, while it would enable them by prudence and good Judgement to reconcile to the American mind, many apparent difficulties—which without extensive Commercial Knowledge it might be often impossible to overcome, that in a country like America which was merely agricultural and commercial and where the trade was carried on by British merchants and natives of Great Britain in every state in the Union, it would seem to be a matter of the greatest consequence to england to establish an accurate consular system with a superintending consul of extensive knowledge and Abilities, whos⟨e⟩ attention would of course be directed to the rise and progress of the Trade between the two countries, and who by the exercise of good Judgement watching every event, might be able to suggest useful hints for rendering the intercourses more beneficial between two Countries whose Language, manners Education & Tastes so perfectly assimulate as those of Great Britain and the United States of America."

His Lordship Said "He perfectly agreed with me with respect to the discription of Characters proper to fill the offices mentioned, but that Candour Obliged him to state, and he spoke as the minister of England that, that part of the Treaty of peace, which related to the Military posts on the frontiers, must become a subject of discussion, as it was not only of great importance to the fur trade of England, and embraced a very respectable part of the Commercial and manufacturing interest of the kingdom but that the subject was also closely connected with the security of the frontiers of Canada and of their influence over the natives, that as to the natives he was very sorry to find The Government of the United States carrying on vigorous hostile measures against them, that in consequence of it the British trade had been very materially effected the two Last seasons & would be totally destroyed unless some measures were taken, to accommodate the differences, and that he had noticed some observations in a late American Paper tending to impress the public mind with opinions, that England countenanced the depredations of the savages on the frontier—which gave him some uneasiness, for he could with truth assure me that the Cabinet of England disclaimed the Idea in the present Situation, but it was his duty to make this impression, that England could not with perfect indifference, see a tribe of indians extirpated, from whom they received such advantages, without endeavouring in some degree to shelter them, but he flattered himself, with the expectation that America would not proceed to too great extremities on this subject"—I must candidly acknowledge to the President that these Last observations produced in me a glow, and roused some former professional feelings, but these being from various circumstances in some measure checked, I answered in such a manner, as fully to convince the minister, that tho on mild questions, I was disposed to cultivate as much benevolence and friendship as the pursuits of peace and tranquility could look for, still on others I nourished feelings capable of meeting points less amicably marked, and in the way (as I think) they ought always to be encountered.

With respect to an investigation of the principles of the Treaty I answerd, "that I had not an Idea that my country, would discover any reluctance in entering into any investigations that should be properly presented by a minister, always haveing in view the perfect fulfilment of the Treaty, in such a manner, as not to bear hard upon either of the contracting parties, or to wound the feeling of either in the explanation of any of the articles of which it was composed, but in this pursuit I doubted not, but the negotiating minister, would be fully convinced, that the fur Trade of England might perhaps be rather benifited than checked, by withdrawing their troops within their own proper Limits—and that in consequence of it, and the rapid encreasing settlements of the frontier of America, that respectable part of the commercial and manufacturing interests of England which his Lordship was pleased to allude to, would be rather extended than injured, and that the connection the subject had with the security of the frontiers of Canada absolutely invited the removal, for then the troops and inhabitants of the United States together with the intermediate lakes would form an insurmountable barrier, between the present belligerent Savages and the British inhabitants both of upper and lower Canada and that it might possibly be a point which america would not object to to enter into a defensive treaty with England as far as it would relate to mutual security against the savages or the frontiers of their respective territories—that with respect to the present hostilities between the United states of America and the Miami tribes of Indians, I doubted not but my Country would readily confide in the assurance his Lordship was pleased to make that the government of Great Britain totally disclaimed the Idea of at present aiding or abetting those Savages in the depredations they had made and were still makeing on some defenceless parts of the American frontier; That I believed those at the head of the Government of America entertained too favourable an opinion of the Characters of the present administration of England to suspect them of being capable, of countenanceing such inhuman and barbarous incursions—but that when in the packs and Haversacks of Indians slain in battle, were found British provisions, it was impossible to ascertain, whether it was procured from the British Garrisons in way of Barter for furs or other articles of indian traffic or whether it was supplyed for the purpose of enabling them to carry on the expedition, in Which those individuals had fallen a Sacrifice, that when those circumstances happened to a printer it might Justify the observations made and the Paragraphs published in the papers to which his Lordship alluded, but I believed he would not Suspect any gentleman in the administration of the Government of America could for a moment believe that the ministers of England could be capable of such measures[7]—That as his Lordships observations pressed on the conduct of America, towards those Savages, I felt no diffidence in asserting that the Conduct of the United States towards the Savages on their frontiers was more strongly marked with Justice & benevolence than that of any power who had ever yet come in contact with them, that this assertion was founded on treaties already made with other tribes, and on simular offers extended with the hand of benevolence to those very indians to whom his lordship alluded, that America was willing at any period to make peace with them upon those express principles, which had produced tranquility to every other nation, and of which she might rather boast than be ashamd and that she felt herself perfectly competent not only to chastise, but even if necessary to extirpate; still she would blush at excercising that power unless authorised by necessity and preceded by every consiliatory proposal that Justice could warrant or the Circumstances of the case admit of—That the war was by no means sought on our part, but being forced into it for the security of our settlements and protection of our frontiers, and in every stage of its progress continuing to hold in one hand mild and honourable terms of peace, while the other grasped the necessary weapons of war, it would be be rather probable that we should pursue the war, with vigour, untill peace the only object of it, was obtained, rather than check those exertions under any apprehension that England would side with Savages in such a cause, particularly if Ministers would but give themselves the trouble of Examining the question and weighing the principles of those treaties I alluded to, but even if they should think proper to take the side hinted at—America could only act one uniform part, Viz. being satisfyed of the Justness of her Career and the integrity of her intentions she doubtless would pursue her measures with firmness and leave the event["]—His Lordship asked me if I could favour him with a perusal of those treaties, I told him ["]I could, they were in the Possession of Mr Colqhoun, & I would request him to send them to his Lordship," He observed he would be glad to peruse them and was "perfectly disposed to think well of the pursuits of the United States, and to nourish every favourable disposition, that he sought this interview that I might on my return to my country communicate to the President of the United states the real friendly dispositions of the Ministers of Great Britain and of the Nation at Large towards him and the Country over which he presided"—He then brought forward the present Constitution of Canada, which after conversing on some time we parted and I immediately set off for Falmouth, where I found the Packet waiting my arrival—There are several other points, than those I have here related, which may be calculated upon to be embrac'd on the propositions which may be expected on the arrival of the English Minister; which tho they were brought forward in a Less pointed manner and in conversations with other persons besides Lord Grenville, still doubtless are such, as we shall find them much Attached to, and perhaps worthy of some deliberate previous Considerations, but this Letter is spun out to such an unrea-

sonable Length that I am apprehensive I have already trespassed too much on the Presidents time and patience, therefore
shall not proceed further than to state, that haveing thus communicated the opinions and dispositions of the present administration of England as received from one of the principal Secretaries of State; it may not be improper to assure the President
that what is called the opposition, nourish equally friendly opinions. on the evening of the 8th of April when the new Constitution of Canada was introduced by the Minister, Mr Fox in oppos-
ing the bill among other reasons said "That the situation of
Canada, with regard to the united States of America was also a
reason why they should be very careful to extend to them every
advantage they were capable of receiving. It was proved by fatal
example unless Canada was restrained by the wish of the People,
it would be in vain for them to think of restraining it by coertion.
Prejudices had now *so far subsided that he might freely confess,* that the
constitution and Government of America was of a structure,
more likely to make a people happy and flourishing than any
other that was ever Established in the world either Ancient or
Modern. It behoved the house therefore to provide that the
people of Canada should never have occation to contemplate
with envy the situation of their neighbours, but that they should
remain subjects of Britain by choice, founded on the experience
of the superior advantage derived from it"[8]—The President will
doubtless perceive, that the Language adopted by me in the
course of my communication with Lord Grenville was perfectly
consiliatory, and as far as my knowledge of the sentiments of the
people goes, I took the Liberty of concluding that they were
favourable to a Liberal Commercial connection with Great Britain and considered myself as conforming to their dispositions
in using such a stile of expression as appeared to me calculated,
to excite favourable dispositions in the person to whom my dis-
cource was addressed. If however, my Zeal on any of the points
here stated may have carried me on the one side or the other,
too far, it must be recollected that it can in no point of view be
considered as a committment of my country or the opinion of
its rulers, but merely a committment of the opinion of a private
individual who as he thinks it his duty to do, freely submitts
them to the perusal of The President of The United States and
with as much Candour as they were given to Lord Grenville

when sought for by him.[9] With sentiments of the highest respect, I have the honour to be the Presidents most Obedient and very Humble Servant

W. S. Smith

ALS, DNA: RG 59, Miscellaneous Letters.

William Stephens Smith, who had served in London in the 1780s as secretary to his father-in-law, John Adams, then American minister to Britain, returned there in December 1790, ostensibly to pursue private business, but he also hoped to position himself for the future appointment of American minister to Britain (see Smith to GW, 21 Oct. 1791). Smith claimed to have completed his business by late March or early April 1791, having obtained the means of further speculating in the public debt by selling some lands and having successfully borrowed $100,000 for Robert Morris from the Pulteney Associates (see n.4 below, and Francisco de Miranda to Henry Knox, 2 Feb. 1791, NNGL: Knox Papers).

1. Smith is referring to his letter of 1 Dec. 1790.

2. Glasgow merchant Patrick Colquhoun (1745–1820) was on close terms with Henry Dundas (1742–1811), member of Parliament from Edinburgh, who became secretary of state for the home office in June 1791 after the incumbent home secretary, Lord Grenville, was appointed secretary of foreign affairs. On 15 Feb. 1791 Colquhoun and William Temple Franklin signed preliminary articles of agreement for the sale of the million acres that Robert Morris had acquired from Oliver Phelps and Nathaniel Gorham in 1790 (see Tobias Lear to GW, 8 May 1791, n.5).

3. After making a copy GW returned to Smith on 13 July the enclosed letter from Colquhoun to Dundas, written from George Street, London, 4 April 1791: "Mr Colquhoun begs leave to remind Mr Dundas of the Circumstances he had the honor to mention to him in his note of last monday—namely, that Colo. Smith has fixd positively to return to America on Tcusday next, or Wednesday at farthest. Did not Mr Colquhoun firmly believe that much useful information to Government would be derived from an interview with this Gentleman, previous to his departure, he would not have presumed to have mentioned this matter again, which he does entirely without Colo. Smith's Knowledge. He has no hesitation to avow his anxiety upon a measure that appears to him of such infinite consequence to the Country, nor his fears that an opportunity extremely critical may be lost by the delay even of a very few day's" (DNA: RG 59, Miscellaneous Letters).

4. Wealthy Scottish member of Parliament William Pulteney (1729–1805) generally supported William Pitt's administration and invested heavily in New York land speculations, acquiring Robert Morris's holdings in the Phelps and Gorham purchase for £75,000 on 17 Mar. 1791. On 6 April Smith wrote to Pulteney: "Just as I am on the point of my departure for america, you have been pleased to inform me, 'that the Gentlemen at the head of the administration of this Country are very desireous of seeing me, as they are investigating those points which may promote a friendly intercourse between Great Britain and the United States of America; But that the pressure of European Affairs

at the present moment, renders it impossible for them immediately to attend to the subject, and therefore as they wish an interview previous to my departure, it would be very agreeable to them, if I could make it convenient to postpone my departure untill the May Packett.' If the Ministers of England perfectly understand that in communicating with me, they communicate with a private Citizen of America, I can have no objection to the proposed interview; neither can I hesitate in Stating to you, Sir, that to my private affairs, a delay, such as is wished, would be of very little importance—But having visited England with the knowledge and approbation of the President of the United States, and having communicated to him my intention of returning in the april packet, I cannot consider myself justified in overstaying that period upon any pretext whatsoever; I must therefore after maturely considering the subjects of our conversation the last evening, decide in favor of a rapid movement to America in the Packet, agreeably to my original arrangements—But at the same time sir, I would suggest, that as I propose sailing in a Vessel under the perfect command of administration, If (as I have been lead to suppose) they wish to see me previous to my departure, and should think proper to detain the Packet untill the object they have in view is answered, and untill my arrival at Falmouth—no arrangements of mine shall interfere with their wishes" (DNA: RG 59, Miscellaneous Letters).

5. "No. 3" was Grenville's letter to Pulteney, dated St. James's Square, London, 6 April: "I mentioned to you when I had last the pleasure of seeing you here, that I had felt desirous of a proper opportunity of conversing with Colo. Smith respecting the present situation of Affairs between this Country and the United States of America, as being pursuaded that such a conversation would afford me much useful information—As it does not fall within the duties of my Department to conduct or direct the details of any Negotiation which may be entered into between the two Countries, it will I am persuaded be easy for you to explain to Colo. Smith, if you would be so good as to undertake it, that such a conversation could not be considered as being in any manner a ministerial one—If under these circumstances it should be convenient to him to allow me the honor of seeing him here on Saturday morning between twelve & one, I shall be at home and disengaged" (DNA: RG 59, Miscellaneous Letters).

6. GW's retained copy of "No. 4" reads: "Lord Grenville presents his compliments to Mr Pulteney has the honor of acquainting him that he has given directions for the detention of the Packet 'till Colo. Smith's arrival at Falmouth" (Grenville to Pulteney, 7 April, DNA: RG 59, Miscellaneous Letters).

7. On 11 April Knox discussed recent newspaper reports published in Albany and elsewhere of the Indians being armed and supplied by British garrisons in the northwest posts, and Madison informed British agent George Beckwith six days later that the president had received conclusive proof of the fact (see Jefferson to GW, 10 April, n.1, and 24 April and note 6).

8. For the speech of Charles James Fox in the British House of Commons seconding the motion to recommit the Quebec Government Bill, see *Parliamentary History of England*, 29:105–11.

9. GW replied on 13 July.

From Robert Troup

New York, 6 June 1791. As an officer of the federal court for the New York district, he has observed the conduct of Justus Bush Smith as deputy marshal both before and during his brother's absence[1] and states "with the strictest regard to truth, that Mr Smith has ever appeared to me to have been upright, vigilant, active and firm in the discharge of the several duties incumbent upon him;" he does not hesitate to declare that Smith "is in every respect well qualified to execute the office of Marshal of this District,"[2] recommending him "in the strongest terms, to your faverable notice."[3]

ALS, DLC:GW.

Robert Troup (1757–1832) graduated from King's College in 1774 and studied law under John Jay before the Revolution. After serving as an officer in the Continental army, Troup resumed his legal studies under William Paterson in the 1780s and practiced in Albany and New York City, where he became a close friend of Alexander Hamilton. For his support of the federal Constitution, Troup was selected as a bearer of the Constitution in New York City's grand procession of 23 July 1788. GW appointed him federal judge for the district of New York in 1796 (GW to the U.S. Senate, 9 Dec. 1796). Troup invested heavily in New York's western lands and was agent for Pulteney Associates from 1800 until his death.

1. In requesting a leave of absence, U.S. marshal for the New York district William Stephens Smith informed GW on 1 Dec. 1790 that he would leave the executive business of the courts in charge of his brother Justus Bush Smith, one of his deputy marshals, "who from being constantly with me in the office is fully competent to the discharge of its duties, and for which I shall consider myself responsible" (GW to William Stephens Smith, 7 Dec. 1790, n.1).

2. The office became vacant after GW appointed William Stephens Smith to the more lucrative post of supervisor of the revenue for New York on 4 Mar., and GW authorized Henry Knox to offer the position to Marinus Willett (see Willett to GW, 31 July). On 5 July Aquila Giles of King's County, N.Y., reapplied for the position that had eluded him since 11 Aug. 1789. GW named Matthew Clarkson marshal, who had unsuccessfully solicited from GW the office of U.S. auditor, and Clarkson acknowledged receipt of his commission on 15 Aug. (Clarkson to GW, 16 July, DLC:GW, 15 Aug., DNA: RG 59, Miscellaneous Letters) GW sent Clarkson's nomination to the Senate after Congress convened, and it was confirmed on 7 Nov. (see Jay to GW, 13 Mar. and note 1, GW to the U.S. Senate, 31 Oct., and *Executive Journal*, 1:86, 88).

3. Although New York district attorney Richard Harrison also recommended Smith this day, probably to GW (DLC:GW), Smith received no appointment from GW.

From Henry Knox

Sir,   War Department [Philadelphia] June 8th 1791.

Colonel Procter has just arrived in this City by the way of Fort Pitt—He was unable to go forward to the Western Indians without an escort of the six nations—He could have obtained such an escort after counselling with them at Buffaloe Creek, from the 23d of April, until the 15th of May—But the Indians could not proceed either in Canoes along the lake, or by land, but required a vessel—He applied to Colonel Gordon, commanding Officer at Niagara for a vessel either public or private, for which he would pay, but he could not obtain one. The design therefore of inviting the hostile Indians to peace, previously to striking them, has been frustrated.[1]

Brant with thirty Warriors having Girty, and McGee with him, set out from Grand River, to the Western indians about the 11th of May—The Senekas say that his design is peace—That he will return in June to the treaty at the painted Post—That in that case one half the Chiefs will attend at the painted Post, and the other go forward to oblige the Western indians to peace.[2]

The Cornplanter continues his attachment to the United States, but he is exceedingly suspected by Brant's people who are in an opposite interest—the six Nations are for peace.

Colonel Procter transmitted from Fort Pitt, a full account of his proceedings to General St Clair—He will therefore be no longer in doubt about pushing forward the Kentucky expedition.[3]

Colonel Procter has not made a written Report yet—but he will soon do it—I have thought it proper to submit the substance of his Mission to you. I have the honor to be With the highest Respect Sir, Your most Obedt hum. servt

H. Knox

LS, DLC:GW; LB, DLC:GW.

1. Col. Thomas Proctor arrived at Philadelphia on 7 June. For his aborted mission to the Miami and Wabash Indians, see Henry Knox to GW, 30 May and note 7.

2. Soon after leaving his home at Ohsweken, or the Mohawk Village, on the Grand River in April, Mohawk sachem Joseph Brant arrived at the Six Nations' council at Buffalo Creek, which authorized him to proceed on a peace mission to the northwestern tribes. Brant left before the arrival of Proctor and

Cornplanter, the Seneca chief who accompanied Proctor on his mission, and reached the foot of the Maumee Rapids by mid-June. An Indian council was meeting there with Alexander McKee, British deputy agent for Indian affairs at Detroit. Brant was unable to interest the council in peaceful propositions; instead it decided to send a delegation to Quebec to solicit from Lord Dorchester the erection of a British fort at the mouth of the Maumee as well as military aid against the American army mustering at forts Pitt and Washington. Brant, McKee, and representatives from the Ottawa, Chippewa, Potawatomi, Huron, Shawnee, Delaware, Tustur, and Iroquois nations arrived at Quebec in early August and conferred with Dorchester before he left for Britain on 18 August. Dorchester remained noncommittal. Instead of returning to Detroit with the rest of the delegation, Brant went home in early October and remained there (see Knox to GW, 4 Oct., and Kelsay, *Brant*, 445–51, 455).

3. Proctor was supposed to have reached Fort Washington to report the results of his mission by 5 May, and Brig. Gen. Charles Scott's expedition was scheduled to commence on 10 May. Scott's first detachment marched from Frankfort one week later, almost a month before Knox authorized Arthur St. Clair to have Scott advance (see Knox to St. Clair, 9 June, *ASP, Indian Affairs*, 1:177).

From Benjamin Lincoln

Boston, 10 June 1791. Recommends for any "opening in the public line" Francis Cabot, his aide during the disorders of 1787 in Massachusetts, "a Gentleman of information & of great probity," who "has justly merited the esteem & confidence of a very extensive acquaintance" and is "a Gentleman of a respectable family, brother to Mr Cabot one of our Senators in Congress." Cabot "left this part of the Union, the last year, with an intention to establish himself at Georgetown in the commercial line; he finds his business small and that more difficulties attend his introduction than he expected."[1]

ALS, DLC:GW.

1. Francis Cabot, Jr. (1757–1832), a son of Joseph and Elizabeth Higginson Cabot and a brother of U.S. Senator George Cabot, was born in Salem, Mass., and invested in privateers during the Revolution. Although he purchased a lot in the Federal City at the first public sale in October 1791 and did business with the commissioners for the federal district and Tobias Lear, Cabot moved to Philadelphia before 1793 and eventually settled in Natchez, Miss. (L. Vernon Briggs, *History and Genealogy of the Cabot Family, 1475–1927* [Boston, 1927], 1:194–96; Arnebeck, *Through a Fiery Trial*, 69–70, 80, 108).

To Tobias Lear

Dear Sir,   Fredericksburgh [Va.] June 1[1]th 1791

Yesterday we arrived at this place in good health, but with horses much worn down.[1] To morrow I expect to reach Mt Vernon[2]—where, even if my horses were able to proceed, I am obliged to remain until the 27th instant—the day appointed by me at the last meeting, to meet the Commissioners at George town, in order to fix on the spot for the public buildings, and for other purposes, arising from the residence Act.

I have, at this place, received your letter of the 30th Ulto; but none of an intermediate date between that of the 15th and it.[3] Your directions to have them sent cross-wise the Country, was unlucky—first, because there are no cross-posts. 2d because my rout back was not irrevocably fixed—and 3d because I had, knowing these circumstances, directed from Charleston all letters which might be following me, to be returned to this place to await my call. The slow movement of the Mail in the three Southern States prevented (I presume) these directions getting to Richmond before the letters were forwarded to Taylors ferry—& my crossing at Carters (a ferry much higher up James River) has been the cause, or causes, I imagine, of my missing them.[4]

Being interrupted by visitors, I shall postpone until I arrive at Mt Vernon, further communications; the principal, indeed the only purpose of this letter being, to advise you of my arrival at this place, and of my intended stay at Mount Vernon, for the reason which I have assigned. My best wishes attend you, Mrs Lear & the Child; and I am sincerely & affectionately Yrs

Go: Washington

ALS, CSmH.

1. GW mistakenly dated this letter 12 June; the date of his arrival at Fredericksburg was 10 June. That evening he dined and lodged with his sister, Betty Washington Lewis, and the next day, 11 June, "After a dinner with several Gentlemen whom my Sister had envited to dine with me I crossed the Rappahannock & proceeded to Stafford Ct. House where I lodged" (*Diaries*, 6:163).

2. Upon his homecoming after a 1,887-mile trip that took sixty-seven days, GW noted laconically in his diary on 12 June: "About Sun rise we were off—breakfasted at Dumfries and arrived at Mt. Vn. to D." (ibid.).

3. GW probably was referring to Tobias Lear's letter of 29 May.

4. For GW's journey from Salem, N.C., to Fredericksburg and his difficult

crossing at Carter's ferry on 9 June, see ibid., 154–63. After leaving Salem on 2 June, GW examined with North Carolina governor Alexander Martin the site of the Battle of Guilford Court House of 15 Mar. 1781 and discussed politics with him, particularly local reaction to the excise tax and the activities of the Yazoo land companies (ibid., 155, 158–59).

From Tobias Lear

Sir,   Philadelphia June 12th 1791

I flatter myself that this letter will either find you at Mount Vernon, or meet you there in a very few days. In either case, I hope I may be so happy as to congratulat you upon a safe return from your southern excursion.

The day before yesterday a Drayman brought 14 Cases of wine here marked G.W. which he said were from on board a vessel which had arrived from Charleston S.C.—There was no letter, bill of lading or any other paper accompanying them, and I have not yet been able to learn by whom, or by whose desire they were sent. They were, however, received & taken care of. The wine which Mr Jefferson sent for to France on your account has likewise arrived; but as the packages all came marked in Mr Jefferson's name, I did not think proper to have any of them brought here until Mr Jefferson's return from his Eastern tour, when he will be able to make a proper division of it, (as I understood him before his departure that a part of the wines which might arrive was for himself.) It was therefore all put into his Cellar.[1]

Mr Fentham, with whom George & Lawrence board, gave me notice a few days ago that he did not think it would be in his power to accommodate them much longer, as he was placed in a very disagreeable situation by two of his boarders, young Gentlemen from Maryland, having left him without paying off their Account of board, which had been of a long standing, and upon which he depended to enable him to dis-charge some debts which were chiefly contracted for the supply of his house of which these young gentlemen had partaken. He expected his Creditors would come upon him immediately & the consequences would be very disagreeable. He thought he should be obliged at least to break up house-keeping. As I had about the middle of April, (at his earnest request) advanced him a quarter's board for George & Lawrence—which quarter will not expire 'till the latter part of this month, I had it not in my power to afford him any relief by a payment on their Acct—and I did not feel authorized to make any further advances even if he had requested it. I immediately acquainted Doctor Smith with these circumstances & requested his assistance in providing other lodgings for Geo. & Lawce in Case Mr Fentham should not be able to keep them. The Doctor told me he did not consider Mr Fentham's case in so desperate a light as he did himself, and that he intended to request the College Treasurer to advance so much of his salary as would enable him to satisfy his Creditors and that he might then go on as he had done. But if it should finally so be that Mr Fentham could not continue them, there would be no difficulty in providing suitable lodgings for them, and that he would take care to give me timely information of a proper place. On this ground the matter rested 'till last evening, when George informed me that Mr Fentham intended to re- move in a short time to Maryland where he had an advanta- geous offer of a School & a Parish. Should he carry his intentions into effect I shall then refer to Dr Smith's offer of providing a place for them. They both express themselves very well satisfied with the fare & treatment which they have met with at Mr Fent- ham's.[2]

Washington has been detained from School this week past by the Chicken pox which he has had pretty severely—and which I expect will keep him at home most of the present week. The early commencement of the vacation (about the middle or latter part of July) with these interruptions, will not allow time to form an opinion of the effects of any new regulations which may have been formed in his School, before he goes to Virginia.[3]

It is here a great subject of inquiry when you will be in this place; but nobody is able say further than that it is probable you will be here towards the last of the month. Mr Brown, however, undertook to fix the 25th of the month in his paper & from him the other printers have taken up that idea.[4]

Some late English papers say that the Attorney General of G. B. has commenced a prosecution agst Mr Paine for some things contained in his Answer to Mr Burke. This, it was ex- pected by many here, would be the case, when they first read his pamphlet, unless Government should be detered from such a step by an apprehension of its exciting a popular commotion; for the book is said to be read with great avidity and much approbation by a large part of the Community in Great Britain— and almost universally in Ireland.[5]

Mrs Lear unites with me in sentiments of the highest respect & in sincere wishes for your heath & happiness, with a respectful remembrance to all friends at Mt Vernon.[6] I have the honor to be, with the greatest respect & most sincere Attachment, Sir, Your Obliged & Affect. Servt

Tobias Lear.

ALS, DLC:GW; AL[S] (letterpress copy), PWacD.

1. The wine from Charleston was that shipped by Fenwick, Mason, & Co. from Bordeaux at the end of March. The original cover letter and invoice had become separated from the shipment, but William Jackson forwarded to Tobias Lear on 17 June copies that had arrived at Mount Vernon (DLC:GW). See also GW to Lear, 19 June 1791. The firm's letter of 28 Mar. informed GW that eleven cases of wine were shipped the previous summer on the *St. James,* Capt. William Van Leuvenigh, for which Wakelin Welch & Son paid £20.13.7, and that the first shipment of wine was still at Brest but would be sent to Philadelphia by the first available conveyance. The letter also covered an invoice for fourteen cases ordered by Thomas Jefferson for GW and charged to Jefferson's account. That wine was sent to Hazelhurst & Co. of Charleston with directions for its forwarding to Jefferson by the first packet (DLC:GW). The accompanying invoice listing the fourteen cases of 710 bottles of wine and their costs as well as various other charges, for a total of £1,697.19, was postmarked "BALT. JUNE 19 FREE" (DLC:GW). On 7 July Lear wrote to Fenwick, Mason, & Co., acknowledging their letters to GW of 9 July, 10 Aug. 1790, and 1 April 1791 and informing the merchants of the arrival of both shipments of wine. Lear added: "Of these wines none have yet been proved except the claret of the first shipment which is pronounced very good—Those ordered by Mr Jefferson are undoubtedly of an excellent quality coming directly from the fountain head" and noted that he had not yet heard anything about the wine then at Brest, which "seems to have passed thro' so many trials that when it does come, if at all, it must either be highly improved or totally spoiled" (DLC:GW). See also Fenwick, Mason, & Co. to GW, 9 July 1790 and note 4).

2. William Fentham was considered one of the best teachers of the academy associated with the College of Philadelphia under Provost William Smith. Lear paid Fentham and his wife $53.34 on 19 April for "a quarter's board in advance for Geo. & Lawce Washington" (Decatur, *Private Affairs of George Washington,* 227). GW sent George Steptoe and Lawrence Augustine Washington, sons of his brother Samuel, to the college the previous year and paid for their education. They graduated after the college merged with the University of Pennsylvania in September 1791 (see GW to Lear, 3 Oct. 1790, nn.5 and 6, and to George S. Washington, 5 Dec. 1790 and notes 1 and 3).

3. According to a receipt of 1 July, Lear paid James Clement of the College,

Academy, and Charitable School of Philadelphia £1.7.6 for one quarter's tuition for George Washington Parke Custis (ViMtV).

4. Andrew Brown's *Federal Gazette and Philadelphia Daily Advertiser*, 6 June, noted: "We are informed that the President . . . is expected at Mount-Vernon, from his southern tour, about the 12th of this month, and that he would immediately proceed to Philadelphia, so that he may be expected in this City about the 25th instant." The *General Advertiser and Political, Commercial and Literary Journal* (Philadelphia) reprinted Brown's notice on 7 June, and the *Gazette of the United States* (Philadelphia) on 8 June. Brown announced in the *Federal Gazette* on 15 June that GW had arrived at Mount Vernon "on Sunday last [12 June]" and "may be expected in town in a few days." GW actually arrived at Philadelphia on 6 July.

5. Lear probably was referring to the notice in the *Federal Gazette*, 8 June, that "By the English Chronicle of April 9, just received by the Editor, it appears that the Attorney General of Great Britain has received instructions to prosecute Mr. Paine for his pamphlet on the Rights of Men." British attorney general Sir Archibald MacDonald stated at Thomas Paine's trial of December 1792 that he had earlier declined prosecuting Paine because "Reprehensible as that book [*Rights of Man*] was, . . . it was ushered into the world under circumstances that led me to conceive that it would be confined to the judicious reader, and when confined to the judicious reader, it appeared to me that such a man would refute as he went along" (Howell, *State Trials*, 22:382). The Irish patriot William Theobald Wolfe Tone noted in October 1791 that the *Rights of Man* had become "'the Koran' of Belfast" (quoted in Parsons, "The Mysterious Mr. Digges," 488). For the popularity of Paine's pamphlet in Ireland, see Keane, *Paine*, 333.

6. GW replied on 19 June.

To Alexander Hamilton

My Dr sir   Mount Vernon, June 13th 1791.

I am arrived at this place and just in time to acknowledge (in a hasty manner by this days Post—the first opportunity that has offered of writing to Philada since I left Savanna—) the receipt of your private letter of the 17th of April by Mr Smith who lodged it at Cambden, through which it was known my rout would be on my return to the seat of the Government.[1]

Mr Wolcott may be informed that it is my intention to appoint him to the office of Comptroller[2]—With respect to his successor as Auditor, I shall suspend any determination, (if no manifest inconvenience will result from it) until my arrival in Philadelphia, which however is not likely to happen before the 5th or 6th of July as (by appointment at the last meeting) I am to meet the Commissioners, undr the residence Act on Monday the 27th inst: at Georgetown, and may, for aught I know to the Contrary, be detained there several days; and afterwards must move slowly, on account of the exhausted condition of my horses.

No letters from the Northward or Eastward of this, bearing date between the 15th & 30th of May have come to my hands—and having abundant evidence before I reached Charleston of the slow movements of the Mail through the three Southernmost States, I did, before I left that place—on the 9th of that month direct that all letters which might be for & following me to be returned to Fredericksburgh as the first place I should touch the post line upon my return—But these directions not arriving in Richmond in time (as I conjecture) the letters of that interval, agreeably to the superscriptions which I am informed were on them, were forwarded from that place to Taylors Ferry, in expectation of meeting me there—but to this circumstance, which was unknown to me—and to finding from better information than I set out with, that it would be more convenient to cross James river higher up than at Taylors; is to be ascribed my missing the communications which were made between the 15— & 30. of May as mentioned before. These dispatches I may be long without, & perhaps never get; for there are no cross Posts in those parts and the letters, which will have to pass through *many* hands, may find *some* who are not deficient in curiosity.

My return to this place is sooner than I expected; owing to the uninterruptedness of my journey by sickness—from bad weather, or accidents of any kind whatsoever—Having obtained before I left Philadelphia the most accurate account, I could get there, of the places & roads through, & by which I was to perform my tour; and the distances between the former; I formed my line of march accordingly; fixed each days journey & the day to halt; from neither of which have I departed in a single instance, except staying, from a particular circumstance, two days in Columbia, and none at Charlotte, instead of one at each—and crossing James river at Carters ferry in place of Taylors, as was the original intention. But the improbability of performing a tour of 1700 miles (—I have already rode more), with the same set of horses without encountering any accident by which a deviation would be rendered unavoidable appeared so great that I allowed eight days for casualties, and six to refresh at this place when I should have returned to it—None of the former having happened, account for the 14. days I shall rcmain here before the meeting with the Commrs; one of whom Mr Johnston chief Justice of the State of Maryland, & living at a pretty considerable distance from Georgetown; having made his arrangements agreeably thereto, would not be able to meet me sooner.

I mention this matter, that if there is anything pressing in either of the Departments, it may be Known where I am. With affectionate regard I am sincerely yours

G: Washington

LB, DLC:GW.

1. The original receiver's copy of Alexander Hamilton's second letter of 17 April has not been found. It probably was delivered by Congressman William Loughton Smith, who left Philadelphia early on 20 April and, traveling overland, reached Camden, S.C., on 9 May (Matthews, *Journal of William L. Smith,* 75, 76n). GW was in Camden on 25–26 May 1791.

2. On 17 June William Jackson wrote from Mount Vernon to Tobias Lear at Philadelphia, sending under GW's direction a commission that Lear was to complete with Oliver Wolcott, Jr.'s name and then transmit to the secretary of state to be countersigned, sealed, and delivered to Wolcott (DLC:GW). The State Department's memorandum book notes that Wolcott's commission was dated 17 June (DNA:PCC, item 187). On 31 Oct. GW presented Wolcott's name to the Senate, which confirmed his appointment on 7 Nov. (*Executive Journal,* 1:86, 88). Hamilton informed GW on 19 June that he had notified Wolcott of GW's intention, adding: "This appointment gives me particular pleasure, as I am confident it will be a *great & real* improvement in the state of the Treasury Department. There can no material inconvenience attend the postponing a decision concerning the future Auditor, till your arrival in this City. . . . There is nothing which can be said to be new here worth communicating; except generally that all my Accounts from *Europe,* both private & official, concur in proving that the impressions now entertained of our government and its affairs (I may say) *throughout* that quarter of the Globe are of a nature the most flattering & pleasing" (DLC:GW). Wolcott wrote GW on 7 July to acknowledge and accept the appointment (DLC:GW).

Letter not found: from Uriah Forrest, 14 June 1791. William Jackson wrote on this day to Forrest from Mount Vernon: "In reply to your letter of this date, addressed to the President of the United States, he directs me to inform you that he yesterday requested the Secretary of the Treasury to inform Mr Wolcott, the present Auditor, that he should appoint him to the office of Comptroller of the Treasury. Your letter of this date is the first and only letter which the President has received" (DLC:GW).

To Thomas Jefferson

Sir,   Mount-Vernon, June 15th 1791.

I acknowledged the receipt of your letter of the 2nd of April from Richmond—since which I have only received two letters from you of the 10th of April and 15th of May.[1]

Concluding that some of your dispatches may have been forwarded to Taylor's ferry (by which route I did not return) I have to request, if that should have been the case, and the communications were of a particular or pressing nature; that duplicates may be addressed to me at Mount-Vernon, where I shall remain until the 27th of the present month, when, by an appointment before I went to the southward, I am to meet the Commissioners at Georgetown. I cannot now determine how long I may be there—but it is probable I shall not make any particular communications to you before my return to Philadelphia.

If the suggestion contained in your letter of the 10th of April, respecting the engravings, can be carried into effect at a moderate expence, I think it may answer a good purpose. I am Sir, Your most obedient Servant

Go: Washington

A letter from Major Shaw, Consul at Canton, of the 7th of December last, with it's enclosures—and a very unexpected address from some Persons styling themselves, "free people of colour of the Island of Grenada," are herewith transmitted for your consideration—and your opinions thereon when I see you in Philadelphia.[2]

Go: Washington

LS, DLC: Thomas Jefferson Papers; LB, DLC:GW; Df, DNA: RG 59, Miscellaneous Letters.

1. GW acknowledged Jefferson's letter of 2 April on 13 April. He received Jefferson's letter of 10 April on 8 May while at Charleston. Jefferson sent his letter of 15 May directly to Mount Vernon.

2. For these enclosures, see Samuel Shaw to GW, 7 Dec. 1790, and Louis Lagrenade et al. to GW, 24 Jan. 1791.

Letter not found: to Henry Knox, 15 June 1791. On 19 June GW referred Knox to "My letter of the 15th inst."[1]

1. William Jackson informed Tobias Lear on 14 June that "The President thinks he may write to the Heads of departments by the next post." In the letter-book copy of GW's letter of 19 June to Knox (DLC:GW), Lear noted

that "The letter of the 15th instant was not among those put into the hands of T. Lear on the President's return from his southern tour" (see GW to Knox, 19 June and note 1).

To Tobias Lear

Dear Sir,   Mount Vernon 15th June 1791

Your letter of the 29th ulto I acknowledged the receipt of from Fredericksburgh—since which, another of the 5th instt has been received.[1]

The Commissions for Whitaker and McDowell were properly issued; as those also are, mentd in yr letter of the 5th, and it was on my Mind, that blank Commissions signed by me, were left with you for the Officers of the Revenue Cutters; This not being the case, quere, if there is not a necessity of sending some to me for my signature, as I shall not leave this before the 27th—may be detained at George town two or three days—and must, after-wards, proceed slowly, on acct of the low condition of my horses. The Secretary of the Treasury will be able to decide on this point, & I wish you to act in the matter accordingly as he shall advise you.[2] I find another of the federal Judges (Hopkinson) has by his death occasioned a vacancy in the district of Pennsyl-vania. As some have, & others unquestionably will apply for the appointment; I wish you would use every *indirect* means in your power, to ascertain the public opinion with respect to the fittest character as a Successor to Hopkinson. Pursue the same mode to learn who it is thought would fill the present Auditors Office (as *he* will be appointed Comptroler) with the greatest ability & integrity. Severals have been brought to my view for the Comptrolers place (who I suppose would accept of the Auditors) as able & meritorious characters; among these are the names of Mr Richmond, the present Comptroler or Auditor of Mary-land—Colo. Pickering—Mr Kean—Colo. Drayton (a Gentn of So. Carolina[)]—Colo. Forrest and others.[3]

It is hardly to be expected by the Trustees of *any* College, that complaints will not be made by the parents or friends of the boys who go to it, if they conceive they are neglected; and if Trustees mean to do their duty, & support the reputation of the Siminary, they ought, I am sure, to be thankful for well founded representations of neglect in the œconomy—police—or inattention of the professors & teachers.

I am glad to hear that the affairs of our own family are going on well—and it might not be improper to hint to the Servants who are with you (before they are joined by those with me) that it will be very idle & foolish in them, to enter into any combinations for the purpose of supplanting those who are now in authority—for the attempt in the first place will be futile & must recoil upon themselves; and because, admitting they were to make the lives of the present Steward & house-keeper so uneasy as to induce them to quit, others would be got to supply their places; and such too, as would be equally, if not more rigid in the exaction of the duties required of Servants. In a word, that these characters are indispensably necessary to take trouble off the hands of Mrs Washington & myself & will be supported; any attempts therefore to counteract them in the line of their duty, whilst they act agreeably to established rules, & their conduct is marked with propriety, will be considered as the strongest evidence they conceive of their own unworthiness, and dispositions to be lazy, if not dishonest. A good & faithful Servant is never affraid, or unwilling to have his conduct looked into, but the reverse; because the more it is inspected, the brighter it shines. With respect to the other matters of a domestic nature—mentioned in your letter of the 5th—I shall postpone touching upon them until I see you. We are suffering in these parts by a severe drought—Grass is scarcely worth cutting—& Oats, if Rain keeps off two or 3 days longer must be ruined—Corn is bad, but it is too early in the year to form an opinion of the yield of it. Remember me to Mrs Lear and be assured of the sincere esteem & friendship of Yr Affecte

Go: Washington

ALS, CSmH.

1. In acknowledging Tobias Lear's letter of 29 May on 11 June, GW misdated it 30 May.

2. For the difficulties Lear had in completing the commissions, see Lear to GW, 19–20 June, postscript, and 23 June and note 5.

3. No direct application for the auditorship or comptrollership by Col. Stephen Drayton (1736–1810) has been found. During the Revolutionary War Drayton served as deputy quartermaster general for the Southern Department of the Continental army under Gen. Horatio Gates. His finances never recovered from the confiscation of his estates by Lord Cornwallis, and in early

1791 he petitioned Congress for compensation for his losses. The House of Representatives referred the petition to Henry Knox, who apparently did not report favorably on it (*DHFC*, 3:713, 729). According to the second of two letters of 2 Aug. 1791 to GW from William Moultrie, GW discussed a federal appointment for Drayton with some of his supporters during the Southern Tour (DLC:GW). On 4 Aug. Gov. Charles Pinckney wrote GW from Charleston upon being requested to mention Isaac Holmes and Drayton "as Naval Officers should Colonel [Isaac] Motte be appointed Collector . . . I am sure that either of them will very ably & faithfully discharge the duties of that appointment" (DLC:GW). In considering Drayton for office GW apparently heard rumors concerning his unsettled quartermaster accounts and asked Alexander Hamilton sometime in the summer of 1791 to investigate the matter. Hamilton replied on 31 Aug.–1 Sept.: "Mr Wolcott respectfully informs the Secretary of the Treasury, that Stephen Drayton Esq: of south Carolina, is charged on the Books of the Quarter Master Department; with between three & four Millions of Dollars in old emissions recd by him, principally during the years 1779 & 1780. Also that certificates of Specie value, to a large amount, were issued by said Drayton & his assistants, which have been settled by the State of So. Carolina, & for which the said Drayton will be held accountable. On enquiry I have full reason to believe that no accounts in documents have been transmitted to the late Commissioner for the Quarter Master Departmt, or to the Treasury, respecting the expenditure of moneys, or the applications of supplies for which certificates were issued; & therefore no opinion can be given of the manner in which Mr Drayton will account" (DLC:GW). Drayton did not receive a federal appointment from GW. He was later president of a Democratic-Republican society and otherwise supported Edmund Genet after the French minister arrived in Charleston in 1793.

From Triol, Roux, & Company

Translation

Sir,   Marseilles [France] 15th June 1791

It is to the Preserver of the liberty of a great Nation, it is to the defender of the rights of Man, as much as to the President of Congress, that we submit the communication of the Memorial addressed by us to the legislature of France, to establish the legality of our debt with the United States of America, and to solicit, by their means, of Congress, a treatment more equitable than that which it would impose upon us, by confounding us with a crowd of Creditors of a different complexion (denomination) from us, as well by the time or the nature of their debt.[1]

Deign, Sir, to cast your eyes upon our suit. We demand justice, not favor. Whatever may be the acknowledged validity of our title, we are far from insisting upon an entire acquittance; but we cannot consent to see ourselves striped of the greatest part of our fortune, vested in the *Cash* of Congress, under the public faith, and by virtue of the most sacred engagement. Whatever arrangement equity may dictate as most analogous to the object of our deposit, we are ready to submit to with a reasonable sacrifice. The bond of fraternity which grows every day stronger between the Americans & French, promises us that Congress will give to our just complaint, the attention which it merits, and that we shall have in particular to thank you for the disposition which your powerful influence & your natural equity will engage in our favor. We are, with Respect, Sir, Your very humble & Obedt Sert

> Triol Roux & Co.

Translation, in Tobias Lear's hand, DNA: RG 59, Miscellaneous Letters. Neither the original receiver's copy of this cover letter, nor Lear's translation of its enclosure, has been found.

In 1778 the Marseilles merchants Triol, Roux, et Compagnie shipped a cargo to the United States in the *Louise-Marie*, Capt. Guillaume Reboul, who sold part of the cargo to the American army at Providence for $56,664. When Reboul attempted to conclude the sale at Boston a short time later, he was dismayed to find that the depreciated Continental currency he had been paid was worth only 30 to 50 percent of the same amount in French notes. He was then obliged to turn in his American notes when Congress issued a new currency emission. Reboul did not receive his funds until eight months later, and the firm claimed the delay prevented profitable investment of those funds elsewhere. Triol, Roux, & Cie had previously attempted to obtain redress through the French consulate at Philadelphia and through Benjamin Franklin at Passy (Franklin to Triol, Roux, & Cie, 12 April 1781, DLC: Franklin Papers, and Triol, Roux, & Cie to Franklin, 21 Feb. 1783, PPAmP: Franklin Papers).

1. The enclosed "Copie du Mémoire adressé à l'Assemblée Nationale par les Sieurs Triol Roux & Compagnie de Marseille," dated Marseilles, 1 June 1791, is in DNA: RG 59, Miscellaneous Letters, and the text appears in CD-ROM:GW. For correspondence concerning the receipt and translation of the letter and memorial, see Lear to GW, 6, 9, 16 Oct., GW to Lear, 14 Oct., and Lear to Alexander Hamilton, 15 November.

From Henry Knox

Sir   War Department [Philadelphia], June 16th 1791.

I write this Letter with the hopes of its meeting you at Mount-Vernon in good health, after your long and fatiguing journey.

By information from Fort Pitt of the 9th Inst., the tranquility of the frontiers is very great.[1]

About Eight hundred of the troops have arrived at Fort Pitt, from the 16th of May to the 5th instant—Major General Butler had distributed these troops in such a manner, as to cover the frontiers from Fort Franklin on the Allegany, down to the Great Kenhawa, and so as to dismiss the Militia which had been called out.

All the Regulars enlisted, from this State to Massachusetts, have been ordered forward—They amount to about Three hundred, but it is expected they will have considerable additions.

There are some deficiencies in the battalions of Levies of this State, Jersey and Maryland, which will be completed it is expected in a few days.

The Virginia battalion is full, and marched the 4th inst., excepting a small deficiency occasioned by desertions.

By Colonel Procter's additional communications, there can be no doubt but that Brant, accompanied by McGee and Girty, has gone to the hostile Indians with the concurrence of the British Officers[2]—and the Indians invariably asserted his object was to effect a peace—If so, the British mean to have the merit of the action, if we could accept of a peace dictated by them.

I do not enter into details, until I shall have the honor to submit them personally to you. I am, Sir, With the highest Respect Your most Obedt hume Servt

H. Knox

LS, DLC:GW; LB, DLC:GW.

1. The "information from Fort Pitt" probably derived from Maj. Gen. Richard Butler's letter of 9 June to Knox, to which Knox replied on 16 June (*ASP, Indian Affairs*, 1:188–89).

2. Col. Thomas Proctor's "additional communications" probably were the dispatches he had sent to Knox on 21 May by Capt. Michael Gabriel Houdin. Proctor himself arrived in Philadelphia on 7 June (see Proctor's narrative enclosed in his letter of 9 July to Knox, and Knox to Pickering, 13 June, *ASP, Indian Affairs*, 1:161–62, 166).

To Robert Morris

Dear Sir,   Mount-Vernon June, 16th 1791.

Your letter of the 21th of April was not received until yesterday morning[1]—*none* of later date than the 15th of that month overtook me on the road to Savannah, and orders were dispatched for all to be returned to this place after I left the post-road—This will account for the late reception of yours.

The very favorable character given of Mr Wolcott before his appointment to the office of Auditor, having been fully vindicated by his talents and attention in the discharge of its duties, I considered his appointment to the vacant office of Comptroller as due to the public service, and to his own merit—and, in conformity to that opinion, I requested the Secretary of the Treasury, in a letter of the 13th instant, to inform Mr Wolcott that I should appoint him Comptroller of the Treasury. with great regard, I am dear Sir, Your most obedient Servant

G. Washington.

LB, DLC:GW.

1. Robert Morris's letter of 21 April to GW has not been found.

To Thomas Jefferson

Sir,   Mount-Vernon, June 17th 1791.

By the last post from the southward I received your letters of the 17th and 24th of April, with their enclosures.

In a letter of the 7th of May, which I wrote to the Secretary of the Treasury from Charleston, I expressed my approbation of what he informed me had been determined by the Vice-President and Heads of Departments, relative to Mr Short's negociation at Amsterdam, and the further progress of the loans in Holland. I am Sir, Your most obedient Servant

Go: Washington

LS, DLC: Thomas Jefferson Papers; LB, DLC:GW; Df, DNA: RG 59, Miscellaneous Letters. Jefferson docketed the cover of the receiver's copy, "Washington Presidt recd June 21."

Letter not found: to Henry Knox, 17 June 1791. GW docketed Knox's official letter of 17 April as answered on 17 June, and Knox wrote on 21 June to GW: "I have the honor to acknowledge the receipt of your favors, of the 15th and 17th instant."[1]

1. Although Henry Knox wrote "17th instant" in his letter of 21 June, he was probably referring to GW's letter of 19 June (which might have been mis-dated 17 June; the original receiver's copy has not been found).

To Henry Knox

Sir,   Mount Vernon June 19th 1791[1]

My letter of the 15th inst.[2] mentioned that I had not received any letters from you between the 15th and the 30 of May—it should have been the 15th of April and 30th of May.

By the last post from the southward I received yours of the 17th of April—which renders a duplicate of that letter unnecessary.[3]

As it appears to be alike requisite to the satisfaction of the public mind and to General Harmar's honor that the enquiry which he requests should be instituted, I herewith transmit to you his letter to me, with its enclosures, in order that you may give the necessary directions for convening a board of Officers.[4]

Being unacquainted with the state of the subject to which the enclosed letters from Messieurs Foster of Rhode Island relate, I refer them to your consideration.[5] I am Sir your most Obedient servant

Df, in William Jackson's hand, DLC:GW; LB, in Tobias Lear's hand, DLC:GW.

1. Jackson first wrote "June 16" in the draft's dateline with a tilde over the number and superimposed a "7" over the "6" before apparently writing "19th" above the obscured numeral.

2. Lear wrote out "instant" in the letter-book copy followed by an asterisk and noted at the bottom of the page: "The letter of the 15th instant was not among those put into the hands of T. Lear on the President's return from his southern tour." GW's letter of 15 June to Henry Knox has not been found but might have been similar to the one he wrote to Thomas Jefferson the same day.

3. Knox sent two letters to GW on 17 April: a private one recommending Oliver Wolcott, Jr., for comptroller of the treasury and an official dispatch from the War Department. GW probably received only the official one.

4. Josiah Harmar's enclosed letter of 28 Mar. to GW from Fort Washington reads: "If the delicacy of the military character is such, that it will not bear to be even suspected, let it be my apology for the liberty I am taking in addressing this Sheet to yourself. Throughout the course of long Service, it has ever been my greatest ambition to deserve your good opinion—I viewed it as an object inseparable from the duties I owed to my Country—If Vanity has sometimes prompted me to imagine that my feeble endeavors to obtain your approbation were not wholly unsuccessful; think, Sir, how great must be my mortification to forfeit, at this time a little of your Confidence. I will not presume to trouble your Excellency here with the justification of my Conduct on the late expedition—All I intreat is, that you would be pleased to suspend for a while your judgment of it. Arraigned, as I feel myself to be, before the bar of my Country; Accused, as I know myself to be, by the tongue of malevolence,

and the machinations of old and designing enemies; I need not hint at the extreme anxiety of my mind to see that day when your Excellency will permit me to call on and dare even the worst of them, to prove a word to my dishonor—Then Sir, shall I confront them with that cheerfulness and perfect indifference, which on such occasions can only flow from the pride of conscious innocence. I beg you, Sir, to gratify me with a board of Officers on my Conduct—I should not object were they taken from among my Kentucky accusers—Prejudged however as I have been, by acquitting me, they would condemn themselves. Among the acrimonious falsehoods which art and malevolence have joined to circulate, I find there is one of a deeper dye. 'General Harmar was in a scene of continual intoxication, during the expedition.' Let the enclosed Copies of letters from such of my Officers as are here, answer to this charge. The Originals are reserved for the Court of Enquiry, should they be thought necessary" (DNA: RG 59, Miscellaneous Letters). Harmar noted in his letter-book copy that the original, which apparently was never received by GW and has not been found, was sent by one Mr. Williams (MiU-C: Harmar Papers). The text is taken from the duplicate, delivered by Capt. John Pratt. The enclosed copies of the letters from his officers have not been identified, but GW also forwarded them to Knox with Harmar's letter. For the background to Harmar's request for a court of inquiry, see GW to Knox, 19 Nov. 1790. Knox replied to GW on 21 June: "Agreeably to your directions, I will by the next Post direct Major General St Clair, upon the subject of Brigadier Genl Harmar's request for a Court of enquiry" (DLC:GW), and on 23 June he sent instructions for instituting a board of inquiry to Arthur St. Clair (*ASP, Indian Affairs*, 1:178). In response to a general order issued by St. Clair on 14 Sept. a military court of inquiry convened at Fort Washington on 15 Sept., presided over by Maj. Gen. Richard Butler. It met daily until 23 September. No Kentucky militia officers served on the court or ever appeared before it to offer evidence. Butler presented the court's findings to St. Clair on 24 Sept. and 3 Oct.: Harmar's personal conduct was "irreproachable," the organization of the army was "calculated to support harmony," the order of march was "perfectly adapted to the country," the order of encampment and battle was "judicious," and the disposition of his detachments were "made on good principles" (*ASP, Military Affairs*, 1:30). Harmar resigned his commission on 1 Jan. 1792 and served as adjutant general of Pennsylvania from 1793 to 1799.

5. The enclosed letters have not been found. Knox's reply of 21 June notes that "The Letter from Messrs Foster, relate to the Rhode Island company which is vacant, and which will remain so until I have the honor to receive personally, your decision upon the subject" (DLC:GW).

To Tobias Lear

Dear Sir,   Mount Vernon June 19th 1791

Since my last to you (from this place) I have received your letters of the 12th immediately from Philadelphia, and those of the 17th & 24th of April after their having taken a trip to the Southward.[1]

I find by Mrs Washington's letters that Mr Frauncis is very desirous of introducing Mrs Read into the family again; this idea it would be well for him to relinquish at once, & forever; for, unless there are reasons inducing it, which my imagination cannot furnish, it never will happen. Herculas can answer every purpose that Mrs Read would do, and others which she will not; and sure I am that the difference in the expence between the two will bear no comparison; besides, supposing Mrs Read to act fairly & honestly (which by the bye I do not believe she is disposed to do) if she is not to be the absolute Mistress of her own conduct, in a word, *uncontroulable,* she would not remain in the family a month. She would also increase the number, and of course the expence of the *second* Table; which under the Administration of Mr Hyde, I believe was equal to the first (public days excepted). But I hope it is a matter clearly understood by Mr Frauncis that Wine is not to be used at it again under any pretence whatsoever; for there can be no line drawn if it be once admitted; either as to the quantity or quality that will be drank at it.[2]

By the last Post, the letter of Messrs Fenwick & Mason, explanatory of the Wine from Charleston, was forwarded to you; & I should be glad to hear that the Wine was recd in good order; for no attempts of that Ho. hitherto, seems to have succeeded well, so far as I am concerned in them. The other Wine to Mr Jefferson will, I presume, be divided, and settled for, as soon as he shall have returned from his Northern tour.

Without going into the detail on the several points of yr letters I can assure you that the measures you have adopted with respect to Washington—George & Lawrence—my black people—& the employment of Mr Fraunces & Mrs Emmerson, as far as they have been communicated, meet my entire approbation; and I wish you to inculcate strongly upon the white Servants of the family, (as mentioned in my last) that it will be vain & idle in them to suppose, that by a combination they will avoid their own duties—or can effect the discharge of those to whom the management of the Household business is committed. They must be sensible, that they have as high wages as are given to any Servants in their respective stations. that they are as well

provided—& perhaps *better* paid than most—and no extra: duties imposed upon them; consequently, that if an attempt of this
sort is made, it will recoil upon themselves. I shall communicate
the same sentiments to those who are with me, that, if they do
sin, it shall be with their eyes open, & under a knowledge of the
consequences.

As I shall have occasion for a number of blanketts for my
people this fall; and as the best time to purchase them, I am
told, is after the Winter's demand is over; I should be glad if you
would make a pretty diligent enquiry after them before I arrive;
that I may know *whether,* and upon *what* terms, I can get supplied. It is probable I may want near two hundred.

The Majr desires me to write for half a bushel of Turnip seed
of the best kind—viz.—a peck of the White Summer—and the
other peck of the red winter; but a good winter, and good Summer Turnip of any other kind, I suppose will do. It must be sent
soon, or both will be useless.

I should like to see Mr Paynes answer to Mr Burke's Pamphlet;
if it is to be had, & could be sent off by the Post on friday, it
would meet me at George Town on Monday the 27th; where I
shall be, & from whence I shall proceed; but on what day is more
than I am able to determine until I go there, and shall see what
is necessary to be done at that place towards carrying the Law
respecting the Permanent residence of the Government into effect. To do this, there are many matters to decide upon; and
some of them not a little difficult. It is not very probable therefore that I shall leave Georgetown before Thursday; but I would
not have such dependence placed on this, as to *expect* letters will
meet me there on Wednesday evening; especially as it is in distant contemplation (if upon enquiry at Georgetown it shall be
found that the difference in the length of the two Roads is not
great) to return by the way of Frederick town, York & Lancaster,
to Philadelphia.[3]

Paris has become so lazy, self willed & impudent, that John
(the Coachman) had no sort of government of him; on the contrary, Jno. say's it was a maxim with Paris to do nothing he was
ordered, and every thing he was forbid. This conduct, added to
the incapacity of Giles for a Pistilion, who I believe will never be
able to mount a horse again for that purpose, has induced me
to find Paris some other employment than in the Stable—of

course I shall leave him at home. A boy, or two may be necessary there, to assist about the horses—Carriages—& harness. but these (dutch ones) it is possible may be had for their victuals & cloaths; especially if there are large importations from Germany (as some articles in the papers say there will be)—I mention the matter now, that in case arrivals should happen before I get back, of these kind of People, you may be apprised of my wishes—low & squat (well made) boys, would suit best. If emigrants are not to be had, there can be no doubt, but that some of the Dutch Servants in the family could easily procure such as are wanted from among the Citizens—& perhaps none readier, or better than by John himself when he arrives. Remember me to Mrs Lear—and be assured of the esteem & regard of Yr Affecte

Go: Washington

ALS, CSmH.

　　1. GW's last letter to Tobias Lear was dated 15 June.

　　2. For GW's long-standing concern over his household's consumption of wine, see GW to Lear, 17, 20 Sept. 1790.

　　3. For GW's meeting of 27–29 June with the commissioners and proprietors, see Commissioners for the Federal District to GW, 30 June and source note, and *Diaries*, 6:164–66. GW returned to Philadelphia in July by a more westerly route through Maryland and Pennsylvania than his homeward-bound trip in March through Delaware and across the Chesapeake Bay.

From Tobias Lear

Sir,　　　　　　　　　　　　Philadelphia June 19[–20]th 1791.

　　I have had the honor to receive your letters of the 12th & 15th of this month. The former of which I should have acknowleged by the last post had I not been absent on a journey to New York when it arrived in this City. The cause of my Journey to New York was to attend my mother to this place where she proposes to spend a week or two on a visit to Mrs Lear & myself. She had a favorable opportunity of coming to New York, from whence (unexpectedly) I received a letter from her requesting that I would, if it was in my power, come to that place & accompany her to Philadelphia. I accordingly sat off in the Stage on Tuesday last & returned with her by the same conveyance, yesterday. I have provided lodgings for her at Mrs Houses which makes it very convenient for Mrs Lear to be much with her.[1]

It is really unlucky, as you did not return by the way of Taylor's Ferry, that Letters were directed to you at that place. Mr Jefferson gave me a list of the Stages by which you proposed to return, but the time of arrival at those Stages was not fixed; he therefore advised directing letters, until the last of may, to Taylor's ferry by the way of Petersburg, between which places he observed there was a constant intercourse & that a week would hardly ever elapse without presenting an opportunity of sending letters from the latter to the former.[2] I accordingly directed three letters to that place for you—viz.—may 15th—22d & 29th. The last, however, with directions to the Post master of Petersburg, if he should have no opportunity of sending it to Taylor's ferry before a certain day, to return it to Fredericksburg to wait your arrival there. That of the 22d appears to be the only one missing. It enclosed one of Mr Paine's pamphlets, & gave the sketch of a conversation which took place between Colo. Beckworth & myself relative to the dedication of that work.

Agreeable to your directions contained in Major Jackson's letter I informed the Secy of War of your arrival at Mount Vernon, and of the necessity there was of transmitting duplicates of such dispatches as he might have directed to you at Taylor's Ferry, provided such dispatches contained anything of a particular or pressing nature.[3] The Secretary of State has not yet returned from his northern tour; but is expected this evening, when I will communicate the above to him. He & Mr Madison arrived in N. York on thursday last, where I saw them. They express themselves very much gratified by their journey & observations, and both appear to have been benefited in their health by it. Mr Madison does not intend to return immediately to this place, and is not certain but that he shall pay a visit to Boston & the maritime parts of the eastern States before he sets his face to the Southward.[4]

In conformity to the opinion of the Secretary of the Treasury I have the honor now to enclose 12 Commissions for the Cutters to receive your Signature.[5]

The persons whom I have heard mentioned as being more likely to come to view in selecting a successor[6] to Judge Hopkinson are, Mr Lewis, the Attorney, Mr Peters, Mr Ingersoll and a Mr Lawrence who married Gen. Sinclair's daughter. Judge Shippen has likewise been spoken of. The first mentioned Gentleman is thought to stand on the highest ground in every point of view. But it is said that his practise at the bar is so much more lucrative that he would not accept it. However it is thought that he will have it in his power to accept or decline. The second Gentleman is pretty generally thought of. Altho' he has not been in the habits of practise at the Courts; yet it is said that he has a good stock of Law knowledge, and his merit is unquestionable. The 3d is spoken of as a gentleman learned in the law—respectable & meritorious. Of the 4th I have heard but little said—and the 5 Gentleman is said to have been respectable on the bench for many years.[7]

Of all the Gentlemen who have been brouqht to view for the Comptroller's place Mr Kean was thought, on every account, to be the most suitable man to fill that office unless the Auditor should be advanced (which was thought the most likely step and such were his merits that few, besides the applicants or their friends, expected any other person). But there seem to be two obsticles to this Character—first a doubt whether he would accept it—and secondly whether he could be removed from his present office without removing at the same time all expectation of having the business of that board brought to a close; for he is considered as the principal agent in that business. He has attended to it closely & indefatigably. Mr L. from New Hampshire went home in the beginning of April and has not yet returned.[8]

I have not heard Mr Richmond spoken of here with a view to either the Comptrollers or Auditors office. Colo. Pickering was mentioned as a person highly qualified for the discharge of either; but whether he would accept the latter or not I have not understood. Colo. Drayton & Colo. Forrest I have not heard named. I have understood that Mr Smith of Baltimore who was in Congress last winter would accept it (the Auditors office) & his qualifications are said to be very competent to the duties thereof. His respectability is well known.[9]

I shall not fail to use every *indirect* means, in my power, to ascertain the public opinion with respect to the fittest Character to fill these offices and shall communicate whatever I may learn on that head.

There has been a Holy day at the College for the week past, and it happend at a lucky season for Washington, for he has been so much indisposed with the Chicken pox, and, since that has left him, with biles, that has not been able to attend his school near a fortnight.[10] Mr Fentham, I am informed, is certainly to quit his place in the latin school, which, it is said, will thereby suffer an almost irreparable loss; for he is considered as a good Scholar, and has more authority in the School than any of the other masters.

I am in hopes that the Servants of the family, finding a steady determination on the part of their immediate inspectors to have regularity & industry established in the house, and an assurance from higher powers that they will be supported in their just & reasonable measures, will be induced to act as they ought.

It is a matter of serious regret that the prospects of the farmer are so bad from a want of rain. Appearances have been rather unfavorable here for a few days past; but we have just now been blessed with a fine & an abundant shower which very much alters the face of things.

Permit me, sir, to do in this part of my letter what I ought to have done in the first line—that is, to congratulate you upon your safe return to Mount Vernon in the full enjoyment of your health to express the pleasure which that event gives me—and to add my prayers & wishes for as happy a termination of your journey at this place.

Colo. Smith arrived from London a short time since, & was in this place last week. He reports that there were strong assurances from the British ministry that a diplomatic Character would be sent out here in a few months. Colo. Beckworth reports also that his letters confirm that Account; but who will be the man was not then known.[11]

Colo. Walker arrived in New York while I was there after a passage of 43 days from Bristol—I saw him.[12] He says the ministerial party in England declare there will be a war between G. Britain & Russia; unless the Empress makes peace with the Turks—upon the terms proposed by the mediating powers; but the people at large beleive no such thing—they reprobate the idea of a war with Russia from which nothing is to be expected— and they have been so much in the habit of a profitable commerce with that Country that such a step would be so unpopular that the minister would fall in consequence of it.

Mr Dandridge will have the small pox very lightly—this is the 15th day of his inoculation—and but two or three pustules have yet made their appearance.

Mrs Lear is grateful for your kind remembrance of herself and the Child—and with me unites in sentiments of the highest respect & most sincere Attachment with which I have the honor to be Sir, Your most Obedt & very grateful Humble Servant

Tobias Lear.

Monday morning 8 O'Clock

P.S. The Commissions which I mentioned within are not sent herewith. All that were struck off for the Cutters were done under Colo. Hamiltons direction & sent to his office, from whence those came which were filled & received your signature. I have sent twice for some of the blanks but as the Office is not yet opened I cannot get them & this is the last moment of the Mail for this day. They shall be forwarded by the next post.[13]

T.L.

ALS, DLC:GW; ALS (letterpress copy), PWacD. Only the receiver's copy has the postscript.

1. Mary Stillson Lear (1739–1829), the widow of Tobias Lear IV (1737–1781) and mother of Tobias Lear, had come to Philadelphia to see her new grandson, Benjamin Lincoln Lear. Lear left the capital on 14 June and returned with his mother on 18 June. The two-week-long Philadelphia visit that followed initiated a lifelong friendship between Mrs. Lear and Martha Washington (Decatur, *Private Affairs of George Washington*, 242).

2. For Thomas Jefferson's unsuccessful attempts to maintain contact with GW during the Southern Tour, see Jefferson to GW, 1, 8 May.

3. William Jackson's letter of 14 June from Mount Vernon reads: "The President of the United States requests that you will inform the Secretaries for the departments of State and war that he is arrived at Mount Vernon, to which place they will address their letters to him until the 27th of this month when he proposes meeting the Commissioners at Georgetown, by appointment with them before he went to the southward. As the letters for the President were sent from Fredericksburg to Taylor's ferry, by which route he did not return, he has not received any Letters from the Secretaries or from yourself between the 15th and the 30th of May—Should the dispatches to him within that time have contained any thing of a particular or pressing nature it will be necessary for his information that duplicates of them should be forwarded immediately, as it is uncertain when he may receive the originals. The President thinks he may write to the Heads of departments by the next post, in the meanwhile he wishes you to acquaint them of his return—He writes to Colonel Hamilton by this post" (DLC:GW).

4. James Madison relinquished his planned trip to Massachusetts because of ill health and a lame horse and remained in New York City until the third week of August, returning to Philadelphia around 23 Aug. with the intention of accompanying Jefferson home to Virginia (see Madison to Jefferson, 24 July,

Daniel Carroll to Madison, 24 July, Jefferson to Madison, 18 Aug., and Madison to Joseph Jones, post 23 Aug. and source note, *Madison Papers*, 14:52–54, 54–55, 71–72).

5. These commissions were not actually enclosed (see postscript, and Lear to GW, 23 June and note 5).

6. Lear inadvertently wrote "succccessor."

7. Jared Ingersoll was a distinguished lawyer of Philadelphia and served as state attorney general. John Lawrence was married to Elizabeth St. Clair, daughter of Arthur St. Clair. Edward Shippen was president of the court of common pleas of Philadelphia County from 1784 to 1791 and sat as a special judge on Pennsylvania's high court of errors and appeals until 1791, when he was appointed to the state supreme court.

8. GW had reappointed John Kean a commissioner for settling accounts between the United States and the individual states in August 1790. See Commissioners for Settling Accounts to GW, 21 July 1790, n.1. Oliver Wolcott, Jr., hoped that Kean would be named auditor (see Lear to GW, 23 June), and Peter Van Brugh Livingston wrote GW from Elizabethtown, N.J., on 1 June "in behalf of my Friend Mr John Kean, whose losses by three recent Insolvencies have been very considerable, as the office he now enjoys *by your favor* is like to be of no long Duration, that your Excellency would be pleased to confer on him one more permanent," specifically, the comptrollership (DLC:GW). GW appointed Kean to neither office, and Kean resigned from the board of commissioners in October to become cashier of the Bank of the United States (see Kean to GW, 31 October). The "Mr L." to whom Lear refers might have been his early patron and his father's cousin, U.S. Senator John Langdon of New Hampshire.

9. GW appointed former congressman William Smith auditor on 16 July, according to the State Department memorandum book (DNA:PCC, item 187) and that day's *Federal Gazette and Philadelphia Daily Advertiser.* Smith declined the office, and GW nominated on 25 Nov. Richard Harrison in place of Oliver Wolcott, Jr., who had been promoted to comptroller (Harrison to GW, 8 May 1789, n.2). The Senate confirmed the appointment of Harrison on 29 Nov. after GW provided, upon request, further information about him (GW to the U.S. Senate, 25, 29 Nov., both LS, DNA: RG 46, Second Congress, 1791–1793, Records of Executive Proceedings, President's Messages—Executive Nominations; U.S. Senate to GW, 28 Nov., DLC:GW; *Executive Journal*, 1:90, 91).

10. Lear reported on 23 June that George Washington Parke Custis had recovered from his illnesses. After GW's return to Philadelphia, however, Custis became so "very ill with a fever" that he was attended by doctors William Shippen, Jr., and Adam Kuhn, and "The President sat up with him last night" (Benjamin Rush to Julia Stockton Rush, 16 July, in Butterfield, *Rush Letters*, 1:599–601). Jefferson wrote Madison on 24 July that Custis "has had a long & dangerous fever. He is thought better to-day" (*Madison Papers*, 14:55). Martha Washington wrote of his recovery to Fanny Bassett Washington on 29 Aug.: "dear little Wash is quite well and has a very good apetite and gains flesh and strength every day he is now well enough to go to school" (Fields, *Papers of Martha Washington*, 233).

11. Maj. George Beckwith had conversed on 15 June with Alexander Hamilton about the appointment of a British minister to the United States (Syrett, *Hamilton Papers,* 8:475–77). He may also have communicated with Lear directly.

12. At the end of August 1790, GW granted Benjamin Walker, federal naval officer for New York, a leave of absence from his post until March 1791, and Walker traveled to Paris as agent for the Scioto Company. William Duer later informed Walker that Hamilton said no notice would be taken of his staying "a few months beyond" the expiration of his official leave (see Hamilton to GW, 28 Aug. 1790 and note 2).

13. For Lear's reasons for not sending the commissions in the next post, see Lear to GW, 23 June and note 5.

From Stephen Hall

Portland [District of Maine] 20 June 1791. Applies for the position of inspector of survey for the District of Maine: "I have so often troubled You with my applications, that I would gladly make *even this* more concise, lest I become tedious."[1]

ALS, DLC:GW.

1. For Stephen Hall's previous applications for office, see Hall to GW, 14 May 1789 and source note. GW did not appoint him to an excise position at this time.

From Thomas Jefferson

Sir   Philadelphia June 20. 1791.

I am honoured with yours of the 15th instant, & not a little mortified with the miscarriage of so many of my letters. they have been of the following dates[:]

Mar. 27.

Apr. 2.

Apr. 10.

Apr. 17.

Apr. 24.

May 1.

May 8.

May 15.

June. 5. from Bennington. of these it appears that only the three first & that of May 15. had come to hand, & probably that of

June 5. has been recieved ere this. those of Apr. 17. & 24. & May 1. & 8. were sent, the two first to Charleston, & the two last to Taylor's ferry. I now send copies of them, tho their contents are not at this time very interesting.[1]

The papers from the free people of colour in Grenada, which you did me the honour to inclose, I apprehend it will be best to take no notice of. they are parties in a domestic quarrel, which I think we should leave to be settled among themselves. nor should I think it desireable, were it justifiable, to draw a body of sixty thousand free blacks & mulattoes into our country. the instructions from the government of the United Netherlands, by which mister Shaw has suffered, merit serious notice. the channel thro which application shall be made is the only difficulty; Dumas being personally disagreeable to that government. however, either thro' him or some other it should certainly be conveyed.[2]

Mr Remsen had unluckily sent off to New York all my letters on the very day of my arrival here, which puts it out of my power to give you the state of things brought by the last packet. I expect they will be returned tomorrow, & that my next may communicate to you whatever they contain interesting.[3]

I recieved yesterday a letter from Colo. Ternan informing me of his appointment & that he should sail about the latter end of May. the court of Madrid has sent over a Don Joseph Jaudenes as a joint commissioner with de Viar, till a Chargé shall be named. he presented me the letter of Credence from the Count de Florida Blanca when I was at New York. he is a young man who was under Secretary to Mr Gardoqui when here.[4]

Our tour was performed in somewhat less time than I had calculated. I have great hopes it has rid me of my head-ach, having scarcely had any thing of it during my journey. mister Madison's health is very visibly mended. I left him at New York, meditating a journey as far Eastward as Portsmouth.[5] I have the honor to be with the most respectful attachment, Sir, Your most obedient & most humble servt

Th: Jefferson

ALS, DNA: RG 59, Miscellaneous Letters; ALS (letterpress copy), DLC: Thomas Jefferson Papers; LB, DLC:GW.

1. Of the duplicates of the missing letters, those of 17, 24 April, 8 May, are in DNA: RG 59, Miscellaneous Letters; that of the 1 May letter has not been found.

2. Instead of having the American agent at The Hague, Charles-Guillaume-Frédéric Dumas, lodge a formal complaint with the government of the Netherlands, Jefferson on 14 July took the matter to Franco Petrus Van Berckel, Dutch minister to the United States (*Jefferson Papers*, 20:629–30).

3. For Jefferson's detailed instructions of 16 May to clerk Henry Remsen, Jr., and their revision on 28 May, see ibid., 419–20, 462.

4. Jefferson probably met José de Jaudenes y Nebot in New York on 16 June, as he recorded receiving a letter of 1 Feb. from Diego de Gardoqui introducing the Spanish *encargado*, a former member of his staff. The *Gazette of the United States* (Philadelphia), 15 June, announced the arrival of Jaudenes on 11 June on the ship *Four Friends*, Captain Volans, from Cadiz. GW and Jefferson formally received Jaudenes on 19 July (Gardoqui to GW, 24 July 1789, n.2, and GW to David Humphreys, 20 July 1791).

5. GW acknowledged this letter on 26 June.

From Henry Knox

Sir.   War-department [Philadelphia], June 20th 1791

I beg leave to congratulate you upon your arrival at Mount Vernon after so lengthy a journey, and at such a sultry season of the year.

Mr Lear has informed me that you did not receive any letters from any of the other secretaries between the 15th and 30th of May, and desired me if any had been written by me during that period to transmit duplicates—But mine of the 30th ultimo of which duplicates were addressed was the first to reach you on your return.

Not having any material information to submit to you in addition to mine of the 16th instant I shall not further intrude upon you by this post—But if any thing of importance should occur previously to your arrival, I shall have the honor to inform you thereof. I have the honor to be Sir, with the highest respect, Your most obedt and very humble Servant

H. Knox

LS, DLC:GW; LB, DLC:GW.

To James Mercer

Dear Sir,   Mount Vernon, June 21st 1791.

When I was in Fredericksburg on my way to the southward I received a letter from Mr Neil McCoull of which, and the letter of his lawyer, referred to, the enclosed are copies.[1] The verbal answer returned to Mr McCoull by his son, was that I had conceived so far as I was concerned in the business, that the matter had been settled long ago—But as it appeared otherwise from the application he had then made to me, I would on my return speak to you on the subject, and inform him of the result. This I accordingly intended to have done; but your duties in Richmond having taken you from Fredericksburg at the time I came thro' it,[2] I am reduced to the necessity of troubling you with a letter, praying that some decision may be had by which I shall be released from this demand—or at any rate, that I may be instructed what answer to give Mr McCoull, who unquestionably will expect one from Dear Sir, Your most obedient and very humble servant

G. Washington.

LB, DLC:GW; ALS, listed in Robert F. Batchelder, catalog no. 9 (n.d.), item 1.

1. The enclosures have not been found but probably dealt with GW's acquisition of the Four Mile Run tract from James, John Francis, and George Mercer in 1774. The surviving Mercer brothers gave GW a bond of indemnification in May 1787 to relieve him from having to pay a £450 bond to Neil McCoull and Alexander Blair, attorneys of the deceased George Mercer. See GW to James Mercer, 12 Dec. 1774 and note 3, 26 Dec. 1774, 19 Nov. 1786 and note 1, and GW to John Francis Mercer, 19 Dec. 1786.

2. GW passed through Fredericksburg on his way south on 8–10 April and upon his return from the Southern Tour on 10–11 June (*Diaries*, 6:107–8, 163).

From Pierre-Charles L'Enfant

sir   George town [Md.] jun 22. 1791

In framing the plan, here anexed, for the Intended federal City I regreted much being induced by the shortness of time from making any particular drawing of the several buildings—squars—and every other Improvement which the smalness of the scale of the general map together with the hurry with which

I had it drawn could not admit of having so correctly lay down as necessary to give a perfect Idea of the effect of the whole in the Execution.[1]

My whole attention was given to the combination of the general distribution of the grand local[e] as to an object of most immediate moment and of Importance to this I yielded Every other consideration & have in consequence to sollicite again you Indulgence in submitting to you my Ideas in an In Compleat drawing only correct as to the situation and distances of objects all of which were determined after a local[e] well ascertained having for more accuracy had several lines run on the Ground cleared of the wood & after wards measured with posts fixed all along, to serve me as certain bases from after the which I might arrange the whole with a Certainty of making Every part fit to the various ground.

having first determined some principal points to which I wished making the rest subordinate I next made the distribution regular with streets at right angle *north-south* & *East-west* but after wards I opened other on various directions as avenues to & from every principal places, wishing by this not mearly to contrast with the general regulariety nor to afford a greater variety of pleasant seats and prospect as will be obtained from the advantageous ground over the which these avenues are mostly directed but principally to connect each part of the city with more efficacy by, if I may so Express, making the real distance less from place to place in menaging on them a reciprocity of sight and making them thus seemingly Connected, promot a rapid stellement over the whole so that the most remot may become an adition to the principal while without the help of these divergent communications such setlements if at all attempted would be languid, and lost in the Extant would become detrimental to the main Establishement.[2]

several of these avenues were also necessary to Effect the junction of several out road which I conceived Essential to bring central to the City in rendering these Road shorter as is done with respect to the bladensburg & Eastern branche Road made above a mile shorter besides the advantage of thier leading from the direction given immediatly on the warfs at george town without passing the Hilly ground of that place whose agrandissement it will consequently check while it will accelerate those over rock

creek on the City side the which cannot fall spreading soon all
along of these avenu forming of themselves a variety of pleasent
ride and being Combined to Ensure a rapid Intercourse with all
the part of the City to which they will serve as doses the main
vains in the animal body to diffuse life trough smaller vessells in
quickening the active motion to the heart.

as to on what point it is most Expedient first to begone the
main Establishment, I belive the question may be easily resolve
if not viewing by part but Embracing under one sight the whole
Extant from the Eastern branch to george town & from the
banck on the potowmack across towards the montagnes. for considering impartially the whole Extant and reflecting it is that of
the Intended City then only one position will appear Capable of
promoting the rapid agrandissment & setlement of the whole.

a cross the tiber up above were the tide water come lay certainly the elligible spot to lay the Fundation of an Establishement of the nature of the one in view, not because this point
being central is the most liekly to diffuse an Equallity of advantages trough the whole territory and in return to derive a benefit
proportional to the rise of its valu but because the nature of the
local[e] is such as will made Every thing Concur to render a settlement there prosperous—there it will benefit of the natural
jalousie which must stimulate Establishements on each of its opposed limits it will become necessarily the point of reunion of
both and soon become populous.[3]

a canal being easy to open from the Entrance of the eastern
branch and to be lead a cross the first settlements and carried
towards the mouth of the tiber were it will again give an issue in
to the potowmack and at a distance not to far off for to admit
the boats from the grand navigation canal from getting in, will
undoubtedly facilitate a Conveyance most advantageous to trading interest. it will insure the storing of markettes which, as lay
down on the map, being Erected all long the canal and over
pounds proper to shelter any number of boats will leave of mart
House from were when the City is grown to its fullest extant the
most distant markets will be supplyed at command.[4]

to these advantages of first necessity to considere to determine
the seat of a City is added that of the positions which there offer
and the which are the most suceptible of any within the limits of
the Intended city of leading to those grand Improvements of

publique magnitude and as may serve as models for all subsequent undertaking and stand to future ages a monument to national genious and munificence.

after much menutial search for an elligible situation, prompted I may say from a fear of being prejudiced in favour of a first opinion I could discover no one so advantageous to Erect the Congressional building as is that on the west end of Jenkins heights which stand as a pedestal waiting for a monument, and I am confident—were all the wood cleared from the ground no situation could stand in competition with this—some might perhaps require less labour to be rendered agreable but after all assistance of arts none Ever would be made so grand and all other would appear but of a secondary nature.

that were I determined the seat of the presidial palace, in its difference of nature may be view as Equally advantageous to the object of adding to the sumptuousness of a palace the convenience of a house and the agreableness of a country seat situated on that ridge which attracted your attention at the first inspection of the ground on the west side of the tiber Entrance it will see *10* or *12* miles down the potowmack front the town and harbor of allexandria and stand to the view of the whole city and have the most Improved part of it made as addition to those grand Improvements for which the ground in the dependency of the palace is so proper.[5]

fixed as Expressed on the map, the distance from the congressional House will not be to great as what Even the activity of business may be no mesage to, nor from the president is to be made without a sort of decorum which will doubtless point out the propriety of committees waiting on him in carriage should his palace be Uncontigous to Congress.

to mak how ever the distance less to other offices, I placed the three grand departments of state Contigous to the presidial palace and on the way leading to the Congressional House the gardens of the one together with the park and other improvement on the dependency are connected with the publique walk and avenu to the Congress House in a manner of most service a whole as grand as it will be agreable and Convenient to the whole City which from the distribution of the local[e] will have an easy access to this place of general report and all long side of which may be placed play house—room of assembly—accademies and all such sort of places as maybe attractive to the larned and afford divertion to the idle.

I proposed Continuing the canal much farther up but this being not to be effectual but with the aide of locks, and from a level obtained of the height of the spring of the tiber the greatest facility being to bring those watters over the flat back of Jenkins I have the more readily a preference to avail of this water to supply that part of the city as it wi⟨ll⟩ promot the Execution of a plan which I propose in this map, of leting the tiber return in its proper chanell by a fall which issuing from under the base of the congress building may there form a cascade of forty feet heigh or more than one hundred waide which would produce the most happy effect in rolling down to fill up the canall and discharge it self in the potowmack of which it would then appear as the main spring when seen trough most grand & majestique avenu intersecting with the prospect from the palace at A point which being seen from both I have designated as the proper for to erect A grand Equestrian figure.[6]

in the present unimproved state of the local[e] it will appear that the height were is marked that monument close intercept this view of the water from the plalace and in fact it is partly the case but it must be observed that having to bound the Entrance of the tiber ⟨*illegible*⟩ breadth of a canal of *200* feet which is the utmost breadth that can be preserve to avoid its being drained at low water. it will require much ground to be trown in to feel up, and at least as much as will Enable to levell that point of heigh ground betwen the tiber and n. yo[u]ng House to almost a levell with the tide water and of Course to procure to the palace and all other House from that place to congres a propect of the powtomack the which will acquire new swetness being had over the green of a Field well level and made brilent by shade of few tree Artfully planted[7] I am with respectfull submission your most Humble a. obeident servant

P. C. L'Enfant

ALS, DLC: Pierre-Charles L'Enfant Papers; copy (with variant text), DLC: Digges-L'Enfant-Morgan Papers. GW docketed the ALS, "From Majr L'Enfant 22d June 1791." GW evidently gave the letter to the commissioners for the federal district, as a second docket, in an unidentified hand, indicates they returned it to GW on 14 Mar. 1792. The wording of the copy, in the hand of Isaac Roberdeau, assistant of Andrew Ellicott and Pierre-Charles L'Enfant, differs substantially from the ALS, although their contents are essentially the same. A docket in an unidentified hand indicates that the letter was dictated to Roberdeau by L'Enfant, and the textual differences reflect Roberdeau's efforts to translate L'Enfant's broken English and clarify L'Enfant's vision for the city. For background to this letter, see Memorandum of L'Enfant, 26 Mar., and GW to L'Enfant, 4 April.

1. The enclosed plan has not been identified but was not the one L'Enfant gave GW on 19 Aug., which shows no marks of haste. The letter and enclosed plan were probably delivered to GW at Mount Vernon, perhaps by L'Enfant himself, on 22 June.

2. L'Enfant's plan of wide diagonal avenues superimposed on a grid of narrower streets was intended to promote rapid settlement, as the lots to be located along these avenues (particularly the broad avenue connecting the Capitol with the President's House) would be developed first.

3. The tidal portion of Tyber Creek ended at the western foot of Jenkins Hill (later Capitol Hill), at the eastern end of the modern Mall. Located about midway between the Eastern Branch and Georgetown, this was the area L'Enfant judged the most eligible for initial development.

4. Tiber Creek was quite shallow and of no value to commerce in its natural state. L'Enfant proposed to transform it and St. James Creek, which enters the Eastern Branch near its mouth, into canals suitable for commercial navigation and to join the canals on the western side of Jenkins Hill at the point where he proposed to center the development of the city.

5. When GW met with the proprietors of land in the federal district in March, he had pointed L'Enfant toward the site on the east side of Rock Creek below Georgetown where he wanted the President's House to be built. The place selected by GW was slightly west of the subsequent site of the White House, closer to the banks of the Tiber, on a low ridge commanding a view down the Potomac toward Alexandria. L'Enfant proposed to place the President's House slightly east of this point.

6. L'Enfant's proposal to have the waters of the Tiber issue from beneath the Capitol in a grand cascade was one of the many Baroque elements in his plan, which bears comparison with Versailles. Like some of the other ambitious aspects of the plan, it was never carried out. The equestrian statue to which L'Enfant alludes was to be a statue of GW, fulfilling a resolution of Congress of 7 Aug. 1783 "that an equestrian statue of General Washington, be erected at the place where the residence of Congress shall be established." Congress had specified that the statue be made of bronze, with GW to be represented in Roman dress, holding a truncheon in his right hand (*JCC*, 24:494–95). See also Giuseppe Ceracchi to GW, 31 Oct. 1791.

7. The high point was located near the modern intersection of 10th Street and Maryland Avenue, S.W., and reached a height of more than thirty feet above tidewater. The point where L'Enfant proposed to place the President's House, due north of this rise on the right bank of Tiber Creek, was slightly lower. The plantation home of Notley Young (c.1736–1802), located on the banks of the Potomac near the modern intersection of 8th and I streets, S.W.,

and acquired by deed from his mother in 1762, was a portion of a larger tract known as Duddington's Pasture. It ran along the Potomac from near the mouth of Tiber Creek to the mouth of the Eastern Branch, extending inland about half a mile.

From Henry Knox

Sir,   War Department [Philadelphia] June 23d 1791.

The Post has arrived from Fort Pitt and brought Letters of the 16th instant, from Major General Butler—Every thing was tranquil—the Levies were posted so as to dismiss the Militia down to the Great Kenahwa.[1]

I have written to Major General St Clair, not to expect more than 2,500 regulars and Levies in addition to the old troops on the Ohio—That if the service should require a greater number, that he must draw them from Kentucky in such numbers, and of such species of troops as he shall judge proper.[2]

Nearly all the troops expected to be of service in the Campaign, are now moving forward.

I have just received a Letter from General Sevier, dated the ceded territory the 5th instant—in which he informs me, that three Companies of his battalion were raised, and would march in a few days for Fort Washington—As dependence was placed upon that district for Rifle-men, this information affords me great satisfaction.

That Governor Blount has informed him, there is likely to be a very large representation of the Cherakees, and that the treaty would probably be opened on the 5th of June.

That the Goods for the treaty, and Soldiers Clothing had all arrived safe some time before. I have the honor to be With the highest Respect, Sir, Your most Obedt hume servt

H. Knox

LS, DLC:GW; LB, DLC:GW.

1. Among other things, Richard Butler's letter of 16 June to Henry Knox, to which Knox replied on 23 June, dealt with problems with the quality of beef supplied to the army by its chief contractor, William Duer (*ASP, Indian Affairs*, 1:189).

2. Knox's letter of 23 June to Arthur St. Clair is in ibid., 178.

From Tobias Lear

Sir,   Philadelphia June 23d 1791

After acknowledging the receipt of your letter of the 19th Inst. with which I have been this moment honored, I have to communicate to you the melancholly account of the death of the good and amiable Doctor Jones. He died this morning! He had for two or three days past been so much indisposed as to be confined to his bed; but his friends had no idea of his being in immediate danger. I saw him the day before yesterday & yesterday. And when I visited him yesterday he thought himself much better than he was the day before, and expressed his hopes & expectations of getting abroad in a few days. Last evening he took 3 grains of opium which not having the desired effect, he, this morning, took some of his own Elixir—and soon after fell a sleep. A short time afterwards Dr Foulke called to see him, and being informed that he was a sleep, he sent his servant up to see if he had not awoke. The Servant found him dead. These are the particulars as they have been related to me.[1]

Fraunces has been strenuous in his endeavours to get Mrs Read into the family; but having met with so peremptory a refusal from Mrs Washington & myself to listen to the matter, I presume he has laid aside the idea of effecting it. Her coming would certainly be attended with all the evils which you suggest; and in addition to them I have no doubt but she would oblige Mrs Emerson to quit the family, which, in my opinion, would be an irreparable loss. Mr Fraunces is stongly guarded in his agreements against the use of any kind of wine at the second Table under any pretence.

I received, by the last Post, a letter from Major Jackson covering a Commission for the office of Comptroller of the Treasury, which I had filled with the name of Mr Wolcott & after the seal was affixed to it & countersigned by the Secretary of State⟨,⟩ I delivered it to that Gentleman. A letter from Messrs Fenwick & Mason, explanatory of the wine from Charleston, was received at the same time. The Cases are agreeable to the Invoice and appear to be in good order; but how their contents are I know not. I intend, however, to have them examined to know whether they may be depended on or not. Mr Jefferson tells me that the wine which he has for you shall be attended to as soon as he can find a little leisure from the business that has pressed upon him since his return from his Northern Tour.[2]

I need not tell you, Sir, how happy I am to find that my doings in your absence, so far as they have been communicated to you, meet your approbation. I entertain strong hopes that the Servants will be fully impressed with the folly of any attempt to frustrate the determination of establishing order & industry in the family. Rhemur has given notice that he shall quit the family at the expiration of the present month; not from any disgust, but that he may live in New York with his wife, whose parents, he says, will not permit her to come to this place. Fraunces says a man in his place is indispensable, and he must therefore get another. This being the case, I am sorry that Rhemur cannot continue; for he has conducted himself in a quiet, peacable, and so far as I can learn⟨,⟩ honest manner since he has been with us.[3]

I shall not fail to pay particular attention to your wishes respecting the Blankets—And the two kinds of Turnip seed (if they can be got) shall be procured and sent to the Major by the first vessel that sails for Alexandria. At present there is no vessel up, but one is expected here every moment from Alexa which will return thither immediately. I will follow the directions respecting boys for the Stable, and if any vessels arrive with Emigrants from Germany I think they may be procured from that quarter; otherwise there is no doubt but they may be obtained in the City.

I do myself the honor to enclose Mr Payne's Answer to Mr Burke. I enclosed one in my letter of the 22d of may which I presume has not yet got to your hands. In Mr Fenno's papers of Saturday last, & this day, are two Numbers signed Publicola, taken from the Massachusetts Centinel, in answer to Mr Payne. The general voice says they are written by Mr Adams; but those who are best acquainted with his style say they are not.[4]

In my letter of the 19th I mentioned my intention of transmitting, for signature, some blank Commissions for the Revenue Cutters; but upon looking over those which had been struck off for that purpose, and of the parcel which had been filled & transmitted to their respective addresses, before you left this place, I found there was an important error, as you will see in the last line of the one enclosed. I shewed it Colo. Hamilton who observed that it would never answer to have these issued, and if

those which had been transmitted to the Officers were of the
same kind it would be proper to recall them and have others
issued without the limiting clause. I then applied to the Office
of State where the Commissions were filled up & recorded—and
found that those which had been transmitted were of this kind.
Mr Jefferson immediately gave directions for striking off a number of Blanks without that clause, which will be ready for your
signature on your arrival in this City—which the Secretary of
the Treasury says will be in season for them. I never before examined one of these commissions. Those which were completed
before your departure came with the Seals affixed from the Office and were returned immediately after being signed, to be
transmitted. There were never any of the Blanks in my possession.[5]

Mr Wolcot received his Commission with expressions of gratitude, and at the same time asked if any person had been fixed
upon for the Auditor's office. I told him I had not understood
that there was; but that several, whose names I mentioned, had
been brought to view. He observed, that knowing as he did the
duties & importance of that office, he did not hesitate to give it
as his opinion that the credit & respectability of the department
of Finance, depended more upon that Officer than upon any
one in the department except the Secretary. He had it more in
his power to give a complexion to the business done at the Treasury than any other officer. Every person who had accounts to
settle there necessarily had more to do with the Auditor than
with any one else; and from the manner in which that officer
did his business they would be led to form their opinion of the
department. The harmony of the department, he added, likewise much depended on that officer; for if his doings were not
so executed as that they could meet the approbation of the
Comptroller it would cause a discord between the two—and unavoidably throw an enormous weight of business on the latter—
more, perhaps, than it would be possible for any man to execute
in addition to the other duties of the Office. After making these
observations he said there was no doubt, but that your mind
would naturally turn itself to the Southward for a Character to
fill that place. In which case he could not help expressing a wish
that Mr Kean might be thought the suitable man; for from the
knowledge he had of his talents & disposition, Industry & Integ-

rity he had no doubt but he would fill the place with much credit. I then expressed the idea which had been suggested by some that he would not accept it. Mr W. said he knew nothing of that, for he had never expressed to him anything which could lead to the discovery of a sentiment on that point. I, afterwards, fell in with Colo. Hamilton, who introduced the subject, & said he had no doubt but Mr Kean would accept the appointment if it should be offered to him, and appeared to speak as if from Authority. I have had no opportunity since my last, of learning anything more of the public opinion respecting a District Judge.

Unless I hear from undoubted authority that you will come through Baltimore I shall not write again, unless some special circumstance should require it. If you come through Baltimore I shall have the honor to address a letter to you at that place.

Mrs Washington is uncertain whether she shall write at this time, and in case she should not she directs me to tell you she is well & to rember her to you in suitable terms. Washington has recovered from the effects of the Chicken pox; but Nelly has been for some days past sadly afflicted with a sore throat. She is now a little better. Mr Dandridge is quite well—Mrs Lear & the child enjoy good health. She unites with me in a grateful & respectful remembrance to yourself & best wishes to all at Mount Vernon. I have the honor to be with the greatest gratitude & respect Sir, Your obliged & Obedt Sert

Tobias Lear

ALS, DLC:GW.

1. The prominent Philadelphia physician John Jones attended GW during his near-fatal illness of May 1790. See William Jackson to Clement Biddle, 12 May 1790, editorial note. On 29 July Jones's brother Edward, a clerk in the Treasury Department, requested from GW appointment to a more responsible position if a vacancy occurred, stating: "By one of those sudden Vicissitudes, to which all mankind are Subjected, I became reduced to the necessity of accepting of a Clerkship in the Treasury to shield a Wife and Children from the evils incident to a State of want. It was natural however to suppose, that in accepting of this place, I was not without hopes, that my own Talents and Industry, seconded by the interest of my friends, would enable me on some future day, to obtain a post of greater emolument. Buoyed up therefore, with the expectation of seeing better times, I submitted with cheerfulness to my lot—until inexorable death steped in and depriving me of my best friend and brother Dr John Jones of this City, has blasted all my future prospects" (DLC:GW).

2. According to Thomas Jefferson's letter of 24 June to Lear, Jefferson had

that morning endeavored "to make a statement of the cost & expences of the President's wines, but not having a full account of the whole from Fenwick he is unable to do it but on sight of the acct rendered by him to the President. if mister Lear the first time any circumstance shall give him occasion of doing Th: J. the honour of calling on him, will put that acct in his pocket, the matter can be completed in two or three minutes. the cloudiness of the present day renders it favourable to remove the 4. hampers of Champagne from Th: J.'s cellar, if mister Lear thinks proper to send for them. it would be well to open a case of every kind & place the bottles on their shelves that they may be settled before the President's return" (owned by Mr. Dudley Stoddard, New York).

3. Liveried houseman Henry Rhemur was replaced by Charles Liddle. See Lear to GW, 10 Oct. 1790, n.4, and Decatur, *Private Affairs of George Washington,* 252.

4. For the first "Publicola" essay reprinted from Benjamin Russell's *Columbian Centinel* (Boston) in "Mr Fenno's papers," see *Gazette of the United States* (Philadelphia), 18 June. The essays, actually written by the vice-president's eldest son, John Quincy Adams (1767–1848) who recently had been admitted to the Boston bar, continued in the *Centinel* on 11, 15, 18, 22, 29 June, 2, 9, 13, 20, 27 July and were widely reprinted.

5. The enclosed cutter commission has not been found. Lear discussed the flawed commissions with Assistant Secretary of the Treasury Tench Coxe, who wrote of the objectionable clause to Lear on 27 June: "I have now before me Captn Montgomery's commission, which contains the error you supposed, being limited by the end of the next session of the senate" (DLC:GW). Lear replied to Coxe on 29 June that "Commissions have been struck off for the Officers of the Cutters without the error contained in those which have been issued; and if the Secretary of the Treasury thinks proper, they shall be filled with the names of those persons who have been appointed, & be ready for the Presidents signature on his arrival, that those which have been issued may be recalled, & these sent in their places. Should this meet the Secretarys idea, I will be obliged to you for a list of the persons to whom commissions have been sent that no error may happen in inserting the names & offices" (DLC:GW). Coxe sent Lear the same day a return of the officers of the revenue cutters whose appointments were known at the Treasury and noted: "the dates of the old commissions cannot be furnished from this office. The Secretary is of opinion that Capt. Cochrans, Capt. Cookes, & Mr Wallaces, commissions should be of the dates of the letters announcing their appointments which are noted at the foot of the return, unless it may contravene the rules in the Department of State" (DLC:GW). On 7 July Coxe further informed Lear that John Howell was appointed commander of the Georgia cutter, with Hendrick Fisher and John Wood, first and second mates, respectively, as evidenced by GW's letter of 20 May in the Treasury Department's files (DLC:GW). The State Department memorandum book notes that on 13 July: "The Officers of the revenue cutters were commissioned anew on account of an imperfection in their first commission, and these new Commissions were sent to the Secretary of the Treasury for transmission; and the expediency of obtaining from the said Officers their first commissions, was suggested to & left with him" (DNA:PCC, item 187, 113). Lear returned unidentified letters to Hamilton on 13 Aug. with commis-

sions for the mates of the Virginia cutter as well as commissions for excise inspectors Thomas Marshall in Virginia, Sylvanus Walker in South Carolina, and Josiah Murdaugh in North Carolina (DLC:GW).

From George Clendenin

Sir,   Philadelphia, June the 25th 1791[1]

On the Eleventh day of May last I Receiv'd your Excellencies favour, directed to me from this City, dated, The twenty first of March, Wherein you inform me that you have disposed of the whole of your Lands On the great Kanawa, and on the Ohio between the two Rivers bearing the name of Kanawa, Drafts of which have been in my hands for A Considerable time. And altho I am purswaded you must have sold them considerably under their Value from their present Expos'd situation, Nothing Could contribute more to the welfair of the place, than the Immediate Sale of the Military Lands, as they are held in Such large Surveys as to prevent the Settlements from taking place, So as to form a Barier against the Indians, Wherefore I am Convinc'd you will consider your loss very Inconsiderable.

On the Receipt of your last mentioned letter I would have Immediately Transmitted you the Drafts In my hands (which you Required) Had I not been coming to this place; therefore brought them with me, & have herewith Inclos'd them free from any Incumbrance whatever, as I was unwilling to take any Steps concerning them, until I had Receiv'd An answer to the letter which I wrote your Excellency last Winter by the Honble andrew Moore, Expressive of the Terms on which I apprehended your Lands might be Seated, to which I Never Receivd an answer or Any Account until you Inform'd me of the late Sale.

And permit me Sir to assure you that I feel abundantly Recompenc'd, for any Indeavours I may have us'd, respecting your property In that quarter, And Contemplate no act of my life with greater pleasure, Then that of rendering you any service in the reach of my Small Abilities. I have the Honr to be with great Respect and Esteem your Very Obt Hble Sevt

                         Geo. Clendinen

ALS, DLC:GW.

1. George Clendenin apparently traveled to Philadelphia to press his claims for reimbursement from the federal government for his expenditures on frontier defense (see Clendenin to GW, 19 July).

To Thomas Jefferson

Sir,   Mount-Vernon, June 26th 1791.

The last post brought me your letter of the 20th instant, and the duplicates of your letters, which were missing when I last wrote to you—the originals of which have since been received—This acknowledgement is all the notice I shall take of them until I have the pleasure of seeing you.

I have selected the letters written by you to me while you were in the administration of the government of this State—and I will take them with me to Philada.

The enclosed letters have been received since my return to Mount Vernon.[1] I am Sir, your most obedient Servant

Go: Washington

LS, DLC: Thomas Jefferson Papers; Df, DNA: RG 59, Miscellaneous Letters; LB, DLC:GW. Jefferson endorsed the LS, "recd June 30."

1. The enclosures have not been identified.

To Tobias Lear

Dear Sir,   Mount Vernon June 26th 1791.

This is the eve of my departure for George town, & being Sunday, ought to have been a day of rest; but it is not so with me, either from company, or business; the latter, occasioned by a constant succession of company during the whole of last week: wch obliged me to postpone many matters until this day, which ought, & but for that reason, would have been done in the course of it—Such time as I have been able to spend in my study to day, has been employed in sorting of the Letters & Papers which have been recd since I left Charleston—part of which I enclose, because my travelling writing desk will not contain them.[1]

I have but little leizure to say much in this letter, if much (as I expect soon to be in Philadelphia) was necessary. I presume all the letters which had been sent to Taylors ferry, and other places have got to me—but that you may judge, the following is a list of them.

April—3d 5th 10th 15th 17th 24th
May—1st 8th 15th 22d 29th
June—5th 12th 19th

What my stay at Georgetown may be, is at present beyond my ken—I go there prepared to proceed, and shall make Herculas take the Waggon box in place of Paris. From that place, so soon as I shall be able to decide on the day of my departure from it, and the rout, I will inform you, or Mrs Washington thereof.[2] I think it was a duty you owed Mrs Lear, your mother, to meet her at New York, for the purpose of accompanying her to Philadelphia. If she is still in that city I request my respects may be presented to her. The last Post came without the Commissions promised in the P.S. to your letter of the 19th or any letter from you—my best wishes attend Mrs Lear &ca and I am Your sincere friend and affecte Servant

Go: Washington

ALS, DLC: Tobias Lear Papers.

1. The enclosed papers have not been identified. Sometime before leaving Mount Vernon at 6:00 A.M. on 27 June, GW drafted a memorandum, probably for George Augustine Washington (see Fitzpatrick, *Writings of Washington*, 31:307, n.4): "The Work which immediately occurs to me to be done is the following; but the order in wch it is to be executed, must depend in part upon the weather, and circumstances; but chiefly upon the Orders of Mr Whiting. viz. A Corn house at the New Barn, at Ferry & French's Plantation exactly of the size and appearance of the one by the Overseers House at the Ferry. Another Corn House at the River Plantation of the size, and similar to the one that is now there. Shingling the side of the Overseers House at the Ferry that leaks, and making it tight. Finishing the well by the New Quarter that the efficacy of the Rope may be tried in drawing Water. Building a Necessary, with two Seats for the use of the New Quarter; It may be shingled with old Shingles, & weatherboarded with old plank ripped of the old Quarter—Isaac knows where it is to be placed. Removing Richards House in the Hollow to Muddy hole for Davy to live in. Huts, or some kind of covering will be wanting at Dogue-run; some of the People at that place complain much of the Leakiness of their Houses and others will be sent there. Setting up the New Gates where wanting; & will be pointed out by Mr Whiting. Muddy hole Barn is to be compleatly repaired; and that in the Neck is to be thoroughly examined; but, if upon examination it is found to be so far gone as to be irreparable—or, that the repairs would be almost as tedious & expensive as building a new one; it must, in that case be only patched & propped so as to serve until a new one can be built. The old Quarter at Mansion House to be taken down; and all the Scantling, Boards and Shingles worth any thing secured—and the nails saved. Frames for Hot beds to be prepared for the Gardener according to his directions if it is not upon an expensive plan. Air, by means of dormant Windows, or doors like the others, to be admitted into the graineries at the New Barn at Ferry & French's. agreeably to directions given. The same thing to be done, and for the same purpose, on the stable at the Mansion House. This also has been explained. The Floor and Sleepers of the Ice House should be

examined & repaired, if they want it before the time for filling it shall arrive. A Screen, or Sieve for separating stone for gravel should be got ready for the Gardener. Preparation should be made, and the materials provided, for making new, and repairing old Harrows—Ploughs—Cradles—Rakes & such like things: As also for the necessary repairs of Houses &ca; In short, every thing of this kind should be looked forward to, as work for weather which would make out-door labour unprofitable & inconvenient. The Houses at the Ferry & French's Plantations are to be removed to the center of both (where marked) as soon as circumstances will admit of it. And, I believe, I shall lay in materials for building a Barn & treading floor at Dogue Run. but this I shall consider of. New Posts for the circle before the door must be thought of, but of what kind is not absolutely resolved on at present. Making gravel Walks in the upper Garden—and in the Pine Labyrinths. Getting up all the ground in the Vine yard Inclosure. Keeping the Shrubberies clean. Planting Trees—in Clumps and otherwise and trimming others. Planting Ivy around the Ice House and at the No. end of the Lawn East of the Ho.—also on the sides by the front gate" (AD, DLC:GW).

2. GW arrived at Georgetown about 9:00 A.M. on 27 June and left there shortly after 4:00 A.M. on 30 June; no letters written by him or William Jackson to Lear or Martha Washington in Philadelphia between those dates have been found, but Lear did inform Clement Biddle in a "Saturday noon" note, probably 2 July, that "the President, having taken the rout through York & Lancaster, does not expect to be in this City sooner than the middle of next week" (PHi: Washington-Biddle Correspondence). Before leaving Georgetown GW decided to proceed by way of Frederick, Md., and York and Lancaster, Pa., as he noted a desire "of seeing the nature of the Country North of Georgetown, and along the upper road" (*Diaries*, 6:166). GW's party arrived at Frederick at sundown on 30 June (ibid., 164, 166, 167).

To Charles Cotesworth Pinckney

Dear Sir,   Mount-Vernon, June 26th 1791
    The enclosed letter, which is under a flying seal, and the plough, which accompanies it, are referred to your inspection—and are addressed to your care, to be transmitted to Mr Chesnut at Camden.[1] With great regard, I am dear Sir, Your most obedient Servant

Go: Washington

LS, privately owned; LS (photostat), PPRF.
    Charles Cotesworth Pinckney had introduced to GW the previous summer his friend John Chesnut, a merchant and planter in Camden, S.C., and GW attended a public dinner at Chesnut's house on 25 May 1791 during the Southern Tour (Charles Pinckney to GW, 4 July 1790, nn.3 and 4).
    1. GW's enclosed letter of this date to Chesnut reads: "In conformity to my

promise, when I saw you at Camden, I have selected one of my drill ploughs, which will be sent to Norfolk, whence it will be forwarded to Charleston, directed to you, and addressed to the care of General Pinckney. The original intention of the drill plough, on the principle of that which is sent to you, was to plant the grain or seed, in rows, at equal distances—the distance to be determined by the space at which the holes were made from each other—their number for corn was only four—but for sowing pease and some other kinds of grain in drills, the holes were encreased to the number now in the barrel. The application of this plough to the planting of indigo will, in my opinion, be productive of dispatch, regularity, and an abridgement of labour. The continuity in which the indigo-seed is sown, in the same row, will only require an additional number of holes—the proportioning of which, and their size, in order that the seed may issue in proper and equal quantity, may occasion some waste at first—but the loss of seed, in determining them, will be no object, compared with the advantages, when the just size and number of the holes are ascertained. You will perceive that the plough, which is sent, is drawn by a swingle-tree—but they may likewise be made with shafts—the barrel may be extended to six feet, or to such length as to answer for any number of rows, that may be thought necessary, so partitioned as to prevent an accumulation of the seed at either end—you will only have occasion to prefix a plough-share to each row of holes, and proportion your force of horses or Oxen to the draught. The foot-stock, to which the truck wheel is fixed, and which may be raised or depressed, is intended to regulate the depth of the ploughs insertion into the ground. The band, which crosses the barrel in a certain direction, was placed, when the grain was to be deposited at equal distances, to prevent its emission at more holes than one—in sowing the indigo seed it will not be wanted. The harrow will be proportioned to the plough or ploughs, and so constructed as effectually to cover the seed, without adding more than is unavoidable to the weight. I hope you will sufficiently comprehend the principles of this plough to render its adoption highly useful to the planting interest of south Carolina. Should the experiment so eventuate, my agency therein will be most agreeably rewarded" (LS, owned by anonymous donor; see also LS [photostat], PPRF). Thomas Newton, Jr., of Norfolk, Va., informed GW on 26 Oct. that he "forwarded your plough to Genl Pinkney but have never heard of its arival" (DLC:GW).

From Henry Knox

Sir.   War-department [Philadelphia] June 27th 1791.
    I have the satisfaction to transmit a copy of a letter received from Judge Innes and the board at Kentuckey relative to his first desultory expedition against the indians[1]—We may soon expect to hear of the result of this incursion.[2] I have the honor to be Sir with perfect respect, Your most obedient Servt
                                                        H. Knox

LS, DLC:GW; LB, DLC:GW.

For background to Brig. Gen. Charles Scott's Kentucky militia expedition against the Ouiatanon (Wea) villages on the Wabash River, see Henry Knox to GW, 22 Feb. 1791 and note 8, 30 May and note 8, and 6 and 8 June.

1. Knox's instructions of 9 Mar. to Scott and Scott's 28 June report of the expedition are in *ASP, Indian Affairs,* 1:129–33. The enclosed copy of the letter of 20 May of Harry Innes, Benjamin Logan, and Isaac Shelby to Knox reads: "The board appointed by your letter to General Scott of the 9th of March took the subject into consideration on the 8th day of April, and it is with real satisfaction we inform you that the propositions contained in the letter were received with pleasure by the inhabitants of the district, and that the first detachment authorised to be raised marched on the 17th instant from Frankfort on the Kentucky in high spirits under the command of General Scott. We shall not be considered vain when we observe that a more choice body of men could not be raised in the United States—young—healthy—well armed—well mounted—and amply provided with provisions—We are flattered that nothing can prevent success unless the enemy should gain information of their approach and evacuate their towns—Of this we have some apprehensions, as two prisoners have been taken since the inlistment of the volunteers commenced. On the return of the army, the board will make to the War-Office a special report of their proceedings—For the present we hope the above information is sufficiently satisfactory" (DLC:GW). Innes's postscript of 30 May adds: "I yesterday received a letter from Mr [John] Brown who is gone on the expedition as a private dated the 23d inst: wherein he says that the detachment will march that day in good spirits with 20 days provision, and this day unless greatly impeded in their march hope to make their stroke—The spies had seen no recent sign of indians near the Camp on the bank of the Ohio opposite the mouth of Kentucky, therefore he concluded that the army had not then been discovered by the enemy" (DLC:GW).

2. Knox received no news of Scott's expedition until Jonathan Williams's letter of 5 July arrived from Staunton, Va., on or about 16 July, when Knox probably had Tobias Lear submit it to GW. Knox wrote that the "circumstances are such; that it appears to me a very considerable reliance may be placed on his success" (DLC:GW). Williams's letter to Knox reads: "Although I think your official dispatches will have given you satisfactory Accounts of Genl Scotts movements & success, yet I presume you will not think it improper to take the chance of this Letters coming sooner to hand. A Mr Bowman passed through this Town 3 days since from the Falls of the Ohio, and reported that at Beards Town he saw 2 men who were in Scotts expedition, who informed him that the Party had recrossed the Ohio on their return, after having destroyed three Indian Towns, killed 32 Warriors, and brought away 50 or 60 Women & Children Prisoners. He left one house for the aged & infirm women, and left them a supply of Provisions with Letters for Indians of other nations who might pass that way. Genl Scott lost no men in the action which appears to have been a surprize, but 3 were wounded, & three more were drowned in crossing the river. As Mr Bowman passed through this place without stopping I had not an opportunity of seeing him, but I have gathered this account from Mr

Buchanan who saw him and who knows his family, which is a very creditable one. There are several other reports in Town, which come much in the same way from other persons of the party, and there is ever uniformity in the whole which gives it credibility in this place; As such I give it to you, and I hope it will be confirmed by more authentic Accounts. I have not been able to fix the dates with accuracy, but as Genl Scott crossed the Ohio in his way out on the 21st of may, they may be tolerably ascertained by those who know the distance, and the time usualy taken for such a march. It seems that the Towns were on the wabash river and are called the Weeyaw Towns. Genl Scott it is further said began his march in a direction towards the Miami Towns, but, having lost some horses, which appeared to have taken that road, he was apprehensive of the Indians taking an alarm, so changed his object. Two of the Towns he destroyed had been abandoned; But one therefore was surprized" (NNGL: Knox Papers).

From the Earl of Buchan

Sir,   Dryburgh Abbey [Scotland] June 28th 1791.

I had the Honour to receive your Excellencys letter relating to the advertisement of Dr Andersons periodical publication in the Gazette of the United States which attention to my reccomendation I feel very sensibly and return you my gratefull acknowledgment.[1]

In the 21st No. of that literary miscellany I inserted a monitory paper respecting America which I flatter myself may if attended to on the other side of the Atlantick be productive of good consequences.[2]

To use your own emphatic words may that Almighty Being who rules over the Universe—who presides in the Councils of Nations—and whose providential aids can supply every human defect, consecrate to the Liberties & Happiness of the American People a Government instituted by themselves for publick & private security upon the Basis of Law & equal administration of Justice preserving to every individual as much civil & political freedom as is consistent with the safety of the Nation. And may He be pleased to continue your Life and strength as long as you can be in any way usefull to your Country!

I have entrusted this sheet enclosed in a box made of the Oak that sheltered our Great Sir William Wallace after the Battle of Falkirk to Mr Robertson of Aberdeen a Painter with the hope of his having the honour of delivering it into yr hands, reccomend-ing him as an honest artist seeking for bread & for fame in the New World.[3] This Box was presented to me by the Goldsmiths Company at Edinburgh, to whom feeling my own unworthiness to receive this magnificently significant present, I requested & obtained leave to make it over to the Man in the World to whom I thought it was most justly due. Into your hands I commit it requesting of you to pass it on the event of your decease to the Man in your own Country who shall appear to yr judgment to merit it best upon the same considerations that have induced me to send it to Your Excellency.[4] I am with the highest Esteem, Sir, Yr Excellencies most Obedt & Obliged humble servt

Buchan.

I beg yr Excellency will have the goodness to send me your Portrait that I may place it among those whom I most honour. Whether Mr Robertson may be equal to the task I know not but I beg leave to reccomend him to yr countenance as he has been mentioned to me favourably by my worthy friend Professor [William] Ogilvie of Kings College Aberdeen.[5]

ALS, PHi: Gratz Collection.

1. For GW's role in the publication of James Anderson's prospectus of the *Bee, or Universal Literary Intelligencer,* see Buchan to GW, 27 Mar. 1790 and notes 1 and 2. David Steuart Erskine, eleventh earl of Buchan, was referring to GW's letter of 30 June.

2. Buchan's essay "On America" was published under his regular pseudonym "Albanicus" on 4 May 1791 in the *Bee,* 3, no. 21, pp. 96–101.

3. Archibald Robertson (1765–1835) was educated at King's College in Aberdeen, Scotland, and studied painting at Edinburgh before returning to Aberdeen to operate a "Drawing Academy." He left for London in 1786, became a student of Sir Joshua Reynolds, and also took lessons from Benjamin West. Robertson soon attracted the attention of the court with his skillful miniatures and earned the appellation of "The Reynolds of Scotland" before returning to his homeland. Robertson decided to settle in the United States and arrived at New York on 2 October. He was presented to GW by Tench Coxe on 30 Dec. and delivered this letter and relic from Buchan (Robertson, *Letters and Papers of Andrew Robertson,* 9, and Stillwell, "Robertson," 1, 16). See also *Virginia Gazette and Alexandria Advertiser,* 12 Jan. 1792.

4. The hinged wooden snuffbox, about four inches long, three inches wide, and two inches deep, was constructed of six pieces of one-eighth-inch-thick finely polished oak, elegantly bound with silver. Mounted upon the inside of the lid was a silver plate bearing the inscription, "Presented by the Goldsmiths of Edinburgh to David Stuart Erskine, Earl of Buchan, with the freedom of their Corporation, by their Deacon, 1791" (described and quoted in Robert-

son, *Letters and Papers of Andrew Robertson,* 9). Not having received an acknowledgment, Buchan wrote GW on 15 Sept.: "Sometime ago I did myself the
pleasure to transmit to you by Mr Archibald Robertson of Aberdeen a testimony of my sincere respect contained in a Box made of the venerable oak
which sheltered our great Wallace after his defeat at Falkirk, which Box was
cut out of the Tree by the propreter & Sent to the Corporation of Goldsmiths
at Edn. & by them presented to me with the freedom of their Company in the
Box abovementioned and which I hope you will receive. It is a respectable
curiosity & will I flatter myself be a relique of long endurance in America as a
Mark of that Esteem with which I have the honour to be Sir, Yr Obedient
humble Servt" (PHi: Gratz Collection; the docket on the Sprague transcript
[DLC:GW] notes that the letter was received on 15 June 1792—the address
cover of the original receiver's copy is missing). Buchan later referred to GW as
"the modern American Wallace" (quoted in Lamb, "Unpublished Washington
Portraits," 278). Sir William Wallace (c.1272–1305) led a Scottish uprising
against Edward I from 1297 until 1305. He was defeated at the Battle of Falkirk in the summer of 1298 by Edward and his forces and retreated with the
remnant of his army to Stirling before seeking aid abroad. After his capture
and execution by the English in 1305 Wallace became the best-known champion of Scottish liberty.

In his final will of 9 July 1799, GW wrote: "Whether easy, or not, to select
the man who might comport with his Lordships opinion in this respect, is not
for me to say; but conceiving that no disposition of this valuable curiosity can
be more eligable than the re-commitment of it to his own Cabinet, agreeably
to the original design of the Goldsmiths Company of Edenburgh, who presented it to him, and at his request, consented that it should be transfered to
me; I do give & bequeath the same to his Lordship, and in case of his decease,
to his heir with my grateful thanks for the distinguished honour of presenting
it to me; and more especially for the favourable sentiments with which he
accompanied it" (ADS, ViFaCt). His executors transmitted the box to Buchan
in February 1800 by British minister Sir Robert Liston, with a copy of GW's
will, and the earl noted on 16 Aug. 1800 at the bottom of their letter that he
himself wished to bequeath the box to "Washingtons University in Columbia"
(Papers of the Earl of Buchan, William Salt Library, Stafford, United Kingdom). Buchan provided details in the "Observations respecting the Will of
General Washington," drafted on 6 May: "With respect to the fourteenth
Clause by which the General recommits to me the Box . . . , I destine it for the
University of Washington with a Golden Pen to which there may be annually
offered medals by the States to the honour of such young Citizens Students
therein as shall be found in comparative trial to have made not only the greatest progress in useful knowledge during the whole of their course of Education
but shall at the same time have been found to be most exemplary in their
conduct & most preeminently posessed of the Principles & knowledge 'most
friendly to Republican Government & to the true & genuine liberties of Mankind' to use the words of the great Founder himself & I deposit this expression
of my Will & intent concerning this Relique Wch you Dr Robert Anderson of
Herriots Green Edinburgh Author of the respectable Edition of the British

Poets & other useful works to the end that in case of my Decease without any
other extant declaration of my will in this respect that my Executors may comply with the same for which this writing will be their sufficient warrant" (Papers of the Earl of Buchan, William Salt Library, Stafford, United Kingdom).
The box was stolen in transit in the nineteenth century, and advertisements
of a reward for its return proved unavailing (Cleveland, "Robertson, and His
Portraits of the Washingtons," 9). It apparently was in the possession of Ian
Keith Mackintosh of Wadhurst, Sussex County, England, in 1958 (*Country Life*,
123 [9 Jan. 1958], 74).

5. For GW's reply and Robertson's portrait of GW, see GW to Buchan, 1
May 1792.

From the Commissioners for the Federal District

Sir   George Town [Md.] 30th June 1791

Turning our attention to Day to the Circumstances of the Carrollsburgh and hamburgh Lots, we are not free from apprehensions of difficulties in Settling with some of the Proprietors—
Many of the Proprietors of the Carrollsburgh Lots have signed
an Engagement to give up one half their Land on having the
other half assigned them as near their original Situation as the
new laying out will permit—According to the new plan, by an
appropriation of ground for public uses, it will be out of the
Power of the Commissioners to assign Land in Compensation
near the former situation the most probable resourse to give
content will be, to give the value in Land which may fall to the
public in a different situation; but it is not likely that this will be
satisfactory in every Instance.

The subscribers for Hamburgh have subjected their lots on a
valuation—the state of the funds will not allow us to go deep in
that way, we have therefore consented as was the Idea whilst you
were here, to put them on the same Footing as the Proprietors
of Carrollsburgh, with this restriction, that where a part of their
own Lots cannot be assigned nor a compensation in other Lands
agreed on, that the old Terms shall be binding to receive the
value. This we expect will a good deal narrow the demand for
money.

Those circumstances have induced us to mention our apprehension to Majr L'Enfant and to remark to him your ideas, as
you were pleased to disclose them, to him and us, of preserving
as much of the Land to the original proprietors as well may be,

and that they more strongly applied to those places than those parts of the plat which occasioned them.

As Majr L'Enfant purposes ⟨soon⟩ to attend you and probably will have the ⟨plat with⟩ him, we much wish, Sir, your attention to those parts and that they may be left in such a state as to lessen as far as possible the difficulties in settling with the proprietors[1]—In consequence of what passed concerning a Treasurer and the probability of circumstances soon arising under which one may be necessary we have proceeded to the appointment of William Deakins Junr.[2] We are Sir with great respect your mo. obedt Servts

Thos Johnson
David Stuart
Danl Carroll

LB, DNA: RG 42, Records of the Commissioners for the District of Columbia, 1791–1925, Proceedings and Letters Sent, 1791–1802.

For background to this letter, see GW to Thomas Jefferson, 2 Jan., editorial note, and Pierre-Charles L'Enfant to GW, 22 June. GW arrived at Georgetown early on 27 June and met briefly with the commissioners for the federal district before calling together the proprietors. He noted that "from some misconception with respect to the extension of their grants," some "had refused to make conveyances and recapitulating the principles upon which my comns. to them at the former meeting were made and giving some explanations of the present State of matters & the consequences of delay in this business they readily waved their objections & agd. to convey to the utmost extent of what was required" (*Diaries*, 6:164). On 28 June GW toured the grounds of the Federal City with Andrew Ellicott and L'Enfant to choose the site for the principal federal buildings, approving L'Enfant's selection of Jenkins Hill for the Capitol but overruling his decision to place the President's House slightly to the north of the site GW had pointed out in March. GW also directed Ellicott to alter the boundaries of the city in order to leave out a spring owned by Benjamin Stoddert (ibid.). Meanwhile, the commissioners and proprietors completed deeds of trust, whereby land was conveyed to trustees Thomas Beall of George and John Mackall Gantt, who were to oversee the division of the city lots in accordance with the agreement of 30 March. The deeds of trust completed by proprietors Stoddert, Anthony Holmead, Jonathan Slater, George Walker, and Clement Woodward are in DNA: RG 42, Deeds of Trust to Beall and Gantt, Trustees, from Proprietors in Carrollsburgh and Hamburgh, with Some from Original Proprietors of Washington City (Dowd, *Records of the Office of Public Buildings*, 17). GW met again with the proprietors on 29 June and made known the locations for the federal buildings, referring to L'Enfant's rough plan. GW added that there would be fewer diagonal avenues than L'Enfant proposed and that an exchange building would be constructed on the eastern side of the city to balance the executive buildings on the west. He observed: "a general approbation of the measure seemed to pervade the whole" (*Diaries*, 6:165). GW set out this day for Philadelphia at about four o'clock in the morning, and the commissioners continued their meeting, turning their attention to the complications of land ownership in the projected towns of Hamburgh and Carrollsburgh (see William Deakins, Jr., and Benjamin Stoddert to GW, 9 Dec. 1790, 3, 17 Feb., and Agreement of the Proprietors for the Federal District, 30 Mar. 1791, source note).

1. L'Enfant did not travel to Philadelphia to meet with GW as soon as expected. The commissioners wrote to GW on 2 Aug. that "L'Enfant purposes to wait on you soon with his drafts for your confirmation," but he still had not appeared by the mid-August, prompting Jefferson to write L'Enfant on 18 Aug., inquiring when, if at all, he planned to arrive (*Jefferson Papers*, 22:47–48).

2. Deakins served as treasurer of the commission until July 1796.

From Thomas Attwood Digges

Belfast 1 July 1791

As I am writing to Mr Fitzgerald I take the liberty under a Cover to Him to inclose Your Excellency a description of Messrs McCabe & Pearce's new invented double Loom for weaving two peices at the same time, & which description is annexd to the Report of a Committee of the Irish House of Commons upon the utility & benefit of such a Loom.[1]

Since Mr Wm Pearces embarkation hence to New York in May last, in order to obtain a Patent from Congress for said Loom, His partner Mr Thomas McCabe has taken no steps in this Country for a premium, But He is now in London endeavouring to obtain a Patent for in England, where He will undoubtedly succeed.

It is necessary for me to mention to Your Excellency, That the drawings & specifications commonly necessary for the obtaining a Patent went out in the Brig Endeavour Capt. Seward to N. York with Mr Pearce and a working Artist Mr Wm Jameson who made the Looms, and together with a set of Temples & Headles Elbow & Shuttles &ca were boxd up, seald, and directed for Your Excellency to the care of Mr Geo. Woolsey Merchnt New York. Mr McCabe as well as myself mentiond this in seperate Letters to Your Excelly, and I gave Mr Peare a seperate introductory Letter. He will be a most valuable acquisition in whatever quarter He may fix, & has I think ere this been at Alexandria & the Falls.

As I had it not in my power then to forward the printed Report of the Committee, I take this oppertunity of forwarding it, And am with the highest Esteem & veneration Yr Excellencys most Obedt & very He Sert[2]

Thos Digges

ALS, DNA: RG 59, Miscellaneous Letters.

For Thomas McCabe, Sr., and William Pearce and their "double Loom," see McCabe to GW, 21 July 1790 and notes 2 and 3. Pearce left Ireland with letters of introduction from Thomas Attwood Digges in May 1791 and arrived at Philadelphia before mid-July (see GW to Thomas Jefferson, 12 July 1791 and note 3). For Digges's reputation, see Parsons, "The Mysterious Mr. Digges," 486–92.

1. The Alexandria, Va., merchant John Fitzgerald was the brother-in-law of Digges. The enclosed description of the loom, in Digges's hand and initialed by him, and the 2-page "REPORT ON THE PETITION OF THOMAS MACABE AND WILLIAM PEARSCE. *Reported to the Irish House of Commons, 14th February, 1791, By the Right Honourable* JOHN O'NEILL," first Viscount O'Neil, are printed in Elias and Finch, *Letters of Digges*, 429–34. Jefferson also received a copy of the report on 16 July from the American consul at Dublin (see William Knox to Jefferson, 19 April, *Jefferson Papers*, 20:241–44).

2. For Digges's previous letters from Belfast to GW and Jefferson in late April 1791, see Digges to GW, c.28 April, letter-not-found entry, GW to Jefferson, 12 July, nn.2 and 3, and Digges to Jefferson, 28 April, *Jefferson Papers*, 20:313–15.

To the Inhabitants of Frederick, Maryland

Gentlemen, [Taneytown, Md., 1 July 1791]

I express with great pleasure my obligations to your goodness, and my gratitude for the respectful and affectionate regard which you are pleased to manifest towards me.[1]

Your ascription of my public services over-rates their value, and it is justice to my fellow-citizens that I should assign the eminent advantages of our political condition to another cause—their valor, wisdom, and virtue—from the first they derive their freedom, the second has improved their independence into national prosperity, and the last, I trust, will long protect their social rights, and ensure their individual happiness.

That your participation of these advantages may realise your best wishes is my sincere prayer.

G. Washington

LB, DLC:GW.

1. GW noted on 1 July: "Received an Address from the Inhabitants of Frederick town and about 7 Oclock left it. Dined at one Cookerlys 13 Miles off & lodged at Tawny town only 12 Miles farther—being detained at the first stage by rain and to answer the address wch. had been presented to me in the Morning" (*Diaries*, 6:167). The address, signed "At the request and in behalf of the inhibitants of Frederick" by George Murdock, William M. Beall, Richard Potts, Dr. Philip Thomas, and John McPherson, reads: "The inhibitants of Frederick take the liberty to congratulate you upon your safe Arrival at this place. And to Assure you that it gives them sincere pleasure to have this opportunity of expressing that veneration and attachment which they have always felt and still feel for your person & character, As A Patriot, a soldier, A Statesman And a fellow citizen. They have Sir a lively sense of gratitude for that long Series of Services which you have so ably exhibited on the public Stage in behalf of your Country, and from which they, in common with the rest of their fellow citizens, have experienced Such Solid Advantages. They consider you, under heaven, as the *chief* Author of their political Salvation; And At the time that they profess their firm attachment to your person as their chief Magistrate, And to that excellent Constitution over which you preside, they are happy in the blessings derived from your Administration; And as republicans have a pride in Admiring that equality that hath been established, and which they hope will ever prevail throughout United America. They gratefully Acknowledge the blessings of Providence conferred by your safe return in good health from your long Southern tour at an unhealthy season of the Year, and pray heaven that it may very long be preserved here, & that you may be finally happy hear after" (DLC:GW).

From George Skene Keith

Sir   Keith hall by Aberdeen N. Britain July 1st 1791

A Clergyman of the Church of Scotland takes the Liberty of writing your Excellency on a subject interesting to mankind— and begs you will accept of the small publication which accompanies this Letter—The subject is at present under discussion in the Assembly of the United States: and the Author would not have troubled your Excellency, if he had not bestowed more labour on that subject than he believes any man existing has done.[1]

A Copy in Manuscript was sent you about 9 months ago to the Care of Dr Nesbit Principal of Carlisle College near Philadelphia as the author has been long in terms of intimacy with that Gentleman—But as it may have been miscarried, a copy of the publication is now forwarded to your Excellency.[2]

The writer of this is Nephew to the late Reverend Mr John Barclay, Rector of St Luke parish Maryland, who was honoured with the Friendship—or at least much indebted to the patronage, of your Excellency—Soon after his first settlement in Virginia he married a couple without the consent of their parents—Your Excellency saved him from the consequences; and though he lived not to see your Glory, in a public character, he spoke and wrote of you in a becoming manner[3]—His Nephew therefore has a private motive for writing you—And has the honour to be with very high Esteem Sir Your Excellencys Most Obedt Servt

Geo: Skene Keith

ALS, DLC:GW.

George Skene Keith (1752–1823), eldest son of James Keith of Aquhorsk in Mar, near Aberdeen, Scotland, was educated at Marischal College and the University of Aberdeen in the late 1760s. After the death of his uncle in 1772, Keith relinquished his plans of moving to America and pursued a clerical career in Scotland. He was ordained in May 1778 to the living of Keith-Hall and Kinkell, Aberdeen, "a very tolerable Benefice" and later claimed that during the Revolutionary War he "was one of the few Scotch Clergymen, who did not pray for the Destruction of the American Rebels" (Keith to GW, 14 Jan. 1792). Keith's investigations into methods for equalizing weights and measures, based upon the adoption of the second's pendulum as a standard, were presented to a committee of the British House of Commons in early 1790 and supported in Parliament by Sir John Riggs Miller on 13 April 1790. Miller's speech was reprinted in the press and consulted by Thomas Jefferson in preparation of his own report on weights and measures (*Parliamentary History of England*, 28:639–49; Jefferson to Speaker of the House of Representatives, 4 July 1790, *Jefferson Papers*, 16:623–24).

1. The enclosure was Keith's 20-page *Tracts on Weights, Measures and Coins* . . . (London, 1791), two copies of which were in GW's Mount Vernon library at his death (Griffin, *Boston Athenæum Washington Collection*, 113–14). GW called congressional attention to the establishment of uniform weights and measures in his two 1790 addresses to that body, and both messages appeared in Britain shortly after they were delivered (GW to the U.S. Senate and House of Representatives, 8 Jan. and 8 Dec. 1790). See also Edward Newenham to GW, 31 Jan. 1791. On 15 Jan. 1790 the House ordered Jefferson to report on the subject, and Jefferson's final draft was submitted on 4 July. The Senate committee to which it was later referred reported on 1 Mar. 1791 "that it would not be eligible, at present, to introduce any alteration in the measures and weights which are now used in the United States" (*DHFC*, 1:517–18, 661, 3:265, 509–10, 634, 641; Jefferson to Speaker of the House of Representatives, 4 July 1790, *Jefferson Papers*, 16:623–24). Keith also sent Jefferson a copy of his pamphlet on 1 July 1791, as well as an unpublished criticism of Jefferson's report (see Keith to GW, 14 Jan., and Jefferson to GW, 14 June 1792).

2. Keith had earlier sent a manuscript copy of his first tract, "Synopsis of a System of Equalization of Weights and Measures of Great Britain," to Charles Nisbet (Nesbit) of Dickinson College in Carlisle, Pa., to be forwarded to GW, which was never done (see Keith to GW, 14 Jan. 1792). On 7 May 1792 Tobias Lear replied to Keith: "The manuscript Copy of this work which you mention in your letter to have been sent to the President some time ago, to the care of Doctor Nesbit, never came to his hands" (DLC:GW).

3. Anglican clergyman John Barclay (d. 1772) served Cumberland Parish, Lunenburg County, Va., after he immigrated to the colony in 1756. He was pastor to All Hallows Parish, Anne Arundel County, Md., in the early 1760s before being appointed rector of St. Luke's Parish, Queen Annes County, Md., in 1763. Barclay dined at Mount Vernon at least twice in August 1769 (see Keith to GW, 14 Jan. 1792, and *Diaries*, 2:174–75). Keith might have been referring to Barclay's reinstatement as minister to the 2d Virginia Regiment mentioned in William Byrd's weekly return of 17 July 1758 (see James Glen to GW, 19 July 1758, n.4).

From Stephen Sayre

Sir   Paris 2d July 1791

I did myself the honor of writing you in octor last—stating, in part, what had been my conduct & situation, during our contest for Independence. You may imagine, it is not a little mortifying to reflect, that I am unworthy the employments I have expected—or, that my Country treats me unjustly.[1]

This is the last time I ever mean to trouble you with importunities.[2]

As I have lately taken a share in a manufactory of Snuff in this City, I must naturally be inclined to have some Employment there—and as you will, probably, soon send a Minister, I wish the Secretaryship. Mr Short tells me, that in case he is the Minister, he should be very happy in my having it—But let me request one of the greatest favours you can do me—Let me have a single Line—promising this, or some other nomination—or, *that I may never expect any appointment whatever.*[3] Mr Short knows my address—but to be more certain, I am fix'd in rue St Denis—No. 413. Monr La Fayette has promised to write to you in my favour: but I expect he will forget to do so. I am with all due Respect & Consideration your obt Servt

Stephen Sayre

ALS, DNA: RG 59, Miscellaneous Letters.

1. For Stephen Sayre's letter of "octor last," which GW referred to Thomas Jefferson, see Sayre to GW, 15 Oct. 1790. See also Sayre to GW, 20 Nov., n.3.

2. Sayre wrote GW again on 13 July 1793, seeking an appointment to negotiate a treaty with Algiers (DLC:GW).

3. Having received no reply Sayre again wrote GW from Paris on 10 Sept.: "I have had the honor of addressing you, perhaps too frequently—with some hopes of a Reply—supposing I might have really deserved that little attention, even from the first Majestrate—But now I am compel'd to the mortifying conclusion that I had over-rated my consequence. I mean no longer to amuse myself with such dreams of expectation—I am not the only man who has sacrificed his independance for an ungrateful Country—Had I felt less, & done nothing, had I pursued the path of my own Interest, & gone over to America with the results which must have attended self⟨ish⟩ness—I should long since have had ⟨*illegible*⟩ for the language of Sollicitation & complaint. I trust you will generously forgive my making these disagreeable Remarks—It is the right of a citizen to complain—my feelings are hurt—my heart is wounded, but my Spirit is neither humbled, or bent to unworthy flattery. You have it in your power to serve me & you must be well persuaded, I can, at the same time, serve my Country—but you have it equally in your power, to employ another, who comes to you with more influence. But, I quit, forever, the loathsome Object that has too often led me into Resentment, or envious comparison. I now write, chiefly to acquaint you—that there are multitudes of discontented people of wealth & consequence, in this Country, who will look for Establishments in America, as soon as the hopes of a counter-revolution are at an end—that period, is not, as I beleive, & hope, far of. I have hinted already to the Secretary of the Treasury, how much our Country might profit, by this disposition: but if Congress should think otherways I would suggest to you Sir, that you form a plan (most suitable to yourself) by which you may dispose of your own lands on the western Waters. I mean the sale of a part of them. It might be done by intervening Lots, or Parcels—selling one—keeping the next—or by taking up a greater quantity, make settlements. by sale to give value to such lands as you now have—Nothing can be easier than to give most favorable ⟨*mutilated*⟩ of ⟨these Lands⟩, & Country where you have, long since made your election. Colon. Blagden is now selling Lands, under many disadvantages, at 6. & 9 Livres—Yours would, I am persuaded, fetch three times as much. If you, upon Reflection, think this Idea worth your puting into practice, & choose to give me your confidence in it; you may join Mr Frederic Peregoux [Jean-Frédéric Perregaux] in the power with me—He is one of the most respectable Bankers here, as Monsr dela Fayette will assure you" (DNA: RG 59, Miscellaneous Letters).

Letter not found: from Rodolf Vall-travers, 3 July 1791. In a letter to GW of 30 Nov., Vall-travers referred to his letter of "July 3d; from Rotterdam; by Captn Trevett of Marblehead; charged with literary Communications to the learned Societies at Philadelphia, Boston" (DNA: RG 59, Miscellaneous Letters).[1]

1. See also Vall-travers to GW, 21 July, n.4.

To the Citizens of York, Pennsylvania

Gentlemen,   [York, Pa., 3 July 1791]
I receive your congratulations with pleasure, and I reply to your flattering and affectionate expressions of esteem with sincere and grateful regard.[1]

The satisfaction which you derive from the congeniality of freedom with good government, clearly evinced in the happiness of our highly favored country, at once rewards the patriotism that atchieved her liberty and gives an assurance of its duration.

That your individual prosperity may long continue among the proofs which attest the national welfare is my sincere wish.

G. Washington.

LB, DLC:GW.
1. GW wrote that he arrived at York about two o'clock in the afternoon on 2 July and the next day "Received, and answered an address from the Inhabitants of York town" (*Diaries*, 6:167–68): "With sentiments of the most perfect esteem and attachment, the citizens of the Borough of York beg leave to present to you their sincere congratulations on your safe arrival here, after an extensive tour thro that country which owes so much to your brave and prudent exertions in War, and to your wise and just administration in peace. We cordially join in the general satisfaction and joy which all the citizens of America feell in seeing you, and in those universal sentiments of regard to your person and veneration for your character which dictate the addresses that in various expressions have been offered to you. We join in the general satisfaction that every friend to human happiness must feel on finding that the people of the united states do now show a great and convincing Proof to all the world that freedom and good government are perfectly compatible— And that a first Magistrate unanimously chosen by the people may at once possess their utmost veneration and most hearty regard. We wish you a safe return to the seat of government, and do sincerely unite with the millions of America in praying that the supreme Governor of the Universe may long continue a life which he has so eminently distinguished in preserving and securing the best rights and happiness of the Citizens of this greatly favoured Country" (DLC:GW).

To the Corporation and Inhabitants of Lancaster, Pennsylvania

Gentlemen, [Lancaster, Pa., 4 July 1791]

Your congratulations on my arrival in Lancaster are received with pleasure, and the flattering expressions of your esteem are replied to with sincere regard.[1]

While I confess my gratitude for the distinguished estimation in which you are pleased to hold my public services, a sense of justice to my fellow-citizens ascribes to other causes the peace and prosperity of our highly favored country—her freedom and happiness are founded in their patriotic exertions, and will, I trust, be transmitted to distant ages through the same medium of wisdom and virtue. With sincere wishes for your social, I offer an earnest prayer for your individual welfare.

Go: Washington

DS, PHi: William Smith Papers; LB, DLC:GW. A later hand noted at the bottom of the receiver's copy: "Preserved by Charles Smith Esqr. of Lancaster."

1. The address, signed "on behalf of themselves & the Inhabitants of the Borough of Lancaster" by burgesses Edward Hand and Paul Zantzinger, and assistants John Hubley, Adam Reigart, Jacob Krug, Casper Shaffner, and Jacob Frey, reads: "On behalf of the Inhabitants of the Borough of *Lancaster*, the Members of the Corporation beg leave to congratulate you on your Arrival at this place. On this joyful Occasion, they approach the first Magistrate of the Union, with hearts impressed with no less grateful Respect than their fellow Citizens of the East and of the South. With them they have admired those Talents, and that firm Prudence in the field, which finally ensured Success to the American Arms. But, at this time, Reverence forbids the Language which would naturally flow from the Recapitulation of the Events of the late glorious Revolution. The faithful page of History will record your illustrious Actions for Posterity. Yet we cannot forbear to mention what we, in our Day, have beheld & witnessed. We have seen you, at the awful Period when the Storm of War was bursting around us, and our fertile plains were deluged with the richest blood of *America*, rising above Adversity, and exerting all the Talents of the Patriot & the Hero, to save our Country from the threatened Ruin: And when, by the Will of Heaven, those Exertions had restored peace and prosperity to the *United States*, and the great Object for which you drew the Sword was accomplished, we have beheld you, adorned with every private social Virtue, mingling with your fellow-Citizens. Yet that transcendent Love of Country, by which you have always been actuated, did not suffer you to rest here; but when the united voice of Myriads of Freemen (your fellow Citizens) called you from the repose of domestic life, actuated solely by the principles of true Glory, not seeking your own Aggrandizement, but sacrificeing the sweets of retired Life

to the Wishes and happiness of your Country, we have beheld you, possessed
of the Confidence of a great people, presiding over their Councils, and, by
your happy Administration, uniting them together by the great political Bond
of one common Interest. It is therefore the Inhabitants of this Borough seize
with Joy the only Opportunity which has offered to them to testify their Approbation of, and their Gratitude for, your Services. Long, very long, Sir, may
you enjoy the Affections of your Fellow-Citizens. We pray for a long Continuance of your health & Happiness, and the choicest Blessings of Heaven on our
beloved Country, and on *You,* its *Father* & its *Friend*" (DLC:GW). The last entry
in GW's 1791 diary ends on 4 July: "At half passed 2 oclock I received, and
answered an address from the Corporation [of Lancaster] and the complimts.
of the Clergy of different denominations" (*Diaries,* 6:169). No entries have
been found between 5 July 1791 and 30 Sept. 1794 (see ibid., 1:xli, xlvi, and
JPP, xi; see also Tobias Lear to John Marshall, 13 Aug. 1803, and "The Missing
George Washington Diary," editorial note, *Marshall Papers,* 6:192–97).

From William Simmons

Philadelphia, 4 July 1791. Presents his qualifications for the post of auditor of the United States and requests the appointment on the ground
of background study and experience.[1]

ALS, DLC:GW.
   William Simmons of 7 North Sixth Street, Philadelphia, was principal clerk
of the U.S. auditor's office (*Philadelphia Directory,* 1791, 119). He petitioned
Congress in January 1791 for a salary increase, which was supported by Alexander Hamilton's report of 24 Feb. to the House of Representatives and
granted by the "Act supplemental to the act 'establishing the Treasury Department,' and for a farther compensation to certain officers" of 3 Mar. (Syrett,
Hamilton Papers, 8:141–42; 1 *Stat.* 215; *DHFC,* 3:659, 735).
   1. Simmons continued serving as chief clerk under auditors William Smith
of Baltimore and Richard Harrison. On 19 Oct. 1792 after GW authorized a
leave of absence for Harrison who planned a trip to Virginia (see Lear to Hamilton, 13 Oct. 1792, DLC:GW), Hamilton observed to GW "that the absence of
the Auditor renders it requisite for the President to designate the person who
shall execute the duty of Auditor in his absence, pursuant to the Eighth Section of the Act making alterations in the Treasury and War Departments. The
first Clerk naturally presents himself to consideration; and will, it is believed,
be adequate to all necessary business" (DLC:GW). Oliver Wolcott, Jr., similarly
recommended Simmons to GW on 12 Feb. 1795. Simmons again applied to
GW for the auditorship on 31 Jan. 1795, when Wolcott was to be nominated
secretary of the treasury and Harrison was likely to be promoted to the office
of comptroller: "I have sir been a number of years employed in public offices,
and ever since the first organization and establishment of the Treasury Department I have acted as Principal Clerk in the office I now solicit; and during
the long interregnum between appointment and acceptance which formerly

happened I had its entire direction. But for my Character and pretensions generally I must beg leave to refer your Excellency to the Secretary of the Treasury" (DLC:GW). Again not receiving the requested appointment, Simmons asked Hamilton on 17 Mar. 1795 to recommend his application for the imminent vacancy of accountant to the War Department, noting that his appointment would be perfectly agreeable to the secretary of war, who recommended he write to Hamilton, and requesting "that you will be pleased to inform me whether the arrangements which you have already made are such as to render a direct application from me to the President unnecessary, and if not; that you will be pleased to furnish me with such testimony in support of an application, as you from a knowledge of my character and qualification may think proper" (DLC:GW). Hamilton forwarded Simmons's letter to GW from Albany on 24 Mar., writing: "I have heretofore had occasion to mention to you the merits of Mr Simmons the writer of the inclosed letter. It is but justice, that I bear in his favour the testimony he desires. I can with truth give my opinion that he is well qualified for the office in question; insomuch that I believe it will be very difficult to find one who has better pretensions—From long service in the Department he understands thoroughly the course of business in it, as well as under the former as under the present Government . . . His intelligence cooperates with his experience to recommend him; and one need not fear to speak too strongly of his assiduity and integrity. So necessary was he in the department from his knowlege of the course of the old business that it cost me repeated pains to prevent his leaving it; and as he had a prospect of doing better in private business than upon a Clerks salary, one of the means employed was to give him the expectation of a recommendation at some future time to some more adequate station, (if an opportunity should occur) for which he was qualified. The present Office is of that nature—and it is but fulfilling my promise to place him before you for consideration. I will only add that if all the considerations proper to be consulted shall appear to you to coincide in him his appointment will give me pleasure" (DLC:GW). GW appointed Simmons accountant to the War Department on 11 April 1795 in place of Joseph Howell, Jr., who had resigned, and presented his nomination to the Senate on 12 June (GW to Simmons, 11 April 1795, copy of commission, DLC:GW; *Executive Journal*, 1:179, 181). Simmons continued in that office until at least 1809 (Syrett, *Hamilton Papers*, 1:192).

From Mary Harding Bristow

Sir   Spring Gardens London 5th July, 1791
     I once more take the liberty of addressing a few lines to Your Excellency, as I am inform'd the Sale of my Son's Brent Town Lands, was finaly set aside by the decree of Your Court of Appeals last december. there fore, the Claims of individuals upon it are entirely wiped away; leaving only that of the State under

the Escheat and forfeiture Laws, made during the War.[1] I some years ago, did myself the honor to write to you, and send a Copy of the Petition, and Memorial Myself, and the other Guardians of my Son had address'd to the Assembly of the States in his behalf, which you had the goodness to acknowledge the receipt of.[2] I shall there fore not trouble you with sending over an other Petition to the Legislature; but rely entirely on Your Excellency's, and their Justice, & Humanity in Restoring to my Son that part of his Estate which it now absolutely is in their power to do—as I am sure they will recollect my *Infant* Son, cou'd do no act to offend! and as the Moderation of Peace, has succeeded the Asperities of War; I will hope: from the known goodness of Your Heart, and the great influence You must have! that I shall be made happy in a favorable Answer to my Request, which will always be acknowledged with great gratitude by Sr Your Excellency's Most Respectfull Humble Servant[3]

M: Bristow

P.St John Taylor Esqr. is in Possession of the affidavits of my Husband's death and the Infancy of my Son. if you Sir shou'd think them of any Use.

ALS, DLC:GW. The letter's cover is addressed to GW at Mount Vernon and is postmarked Norfolk, 5 Sept. 1791.

For previous correspondence concerning Virginia's confiscation in 1779 of Robert Bristow's Prince William County tract and his wife's attempts to have it restored to her son, Richard, see Mary Harding Bristow to GW, 22 Oct. 1790.

1. After the Virginia Court of Appeals confirmed a High Court of Chancery decree and the state's title to Robert Bristow's Prince William County lands in December 1790, the governor appointed Thomas Lee, Jr., agent to collect rents from the tenants of the remaining 7,000 acres that had not been sold during the Revolutionary War and to recover money from the former county commissioners of escheated property and, later, to sell the tract. In March 1794 Mary Bristow's attorney, Richard Marshall Scott of Dumfries, Va., presented a memorial to the governor in the name of Richard Bristow requesting suspension of the sale of the property scheduled for 5 May 1794 until the High Court of Chancery considered an injunction bill presented by the Bristow tract tenants. An injunction was granted, and the sale was postponed, but the Bristows were ultimately unsuccessful. The tract was divided and sold at auction in the nineteenth century. See *Journals of the Council of State of Virginia*, 5:257, 272, 278, and *Calendar of Virginia State Papers*, 5:257, 269, 6:643–44, 7:20, 63–64, 65–66, 79, 8:417–18, 9:392.

2. Mary Bristow's letter of 27 Nov. 1783, forwarded to GW by George William Fairfax on 9 Dec. 1783 and received on 10 June 1784, is in DLC:GW. See

GW to Benjamin Harrison, 14 June 1784 and note 1. For GW's acknowledgment, see his letter to Mary Bristow of 15 June 1784.

3. GW answered this letter on 14 Nov. and enclosed the original of his letter of February 1791 (see Bristow to GW, 22 Oct. 1790, n.1), which had been sent to London and returned as undeliverable: "I have received another letter from you to the same effect as the former dated July 5th 1791. and as circumstances continue to be the same with me as when the enclosed letter was written, that will serve as a reply to both—I will take the liberty to add that if your application should be made to some Gentleman in Virginia, on whose good offices you could depend, it might be the means of satisfying your enquiries on that subject" (LB, DLC:GW). It was probably GW's letter of February 1791 to Bristow that New York City postmaster Sebastian Bauman returned to GW on 20 Aug., writing: "I have taken the liberty to inclose to Your Excellency a letter which came to hand by the British Paket Duck of Cumberland. It appears somewhat Extraordinary that the Post Office in England should return a letter directed for London, when there is no such place on the Charts of the United States" (DNA: RG 59, Miscellaneous Letters).

From Pierre Huet de La Valinière

Lake Champlain 6th July—1791—2 O'clock P.M.
To the Great General, the Preserver & Protector of the most admirable Country in the world—Safety!

I do not know enough of the English language to write it in one quarter of an hour as it is necessary for me to do. I have just learnt that you charity, joined to your justice, leads you to wish to be informed of those who have not been rewarded according to your good intentions. I beleive I am one of that number. In October 1784 I returned from the prisons of Europe, where the cause of America had been my ruin. I ventured to present a memorial to Congress, at least to the President & secretary of it, and receiving no answer I presented one to Genl Knox, who, assured of my suff⟨*mutilated*⟩gs, gave me a living as a Refugee for 6 months.[1] I then sought to obtain a living for 3 years in the cause of America in the Illinois Country, where I in vain sought to make the Tories return to their duty, who deceived & deceiving, as I think, Genl Harmer. I was not able to bring it about, on the contrary the goodness & integrity of his heart made him give faith to all their deceptions accompanid with their liquor.[2] I then returned by sea, after having passed though a thousand dangers—losses & afflictions. I am at present with the Canadian Refugees; but more than ever suspected by the English, who will not suffer me to put my foot in Canada about my own affairs. Time will not permit me to develop my misfortunes—But waiting 'till it will, I take the liberty to assure you of the humble respects with which I have the honor to be Your Excellency's most Obed. & Hbe Sert

P. Huet[3]

Translation, DNA: RG 59, Miscellaneous Letters; ALS, in French, DNA: RG 59, Miscellaneous Letters. The text is taken from a translation prepared for GW by Tobias Lear; the receiver's copy, in French, appears in CD-ROM:GW.

Pierre Huet de La Valinière (Valliniere; 1732–1806) was born at Varades, France, to Charles Huet de La Valinière and Olive Arnaud. After studying at Nantes and Paris, he was ordained in Montreal in 1755 and served five parishes in and around Quebec until 1779. Suspected by the British colonial administration during the American invasion of Canada, he was deported and imprisoned in England before being allowed to return to France. La Valinière later served in the French West Indies and ministered to French-Canadian refugees in New York. After becoming vicar-general to the Illinois Country in April 1786, the disputatious priest left for New Orleans between 1787 and 1789 and then returned east. In October 1790 he was again at Montreal but shortly thereafter settled at Split Rock, N.Y., on Lake Champlain, and wrote an autobiographical poem, published in Albany in 1792. Soon afterwards, La Valinière's church and presbytery burned down, and he returned to Canada, where he remained until his death (Alvord, *Kaskaskia Records, 1778–90*, xxxvii–xlix; "Father Peter Huet de la Valiniere," *American Catholic Historical Researches*, n.s., 2 [July 1906], 203–39; Evans, *American Bibliography*, 8:309).

1. On 17 Oct. 1785 the Confederation Congress referred to the Board of Treasury La Valinière's petition "stating his losses and sufferings & offering his services & praying for an answer. 1 concerning some succour, 2d concerning the recovery of his baggage which he left last spring at Newbury & 3dly concerning his being employd at Ilinois or some other place." No report on the petition has been found (DNA:PCC, item 180, 9; see also *JCC*, 29:837). La Valinière's memorial to Henry Knox might be the MS account of his conduct in the Illinois Country in MHi, a copy of which is in the Public Archives of Canada. La Valinière wrote from Kaskaskia to Charles Thomson, secretary to Congress, on 3 Feb. 1787: "After having presented a memorial to his Excellency the President of Congress on the 8th October 1785. (on which you had the goodness to tell me to address myself to Mr [David] Howell at that time a member of Congress for the State of Rhode Island) seeing it would take up too much time to wait for an answer I left New York in May 1786 to come hither—I have received from Congress but very little provisions on account of the excessive persecutions which I have endured in Canada and in Europe for the American cause—However I am come here to continue to render you all the service in my power." He also described the Illinois Country, recommended building a fort there, and mentioned that he sent Knox "a piece in french & English which you might have printed" (NNGL: Knox Papers).

2. On 25 Aug. 1787 La Valinière notified Congress through Thomson of

the difficulties that the French inhabitants of Kaskaskia had faced since their last petition of 2 June 1786 and James Monroe's committee report of 23 Aug. 1786 (see *JCC*, 31:563) and described Josiah Harmar's 16–27 Aug. 1787 visit to Kaskaskia: John Dodge "deceived him in their way as he was deceived himself he made him stay, live, drink, and dwell only in the houses of the friends of Dodge, he [Barthélemi Tardiveau] accompanied him every where like his interpreter, but he could not shew him the truth being himself very ignorant of it, and he gave allways an evil idea to every word proceeding from those whom Dodge thought be his enemies. . . . The Colonel prefered to drink day and night with the said Dodge himself" (Alvord, *Kaskaskia Records, 1778–90*, 381–83, 424–29). Harmar's own report to Knox of 24 Nov. 1787 is in Smith, *St. Clair Papers*, 2:30–35.

3. The signature on the original receiver's copy reads, "P. Huet dela Valinière prêtre."

From Cezar Du Buc

Monsieur   Cambridge prés de Boston Le 7. Juillet 1791

Chargé Par Le Gouverneur Général de st Domingue de Remettre á Votre Excellence La Lettre Cy jointe[1] et animé du desir de méler, Comme ami de L'humanité, mes hommages á Ceux que vous rendent tous Ceux qui Sâvent apprécier Les services qu'elle a Recu de vous, je me promettais de ne pas Laisser Echapper L'heureuse occasion que m'en fournissait Mr de Blanchelande, mais des Combinaisons de hazard me plaçant hors de mesure de pouvoir Realiser mon projet sous le moment j'ay L'honneur d'Envoyer á Votre Excellence la dépêche du Gouverneur de st domingue, et de La prier de me permettre de lui offrir en personne mes Respectueux hommages Lorsque voyageant dans Le Continent je me trouveray á portée d'elle. Je suis avec Respect Monsieur De Votre Excellence Le trés humble et trés obeissant serviteur

Cezar Du Buc

ALS, DNA: RG 59, Miscellaneous Letters; no contemporary translation of the receiver's copy has been found, although Tobias Lear translated its enclosure (see n.1 below).

Cezar Du Buc (César Dubuc), sieur Saint-Olmype (Olimpe), was a Creole resident planter of La Croix des Bouquets who opposed the autonomous Saint Marc Assembly of Saint Domingue. Du Buc later corresponded with the émigré prince de Condé and requested in a petition to the British government during its occupation of the island that French citizens be allowed to adopt the British law of debt (see Geggus, *Slavery, War, and Revolution*, 76, 425, n.207).

1. Philibert-François-Roussel (Rouxel), vicomte de Blanchelande (1735–1793), the French governor of Saint Domingue, fled Port-au-Prince the same day Col. Thomas-Antoine, chevalier de Mauduit du Plessis, the commander of the city's French army garrison, was assassinated. Blanchelande was blamed for the colony's unrest and was sent to France in chains in 1792, condemned to death, and guillotined. Lear's translation of Blanchelande's enclosed letter to GW of 9 May, written two months after the governor's flight to Cap Français, reads: "An old Soldier, who glories to have appreciated the talents of Your Excellency, could not have been engaged in all the last war in the windward islands without being animated with the liveliest desire to have an opportunity of personally paying you that tribute of admiration which is due to you—but the discharge of my duties have been constantly opposed to this intention, but I hope that on leaving the government of St Domingo it will be in my power to carry this intention into effect. If one, Sir, might, on such an occasion, employ a substitute, it would certainly be the Person who is dearest to us—under this title I could not refuse to the solicitations of Mr Cesar Dubuc, who meditates a voyage, and perhaps an establishment in America, the means of being introduced to him, whose virtues have opened an Asylum, in the vast Continent, to the oppressed. Mr Cesar Dubuc (formerly the Sieur Olimpe) in mingling my homage with that he shall render to your Excellency himself, will not lessen the desire which I have to offer it in person. I will have to add thereto my expressions of gratitude should you deign a reception to Mr Dubuc—he is possessed of large estates in St Domingo, and his conduct in public affairs since the revolution have constantly proved his disinterestedness and the purity of his views. You will soon perceive, Sir, that Mr Dubuc unites with extensive knowledge and invariable honor the embellishments of mind and of society. I shall be the more obliged by Your Excellency's goodness to Mr Dubuc as he is dear to me by the tenderest friendship" (DNA: RG 59, Miscellaneous Letters; a transcription of the ALS, in French, of this letter is in CD-ROM:GW).

From Alexander Hamilton

Philadelphia, 8 July 1791. Respectfully submits a contract between the superintendent of the establishments on the Delaware River and John Wilson for building a beacon boat for its shoals[1] and humbly gives his opinion, after comparing Wilson's contract with that of Warwick Hale, enclosed,[2] and after inquiring into the proportional value of a similar boat already built and into the present rates of constructing vessels in Philadelphia, "that a contract, more beneficial to the United States with a workman of competent ability would be difficult to effect."[3]

LB, DLC:GW.

1. Superintendent William Allibone, the master warden of the port of Philadelphia, had forwarded to Alexander Hamilton on 22 April Philadelphia boat-

builder John Wilson's contract of 19 April for building a replacement beacon boat at Brown Shoal for £78.2.6 (Syrett, *Hamilton Papers,* 8:304). GW approved the contract on 9 July and approved a similar contract with Wilson in March 1793 (DNA: RG 26, Lighthouse Deeds and Contracts, Vol. A, 5, 29).

2. The enclosure has not been found.

3. No reply has been found. Hamilton wrote a second letter to GW this day concerning federal coastal establishments in Pennsylvania, submitting a contract of 20 April made between Allibone and Joseph Anthony & Son of Philadelphia for a year's supply of "Winter pressed or strained Spermaceti Oil" at 3s. 7d. Pennsylvania currency a gallon for the Cape Henlopen lighthouse. On 22 April Allibone forwarded that contract to Hamilton, who favored its terms, and GW approved it on 9 July. The firm continued to supply the lighthouse with fuel through 1797 at least (see Hamilton to GW, 8 July, DLC:GW, and DNA: RG 26, Lighthouse Deeds and Contracts, vol. A, 7–8, 17, 61).

From Alexander Hamilton

Philadelphia, 8 July 1791. Presents his respects to the president and transmits a dispatch just received from Georgia.[1]

LB, DLC:GW.

1. The enclosed dispatch, probably from John Habersham, federal customs collector at Savannah, to Alexander Hamilton, has not been identified. It apparently covered a letter of 2 June from Maj. Richard Call to army contractors Speirs, McLeod, & Co. (see Knox to GW, 9 July and note 1).

From A. Hammond

Respected Sir,   Saturday Morng July 8th 1791.

The knowledge of the benevolence of your heart has prompted me to trespass a little on your time; for which I can plead no other excuse than my hope that your Excellencys indulgence will extend to the Gratification of not only my wish but the wish of many who justly entertain a great veneration for your virtues.

Could your Excellency be prevail'd on to honor the Theatre with your presence on Monday Evening, the writer of this (who respectfully waits your determination) would esteem it as a pleasing satisfaction and an essential piece of service as the Play was announced for his Benefit.[1]

It may probably be an inducement to your Excellency to honor my request with your particular attention when I inform you I am Grandson to an old Gentleman (Mr Christopher Ludwick) whom you have often distinguish'd with your notice and favord with marks of your esteem & approbation.[2] Real necessity, combin'd w'th an inclination for the stage were the causes of my embracing my present profession; and being but young in the Theatrical world is one reason for my earnestly soliciting your Excellency's Patronage as an introduction to that of the Public. But, I fear I intrude on your patience and will therefore conclude.

Should I be fortunate enough to merit a compliance with my request, It shall ever be rememberd with heartfelt Gratitude by your very humble Servant[3]

A. Hammond.

ALS, DLC:GW.

A. Hammond's name appears in neither the 1791 Philadelphia city directory nor the 1790 U.S. Census, but he might have been a resident of his grandfather's Germantown, Pa., household, which included two white males over age fifteen (*Heads of Families* [Pennsylvania], 196). Hammond probably joined Lewis Hallam, Jr., and John Henry's Old American Company in late 1790 or early 1791. GW attended its performances at Philadelphia's Southwark Theater in January and February 1791, and the company held a benefit for Hammond on 9 June, before GW returned to the capital (William Dunlap, *A History of the American Theatre* [New York, 1832], 88, 91; Seilhamer, *American Theatre*, 2:316–18, 320–21, 325). One critic of Hammond's performance as "Don Pedro" in *Recess* in April and May noted that "with application he will improve. There is room" (*General Advertiser and Political, Commercial and Literary Journal* [Philadelphia], 2 May). In July Hammond was playing "The Fop" in *The Birth of Harlequin; or, The Witches Frolic* at Sadler's Wells (*General Advertiser and Political, Commercial and Literary Journal* [Philadelphia], 11 July). He later accompanied Hallam and Henry's troupe to New York, where it opened in the John Street Theater on 10 Oct., and he closed the season with another benefit on 14 May 1792. He appeared in neither of the two plays that GW attended at the Southwark Theater on 14 Nov. 1792. Hammond played several minor roles after the company was reorganized and before it ended its last Philadelphia season in November 1794. His name does not appear on any of the company's play lists after it came under new management in 1795 (Seilhamer, *American Theatre*, 2:340, 3:104; *Federal Gazette and Philadelphia Daily Advertiser*, 17 Nov. 1792).

1. "(Mr. Hammond's Night.) At the Theatre in Southwark" was announced in the *General Advertiser and Political, Commercial and Literary Journal* (Philadelphia), 11 July. The evening's main performance was a comedy, *The Clandestine Marriage*, after which Hammond presented "An occasional ADDRESS," which was followed by a new two-act "Pantomine Entertainment." The evening's performances closed the season for the company (Seilhamer, *American Theatre*, 2:322).

2. GW had met Christopher Ludwick (Ludwig, Lodwick, Lodowick; 1720–1801) during the Revolutionary War, when the German immigrant undertook a secret mission to Staten Island, attempted to persuade Hessian prisoners of war to defect to the American cause, and served as the superintendent of bakers and director of baking for the Continental army. Ludwick framed and hung on the parlor wall of his farmhouse near Germantown the certificate that GW wrote in April 1785 in support of Ludwick's memorial to Congress of March 1785 (Hugh Mercer to GW, 19 Aug. 1776, n.1; Ludwick to GW, 29 Mar. 1785 and note 1). See also "Christopher Ludwig, Baker-General in the Army of the United States during the Revolutionary War," *Pa. Mag.*, 16 [1892], 343–48.

3. GW apparently did not reply to Hammond's letter, and no evidence has been found suggesting that he attended the Southwark Theatre on 11 July. According to the *General Advertiser and Political, Commercial and Literary Journal* [Philadelphia], 7 July, GW arrived in Philadelphia on 6 July "in good health." Sometime between 6 and 24 July, probably closer to the latter date, a tumor appeared on GW's thigh similar to the one that was removed in mid-June 1789 (see James McHenry to GW, 28 June 1789, source note), after which his activities were generally confined to his residence. Thomas Jefferson wrote to James Madison from the capital on 24 July: "The President is indisposed with the same blind tumour, & in the same place, which he had the year before last in New York. As yet it does not promise either to suppurate or be discussed [dissipated]. He is obliged to lye constantly on his side, & has at times a little fever." Three days later Jefferson reported that GW "is much better. An incision has been made, & a kind suppuration is brought on." Henry Lee wrote to Madison on 29 July that GW had nearly recovered, and Jefferson added on 3 Aug. that "The President is got well" (*Madison Papers*, 14:55–56 and note 1, 58, 59, 62). GW himself reported to William Moultrie on 9 Aug.: "I am now recovered." The following month Frances Bassett Washington reported from Mount Vernon to her father: "the President looks better than I expected to see him, but still there be traces in his countenance of his two last severe illnesses, which I fear will never wear off" (Frances B. Washington to John Bassett, 21 Sept., ViMtV).

From Michael Shubart

Philadelphia July 8th 1791.

Your Memorialist Michael Shubart of this City Distiller, humbly sheweth.

That by the free Choice of his Fellow Citizens he has heretofore served in several Offices of this Commonwealth, amongst which a Representative in the Assembly & County Commissioner each for three Years, but by losses and Misfortune became so far reduced that he was obliged to give up all he had, and is out of Employ ever since, having no means to begin any Thing

He has applied to Mr Delany two Years ago, and often since for the Office of Gauger or Inspector but never succeeded, He has since applied to Mr Clymer for an Employ under him, and as he has been a Distiller and well versed in that Occupation, he was in great hopes, but was likewise disappointed. He now Applies to the President for some Office or public Employ by which to get a Livelihood for a Numerous Family in his advanced Years. For his Personal Character he refers to Robert Morris & Fredrick August Muhlenberg Esqrs.[1] And your Memorialist will ever pray &c.

Michael Shubart

ALS, DLC:GW.

The household of Michael Shubart, distiller, at 29 North Seventh Street, Philadelphia, consisted of five white males over fifteen years old, two under sixteen, and six white females (*Philadelphia Directory,* 1791, 118, and *Heads of Families* [Pennsylvania], 224).

1. GW did not appoint Shubart to a federal office. Shubart again wrote to GW, on 11 Dec. 1792, unsuccessfully soliciting the "Office for Registering of Ships &c. . . . for the Port of Philadelphia," which he claimed would "soon be open" (DLC:GW). Frederick Phile, whom GW had appointed naval officer for the port of Philadelphia in August 1789, died in 1793, but Shubart did not replace him (see GW to the U.S. Senate, 3 Aug. 1789).

To Thomas Smith

Sir,   Philadelphia, July 8th 1791

I received your letter of the 20th of April, while I was on my journey to the southward, and until my return to this place it has not been in my power to acknowledge the receipt of it.[1]

I must now beg, Sir, that you will receive my best thanks for the particular attention which you have paid to such business as I have had occasion to place in your hands, and to be assured that you have accomplished it entirely to my satisfaction.

The sum of 276²⁰/₁₀₀ dollars which you mention to have lodged in the Bank of North America, subject to my order, I find is there. With very great esteem and regard, I am, Sir, Your most obedient Servant

G. Washington.

LB, DLC:GW.

1. GW returned to Philadelphia on 6 July. Thomas Smith's letter of 20 April has not been found, nor has the business entrusted to him been positively

identified. Smith had previously acted as GW's attorney in ejectment proceedings against squatters on GW's western Pennsylvania lands (see GW to Smith, 26 Dec. 1788).

From Agricol Billion

at Mr James Mercier No. 15 North Water Street
Mr President   Philadelphia July 9th 1791

The satisfaction which the News of your return to Philadelphia has spread through the public mind manifested itself in such a manner that strangers, even those unacquainted with the english language, could not be ignorant of it; and altho I am of this last description, I have proved, as well as your Citizens, the sentiments of sensibility and admiration which all Europe expresses for your social & military virtues, and mingle my acclamations with those of this fortunate and grateful people whose fetters you have broken.

I had proposed, Mr President, before your arrival was announced, to invite, through the medium of the public papers, the Amateurs of the fine Arts, to make a purchase of three precious peiccs which I have brought here, They consist of two Busts of white marble as large as the life, one representing the effigy of John James Rousseau, and the other that of Montesque, and a small time piece for a Hall—supported by 4 Columns of white marble—covered by a chinese canopy & gilt with gold in the manner of the famous Baillon.[1] This Time piece is about 18 inches high and may be placed either on a Chimney Piece or on a Table, it has a glass case which wholly covers it.

The epoch of your return being indicated to me, I have therefore suspended the insertion of these things in the public Papers, flattering myself that you woud not dissapprove, Mr President, of my having the honor to offer them to you—in order that they might not be advertised in the papers until you had the refusal of them.[2] I am, with Respect, Mr President, Yr most Huble & Obet Sert

Agricol Billion

Translation, DNA: RG 59, Miscellaneous Letters; ALS, in French, DNA: RG 59, Miscellaneous Letters. The text is taken from a translation prepared for GW; the receiver's copy, in French, appears in CD-ROM:GW.

Agricol Billion has not been further identified. A Charles Billon was a principal of a watchmaking firm located at 12 South Third Street, Philadelphia, in 1795, and was listed in city directories as a clockmaker, watchmaker, and jeweler in the late 1790s and early 1800s (Eckhardt, *Pennsylvania Clocks and Clockmakers*, 170).

1. Before his death in the early 1770s, Jean-Baptiste Baillon of Paris was clockmaker to Marie-Antoinette.

2. After figuring on the cover of the original receiver's copy the costs of the pieces, Tobias Lear noted that Billion's offer was "Answered in the negative"; no reply has been found.

Tobias Lear to Alexander Hamilton

Philadelphia, 9 July 1791. "The President has received a letter from Mr Rue, who was appointed second Mate of the revenue Cutter on the Delaware station, declining his appointment & returning his commission."[1]

LB, DLC:GW.

1. The letter of resignation from Benjamin Rue to GW has not been found but must have been written between 28 June and this date. Tench Coxe wrote to Tobias Lear on 28 June that Rue, "of the Pennsylvania Cutter, called at the Treasury a few days ago for the purpose of resigning; as he only mentioned the matter verbally, and was not prepared with a proper letter, he proposed to make his resignation with due form & respect in writing, to the President, of the honor of whose confidence he appeared to entertain a lively sense. His sole reason for not entering on the duty assigned him is, that since the appointment of Capt. Montgomery he has made engagements in another line from which it is not in his power to absolve himself" (DLC:GW). On 29 July Lear sent Rue's letter and commission to Thomas Jefferson, along with those of Edmund Pendleton, Thomas Johnson, Thomas Pinckney, John Marshall, Robert Hanson Harrison, George Nicholas, Nathaniel Gilman, Richard Stockton, and John Rutledge, Sr., to be filed in the records of the State Department (DNA: RG 59, Miscellaneous Letters).

From Henry Knox

War Department [Philadelphia] the 9th of July 1791
The Secretary at War having by order of the President of the United States, taken into his serious consideration, a Letter written by Major Richard Call, commanding Officer of the troops of the United States, to Messrs Speir and McLeod & Company dated the 2d of June—humbly Reports.[1]

That all evidence whereon the said Letter may have been been grounded is entirely wanting, and therefore no conclusive opinion can be found thereon.

That the said Letter however seems to indicate on the part of the said Major Call, that he is under an influence independent of the immediate executive of the United States, and therefore liable to take measures inconsistent with their true interest and dignity. That under this impression, it would be proper that he be replaced immediately by another commanding Officer, and that he be ordered to join the troops on the Ohio.[2]

That upon receiving more full information, the Secretary of War will, conformably thereto, submit a further report.[3]

All which is humbly submitted to the President of the United States.

H. Knox

LS, DLC:GW.

1. This was probably the letter that Tobias Lear transmitted to Henry Knox on 7 July, with GW's wish that he "take into his serious consideration," the enclosed letter "relative to some misunderstanding which has taken place between the Creek Indians & the Inhabitants of Georgia" (DLC:GW). The letter, probably from John Habersham, that Knox asked Lear on 30 Aug. to submit to GW might have been related to the Creek situation (DLC:GW).

2. Call was not transferred to the Ohio frontier at this time and continued as commander of federal troops in Georgia. James Seagrove reported to GW on 5 July 1792 that Call "hath resigned himself to so continual a state of intoxication with strong liquors, as to render him totally incapable of acting, or even judging, of what is proper in the line of his duty."

3. On 13 July Knox submitted to GW three letters he drafted that day for Gov. Edward Telfair of Georgia, Creek leader Alexander McGillivray, and Call, and he informed GW that "Tomorrow morning I shall wait upon you to receive your commands relative to these letters & to make any necessary explanations" (DLC:GW). He also enclosed a copy of an unidentified letter from John Heth to McGillivray regarding Georgia-Creek relations and the implementation of the Treaty of New York of 1790. For the texts of Knox's letters to Telfair, McGillivray, and Call, as approved by GW, see *ASP, Indian Affairs*, 1:125, 127–28.

Tobias Lear to Edmund Randolph

[Philadelphia] 9 July 1791. By the president's command, returns the enclosed letter with the thanks of the president for the attorney general's

attention in submitting it for his perusal and notes that "The President expresses his pleasure at its contents."[1]

LB, DLC:GW.
   1. The enclosed letter has not been identified.

From Henry Knox

Sir   War department [Philadelphia], 11th July 1791.

  Agreably to the powers you were pleased to vest in me on the ninteenth of March last, I have filled, the following vacancies, on the condition that you should approve thereof.[1]

Second Regiment.

Captain Samuel Newman, vice Pray declined.
        Jonathan Haskell, vice Freeman declined.
Lieutenant Martin Brimmer Sohier, vice Newman, promoted.
        Cornelius Lyman vice Higginson declined.
        Joseph Dickinson, vice Huger declined
Ensign William Balch, vice Sohier promoted.
        John Sullivan, vice Edwards declined.
        John Tillinghast vice George Tillinghast, declined.
        Daniel Tilton, vice Joseph Smith Gilman, declined.
        Samuel Andrews, vice Joseph Pierce junr declined.
        John Bird, vice Dickinson promoted.
        Micah McDonough, vice Duff, declined.
Surgeon's mate, Elijah Tisdale, vice Sumner declined.

  I have also to inform you Sir that the following vacancies exist.

  One Lieutenant Colonel Commandant, One Captain, One Lieutenant and One Surgeon.

  I humbly propose that the senior surgeon's mate of the first regiment, to vizt John Elliot shall be appointed surgeon of the second regiment, and that the vacancy be filled by John Lynch, of New York, who is recommended by Dr Cochran.

  That Captain Hughes have the vacancy of the Rhode Island company: He was formerly of that line, and has the reputation of a good officer.

  For the vacant Lieutenancy in the second regiment, I submit John Heth, an Ensign in the First regiment, and at present employed on a mission to the Creeks.[2]

That vice Heth, I submit Hastings Marks of Charlottesville, Virginia, to be an Ensign, who is recommended by Mr Jefferson.[3]

I have also the honor to submit that Captain McCurdy of the First regiment, and Lieutenant Ernest of the Artillery have tendered their resignations—The former is at Lancaster, and in arrest, and will not probably be any loss to the service. The latter having been on the recruiting service has injured himself in such a manner as to be unfit for military duty.

I have informed these officers, that their resignations should be submited to the President of the United States, and would probably be granted.[4]

In this case the eldest Lieutenant of the First regiment will fill Captain McCurdy's place, and the eldest Ensign the place of the Lieutenant—This will occasion a vacancy of an Ensign, which it is submitted should be filled by a young gentleman at present serving as a cadet on the frontiers, by the name of Elijah Strong son of Captain Strong, who is in actual service on the Ohio, or John Bertlee Shee, son of Colonel Shee of Philadelphia.

The vacant lieutenancy in the Artillery to be filled by Staats Morris of New York. I have the honor to be with great respect Sir Your most obedient and humble servant

H. Knox
secy of War

LS, DLC:GW; LB, DLC:GW.

1. For GW's authorization of Henry Knox's arrangements for the military expedition against the hostile northwestern Indian nations, see Knox to GW, 14 Mar. and enclosures, and 18 Mar. (first letter), n.2. GW approved most of Knox's suggestions and submitted the names of all except John Lynch, Elijah Strong, and John Bertles Shee to the Senate on 1 Nov. (see GW to the U.S. Senate, 31 Oct. 1791 [first letter], and *Executive Journal*, 1:85–87).

2. For John Heth's mission, see Knox's instructions to him, dated 31 May (*ASP, Indian Affairs,* 1:125–26).

3. Thomas Jefferson forwarded to Knox on 24 Nov. 1790 certificates recommending his sister Anna's (Nancy) nephew, Hasting Marks of Charlottesville, "who would be glad of some commission in the federal troops to the Westward" (*Jefferson Papers,* 18:69; see also Marks to Jefferson, 10 Jan. 1792, ibid., 23:33–34). The Senate confirmed his appointment as ensign of the 1st Regiment of Infantry on 7 Nov. 1791 (*Executive Journal*, 1:86, 88).

4. No resignation letter to GW from either William McCurdy or Matthew Ernest has been found.

Henry Knox to Tobias Lear

Philadelphia, 11 July [1791]. Requests that "some information just received by express" be submitted to the president; "After he shall have perused them I will wait upon him to receive his orders."[1]

LS, DLC:GW; LB, DLC:GW.

1. A docket on the original receiver's copy and a note at the bottom of the letter-book copy identify the enclosures as dispatches from Maj. Gen. Richard Butler at Fort Pitt. Henry Knox's reply of 12 July to Butler's dispatch states: "Yesterday morning, at eight o'clock, I received your favor of the 2d instant, by express, James McClellan. The information of Thomas Rhea, whose affidavit you transmitted, was, indeed, of the importance to justify a special express. It has been submitted to the President . . . , who will take it into his most serious consideration. To quarrel, and come to an open rupture with the crown of Britain, would, in the present situation of this country, be a very serious affair, and to be avoided, if possible, consistently with national honor and dignity. . . . Indeed, it is hardly to be doubted, if the facts alleged by Rhea be true, but this instance of aid to the Indians, will be followed by others" (*ASP, Indian Affairs*, 1:190–91). After George Beckwith read in the *Gazette of the United States* (Philadelphia), 13 July, about Rhea's capture by Indians whom he later witnessed receiving military supplies from the British, he protested to Alexander Hamilton that "Insofar as Ray's declarations may have a tendency to excite any suspicions of an unfriendly nature on the part of the King's government, they are totally devoid of truth, and as such, I trust will not be credited" (Syrett, *Hamilton Papers*, 8:544–46). Rhea's narrative appears in *ASP, Indian Affairs*, 1:196–97.

From Samuel Osgood

Sir   Philadelphia July 11th 1791.

In the Execution of the Duties incumbent on the Postmaster General, I am sensible from Experience of the Propriety of his residing at the Seat of Government.

From a Consideration of the Inconveniences that would result to me by a Removal to Philadelphia, I am induced to make a Resignation of the Office of Postmaster General with which you were pleased to honor me, and for which, I beg leave to make my most grateful Acknowledgements. Whenever a Successor may be appointed, I shall be ready to deliver over the Office.[1]

Permit me, Sir, to mention Mr Burrall, who has been my Assistant in the Office; His Knowledge of the Business of the Department—His attention & Accuracy in keeping the Accounts of the same, as well as his long Services in other Departments under the late Congress of the united States, are Circumstances in his favor, which, I have no doubt, will have that weight given to them, which they may Justly merit.

sincerely wishing you a long & prosperous Continuance in your present important and arduous Station. I have the honor to be With the greatest Respect Sir, your most obedient Servant

Samuel Osgood

ALS, DNA: RG 59, Miscellaneous Letters.

1. Rumors of New York resident Samuel Osgood's impending resignation as postmaster general had circulated ever since the federal capital moved from New York to Philadelphia in 1790 (see Timothy Pickering to GW, 3 Sept. 1790 and note 2) and resurfaced in the spring of 1791. When John Moylan recommended his brother Stephen for the vacancy to Robert Morris on 17 July 1791, he mentioned that "a few months ago" Osgood's resignation "was talked of as soon likely to take place" (DLC:GW). See also Lear to GW, 17 April. For GW's appointment of Pickering as Osgood's replacement, see Pickering to GW, 27 August.

To Thomas Jefferson

[Philadelphia] Tuesday 12th [July] 1791[1]

The enclosed I send this afternoon, for your perusal.[2] Tomorrow, 8'Oclock, I shall send the person who was the bearer of it, to you. It being the hour, he left word, when he left the letter, that he should call upon me. If Mr Pearce merits the character given him by T: D. he will unquestionably merit encouragement, & you can put him in the way to obtain it.[3] Yrs ever

G.W.

ALS, DLC: Thomas Jefferson Papers. Jefferson endorsed the letter as received on 13 July.

For the background to this letter, see Thomas McCabe, Sr., to GW, 21 July 1790 and notes 2 and 3, and Thomas A. Digges to GW, 1 July 1791.

1. Jefferson wrote "July" under GW's erroneous "June."

2. The enclosure, most likely Digges's letter of c.28 April 1791 introducing William Pearce to GW, has not been found.

3. Only after being so advised by Jefferson and Edmund Randolph had the president declined further involvement in a state plan to establish a woolen manufactory in Virginia. GW was told that "it is felony to export the Machines which it is probable the Artist contemplates to bring with him [from Britain], and it certainly would not carry an aspect very favorable to the dignity of the

United States for the President, in a clandestine manner, to entice the subjects of another Nation to violate its laws" (see GW to Beverley Randolph, 13 Jan. 1791 and note 1). For British laws prohibiting the export of textile machinery and the emigration of skilled mechanics and artisans, see Thomas Howells to GW, 14 July 1789, source note, and Arthur Young to GW, 25 Jan. 1791, n.2. One week after GW's recommendation in his address to Congress of 8 Jan. 1790 that the safety and interest of a free people required the promotion of manufactories of military supplies and other necessities, the House ordered Alexander Hamilton to prepare a plan for the encouragement and promotion of American manufactures, and his new assistant, Tench Coxe, began work on the report shortly after his appointment in May 1790 (*DHFC,* 3:265; Cooke, *Coxe and the Early Republic,* 183). Jefferson had learned of Coxe's interest in American manufactures when Coxe had sent him on 15 April a copy of his plan for a manufacturing center to be established near the new Federal City (*Jefferson Papers,* 20:215–18). Unwilling to approach Hamilton directly (who was then organizing the Society for Establishing Useful Manufactures with William Duer and other speculators) in order to fulfill GW's command to put Pearce "in the way to obtain" encouragement, Jefferson instead referred Pearce to Coxe. The inventor delivered to Coxe on 13 July Digges's letter of introduction to GW, and Coxe reported back to Jefferson the same day (see ibid., 623). Coxe then brought Pearce to the attention of Hamilton, who became the artisan's patron. According to a receipt of 20 Aug. 1791, Hamilton gave Pearce $100 "towards providing the use of Society for the establishment of Manufactures in the State of New Jersey certain machines & models of Machines to be delivered to the said Alexander Hamilton" (Syrett, *Hamilton Papers,* 9:85–86). With Hamilton's continued financial support, Pearce constructed looms in two Philadelphia shops owned by John Nixon, and his cotton manufactory at 13 Penn Street was fully operational by the time Congress considered Hamilton's report on manufacturers, which was presented to the House on 5 Dec. (see ibid., 10:230). It undoubtedly was Hamilton who was behind GW's visit to the establishment in June 1792 (see McCabe to GW, 21 July 1790, n.2, and *Gazette of the United States* [Philadelphia], 9 June 1792).

From Edmund Randolph

Sir   Philadelphia July 13. 1791.

Having been engaged in court from the time of my leaving you yesterday, for the greater part of the day, I had not an opportunity of conversing with Mr Lewis, until the evening. He has committed to paper the result of his mind, in consequence of my interview with him, and I do myself the honor of inclosing it to you. I was indirectly informed that Judge Yeates would not be induced, upon any consideration, to live in this city; a place, from which the district-judge could not well be absent.[1]

I also made a distant inquiry as to Mr Fitzsimmons's inclination to the Auditorship. But I find, that he considers the employment, insufficiently compensated for the interruption, which his private business must sustain.

In revolving the subject of the Postmaster generalship, I have been impressed with the importance of its duties, and the skill, necessary for their execution. In both these, however, I do no more, than concur with you. I beg leave to repeat, what I yesterday took the liberty of suggesting, that the opinion of many respectable men has been strenuous in favor of relaxing that delicacy, which is supposed to have restrained you in the distribution of offices, with respect to those, who are around you. I shall not dissemble my genuine sentiment, that the propriety of departing from it seems to depend on the obvious fitness of the character nominated. By obvious fitness, I mean something, arising from acknowledged talents, habits of business, and public estimation, which will cut off every possible suspicion of an undue predilection. I do not apprehend, that it was your wish, that I should go farther than this. But that some scope of choice may be presented to you, I will submit to your consideration the following names:

Thomas Paine[2]

Richard Peters.

Wm Smith, Baltimore

Thos Fitzsimmons.

Charles Thomson.

—— Huston of Jersey, if living He was a member of congress.[3] If the salary would attract candidates at a farther distance, I have no doubt, that you will have a great range for appointing to the office.

I delivered yesterday to the secretary of state the two subjects, with which you charged me for him. I have the honor, sir, to be with the highest and most sincere respect yr mo: ob. serv.

Edm: Randolph

ALS, DLC:GW.

1. The enclosure has not been further identified. William Lewis had written earlier to GW, on 8 July 1791: "I am honored with a Communication, very grateful to my feelings, which you have been pleased to make to me through Major Jackson, relative to the office lately held by the honorable Mr Hopkinson, and under the impressions which it has occasiond, am truly sorry that

Circumstances oblige me to decline the proposed appointment. Altho' it would be wrong in me to trouble you with many observations on the Subject, the respect which I at all times feel for you, calls upon me to mention, that being in a very eligible Situation at the Bar in point of Emolument, as well as respectability of employment, and of an age perhaps best suited for it, the meditated Change would hardly be Consistent with the duty which I owe to my family" (DNA: RG 59, Miscellaneous Letters). Lewis shortly thereafter changed his mind, and according to the State Department's memorandum book, a commission as Pennsylvania district judge was issued to him on 14 July (DNA:PCC, item 187, 113). See also Thomas FitzSimons to GW, 10 May, n.1. Jasper Yeates of Lancaster, Pa. (1745–1817), had been appointed an associate justice of the Pennsylvania supreme court in March 1791.

2. It appears that Edmund Randolph later inserted Thomas Paine's name here at the top of the list as an afterthought. On 21 July Randolph wrote to James Madison: "Mr. J[efferson] and myself have attempted to bring Paine forward, as successor to Osgood. It seemed to be a fair opportunity for a declaration of certain sentiments. But all, that I have heard, has been, that it would be too pointed to keep a vacancy unfilled, until his return from the other side of the water. The contest seems to lie between Pickering, Peters, and *F. A. Muhlenberg,* who most probably cannot be reelected" (*Madison Papers,* 14: 51–52).

3. South Carolina native William Churchill Houston (1746–1788) graduated from Princeton College in 1768 and served as a member of the Continental Congress from New Jersey from 1779 to 1781 and 1784 to 1785. He was a delegate to the Annapolis Convention of 1786 and the Federal Convention of 1787.

To William Stephens Smith

Sir,   Philadelphia July 13th 1791.

I have received since my return to this place the letter which you were so kind as to write on the 6. of June, and am now to make you my acknowledgements for the information it contained.[1] Very soon after I came to the government I took measures for enquiring into the disposition of the british cabinet on the matters in question between us: and what you now communicate corresponds very exactly with the result of those enquiries.[2] Their intention indeed to send a minister is more strongly indicated on this occasion as one of the Secretaries of State has come forward voluntarily to say so[3]—how far they may be disposed to settle the other points which are really interesting to us is still a subject of conjecture—in all events we are to thank you for the trouble you have taken, & the lights you have contributed to throw on this subject.

Having taken copies of the documents, which accompanied your letter I herewith return the originals.[4] I am Sir, with great regard, Your most obedient servant[5]

G. Washington

LB, DLC:GW; Df (letterpress copy), in the hand of Thomas Jefferson, DLC: Thomas Jefferson Papers.

1. William Stephens Smith left England immediately after meeting with British home secretary Lord Grenville and reached New York on 5 June. After writing his report of 6 June to GW, he traveled to Philadelphia to meet with Alexander Hamilton, John Jay, Rufus King, and others who shared his pro-British sentiments, arriving on 12 June. He sent his father-in-law, John Adams, on 5 Aug. a copy of his report to GW, noting: "Mr Jay. Hamilton and King, were much pleased with the contents of it, But I believe The President Mr Jefferson & Mr Maddison would have rather I had stayed at home" (MHi-A).

2. The first part of this sentence is similar to the relevant part of GW's message of 14 Feb. to Congress, which Jefferson had also drafted.

3. For rumors of the appointment of a British minister to the United States, see Hamilton to GW, 11 April. George Hammond was not named to that post until September. He arrived in America the following month but did not immediately present his credentials. See George III to GW, 2 Sept. 1791.

4. This sentence appears only in the letter-book copy.

5. Upon receipt of this letter, Smith drafted an angry reply, which was not sent and has not been found. As Smith wrote to Adams on 5 Aug.: "Inclosed I send you the Presidents answer to that Letter, and my reply to it, but being advised by Colo. Hamilton to take no notice of it, but leave it to its own operation on the minds of the Government, I reluctantly withheld it, and only replyed, Thus 'I have the honor, to acknowledge the receipt of the Presidents Letter of the 13th of July in answer to the Communications I thought it my duty to make on the 6th of June after my return from Europe'" (MHi-A).

From Martinus van Doorninck

Sir   New York Júlÿ 13 1791.

Disgusted with the revolution of Holland, i resolved to cross the Atlantic, to settle me in this coúntrÿ of libertÿ, and was provided with the inclosed bÿ one of its most Strenuous assertors, the Gallant Marqúis de La Faÿette. At mÿ arrival i had the design to go to Philadelphia, and deliver the letter to Yoúr Exe:, but informed, that Yoúr Exe: was on a toúr throúgh the Soúthern States, i was obliged to give úp for that time anÿ intention, bút Since some daÿs hearing Your Exes: retúrn from his voÿage, i am compelled to Send the letter by the mail, becaúse i find, i can't stand the súffocating hotness, which reigns in this Season,

bÿ which i, and the most of mÿ familÿ, have not enjoÿed a good
health Since the daÿ of oúr arrival: bÿ this i'm indisposed to wait
on Yoúr Exe:, nevertheless i shall be for ever the Admiror of the
Foundator of American Independencÿ and am Sir Yoúr Excel-
lencÿ's Most humble and devoted Servant
                                    Martinus van Doorninck

ALS, DNA: RG 59, Miscellaneous Letters.

To Thomas Johnson

Dear Sir   Philadelphia July 14th 1791.
   Without preface, or apology for propounding the following
question to you—at this time—permit me to ask you with frankness, and in the fullness of friendship, whether you will accept of
an appointment in the Supreme Judiciary of the United States?
   Mr Rutledge's resignation has occasioned a vacancy therein
which I should be glad to see filled by you. Your answer to this
question by the Post (which is the most certain mode of conveying letters) as soon as you can make it convenient, will very
much oblige Dear Sir Your most Obedient & Affectionate Hble
Servt[1]

                                    Go: Washington

ALS, PHi: Dreer Collection; photostat of ALS (duplicate), MdHi; LB,
DLC:GW.
   1. GW probably posted the original receiver's copy of this letter and then
on 17 July sent a duplicate enclosed in a letter to William Deakins, Jr., who
replied from Georgetown, Md., on 22 July: "Your much Esteem'd favor of the
17th Current, I had the Honor to receive, yesterday, & the letter for Mr Johnson was forwarded this day by a safe hand" (DNA: RG 59, Miscellaneous Letters). Thomas Johnson answered GW on 27 July, writing from Spurrier's Tavern in Anne Arundel (later Howard) County, Md.: "I write this in my way from
Annaps to Frederick to acknowledge the Receit of your kind Letter of the
fourteenth Instant and the Duplicate of it; they reached me so early as the
twenty second and twenty third the last on my Way to Annapolis. Your earnestness that I should accept so strongly marks the Rank I hold in your Regard
that I cannot but be in good Humor with myself and a Conversation with Mr
Carroll, which I hoped to have had at Annapolis would probably have informed me in some particulars that might lead my Determination—amongst
others and not the least whether the southern Circuit would fall to me; if it
would at my Time of Life and otherwise circumstanced as I am it would be an
insurmountable Objection. Mr Carroll is at his Manor where I purpose to call

on him Tomorrow—soon after I intend to trouble you with another Letter"
(DNA: RG 59, Miscellaneous Letters). Johnson wrote again to GW from Frederick, Md., on 30 July: "I wrote to you the other Day from Spurriers on my
way from Annapolis undecided as to accepting the Office of Judge and expecting Mr Carroll could assist with Lights to determine me but he could not.
I now write to Mr Jay, who is probably not in Phila., and also to Mr Wilson to
inform you whether by the subsisting or designed Arrangement, which I suppose the Judges agree on amongst themselves, the next Southern Circuit
would fall to me; if it would, I neither expect or desire any Alteration to acco-
modate me but my weak Frame and the Interest my Family have in me forbid
my engaging in it: Let this Single Circumstance if you please, determine the
one Way or the other for my Answer. I had almost resolved to see you at philadelphia but Potomack Affairs and Mr D. Carroll's Letter call me to George
Town on Monday, from whence it is likely this Letter will go. I feel real Unesi-
ness that my Embarrassment should occasion delay in your filling up this Office as the Time is now so short: impute it to the true Occasion and believe me
that whether I receive the Commission or not the Manner in which you have
been pleased to offer it is the greater part of it's Value and will with the many
other Instances of your Confidence and Friendship be remembered with pleasure." Before sending this letter Johnson added a postscript when he was at
Georgetown on 1 Aug.: "It never occurred to me 'till Yesterday that the supreme Court was to sit as to day, I imagine you found yourself obliged to fill
up the Office I do not regret my Inattention for any Thing so much as keeping
you in Suspence for which indeed I am sorry" (DNA: RG 59, Miscellaneous
Letters). After receiving Johnson's two letters, GW consulted with the justices
of the Supreme Court about Johnson's appointment and issued Johnson a temporary commission as associate justice on 5 August. GW presented his name
to the Senate when the Second Congress convened, and Johnson's appointment was confirmed on 7 Nov. (see GW to Johnson, 7 Aug., and to the U.S.
Senate, 31 Oct., and *Executive Journal*, 1:85–86, 88).

From John Brett Kenna

Friday 11. O Clock [14 July 1791][1]
May it please your Excellency
I am very Certain my Letter demands more Apologies than
Words Can Make. I must rely on your Innate Goodness of heart
being a Mason to pardon me. I am in Great Distress. I had the
Honor the War before this of being an Officer in the 54th Regt.
I am known to General Spotswood, & young Mr Lewis of Fred-
ericksburgh.[2] I have been Assisted by Some of the Masons, &
J.B. Smith ∴ G.M. of Pennsylvania,[3] I most Humbly & Sincerely
beg pardon for the Liberty I have taken, & am with Great Re-

spect, your Excellencys, most Obedt most devoted very humble Servant[4]

John Brett Kenna ∴

ALS, DNA: RG 59, Miscellaneous Letters.

John Brett Kenna has not been further identified. GW joined Fredericksburg Masonic Lodge No. 4 in November 1752, was raised to the third degree in August 1753, and appears in the lodge records only twice more, in September 1753 and January 1755. The lodge was the third "Ancient" lodge in Virginia and received its charter from the Grand Lodge of Scotland on 21 July 1758 (see Ronald E. Heaton and James R. Case, comps., *The Lodge at Fredericksburgh: A Digest of the Early Records* [Norristown, Pa., 1975], 2, 91; Tatsch, *Freemasonry in the Thirteen Colonies*, 133–34).

1. A later hand added the dateline "July 14. 1791," which was derived from the contemporary docket: "From Mr John Bret Kenna for some relief—July 14th 1791," in Tobias Lear's hand.

2. Alexander Spotswood (1751–1818), who served in the Revolutionary War as colonel of the 2d Virginia Regiment from 1776 to 1777 and was appointed brigadier general by the state in 1781, was married to the eldest daughter of GW's half brother Augustine. GW occasionally visited Spotswood's Spotsylvania County estate on the Rappahannock River and corresponded with him about agricultural topics (*Diaries*, 4:131n). "Young Mr Lewis of Fredericksburgh" was probably GW's nephew Robert Lewis, who later joined the Fredericksburg Lodge (Brown, *George Washington, Freemason*, 15–16).

3. In addition to being grand master of the Pennsylvania Masons, Jonathan Bayard Smith was a member of the American Philosophical Society and the St. Tammany Society. The "tri-con" symbol after his and Kenna's names was first used by French Masons as a terminal point of punctuation for abbreviations in the mid-1770s and came to denote a Masonic official (see Albert G. Mackey, *A Lexicon of Freemasonry* . . . [5th ed., Philadelphia, 1866], 11).

4. No evidence has been found suggesting that GW ever replied or contributed to Kenna's relief.

From Thomas Irwin

Sir,   Philadelphia 15th July 1791

I hereby take the liberty of Congratulating your Excellency on your safe arrivall from the Southern Tour of the United States over which I hope you will long, and happily preside.

I must beg your Excellencys permission to state a few facts and make a request. I have been a Merchant of this City Twenty Years, in the course of the late Revolution, few owned more private Vessells of War than I did, and no persons Vessells delivered more English Prisoners to the American Commissary, either in the American and French Ports than mine did, towards the conclution of the War Fortune proved unkind, and I had not less than 13 or 14 well equiped Letters of Marque (in all of which I was largely concearned) Captured by the Enemy, since the Peace I owned a part of a large Ship which was Captured by the Algerines. I have lately made a Voyage, to the West Indias where I have also been unfortunate and at the Havana I lost near 20,000 Dollars, from such a Train of missfortunes your Excelly will naturly conclude that my Finances are exausted, that being the case, and being informed, that an Office is Vacant, that requires an accomptant to fill it. I mean that of Auditor. I take the Liberty of Offering your Excellency my service and of assuring you that should I be so happy as to meet your Excellencys Approbation, unremitting care attention and Fidelity shall be used by me in the Execution of the Business—should an information respecting my Character be necessary, I will be much Obliged to your Excellency If you will please to inquire of the Govornor of this State the Governor of New Jersey, The Honable Judge Wilson, Robt Morris and Blair McClenachan Esqrs. or Genl Irvine— If I should not be so happy as to meet your Excellencys choise in this appointment I request you will please to remember me, when a future opportunity may Offer.[1] I have the Honor to be with every sentiment of regard &c. &c. &c. Your Excellencys Most Obt most Huml. servt

Thomas Irwin

ALS, DLC:GW.

Philadelphia merchant Thomas Irwin invested in the following Revolutionary War privateers: the sloop *Queen of France,* schooners *Chance* and *Concord,* brigs *Delaware, Hetty, Impertinent, Lady Gates, Neptune,* and *Susannah,* and ships *Congress, Minerva, Revolution,* and *Washington.* For Mathew and Thomas Irwin & Company's troubles with Algerian corsairs, see Mathew Irwin to GW, 9 July 1789.

1. Thomas Irwin again solicited the auditor's office from GW on 22 Aug., enclosing an unidentified "further Information of my Character" (DLC:GW), which might have been the letter that Blair McClenachan sent GW on 15 July recommending Irwin as a capable merchant, good accountant, and an honest and industrious man whose best exertions in support of his country's liberties during the Revolutionary War were not wanting (DLC:GW). In later recommending "Irvine's" application for the auditorship, New Jersey federal marshal Thomas Lowrey wrote to GW on 25 Oct. from Trenton, referring him to an enclosed letter of 11 Oct. to Lowrey, in which New Jersey governor William Paterson stated that "Mr Irwin's Character, both in a moral and political View,

is extremely fair. He is honest, sober, industrious, attentive to Business, and well-versed in Accounts: he was a Merchant regularly bred. He was an early, decided, active, and persevering Whig during the late Contest, and is in Principle closely attached to the present Frame of Government. Mr Irwin was at one Period a Man of very considerable Property, but by a Series of untoward Events is now reduced and in narrow Circumstances. Poverty, however is no Crime. But why need I be particula⟨r⟩ on the Subject—You know Mr Irwin well—Let me then entreat your kind Offices in his Favor; they will be conferred on a meritorious Man" (DLC:GW). Irwin did not receive the desired appointment and again wrote GW the following year, unsuccessfully soliciting the position of treasurer of the U.S. Mint (Irwin to GW, 24 April 1792, DLC:GW).

From Frederick A. C. Muhlenberg

Philadelphia, 15 July 1791. Offers himself as a candidate for the office of postmaster general, Samuel Osgood having resigned. "This State having been divided into Districts & I having changed my place of Residence, renders it uncertain whether I shall be returnd a Member of the next Legislature, which Consideration induces me to take this Step."[1]

ALS, DLC:GW.

1. Congressman Frederick Augustus Conrad Muhlenberg did retain his seat in the U.S. House of Representatives and served through the end of the Third Congress, but he was not reelected as Speaker of the House when the Second Congress convened in October 1791.

Letter not found: to William Deakins, Jr., 17 July 1791. On 22 July Deakins referred to GW's "much Esteem'd favor of the 17th Current."[1]

1. See GW to Thomas Johnson, 14 July, n.1.

Letter not found: to George Augustine Washington, 17 July 1791. GW's nephew wrote to him on 1 Aug., acknowledging "rect of Your favor of the 17th Ulto."

From Sebastian Bauman

New York, 18 July 1791. Since Postmaster General Samuel Osgood is resigning, begs to "impress into" his successor, "under whom I must hold my Office," and "to whom I may be a stranger, . . . sentiments favourable of me. I am competent for the Office in all its shape. Your

Excellency may rely not to be Disappointed in your recommendation, for non shall Exceed me in the duty of my Office, Both in integrity and Punctuallity."[1]

ALS, DNA: RG 59, Miscellaneous Letters.
1. Sebastian Bauman (1739–1803) retained his federal office as New York City postmaster until his death.

Letter not found: from William Linn, 18 July 1791. In a letter to William Linn, 21 Oct. 1791, Tobias Lear wrote: "The President likewise desires you will accept his thanks for the sermon which you had the goodness to send to him on the 18th of July."[1]

Presbyterian and Dutch Reformed clergyman William Linn (1752–1808) was born in Cumberland County, Pa., and graduated from the College of New Jersey (Princeton) in 1772. Licensed to preach in 1775, he served as a chaplain in the Continental army before resigning and filling the pulpit of Big Spring Church in Cumberland County in 1777. In the mid-1780s Linn was head of Washington Academy in Somerset County, Md., before accepting a call to be associate pastor of the Collegiate Dutch Reformed Church in New York City in 1786. Linn was elected first chaplain of the U.S. House of Representatives in May 1789 and was reappointed in 1790. He also acted as president of Queen's College (Rutgers University) from 1791 to 1794. Linn was invited to deliver the eulogy for GW before the New York Society of the Cincinnati on 22 Feb. 1800 (*Princetonians, 1769–1775*, 231–35).
1. Linn probably sent GW a copy of his *The Blessings of America. A Sermon, Preached in the Middle Dutch Church, on the Fourth July, 1791, Being the Anniversary of the Independence of America: at the Request of the Tammany Society, or Columbian Order* (New York, 1791) which condemned Edmund Burke and praised the spirit of revolution in Europe. This was bound with other pamphlets in a volume entitled "Cincinnati" in GW's library at Mount Vernon at his death (Griffin, *Boston Athenæum Washington Collection*, 47, 125). Lear wrote Linn on 21 Oct. that "the multiplicity of business" after GW's "return from his southern tour" and "his late absence from the seat of government" delayed acknowledgment of Linn's letter (DLC:GW). The copyist mistakenly addressed this letter to William Lind. Lear also acknowledged in the same letter the volume of sermons Linn sent to Mrs. Washington, probably his *Sermons Historical and Characteristical*, copyrighted on 1 June 1791 (Evans, *American Bibliography*, 8:171).

From Thomas Mifflin

Sir   Philadelphia 18th July 1791
I think it proper to lay before you, copies of the various documents respecting an application, which I have recently made to the Governor of Virginia,[1] requiring, agreeably to the provision

contained in the second section of the fourth article of the Constitution of the United States,[2] that he would take proper measures for apprehending Francis McGuire, Absalom Wells, and Baldwin Parsons, as fugitives from justice, in order that they might be delivered up to this State, having jurisdiction of their crime. The opinion which the Attorney General of Virginia has given upon this subject,[3] as far as it respects the nature of the offence, is, I conceive, inaccurate, and could not have been given with a previous knowledge of the law of Pennsylvania on the subject: For, by an Act of Assembly, passed on the twenty ninth day of March, in the year one thousand seven hundred and eighty eight, the offence, charged in the several indictments, is rendered highly criminal, and the perpetrators, on conviction in any Court of Quarter Sessions (a Court of criminal jurisdiction exclusively) are not only condemned to forfeit the sum of one hundred pounds, but are subject, likewise, to be confined at hard labour, for any time not less than six Months, nor more than twelve Months. The fact charged, therefore, is a crime, made such by the laws of Pennsylvania; partaking of the nature of a felony, it is certainly included in the Constitutional description of "treason, felony, *or other crime*;" and, altho' an action of trespass might be maintained in Virginia, by the injured individual to recover damages for his personal wrongs, yet, it is obvious, that no indictment, no trial, no conviction, no punishment, in the public name, could take place, according to the provisions of our Legislature, but under the authority of Pennsylvania, within her jurisdiction, and in the County where the offence was committed. It is equally certain, that the laws of the State, in which the act is committed, must furnish the rule to determine its criminality, and not the law of the State, in which the fugitive from Justice happens to be discovered.

I mean not, however, Sir, to enter into any farther controversy upon this point; it is sufficient to explain it: But as the Attorney General of Virginia has suggested another difficulty, with respect to the mode of arresting persons demanded as fugitives from Justice, I have thought the present, a proper, occasion to bring the subject into your view, that, by the interposition of the Fœderal Legislature (to whose consideration you may be pleased to submit it) such regulations may be established, as will, in future, obviate all doubt and embarrassment, upon a constitutional question, so delicate and important.[4] I have the honor to be, with perfect respect, Sir, Your most obedient humble Servant

Thomas Mifflin

LS, DNA:PCC, item 69; copy, DNA: RG 46, Second Congress, 1791–1793, Records of Legislative Proceedings, President's Messages; copy, Vi.

The controversy between Pennsylvania and Virginia that began with the murder by Virginians of peaceful Indians on Pennsylvania territory in March 1791 (see Henry Knox to GW, 31 Mar. 1791 and notes 1 and 2) was exacerbated by the case of the kidnapping of a free black man in Washington, Pa., in which two of the Indian murderers were also implicated. The complex dispute was soon brought to the attention of the federal government and eventually contributed to passage of the first Fugitive Slave Act in 1793. According to the memorial of 13 May to the governor of Pennsylvania from the Pennsylvania Society for Promoting the Abolition of Slavery, John, a free black citizen of Washington, Pa., was on 10 May 1788 assaulted, seized, and carried away by disguised persons intent on selling him into slavery. These men were later identified as Francis McGuire, Baldwin Parsons, and Absalom Wells, who fled into Virginia, where they sold John as a slave to Nicholas Casey, near Romney, Va., on the south branch of the Potomac (DNA:PCC, item 69). The Ohio County delegates to the Virginia assembly later explained to Virginia governor Beverley Randolph that a Mr. Davies of Maryland had settled in western Virginia near the Pennsylvania line in the 1770s with his slave John, and when the commissioners appointed to ascertain the Pennsylvania-Virginia border completed their work, Davies discovered that he was a citizen of Pennsylvania. In an attempt to avoid the ramifications of the Pennsylvania slave law of 1780 (see Tobias Lear to GW, 5 April and note 3, and GW to Lear, 12 April 1791), Davies hired John out to a Mr. Miller on the Virginia side of the line. After John escaped, seduced by the "Negroe club," an arm of the Pennsylvania abolition society, according to the Ohio County delegates, Miller advertised for his return, and McGuire, Parsons, and Wells searched for him, found him in Washington, Pa., and brought him home (see Thomas Jefferson to GW, 20 Dec. and enclosure, DNA: RG 59, Miscellaneous Letters, and *Calendar of Virginia State Papers,* 5:396–98). Only Wells was taken into custody. McGuire, who with Capt. Samuel Brady and others had retaliated against the murder of a white family near Buffalo Creek by killing the alleged Indian perpetrators at Big Beaver Creek, escaped, and Parsons remained at large.

1. The various enclosures included copies of Pennsylvania governor Thomas Mifflin's letter of 4 June to Virginia governor Randolph and the documents it covered (the memorial of 13 May from the Pennsylvania abolition society to Mifflin and copies of Washington County court clerk and prothonotary Edward Burd's certificates of 24 May of the fugitives' indictments) and Randolph's reply of 8 July to Mifflin, enclosing the Virginia attorney general's opinion on Mifflin's demand (see n.3 below). Most of these enclosures (DNA:PCC, item 69) appear in *Calendar of Virginia State Papers,* 5:320–22, 326–28, 340–41, except Mifflin's letter of 4 June to Randolph: "I am under the

necessity of troubling your Excellency with authenticated copies of a representation which has been made to me, by the incorporated Society for the gradual abolition of Slavery &c., respecting the illegal and forcible seizure and carrying away from the County of Washington in this Commonwealth a certain free Negroe Man named John, with an intention To sell him as a slave in another State, and of transcripts from the records, of a Court of Oyer and Terminer, held in and for the said County of Washington, from which it appears that Indictments, have been duly found, charging this Violence to have been committed by Baldwin Parsons, Absalom Wells, and Francis McGuire who fled from Justice into the State of Virginia. Permit me therefore to request, that your Excellency will be pleased to take the proper measures, to cause the said Baldwin Parsons, Absalom Wells and Francis McGuire, to be delivered up to this State, having jurisdiction of their crime, agreably to the provisions, contained in the second Section of the fourth Article of the Constitution of the United States. And, I am persuaded that your Excellency's regard for Justice, and humanity will prompt you to extend your interference on this occasion, as far as it may be expedient, to restore the Negroe to his freedom" (DNA: PCC, item 69).

2. "A person charged in any State with treason, felony, or other crime, who shall flee from justice, and be found in another State, shall, on demand of the executive authority of the State from which he fled, be delivered up, to be removed to the State having jurisdiction of the crime" (U.S. Const., Art. IV, sec. 2).

3. On 14 June Governor Randolph laid Mifflin's letter of 4 June before the Virginia state executive council, and the council advised submitting it to Virginia attorney general James Innes for his opinion (*Journals of the Council of State of Virginia,* 5:295–96). Innes's report of 20 June is in DNA:PCC, item 69. When forwarding Innes's opinion to Governor Mifflin on 8 July, Randolph wrote: "Your Excellency will readily perceive that the opinion of the first law officer of the State must preclude the Executive from taking any measures for apprehending and delivering the persons demanded by you. It is to be lamented that no means have been provided for carrying into effect so important an Article of the Constitution of the United States. This case will, however, we hope be the means of calling the Attention of the Legislature to a subject of such consequence" (*Calendar of Virginia State Papers,* 5:340–41). The Pennsylvania governer acknowledged Randolph's letter on 19 July, enclosing a copy of Mifflin's letter of 18 July to GW as well as an extract of the 29 Mar. 1788 Pennsylvania act amending the act for the gradual abolition of slavery and noting that "I have submitted the subject to the consideration of the President of the United States, in hopes that by an interposition of the Federal Legislature, the difficulty with respect to the mode of arrest may for the future be removed" (ibid., 345).

4. After receiving this letter GW referred it and its enclosures to Edmund Randolph on 23 July.

To Aedanus Burke

Sir,   Philadelphia July 19th 1791

Your letter of the 6. of May covering one from Colo. Philemon Waters, was put into my hands while I was in Charleston[1]—During my journey, you will readily conceive, it was not in my power to attend to, and answer the subject of Colo. Waters's letter, which is the cause of this late acknowledgement of it—and I must now request, Sir, as his letter came thro' your hands, and as a letter to him might meet some difficulty in getting to him across the Country, that you will be so good as to convey this reply to Colo. Waters whenever an opportunity occurs.

That the 200,000 acres of land granted by Dinwiddies proclamation in the year 1754 to the Officers and Soldiers of the Virginia Troops (a part of which Colo. Waters claims for having been a soldier at the battle of the Great Meadows in that year) having been surveyed, distributed, and patents issued in the names of those, who put in their claims before the close of the year 1773, there does not appear to be the smallest prospect of his receiving any benefit from his claim—and further that it is not possible for me to afford him any relief in this case either in the capacity of President of the United States (from which he seems to expect assistance) or in any other character. I am Sir, Your most obedient Servant

G. Washington.

LB, DLC:GW.

For the background to this letter and Philemon Waters's claim under Virginia governor Robert Dinwiddie's proclamation of 1754, see Waters to GW, 3 July 1790.

1. GW was at Charleston from 2 to 9 May. Former congressman Aedanus Burke's letter of 6 May to GW reads: "The letter which I have the honor of inclosing, was sent down to Charleston last year, inclosed in a Letter addressed to me, by Coll Philemon Waters, with his request to deliver it to you then at New York. Thro' the negligence of some person to whom the Letter to me was entrusted, I never received it until Yesterday. I have only to observe that Coll Waters lives within a few miles of Cambrige in the District of Ninety Six has a family, as is I believe a deserving man" (DNA: RG 59, Miscellaneous Letters).

To Richard Champion

Sir,   Philadelphia July 19th 1791

While I was on my Journey through the Southern States it was not in my power to acknowledge the receipt of your letter of the 24th of May,[1] which was put into my hands at Camden,[2] and to make a proper return of my thanks for the Manuscript reflections upon our present situation &c.[3]—and the printed Volume of your Observations on the Commercial Connexion between Great Britain and the United States, which accompanied your letter.[4] You will therefore, Sir, be pleased now to accept my acknowledgements for these, as well as for the very polite terms in which you express yourself towards me in your letter. To endeavour to diffuse a knowledge of the true interests of our Country in a commercial or political view is certainly a meritorious attempt, and in this age of free inquiry every one has a right to submit to the consideration of his fellow-citizens such sentiments or information as he thinks may conduce to their interest or happiness. I am, Sir, Your most Obedt Servt

Go: Washington

LS, Sheffield City Library, Great Britain; LB, DLC:GW.

Bristol-born ceramist Richard Champion (1743–1791) was the chief competitor of Josiah Wedgwood's manufacturing enterprises in the 1770s and early 1780s. Champion was a staunch Whig and supported the American cause during the Revolution, often sending political intelligence to his brother-in-law John Lloyd, an agent in Charleston since 1777. After the war disrupted his business ventures Champion accepted an appointment as a deputy paymaster, which office he resigned under suspicion of embezzlement in 1784. That October he sailed for America with his wife and children and settled on land purchased for him by Lloyd about ten miles north of Camden, S.C., on Rocky Branch, a tributary of Grannys Quarter Creek, where Champion had discovered fine-quality clays. Champion was appointed clerk to the Camden Court of Common Pleas and General Sessions in 1786, served in the South Carolina general assembly from 1789 to 1790, and was a delegate to the state constitutional convention of 1790. From March 1791 until his death that October, he was commissioner in equity and register of the court of equity in Cheraw, Camden, and Orangeburg districts (see G. H. Guttridge, ed., *The American Correspondence of a Bristol Merchant, 1766–1776: Letters of Richard Champion* [Berkeley, Calif., 1934], 1–8).

1. Champion's letter to GW, dated Rocky Branch, S.C., 24 May, reads: "Although your Fellow Citizens felt the full force of the invigorating Hand which first secured to them their Liberty and their Peace, and which has since, by its wise Administration, supported their Rank amidst the Nations of the Earth,

there still remained, amongst many of them, an unsatisfied Desire, an anxious Wish to behold the face of their Benefactor, to whom, as the first and best Instrument of a merciful Providence, they are indebted for these Blessings. It was an Event which seemed necessary to the Consummation of their Happiness. They have now obtained the Gratification of their Wishes. For this auspicious Day has brought with it its full accomplishment. Amidst the Congratulations which surround you on this happy Occasion, suffer me, Sir, a Sharer in the Distress, a partaker in the Joys of my Country, to pay my humble Tribute of affectionate Duty and respectful Acknowledgment. United, Sir, to this Country by Blood, by Affinity, and by an early and zealous Attachment to Liberty, the most active Exertions within the Compass of my small Power and Ability, and upon the purest principles, was made by me during the War; in the earlier part of it to promote Reconciliation, in the latter Stage, Peace. It was equally Patriotism both in England and America (yet few in England felt the force of this Duty) to oppose Attempts alike tyrannic and unjust, unpolitic and absurd, upon the success or failure of which depended the Ruin or Preservation of their Liberty. The Attempt failed, and the Sovereignty of the United States was acknowledged. This awful Separation of a great Empire, whose united Efforts had equalled the most powerful Exertions of antient or modern Times, made a deep Impression upon the Minds of those, who conceived at least the possibility of converting the antient Affection of Fellow Citizens into the Attachment of faithful Allies. Under this Impression a Work was offered by me to the Public, with a View to point out the true Interests of a People, who had too long unhappily forsaken them. But the offering was fruitless Our Separation appeared to be confirmed. Yet the Distance preserved by Great Britain was not without its Utility to this Country. It demonstrated to us, that from her own Exertions, America should derive her Strength. Of this Work, I beg, Sir, the Honour of your Acceptance. I have since published another, which is in some Measure a Continuation, but unfortunately I have no Copy. Many Years have now elapsed since I became a Citizen of this State. A Period, almost wholly spent in Retirement devoted to literary Pursuits. The Manuscript which accompanies this, and of which I likewise beg Sir, your Acceptance, contains some cursory Reflections upon the Country, which you now honour with your Presence. It is a mere Sketch, written upon a temporary occasion, never published, and is intended for a large work; of which I have many Materials, and which a very perfect Knowledge of the Court of Great Britain, during the reign of its present Monarch, has afforded me. Vanity is said to be, probably with Truth, the ruling Passion of an Author. But, Sir, Vanity on this Occasion almost ceases to be a foible. Affection, Duty, Veneration, and Every Incitement which can warm the Heart of a Man in private Life, at the Sight of his Benefactor, must operate in the highest and most powerful Degree at the Sight of the Benefactor of Millions. The Widow, Sir, will throw in her Mite. And even the feeble Voice of an humble Individual will be heard, when, amidst a whole People, he turns to you, Sir, who, under Providence, was our greatest Benefactor; when in imploring for you all manner of Happiness and Prosperity, and in that Prayer is included the Happiness and Prosperity of the United States, he joins the universal Cry in saluting you, the Father of your Country. History, Sir, is sparing of Characters in which the Virtues of public and of private Life, conspicuously shewn in the various and trying Occasions which you have experienced, have been so fully proved, and so strikingly exerted. You was drawn, Sir, from the Privacy of Retirement by Nations who, differing in Principles and discordant in manners, were unanimous in their Call upon you. The Integrity of your Principles, the Mildness of your Manners, converted their Austerity or their Licentiousness into union of Sentiment, and Liberality of Opinion. And when in an unequal and unexpected Contest, you were devoid of every other Resource, than those which you drew from the greatness of your Abilities, the firmness of your Mind, unappalled in Danger, and prepared for Events, your Caution and Prudence secured our Safety, your Activity and Valour established our Independence. Yet, Sir, whilst the Plaudits of a well-earned Triumph were sounding in your Ears, you lost not the Relish of Retirement, of those solid Satisfactions which your Integrity and your Patriotism had so justly and dearly purchased. Such however was the Situation of your Fellow Citizens, that your Absence from the Administration was incompatible with their Safety. They were constrained, Sir, to do violence to their feelings, in requesting of you the Sacrifice of the Sweets of Retirement; in which at an advanced Period of Life, we can alone be said to live. But the Prosperity of your Country, the fate of future Millions depended upon your Compliance. And you hesitated not, even at the Greatness of this Sacrifice. You, Sir, chearfully obeyed the Call of your fellow Citizens, and assumed the Administration. And now, Sir, tried as you have been in the most critical Situations—in Adversity, whose rugged Brow has only served to illustrate your Virtues; in Prosperity whose swelling sails have not disturbed the Serenity of your Mind, in the Administration of Government, which has proved a Source of Blessings to your Country, what more have we to ask of the most high God, than a Continuance of the Happiness which we enjoy under your Government. And that, when full of Days and full of Honour, it shall please his Providence to remove you into the Regions of Eternity, you may leave the People of these United States, which first formed under your Auspices, and now nurtured by your Care, are rising into a great and powerful Nation, happy in themselves, and happy in the Remembrance of those Virtues, to which they owe these Blessings—In the Remembrance of those Actions which will be faithfully recorded by Posterity, for the Benefit and Instruction of the future Ages of the World. It is for them, Sir, that your Labours have been employed, and by them your Actions will be approved" (DLC:GW).

2. Champion's letter to GW and its enclosures were given to William Jackson at Camden, according to Champion's 25 May letter to Jackson: "Mr Champion presents his Compliments to Major Jackson, and requests the favour of him to present the Letter, Book and parcel which accompanies this, to the President. Mr Champion has taken the Liberty to intreat the Honour of the President's acceptance of a Book, and a Manuscript enclosed. And he will trespass on the Indulgence of Major Jackson to beg him to procure the President's acceptance of the Parcel. It contains two Reliefs in a very fine Porcelain, exquisitely wrought round with flowers. The one of Dr Franklin. The other taken from a Relief, (a good likeness, as he was informed of the President when young,) which Mr Champion directed a Statuary to make. But in the likeness Mr

Champion finds himself disappointed. He therefore merely presents it as a Curiosity, made from a beautiful native Porcelain, which is to be found in America. Mr Champion took a similar Liberty during the War, in sending these Reliefs to the President, by way of Paris, but he never knew whether they arrived safe. These were finished, the ornaments having been enamelled with gold, which he laments is not the Case with these. But being two which he had by him he brought them out England with him, and through forgetfulness, or accident Omitted it. Mr Champion begs Major Jackson will pardon the Trouble he has given him, and will do him the Honour to accept one of the Covered creations himself, which accompanies the other. Mr Champion meant to have trespassed further upon Major Jackson's Indulgence in requesting to know Whether the President had a Levee, but he finds that his Stay will be short, and therefore is unwilling to break in upon the hour before Dinner, as the President must necessarily be fatigued, but will hope at that time to have the Honour of being presented to him" (DLC:GW).

No acknowledgment of GW's receipt of the relief portraits has been found. High-relief biscuit-porcelain plaques ornamented with delicate flowers and ribbons were a unique product of Champion's Bristol manufactory from 1774 to 1778. The pieces given to GW in 1791 were hung over the fireplace in Mount Vernon's "sitting parlor" after GW's presidency and became Martha Washington's property at his death. The GW plaque, which may have been modeled after Alexander Campbell's fictitious mezzotint of GW published in London in September 1775 or an undated engraving by Justus Chevillet or other early French engravings based on Charles Willson Peale's 1776 portrait of GW, was acquired by Martha's granddaughter Martha Parke Custis Peter and descended to W. G. Peter, who loaned it to the National Art Gallery in 1923. It was owned by her descendants in 1982 and returned to Mount Vernon in 1995 on loan from an anonymous donor (see frontispiece; Kirkland and Kennedy, *Historic Camden*, 363; Detweiler, *George Washington's Chinaware*, 147–49, 195 nn.275, 279, 280; Prussing, *Estate of George Washington*, 106, 107 n.5; *Mount Vernon Ladies' Association Annual Report*, 1995 [Mount Vernon, Va., 1996], 39).

3. The draft of Champion's 17-page "Manuscript reflections" to which GW referred is in DLC:GW. The text of the piece, entitled "Cursory Reflections upon our present Situation, together with the probable relative Consequences of the Federal Government to the Municipal Privileges of the several States," appears in CD-ROM:GW.

4. The volume that Champion presented to the president, which GW autographed on the title page and which was part of the Mount Vernon library at his death, was actually entitled *Considerations on the Present Situation of Great Britain and the United States of America, with a View to Their Future Commercial Connexions* . . . (2d ed., London, 1784). Champion's earlier edition of the book, which argued for American free trade with the West Indies, was published anonymously in England in 1784. He also published *Comparative Reflections on the Past and Present Political, Commercial and Civil State of Great Britain: with Some Thoughts concerning Emigration* (London, 1787), which is probably the volume Champion referred to in his letter of 24 May to GW (see Griffin, *Boston Athenæum Washington Collection*, 42–43).

From George Clendenin

Sir   Indian Queen Philadelphia. July the 19th 1791

In May 1790, I Receiv'd Instructions from the Secretary of War (Copy of which I herewith enclosed)[1] to raise a Certain Number of Scouts for the Safety of the Frontier pursuant to which I did Raise the number required and Subsisted them by Actual Disbursment out of my Own property, by the tenor of the Secretaries letter of Instructions I conceived that prompt payments wa⟨s⟩ to be made for the Services perform'd and Contingincies annaxed on proper Vouchers being produced Agreeably to which Instructions I Transmitted to (Genl Harmar) the documents Required and came to this place with the prospect of Receiving Compensation without Delay. On my application I found that the Accounts had not been Transmitted to this place by Genl Harmar, but having Retain'd the Originals of Said Accounts In my hands, I have presented them for payment, They have been passed upon by the Auditor of Army Accounts and Reported to the Secretary of War to Amount of 968 Dollars as by the Secretary's letter herewith will appear, but by the Same letter It also appears that payment Cannot be made Until provision is made by Congress for that purpose⟨.⟩ This is a Demur which I did not expect; I have now been on this business a Considerable time, on heavy expences, and If I am Constrain'd to remain here until the meeting of Congress will amount to more than I am to Receive (I mean the amount of Supplies).

I have therefore to Solicit that you will Take the premises under your Consideration and Grant that payment be made me on the Accounts, or that the amount be advanc'd me, to be accounted for, The peculiar Situation I am in I conceive will Justify me for making this application, first from having disbursed out of my own property the whole of the Subsistance, secondly by having Gaurantee'd to the men their pay which they will demand of me Immediately On my Return home, Thirdly the Expences which must accrue on my Remaining here, or the fatigue of my going home and Returning.

In making this application to you, Sir I must beg permission to add that the Secretary of War by his conduct toward me in this Business merits my warmest thanks, I am Convinced that he would have Rendered this Application unnecessary had it been in his power, or if the practice of his Department would have admitted it—why Genl Harmar has not Transmitted the papers to this place may be assigned a Variety of Causes, The dista⟨nce⟩ from the Capitol the miscariages which dispatches a⟨re⟩ Subject to, are not the least.

It may perhaps with Some propriety be added among the other appologies for this Applicatio⟨n⟩; The Extream anxiety and distress of Mind I feel as a husband and father, in being absent from my family at a period when Surrounded by Savages and depr⟨i⟩ved of my Company and protection when the most Require it; On this Subject I would be Silent but I feel it too much, Nor can I urge reasons for making this application to you without Adverting to this. I have the Honr to be with the Highest Respect and Esteem your Obt Hble Sevt

Geo. Clendinen

P.S. I hope The enclosed papers will be Return'd to me at the Indian Queen fourth Street.

G.C.

ALS, DNA: RG 59, Miscellaneous Letters.

For correspondence concerning federal support of frontier scouts in 1790, see Henry Knox to GW, 26 Feb. 1790, 5 Jan. 1791, and Beverley Randolph to GW, 29 Nov. 1790 and source note.

1. The enclosed copy of the instructions that Knox sent on 13 April 1790 to George Clendenin, the county lieutenant of Kanawha County, Va., has not been found. GW probably returned it and the enclosed accounts to Clendenin, as requested in his postscript, or they burned in the War Department fire in 1800. For similar instructions, see Knox to David Shepherd, lieutenant of Ohio County, Va., 13 April 1790, WHi: Draper MSS, Shepherd Papers (the editors acknowledge the assistance of Theodore J. Crackel of the Papers of the War Department, 1784–1800, East Stroudsburg, Pa., in locating these instructions).

To Hannah Meredith Gordon

Madam, Philadelphia July 19th 1791.

In reply to your letter of the 3rd of march with which I have been honored, I am under the necessity of observing, that circumstances put it out of my power to afford you any assistance in recovering your lands which you mention to have been confiscated during the late war in the State of Pennsylvania.

Situated as I am in respect to the General Government of this country, you must yourself, Madam, be fully sensible of the impropriety there would be in my interfering with the laws of any particular State; and more especially in a case of an individual or private nature. You will therefore, I trust, have the goodness to believe that my conduct on this occasion is governed by a sense of public duty, which with me has ever been superior to every private consideration.

To the Courts of Justice I must beg leave to refer you, Madam, for the recovery of such bonds or debts as may be due to you in this country—They are open to foreigners of every description, and I flatter myself in no country will justice be found to be more equally or impartially administered. I have the honor to be, very respectfully, Madam, your most obedt Servant

G. Washington

LB, DLC:GW.

For the background to this letter sent to Aberdeen, Scotland, see Hannah Meredith Gordon to GW, 3 Mar. 1791.

To William Gordon

Dear Sir,   Philadelphia July 19th 1791

As it has ever been a rule with me to make my private concerns give way to my public duties, when both cannot be accomplished, I now find myself under the necessity, from the weight of public business, which is at this time much encreased by an absence of more than three months, [(]on a tour thro' the southern States) of refraining to enter so fully into my private correspondencies as my inclination would lead me to do.

I am therefore only able to acknowledge the receipt of your letter of the 31. of January—and refer you to a letter which I wrote on the 9 of March on the subject of the subscriptions to your history, and which contained the accounts of the subscription and a bill of exchange of £29. 15/3. Sterling for the ballance of that account.[1]

I now enclose the 3 bill of the set which accompanied your account, and shall only add my thanks for the prayers and good wishes which you offer for my happiness, and assure you that I reciprocate them with very great sincerity. I am dear Sir, with much esteem, Your most obedient Servant

G. Washington

LB, DLC:GW.

For the background to GW's involvement with William Gordon's *History of the Rise, Progress, and Establishment, of the Independence of the United States of America*, see Gordon to GW, 8 Mar. 1784, source note, 24 Sept. 1788, source note and note 5, 28 Oct.–1 Nov. 1788, 16 Feb. 1789, and 20 Feb. 1790, GW to Gordon, 20 April 1786, and 25 Feb. 1791 and note 1, and GW to James Mercer, 20 Jan. 1786, n.3.

1. No letter of GW to Gordon dated 9 Mar. 1791 has been found; GW wrote on 25 February.

To Catharine Sawbridge Macaulay Graham

Madam,   Philadelphia, July 19. 1791.

At the same time that I acknowledge the receipt of your letter of the first of march with which I have been honored, let me request you to accept my thanks for your polite attention in sending me the pamphlet which accompanied it.[1] The importance of the subject, which has called forth your production and numerous others, is so deeply interesting to mankind that every philanthropic mind, however far removed from the scene of action cannot but feel anxious to see its termination, and it must be the ardent wish of every good man that its event may encrease the happiness of the human race.

I often regret that my public duties do not allow me so much time as my inclination requires to attend to my private correspondencies, especially with you Madam—But I persuade myself your goodness will lead you to place the brevity of this letter to its proper account, particularly when I add that I am but just returned from a tour of near 2000 miles thro' the southern States, to perform which took me more than 3 months. I shall only further add to it what I know must give you great pleasure, that the United States enjoy a scene of prosperity and tranquillity under the new government that could hardly have been hoped for under the old—and, that, while you, in Europe, are troubled with war and rumours of war, every one here may sit under his own vine and none to molest or make him afraid. I have the honor to be &ca

G. Washington.

LB, DLC:GW.

1. Catharine Sawbridge Macaulay Graham had enclosed a copy of her pamphlet *Observations on the Reflections of the Right Hon. Edmund Burke, on the Revolution in France, in a Letter to the Right Hon. the Earl of Stanhope* (London, 1790) in her letter to GW of 1 March.

To David Humphreys

My dear Sir,   Philadelphia July, 20. 1791.

I have received your letters of the 16 of February and 3 of may, and am much obliged by your observations on the situation, manners, customs and dispositions of the Spanish nation—In this age of free enquiry and enlightened reason it is to be hoped that the condition of the people in every Country will be bettered and the happiness of mankind promoted. Spain appears to be so much behind the other Nations of Europe in liberal policy that a long time will undoubtedly elapse before the people of that kingdom can taste the sweets of liberty and enjoy the natural advantages of their Country.

In my last I mentioned my intention of visiting the southern States, which I have since accomplished, and have the pleasure to inform you, that I performed a journey of 1887 miles without meeting with any interruption by sickness, bad weather, or any untoward accident—Indeed so highly were we favored that we arrived at each place, where I proposed to make any halt, on the very day I fixed upon before we set out—The same horses performed the whole tour, and, altho' much reduced in flesh, kept up their full spirits to the last day.

I am much pleased that I have taken this journey as it has enabled me to see with my own eyes the situation of the country thro' which we travelled, and to learn more accurately the disposition of the people than I could have done by any information.

The country appears to be in a very improving state, and industry and frugality are becoming much more fashionable than they have hitherto been there—Tranquillity reigns among the people, with that disposition towards the general government which is likely to preserve it—They begin to feel the good effects of equal laws and equal protection—The farmer finds a ready market for his produce, and the merchant calculates with more certainty on his payments—Manufacturers have as yet made but little progress in that part of the country, and it will probably be a long time before they are brought to that state to which they have already arrived in the middle and eastern parts of the Union.

Each days experience of the Government of the United States seems to confirm its establishment, and to render it more popular—A ready acquiescence in the laws made under it shews in a strong light the confidence which the people have in their representatives, and in the upright views of those who administer the government. At the time of passing a law imposing a duty on home made spirits, it was vehemently affirmed by many, that such a law could never be executed in the southern States, particularly in Virginia and North Carolina. As this law came in force only on the first of this month little can be said of its effects from experience; but from the best information I could get on my journey respecting its operation on the minds of the people (and I took some pains to obtain information on this point) there remains no doubt but it will be carried into effect not only without opposition, but with very general approbation in those very parts where it was foretold that it would never be submitted to by any One.[1]

It is possible, however, and perhaps not improbable that some Demagogue may start up, and produce and get signed some resolutions declaratory of their disapprobation of the measure.

Our public credit stands on that ground which three years ago it would have been considered as a species of madness to have foretold. The astonishing rapidity with which the newly instituted Bank was filled gives an unexampled proof (here) of the resources of our Countrymen and their confidence in public measures.[2]

On the first day of opening the subscription the whole number of shares (20,000) were taken up in one hour, and application made for upwards of 4000 shares more than were granted by the Institution, besides many others that were coming in from different quarters.

For some time past the western frontiers have been alarmed by depredations committed by some hostile tribes of Indians; but such measures are now in train as will, I presume, either bring them to sue for peace before a stroke is struck at them, or make them feel the effects of an enmity too sensibly to provoke it again unnecessarily, unless, as is much suspected, they are countenanced, abetted, and supported in their hostile views by the B——h. Tho' I must confess I cannot see much prospect of living in tranquillity with them so long as a spirit of land jobbing prevails—and our frontier-Settlers entertain the opinion that there is not the same crime, (or indeed no crime at all) in killing an Indian as in killing a white man.

You have been informed of the spot fixed on for the seat of Government on the Potomac, and I am now happy to add that all matters between the Proprietors of the soil and the public are settled to the mutual satisfaction of the Parties, and that the business of laying out the city, the grounds for public buildings, walks &ca is progressing under the inspection of Major L'Enfant with pleasing prospects—Thus much for our american affairs— and I wish I could say as much in favor of circumstances in Europe—But our accounts from thence do not paint the situation of the Inhabitants in very pleasing colours. One part exhibits war and devastion—another preparations for war—a third commotions—a fourth direful apprehensions of commotions— and indeed there seems to be scarcely a nation enjoying uninterrupted, unapprehensive tranquillity.

The example of France will undoubtedly have its effects on other Kingdoms—Poland, by the public papers, appears to have made large and unexpected strides towards liberty, which, if true, reflects great honor on the present King, who seems to have been the principal promoter of the business. By the by I have never received any letter from Mr Littlepage, or from the King of Poland, which you say Mr Carmichael informed you were sent to me last summer.[3]

I yesterday had Don Jaudennes, who was in this country with Mr Gardoqui, and is now come over in a public character, presented to me, for the first time, by Mr Jefferson. Colonel Ternant is expected here every day as Minister from France.

I am glad to learn that the air of Lisbon agrees so well with you—I sincerely hope you may long, very long enjoy the blessing of health accompanied with such other blessings as may contribute to your happiness.

I have been in the enjoyment of very good health during my journey, and have rather gained flesh upon it.

Mrs Washington desires her best wishes may be presented to you—You are always assured of those of my dear Sir, Your sincere and affectionate friend

G. Washington.

LB, DLC:GW.

1. For the 3 Mar. 1791 Excise Act, see GW's Executive Order, 15 Mar. and source note, GW to Alexander Hamilton, 15 Mar. (first letter), and 1 *Stat.* 199–214. Tobias Lear wrote to David Humphreys on 12 April: "I hope his [GW's] presence may have the same happy effect to the Southward as it did to the eastward in the fall of 89—something of a soothing nature is much wanted in the Southern States. The Law imposing an additional duty on distilled Spirits—and that establishing the Bank of the U.S. (two of great importance) are said, by the Representatives from that quarter, to be extremely disagreeable there. But it is to be hoped that the presence of our chief Magistrate will, like the vivifying influence of a vernal sun, dispel the gloom of discontent and give a new spring to that spirit which can alone conduct us to tranquility and greatness" (PPRF).

2. For the background to the establishment of the Bank of the United States, authorized by the "Act to incorporate the subscribers to the Bank of the United States" of 25 Feb. 1791 and a supplementary act of 2 Mar., see Edmund Randolph to GW, 12 Feb., source note, and 1 *Stat.* 191–97.

3. Humphreys wrote GW on 16 Feb. that American chargé d'affaires William Carmichael at Madrid had informed him that Lewis Littlepage (1762–1802) of Hanover County, Va., who had visited Mount Vernon and received letters of introduction from GW in November 1785 before leaving for Poland to accept a position in the court of Stanislas II Augustus, "gave you a clear, interesting & intelligent view of affairs in the North in a letter written from Madrid last Summer, and sent at the same time with one written to you by the King of Poland in his own hand." See also Patrick Henry to GW, 14 Oct. 1785, n.1, and *Diaries*, 4:220–21. Neither letter has been found.

From Thomas Lang

Philadelphia, 20 July 1791. Presents a copy of *An Essay on Commerce and Luxury* which he has published this day.[1]

ALS, DLC:GW.

1. A copy of the enclosed work, *Of Commerce and Luxury* (Philadelphia, 1791), was bound with miscellaneous pamphlets in the Mount Vernon library before GW's death (Griffin, *Boston Athenæum Washington Collection,* 558). The notice

appearing in the *General Advertiser and Political, Commercial and Literary Journal* (Philadelphia), 29 July, stated that Thomas Lang's "An Essay on Commerce and Luxury" was published on that day. The city directory gives the printer's address as 21 Church Alley (*Philadelphia Directory*, 1791, 74).

From Thomas Paine

Dear Sir   London July 21st 1791

I received your favour of last Augst by Col. Humphris, since which I have not written to, or heard from you.[1] I mention this that you may know no letters have miscarried. I took the liberty of addressing my late work—"Rights of Man," to you; but tho' I left it, at that time, to find it's way to you, I now request your acceptance of fifty Copies as a token of remembrance to yourself and my Friends.[2] The work has had a run beyond any thing that has been published in this Country on the subject of Government, and the demand continues. In Ireland it has had a much greater. A letter I recd from Dublin 10th of May mentioned, that the fourth edition was then on Sale, I know not what number of Copies were printed at each edition except the second, which was ten thousand. The same fate follows me here as I *at first* experienced in America, strong friends and violent ⟨*mutilated*⟩- nemies, but as I have got the ear of the Country, I shall go on, ⟨*mutilated*⟩nd at least shew them, what is a novelty here, that there can be ⟨*mutilated*⟩ person beyond the reach of Corruption.[3]

I arrived here from France about ten days ago. M. de la Fayette was well. The affairs of that Country are verging to a new Crisis, whether the Government shall be Monarchical and hereditary or wholly representative? I think the latter opinion will very gene⟨r⟩ally prevail in the end. On this question the people are much forwarder than the National Assembly.

After the establishment of the American Revolution, it did not appear to me that any object could arise great enough to engage me a second time. I began to feel myself happy in being quiet; but I now experience that principle is not confined to Time or place, and that the ardour of Seventy six is capable of renewing itself. I have another work in hand which I intend shall be my last, for I long much to return to America.[4]

It is not natural that fame should wish for a rival but the case is otherwise for me, for I do most sincerely wish there was some person in this Country that could usefully and successfully attract the public attention, and leave me with a satisfied mind to the enjoyment of quiet life: but it is painful to see errors and abuses and sit down a senseless spectator. Of this your own mind will interpret mine.

I have printed sixteen thousand copies; when the whole are gone, of which there remain between three and four thousand I shall then make a cheap edition, just sufficient to bring in the price of printing and paper, as I did by Common Sense.

Mr Green who will present you this, has been very much my friend. I wanted last October to draw for fifty pounds on General Lewis Morris who has some Money of mine, but as he is unknown in the Commercial line, and american Credit not very good, and my own expended, I could not succeed, especially as Gov. Morris was then in Holland. Col. Humphries went with me to your Agent Mr Walsh to whom I stated the Case, and took the liberty of saying—that I knew you would not think it a trouble to receive it of Gen. Morris on Mr Walsh's account; but he declined it. Mr Green afterwards supplied me and I have since repaid him. He has a troublesome affair on his hands here, and is in danger of losing thirty or forty thousand pounds, embarked under the flag of the united States in East India property, The persons who have received it with hold it and shelter themselves under some law contrivance. He wishes to state the Case to Congress, not only on his own account, but as a matter that may be nationally interesting.[5]

The public papers, will inform you of the riots and Tumults at Birmingham, and of some disturbances at Paris, and as Mr Green can detail them to you more particularly than I can do in a letter I leave those matters to his information.[6] I am Sir, with Affectionate concern for your happiness and Mrs Washington, Your much Obliged Humble servant

Thomas Paine

ALS, DLC:GW.

1. GW last wrote Thomas Paine on 10 Aug. 1790.

2. For the background to the reception and republication of Paine's *Rights of Man* in the United States, see Thomas Jefferson to GW, 8 May 1791. Paine's dedication "TO *GEORGE WASHINGTON*, PRESIDENT OF THE UNITED STATES OF AMERICA," first reprinted in America in the *General Advertiser and Political, Commercial and Literary Journal* [Philadelphia], 22 April, reads: "SIR, I PRE-

SENT you a small Treatise in defence of those Principles of Freedom which your exemplary Virtue hath so eminently contributed to establish.—That the Rights of Man may become as universal as your Benevolence can wish, and that you may enjoy the Happiness of seeing the New World regenerate the Old, is the Prayer of SIR, Your much obliged, and Obedient humble Servant, THOMAS PAINE" (London, 1791). GW received Paine's fifty copies in late 1791 or early 1792 (see n.5 below) but did not acknowledge their receipt until the spring of 1792, after receiving from Paine copies of the second part of the *Rights of Man,* published in February 1792 (see GW to Paine, 6 May 1792). Forty-three copies of part 1 remained at Mount Vernon at GW's death (Griffin, *Boston Athenæum Washington Collection,* 523).

3. For the phenomenal popularity and sales of early editions of *Rights of Man,* see Keane, *Paine,* 307–8, 324, 331, 333. British authorities hesitated bringing legal action against Paine for fear that the publicity of a trial over the relatively expensive three-shilling first edition would increase demand for the book and hasten publication of cheap editions aimed at a wider audience (see Lear to GW, 12 June 1791 and note 5). They did, however, keep the author under surveillance and moved against him after publication of the second part of the *Rights of Man,* when Paine was charged with seditious libel and fled to France. He was found guilty at the trial held in absentia in December 1792 (see Keane, *Paine,* 334–44, and Howell, *State Trials,* 380, 471).

4. Paine's work in progress was an assault on European despotism tentatively entitled *Kingship,* which he commenced in May 1791 while at Versailles and completed in London in February 1792 and published as *Rights of Man, Part the Second.* Jefferson and Edmund Randolph attempted to obtain for Paine the vacancy of postmaster general, and Paine tried to return to America in 1795, 1797, and 1799, but he did not land at Baltimore until October 1802 (see Randolph to GW, 13 July 1791, n.2).

5. For the claims against the British of English native and New York merchant William Green, see Jefferson to GW, 17 April, Green to Jefferson, 21 Jan., and notes and documents in "The American Consul at London: Joshua Johnson and the Brigantine *Rachel," Jefferson Papers,* 18:580–82, 20:482–522. Green reached New York by early December (see Green to Jefferson, 6 Dec. 1791, ibid., 519–22) and forwarded to GW two weeks later Paine's letter and pamphlets on 19 Dec., writing: "The letter which is inclosed, I promised the writer, I would deliver in person, but, not having left England, so soon as I expected, having had a long passage, and my affairs since my return here, having demanded a very close and attentive application to put in some order, I am unable to visit Philadelphia until next month. Anxious therefore that it may not have any farther delay, and having no other opportunity so proper, I forwarded it on by the common post. It is a particular comfort to the mind of Mr Paine, to beleive, that Your Excellency entertains a kindness for him, and that, nothwithstanding the high & important matters, constantly under your consideration, ⟨*mutilated*⟩ condition might be happy enough, to catch a moment of Sympathy, It is a little singular, that, whilst his ardent mind, and benevolent heart, has embraced, and asserted the cause, and the rights of humanity, with such uncommon ability, he, himself, has been exposed to all the

little sufferings of common distress, whilst old age, and its concomitant infirmities, are advancing upon him fast. The Publication of his book, of which, I forward on a box of Copies, has barely paid his debts, which were nevertheless inconsiderable. I mention this circumstance, merely to prevent Your Excellency from Supposing otherways. I beleive Mr Paine flattered himself, that your Excellency would ⟨m⟩ake some inquiries of me, respecting his fate & circumstances, of which, from my knowledge of him, and my friendship for him, I might be able to make as sincere a request, as any of those persons, who have the honor of approaching your Excellency, and this was one motive, Why I did not sooner forward his letter. I send it now, lest any longer delay, might be injurious to him" (DNA: RG 59, Miscellaneous Letters).

6. Accounts of the destruction of two meetinghouses in Birmingham and the house of Unitarian minister and scientist Joseph Priestley by royalist mobs on 14–16 July reached London by 18 July and were reprinted in Philadelphia two months later (see, for instance, the *Times* [London], 18, 19 July, and the Philadelphia papers *General Advertiser and Political, Commercial and Literary Journal*, 14 Sept., and *Gazette of the United States*, 17 September).

From Rodolph Vall-travers

Copy. No. 1 ⟨*illegible*⟩
May it please Yr Excellcy!
Sir!   Roterdam, July 21. 91.

Humbly flattering myself with your safe & kind Reception of my Letter & Packet dated from Hamburg, the 15th of March, & conveyed by Captn Bell of Philadelphia, with Maps, & several Memoirs (No. 2.) collected for the Use of yr assiduous Surveyor & Geometer, John Churchman of Philadelphia;[1] and, under Yr Excce's Approbation, with my humble Offers of further Services from this Continent, in communicating & promoting as much useful Knowledge, as may still lay within the narrow Circle of my literary Connections with most of the learned and patriotic Societies in Europe, in Behalf of your several similar encouraging Institutions: I now beg Leave to transmit to Yr Exccy a Work of mine, composed in English, from dutch & german Materials, collected these 20. years, on the Spot, by Mr Eshelscrown, dutch & danish Residt in the East Indies; disclosing a succinct Account of the actual *State of European Setlements throughout the East-Indies,* and many material Circumstances and Mysteries of their Trade, both with the Natives and with Europe.[2] This Branch of the mercantile Industry of the american States, wisely laid open to reciprocal Emulation, must reap signal advantages from their situation, Frugality & Freedom in their Competition with all the monopolising, expensive, restrained and over-whelmed Companies with Debts, Militairies, & Taxes, estab-lished by the several maritime Powers in Europe. The dutch East India Company, tho' the most oeconomical & industrious of all, groaning under an avowed Debt of near 100 Millions of Florins, is now sending Mr Nederborg, as their Plenipotentiary, to all their asiatic setlements; to investigate the Sources of their Decay, to correct abuses, and, on his Report, either to apply proper Remedies; or, if incurable, to suppress their Charter, and to lay that Trade as open, as they lately did that to the West Indies.[3]

Thus circumstanced, and wishing to contribute my litle Mite to the Prosperity of the worthy american Assertors of their un-doubted natural Rights and legal Liberties: I thought, a speedy Publication of an autentic, impartial Display of all the particu-lars of that extensive and intricate Commerce, as it now exists in all Parts, & in all its Branches, exhibited in N. america, under Yr Exccy's Approbation, Patronage & Encouragement, might not be unwelcome to your sagacious Fellow-Citizens? In this Per-suasion, I this Day deliver my Manuscript to Captn F. Folger, related to my late venerable Friend, Dr Bn Franklin,[4] ready to sail to Baltimore, his native Country; desiring him, to present this small Tribute of my Zeal & sincere attachment to Yr Excel-lence's previous Inspection & subseqt Disposal.

Shou'd Yr Exccy kindly complying with my humble Offers of the 15th of March, by Captn Bell, be pleased to honor me with yr Commands, and Instructions, and appoint me, in any official Caracter, as Agent, Consul, or Resident, with the necessary usual Support: it wou'd be the Heigth of my Ambition, to answer the Trust to the Satisfaction of my Superiors, and to the utmost Emolument of your illustrious confederate States; that great Pat-tern of a well constituted, wisely combined, truly free and happy Commonwealth.[5] I am, with unfeigned Admiration, most re-spectfully Sir! Your Excellency's most sincerily devoted humble Servant

I. Rodolf Valltravers.

ALS (copy), DLC:GW.

For the correspondence of Rodolf Vall-travers with GW, see Vall-travers to GW, 20 Mar. 1791. Vall-travers sent this letter from Rotterdam the last week of July by Capt. Frederick Folger of Baltimore, a near relative of Benjamin

Franklin, whom Vall-travers claimed as his "immortal Friend" (see n.4 below). Vall-travers later noted that Folger arrived at Baltimore in September (Vall-travers to GW, 1 Aug. and 30 Nov. 1791, both in DNA: RG 59, Miscellaneous Letters).

1. No letter of 15 Mar. from Vall-travers to GW has been found; he may have been referring to his letter of 20 March.

2. In his letter of 1 Aug. to GW (see nn.3 and 4 below) Vall-travers described his enclosure as "a Manuscript Work of mine, lately finished, & entitled: 'A new and autentic Account of all the European, especially the Dutch, mercantile Setlements in the East-Indies; their present military, civil, political and mercantile State, and their respective Trade in Asia, and with Europe; collected from ample Materials, furnished me in the german Language, by Adolph Eshelscrown, Esqe, late Resident of the Dutch East-India-Company in Sumatra, and since in the Denish Asiatic Company's Service; With a Plan for settling the Nicobar-Isles. In 3. 4ô Vols. MSt with an alphabetl copious Index: 1791.'" Thomas Jefferson returned this work to Vall-travers on 2 April 1792, noting that it contained much useful matter, but since the president did not concern himself with publishing such materials, he was returning them "with the hope that the world may have the benefit of their publication and yourself that of their sale" (*Jefferson Papers,* 23:366–67). Vall-travers also sent GW on 21 July "the 12th last Vol[um]e 8ô of mÿ Friend, Arthur Young⟨'s⟩ select annals of Agriculture, for yr encouraging Society" (Vall-travers to GW, 1 Aug., DNA: RG 59, Miscellaneous Letters). Captain Folger transmitted the letter of 21 July and volumes to GW from Baltimore on 6 Feb. 1792, noting that Eshelscrown, a Danish gentleman, had resided in the East Indies eighteen years and concluding: "Your Excellency will permit me to say: that, while I enjoy the Satisfaction of performing my Promise to an Individual, attended with the Honor of communicating with Yr Excy Yet at the same Time, I feel a Regret at being an Instrument to trespass on that precious Time, which is every Moment involved in Contemplation for the Good of Millions" (DLC:GW).

3. Vall-travers on 1 Aug. again wrote to GW about the East Indies trade (DNA: RG 59, Miscellaneous Letters).

4. Ever since he visited Franklin at Passy, France, in 1777, Vall-travers had been an indefatigable correspondent of the American diplomat (Vall-travers to Franklin, 25 April, 2 July 1777, *Franklin Papers,* 23:610–11, 24:254–55). The purpose of Vall-travers's letter to GW of 1 Aug. 1791 was: "besides informing Your Excellcy of the Conveÿances used in forwarding the two first, to point out another Line, in which I have humbly endeavored to Serve the N. american States, as directed bÿ Dr Franklin, and still confirm with the same Zeal; by translating into german, the worthy Cosmopolite's excellent Instructions to all those, who have some Thoughts of quitting Europe, to Settle in N. America; imparted to me in English, when at Paris; which I got printed in Germany, dispersed, inserted in Almanacks, and Several News-papers, at mÿ own Expence. The good Effect of this Measure has been visible, not only by an Increase of Emigrants of various Descriptions, but by deterring all those useless & burdensome Vagrants, whose restless, vicious, idle Lives, from a total Neglect of their Education, rendered them even dangerous to everÿ Society.

From this Branch of my Attention to the Wellfare & Prosperity of the Worthy American Confederates, I humbly flatter myself, no small Advantages will derive" (DNA: RG 59, Miscellaneous Letters). A German translation of Franklin's *Information to Those Who Would Remove to America* (Passy, 1784) was published in Hamburg in 1786 (Van Doren, *Franklin*, 706).

5. Vall-travers's letter of 1 Aug. also stated: "What other Measures, the Wisdom of Congress, and of the Several States, maÿ judge proper to adopt and to prescribe to me, when honored with their Commands and Support, shall be diligently pursued, to the utmost of mÿ poor ability." He concluded: "My Stay at this Place being only temporary till I am made acquainted with Yr Excellys Pleasure, in disposing of my humble Services, Your Commands will reach me Safest, under Cover to Mr Dumas, the American Agent at the Hague; to whom I shall leave mÿ further Directions, whenever I depart from Rotterdam, to fix, perhaps, at Bruxelles" (DNA: RG 59, Miscellaneous Letters). Never having received a reply from GW, Vall-travers wrote again from Rotterdam on 30 Nov., listing his previous letters, their conveyances, and their enclosures: 20 Nov. 1789, by Capt. John Bell of Philadelphia, sailing from Hamburg in June 1790 (letter not found); 20 Nov. 1789, by the ship, *Liberty,* Captain Paddock, for New York, from Hamburg (letter not found); 15 Mar. 1791, by Bell, from Hamburg, with two packets containing several memoirs and maps for John Churchman and the American Philosophical Society (letter not found); 3 July 1791, by Captain Trevett of Marblehead, Mass., from Rotterdam, with literary communications to the learned societies at Philadelphia, Boston, and elsewhere (letter not found); 21 July 1791, by Capt. Frederick Folger of Baltimore, for Baltimore, from Rotterdam, with manuscript works in English; 1 Aug. 1791, by Captain Stuart of Baltimore, for Baltimore, from Rotterdam, with six copies of his German publication of Franklin's advice to American settlers; 17 Aug. 1791, by the *Pringle,* Capt. William Callahan, for Charleston, S.C., from Rotterdam, with a packet for Henry Laurens containing proposals for Congress and for several patriotic societies in the Carolinas (letter not found); copy of 30 Nov. 1791, by the ship *Massachusetts,* Capt. William Dolliver of Boston, to Savannah. Vall-travers also begged leave on 30 Nov. "to add a few further Thoughts, occasioned by Subsequent Occurrencies. Most of the above Dispatches having reached N. America in the Summer-Season, when the Assemblies of the Congress, and of your several encouraging Societies happen to be prorogued and dispersed till about Christmas, no Answer cou'd be reasonably expected before they meet. Supposing therefore their safe Arrival, punctual Delivery and favorable Reception, I need not repeat in this Letter all the particulars of their several Contents. Suffice it to say, that: 1° Besides my literary Services, offered to your respective philosophical Societies, for the Encouragemt and Progress of all useful Arts & Sciences, by Means of a regular Communication, from all Parts of this Continent, extracted & transmitted in English, of new, interesting Publications, Discoveries, Inventions, or Improvements; in occasional Aquisitions of Select Libraries, mathematical Instruments, Tools, & useful Machines, with their Explanation; Collections of instructive natural Productions, in the mineral, the vegetable & animal Kingdoms; of Patterns from the best Antiques, for erecting an Academy of

Drawing, Engraving, Painting & Sculpture, to improve yr own Artists, Trades and Manufactures. And 2° Besides the Supplies offered of useful Handicraftmen; agricultors; of People well-skilled in the Art of Mining, Metallurgy, or other, either industrious or opulent Emigrants, in Quest of a secure peaceful Shelter from civil & religious Oppression and from the Horrors of anarchy & civil Wars: 3° It wou'd not less be in my Power, when duely authorised and supported, to negociate with several mercantile States in Europe, not yet fettered with exclusive Asiatic & Westindian Companies, Treaties of mutual Amity, Defense, & mercantile Advantages similar to that, which H. E. John Adams, Esqre your worthy Vice-President, has so happily concluded with the 7. united States of this Country, in Octr 1782. 4° With this View, I mean to repair from hence to Bruxelles, the Capital of the Emperor's belgic Dominions; with an Intention of being minutely informed, concerning the present forlorn & expiring Condition of their Asiatic Company, trading from Ostend & Trieste to the East Indies, with the worst Success; to Sound their Disposition towards a mutually beneficial Treaty, and Admittance of North-American Ships, with Indian & other Goods, not restrained by the too Selfish British Navigation-Act, into the aforesaid two Harbors; and to procure an autentic Copy of their present Duties on all foreign Imports and Exports, to compare & to adapt them to those of your united States. . . . 5° An active public Resident, furnished with the usual Credentials & proper Instructions, might successively answer all the above Objects, not only at Bruxelles: but likewise in Switzerland, at Zürich; in Piedmont, at Turin; for Sicily, at Naples; for Toscany, at Florence; and in the Republics of Lucca, Genoa, Maltha, and Venice: All which wou'd gladly recieve Indian & other Commodities, at the cheapest Rates, introduced by well armed American Vessels, 2 or 3. in Company, to face all the piratical States, & their Encouragers. From all which Places he cou'd engage a Variety of colonising Artists, to accelerate the Accomplishment of the N. american Capital of Washington, in its great Founder's Lifetime, as an everlasting Monument of his Fellowcitizen's well carried Veneration and Gratitude! They wou'd also facilitate pecuniary Negociations, on the same liberal Terms, lately proposed by Congress, at Amsterdam. These wou'd, I make no Doubt, induce the opulent Capitalists of Geneve, Bern, Zürich, Basil, Genoa & Venice to trust their superfluous Wealth, rather to the frugal & laborious united States of America, than to arbitrary, profligate & deeply involved, less congenial Sovereigns; and promote thereby a more intimate Intercourse among the several republican States, for their common Interest, Respectability and Security. This was the Plan, I recommended to my great Friend, Dr Franklin, when at Passy, in 1777; who, at that Time, found it rather premature. But now, nothing cou'd be more seasonable, in the present fermenting State of all Europe, contending, after your Example, for the Rights of Social Men, and for the just Enjoyment of legal Liberty. How long I may still be able to co-operate in promoting such Philanthropic Labors at my advanced Age, born in 1723, when Seconded by Yr Exccy's & Mr Jn Adam's patriotic Directions and generous Protection? God knows!" (DNA: RG 59, Miscellaneous Letters). The 30 Nov. reference of Valltravers to the "Capital of Washington" is the earliest such usage of GW's name for the Federal City by a foreigner yet discovered.

Sometime in early 1792 GW referred Vall-travers's letters of 15 Nov. 1789 and 20 Mar., 21 July, 1 Aug., and 30 Nov. 1791 to Jefferson, who replied to Vall-travers on 2 April 1792: "On the other subjects of your letters I am not authorised to say any thing in particular" (*Jefferson Papers*, 23:366–67).

To Henry Knox

(Confidential)
Dear Sir,   Philadelphia July 22d 1791
If, without disclosing the object in the smallest degree, you can come at (from Mr William Houston or through any other channel by the time you return) the rate of abilities possessed by Colo. (Joseph) Habersham—to what they would most usefully apply—whether he is a man of arrangement—or Industry— &ca you would oblige me in making the enquiry.[1] I wish also to be informed, if the means of accomplishing it should be within your reach of the *law* abilities and knowledge *generally* of Mr *John* Houston, in case circumstances might envite me to look to that quarter for an *Associate* Judge for the Supreme Court of the United States.[2] Yours sincerely

Go: Washington

ALS, NNGL.

1. Joseph Habersham (1751–1815) was a planter and merchant of Savannah who attended the College of New Jersey (Princeton) in 1767 before completing his education in England. He was an early supporter of the American Revolution and served as a major in the Continental army. After the war he served as a state legislator and supported ratification of the federal Constitution. Although Habersham did not receive an appointment at this time, GW named him postmaster general in 1795.

2. John Houstoun (1744–1796) was a former governor of Georgia. Knox replied this day to GW from his temporary residence of Bush Hill, John Adams's Philadelphia home: "I have received the confidential letter with which you have been pleased to honor me. I will pay all the attention thereto which my opportunities shall admit, and report the result I most ardently hope on my return to find you entirely free from pain and in perfect health" (DLC:GW). Knox was leaving for New York to consult with William Duer on their speculations in Maine lands. During his absence Tobias Lear wrote to the principal clerk of the War Department, Maj. John Stagg, Jr., on 28 July that GW "directs me to inform you, that he thinks it best for the letters & papers from Colo. Pickering to Genl St Clair, to be sent to General Butler without a seal, that he, seeing the necessity of their getting to General St Clair as soon

as possible, may use the best means of conveying them to him with dispatch & safety" (DLC:GW). After his return to Philadelphia, Knox sent to Arthur St. Clair on 8 Aug. a duplicate of Timothy Pickering's letter of 8 July to St. Clair informing the general that it was impractical to request the Seneca to join the expedition against the hostile northwestern Indian nations (*ASP, Indian Affairs*, 1:180–81).

From Edmund Randolph

Sir   Philadelphia July 23. 1791.

In preparing the letter, which I had the honor of addressing to you on the 20th instant, respecting the controversy between the governors of Pennsylvania and Virginia, I kept in view the propriety of saying something of a reference to congress, and of ascertaining the time, when you would probably choose to interpose in such disputes.[1] Presuming, that you would not wish to confirm more of the report of a public officer, than may be necessary, and not perceiving any immediate reason in this case for your deciding on the fit time for your interference, the subjoined draught of a letter to Governor Mifflin goes upon the idea of a reference to congress only.[2] Should I be wrong in this conjecture, I shall with great readiness submit another draught upon any plan, which you may be pleased to suggest. I have the honor, sir, to be with the highest respect yr mo. ob. serv.

Edm: Randolph.

ALS, DNA:PCC, item 69.

For background to this letter, see Thomas Mifflin to GW, 18 July, and notes to that document.

1. Edmund Randolph's letter of 20 July to GW reads: "The secretary of state yesterday submitted to me, by your instruction, copies of the letter from the governor of Pennsylvania to you, and of his correspondence with the governor of Virginia, on the demand of Francis McGuire, Baldwin Parsons, and Absalom Wells, as fugitives from justice.

"This demand is founded on that article of the fœderal constitution, which directs, that 'a person, *charged* in any state, with treason, felony or *other crime*, who shall *flee from justice*, and be *found* in another state, shall, on demand of the executive authority of the state, from which he fled, be delivered up, to be removed to the state, *having jurisdiction* of the crime.'

"He must be *charged*. This term is sufficiently technical, to exclude any wanton or unauthorized accusation, from becoming the basis of the demand. It would, in the language of mere legal entries be applicable, where a bill had been found by a grand jury. It must be interpreted under the constitution, as at least requiring some Sanction to be given to the suspicion of guilt by a previous investigation. In the present instance a grand jury, convened before two of the justices of the Supreme court of Pennsylvania have made it; and thus have furnished a ground for bringing the foregoing persons to a formal trial. Should such a procedure, as this, be declared to be incompetent, as a charge, the object of this article in the constitution must be either defeated, or be truly oppressive. For between an indictment and an actual trial there is no intermediate examination of the fact; and to wait for the condemnation of an absent culprit before a demand, would compel a judgment to be rendered behind his back. Outlawry indeed may be practised in sometimes; but it cannot be always pursued: and even where it is pursued, it Stamps the offence with no higher appearance of truth, than a true bill, received from the grand jury.

"The person charged must be also charged with a *crime*. That the supposed conduct of Mcguire and others is a crime under the laws of Pennsylvania, the very respectable attorney-general of Virginia has not been informed. It is punishable by a fine and hard labor. The first process is a capias: outlawry is inadmissible on it, and the offender cannot appear by his attorney. Some doubt may perhaps be entertained, whether according to a known rule of construction, the words 'or other crime,' being associated with treason and felony, ought not to be confined to crimes having some quality, common to them and treason and felony. Such a common quality does not exist, unless it be that of felony itself. Why then are the words, 'or other crime,' added, if felonies alone were contemplated? In the penal code of almost every state, the catalogue of felonies is undergoing a daily diminution. But it is not by the class of punishment, that the malignity of an offence is always to be determined. Crimes, going deep into the public peace, may bear a milder name and consequence; and yet it would be singular to shelter those, who were guilty of them, because they were not called and punished as felonies.

"The person, charged with a crime, must also *flee from justice*. Some species of proof is indispensable. Otherwise the most innocent citizen may be carried in chains from his own to another state. It cannot be denied, that every assertion of a governor ought to produce assent. But upon a judicial subject, testimony according to the judicial course is alone adequate; and the demand is the only thing, which is referred to an executive absolutely. The governor of Virginia is responsible for the just use of his discretion; and if he should yield to informal evidence, he must yield at his peril. With every respectful deference therefore for the communications of the governor of Pennsylvania, he ought to exact the return of a public officer on some process, or an affidavit, before he takes measures for apprehending McGuire and others. On this occasion, however, the governor of Pennsylvania builds his demand on the documents, transmitted to the governor of Virginia; not one of which has the semblance of proof, that they do flee from justice. Permit me too, to observe, sir, that the governor of Pennsylvania is perhaps not apprized of a fact, which the prothonotary of the supreme court of Pennsylvania has this moment stated to me in writing; to wit: that in the spring of 1790 he issued writs of capias against them: that it was returned, that McGuire and Parsons *were not found,* and that Wells was taken and committed; and that nothing was done at the last session in these cases. Now this is no complete proof, that even Mcguire and Parsons have *fled* from justice: it manifests, that Wells has not fled; and it evinces the necessity of caution in branding a man, as a deserter of a fair trial.

"The person, charged with a crime, must not only flee from justice, but he must be *found* in another state. At first it may seem unimportant, whether he be so found or not; because if he be not there, he can sustain no injury from an arrest. I will not decide, how far his character may suffer, if he proclaimed throughout a state, as a fugitive, when he may have have entered it; nor yet what other inconveniences he may undergo. But if the probability of these be striking, he ought not to be hunted for by public authority at random. The offence, altho' afterwards repaid, and the trouble, which cannot be avoided in the pursuit, ought not to be causelessly thrown on a sister state. Hence is it made a prerequisite to a demand, that the culprit shall be *found* in the state: that is, that some satisfaction be given, that government will not be put upon a frivolous search. In this case no legal exhibit is shewn to this effect: nay it is presumable, that Wells remains in the custody of Pennsylvania.

"The person, charged with a crime, fleeing from justice, and found in another state, is to be delivered up, to be removed to the state, *having jurisdiction*. In this place, I am compelled to differ from the attorney general of Virginia in two points. He is pleased to affirm, that to support the demand, 'there must be a defect in the jurisdiction of the state, from which the demand is made, and an exclusive jurisdiction in the state, making the demand'; and that 'the executive of Virginia cannot comply with such a demand, until some additional provisions by law shall enable them to deliver up the offenders.'

"It is notorious, that the crime is cognizable in Pennsylvania only; for crimes are peculiarly of a local nature. Therefore his two conditions are here fulfilled; namely a defect of jurisdiction in Virginia, and an exclusive jurisdiction in Pennsylvania. But if it were conceived, that Virginia might chastize offences against Pennsylvania or that an action might be maintained in Virginia for what is a crime in Pennsylvania, it would not follow, that the latter could not demand a malefactor from the former; for the clause in the constitution was obviously dictated by a wish to prevent that distrust, which one state would certainly harbour against another in situations, so capable of abuse. Besides, it corresponds with the words of the constitution, if the state demanding *has a jurisdiction;* altho' it might not be an exclusive one. And these observations would have equal weight, if the fœderal courts in Virginia could animadvert on crimes, arising within the limits of Pennsylvania. But the constitution directs, that trials 'shall be held in the state, where crimes shall have been committed.'

"I differ farther; in not discovering the disability of Virginia to deliver up the offenders. It has been sometimes fancied, that by delivering up is meant, only that the state, from which the demand is made, should express an approbation, that they may be apprehended within its territories. But as a state cannot be said to deliver up without being active; and it might disturb the tranquillity of one state, if the officers of another were at liberty to seize a criminal within its limits, the natural and safe interpretation is, that the delivery must come from Virginia.

"To this duty the executive of that state offer no objection; but they contend, that her own constitution and laws, and those of the United States being silent as to the manner and particulars of arrest and delivery, they cannot, as yet, move in the affair.

"To deliver up is an acknowledged fœderal duty: and the law couples with it the right of using all incidental means, in order to discharge it. I will not inquire here, how far these incidental means, if opposed to the constitution or laws of Virginia, ought notwithstanding to be exercised; because Mcguire and his associates may be surrendered, without calling upon any public officer of that state. Private persons may be employed, and clothed with a special authority. The attorney general agrees, that a law of the United States might so ordain; and wherein does a genuine distinction consist, between a power, deducible from the constitution, as incidental to a duty, imposed by that constitution; and a power, given by congress, as auxiliary to the execution of such a duty? Money indeed must be expended; and a state may suspend its exertions, until the preliminary proofs are adduced. I cannot undertake to foresee, whether the expending state will be reimbursed. If the constitution will uphold such a claim, it will doubtless be enforced. If it will not, it must be remembered, that that instrument was adopted with perfect free-will.

"From these premises I must conclude, that it would have been more precise in the governor of Pennsylvania to transmit to the governor of Virginia an authenticated copy of the law, declaring the offence: that it was essential, that he should transmit sufficient evidence of Mcguire and others having fled from the justice of the former, and being found in the latter: that without that evidence the executive of Virginia ought not to have delivered them up: that with it they ought not to refuse. The governor of Pennsylvania, however, appears to be anxious, that this matter should be laid before congress; and perhaps such a step might content all scruples.

"But at any rate I can find no obligation nor propriety, which can warrant the interposition of the President at this stage of the business. A single letter has gone from the governor of Pennsylvania to the governor of Virginia. A compliance has been denied; and the denial has proceeded from a deficiency of proof in two instances, from a misapprehension of fact in another, and probably untenable reasoning in some others. This deficiency then ought to be supplied by the governor of Pennsylvania; and the fact, which has been mistaken, placed on its true footing. As to any inaccuracy of reasoning, the President can do no more, than shew to the governor of Virginia, where it lies: he cannot be authoritative: nor would he, I presume, even if he had power, choose to exert it, until every hope should be lost of convincing the judgment of the state. But this argumentative intercourse belongs to the governor of Pennsylvania; and ought to be managed by him, until the prospect of satisfaction shall disappear. At such a period it may perhaps be seasonable for you to interfere. But *now* to interfere would establish a precedent for assuming the agency in every embryo-dispute between states: whereas Your mediation would be better reserved, until the interchange of their sentiments and pretensions shall fail in an accommodation" (DNA:PCC, item 69).

2. The "subjoined draught" in Randolph's hand of GW to Mifflin, 23 July, reads: "The papers, which your excellency lately transmitted to me, concern-

ing your demand from the governor of Virginia, of certain persons, supposed to be fugitives from justice, were submitted to the attorney general of the United States for his opinion. A copy of that opinion is now forwarded; and I shall take an opportunity of laying before congress all the documents, of which I am possessed, on this subject" (DNA:PCC, item 69). Mifflin wrote to GW on 2 Aug.: "I find, on referring to the Records of the Supreme Court of this Commonwealth, in the case of McGuire, Parsons, and Wells, which I lately submitted to your consideration, that the last of these persons was apprehended. I have, therefore, in addition to the other documents, inclosed to you a transcript of the Record; a copy of which I shall, likewise, transmit to the Governor of Virginia, together with the necessary evidence (as soon as it can be procured) to prove that McGuire and Parsons, have actually fled from the justice of Pennsylvania into that State, agreably to the form suggested in the opinion of the Attorney General, which you have been pleased to communicate" (DNA:PCC, item 69). For GW's submittal of the matter to Congress when it convened, see GW to the U.S. Senate and House of Representatives, 27 Oct. (second letter).

To the Commissioners for the Federal District

Gentlemen,   Philadelphia July 24th 1791.

I have received from Mr Peter the inclosed letter proposing the erection of Warves at the New City, between Rock Creek and Hamburg. My answer to him is, that the proposition is worthy of consideration, and that the transaction of whatever may concern the public at that place in future being now turned over to you, I have inclosed the letter to you to do thereon whatever you may think best, referring him at the same time to you for an Answer.[1]

The consequences of such Wharves as are suggested by Mr Peter will no doubt, claim your first attention—next, if they are deemed a desireable undertaking, the means by which the work can be effected with *certainty* and dispatch—and lastly, the true and equitable proportion which ought to be paid by Mr Peters towards the erection of them. I am, Gentlemen, with perfect consideration Your most Obedt Servt

Go: Washington

LS, DLC: Presidential MSS, General, Letters of the Presidents of the United States; LB, DNA: RG 42, Records of the Commissioners for the District of Columbia, 1791–1925, Proceedings and Letters Sent, 1791–1802.

1. Robert Peter wrote to GW from Georgetown, Md., on 20 July: "Col. L'Enfant, I understand has expressed a wish that I woud make propositions to join

the public in the expence of Erecting wharves to extend from the Mouth of Rock Creek, to the point above Hamburg, called Cedar point, being about three Thousand feet—It is a work of great Magnitude for an Individual to engage in, but as I have the wood adjoining the Shore, & coud spare some labourers, & by furnishing such matters, might have, but little Money to Advance—And as I really believe the expence woud be more than compensated by the Increased Value of the Lots, and as it woud assist in Satisfying the World, that the great work of the Federal City was going on in earnest, I have made up my Mind to enter into the Business in Earnest, if you Sir think it an Object deserving attention. The Channel running very near the Shore, it woud not be Necessary to extend the Wharves far into the River. I woud propose that the best and most frugal mode for Compleating the whole, be adopted immediately, and the work set about without any delay, so as to Compleat the whole this Fall, if Practicable, and if possible to have a good part effected by the time of the Sale of the Lots in October—That the Wood should be furnished by me on the same terms that it could be had from others, and that the whole Expence shoud be divided between the public & me, in proportion to the property held by each, on the Water—The Streets I Consider as belonging to the public & one half the Lots—so that I suppose somewhere about one third of the Expence would be mine & about ⅔ds the Publics—Perhaps this Letter woud have been more properly addressed to the Commissioners, but as I presume they woud do nothing without your Concurrence, and as they are so dispersed that a good deal of delay might take place, I have thought it best to address myself immediately to you" (DNA: RG 42, General Records, 1790–1931, Correspondence, 1791–1931, Letters Received). GW replied to Peter on 24 July: "I have received your favor of the 20th Inst: proposing the building of wharves at the New City, between Rock-Creek & Hamburgh; the proposition Certainly is worthy of consideration, and, as the transaction of what may concern the public at that place in future is now turned over to the Commissioners, I enclose your letter to them, to do thereon what they shall think best. To them therefore I take the liberty of referring you for an answer" (copy, DLC: Presidential MSS, General, Letters of the Presidents of the United States). The commissioners replied to GW on 2 August.

From Thomas Jefferson

[Philadelphia] July 27. 1791.

Th: Jefferson has the honour to inclose to the President his letter to G. Morris, to which he will add any thing the President pleases by way of Postscript or by incorporating it into the letter. a ship sailing from hence for Havre on Monday Th: J. proposes to send his letters for France by that rather than by the French packet.[1]

LS, DNA: RG 59, Miscellaneous Letters; LB, DLC:GW.

1. The enclosure was Thomas Jefferson's letter of 26 July 1791 to Gouverneur Morris, in which Jefferson approved Morris's measures with the British ministry and sent a remittance for a thousand dollars to supplement Morris's previous payment. GW apparently approved the letter on 28 July, and Jefferson enclosed it in a letter to William Short of 28 July for forwarding to Morris (*Jefferson Papers*, 20:680, 685; see also 691–93).

To Thomas Jefferson

Dear Sir, [Philadelphia] Thursday Afternoon, 28th July [1791]

I have just given the enclosed Letters an acknowledgment, & was about to file them; but not recollecting whether I had ever shewn them to you, or not—I now, as they contain information, & opinions on Men & things, hand them to you for your perusal.[1] By comparing them with others, & the predictions at the times they were written with the events which have happened, you will be able to judge of the usefulness of such communications from the person communicating them. I am Yrs sincerely

Go: Washington

ALS, DLC: Thomas Jefferson Papers.

1. The enclosures probably included Gouverneur Morris to GW, 22 Nov., 1, 24 Dec. 1790, and 9 Mar. 1791 (see GW to Morris, 28 July 1791).

To Lafayette

Philadelphia, July 28. 1791.

I have, my dear Sir, to acknowledge the receipt of your favors of the 7 of March and 3 of May, and to thank you for the communications which they contain relative to your public affairs.[1] I assure you I have often contemplated, with great anxiety, the danger to which you are personally exposed by your peculiar and delicate situation in the tumult of the times, and your letters are far from quieting that friendly concern. But to one, who engages in hazardous enterprises for the good of his country, and who is guided by pure and upright views, (as I am sure is the case with you) life is but a secondary consideration.

To a philanthropic mind the happiness of 24 millions of people cannot be indifferent—and by an American, whose country in the hour of distress received such liberal aid from the french, the disorders and incertitude of that Nation are to be peculiarly lamented—we must, however, place a confidence in that Providence who rules great events, trusting that out of confusion he will produce order, and notwithstanding the dark clouds which may threaten at present, that right will ultimately be established.

The tumultous populace of large cities are ever to be dreaded—Their indiscriminate violence prostrates for the time all public authority—and its consequences are sometimes extensive and terrible—In Paris we may suppose these tumults are peculiarly disastrous at this time, when the public mind is in a ferment, and when (as is always the case on such occasions) there are not wanting wicked and designing men, whose element is confusion, and who will not hesitate in destroying the public tranquillity to gain a favorite point—But until your Constitution is fixed—your government organised—and your representative Body renovated—much tranquillity cannot be expected—for, until these things are done, those who are unfriendly to the revolution, will not quit the hope of bringing matters back to their former state.

The decrees of the National Assembly respecting our tobacco and oil do not appear to be very pleasing to the people of this country; but I do not presume that any hasty measures will be adopted in consequence thereof; for we have never entertained a doubt of the friendly disposition of the french Nation towards us, and are therefore persuaded that if they have done any thing which seems to bear hard upon us, at a time when the Assembly must have been occupied in very important matters, and which perhaps could not allow time for a due consideration of the subject, they will, in the moment of calm deliberation, alter it, and do what is right.[2]

I readily perceive, my dear Sir, the critical situation in which you stand—and never can you have greater occasion to shew your prudence, judgment, and magnanimity.

On the 6 of this month I returned from a tour through the southern States, which had employed me for more than three months—In the course of this journey I have been highly gratified in observing the flourishing state of the Country, and the good dispositions of the people—Industry and economy have become very fashionable in those parts, which were formerly noted for the opposite qualities, and the labours of man are assisted by the blessings of Providence—The attachment of all Classes of citizens to the general Government seems to be a pleasing presage of their future happiness and respectability.

The complete establishment of our public credit is a strong mark of the confidence of the people in the virtue of their Representatives, and the wisdom of their measures—and, while in Europe, wars or commotions seem to agitate almost every nation, peace and tranquillity prevail among us, except on some parts of our western frontiers where the Indians have been troublesome, to reclaim or chastise whom proper measures are now pursuing—This contrast between the situation of the people of the United States, and those of Europe is too striking to be passed over even by the most superficial observer, and may, I believe, be considered as one great cause of leading the people here to reflect more attentively on their own prosperous state, and to examine more minutely, and consequently approve more fully of the government under which they live, than they otherwise would have done. But we do not wish to be the only people who may taste the sweets of an equal and good government—we look with an anxious eye for the time when happiness and tranquillity shall prevail in your country—and when all Europe shall be freed from commotions, tumults, and alarms.

Your friends in this country often express their great attachment to you by their anxiety for your safety.

Knox, Jay, Hamilton, Jefferson remember you with affection—but none with more sincerity and true attachment than, My dear Sir, Your affectionate

G. Washington.

LB, DLC:GW.

1. Lafayette's letter of 3 May from Paris, which enclosed a copy of his speech of 22 April to the Paris commune and national guard (see Lafayette to GW, 6 June 1791, n.2), reads: "My dear General I Wish it Was in My power to Give You an Assurance that our troubles are at an End, and our Constitution totally Established—But altho dark clouds are Still Before us, We Came So far as to foresee the Moment When a Legislative Corps Will Succeed this Convention, and, Unless Foreign Powers interfere, I Hope that Within four Month Your friend Will Have Reassumed the life of a Private and Quiete Citizen. The Rage

of Parties, Even Among the Patriots, is Gone as far as it is Possible, Short of Blood shed—But Altho' Hatreds Are far from Subsiding, Matters don't Appear So Ill disposed as they formerly were towards a Coalition Among the Support-ers of the Popular Cause—I Myself am Exposed to the Envy and Attacks of all parties for this Simple Reason, that Who Ever acts or Means wrong finds me an insuperable obstacle, and there Appears a kind of phœnomenen in My Situation, all Parties Against me, and Yet a National Popularity Which in Spite of Every effort Has Been Unshakable—a proof of this I Had lately when dis-obeïed By the Guard, And Unsupported By the Administrative Powers Who Had Sent me, Unnoticed By the National Assembly Who Had taken fright, the King I do not Mention, as He Could do But little in the Affair, and Yet the little He did Was Against me, Given up to all the Madnesses of licence, faction, and Popular Rage, I Stood alone in defense of the law, and turned the tide Up into the Constitutional Channel—I Hope this lesson Will Serve My Country, and Help towards Establishing the Principles of Good order—But Before I Could Bring My fellow Citizens to a Sense of legal Subordination I Must Have Conducted them through the fear to loose the Man they love—inclosed is the Speech I delivered on the occasion—I send it Not for Any Merit of it, But on Account of the Great Effect it Had on the Minds of the People, and the disci-pline of an Army of five and forty thousand Men, Upwards of thirty of Whom are Volonteers, and Who to a Man are Exposed to all the Suggestions of a dozen of Parties, and the Corruptions of all kinds of pleasures and Allurements. The Commitee of Revision is Going to distinguish in our Immense Materials Every Article that deserves to Be Constitutional, and as I Hope to Convene in a tolerable State of Union the Members of that Committee, as their Votes Will in the House influence the popular Part of the Assembly, I Hope that Besides the Restoration of all Natural Rights, the destruction of all the Abuses, We May Present to the Nation Some Very Good institutions of Governement, and organise it so as to Ensure to the people the Principal Consequences, and Enjoïements of a free Constitution, leaving the Remainder to the legislative Corps to Mend into well digested Bills, and Waïting Untill Experience Has fitted us for a More Enlightened, and less Agitated National Convention. in the Mean While our Principles of liberty and Equality are invading all Europe, and Popular Revolutions Ripening Every Where. Should foreign Powers Em-ploy this Summer with Attaks Against our Constitution, there Will Be Great Blood shed, But our liberty Cannot fail us—we Have done Every thing for the General Class of the Country people, and in Case the Cities Were frightened into Submission, Yet the peasants Would Swarm Round me, and fight to death, Rather than Give up their Rights. Adieu, My Beloved General, My Best Respects Wait on Mrs Washington—Remember me to Hamilton, jay, jefferson, Knox, and all friends" (PEL).

2. Lafayette informed GW on 7 Mar. of the French National Assembly de-crees of 1 and 2 Mar. 1791 that increased the duties on American imports of tobacco and whale oil. Gouverneur Morris similarly wrote GW on 9 Mar. stat-ing his hopes that Congress would not react precipitously, as the acts were not a deliberate movement of the national will, and that representations by the United States at the proper time would effect a change. GW probably dis-

cussed the matter with Thomas Jefferson after GW returned to Philadelphia on 6 July, as Jefferson had received on 22 June 1791 a dispatch on the subject from William Short dated 11 March. A policy was formulated before 28 July, when Jefferson sent instructions to Short (*Jefferson Papers*, 19:532–34). See also Lafayette to GW, 7 Mar. and note 1, Jefferson to GW, 30 July 1791 and note 1.

To Gouverneur Morris

Dear Sir,   Philadelphia July 28th 1791.

I have now before me your favors of the 22d of November—the 1st & 24th of December 1790—and of the 9th of March 1791.[1]

The Plateaux which you had the goodness to procure for me, arrived safe; and the account of them has been settled, as you desired, with Mr R: Morris. For this additional mark of attention to my wishes, I pray you to accept my thanks.[2]

The communications in your several letters, relative to the state of Affairs in Europe, are very gratefully received; and I should be glad if it was in my power to reply to them more in the detail than I am able to do. But my public duties, which are at all times sufficiently numerous, being now much accumulated by an absence of more than three months from the Seat of Government, make the present a very busy moment for me.

The change of systems, which have so long prevailed in Europe, will, undoubtedly, affect us in a degree proportioned to our political or commercial connexions with the several nations of it. But I trust we shall never so far lose sight of our own Interest & happiness as to become, unnecessarily, a party in their political disputes. Our local situation enables us to maintain that state with respect to them, which otherwise, could not, perhaps, be preserved by human wisdom. The present moment seems pregnant with great events; but, as you observe, it is beyond the ken of mortal foresight, to determine what will be the result of those changes which are either making, or contemplated in the general system of Europe. Although as fellow-men we sincerely lament the disorders, oppressions & incertitude which frequently attend national events; and which our European brethren must feel; yet we cannot but hope, that it will terminate very much in favor of the Rights of Man. And, that a change there, will be favorable to this Country, I have no doubt. For under the former system we were seen either in the distresses of War, or viewed after the peace in a most unfavorable light through the medium of our distracted State. In neither point could we appear of much consequence among nations. And should affairs continue in Europe in the same state they were when these impressions respecting us were received, it would not be an easy matter to remove the prejudices imbibed against us. A change of system will open a new view of things—& we shall then burst upon them as it were with redoubled advantages.

Should we, under the present state of Affairs, form connexions, other than we now have, with any European Powers, much must be considered in effecting them, on the score of our increasing importance as a Nation; and at the sametime, should a treaty be formed with a nation whose circumstances may not at that moment be very bright, much delicacy wd be necessary in order to shew that no undue advantages were taken on that account. For unless treaties are mutually beneficial to the parties, it is vain to hope for a continuance of them beyond the moment when the one which conceives itself over reached is in a situation to break off the connexion. And I believe it is among nations as with individuals—the party taking advantage of the distresses of another will lose infinitely more in the opinion of mankind, & in subsequent events, than he will gain by the stroke of the moment.

In my late tour through the Southern States, I experienced great satisfaction in seeing the good effects of the general Government in that part of the Union. The people at large have felt the security which it gives, and the equal justice which it administers to them. The Farmer—the Merchant—and the Mechanic have seen their several Interests attended to, and from thence they unite in placing a confidence in their representatives, as well as in those in whose hands the Execution of the Laws is placed. Industry has there taken place of idleness, and œconomy of dissipation. Two or three years of good crops, and a ready market for the produce of their lands has put every one in good humour; and, in some instances they even impute to the Government what is due only to the goodness of Providence.

The establishment of public credit, is an immense point gained in our national concerns. This, I believe, exceeds the expectation of the most sanguine among us. and a late instance, unparalleled in this Country, has been given of the confidence reposed in our measures, by the rapidity with which the subscriptions to the Bank of the United States were filled. In two hours after the Books were opened by the Commissioners the whole number of shares were taken up, & four thousand more applied for than were allowed by the Institution; besides a number of Subscriptions which were coming on. This circumstance was not only pleasing as it related to the confidence in Government; but as it exhibited an unexpected proof of the resources of our Citizens.

In one of my letters to you, the account of the number of Inhabitants which would probably be found in the U. States on enumeration—was too large. The estimate was then founded on the ideas held out by the Gentlemen in Congress of the population of the several States—each of whom (as was very natural) looking through a magnifier would speak of the greatest extent to which there was any probability of their numbers reaching. Returns of the Census have already been made from several of the States, and tolerably just estimate has been formed (now) in others; by which it appears that we shall hardly reach four millions; but this you are to take along with it, that the *real* number will greatly exceed the *official* return; because, from religeous scruples, some would not give in their lists; from an apprehension that it was intended as the foundation of a tax, others concealed or diminished theirs; and from the indolence of the mass, & want of activity in many of the deputy Enumerators, numbers are omitted. The authenticated number will, however, be far greater I believe, than has ever been allowed in Europe; and will have no small influence in enabling them to form a more just opinion of our present growing importance than has yet been entertained there.[3]

This letter goes with one from the Secretary of State, to which I must refer you for what respects your public transactions,[4] and I shall only add to it the repeated assurances of regard and affection with which I am Dear Sir, Your Obedt & Obliged

Go: Washington

ALS, NNC; LB, DLC:GW.

1. GW presented to Thomas Jefferson this day the letters Gouverneur Morris had addressed to the president.

2. For the additional plateaux that Gouverneur Morris sent to GW on 19

Nov. 1790, see GW to Morris, 1 Mar., 15 April, and Morris to GW, 22 Nov. 1790 and note 1. Robert Morris was paid five guineas for them on 25 April 1791 (Decatur, *Private Affairs of George Washington*, 229).

3. GW had written to Morris on 17 Dec. 1790: "The numbers of our people as far as they can be ascertained from the *present* stage of the Census, will not fall short, it is said, of five millions—some think more." By late July 1791 GW had received and reviewed census returns from the states of New Hampshire, Massachusetts, Connecticut, Delaware, and Georgia and the districts of Kentucky and Maine (which totaled 1,070,477 persons) and probably discussed population estimates with Jefferson, who was also concerned that summer with circulating the census figures in Europe in their best light (see Jefferson to David Humphreys, 23 Aug., to William Carmichael, 24 Aug., and to William Short, 29 Aug. 1791, *Jefferson Papers*, 22:61–64, 95–97). John Parker, the federal marshal for New Hampshire, completed his returns sometime before Tobias Lear wrote to Oliver Wolcott, Jr., on 11 July of "an error in his census returned to the president" (DLC:GW). The next day Lear gave the corrected New Hampshire returns to Thomas Jefferson, along with those of Delaware (completed 4 May), Maine, Connecticut, Georgia (completed 25 June), and Kentucky (DNA: RG 59, Miscellaneous Letters). After returning to Philadelphia GW discussed the census returns with Lear, who drafted two circular letters to the several marshals on 13 July. Lear requested those marshals whose aggregate returns GW had already seen (New Hampshire, Massachusetts, Connecticut, Delaware, Georgia, and Kentucky), to provide GW with a population breakdown by town and county, if convenient, "merely to gratify his private curiosity" (DLC:GW; the only receiver's copy found, Lear to Allan McLane, 13 July 1791, NHi: McLane Papers, differs only slightly from the retained copy). In his circular to the marshals from whom GW had yet to receive returns (Rhode Island, Vermont, New York, New Jersey, Pennsylvania, Maryland, Virginia, and the Carolinas), Lear requested the same breakdown for GW: "he desires you may transmit it to him either when you make your general return, or at any other time that may be convenient to you" (the retained copy in DLC:GW is dated 13 July, but the only receiver's copy found, to Clement Biddle of Philadelphia, in PHi: Washington-Biddle Correspondence, is dated 14 July). For the responses of the marshals to this personal request, see Biddle to Lear, 19 Aug., PHi: Clement Biddle Letter Book, and Lear to Edward Carrington, 29 July, DLC:GW. The population of the United States (excluding South Carolina's figure of 249,073) finally reported by Jefferson on 24 Oct. totaled 3,893,635 (ibid., 227–28). For the noncompletion of the South Carolina census, see Thomas Bee to GW, 2 October. "Religious scruples" against census taking were reactions against the "sin of David" presented in the Old Testament (1 Chronicles 21 and 2 Samuel 24), which describe King David's provocation by Satan to number Israel and Judah, after which the Lord sent a punishing plague that carried off 70,000 men.

4. For Jefferson's letter of 26 July to Morris, see *Jefferson Papers*, 20:680. Morris replied to GW on 30 September.

From Humbert Droz

No. 93 south front street
Monsieur;   Philadelphie Le 29 Juillet 1791

L'amour des arts m'a fait quitter la Suisse ma Patrie J'ai exercé 25 ans à Paris sous les plus brillans artistes, je puis dire avec succés, celui de L'horlogerie.

Ayant toujours vecu jour le jour, l'emigration des Contrerevolutionaires, et le plaisir Cruel que se font Les ¾ des grands, Je veux dire des Gens riches, de ne rien faire m'ont fait penser à un autre pays; l'Abbé Reinal le Cultivateur ameriquin m'ont decidé pour Celui ci.[1]

J'ai laissé ma femme et mon fils Jusqu'a ce que je Sache en m'etablissant ici, si j'y trouverai une existence plus assurée à la fin de mes jours, qu'en france, alors je les ferai venir, sinon, J'irai Les rejoindre.

Je Croirois ne pas faire l'usage que je dois faire de mes talents si je ne Les offrois particulierement, à l'homme, que tout le monde envisage Comme le plus meritant des 13 Etats unis Q'il m'honore de sa Confience, et je jure foi de suisse qu'il ne sera pas trompé.

Voici 8 ans que je n'ai été occupé qu'a mettre l'harmonie, dans les ouvrages les plus Compliqués, montres à masses, repetant Les minutes, à Equation ayant toutes Sortes de quantiemes Echapements à vibrations libres &ca qui s'executoient Chez Mr Breguet, premier artiste de Paris et je Crois du monde Entier.[2]

desorte que la plus mauvaise montre, si on veut faire le sacrifice de me payer mon travail, je la mettrai dans le Cas de servir Comme une bonne, en donner mon billet de garentie pour 10 ans; et si on peut prouver au bout d'un an—qu'elle a mal eté, sans qu'on l'ait laissé tomber ou d'autres accidents, Je m'engage à rendre L'argent reçu pour Cela.

bien entendu qu'il faut renouveler Les huilles tout les 3 ans dans Les montres plates ou à repos, et tout Les 7 dans les hautes à roue de rencontres.

Attendant Vos Ordres Je Suis trés Respectueusement Monsieur Votre trés humble Et obeissant Serviteur

A Lis Humbert Droz

LS, DNA: RG 59, Miscellaneous Letters.

Humbert Droz (Lambert Dros; d. 1813) might have been a member of the

Droz family of Neuchâtel, Switzerland, which was noted in the eighteenth century for its watchmakers. According to Philadelphia directories, clockmaker
and watchmaker Droz lived on Mulberry Street in the 1790s and early 1800s,
and he apparently was in business with his sons from 1806 to 1813 (Eckhardt,
Pennsylvania Clocks and Clockmakers, 175).

1. Droz misattributed authorship of Michel-Guillaume-Jean de Crève-
coeur's *Letters from an American Farmer* (London, 1782), French editions of
which were published in Paris in 1784 and 1787 as *Letters d'un Cultivateur
Américain,* to Abbé Guillaume-Thomas-François Raynal (1713–1796), who
published *Révolution de l'Amerique* in London in 1782.

2. Abraham-Louis Breguet (Louis-Abraham Bréguet; 1747–1823) of Neuchâtel perfected in his Paris workshop the movements of pedometer winding
systems that made the production of "perpetuelle" or self-winding watches
more practical. He enjoyed the patronage of George III and later of Napoleon
and became *horloger de la Marine* and a member of the French Academy of
Sciences before his death.

From Alexander Hamilton

Treasury Department [Philadelphia] July 29th 1791
The Secretary of the Treasury has the honor respectfully to
submit to the President of the United States, a contract made by
the Collector of the District of Washington in North Carolina,
for the stakage of all the shoals & channels of that State to the
Northward of the District of Wilmington, which have been heretofore thus designated.[1] The former stakes having generally
fallen to decay, or being washed away for want of attention, the
expence will be necessarily greater in the re establishment than
it probably will be in the future preservation of the stakeage now
intended to be executed. It is stated by the collector that the
contracts for the renewal of the stakes on these waters shortly
after the late war, was made at the rate of 250 Dollars pr annum, & that tho' the expiration of so considerable a part of the
current year had given rise to an expectation that he should be
able to contract for less money, yet he found it impracticable to
provide for the execution of the business on more favourable
terms. Tho' there does not appear to be any thing particularly
advantageous in this agreement, the Secretary begs leave to suggest an idea that the interests of the United States may be more
advanced by the immediate accommodation to the navigation,

than it might be, by an uncertain experiment of forming a more reasonable contract.[2] All which is humbly submitted

Alexander Hamilton
Sey of the Treasury.

LB, DLC:GW.

1. John Gray Blount and Charles Cook on 6 June contracted with the customs collector of Washington, N.C., Nathan Keais, to stake channels through the Swash, Royal Shoal, Portsmouth Channel, and the Pamlico, Pongo, and Tar rivers in North Carolina (DNA: RG 26, Lighthouse Deeds and Contracts, vol. A, 6). Keais forwarded the original contract to Alexander Hamilton on 16 June (Syrett, *Hamilton Papers*, 8:483).

2. Tobias Lear returned the contract to Hamilton this day with GW's approval (DLC:GW).

From Alexander Hamilton

Treasury Department [Philadelphia] July 29th 1791.
The Secretary of the Treasury having had the honor to lay before the President of the United States, the correspondence of Mr Short respecting the loans made, & to be made, pursuant to the several Acts of Congress for that purpose; begs leave to note particularly for his consideration two circumstances which appear in that correspondence.[1]

First, that there are moments when large sums may be borrowed in Holland with more facility & advantage than small sums at other times.

Secondly, that there is some prospect of opening loans with success in other Countries than the United Netherlands.

These circumstances appearing, the Secretary respectfully requests the consideration & instruction of the President of the United States; whether it may not be expedient to remove the present restrictions upon Mr Short, so as to enable him to embrace favourable moments, and open at his discretion, loans at such times & places and for such sums, as he may find adviseable, within the limitations of the respective laws authorising the Loans.[2] which is respectfully submitted by

Alexander Hamilton
Secy of the Treasury.

LB, DLC:GW.

For background to this letter, see Alexander Hamilton to GW, 26 Aug. (second letter), 3 Sept. 1790, and 10 and 14 April 1791, GW to Hamilton, 28 Aug. 1790 and note 1, and 7 May 1791, GW to the U.S. Senate and House of Representatives, 8 Dec. 1790, Jefferson to GW, 17 April, 1 May 1791, and GW to Jefferson, 17 June 1791. For William Short's original instructions to negotiate American loans in Holland, see Hamilton to Short, 1 Sept. 1790, Syrett, *Hamilton Papers,* 7:6–14.

1. Tobias Lear returned the enclosed correspondence to Hamilton this day (DLC:GW).

2. Lear also probably transmitted to Hamilton this day GW's approval of Hamilton's proposal: "Upon a full consideration of the reasons offered by Mr Short, in his correspondence with you, for removing the restrictions laid upon him by his present instructions, so far as relates to his not opening a loan for more than a certain sum—and not being allowed to open a new Loan until the terms of the preceding one shall have been ratified here—I have thought it expedient & for the interest of the United States that those restrictions should be removed—And I do hereby authorise you to inform Mr Short that he may open at his discretion loans for the United States, at such times & places, & for such sums as he may find adviseable within the limitations of the respective Laws authorising these Loans" (LB, DLC:GW). Hamilton provided Short new instructions on 1–2 Aug. (Syrett, *Hamilton Papers,* 9:1–4).

From Thomas Jefferson

Sir   Philadelphia July 30. 1791.

I have the honour to inclose for your perusal a letter which I have prepared for mister Short.[1]

The ill humour into which the French colonies are getting, & the little dependence on the troops sent thither, may produce a hesitation in the National assembly as to the conditions they will impose in their constitution. in a moment of hesitation small matters may influence their decision. they may see the impolicy of insisting on particular conditions which operating as grievances on us, as well as on their colonists, might produce a concert of action. I have thought it would not be amiss to trust to mister Short the sentiments in the cyphered part of the letter, leaving him to govern himself by circumstances whether to let them leak out at all or not, & whether so as that it may be known, or remain unknown, that they come from us. a perfect knowledge of his judgment & discretion leave me entirely satisfied that they will be not used, or so used, as events shall render proper. but

if you think that the possibility that harm may be done, over-
weighs the chance of good, I would expunge them, as in cases
of doubt it is better to say too little than too much.² I have the
honour to be with the most perfect respect & attachment Sir
Your most obedient & most humble servant

Th: Jefferson

ALS, DNA: RG 59, Miscellaneous Letters; ALS (letterpress copy), DLC:
Thomas Jefferson Papers; LB, DNA: RG 59, Domestic Letters; LB, DLC:GW.

1. Jefferson's letter of 28 July to William Short opened "some new and important matters," particularly the administration's policy on the new French
navigation acts and trade with the French colonies in the Caribbean. Jefferson
encoded one paragraph, which concludes: "An exchange of surplusses and
wants between neighbour nations, is both a right and a duty under the moral
law, and measures against right should be mollified in their exercise, if it be
wished to lengthen them to the greatest term possible. Circumstances sometimes require that rights the most unquestionable should be advanced with
delicacy. It would seem that the one now spoken of would need only a mention
to be assented to by an unprejudiced mind: But with respect to America, Euro-
peans in general have been too long in the habit of confounding force with
right. The Marquis de la Fayette stands in such a relation between the two
countries, that I think him perfectly capable of seizing what is just as to both.
Perhaps on some occasion of free conversation you might find an opportunity
of impressing these truths on his mind, and that from him they might be let
out at a proper moment, as meriting consideration and weight, when they
shall be engaged in the work of forming a Constitution for our neighbours. In
policy, if not in justice, they should be disposed to avoid oppression, which
falling on us, as well as on their Colonies, might tempt us to act together"
(*Jefferson Papers*, 20:686–91). The editors of the *Jefferson Papers* suggest that
Jefferson might have contrived the degree of discretion permitted Short as an
opportunity to express full confidence in the abilities of his protégé, whose
pretensions for appointment as minister to France Jefferson wished to advance
(ibid., 691n). For background to the French National Assembly acts affecting
the American tobacco and whale oil trades, see Lafayette to GW, 7 Mar. and
note 1, and GW to Lafayette, 28 July and note 2.

2. GW replied to Jefferson this day: "I have given your letter to Mr Short,
dated the 28th instt an attentive perusal. As you place confidence in his judgment and discretion, I think it is very proper that the sentiments which are
expressed in the cyphered part of it, should be handed to him; and approve
the communicating of them to him accordingly" (ALS, DLC: Thomas Jefferson Papers).

To Charles Carroll (of Carrollton)

Dear Sir,   Philadelphia, July 31. 1791.

Your favor of the 16 only got to my hands on friday last[1]— Not having my private papers at this place, to refer to, I can say nothing with precision as to the sum, or sums which is due from me on account of my purchase of Clifton's land—It is highly probable, however, that the information given to you by your Attorney is right—Be the amount, however, what it may, I shall be ready at any moment, to pay the same in cash at this place, or in post notes at Baltimore, or Alexandria, as you shall direct.

But you will please to recollect, my dear Sir, that there is a prerequisite to this payment, which was the original cause, why the money was not paid at the time of the sale—I mean a release of the mortgage, or some conveyance by which the Purchaser should be assured of the legal, or a secure title to the land.

The particulars relative to this transaction are a little out of my recollection at present—but in substance I believe they stand thus—That the land belonging to Clifton, now held by me, was mortgaged as security to—among others—Mr Ignatius Digges who, in this case, acted under, or would take no step without applying to, Mr Carroll, your father; and was the only one of several Mortgagees who refused to quit claim of the land—by which means my legal title to it is yet incomplete.

By to-morrow's post I will write home for these papers; and, as I have observed before, as soon as the impediment is removed, or I am in any manner made secure, the money shall be paid in either of the ways before mentioned; for it cannot be more your wish than it is my desire to bring the matter to a close.[2] With much esteem and regard, I am dear Sir, Your most obedient humble Servant

                                                   G. Washington

LB, DLC:GW.

U.S. Senator Charles Carroll of Carrollton (1737–1832) was the last surviving signer of the Declaration of Independence. Considered one of the richest men in America, he had invested in the Potomac Company and the Baltimore Ironworks Company, as well as in government securities. For an introduction to the long and tangled legal dispute over William Clifton's land on Clifton's Neck, on which GW's River farm was located, see GW to Benjamin Waller, 2 April 1760, n.1.

1. Carroll's letter of 16 July from Doughoregan Manor, Anne Arundel

County, Md., reads: "The long chancery Suit commenced by my Father against his partners in iron works, is at length determined, and I am now at liberty to make use of the money, which was decreed to my father by the courts in Virginia, and deposited in your hands, subject to his order. My attorney acquaints me this money amounts to £243.13.1 Sterling, & £67.4.7 Virga currency; I Suppose him to be correct in this assertion, because the late decree of our chancery Court, copy of which I have by me, States that those two Sums were decreed my father, and not received by him; I therefore presume they remain in your hands. You would oblige me very much by paying those Sums to Messrs Richard Lawson & Co. of Baltimore town in two months from this time; Should it be inconvenient to you to pay the money to those gentlemen, you will be pleased to direct it to be paid to Messrs Josiah Watson & Co. of Alexandria. I request the favor of an answer informing me to which of those companies you will direct payment to be made, and at what time . . ." (PHi: Gratz Collection).

2. Carroll replied to GW on 11 August. No letter of August 1791 from GW to George Augustine Washington at Mount Vernon dealing with Clifton's land has been found, but GW wrote Carroll on 28 Aug. that he had received the papers for which he had written to Mount Vernon.

From Marinus Willett

Sir,   New York 31st July 1791

By General Knox I had the honor of being advised that your Excellency was disposed to confer on me the appointment of Marshal for this District If I so inclined. This measure I suppose to have proceeded from my former application for that office and my subsequent wish to have some appointment in the General Government.

I beg leave to return my most sincere thanks for your Intention to serve me, But as from the best Information I was able to Collect the short time General Knox was here it appeared that my famaly could receive little or no support from the office and as my situation is such as to require that whatever business I pursue must assist in the support of my famaly, and having received encouragement to think That as by the Constitution of this state a new Sheriff for this County must be appointed the 29th day of September next I should have that office confered on me I became considerably embarrased; Whilst on the one hand a wish to be in the service of the General Government seemed to preponderate, The calls of my famaly Increased by a very aged Parent and an elderly maiden sister whose Intire dependance are on me led me to conclude it best to look to that appointment which promised most towards their support.

My desire of having some appointment under the Union still remains, and if I could have any office there that would promise a very reasonable support it should have by far the preference of the appointment I expect to receive from this state.

I feel Sir, a most gratefull sence of the honor Intended me by your Excellency—I am very sure that in all your appointments you are governed by the best of motives, and that as I once had the honor of hearing you express yourself, You carefully avoid, *"Errors of the heart"*.

I am very sure Sir, You will pardon notwithstanding your most justly exalted situation whatever in this may look like Intrusion—Your knowledge of me for fourteen years past will help you to believe even before I speak that no man has served the public with more diligence and Integrity then I have—The early Impressions my mind received in favour of Liberty Joined to an enthusiastic love of my Country produced habits of the strictest attention to her service during the revolution—Many served the public with more brilliancy and greater abilities—But for attention diligence and exertions not altogether unsuccessfull I give way to none—The political motto of *"Sining beyond forgivness"* was a favorite of mine—I regularly viewed the worst situation I could possibly be plased in without concern, And in case of a general failure in the Opposition I ever felt a raidiness to embrase wretchedness in its most distressing forms. Forgive me Sir, whilst I declare that this led me, (perhaps vainly led me) to suppose that in case of success I might expect to rise in proportion with the common cause.

Under this impression it was that I first applied for the offise of a Marshal, An office which from the universal acceptation I had found in the exercise of a four years Sheriffilty I promised myself I bid fair to receive. Having failed in this and being once more called to execute a Commission from Your Excellency, The same ardor that had hitherto governed my public actions induce me to execute it. The efforts I made on that occasion were succesfull eaqual to my most sanguin hopes, And one very Pleasing effect was the particular approbation I received from you, and an Intimation through General Knox of your readiness when opportunity should offer of affording me servise—Incouraged by this Intimation on hearing of the Creation of an offise which promised a decent support under the belief that the public would be as well served by me as by any other man I was induced to make an application—However great in favour of myself my prejudise may be, I am convinced that the purest motives directed your appointment; And in this perswasion nothwithstanding the greatness of my disapointment, I am satisfied.

Yet Sir, Lest from some misinformation respecting my circumstances I might have been prejudised. I beg leave to assure you that altho I have always been in the habit of exercising strict oconomy, and tho I have never been accostomed to eat the bread of Idleness, I am at the age of fifty years called on to be very circumspect least in the decline of life I should experience difficulties to which hitherto I have been a stranger.

My duty to myself and my duty to my famaly and others whose dependance are on me have urged me therefore to intrude on your patience—To receive some appointment under the Union to assist me with those whom providence has Plased under my charge to go comfortably and decently through life is still the great wish of my heart.

It is not an avidity for gain tha⟨t⟩ spurs me on to this wish—I feel Sir a Constant desire to be employed by the public, Yet in that employment my circumstances require a compensation—And while I frankly confess that from reflections on the hazards & difficulties I have passed I feel a kind of Conscious merit in having performed an upright part thus far. I feel likewis⟨e⟩ an Assurance that any public trust commited to my care in future will not suffer Injury.

Your Soul I am sure is too good, And your heart sufficiently Attached to old servants of the public to think it an unreasonable thing in them to wish that their latter days may not be worse then their begining.

The Offise of Sheriff for this County which I am led to believe I may receive in September next will be fully eaqual to every thing I could desire for the four years it may endure—But at the expiration of that time it must pass from and leave me where it has once already done; For this among other Causes I should prefer an apointment under the General Government which provoided it is perminant I would make choise of tho it may not be half as lucrative.

After being thus particular, I beg to plase myself before you, And to assure you that such is my Confidence in your *Superiour tallents at doing right,* And such my veneration for you—That if your Excellency should think fit to name me to any office whatever, I will with Pleasure receive it—If therfore the thing proposed to me through General Knox (which in my embarrasment I was Indused to decline) should not be disposed of and it is still your inclination to confer it on me it shall be thankfully received as a Pledge of your regarde and the most pointed care taken to guard against its receiving Injury under my charge.[1] With the most profound veneration and respect I have the honor to be Sir, Your most Obedient and very humble Servt

                                                        Marinus Willett

ALS, DNA: RG 59, Miscellaneous Letters.

For Marinus Willett, his previous applications, and his previous employment by the federal government, see Leonard Bleecker to GW, 4 June 1789, n.2, Henry Knox to GW, 15 Feb. 1790, n.5, and Willett to GW, 7 July 1789 and source note, and 29 Mar. 1790.

1. Matthew Clarkson was appointed to the office of federal marshal for the New York district vacated by William Stephens Smith. GW later offered Willett a commission as brigadier general of the army, which he declined (see Willett to GW, 14 April, and GW to the U.S. Senate [second letter], 3 May 1792).

From Thomas Hill Airey

                        Maryland Dorchester County Near Cambridge
Honour'd Sir.   August 1st 1791.

Please to permit a person at the distance of near two Hundred miles from your Excellencies temporary place of residence, and unknown to your Excellency, to intrude on your precious moments while I attempt to impart a matter, that may appear of some importance, & at the same time a mistiry that has evaded the deepest reserches of the Learned, in expounding the Prophetick writings. it is contained in the 7th Chapr of Daniels Prophecy, and expounded by the Prophet that succeeded him while the Jews were in captivity in Babilon. In one of the preceeding chapters, the King of Babilon has an Image presented him in Sleep, composed of several kinds of metal and part of Clay, which alarm'd the King, and caused him to have all his wise men assembled to make known to the King his dream; and the interpretation thereof. but none were able to make it known, till Daniel came before the King, and made known the full exposition of the dream; and shewed the King the fall of his own great Empire, and that there would be three other, great Empires that would succeed his, and that the rise of the one would be the downfall of the preceeding one, and that the fourth would likewise have an end by the Stone cut out of the mountain that would overturn all those Kingdoms and stand for ever. In the 8th Chapter Daniel has a full interpretation of the Image that had appeared to the King, conveyed to him in the similitude of Beasts; the Ram with two horns denoting the Meeds and Percians, and the Hee Goat the Grecian Kingdom and it's division into four Kingdoms after the death of Alexander, which Kingdoms was to be subdued by the Roman Empire.

As God has almost invariably used Similitude to convey the knowledge of his great and divine Misteries of futurity to the Prophets, and through them to the rulers and people in past ages. So God has been pleased, to make known, to his Ancient Prophets, the great events that was to be fulfilled in our day, by the same method of similitude; and has been pleased to give so plain an Interpretation of the similitude of the Eagle, to the American Standard; that there is shewn in the device, the number of Kings that are to succeed each other, the defections that will arise, and the causes of them, the number of Petty Kings that will arise and overturn the union, the devision of America into three Kingdoms, the conflicts that will arise during their continuance, and at last the final disolution of America. There are but two instances prior to this recorded in the Sacred Pages where the Great Supreme Ruler of the universe has Honour'd his Vicegerents on earth, with the foreknowledge of what would befall the People he had placed under their care.

And the third Instance, is an honour reserv'd for your Excellency, for the faithfull discharge of the Great and important trust reposed in you, in being the happy instrument, under God, of delivering so extensive a Continent, with it's numerous inhabitants from under the yoke and tiranny of Brittish Bondage.

Shou'd your Excellency condicend to think the foregoing relation, of that importance, as to merit your attention; so as to wish a full investigation of all the Proofs, necessary to gain your Excellencies belief of what I have related; the honour of a line from you, appointing the place where to attend, wou'd chearfully be obey'd. There is but one thing more and will ceas to intrude on your Excellencies patience, and that is, as the mistery to be made known is of that nature to be out of the reach of common observers, being dictated by the Sperit and gift of Prophecy, and we live at a time when Infidelity and Satire prevale much in our Land; wou'd wish to be as private in imparting it to your Excellency, as I can not so much on my own account as my connections, should it be known that I attempted to impart to your Excellency a matter that appears so far above the reach of their and others comprehension.[1] Permit me the honour to subscribe myself, with the greatest esteem, your Excellencies Most devoted & most Obedient Humbl. Servt

Thos: Hill Airey

ALS, DLC:GW.

Thomas Hill Airey of Dorchester County, Md., the son of an Anglican minister, freed thirty slaves in the spring of 1790 because "the practice of holding Negroes in perpetual bondage and slavery is repugnant to the pure precepts of the Gospel of Jesus Christ" (deed of manumission, 8 April 1790, MdAA). About the same time he and his wife Mary Harris Airey deeded a site to the local Methodist congregation for a church (Jones, *Dorchester County*, 141, 148, 276; Brumbaugh, *Maryland Records*, 2:109).

1. Airey wrote to GW on 17 July 1792, again drawing his attention to "the observance of the Prophetick writings," particularly Daniel, chap. 7, and the apocryphal Second Book of Esdras, chaps. 11–16, which Airey contended had special significance for the United States. Airey acknowledged the "surprise and the exercise of mind, your Excellency will have on perusing a Letter on so uncommon a subject from a person utterly unknown, & may aptly conclude me to be a person of very great weakness, or of the highest presumption" but assured GW of the "purity & disinterestedness of my intention" to make known "the important point of view in which the Prophecies appear to me, which he hoped would be "a sufficient appology, for intruding on your Excellencys invaluable moments." Airey contended that symbols used by the Prophets bore "a very striking resemblance" to the situation of the United States: "Daniel has a view of the number of Presidents that are to succeed each other in America, under the emblem of Horns, . . . but the Prophet Esdras, has a more conspicuous view, of the American Kingdom under the emblem of the Eagle: in the 12th Chapr and gives a full exposition, of it's extensive dominion, it's many revolutions, and its final end. which Prophecy respecting its end, is confi[r]m'd by St John . . . who compares the whole World, to a great City, and it's division into three parts; by that great & general Earthquake, which immediately preceeds that Glorious and happy reign of the Saints on Earth for a thousand years." Airey concluded: "There are many important Prophecies, that are

shortly to be accomplished, of a very interesting nature, but I forbare to mention them" (DLC:GW).

From the Officers of the Mero District

Mero District—Augt 1st 1791.[1]

Our remote Situation from the Seat of Your residence hath Prevented us from Steping forth so early as many have, to Congratulate Your Excellency on the Completion of the union of all the States, an event Productive of many Salutary Consequences, even at this Period, and to declare the attachment and veneration we have for Your charector and many Virtues.

We Know to promote, the Welfare of the Citizens of America in General is Your Strongest desire, an evidence of this we have in the Appointment of those Officers of the Ceded Teritory made immediately by Yourself, They meet with General Approbation. Govenor Blount we are Consious at the late Treaty hath done every thing that a man could do to restore Peace to the Teritory.

We are Situate in a part of Your Teritory which is more liable to the inroads and depredations of a Number of the Indian Tribes than Perhaps any Other People. Since the last week of May when the Cherokees were invited to a treaty, and while the talks were actually holding, the Indians Killd nine of Our Citizens and Stole fifty or Sixty head of Horses, and Still Continue their depredations, these Murders for the most part have been Commited on Persons who were Cultivating thier Plantations for the Support of their families.[2] The Cherokees at the Treaty informd that this Mischief was done by the Creeks altho they Acknowledged that some of their Young men were with them, the Chicasaws also with whom we are in Perfect Amity tell us and we have every reason to believe the Creeks and Cherokees Combined are the Perpetrators of those Murders. We implore Your interposition, fully hoping to meet with a more ample Protection than we have hertofore receivd from the State of North Carolina—the expectation of which was a Powerful incentive inducing us to use Our utmost influence to obtain the Act of Cession.

That You may long and Prosperiously Preside over these States: with Satisfaction to Yourself and Still Merit the Grateful Applause of a free People is the fervent wish of

John McNairy J. S. C. L. E.   Jno Rains Capt. Dn
Dan Smith Secy   Daniel Rowan Ensin
Jas Robertson B: G.   Thomas Maston J. P.
J. Winchester L. C. C. S.   Thos Johnson Capt. T. C.
Elijah Robertson L. C. C. D.   A. Hardin Insign
Robt Hays L. Colo. Cavalry   James McKa⟨in⟩ Capt.
Casper Manscer Lt Colo. S.   Alexr Walker Capt.
David Hay 1st Majr D.   Robt Ewing J. P.
Anthy Sharp Majr   Robt Edmondson J. P.
Edwd Douglass Majr   John Shannon C. D.
William Edmiston Majr C.   John Caughran ⟨Leu.⟩
William Don⟨el⟩son Mag.   William Mares Lieut.
Willm Blackmore Capt. L. D.   Henry Bradford Majr B⟨rigd.⟩
Josiah Ramsey Magr T. C.   Jas Ford L. C. of T. C.
Jacob Pennington Majr T. C.   Isaac Titsworth Lt C. ⟨T.⟩ C.

DS, DNA: RG 59, Territorial Papers, Territory Southwest of the River Ohio. The cover is docketed: "Territory U.S. south of the River Ohio—Sept. 20 1791. From—Gov: Blount Encloses a memorial from the Officers of Miro District—The Memorial ⟨answerd⟩ by the Secy of War Oct. 28th 1791." The cover letter, William Blount to GW, 20 Sept., has not been found but was offered for sale in the *Collector*, 55, no. 3 (Jan. 1941), item 631. Both may have been delivered by John Sevier, Jr., whose name appears on the cover of the memorial.

The signers were civil, judicial, and militia officers of Davidson, Sumner, and Tennessee counties of the Mero District.

1. This dateline was added by a later hand.

2. The memorialists may be referring to the Indian attack of May 1791 on a house on the Rolling Fork of the Cumberland River in which the owner and his family were murdered (Ramsey, *Annals of Tennessee,* 557).

From Winthrop Sargent

Fort Washington County of Hamilton and Territory
of the U. States North west of the River Ohio
Sir   August 1st 1791

I enclose to your Excellency a Copy from the Records of the Proceedings of the governour of the Western Territory in the Executive Department of Government for the Month of July

1791—To delay it until my next periodical communications, which must include the whole of the present year would be (most probably) detaining it beyond the next Sessions of Congress, when some Questions and Applications upon the Subject of Lands in this Country may make a Reference thereto, proper and necessary[1]—with every Sentiment of most perfect Respect I have the honour to be Your Excellency's obedient Humble Servt

Winthrop Sargent

ALS, DNA: RG 59, Territorial Papers, Territory Northwest of the River Ohio; copy, DNA: RG 59, Territorial Papers, Territory Northwest of the River Ohio.

1. The enclosed proceedings for July of the executive department of the Northwest Territory appear in Carter, *Territorial Papers*, 3:347–56. On 9 Nov. Tobias Lear transmitted them and their covering letter to Thomas Jefferson (DNA: RG 59, Miscellaneous Letters), who, according to the State Department memorandum book, received them on 14 Nov. (DNA:PCC, item 187, p. 119) and reported on them to GW the same day.

From George Augustine Washington

Honored Uncle   Mount Vernon Augt 1st 1791.

Such is my situation at this time that I can do little more than enclose the Report and acknowledge the rect of your favor of the 17th Ulto the directions therein given I shall have attended to and will reply to it and give you every necessary information before I leave this if I am able.[1] but at this time I do not flatter myself to be able to undergo the exercise of a journey in less than a fortnight—as soon as the Brickmakers and Bricklayers with there attendants finished harvest and grass cuting I had them put to work—Davis is now diging out the foundation for the wall in front of the house and will proceed to geting up the wall[2]—I purchased of a Vessel yesterday some shells which is landing to day tho' not more than abt 200 Bushls the first that I have been able to get tho' I have used every means possible. I have at different times engaged these Vessels expressly for the purpose the two first have disappointed me the last which engaged under the penalty of 20£ was to be here next week[.][3] We had on Tuesday last a light sprinkle of rain in the four noon and afternoon but insufficient to conduce to the relief of any thing there is no more the appearance of verdure in the enclosures about this house than if the whole had been consumed by fire.

Whiting tells me that the prospects for Corn is deplorable indeed unless we are favord with immediate and abundant rains there can be but very little made and present appearances are unfriendly to it very shortly we are in order for sowing wheat but Whiting says unless there comes rain it would be attended with the loss of the seed to sow for it would vegetate and perish for their is not moisture in the earth to bring it up and nourish it this I know was the case with the first sown wheat in the neck and D: Run last year. Your letter which I expect to recieve by the return of the Servant from Alexa to night will speak something on this subject as I mentioned in a letter written sometime since the sowing of the fallowed field at D: Run[4]—as I expected you might for some particular purpose wish immediate forma[tion] of the hights of the Jacks as I was not able to do it myself desired Whiting and to be very accurate, had them brought into the Piaza as the best place—the hights as here discribed I believe are just tho' they fall short of what they had been supposed to be and what the Spanish Jack had once been determined to be by measurement—Royal Gift 14 hands 1½ Inch. his Ears 14 Inches[.] Knight Malta. 13 hands. 1½ Inch. his Ears. 12½ Inches[.] Young Jack 3 Years old this spring— 12 hands. 1¼ I: Ears 12 I.—I think You mention'd that Colo. Washington would in September send for Royal Gift I shall leave directi⟨ons⟩ should I be absent to have him deliver'd if the Person who applies is authorised[5]—I have recieved from Doctr Stuart £525—part of which to the amt of £265.18.10¼ I applied to the discharge of the Ball: due on Your several Bonds to Mr Triplett meaning the original Bond and two which You had given him for interest[6]—I have settled the specie tax with the Sherriffs and shall the Levies I shall when I am setg out pay Ball for all the work he may have done at that time and leave money to pay the Bal: which in the whole will I expect amt to abt £100. settle such accts as are in Alexandria—and have all the accts posted up so as to leave all my monied transactions clearly to be understood as my first object is to discharge with satisfaction and strict justice the trust You have imposed in me[7]—it is but prudent to be at all times prepared for an event that is uncertain and the present state of my health being unfavorable to long life unless a change should take place points out to me the propriety of such arrangements as may illucidate all my transa⟨cti⟩ons—as they neither tend to protract or curtail life they need produce no unfavorable opperation on the spirits or mind it has a contrary tendency because I possess a mind capable of reflection and the fewer embarssments I have to contend with the greater fortitude I shall possess to support misfortune—I hope with care and the change of air to be restored but I fear not in a short time so as to enable to undergo so active a life as I wish the day before yesterday the spiting of blood left me yesterday it returned to day it has lessen'd—on Thursday the pain in my breast was troublesome attended with severe pains throughout my body which induced me to apply a large Blister to my breast which had been recommended by Doctrs Stuart & Craik—it drew well and I have kept it runing since and if I find advantage from it which I hope I shall will repeat the Blister to increase and continue the discharge—it is painful and disagreeable particularly in the attitude of writing[8]—therefore beg leave to conclude with assurances of the tenderist attachment to You my Aunt and Children and good wishes for Mr Lear & Lady and Majr Jackson—I am Your truely affectionate Nephew

Go. A. Washington

ALS, DLC:GW.

1. No letter from GW to George Augustine Washington of 17 July has been found. The enclosed "Report" was probably Anthony Whitting's farm report of 24–30 July (DLC:GW), the text of which appears in CD-ROM:GW.

2. The ha-ha on the east side of the mansion was constructed by Tom Davis, a dower slave and skilled bricklayer, who also harvested grain, painted exteriors, hung wallpaper, cut grass, and worked at GW's fishery. In his off-duty hours Davis raised watermelons, which he sold to GW, and provided waterfowl and game for the Mount Vernon table with the help of a Newfoundland dog named Gunner (Ledger B, 344, 346; Custis, *Recollections*, 458).

3. On 19 July William Dunnington formally agreed with George A. Washington to deliver between six and eight hundred bushels of "good clean live Oyster shells . . . above high water mark" at GW's lime kiln for twenty-four shillings per hundred bushels (DLC:GW). GW's accounts record the payment of £2.5 to William Batline for two hundred bushels of oyster shells on 1 Aug. and £6.10.3 to William Dunnington for 542½ bushels on 5 Aug. (Ledger B, 329).

4. No such letter from GW to George A. Washington has been found, nor has Washington's letter "written sometime since the sowing of the fallowed field" at Dogue Run been found. His most recent letter to GW of 7 Mar., does not discuss sowing wheat.

5. During the Southern Tour GW discussed with his kinsman Col. William Washington the possibility of having Royal Gift stand to stud in the neighborhood of Charleston (see Tobias Lear to GW, 15 May, n.6).

6. GW's accounts record this payment on 22 July to William Triplett (Triplet), executor of the late Harrison Manley (Ledger B, 329).

7. George A. Washington settled outstanding accounts with Alexandria merchants this week and left £22.10.6 with William Wilson to be delivered to the sheriff for the Fairfax County and Truro Parish levies (Ledger B, 329, and receipt, 5 Aug., ViMtV).

8. George A. Washington wrote to Burwell Bassett, Jr., on 4 July, "having just wrose from my bead having been confined to it since Saturday evening. I was most violently attacked with the headach which I am frequently afflicted with attended with a severe and excruciating puking which has left me very feeble and disordered—if I recover my strength sufficiently shall leave this the last of the week with Fanny and the Children who have not been well for Berkley" (ViMtV).

From the Commissioners for the Federal District

Sir   George Town [Md.] 2d August 1791

We have your communication of Mr Peter's proposals for wharfing and To day had propositions from Mr George French to cut the Canal from James's to Goose Creek and wharf the sides of the Creek, fill in and compleat the work for twenty two thousand pounds—We are not furnished with Mr Peter's Estimate, but suppose it would amount to a large sum—On a rough estimate we expect in October we must pay between five and six thousand dollars for expences not including the compensation to be made to Majr L'Enfant for his personal Services.[1]

Advice from the Governor of the low state of the Treasury of Virginia and the objection by the Treasurer of Maryland against issuing before the first of January, which we have attempted to obviate, make it probable that we must have recource to private credit to defray the Current expences. With this unpleasant Prospect and the uncertainty of the produce of the sales in October, we have resolved to decline entering into engagements respecting the Canal or wharfing.[2]

The survey and Plan of the City is not in the forwardness we wish: We have hopes still given us that they will be in such a State tho not compleat, as to begin the Sales the 17th of October, especially as Mr Ellicot can be spared a month longer as he purposes with your leave. Majr L'Enfant purposes to wait on you soon with his drafts for your confirmation, and we cannot help repeating our wish that in the new laying out Carrollsburgh and Hamburgh as little alteration and appropriation as may be, may take place, for we shall unavoidably have difficulties enough, to reconcile private interest with public views[.] The regulations for improvements must be fixed before the sales; We conceive it to be a work of some Delicacy, and we should be happy that we could furnish any useful remarks on that subject. Pressed as you are with so many different things; we cannot without reluctance request your attention to this object, but we wish to be in possession of the system in time so that we may fully understand and be able to justify it, or propose our doubts. We are Sir, with truth and respect your mo. obt Servts

Thos Johnson
Dd Stuart
Dl Carroll

LB, DNA: RG 42, Records of the Commissioners for the District of Columbia, Letters Sent, 1791–1802.

1. For the proposal of Robert Peter, see GW to the Commissioners for the Federal District, 24 July. Pierre-Charles L'Enfant proposed to GW on 22 June that a canal be cut between St. James Creek and Goose, or Tiber, Creek.

2. At GW's request Thomas Jefferson on 22 Aug. asked Thomas Harwood, treasurer of Maryland, if he would accept GW's "draught for the first installment of the money granted by the state of Maryland" (*Jefferson Papers*, 22:58). For the payments by Virginia and Maryland for construction in the Federal City, see Daniel Carroll to GW, 22 Jan., and Beverley Randolph to GW, 15 Feb. 1791.

From Pierce Butler

Charleston [S.C.] 3 August 1791. Encloses an application for a federal customs appointment from the lieutenant governor of this state and assures GW "that No Gentleman in Carolina can have a stronger Claim to Your Attention, or is better suited for the Station than Mr Holmes; And I am persuaded that His Appointment woud give general satisfaction."[1]

ALS, DLC:GW.

1. The enclosed letter of Lt. Gov. Isaac Holmes (d. 1812) of 3 Aug. to GW solicited appointment either to the federal collectorship for Charleston, vacated by the death of George Abbott Hall on 1 Aug., or to Abraham Motte's

position as naval officer for that port if Motte was promoted to collector (DLC:GW). On 3 Aug. Richard Hutson also recommended Holmes to GW (DLC:GW). Motte applied to GW for the collectorship on 3 Aug., "stimulated to it by the assistance which it will enable me to render an aged & amiable mother, who from a state of opulence is much injured in her circumstances by having large payments made her in depreciated Continental money." Edward Weyman, surveyor for the port, applied to GW on 3 Aug. for the post of naval officer in the event of Motte's promotion (DLC:GW), and on 4 Aug. Charles Pinckney recommended to GW Holmes and Steven Drayton for that office (DLC:GW). GW also received an application dated 3 Aug. from John Mitchell for the collector's post (see Mitchell to GW, 20 May 1789, n.1). GW apparently appointed Holmes collector, who served until he was removed in 1797 for his inability to collect delinquent accounts (see GW to the U.S. Senate, 31 Oct. 1791).

Letter not found: from Daniel Carroll, 5 Aug. 1791. Thomas Jefferson wrote to the commissioners for the federal district on 28 Aug.: "Your joint letter of the 2d. inst. to the President, as also Mr. Carrol's separate letters of the 5th. and 15th. have been duly received" (*Jefferson Papers*, 22:88–89).[1]

1. One or both of Daniel Carroll's letters concerned title to lots in Carrollsburgh and covered a plat of the town, all of which GW referred to Thomas Jefferson, who replied to Carroll and the commissioners of the federal district on or about 28 Aug. (see Jefferson to the Commissioners, 28 Aug., *Jefferson Papers*, 22:88–89, and GW to Jefferson, 29 August).

From Simon Wilmer

Sir   Chester Town Maryd 5th Aug. [17]91

Mr Lewis who lately fill'd a department in your Excellencys house hold suggested to me, that one or more assistant Secretaries must necessarily be appointed this Fall, in consequence of his retirement and the probability of Major Jacksons translation to some other Office; If such Vacancies have taken place, and are still to be filled, I must beg permission to approach your Excellency as an applicant, altho I fear my pretensions are not commensurate with the honor I now Solicit, yet I am impell⟨'d⟩ to enforce my wishes from a conviction that my claims will be properly measur⟨'d⟩ by your condescension.[1] My age does not exceed 23 years and near five of that term have been devoted to business in Europe from whence I have lately return⟨'d.⟩ My fortune is small but Independent and I flatter myself that neither my manners or Person will found exceptionable and as your

Nephew infor⟨m'd⟩ me that it requir'd an association of the man of business with some Personal address, I can only assure you Sir, that I am perfectly prepar⟨ed⟩ for the first qualification and shall be ambitious to improve the latter in your School of refinement. Mr James Tilghman of this County with whom I have the honor to be distantly related, will furnish me with the necessary recommendations, but If I deserve your Scrutiny, Sir, I hope an intermediate application to Major Richmond of this State will prove Satisfactory.[2] I am fearful my prayer will be found extremely informal, but I concluded that a simple illustration of facts woud be preferable to all the Sophistry of adulation which fancy cou'd devise. I have the honor to be Sir With the most profound respect & Esteem your most devoted and very Humble Servant

Simon Wilmer

ALS, DLC:GW.

Simon Wilmer (born c.1768) belonged to a prominent family of Kent County, Md., numerous members of which had the same given name, including two contemporaries of the letter writer, who at this time were serving in the state legislature.

1. GW's nephew Robert Lewis left GW's official family early in 1791 (see Lewis to GW, 10 January). William Jackson applied to GW for the postmaster generalship, writing sometime before Samuel Osgood's resignation of 11 July: "I beg leave, with the greatest deference, to submit myself to your consideration as his successor. Could I believe, Sir, that your approbation of my wish (should I be so happy as to obtain it) could be construed into an act of partiality towards a person of your family—interesting as the completion of this wish is to my happiness—I would not desire it. No, Sir, I would not consent that, in this only instance, you should be supposed to depart from that impartial justice, which characterises all your actions, and has given unlimited confidence to your administration: But, beneficent as you have been to me, it is not to your goodness alone, on the present occasion, that I address my application—I refer myself, with some degree of confidence, to your knowledge of my public services, to your acquaintance with my capacity: and to your opinion that my talents and my disposition will be united in exertion, to merit what you may be pleased to think me worthy to receive. If to the consideration of my military service, during the whole war, and the faithful discharge of some important civil duties, your friendship and your sense of propriety should be agreed to add the desire of making me happy, I shall indeed regard myself as being completely so. To the obligations of fidelity and attention, which my duty to the public would impose, will be superadded an ardent desire to manifest my sense of your goodness by rendering justice to your favorable opinion" (DLC:GW).

2. Major Richmond was Christopher Richmond, auditor general of Maryland.

From Henry Knox

Sir   War Department [Philadelphia], 6th August 1791.

I have the honor to submit to you, Governor Blount's report, relative to the treaty with the Cherokees, which he formed on the 2d instant—and also his request for leave of absence.[1]

I shall have the honor to wait upon you personally relative to this business, after you shall have read the papers.

I have also the honor to submit Copies of the Instructions and Letters to Major General St Clair, Major General Butler and Mr Hodgdon the Quarter Master; and also to Brigadier General Scott, and the Board in Kentucky.[2] With the highest Respect I have the honor to be Sir, Your most Obed. huml. servt

H. Knox

LS, DLC:GW; LB, DLC:GW.

1. No copy of William Blount's report on the Treaty of Holston of 2 July has been found. See Carter, *Territorial Papers*, 4:65, n.69. For Blount's letter to Henry Knox of 17 July requesting a leave of absence, see ibid., 70–71. GW referred Blount's request to Thomas Jefferson, who informed Blount on 12 Aug. of GW's "consent to the absence you therein ask from the 15th. of September to the 20th. of November" (*Jefferson Papers*, 22:29–30).

2. Knox's instructions of 21 Mar. to Arthur St. Clair are in *ASP, Indian Affairs*, 1:171–74. The enclosed letters to St. Clair probably included Knox's letters of 21 July stating that GW "has commanded me to urge, that, as soon as your troops are assembled, or such portion thereof as you may judge proper, that you commence the establishment of such of your posts of communication, to which your force may be adequate. He is greatly anxious that the campaign be distinguished by decisive measures, so that the expense incurred may be manifestly useful and important" (ibid., 179–80) and of 4 Aug., which mentioned GW's anxiety for the commencement of operations (ibid., 180–81). For Knox's instructions of 5 April to Richard Butler, see ibid., 184–85. On 21 July Knox wrote Butler that GW "is exceedingly anxious that Major General St. Clair should commence his operations at as early a period as possible; and he has commanded me to urge that you, and all the troops within your orders, descend the Ohio immediately" (ibid., 191). Knox informed Butler on 4 Aug. that GW "is extremely anxious that the troops should be immediately assembled at fort Washington. I am persuaded, from your former letter, that they have all descended the Ohio," which was not the case (ibid., 192). For Knox's instructions of 31 May to Quartermaster Samuel Hodgdon, see ibid., 193. The enclosed copies of Knox's letters to Hodgdon were those of 9, 23, 30 June, 7, 14, 21 July, and 4 Aug. (ibid., 193–95). For Knox's instructions to Charles Scott, dated 9 Mar., see ibid., 129–30. Knox's communication to the "Board in Kentuckey" has not been found but was probably in response to its letter to him of 20–30 May (Knox to GW, 27 June, n.1).

From Hugh West

Sir, [Philadelphia, 6 August 1791]

I took occasion to wait upon your Excellency this fore-noon, but was unable to gain personal access, by reason of your then present Engagements. It was alledged, that my Business might be imparted, by means of a Secretary, to your Excellency: but which for a very obvious reason, I declined. It is of such a nature, I presume, as to suit your Excellency's ear alone. It is not improbable, that while you are prompt, from the exalted consideration of the common Interest, to the most arduous vigilance and noblest care; you may deem it an intrusion upon your Excellency to be addressed by a Stranger to your Person, for the purpose of a private Interview with your Excellency. For had I not all along anticipated this mode of communication to your Excellency, it would have behoved me to have premised certain particulars by which to make myself known in a satisfactory manner. But lest your Excell. should think it proper to refuse me the honour of your presence upon this occasion, I proceed to subjoin a few circumstances relative to my last design. I am the youngest Son of John West jun. (Deceas'd) of Virginia, with whom, in his life-time, your Excel. had some acquaintance.[1] For several years I enjoyed a small paternal Estate in the vicinity, of Alexa. near which I was born: but having, in part expended it in order to consummating the study of a medical profession to which I was designed; it hath become expedient that I should now engage in some certain Employment, whereby to acquire a subsistance for my family. Herein I have been exceedingly perplexed. A few days ago I applied to a Mr Nourse, Register: with whom I deposited a specimen of my Hand-writing (having had a previous Recommendation from Dr B. Rush) of which he approved. But there being no vacancy at that time, I have the promise of only succeeding to the first that shall take place in that Office—However he was candid enough at the same time to suggest, that there was but little probability of it at all. While I am unwilling to prescribe a sentiment of Hospitality to the President of the U. States; with all humility, I present a picture of my complicated distress—It is enough, that my wife (to whom I have been united for a bout 18 months) and myself have been uniformly subject to a wretched dependance on our Relations.

I would farther beg leave to observe, that having learnt there will be an Auditor appointed in a short time, His Excellency may ⟨do every⟩ necessary service to me by a Letter recommendatory to *him*, for such employment as he may esteem me to be capable of. His Excel. will be pleased to decide this matter agreeably to his leisure; he either to appoint any hour determinately at which I may see him upon the subject abovementioned, or give me such general recommendation as may ensure success to my undertaking, who have the honour to be, His Excellency's most obedt & Devoted Servant

Hugh West

ALS, DNA: RG 59, Miscellaneous Letters. The dateline is supplied from a later notation on the letter: "File Aug. 6. 1791."

The application of Hugh West (c.1755–1801) was supported by a lukewarm recommendation of 1 Aug. from William Herbert of Alexandria: "My knowledge of this young Gentleman, these two last Years, will not warrant my saying much of him, farther than, that I have been credibly informed, that he is greatly altered for the better, for it must be confessed his Conduct, prior to that period, was that of an extravigant & dissipated young Man—but I hope & believe he has discover'd his error & that he is thoroughly Reclaimed & that in case he should be nominated to any place, by which he could Obtain a livelihood, he will conduct himself with Care & fidelity in the discharge of the duties of his Office & thereby merit any favor done him" (DNA: RG 59, Miscellaneous Letters). Roger West of West Grove, Va., on 10 Aug. also assured GW: "It is with peculiar pleasure I have marked the change in Mr Wests Conduct for these two years past for the better; indeed, I verily believe that a thourough reformation has succeeded in him, and that he sees with horror and detestation the impropriety of his former Idle and dissolute habits, and resolves with Religious firmness in future, to abandon them, and to Seek usefull and honorable imployments wherever He may find them. If you should be dispos'd to interest yourself for this Young Gentleman I have no doubt but He will with an honest Zeal discharge any trust reposed in him to your Satisfaction, and thereby merit a continuance of your favor" (DNA: RG 59, Miscellaneous Letters). On 11 Aug. James Craik also reported to GW that he had no personal acquaintance with West "and therefore am at some loss how to present him to you, yet from the opinions of Some which I think I can rely upon, Am induced to think him qualified to transact Business that will Occur in the Subordinate Grades" of the Treasury Department. "There are two Circumstances attending this Gentleman that are matters of Notoriety at this place. in the early part of his life he was an extravagant, and a Dissipated young man which led him to dispose of all his Patrimoneal Estate. And that for these two years past he has manifested a desire to be usefully imployed, which I beleive to be truly the case—Should it be agreeable to you to interest yourself for his advantage I think he will Act with Circumspection & propriety" (DNA: RG 59, Miscellaneous Letters). GW immediately employed West as a recording clerk under the direction of Tobias Lear. West remained in GW's official household until 1792, when GW certified on 15 Aug. his sobriety, diligence, prudence, and integrity (GW to West, 11 April 1798, n.2). West wrote GW on 20 Sept. 1792 that, having failed to find employment in one of the executive departments, he had decided to open a grocery store. His brother Thomas West had given him a house, and other relatives "will afford me some present assistance, but they can not immediately advance a competent sum: I have therefore to request the loan of 100 Dollars from you Sir—upon the most Satisfactory security you may demand. You may possibly be surprized after *all* that you have done for me, that I should ask so considerable a favor: but, Sir, permit me just to remark, that, as by means of the abovementioned business I shall be enabled both to support my family in Philadelphia, which are very destitute, as well as to discharge the sum I am now solliciting; you will do me a great service, without affecting (I hope) your own interest. But, Sir, relying that your determination will be equally founded in the proper regard to your benefit, and the nicest principles of humanity, as it relates to my truly calamitous situation; after mentioning that, should it better suit your convenience to furnish me with *any* less sum than that cited in the former part of this letter it will be most gratefully received" (DLC:GW). GW responded on 21 Sept. 1792: "Your Letter of this date is now before me. I am very sorry that your endeavours to be employed in some one of the public Offices in Philada, have been unsuccessful; & hope the business which you have now in contemplation to undertake, may be attended with advantage. if, therefore, I can make it comport with my own numerous calls for money, I will furnish you with the sum requested in your Letter, before my return to Philadelphia" (LB, DLC:GW).

1. John West, Jr., of Fairfax County was GW's coexecutor of the estate of Thomas Colvill (see James Tilghman, Sr., to GW, 6 Oct. 1790, n.2).

From Thomas Jefferson

[Philadelphia] Aug. 7. 1791.

Th: Jefferson has the honour to send for the President's perusal, his letters to Govr Sinclair & Judge Symmes: as also letters received from the postmaster at Richmond on the subject of the two cross posts.[1] he has gone further as to that towards the South Western territory, than Th: J.'s letter authorized, as he only submitted it to his enquiry & consideration whether a post along that rout could maintain itself. he has advertized it as if decided on. however there is doubtless time enough to correct the rout, if it be not what the President would wish.

AL, DNA: RG 59, Miscellaneous Letters; LB, DLC:GW.

1. Thomas Jefferson's letters to Arthur St. Clair and John Cleves Symmes of 6 Aug. concern the dispute over the eastern boundary of Symmes's purchase in the Ohio country (*Jefferson Papers*, 22:8–9). At GW's command Tobias Lear

returned them to Jefferson this day (DLC:GW). The enclosed letter of 1 Aug. to Jefferson from Augustine Davis, postmaster at Richmond, covered a "Proposal for the Establishment of Cross-posts in Virginia" (*Jefferson Papers*, 20:711–12).

To Thomas Johnson

Dear Sir,   Philadelphia August 7th 1791.

I have been duly favored with your letters of the 27 & 30 of July; the last of which came to hand while the Judges of the Supreme Court were with me on an invitation to dinner.[1]

I took this opportunity of laying your letter before the Chief Justice, (as you mentioned your having written to him and to Mr Wilson on the subject) in order that it might be communicated to the other Judges—After a few minutes consultation together, the Chief Justice informed me that the arrangement had been, or would be so agreed upon that you might be wholly exempted from performing this tour of duty at that time—and I take the present occasion to observe that an opinion prevails pretty generally among the Judges, as well as others who have turned their minds to the subject, against the expediency of continuing the Circuits of the Associate Judges, and that it is expected some alterations in the Judicial system will be brought forward at the next session of Congress, among which this may be one.

Upon considering the arrangement of the Judges with respect to the ensuing circuit and the probability of future relief from these disagreeable tours, I thought it best to direct your commission to be made out and transmitted to you, which has accordingly been done, and I have no doubt but that the public will be benefitted, and the wishes of your friends gratified by your acceptance.[2] With sentiments of very great regard, &ca

G. Washington.

LB, DLC:GW.

1. GW probably dined with the justices of the Supreme Court on 4 Aug.; the next day he signed a temporary commission for Thomas Johnson as associate justice.

2. Tobias Lear forwarded this letter to Thomas Jefferson on 7 Aug. (DLC: GW) with the instruction that it be sent with Johnson's commission, which Johnson acknowledged in a letter to GW of 13 August.

To Thomas Johnson

Dear Sir, Philadelphia August 8th 1791

It appearing to me proper that the Commissioners should be apprised of the pretensions—signified in the enclosed letter—I send it to them accordingly, that such prudent use may be made of the information as to them shall seem fit.[1]

I have not given, nor shall I give any answer—at least for the present—to the writer of it; and no person is knowing to my having received such a letter. I am—Dear Sir, Yr Most Obedt Servt

Go: Washington

ALS, DLC: Presidential MSS, General; LB, DLC:GW; LB, DNA: RG 42, Records of the Commissioners for the District of Columbia, Letters Sent, 1791–1802.

1. The enclosure was a copy of Robert Douglas's letter to GW of 15 April asserting ownership of a fifty-acre tract in the federal district. Johnson replied to GW on 13 August.

From Jacob Milligan

sir Philadelphia August 8th 1791.

My feelings being much hurt by what General Moultrie told me, was Said disrespectfull of my Charactor—In consequence of which I left all my Business and came to this Place with a Certificate which I beg leave to hand to Your Excclency which I hope Will be Sufficiant to shew that I am not the person represented.

Being informed by some of signers that there was Several Vacances—such as Port Master for the Port of Charlestown Keeper of the light for ditto—and Keeper of the Light of Cape Henry in Virgina.

If Your Excelency should think proper to appoint me to any of those Offices or any Other it will be a favour Confered On Your Excelencys Obliged and very Hume Servt

Jacob Milligan

ALS, DLC:GW.

Jacob Milligan bore a recommendation from Pierce Butler to GW, dated Charleston, 6 July, noting that Milligan wished to obtain "a small place in the Revenue Arrangement of this State" and that he had distinguished himself in several engagements during the Revolutionary War, "particularly in One with a British Galley Shewed a Cool and determined Bravery not to be Surpassd" (DLC:GW). Milligan received no appointment from GW but was later employed as harbor master of Charleston and assistant to Isaac Huger, U.S. marshal for the South Carolina district.

From Ebenezer Tucker

Surveyors Office Port of Little Egg h[arbo]r [N.J.]

Dear Sir　　　　　　　　　　　　　　　⟨Au⟩gst the 8th 1791

as the Law of the Nation Requires Cutters to be Fitted & mannd for the Aid of the Customs, Permit me Sir to Observe that it's my Oppinion that the Cutter that Cruzes on this Coast Shoud have an Officer On Board that understands the Coast harbours Creeke &c. Vary well. Capn Dennis of the Vigalant who paid our port a Visset a few Days Since, informs me that his first officer is not yet appointed, he also told me he wished a man On Board acquainted with the Coast as it woud tend to the Advantage of the Revanue, as on this Coast Between the two Oppulant Citties of Phila. & N. York Great Attention to the Inlets Creekes &c. Shoud be paid to Prevent Illicit Practices which is Vary Eassy to be Excuted in this port. Unless a good lookout is kept—which is my Desided Oppinion on also—I have a Brother by the name of Stephen Tucker about 22 Years of age thats a tollerable Good Seaman & Pilot, is active & Smart, & wishes to Engage in the Service, & from his knoledge of the Coast Inlets &c. I think he woud Suit Capn Dennis Vary well. I have also wrote the Secraty of the Treasury On this Subject. Should the President be pleased to Honor Mr Tucker with the appointment I am Confident he will be Servicable to Government, & will Receaive the favour with Gratitude, as well as Your Most Oblieged & Vary Humble Servant

Ebenr Tucker

N.B. I have Recd & accepted the Comission as inspector of the Revanue of this Port, & am Yours with all Posable Esteem.

E.T.

ALS, DLC:GW. Ebenezer Tucker noted on the cover: "To the Particular Care of Mr H. Drinker."

To William Darke

(Private)

Dear Sir, Philadelphia August 9. 1791.

I have received your letter of the 24 ult.[1]—Regarding its contents, altho' relating to objects of public import, as private communication, I shall reply to, and remark upon them, with that candor which my personal esteem, and my public wishes strongly enjoin.

I need not tell you that my regret is seriously excited by learning that any cause of discontent should exist, either on your own part, or that of your Officers, with General Butler, and it is hardly necessary to express my earnest wish that it may speedily subside, and be entirely done away—But, as I rely greatly on your disposition to advance the public interest, tho' even by the relinquishment of private opinions, I shall offer to your consideration some remarks which I am persuaded will have weight with you, and induce your influence with your Officers to dismiss their discontents, and to think only of their public duty.

Let it in the first place be remembered that one common cause engages your service, and requires all your exertions—it is the interest of your country—To that interest all inferior considerations must yield. As an apology for the seeming inattention of a commanding Officer it should be considered that the variety of objects, which engage him, may produce an appearance of neglect, by no means intended—In General Butler's particular instance some allowance should be made for the effects of bodily indisposition, combined with the cares of his station—and I am satisfied no one, either from temper or reflection, will more cheerfully make this allowance than yourself.

On this belief I rest an expectation that every uneasiness will be composed, and that the public service will be proceeded in with harmony and zeal.

The Secretary of War has directed a board of Officers to decide the question of rank between you and Colonel Gibson and others.[2] I shall at all times be happy to evince the sincere esteem, with which I am Dear Sir, Your most obedient Servant

G. Washington

LB, DLC:GW.

1. William Darke's letter of 24 July from "Six Miles from pitsburg" reads: "I

after Completing the Virginia Battalion and Geting the maryland Batalion as forward as I could, Arived at pitsburg the first day of this Month, and have bean since that time about pitsburg and down the River about a hundred and fifty miles at the Several places where the Virginia troops are Stationed, and am very Sorey to find that the officers in General are exceedingly discontent, dont like the treatment of the General and Several of them Talk of Resigning. I confess I cannot Rightly understand the General. I have bean in the service of my Country in allmost all the wars Since the year 1755—in one Capasety or other—and Never Served under any officer be fore that I had So little Satisfaction with In deed, I have had no duty to do nor bean on any Command farther than to turn out a bullock Guard of twelve men. I wish to Get to hed quarters and have writ to General St Clear but being in Grate haest as the Botes were Set off before I began to write I did not Give the General my Reasons as fully as I wished to do. The Virginians think General Butler does not like the Virginians, this is allso the opinion of all the principle Inhabitance about where the ⟨*illegible*⟩ Stationed and they in Concequence dislike him, and think he is partial. I aknoledg I have Noticed Some Same things in the Generals Conduct that I thaught had the apearence of it, but very like may be mistaken—I confess I would Gladly be out of the Service for No other Reason then this, I think I cannot be happy under the Command of Genl Butler except he alters Grately, and have had difficualty to pervail on Several of the officers to Continue, I writ to Genl Butler yusterday—as the Melitia are ordered to the Stations wher the Virginions are to morow—As the River is falling fast—for permition to Go on to head quarters but did not Get the least Satisfaction whether we Should ever Go or not, he did not even Give me as Much Satisfaction as he did one of my officers onst before, which was, as I am Informed he would know when he Saw it in Genl orders—The desertions have bean Grate I beleive twenty have deserted from Captain Hannah, who I think a good officer Some have deserted from the other Companys So that I beleive the Batalion is not quite full Some died with the Small pox two were drownded and Some discharged—so that allthough there were 25 or 26 more then the full Batalion enlisted there is Some wanting to make the Battalion Compleat, the Maryland Batalion has not bean full by about 30, and as many have deserted from that, I beleive there are but about 280—I can give No Account of the other battalion from the Southward. The Indians have done no damage Sinc the fourth of this Month except Killing Some Cattle where Captain hannah is Stationed they flashed a gun and Shaped an other at one of his Men who was on his post at the mout of Wheeling, on the Indian Shore but it having Rained all day their Guns mised fire, they went a few miles up the River and Killd Some Cattle—it Seems by what I have heared to be Likely to be a despute between Colonel Gibson and me which is to take Rank Genl Butler I hear Say Colonel Gibson was a Colo. before I was, Colo. Gibson was never an officer in the Continantal line, he was a State officer and I believe as a Colonel of a Small Regement that was never Compleat. but as for his Clameing any thing from that I dont think he has the Least Right. you that apointed us both must know which is to take Rank. I commanded as a Lieutenant Colo. Commandant in the Continantal line. My late Commition is for the first Regiment and Colo. Gibsons the Second which I Conceived would not have bean the Case if Gibson was to have bean first in Command as the Regiments were only forming But if you intinded Colonel Gibson Should Command, I shall Cheerfully agree to be Commanded by him. I Should be very happy to Receive a line from you on the Subject. . . . I hear there are Several Deserters in the Goals in Virginia and have mentioned Somthing of it to Genl Butler, though but very Slitely, as I find nothing that I think of Seems to meat his approbation Nor did I expect to Stay So long about this place the Regiment I Expected to Command is Scatered from fort frankling to fort washington I Sopose about 700 Miles by water, apart, So that it Seems impossible to teach them much Desapline" (DNA: RG 59, Miscellaneous Letters).

2. GW transmitted this letter to Henry Knox on 10 Aug. with the instruction that "After you have read the enclosed private communication of my sentiments to Colo. Darke, please to seal & forward it, along with your dispatches to the Army" (Madigan, *Autograph Letters*, n.d., 59, item 332).

To William Moultrie

Philadelphia August 9th 1791

I have had the pleasure, my dear Sir, to receive your friendly letter of the 10th of last month—and I reply with affectionate regard to your congratulations & kind wishes.[1]

A slight indisposition (occasioned by a tumour—not much unlike the one I had in New York in the year 1789—) since my return, of which I am now recovered, does not forbid the expectation that my health may be ultimately improved by my tour through the Southern States[2]—my happiness has certainly been promoted by the excursion, and no where in a greater degree than while resident among my fellow-citizens of South Carolina. To their attentions (yours in particular) I shall always confess myself much obliged, and particularly flattered by the regards of your fair compatriots, to whom I wish upon every occasion, to be remembered with grateful respect.

I shall realise your promise of a visit with sincere satisfaction— till then, and always, I beg you to believe me with the greatest regard & esteem, My dear Sir, Your Most Obedt Hble Servt

Go: Washington

ALS (photocopy), DLC:GW; LB, DLC:GW.

1. William Moultrie's letter to GW of 10 July from Charleston congratulating him on his return to Philadelphia and wishing that "your friendly visit to these southern States will not be attended with any evil consequences to your

constitution, but that the long journey and the very great change of climate may establish your health & lengthen your days in peace and happyness" is in DLC:GW.

2. For GW's tumor, see A. Hammond to GW, 8 July 1791, n.3.

Letter not found: from John Cannon, 10 Aug. 1791. In a letter of 7 Sept. to Cannon, GW referred to Cannon's letter "of the 10 of August."

From Charles Carroll (of Carrollton)

Dougheragen [Anne Arundel County, Md.]
Dear Sir   11th Aug. 1791

I was honored with your letter of the 31st past, on the 3d instant; until then I was unacquainted with the defect of your title in the lands purchased of Clifton: I had always understood that my father had let the balance decreed to him remain in the hands of the Commissioners, from a different cause than the one assigned in your letter. He had instituted a suit in chancery against his partners in iron works for an indemnification of the losses incurred by Mercer's attachment, & the subsequent decrees in Virginia, & was advised by his lawyer (Mr Thos Johnson) not to draw the money out of the Commissioner's hands without the consent of his partners; that consent he could never obtain; Some of them returned no answer to his written application for their directions, & consent; others replied that they were no ways concerned in the transaction, & refused to give any direction about the money.

Immediately on the receipt of your letter, I wrote to Mr Cooke on the subject; subjoined you have a copy of his answer.[1] I have this day written again to Mr Cooke requesting him to draw the deed of release to complete your title, and to Mrs Digges, desiring her to execute it with all convenient dispatch; to this request she can not possibly object, as the chancry suit between the late Mr Digges & my father has long since been compromised & settled.[2]

Mr Cooke, you will observe, is of opinion that a deed from Mrs Lee, heiress of Mr Ignatius Digges, is not essential to the completion of your title; I presume therefore, if his opinion be well founded, you would not wish for a deed from Mrs Lee.[3]

When Mrs Digges has executed the deed, and your title is thereby completed, I should be glad to receive payment of the sums mentioned in my former letter in post notes at Baltimore, in preference to any other mode. I remain with sentiments of the highest respect and esteem Dear Sir Yr most obedt hum. Servant

Ch. Carroll of Carrollton

ALS, PPRF.

1. Charles Carroll enclosed a copy of a letter dated 9 Aug. from Maryland attorney William Cooke (c.1746–1817) stating that the decree of the General Court in the matter of Clifton's land directed William Digges, James Addison, Benjamin Farmer, and Ignatius Digges and his wife (William Clifton's creditors) to convey the lands to the purchaser in fee simple in return for a specified payment from the commissioners to be realized from the sale of Clifton's land. The order compelled Digges to accept £634.5.1 as final settlement of a bond of £1268.10.8, and Cooke concluded: "You will perceive that by the decree Mrs Digges, as one of the Defendants, & also as Executrix of her late husband must convey to the President all the right of her late husband, as well as her own in the mortgaged premises with a covenant of Special warranty agt all persons claiming under her, or the late Mr Digges, & deliver w[it]h the bond; this being tendered to the President, he will pay the money. If he requires that Mrs Lee, as the heir of Mr Digges, Should also convey, which I do not think essential, as a release by the Executor of a mortgagee is good without joining the heir, yet there can be no difficulty in getting Mr Lee & his lady to convey" (PPRF).

2. Mary Carroll Digges was the widow of Ignatius Digges (1707–1785), who, with the elder Charles Carroll in 1762, had refused to accept the settlement of the mortgages they held on Clifton's land prescribed by the General Court. GW's title to the land he had acquired at the court-ordered auction in May 1762 was not fully secured until Mary Carroll Digges delivered him an indenture, dated 22 Aug. 1791, relinquishing all claim to the land "in pursuance of the said Decree as also in consideration of the sum of five shillings Current Money to the said Mary Digges in hand paid by the said George Washington at and before the Ensealing and delivery of these Presents" (NjWoG).

3. Mary Digges Lee (1745–1805), the only child of Ignatius Digges, was married to Thomas Sim Lee (1745–1819) of Prince Georges County, Maryland.

From Henry Knox

War Department [Philadelphia] 11th August 1791.

The Secretary of War humbly reports to the President of the United States.

That previously to the 4th day of March 1789, the military invalids throughout the United States, had certain rates of allowance made them on account of their disability, under certain regulations established by Congress—The States respectively in which such invalids resided, were the judges of the disability, and the sums allowed, the amount of which was deducted from the existing requisitions made by Congress on the said States.

That since the operation of the present general government, the payment of the Invalids has been assumed by Congress, who have by Law directed, "That the Military pensions which have been granted and paid by the States respectively, in pursuance of the acts of the United States in Congress assembled, to the Invalids who were wounded and disabled during the late war, shall be continued and paid by the United States, from the fourth day of March last, for the space of one year, under such regulations as the President of the United States may direct."

That three laws to this effect have been passed, to wit: on September the 29th 1789—on the 16th of July 1790—and on the 3d of March 1791.[1]

That the lists which have been received at this Office from the States respectively, have been in several instances incorrect and defective, and that subsequent additions have been made to said lists by several of the States.

That these additions are generally of such Invalids as were originally entitled and provided for by the States—But have been either by accident struck off the list, or for the cause herein after enumerated, by State authority, and now replaced by the same authority.

That on the 11th day of June 1788—the then Congress resolved, "That no person shall be entitled to a pension as an invalid, who has not, or shall not before the expiration of six months from this time make application therefor, and produce the requisite evidence to entitle him thereto."[2]

It is evident from the above resolve, that no additional invalid can be admitted in opposition thereto. But it is presumed by the Subscriber, that each State has a right to correct the list, before transmitted to this Office, shewing the evidence whereon such corrections are grounded.

The States of Massachusetts and Pennsylvania, appear to have struck off several invalids from the list, because they refused to do garrison duty—The States had a right to order such duty to be performed, but the right of punishing by striking off the list upon refusal, may be questioned—But the same States have lately upon re-consideration, thought proper to replace several on the list again, from the time they were struck off—It appears that the said two States have been singular in the requisition for garrison duty, and have replaced the invalids on the list on considering the inequality, and hardship of requiring them to perform garrison duty, which they were not required by any other State to perform.

The question now is, shall the general government give validity to this correction of the States to their own acts, by admitting on the list, such invalids as were so struck off?

On this point the Subscriber humbly conceives, there can be no doubt that such invalids ought to be admitted—for by referring to the original establishment for the invalids, it will appear it was intended for their comfort, and as a mark of public gratitude and justice, and not for their oppression.

If therefore any State has acted with severity towards its invalids, and thinks proper of itself to correct its own conduct, every facility should be afforded by the general government in favor of those unfortunate men, whose services to their country have been the cause of the loss of limbs and health, and all the happiness consequent thereon.

The Subscriber therefore submits as a general principle, the propriety of which he has not a doubt—"That the corrections of each State of the list of invalids, residing therein and provided for thereby, conformably to the acts of the United States in Congress assembled prior to the 4th day of March 1789, be received by the Secretary at War, as if such list had been presented perfect in the first instance."[3]

H. Knox
secy of War

DS, DLC:GW; LB, DLC:GW.

1. These laws are printed in 1 *Stat.* 95, 129–30, 218. Henry Knox is quoting from the act of 29 Sept. 1789.

2. This resolution is printed in *JCC*, 34:210.

3. Tobias Lear noted at the bottom of this document: "Approved by the President of the United States 11th August. 1791."

From Edward Church

May it please Your Excelency   Bourdeaux 12th Augst 1791
   Impressed with the warmest gratitude for the honor of being remembered by you in the nomination of Consuls, and no less grateful for the singular favor thereby conferred on myself and family; more particularly in your having proposed an healthful pleasant Country for our residence, which at the same time held out the most flattering prospects of other advantages from the valuable and important exports from the United States of Amca to Bilboa: I made no delay after the receipt of my commission and orders to embark with my family for this port, there being no probable prospect of an opportunity from Savannah of a more direct conveyance.[1] In considering also the multifarious duties of a Consul as prescribed by the Honble the Secretary of State, with other incidental Calls from my fellow Citizens equally obligatory, that wou'd probably frequently have occurred and of course occupied a large portion of my time, and attention, I will own, that my confidence in a competent reward from my Country was greatly confirmed, and was therefore no small additional incitement to my proceeding immediately, and without hesitation with my family, to the place of my destination.
   Finding on our arrival here that the dangerous indisposition of one of my daughters would probably detain me at least a few weeks; and being greatly alarmed by frequent intimations purporting that no Consu⟨ls⟩ from any nation were admitted as such at Bilboa; I wrote to the American Minister at the Court of Madrid for information on this subject, preparatory to the sending forward my Commission to obtain his Catholic Majestys sanction thereto; Mr Carmichael kindly honoured me with an immediate answer, unfortunately confirming the report; Copies of which I have taken the liberty to transmit to your Excellency; and to his Honor, the Secretary of State.[2]
   Still conscious of the favor intended, the disappointment is not more painful to me, than the idea of again presuming to present myself to your Excellency as an humble Petitioner; and the more, lest by seeming to represent an act of benevolence as the cause, though involuntary, of new and aggravated misfortunes, I shou'd appear to be ungrateful; and rather than hazard the possibility of appearing to be guilty of what I most abhor,

I wou'd most assuredly have concealed the most fatal consequences of such an event, provided they wou'd have affected me
alone; but when the fate of a much loved Wife, four daughters,
one Son, and other dependents, hangs on the same thread; I
dare not be governed by my feelings; and therefore consider
myself indissolubly bound to inform your Excellcy, that a compliance with my duty, and a ready obedience to orders, with the
indulgence at the same time of my own inclinations, were the
joint causes of my removal from America; the which decently
to accomplish, with ⟨a⟩ large family, necessarily required such
exertions as have exhausted all my resources; and now, when
arrived at the door, I am not permitted to enter, nor have I the
means remaining to return home; nor object of support left to
invite me thither.

I conceive it as unnecessary, as it wou'd be difficult, to describe
all that I must naturally feel, and fear, upon such an occasion;
but beg leave to hope, if any excuse can possibly be admitted for
presuming to reiterate my application to your Excellency, that it
may be found in the magnitude of the dangers which hang over
me, and in the feelings of a fond Husband, and Father, in such
a critical situation.[3]

With ardent and unremitted prayers for the long continuance
of your life and health, for the publick Weal, I humbly beg leave
to subscribe myself. May It please your Excellency. Your Excellency's ever faithful and most devoted Servant

Edwd Church

ALS, DNA: RG 59, Despatches from Consular Officers: Bilbao.

1. The Senate had confirmed GW's nomination of Edward Church on 17
June 1790, but on arriving in Bordeaux on his way to his new post, Church
learned that foreign consuls were not admitted at Bilbao. Church remained in
Bordeaux and successfully solicited through Congressman Paine Wingate a
consular appointment at Lisbon or Cádiz. GW nominated Church consul at
Lisbon, which the Senate approved on 5 May 1792 (see GW to the U.S. Senate,
3 May 1792, and *Executive Journal*, 1:122).

2. The enclosed copy of William Carmichael's letter of 4 Aug. 1791 to
Church has not been found but was transmitted by Tobias Lear to Thomas
Jefferson on 9 Nov. (DNA: RG 59, Miscellaneous Letters). Church also wrote
a similar appeal to Jefferson this day, enclosing another copy of Carmichael's
letter (*Jefferson Papers*, 22:30–31).

3. Church wrote again to GW from Bordeaux on 8 Sept., sending a duplicate of this letter (DNA: RG 59, Despatches from Consular Officers: Bilbao).

Letter not found: to Timothy Pickering, 12 Aug. 1791. Timothy Pickering wrote to his brother on 12 Aug.: "this day the President sent me a note, desiring to see me" (Upham, *Pickering*, 2:496).

From William Deakins, Jr.

Sir   Geo. Town [Md.] Augt 13: 1791
At the Earnest solicitation of Captain Benja. Ellingwood, I am Induced to take the Liberty to Address you in his favor, he came from Beverley & settled here about two years ago in the Mercantile Line, but finding it Very unprofitable, he wishes to get the Command of one of the Armed Cutters.[1] I beleive him to be a Man of true Honor & great Integrity & well Qualified for such a trust, he served on board the Dean Frigate Capt. Saml Nicholson as Masters Mate, as Early in the War as 1777, after which he took the Command of an Armed Ship belonging to Messrs John & Andrew Cabot in whose employ he Continued untill the End of the Warr.[2] Mr George Cabot, who is well acquainted with Capt. Ellingwood, will give you his Charactor & Qualifications— I hope you Sir, will excuse the Liberty I have taken as it is Meant to serve a good Man. I am with the greatest respect Sir Your Obt Hble Servt

Will. Deakins Junr

ALS, DLC:GW. The cover indicates this letter was sent "By Mr Cabot."
1. Benjamin Ellinwood served under Samuel Nicholson on the Continental frigate *Deane* in 1777 before being commissioned to command the ship *Sebastian* in September 1779 and the brig *Active* in May 1780.
2. Capt. Samuel Nicholson (1743–1811) distinguished himself in the Continental navy during the Revolutionary War and was recommissioned in 1794. In 1798 he was given command of the frigate *Constitution*.

From Thomas Johnson

sir.   Frederick [Md.] 13 August 1791.
This morning I recieved your Letters of the 7th & 8th Instant and one from Mr Jefferson covering my Commission—I forward yours of the 7th and it's Inclosures to Doctr Stuart and Mr Carroll[1]—I am a Stranger to all that they relate to farther than that Mr Peters signed the paper for Cession of Land as Agent or

Attorney for one Mr Douglass who I suppose is the Father or Son but I never heard the least Surmise that it was not effectual to bind the Land.

I feel myself obliged by the Circumstance attending your Appointment of me to Office—it is difficult to restrain warm Expressions—suffice it that your Choice or Earnestness in my Favor shall not be disgraced by the Heart I cannot so well answer for my Head. I am my dear Sir With Truth and Affection Your obliged obedt Servant

Th. Johnson

ALS, DNA: RG 59, Miscellaneous Letters.

1. The letter of Robert Douglas to GW of 15 April was enclosed in GW's letter to Thomas Johnson of 8 August.

Letter not found: to James Craik, 14 Aug. 1791. In a letter to GW of 31 Aug., James Craik referred to GW's letter to him "of the 14th Inst."

To Benjamin Lincoln

(Private)

My dear Sir,   Philadelphia August 14th 1791

As it never has been my intention to bestow double Offices on the same person, and my design that those Marshalls who have received Appointments under the late Revenue Act should hold the former (i.e. the Marshalls office) until the first of the present month (the time by which the Census was to be returned, or until this business should be accomplished) and no longer, it behooves me to look for a successor to Mr Jackson in the Office of Marshall, for the District of Massats.[1]

How beneficial this Office may be, I know not—At present, the mere emolument of it cannot be, I should suppose, an object; but as a step, it may be desired by such as have nothing better in prospect.

The purpose of this letter, my good Sir, is to request the favor of you to discover—first—whether General Cobb would accept of the Appointment—and 2dly, in case he is disinclined to it, if General Brooks would Act in it.[2] I do not incline to issue the Commission to either of them, or to any other on an uncertainty; because, the refusal of Commissions make a bad impression on the public mind. Having observed this, and it occurring to you that the first of August is passed, the expediency of an early answer will readily appear; and I shall be thankful for receiving it accordingly.[3] I am always—and sincerely Your Affectionate

Go: Washington

ALS (photocopy), PU: Armstrong Photostats; LB, DLC:GW.

1. On 14 June Christopher Gore recommended to Tobias Lear Deputy Marshal Samuel Bradford for the post of U.S. marshal for Massachusetts, describing him as "a firm federalist" and "a gentleman of education, improvd by a visit of Several years . . . to most of the civilized parts of Europe." After returning from Europe in 1780, Bradford had established himself as a merchant; commercial misfortunes "deprived him of his estate, but left his honor unsullied—and his character elevated in the minds of even those, who, by being his creditors became involved in his losses." Gore referred Lear to John Jay and William Cushing for additional information and asked him to place Bradford's "character in a favorable light before the illustrious President" (DLC:GW).

2. David Cobb (1748–1830), speaker of the Massachusetts house of representatives from 1789 to 1793, was a surgeon with a Massachusetts regiment before being appointed lieutenant colonel in the Continental army in 1777. Serving to the end of the war, he was brevetted brigadier general in 1783. He served in Congress from 1793 to 1795. John Brooks (1752–1825), a physician from Reading, Mass., led a company of minutemen in April 1775 before being commissioned major and lieutenant colonel in the Continental army in 1776. GW appointed him subinspector under Inspector General Baron von Steuben in 1778, and Brooks resigned in 1783 to resume medical practice in Medford, Massachusetts. On 11 Sept. Lear requested Henry Remsen, Jr., at the State Department to complete a marshal's commission for Brooks and date it 12 Sept. (DNA: RG 59, Miscellaneous Letters), and Lear sent the temporary commission to Brooks on 12 Sept. 1791 (DNA: RG 59, Miscellaneous Letters). GW formally nominated Brooks marshal after the Senate convened (see GW to the U.S. Senate, 31 October). GW appointed him a major general of the U.S. Army in 1792.

3. Lincoln apparently replied to GW on 25 August. See Lincoln to GW, 25 Aug., letter-not-found entry. Lincoln also wrote to Lear sometime in the summer, as Lear transmitted to Alexander Hamilton on 7 Sept. a "letter from Genl Lincoln to T. L. (which has been submitted to the President's inspection) to be laid before the Secretary, as it points to the same subject [uncompensated duties of port inspectors] relative to the Inspector of the port of Boston" (DLC:GW).

To Anthony Whitting

Mr Whiting, Philadelphia August 14th 1791.

From the last letter I have received from my nephew the Major, I presume he is, 'ere this, on his tour to Berkeley; I shall therefore, during his absence, address my letters on matters which relate to my concerns at Mount Vernon, to you.[1] And do request that the weekly reports may be transmitted to me as usual—with such other accounts of your progress in sowing &ca; prospects (with respect to the growing & harvested Crops); and seasonableness of the weather as you may conceive it will be satisfactory for me to be informed of.[2]

From the heat and drought of the Summer, I should conceive that the rare ripe Corn in the Meadow at the Mill, now is, or very soon will be, hard enough to gather. Under this persuation, & that the ground would be better sown with grass-seeds, and would lay more smooth & fit for the scythe thereafter, I suggest it to you (if you find it can be done in time, and with tolerable convenience) to gather the Fodder that is on *that* Corn as soon as possible, & Immediately after doing so, to remove both Corn & stalk, as they are left standing, to the edges of the field, to be there stacked or set on end, if the first (that is the Corn) cannot at that time be taken from the latter (that is the stalk) with safety; and then, with the heavy Oxe Harrow to level the ground before it is sown with grass-seeds. My reasons for desiring that both Corn & stalks may be taken off together are, first, because if the Corn is not sufficiently hard & dry when this happens, their will be nutriment sufficient in the stalks to effect it, without suffering it to dry too fast—and 2dly because by such removal the ground may be laid perfectly level, & freed from every thing that will incommode the sowing of the Seed, and the cutting of the grass, thereafter. Do not suffer it to escape you, that the grass-seeds in that meadow ought by all means to be sown by, or before the end of this month, that the plants may be up and obtain strength before Winter; Other wise, the ground being low and apt to heave, they might perish in the course of the Winter by the wet & frosts.

It is my earnest wish (as I presume you have already been informed by the Major) that all my Grain & grass-seeds intended for Autumn sowing should now be got into the ground as soon as possible. I am fully satisfied that every moment this business is delayed after the present period, will prove injurious to the ensuing Crop; especially in ground that is not highly manured—or which is not fresh—or naturally very strong. I shall readily grant that where there is but little to sow, the temperature of the weather and state of the ground may be consulted; but where much is to be put in, the season, be the weather as it may, ought not to be slipped. Besides, as the weather has been dry hitherto, the probability of a wet autumn is the greater.

If the Major did not engage an Overseer for Dogue run before he left home, it wd be proper for you to do it, in case one should offer in his absence who can be well recommended. A Man having a wife with a small family would be prefered either to a single man, or one with a large family. The Major has informed me of the terms on which he proposes to agree, & I agree to them.[3] I am of opinion if the old house on No. 2 at that Plantation cannot be made to answer for the accomodation of the Overseer, that the one at the Mansion house (commonly called Richards, which originally came from that place) should be carried back, & fixed on the spot marked for it by the Major. The materials of this House are good, & the house itself is of sufficient size, & can be removed with much more ease than the frame of a new one can be got. It is of no use where it is, & must soon go to decay without an Inhabitant; a removal of it therefore is proper, & desirable in any point of view. A Brick chimney must be put to it after it gets to Dogue run instead of the wood one it now has; and when undertaken, a Bricklayer more skilful than Tom Davis must assist him and Muclus in the erection of it.[4]

When Davis goes about the other Wing of the Green house, direct him to be careful that the ground is truly leveled, and to see also that the joints of the new and old brick work range exactly; and moreover, that the walls are carried to the same height at both ends, and are extend to the Garden Gate; into the Jamb of which the end wall is to be worked.

If Will is not likely to provide Shoes enough for the Negros in due Season, aid must be had elsewhere; and I desire, if the clover which was sown with the Wheat at the Mansion house is not sufficiently thick on the ground, that you will not spare seed in making good the dificency.

I perceive by the last report which has been received, that

Wheat has been tread out in a yard at the Ferry; where a good Barn floor is, I did not expect this would be the case—& I perceive also that Harrows have been carried to Mr Lund Washington's Smith—this ought not to be—nothing should go there that my own Smiths can do—and for Harrows, I should suppose they are competent.

How is your Wheaten crop likely to turn out? Is the 335 bushls as reported to have been deposited in the Grainery at the Ferry & French's, all that was made at those Plantations? If so, the Crop must be short indeed. I am Your friend &ca

Go: Washington

P.S. In the body of this letter I mentioned getting Fodder in the Mill meadow *only* for the reason assigned—but it is of most essential importance, considering the scarcity of Hay, that the whole of it should be got in the greenest & most perfect state possible, without injuring the Corn.

ADfS, ViMtV.

1. For GW's nephew and his trip to Berkeley Springs, see George Augustine Washington to GW, 1 Aug. and note 8.

2. Anthony Whitting sent GW on 29 Aug. a farm report for the preceding week, but neither cover letter nor report has been found. The earliest surviving farm report in Whitting's hand is for 11–17 Sept. 1791, which appears in CD-ROM:GW.

3. On 23 Aug. George A. Washington signed an agreement (witnessed by Whitting) with Henry Jones to act as overseer at Dogue Run for a one-year term beginning 25 Dec., during which Jones would "conduct himself with the utmost Industry Sobriety and Honesty. That he will (when not necessarily called off for other purposes) be constantly with some part or other of his people at their work. as the said President conceives that is the only means of getting work done, and well done, and this too in piece and quietness and to the satisfaction of all concern'd and this his great Object of procuring and Overseer. The said Henry Jones doth further promise and agree that he will not absent himself from said plantation without permission. That he will strickly and indefatigably pursue the plans and obey the orders which he shall receive from the said President or those who manage for him for conducting the business of said plantation. That he will be very particularly attentive to the Stock of every kind not only seeing that they are properly fed but properly Sheltered. and in a particular manner will attend to the plow Horses and working Oxen to see that their allowance is given them in due season and without embezzlement or waste. That he will take a regular account of all Tools of every kind and plantation Utensils and see them forth coming where called for and that the latter are not unnecessarily exposed to the weather—That he will discourage company from resorting to the plantation unless it may be his

relation now and then and will prevent all gunning and fowling within his inclosures, that he will be particularly attentive to the fences of the several Inclosures especially those of the out lines suffering no Stock but his own to be within them—nor his own to be in any Inclosure but such as are allotted for them. That he will provide in due Season meal for the Negroes and see it regular delvered to them and also that they have (if Butter is made) the butter milk after the milk is churned—and when Occation requires it for sick persons or Negro children, that they more over have Sweet milk given them—That he will be very careful of the Negroes in Sickness—that he will repair his plows, Gates and other things when they riquire it, in the best manner he is capable and to avoid further enumeration it is expected that he is to perform every thing within the compass of his power that will most condue to the Interest of his implower—and to sum up the whole that he will act the part of an honest Sober and industrious man—And in failure of either that the said President or his Agent may discharge him at any Season of the Year." Jones's wages would be £30 Virginia currency paid at the end of the year, and he also would receive 300 pounds of fresh pork, 200 pounds of beef, 100 pounds of flour, five barrels of corn, the use of a milk cow, and the privilege of raising fowl for his own consumption (DLC:GW).

4. The plan to move this house was not carried out, and a new one was built at Dogue Run instead. See GW to Whitting, 29 August. Muclus (Mucles) was one of GW's slaves at Mansion House farm who worked as a bricklayer. GW apparently was later provoked to threaten to place Muclus "under one of the Overseers as a common hoe negro" (GW to Whitting, 19 May 1793; see also GW to Whitting, 4 Nov. 1792, 2 June 1793).

Letter not found: from Daniel Carroll, 15 Aug. 1791. Thomas Jefferson wrote to the commissioners for the federal district on 28 Aug.: "Your joint letter of the 2d. inst. to the President, as also Mr. Carrol's separate letters of the 5th. and 15th. have been duly received" (*Jefferson Papers*, 22:88–89).[1]

1. The letters from Daniel Carroll were almost certainly addressed to GW. See Carroll to GW, 5 Aug. (letter-not-found entry), n.1.

From Alexander Hamilton

Treasury Department [Philadelphia] 15 August 1791. Communicates a letter from the superintendent of lighthouses in South Carolina, "by which it appears that the Lantern Story and all the wooden work of the Light house in that state have lately been consumed by fire," with two proposals for rebuilding the lighthouse, the more favorable one from Conrad Hook & John Naverson, the terms of which, "Upon enquiry into the expence attending a similar repair in the Case of the Light house at Cape Henlopen, & making due allowance for local differences (so far as there are materials for comparison) . . . do not appear extravagant," and concludes: "as great inconveniencies may result from delay, it is respectfully submitted as not inconsistent with the interests of the United States to authorise the acceptance of the contract proposed by them."[1]

LB, DLC:GW.
    1. Alexander Hamilton wrote again to GW this day, submitting a proposal made to Hollingsby by Robert McMahin for plastering or "rough casting" it (DLC:GW). Tobias Lear replied to Hamilton this day, indicating GW's approval of the contracts for carpentry and plaster work (DLC:GW).

From Henry Knox

Sir   [Philadelphia] August 15th 1791
    I have traced the report relative to the powder to its fountain head. At present it has rather the complexion of rivalship in Trade. The persons who have originated the Report, own powder Mills, and are of opinion that Jacob Lush who works for them, makes better powder than Jacob Keyser, who works for Joseph Miller from whom the powder in question was Obtained.[1]
    I shall however tomorrow, have Miller's powder proved by the method least liable to error, and report to you the result. In the meantime I have not much doubt of its goodness. I have the honor sir to be with perfect respect Your humble Servant
                                                                    H. Knox

ALS, DLC:GW; LB, DLC:GW.
    1. The War Department had contracted with Joseph Miller (1757–1825) of Germantown, Pa., to supply the army with gunpowder. Jacob Losch operated a powder mill on Mill Creek in Lower Merion, Philadelphia County, during the Revolutionary War. Thomas Roberts revived Losch's mill after the war, and it continued to operate under different owners until destroyed by an explosion in 1792.

From Elhanan Winchester

Dear and most renowned of men,   London August 15. 1791.
    I send you with this a sett of my Lectures upon the prophecies that remain to be fulfilled; which I present to you as a small

token of that sincere respect which I, among many millions of the human race, feel towards the deliverer of my Country, and the friend of mankind. I have mentioned your name and Character with the highest respect in this work (see vol. IV. page 390) in a connexion that will be no disgrace to your very exalted merit.[1]

It has pleased the Great Supreme, the Sovereign of the Universe, to raise you to the greatest dignity that any Man on earth enjoys at present; the happiness of presiding over a free and united people, the object of their free unbiased Choice. you do not only preside over them, but like him whom you so much resemble, you rule in their hearts, and feel in yourself the sublime pleasure of making a considerable portion of mankind happy.

I believe firmly that the blessed period will at last arrive when the glorious Redeemer shall subdue, humble and restore all his Creatures; when every knee shall bow to him, and every tongue shall swear allegiance to his name and Government and confess him to be Lord, to the Glory of God the Father. When the morning Stars shall sing together, and all the sons of God shall shout for joy! When the Whole Creation shall be delivered from the bondage of Corruption, into the glorious liberty of the Children of God. These are the sentiments which you will find dispersed in the volumes before you; they have been well received in this Country, and I hope will not be altogether unacceptable in my native Land.

May the blessings of God attend you all your days, and when you shall be called to depart from this mortal stage, whereon you have acted such a glorious and conspicuous part, may you have the Approbation of the Great Judge of all, and in the bright and blooming morning of the resurrection be raised in the likeness of your Saviour, and receive from his hand a Crown of righteousness, life, and Glory, which shall never fade away.[2] This is, Most Respected Sir, the sincere wish, of your most Humble servant

Elhanan Winchester.

ALS, DLC:GW.

Elhanan Winchester (1751–1797), a native of Brookline, Mass., was a principal founder of the Universalist Church in the United States. In 1780 he became pastor of the First Baptist Church in Philadelphia. Winchester left Philadelphia in 1787 to preach in London, where he published a number of widely read theological works and edited the *Philadelphian Magazine* before his return to America in 1794.

1. The accompanying four octavo volumes of Winchester's *A Course of Lectures on the Prophecies That Remain to Be Fulfilled* (London, 1789) were in GW's library at his death (Griffin, *Boston Athenæum Washington Collection*, 502). Winchester's citation compared GW's relinquishment of military command to the voluntary recession of power made by Joseph the Patriarch and to be made by Jesus Christ at his Second Coming.

2. Tobias Lear conveyed to Winchester on 14 Nov. GW's "best thanks for your polite attention in sending these volumes to him" (DLC:GW).

To Arthur Young

Sir,   Philadelphia August 15th 1791.

That I may not be thought inattentive to your favor of the 25th of Jany—which came to my hands about ten days ago only—I avail myself of the first Packet since the receipt of it to inform you that the Annals, and Chicorium Intybus have got safe to my hands. A set of the former I have presented in your name, agreeably to your request, to the Agricultural Society in this City.[1] For the other sett; for the Seeds; and for the manufactured Wool from the fleece 1 sent you, I pray you to accept my best thanks.

With astonishment hardly to be conceived, I read in No. 86 of your Annals, the account of the taxes with which you are burthened. Had the account come from dubitable authority, the reality of such a tax would not only have been questioned but *absolutely* disbeleived; for I can assure you, Sir, that there is nothing in this Country that has the semblance of it.

I do not, however, mean to dwell on this, or any other part of your letter at this time—the purpose of my writing to you now, is to acknowledge the receipt of the things you had the goodness to send me—and to assure you, that with great pleasure I will forward, in a short time, such information with respect to the prices of Lands, Stock, Grain—amount of taxes &ca, &ca as will enable you to form a pretty accurate idea of the present state and future prospects of this Country.[2]

In the meanwhile, I believe I may confidently add—that although our Agriculture, Manufactures & Commerce are progressing; although our taxes are light; although our laws are in a fair way of being administered well, and our liberties & properties secured on a solid basis by the general Government having acquired more & more consistency, strength and respectability as it moves on; yet, that no Material change in the prices of the above articles has taken place, except in a few instances of Land, under peculiar advantages; nor is it probable there will be in the latter whilst there is such an immense territory back of us for the people to resort to. In a word, Sir, when you come to receive full answers to your several enquiries, I am inclined to believe that you will not be unfavorably impressed, or think an establishment in the United States ineligible to those whose views are extended beyond the limits of their own Country.

Having closed my corrispondence with Wakelin Welch Esqr. & Son—I have to request that your communications to me in future may pass through the hands of Mr Johnson—Consul for the United States in London.[3] With best wishes, and sentiments of much esteem I am—Sir Your most Obedient and very Hble Servt

Go: Washington

ALS, PPRF; LB, DLC:GW.

1. Upon receiving Arthur Young's package, GW wrote Samuel Powel, president of the Philadelphia Society for Promoting Agriculture, on 2 Aug., quoting from Young's letter of 25 Jan.: "You will receive the Annals continued, two setts: one of which I take the liberty of requesting your presenting to the Agriculture Society as before." GW sent numbers 61 through 86 of Young's *Annals of Agriculture* with the request that Powel present them to the society (AL, ViMtV). For GW's presentation of previous volumes of the *Annals* to the Philadelphia society, see GW to Powel, 30 June 1787 and note 2.

2. GW apparently discussed with Thomas Jefferson Young's request of 25 Jan. "for a few particulars of general guidance" for his son, "who urges me to let him try a plough in America." Jefferson sent to GW on 3 Aug. two pages of notes on central Virginia soil conditions, labor costs, and prices of agricultural products, "as he supposes will be interesting to Mr Young, so far as he is enabled to do it with some degree of certainty" (DLC:GW). GW forwarded a copy of Jefferson's notes in this or a later letter to Young and probably used them as the basis of queries in a circular letter of 25 Aug. that he sent to several gentlemen of the mid-Atlantic states with the intention of securing more complete favorable information about American agriculture for the English agriculturalist. See also "Notes on Virginia Lands," 3 Aug. 1791, in *Jefferson Papers*, 20:716–17, and GW to Young, 5 December.

3. The last extant letter of Wakelin Welch & Son to GW, dated 6 May, transmitted to GW Young's letter of 25 Jan. and its accompanying package.

Letters not found: from James Seagrove, 16 Aug. 1791. GW wrote to Seagrove on 14 Sept. of "Three letters of yours—two bearing the 16th and other the 25. of August."

From Henry Knox

War Department [Philadelphia,] 17th August 1791.

The Secretary of War having examined the Report of Colonel Timothy Pickering, Commissioner at a late Council or treaty of the five Nations of Indians, so called, at Tioga Point—humbly Reports to the President of the United States:

That the main object of the said Council was to conciliate the said Indians, to prevent their listening to the invitations of the western hostile Indians, by withdrawing them to a greater distance from the theatre of the war, and to fix their minds, particularly of their idle young men, upon some important object, which by employing them for a critical period, would render them less liable to the temptations of committing depredations.

That from the proceedings it appears, that the Commissioner has with great ability and judgment, carried into effect the objects of his appointment, by cementing the friendships between the United States and the said Indians; and it is to be expected the good effects flowing from this Council, will be hereafter manifestly conspicuous.[1]

But it is to be exceedingly regretted that his desire to accord to the wishes of the Indians, led him to confirm a lease of certain lands belonging to the Cayuga Nation of Indians, to John Richardson. This measure was entirely unauthorized by his instructions, is contrary to the constitution and laws of New York, and to the constitution and laws of the United States.

That the State of New York possesses the undoubted right of pre-emption to the lands of the Cayugas, and that this right embraces every possible modification of said lands, with the concurrence of the United States, whether by sale, lease or otherwise.

That it is also to be regretted, that the Commissioner did not obtain and keep a copy of the instrument of the lease of the Cayuga lands, and his ratification thereof; neither of which are among his papers, or in his possession as he has informed the subscriber.

That the effect of the confirmation to Allan's children is the same as that of the Cayuga lands, although it is presumed the right of pre-emption has been conveyed by the State of Massachusetts to an individual.[2]

The subscriber humbly conceives that it would be proper, in order to avert any evil consequences which might arise upon this subject, to transmit an extract of his proceedings relative thereto, to the Governor of the State of New York, and to disavow explicitly the said transaction as being founded in error; unless it should be judgment of the said State, to avail itself of any benefit that may arise therefrom.

That if this should be the case, which however must be entirely optional with the said State, it would have the effect to keep the said Indians tranquil, by preventing that confusion which must arise in their minds from the disavowal of a transaction formally concluded at a public treaty.

That the letter which accompanies this report is submitted, as proper to be transmitted to the Governor of New York, on the occasion.[3]

H. Knox
secy of war

LS, DLC:GW; LB, DLC:GW.

1. Timothy Pickering met with the Iroquois in early July near Newtown (Elmira), N.Y., not far from Tioga, Pa., after waiting three weeks for the Indians to assemble. He estimated that nearly one thousand were present when the council officially opened on 2 July. Quickly concluding that reports that the Six Nations were preparing for war had been greatly exaggerated, Pickering spent much of the council assuring the assembled chiefs of the peaceful intentions of the U.S. government and urging them to encourage their people to adopt a sedentary agricultural life. Pickering's efforts to persuade the Indians to abandon their traditional culture were met with resistance from the Seneca chief Red Jacket that threatened to undermine the treaty conference. Pickering's journal of the affair is in MHi: Pickering Papers. The papers he sent to GW arrived shortly after the conclusion of the council on 17 July, and Tobias Lear forwarded them on 25 July to clerk John Vanderbrock at the War Department with GW's wish to see Henry Knox about them as soon as Knox returned from New York (DLC:GW).

2. At the final session of the treaty council, some Seneca chiefs asked Pickering to confirm officially the legitimacy of two land cessions they wished to make to John Richardson and to the two daughters of Ebenezer Allen, who had married a Seneca. Pickering had opened the council with the assurance that

under federal law the Indians could dispose of their lands as they wished. As he wrote Knox on 16 Aug. that refusal to accede to them in these cases "would lead them to think that the solemn assurances of the President were made but to amuse & deceive them" (MHi: Pickering Papers), Pickering certified the Richardson grant but objected to the original size of the Allen grant. Under pressure from the chiefs, Pickering reluctantly accepted a smaller grant of some four square miles.

3. Knox's enclosed letter of this day to Gov. George Clinton of New York covered an extract of Pickering's report to GW and noted: "It appears that the Commissioner's desire to accomplish the objects of his commission in the greatest degree, has led him incautiously, at the earnest request of the Cayugas present to ratify and confirm a certain lease of lands belonging to the Cayuga nation of indians, to John Richardson, and to certify that a certain assignment of the Seneka indians to the daughters of Ebenezer Allan was done at a public treaty, held under the authority of the United States. No copies however of either instruments have been retained or produced by the said Commissioner. The right of the State of New York to the pre emption of the Cayuga lands is unquestioned, and also that the said right embraces all possible alienations of said lands by the Indians with the concurrence of the United States according to the Constitution and Laws. Therefore I do by the command of the President of the United States, hereby transmit to your Excellency an explicit disavowal of the conduct of the said Commissioner, relative to the said lease of the Cayuga lands to John Richardson; and also of the Certificate relative to the Senekas assignment of lands to the children of Ebenezer Allan—and I am further ordered to inform your Excellency, that the said acts of the said Commissioner were unauthorized by his instructions, and will be considered as entirely null and void by the United States. But if however the State of New York should judge that it would derive any benefit from the due execution of said lease, the executive authority of the United States will do every thing which may be proper upon the occasion. Colonel Pickering who is going to New York, will personally wait upon your Excellency to give you any further explanation which you may request" (DLC:GW). Lear informed Knox this day that the letter met GW's approbation and that GW requested it be forwarded without delay to Clinton (DLC:GW), who received it before his meeting with Pickering in New York. See Pickering to GW, 27 Aug. 1791.

Letter not found: from Rodolf Vall-travers, 17 Aug. 1791. Vall-travers described to GW on 30 Nov. his letter to GW of "Augt 17" from Rotterdam "by Captn Wm Callahan."[1]

1. Vall-travers noted that Callahan's vessel, the *Pringle,* was "bound for Charlestown; charged with a Packet for my old Friend, H. Laurence, Esqre containing Proposals for the Congress, & for several patriotic Societies established at Charlston, Newbern, Cambridge" (Vall-travers to GW, 30 Nov., DNA: RG 59, Miscellaneous Letters). See also Vall-travers to GW, 21 July, n.5.

From Charles Pinckney

(Duplicate)

Dear Sir   Charleston [S.C.] 18th August 1791.

I am much pleased to find by our last vessels from Philadelphia that you are safely arrived & escaped the dangers which might have been expected from a tour of such length & at so hot a season—hearing after you left us that it was your intention to have taken Ninety Six in your Route from Augusta & that you could not be at Columbia before the 25th I postponed setting out for that place until the twenty first & arrived there the morning after you left it—I regretted very much missing you by a single day as it was my wish to have seen you there & to have accompanied you to Camden—I hope you found Mrs Washington & your friends well & that your tour has given you a favorable opinion of the States you have passed through.

Mr Rutledge our Chief Justice was extremely sorry that from the necessary avocations of his Office he was absent—I once took the liberty of mentioning to you our wish that his vacancy might be filled up by some Gentleman from this State but as there does not appear a disposition in those Gentlemen whom you have been the best acquainted with to accept—& as my having mentioned it may perhaps be in some measure the means of your wish to confine it to this State—it is proper in me to say that I am sure any Gentleman that may be appointed from either of the Southern States will be perfectly agreeable to us.[1]

The Excise Law has at length began to operate—The interior parts of the Country are in a great degree at present opposed to it but when they reflect how necessary it was for Congress after having assumed the State debts to provide every mode in their power which would enable them to avoid direct taxation & how advantageously this tax must operate in favour of this State as the northern States will pay infinitely more towards it than we shall I trust their fears will be quieted & they will consider it as an unavoidable measure.

The great misfortune of this country & indeed of every part of the United States at this time is the Depreciation of property arising from the too great scarcity of a circulating medium—the Establishment of a national Bank & the consequent increase of money arising from the circulation of their Bills will I hope remove this inconvenience—the Objections on account of its unconstitutionality being done away I apprehend the evils which were feared from it to the agricultural interest will be discovered to have been visionary & that it will be found our Commerce & Agriculture are happily so firmly united that an Institution which is of service to the one can never fail to encourage & indeed to promote the other—I wish sincerely that this City may have a Bran⟨ch⟩ of it—in point of Commercial consequence it certainly is entitled to one for I believe with respect to the Sterling value of our own productions this State will in all probability have a right to be considered among the first in the Union—perhaps the very first.[2]

I have already I believe personally mentioned the great inconvenience the people of this & the neighbouring State labour under in having so near a receptacle for their fugitive Offenders, Debtors, & even Slaves at St Augustine—the great number of people some of them of large fortunes who have secretly removed themselves to that place with their properties—the number of Negroes who have been countenanced there & the ready Asylum which it affords to those who fly from the public Justice of their Country render it particularly injurious to the States which are near it.[3]

Conceiving it to be of great importance that an attempt should be made to put a Stop to so growing an evil—the Attorney General of this State has had a Bill of Indictment found against two very notorious Offenders who have taken refuge there & officially applied to me to make a demand for their delivery in order that they may be brought to trial here—In consequence thereof I have transmitted to the Attorney General a copy of the inclosed Letter for the purpose of being sent to St Augustine[4]—I do not suppose the Governour will consider himself authorised to deliver the fugitives; but it may in its event be useful by leading to the establishment of instructions which may authorise him in future to do so & may hold out an idea to offenders that the justice of their Country will pursue them as far as it possibly can.

I inclose you a Copy of a Proclamation of the Governour of East Florida & as the arrival of a Spanish Minister, at Philadelphia makes it probable that some arrangements may be established between the United States & the Court of Spain I thought this the proper time to make the communications I have the honour to submit.[5]

I shall certainly attend to your request respecting the plants & seeds you wish sent from hence at the proper season & have the Honour to remain with esteem & regard Dear Sir much obliged yours truly

Charles Pinckney

ALS, DNA: RG 59, Miscellaneous Despatches, Duplicate Despatches; ALS, DNA: RG 59, Miscellaneous Letters. The text is taken from the duplicate as the original receiver's copy is too faded to read.

1. Charles Pinckney had urged GW on 8 Mar. to appoint a South Carolinian to the vacancy created on the U.S. Supreme Court by the resignation of John Rutledge, Sr., on 5 March.

2. Under the leadership of William Loughton Smith, leading citizens of Charleston obtained pledges to purchase between 650 and 1,000 shares in the Bank of the United States with the explicit purpose of having a branch located there. The directors in Philadelphia voted in November to establish branches in New York City, Boston, Baltimore, and Charleston.

3. For efforts to resolve the American fugitive slave and refugee criminal and debtor problems in Spanish Florida, see Thomas Jefferson to GW, 2 April, and GW to James Seagrove, 20 May.

4. A copy of Pinckney's enclosed letter to Governor Juan Nepomuceno de Quesada of this day is in DNA: RG 59, Miscellaneous Letters. GW apparently referred it with its covering letter to Jefferson, who reported on 7 Nov. (*Jefferson Papers*, 22:266–68).

5. The enclosure, which has not been found, was probably a copy of Quesada's proclamation of 20 Nov. 1790 outlining terms under which settlers might take up land in Florida.

To William Tilghman

Sir,   Philadelphia August 18th 1791.

Your favor of the 14th Ulto came duly to hand—but a confinement of some weeks, and much business since, has prevented my acknowledging the receipt of it until now.[1]

It has not appeared from any Papers I have yet seen that the settlement which seems to have taken place between Messrs Chalmers & George was ever communicated to Mr West. To me it never was. I will, however, again write to the Gentleman who has them in keeping to make a further search, and as soon as his answer is received I will trouble you with another letter on this subject.[2]

In the meanwhile, I offer you my thanks for the trouble this business must have given you & for the assurance of your readiness to prosecute it further. I am—Sir Yr Most Obedt Hble Servt

Go: Washington

ALS, RPJCB; LB, DLC:GW.

1. For background to this letter, see GW to William Tilghman, 3 April. For the recent illness of GW, see A. Hammond to GW, 8 July, n.3, and GW to William Moultrie, 9 August.

2. GW sent attorney James Keith on 19 Aug. a copy of Tilghman's letter of 14 July, writing: "You will perceive by the enclosed letter how the matter stands between the Executors of Colonel Thomas Colvill and Mr Sydney George. If you think it will be of any avail to make further research among the papers of the deceased Mr West for an entry of this transaction—or, to prosecute any new enquiry of his Son respecting it, I would thank you for so doing. At any rate please to advise the steps you think I had best pursue to bring this *particular* matter to a close—and to inform me whether a judgment has been obtained against the Assignees of Semple upon their bond? In that case, whether for principal and interest or principal only? and, when you think I shall be able to close my administration of that estate, it being a matter I am exceedingly anxious to effect" (LB, DLC:GW). No reply from Keith has been found, and when GW wrote Tilghman on 21 July 1793 he did not mention the Colvill estate. In his reply of 25 July to that letter, however, Tilghman wrote GW that Sydney George, Jr., had promised to pay his outstanding bond to John West out of the proceeds of his present crop of tobacco, provided that GW would indemnify him for the payments. See also Tilghman to GW, 16 Aug. 1793.

From Pierre-Charles L'Enfant

Ser   [Georgetown, Md., 19 August 1791]

The heigest of my embition Gratified in having met with your approbation in the project of the Plan which I have now the Honor of presenting to you altered agreeable to your direction, Steel leaving me some thing to wish for until I see the execution of that plan effected to the full attainement of your object.[1]

I shall here beg the permission of fixing for a moment your attention on matter which I conceive of most Importance to the advancement of the business.

The Inspection of the anexced map of doted lines being sufficiently explanatory of the progress made in the work will I hope leave you satisfied how much more has been done than may have been expected from hands less desirous of meriting your applause and I shall confire on this subject with express the obligation I feel to be under for the frindly assistance given me by Mr Ellicott—& to request if circumstances may admit of a delay in the procecution of business he his charged with on the frontier of Georgia that his going there be differed until the latter end of november next, his assistance till then being most Indispensable to compleat the work begone as is necessary to have a number of lots for Houses measured and marked before the time when the first sale is Intended.[2]

this business has proved more tedious than at first considered owing to the multiplicity of operations Indispensable to determine the accute angles & intersect lines with exactness on points given at great distances in which process much difficulties was encountered on account of the great encumbering of timber cut down in every direction, the which the proprietor are avare to preserve and unwilling to remove and most consequently Increase obstacles in the way to a degree as I am well convinced will in the end cause me the regret of falling much short from what I proposed and what is indeed most essentiel to performe previous a sale take place.

brought to the point as matter do now stand enough is done to satisfy every one of an Eanerstedness in the process of execution—and the spots assigned for the Federal House & for the President palace in exibiting the most sumpteous aspect and claiming already the suffrage of a croid of daily visitor both natives & foreigners will serve to give a grand Idea of the whole, but nevertheless it is to be wished more may be done to favour a sale—this being to serve very little towards evidencing the beauties of local[e] reserved for privat setlements all being absolutly lost in the chaos of pulled timber without possibility to juge of the advantages of relative convenincy much less of agreement, to be derived from Improvements Intended in a surrounding local[e] of which but few can form an Idea iven after Inspecting a map.

the grand avenu connecting both the palace & the federal House will be most magnificent and most convenient—the streets runing west of the upper squar of the federal House and which terminate in an easy slope on the canal through the tiber which it will over look for the space of above tow mile will be beautifull above what may be Imagined—those other streets parallel to that canal, those crossing over it and which are at many avenus to the grand walk from the water cascade under the federal House to the president park and dependincy extending to the ban⟨k⟩ of the potomac, and also the severals squar or area such as are Intended for the Judiciary court—the national bank—the grand church—the play House, market & exchange—all through will offer a variety of situations unparalleled in point of beauties—suitable to every purpose and in every point convenient both are devised for the first ofset of the city and combined to command the height price in a sale.

but as I observed before these advantages lost in the present encumbering of the local and not being possible to be made perceptible within the short period left—A sale at a moment so premature will not bring the ten part of what it will at some more suitable season after a rough-hewn of the proposed Improvements may help to the better appreciating the merits of situation.

besides a sale made previous the general plan of distribution of the city is made publique and befor the circumstance of that sale taking place has had time to be know through the whole continent, will not call a sufficient concurence and most be confined to few individuals speculating wanting means or Inclination to Improve and the consequence of a low sale in this first Instance may prove Injurious to the subsequent ones by serving as precedents to under valu the remaining lots at so much less in proportion to the lessening of advantage of situation—on an other part I apprehend the under saling of lots far from prompting a speedy settlement and as many people argue of gaining frind to the Establishment in Inducing Influencial men in those states as may continue opposed to it to become Interested in the succes—will rather disgrace the whole business.

it will I am convinced favour schems already encouraged in consequence of the mediocrity of the deposit required—it will favour the ploting of a number of designing men whom In Georgetown in particular are more active than ever and use of every means to set themselves in a situation to cross the opperation of the plan adopted—and whom in concert with society forming in baltimor and in other places unfrindly promise to engross the most of the sale and master the whole business.[3]

with these apprehension and seeing on an other part nothing to be gained from a sale which at best if taking place this season will only be making the transfer of a most valuable property in to the hand of speculator without a prospect even of deriving from it a mean for to engage with any security in the Intended work to whose first demand a Fund resting on the produce of a deposit most prove inadequate.

I conceive the postponing of that Sale a measure which will be both expedient and advantageous to the business—as it is constant but people realy Inclined to purchase and earnestly disposed to erect Houses will not be on this account dissuaded from their coming on the spot tho' for the Instant disappoint⟨ed⟩ in the object giving them a better Idea of the local[e] woud I presum rather serve to prompt them to greater Exertion and the Idea which they will carry back most greatly serve to Influence other to come and to Increase a competition for lots at the time when the sale may be put off.[4]

this measure in some respect forced by circumstances may I presum take place consistantly by alleging the fact of an Impossibility of having matter ready for it—owing to the necessity of taking the previous and necessary steps of making an Equal division of property betwixt the Individual owner and the publique.

The Impossibility of doing this will not only result from the difficulties encontered in the mesuration of lots but will most evidently from a circumstance not yet mentioned of the proprieter of territory having not returned the survey of ther possession as was repeatedly required of them and which they declined to do until disputs arrosed amongst them respecting to boundary are setled. this not likely to be so soon done most preclud for some time From making the necessary division of property and will prevent the devising of a mode to effect that of those lots which will be found laid across the lines of tow or three different territory which most be frequent on account of the bifarous way the whole property is Intermingled.

Convinced no time will be found lost for to procure the necessary accomodation for congress my Intimacy with plans already forming relating to Establishment on the Eastern branch— on the proposed canal and in various other parts made me not

Esitate in ascerting that settlements will soon be spread through—provided a due attention is given to the carrying on & speedily in every part those Improvements as are combined for the convenance and agreableness of the most distant situation as they are meant to had to the sumptousness of the more centrals. when I observe—provided a due attention is given it is becaus notwithstanding I Indulge the Idea of seeing soon the progress of the Establishment become the wonder of all, I am sensible of the consequences of a ⟨scheck⟩ its progress may receive and am well persuaded that Individuals exertions will wait the signal and model thier process on the sperit with the which the publick business shall be conducted.

it being therefore essential to be begin well and with an assurance of continuing with a progressive degree of activity to the end—considering that a relaxation of motion would greatly more Injure the business than will a delay in mouving I to this effect—under the Head of publick Exertions conceive it Important not to confine the Idea to the erecting of a congress House & a presidial palace other exertions being necessary to prompt and encourage private undertaking.

them alone can form the establishment enswerable to its objects, and to rise the city a city in fact it is Indispensable to consider Every of the Improvements proposed in the plan as being part most essential to the framing of the principal and how ever differential & unconected as they may appear to effect them at a same time and with a proportional degree of dispatch.

it is most Essential to push with the utmost activity Every Improvement as may serve to marcantile Interest. the canal through the tiber a cross to the eastern branch were an aditional branch of it is marked in the plan, is of absolut necessity to determine and Insure a speedy settlement in that part were it is most desirable to help the conveying of material to the tow grand Edifice.

the making of the publick walk from under the federal House as far as it is carried on the potomac and connected with the palace is an objet which so ever trivial as it may appear to the ayes of many will be productive of as much advantage as the first mentioned objects in giving to the city as its first offset a superiority of agr⟨eem⟩ents over most of the city of the world as it will gaine one over them all in point of convenience of dist-

ribution after bringing the various Squar or area to thier Intended Shape and giving aregular and well combined slop to
and leveling every grand avenu and principals streets—begining with the most transversal and were settlements are most
essential—not however ending them were house end but Indescriminatly Extending those Improvements all over accellerating
them on those parts the less attractive to prompt seltements
thereon. no need being of hastening to encourage them on more
advantageous situation the which it may be well to preserve until
the great rise of thier value make it worth the sacrifice.

these Idea already held to your consideration and the which
met your approval at the first begining of the business—having
directed my attention in devising a plan of distribution of local[e] as I conceived to be the best calculated to this effect, made
me consider an appropriation of the several squar as ⟨are⟩ proposed in the plan to be alloted to each of the Individual states
as also the making of a free donation to Every particular religious society of a ground for House of worship a mode from
which Infinit advantages most result.

each of those Establishments tho' probably small at first being
Equally distenced and near situated will by a gradual accroissement soon connect and will from their begining forme a chaine
of Improvements round the principal part of the city which will
extand by a scatering of settlements all along of those transversal
and divergent avenues were none of them will be lost nor will be
to distant from the federal House or the president palace.

Betwixt these tow Edifices in the streets from the grand avenu
to the palace toward the canal there will be a proper stand for
shop—for mechanique and every people in various business,
and the stimulate to builth houses in those part being so great
it is not to be doubted but they will be erected contigeous to each
other and in a short time will increase to a number sufficient to
afford a convenience in the Intercourse of business and to procur proper accomodation to congress member and every officers & other people attach to the Executive.

a marche so wholy different from the ordinary way of forming
a town it is presumable will meet with oposer and be much objected by people who will compute the accroissement of towns
existing and draw Inference from them in concluding aginst the
plan I propose.

it will also, as far as, it may affect speculation on publick property incite many to disclaime against, but upon the whole every objection as may tend to a contraction of the operation of the sisteme most likly to arrise from people Interested in lowering the value of property or perhaps ⟨led⟩ from motives whose good Intent to the whole business may be questioned, I am in hope people actuated from more Independant principle will consider and that how ever prejudice may blind them on the advantages while they enumerate the Inconveniency in this Idea likly to result from the process—they will own that a succes in the attainement of the end the sisteme is combined to promote would be most prosperous—and confident in that succes I Feel the more encouraged to submit my Idea there on to your jugement.

as to the question of what are the means necessary and how to procure them I will observe that those means most be extensive proportioned to the magnitude of the undertaking. and that so ever large as I conceive they ought to be I consider the property at your disposal fully proportionated to the object if attention is given in managing it.

15.000 lots will fall in the share of the publick as half of the property left for Improvements after deduction made of streets and of ground appropriated to publick purposes—these lots will be of various sise from *66* feet to ⟨*57*⟩. in Fronts and from *four* to *seven* in an acre—the sum that will arise from the sale most be immense but as I observed it will only be so if cautiously menaged—for notwithstanding the amount of them lots most be Enormous I fear that under this Idea and when undervaluing the magnitude of the work proposed or not being well convinced of the Importance of having the Improvements carried on on the liberal scale I propose it may induce to a prodigality of those means in saling on low termes the most valuable part of lots a circumstance which in my opinion prove as destructive to the attainement of the grand object as would a contraction of measure determined after a timorous survey of the mass of the undertaking the which in offering a labyrinth of difficulties would soon magnify them to a deffidence of power to surmount.

therefor it is of Importance the whole matter should be contemplated cooly and that so ever short of the time left to effect it may appear not be hurry'd in to process nor to engage in it but after having secured effectual mean to supply the daily Expendit⟨ure.⟩

those means at your disposal I said were proportionated to the object and I considere them so if other means are first exerted to rise the property to tis proper valu.

for to look upon that property at this moment as a mean of supply and to use of this mean to deffray the first expenditure of the begining of the work would indeed be to expunge all resource befor the moment is come for availling of them.

be cause admiting the disadvantageous terms of the sale is advertised as may be altered and iven supposing the sale to be productive from the begining the produce most be various and a fund mearly depending on it will never Insure a timely Supply to daily Expenditure a circumstance which would necessitate a frequent change in the mode of conducting matter, would delay the progress of works begon consequently occasion a loss and a misapplication of means and of time which in the course of every grand undertaking but most unavoidably in one of the magnitude of that under consideration would work a dissipation of every means to an absolut disappointment in the object to obtain.

from these consideration a better security of funds being necessary to combine a plan of operation the good of which can only be Insured aided by punctual payements and regular and plentifull supply of Materials it will expedient first to devise the necessary means considering that Economie in a poursuit of this nature lay in being aided with numerous hands with a power of pouring means there were they may accelerat the leveling of difficulties frequent to enconter.

viewing matter in this light and being convinced money is the principal wheel to give and continu the motion to the machine left to organise I shall make it the oject of this adress to call your attention on the advantages which may be expected from borowing a sum on the credit of the property it self.

under the facility of a loan no hurry being to dispose of the lots since a possibility may be for the publick to erect houses for privat accomodation which would be a measure but expedient and beneficial—it will become possible to appropriate a sum to each particular object to performe and to carry on regularly and at a same time Every of those object, forwording them yearly in proportion to the money alloted for them respectivly.

in that way every Improvement may be easily compleated and without being restrained by little saving consideration they may be carried through the whole city Indescriminatly aiding and assisting every privat undertaking were a reciprocity of benefit may ensu—a mode of process which I may venture to assert would in the end bring three to one for the money they liberally expended and which emply repaying for a loan on what ever termes it might be obtained would be rising the reputation of the undertaking to a degree of splendour and greatness unprecedented contribut most effectually to the increase of popula-t⟨ion⟩ to the accroissement of commerce and would in a short time rise the City one of the first the world will contain.

it is in this manner and in this manner only I conceive the business may be conducted to a certainty of the attainement of that succes I wished to promot in the deliniation of a plan wholy new, and which combined on a grand scale will require Exertions above what is the idea of many but the which not being beyond your power to procur made me ⟨promise⟩ the securing of them as I remain assured you will conceive it essential to pursu with dignity the operation of an undertaking of a magnitude so worthy of the ⟨concern⟩ of grand Empire in the compleat achevement of the which the Honor of this is become so eminently concern and over whose progress the ayes of every other nation envying the opportunity deny'd them will stand juge. I have the Honor to be with respect & submission your most ob⟨*illegible*⟩ & most Humble obedient servant

P.C. L'Enfant

ALS, DLC: Pierre-Charles L'Enfant Papers. The dateline derives from the partially mutilated one added by another hand to the top of the letter: "George Town August 1⟨9⟩ 17⟨91⟩" and from a later docket.

1. L'Enfant apparently presented the enclosed 30-by-40-inch plan (DLC: Map Division) and this letter to GW in person in Philadelphia at the end of August (see n.4 below).

2. For Andrew Ellicott's surveys of the federal district and the border between the Creek Indians and the state of Georgia, see Ellicott to GW, 1 Feb. and note 1, and GW to Thomas Jefferson, 1 Feb. and note 1.

3. The concern of L'Enfant that the lots would be purchased in blocks by syndicated speculators proved unfounded. Most buyers at the October sale were individuals who purchased only one or two of the thirty-one lots sold, except for Jacob Walsh of Boston, who as agent for Samuel Blodget purchased five lots, James Gilchrest of Philadelphia, who bought four, and Nicholas Kirby of Baltimore, who bought three.

4. L'Enfant was unable to persuade GW to postpone the initial sale of lots even though he argued his case in person. L'Enfant arrived in Philadelphia

sometime before 27 Aug. and met with GW, Jefferson, and James Madison on that date. See GW's Memorandum for Jefferson, 27 Aug. and note 1.

From Henry Laurens, Sr.

Mepkin Plantation [St. Johns Parish, Berkeley County]
Dear Sir.   so. Carolina 20th August 1791.

I congratulate with yourself & Mrs Washington on your happy return to Mount Vernon & with my fellow Citizens in general on your arrival at the Seat of Government, events which have gladned many Hearts.

I have been inform'd Sir there will be appointments of Ministers to foreign Courts at the next Session of Congress, should so. Carolina be entitled to one, I would beg leave to name Charles Pinckney Esquire present Governor of the State, his abilities are well known, his honor and integrity stand clear & unimpeach'd.

I do not presume Sir to trouble you by Solicitation but barely to mention the name of Mr Pinckney who will soon be at leisure from his present Commission & who is earnestly disposed to serve his Country.[1] With the most sincere Esteem & Respect I have the honor to be Sir Your much obliged & most obedient servant

Henry Laurens.

ALS, DLC:GW.

1. Charles Pinckney, who was married to Henry Laurens, Sr.'s daughter Mary Eleanor, desired to be minister to Great Britain. GW instead named Thomas Pinckney to that post (see GW to the U.S. Senate, 22 December). Charles Pinckney later was appointed minister to Spain by Thomas Jefferson.

To Thomas Jefferson

Dear Sir,   [Philadelphia] Sunday 21st August [1791]

At eight 'oclock A.M. tomorrow, I set out for Mr Powells farm, to see the operation of Colo. Anderson's threshing Machine.[1] I Break fast, you know, at half past Seven; if it is convenient to take that in your way, I should be glad to see you at it.

When you have read the enclosed letters I will converse with you on the subject of them.[2] I am always yours

Go: Washington

ALS, DLC: Thomas Jefferson Papers.

1. The farm of Samuel Powel on the Schuylkill River was west of the Market Street bridge. Jefferson accompanied GW there on 22 Aug., and they observed the operation of the new threshing machine developed by Alexander Anderson (c.1754–1824). Powel described the machine in a letter of 25 Nov. 1791 that Arthur Young published in his *Annals of Agriculture,* 17 (1792), 206–8.

2. The enclosed letters have not been identified.

From Battaile Muse

Honorable sir.   Berkeley County [Va.] Augt 22d 1791

About ten Days ago I went to Winchester To see one Rowsey who was in Prison bounds at your Suit against Charles Rector for upwards of £105 besides cost.[1] while I was in Winchester a Nephew of yours a Mr Lewis informed me that he was about to forward to you a Petition in favour of Rowsey. I told him of the generous terms offered to him from time to time of his obstinacy & how the Debt arose. Notwithstanding the Petition I expect will be presented.[2] Under the circumstances of the Case I think it my duty to inform you in what manner Mr Rowsey has behaved. When I put him in Jail in June 1790 after a long expensive Lawsuit I offered to let him Replevy for twelve Months in the sum of one half the Debt, he to pay Cost. he repeatedly replyed that he would stay in Jail untill he Spent his Estate before he would condescend to pay one Shilling. in fall 1790 I repeated at Sundry times the same proposals and he was advised by several Gentlemen to comply but he absolutely refused: untill Late Last winter at march Court last I attended him five Days at your Expence & loss of my time for his giving a Twelve months Replevy Bond for half the Debt and Cost. the Bond was Drawn at his request, and by his repeated applications detained me with the promise Every Day of giving me security for the payment on Tomorrow. I waited from Tuesday untill satterday, found he could not be depended on, left him under the promise of his complyance with the Sheriff the next week. Instead of which he gave Security for the Bounds and Resolves to spend his Estate in the Bounds. the length of the time has I suppose accumulated the expences to near £30 perhaps. which sum you will have to pay if you release him. altho' the example would have encouraged evil practices yet I had a Heart to discharge him but could not do it at your expence. he is a poor Man. I know not his Character. I fixed my opinion on his being Security for a Man who was about to deprive you of a Large & Just Debt. he refused to comply with his Security-Ship after very generous terms had been offered him. upon this statement of the case I hope I shall be acquited of any Charge of neglect or disobedience. your Letter in favour of Mrs Lewis respecting Winzors Lease came to hand.[3] nothing has taken place as Yet. the Death of Robin Scott has occasioned the Land Suit to abate.[4] It will revive as soon as possable—I closed my Accots of last years Collection of Rents with Major Geo: A. Wash⟨ing⟩ton the 12th Day of this month. there is a ballance due in Fauquier County by the Tenants of £85.12.3 which Debts are under the Law. the Vileness of the Fauquier Sheriff detains the Collection altho' he has been presented to the Court for his delinquency yet his unwarrantable conduct still prevails—I shall pursue him and endeavour to make him pay up what is in his hands as soon as possable. I wanted to Ballance the Rental before I settled but the Sheriff failing in his Duty prevented it. Major Washington is at his Fathers in this County on a Visit to restore his health Your Brothers & Fairfield Families are as usual.[5]

Colo. Fairfaxes Ledger & Accts have been put Into my hands by the Executor to settle. there is an Acct Agt you and also Agt your Brother Colo. Sa[mue]l Washingtons Estate. I shall be much obliged to you Sir to inform me whether the Accts ever were settled and advise me thereupon.[6] there has been the greatest drought in this Country ever known. the crops of Wheat in quality good but Short. the Crops of Corn & Tobacco are considerably worse than ever known here before. I am Sir with every Sentiment of Esteem your Most devoted Humbe Servant

Battaile Muse

ALS, DLC:GW.

1. Battaile Muse, acting as GW's agent, had obtained judgment against Reuben Rowsey (Reubin Rowsy; Rowzy) at the March 1790 session of the Frederick County court for £156.18.6, 687 pounds of tobacco and 16s. 6d., and his court costs (Frederick County Virginia Court Order Book, 22 [1789–91], 167–68). See also Muse to GW, 28 Nov. 1785, n.5, and 20 July 1790 and note 5.

2. "Mr Lewis" was GW's nephew George Lewis who lived in the vicinity of Winchester, Virginia.

3. The letter was GW to Muse, 6 February. For the land GW had leased to Joseph Windsor that Betty Washington Lewis wished to acquire, see GW to Muse, 28 July 1785 and note 1.

4. For GW's long-running boundary dispute with Robert Scott, see Muse to GW, 20 July 1790 and notes 1 and 2.

5. George Augustine Washington was visiting Happy Retreat, the estate of his father, Charles, GW's brother. Nearby Fairfield was the home of GW's cousin Warner Washington, Sr., who had died in 1790, and of his widow, Hannah, sister of George William Fairfax.

6. For GW's accounts with Fairfax, see GW to Fairfax, 30 June 1786 and note 4.

From Frances Ramadge

Charleston [S.C.] August 22th 1791.

I Must beg leave to Congratulate your excellency on your safe arriveal and good Health afte so long and hazardous a Journey through our barren Country[.] I have sent a small Cask of our Carolina potatoes which beg your exceptance: as I hear the are much better than you have to the Norward. I will send some every opportunity if agreeable—the Shrubs and roots will be fit next month, which I will be very careful in sending: the Soap tree, and Tallow tree seed I Shall get; the sweet scented shrubs and what I Can find will be a rarity: any thing of that kind your Excellency would wish to have, Command me I will be happy, and take pleasure in procure it[.] I have sent a sample of saloop of my own manufacture which you had not room for on your departure from Charleston, it has been approved by the gentlemen of the Faculty in the Physical line, I have made a Quantity of it, and will ship some to New york and Philidelphia if it meets with encouragement[.][1] I most Earnestly pettion your excellency to present it to the Society of Arts and Sciences—my Daughter Sarah present her most respectful Compliments and Joins me in good wishes for Health and happiness to your good family[.] I remain with the greatest respect your excellency most Humble Servant

Frances Ramadge

ALS, DNA: RG 59, Miscellaneous Letters. Tobias Lear docketed the cover of the letter: "Answered September 9th 1791," but no reply from GW or his secretaries has been found.

Frances Ramadge (Rammage) of St. Phillips and St. Michaels Parish served as GW's housekeeper during his stay in Charleston (*Heads of Families* [South Carolina], 40; Lipscomb, *South Carolina in 1791*, 26).

1. Saloop or salep was a medicinal meal, starch, or jelly made from the dried tubers of plants of the genus *Orchis*.

From Nathaniel Russell

Charleston [S.C.] 22 August 1791. Sends a bottle of olives, from a garden of Mr. Bull's about two miles from Charleston, which were cured and pickled by a lady in this city.[1]

ALS, DLC:GW.

Nathaniel Russell (1738–1829), a native of Rhode Island, moved to Charleston before 1770 and established himself as a leading merchant.

1. Tobias Lear replied to Russell on 9 Sept. that GW was "much pleased to find that this valuable fruit is cultivated and brought to such perfection in the united States, and begs you will accept his best thanks for your polite attention in forwarding him this sample. The Lady who cured and pickled them will likewise be so good as to accept his acknowledgments" (DLC:GW).

Letter not found: from Anthony Whitting, 22 Aug. 1791. GW wrote to Anthony Whitting on Monday, 29 Aug., that he had "acknowledged the receipt of yours of the 22d" in a letter he "wrote to you on friday last."

From Thomas Jefferson

[Philadelphia] 23 August 1791. Reports on the official communications from the secretary of the Northwest Territory from 1 Jan. to 30 June that "none of the said communications appear to require any thing to be done on the part of the Government of the United States; That they contain indeed the titles of several acts passed by the Territorial Legislature; but the Acts themselves not being yet communicated, no opinion can be given on them."

LB, DLC:GW; ADf, DLC: Thomas Jefferson Papers; copy, DNA: RG 59, Miscellaneous Letters; copy, DNA: RG 59, Reports of the Secretary of State to the President and Congress.

Tobias Lear had transmitted to Jefferson on 18 Aug. the official communications of Winthrop Sargent with GW's request that Jefferson report on them if necessary (DNA: RG 59, Miscellaneous Letters). Jefferson received them the next day, according to the State Department memorandum book (DNA:PCC, item 187, 115).

Circular on the State of American Agriculture

Dear Sir,   Philadelphia, August 25th 1791

Some enquiries having been made of me by important Characters on the state of agriculture in America, comprehending its Several relations, and intended to ascertain the value of our lands, with their yield in the several kinds of grain, grass &ca—the prices of farming stock, the prices of produce &ca together with a list of the Taxes in the different States, which may in any way affect the Farmer—As an object highly interesting to our country, I have determined to render the most just and satisfactory answers that the best information, which I can obtain from different parts of the United States will enable me to give.

With this view my confidence in your disposition and knowledge leads me to offer to your enquiry and to request from your intelligence as early information as may be convenient on the following heads.

1. The fee simple prices of farming lands in such parts of the State of Virginia, as are neither so near to large Towns as to enhance their value, nor so distant from market as greatly to reduce it, or to make the situation inconvenient—In your answer to this enquiry, be pleased to note, general⟨ly⟩ the situations, the soil, and if it be practicable⟨,⟩ the proportions of arable, pasture, and wood land.

2. The rents of the same lands, when leased, and, generally, the terms of lease.

3. The average product of the same lands in wheat, rye, barley, oats, buckwheat, beans, pease, potatoes, turnips, grasses, hemp, flax &ca—in the common mode of husbandry now practised.

4. The average prices of these articles when sold at the Farm, or carried to the nearest market.

5. The average prices of good working horses, working Oxen, milch-cows, sheep, hogs, poultry &ca.

6. The average price of beef, pork, mutton, veal, and butter and cheese in the neighbourhood, or at the nearest market-Towns.

7. The price of wrought iron, whence the prices of farming utensils may be inferred.

8. A list of the Taxes laid in the State of Virginia.

The tendency of this enquiry will be my apology for the trouble it may give you. With great regard, I am dear ⟨*mutilated*⟩ Your most obedient servant

Go: Washington

LS (photocopy), in the hand of William Jackson, DLC:GW; LB, DLC:GW. According to the letter-book copy, GW sent this circular to David Stuart of Virginia, Philip Schuyler of New York (copy, MH: Sparks Transcripts), Thomas Johnson of Maryland, Thomas Hartley of Pennsylvania, and Thomas Lowrey of New Jersey. The copies sent to the last three men have not been found. GW added a postscript to Stuart's letter: "If you were to confine yourself to the Counties of Fairfax, Loudoun, Berke⟨ley,⟩ Prince William & Fauquier—or even to the three first, my object will be answered by these enquiries of *you.*" Apparently in similar postscripts, GW also asked Johnson to focus on Montgomery, Frederick, and Washington counties, Md., and Hartley on York and Franklin counties, Pennsylvania.

For background to this circular, see Arthur Young to GW, 25 Jan., and GW to Young, 15 Aug. and note 2. For extant replies to it, see Schuyler to GW, 3 Sept., Hartley to GW, 24 Sept., Johnson to GW, 10 Nov., and Stuart to GW, 18 November. GW sent a copy of the circular, with copies of the answers of Hartley, Johnson, and Stuart, to Young on 5 December. After GW's death Young published GW's correspondence with him, including this circular and its responses, as well as Thomas Jefferson's notes to GW of 3 Aug. (see GW to Young, 15 Aug., n.2).

Letter not found: to Thomas Hartley, 25 Aug. 1791. Thomas Hartley wrote to GW on 24 Sept. that he was "highly honoured by your favour of the 25th ult."

Letter not found: from James Seagrove, 25 Aug. 1791. GW wrote to James Seagrove on 14 Sept., acknowledging receipt of Seagrove's letter of "the 25. of August."

To Samuel Vaughan

Dear Sir,   Philadelphia, August 25. 1791.
At the same time that I acknowledge the receipt of your letter of the 10th of may, I must beg your acceptance of my best thanks for the publications which accompanied it.[1]

I am glad to learn that the good opinion first entertained of Mr Rumsey and his inventions still continues, and I sincerely hope as well for his own emolument and the benefit of mankind, as for the credit of our country that he may surmount the obstacles thrown in his way, and receive such consideration as his merits demand.[2]

It is with peculiar satisfaction I can inform you that our public affairs are still in a prosperous train, unclouded by any gloomy prospects of interruption—The convulsed state of Europe at the present moment cannot fail of attaching every American more strongly to his own country—and government; while every heart must be impressed with lively gratitude towards the supreme Ruler of events upon a recollection of the circumstances which have brought us to our present political situation. Wishing that health and uninterrupted tranquillity may attend you to the close of your days.[3] I am dear Sir, with great esteem, your most obedient Servant

G. Washington

LB, DLC:GW.

1. London merchant Samuel Vaughan wrote GW on 10 May: "Permit me to present to You some publications respecting the French Revolution & the English partizans of it, &ca &ca I presume they cannot be unacceptable to Your Excellency, as most of them are but just published. The great cause of Liberty goes on rapidly here, which cannot be wondered at considering that even Poland has taken fire, so as to enduce its Nobility to give up their prejudices against an equality with those hitherto not noble. My eldest Son Benjn desires me to say, that he retains his first opinion of Mr Rumsey & his Inventions; that his only difficulty has arisen from want of capital; & that he is now on a visit to Ireland, to give his opinion respecting a very considerable canal undertaken there, till the termination of some Law disputes allow him to proceed in his operations here" (DLC:GW). The accompanying books and pamphlets, all published in London in 1791, were listed on the verso of the letter: James Mackintosh, *Vindiciae Gallicae. Defense of the French Revolution and Its English Admirers, against the Accusations of the Right Hon. Edmund Burke;* Thomas Christie, *Letters on the Revolution of France, and on the New Constitution Established by the National Assembly: Occasioned by the Publications of the Right Hon. Edmund Burke, M.P., and Alexander de Calonne . . .* ; George Rous, *Thoughts on Government: Occasioned by Mr. Burke's Reflections, &c., in a Letter to a Friend* (4th ed.), and *A Letter to the Right Honourable Edmund Burke;* John Paradise, *Serious Enquiries into the Motives and Consequences of Our Present Armament against Russia;* John Williams, *An Enquiry into the Truth of the Tradition, concerning the Discovery of America by Prince Madod ab Owen Gwynedd, about the Year 1170;* Joseph Priestley, *The Proper Objects of Education in the Present State of the World, Represented in a Discourse, Delivered on Wednesday, the 27th of April, 1791, . . .* , and *A Discourse on Occasion of the Death of Dr. Price;* and Andrew Kippis, *An Address Delivered at the Interment of the Late Rev. Dr. Richard Price on the Twenty-sixth of April 1791.* All were in GW's library at his death (Griffin, *Boston Athenæum Washington Collection,* passim). Vaughan also sent *Unitarian Society* (London, 1791), published by the Unitar-

ian Society for Promoting Christian Knowledge and the Practice of Virtue. Neither this pamphlet nor "Debates on the 7th May on the Quebeck Bill" and "Ditto [on the] 10[th of May] on the Test Act" that Vaughan also listed as enclosed were found in GW's library at his death.

2. At the urging of his supporters in the American Philosophical Society, who had formed the "Rumseian Society," James Rumsey had traveled to Britain to obtain patents for his steam-powered inventions and to interest English capitalists in them. Rumsey's improved steamboat was almost completed when he died in London in December 1792. See David Humphreys to GW, 31 Oct. 1790 and note 11.

3. GW asked Thomas Jefferson on 29 Aug. to transmit this letter to Vaughan with diplomatic correspondence.

From William Nelson, Jr.

Westover [Va.] 26 August 1791. Resigns as U.S. attorney in expectation of a state judicial appointment that Virginia law rendered "incompatible with an office under the foederal government."

ALS, DNA: RG 59, Miscellaneous Letters.

Letter not found: to Anthony Whitting, 26 Aug. 1791. In writing to Anthony Whitting on Monday, 29 Aug., GW referred to his letter to Whitting of "friday last."

Memorandum for Thomas Jefferson

[Philadelphia, c.27 August 1791]

Will circumstances render a postponement of the Sale of Lots in the Federal City advisable? If not

Where ought they to be made

Will it in that case, or even without it, be necessary or prudent to attempt to borrow money to carry on the difft works in the City?

Whether ought the building of a bridge over the Eastern branch to be attempted—the Canal set about—and Mr Peter's proposion with respect to wharves gone into *now*—or postponed until our funds are better ascertained & become productive?[1]

At what time can the several Proprietors claim, with propriety, payment for the public squares wch is marked upon their respective tracts?

Ought there to be any wood houses in the town?

What sort of Brick or Stone [Houses]² should be built—& of wht height—especially on the principal Streets or Avenues?

When ought the public buildings to be begun, & in what manner had the materials best be provided?

How ought they to be promulgated, so as to draw plans from skilful Architects? and what would be the best mode of carrying on the Work?

Ought not Stoups & projections of every sort & kind into the Streets to be prohibited *absolutely?*

What compromise can be made with the Lot holders in Hamburgh & Carrollsburgh by which the plan of the Federal City may be preserved?

Ought not the several Land holders to be called upon to ascertain their respective boundaries previous to the Sale of Lots?

Would it not be advisable to have the Federal district as laid out, (comprehending the plan of the Town) engraved in one piece?

AD, DLC:GW. These queries are in GW's hand, but the page also bears later replies written by Thomas Jefferson, who also numbered some of the queries and wrote seven additional notes, numbered 14–20, at the bottom of the page before returning the document to GW under cover of a letter from Georgetown, Maryland. See Jefferson to GW, 8 Sept. and note 1.

When Pierre-Charles L'Enfant arrived in Philadelphia sometime during the last week of August, he presented to GW his plan of the Federal City and his letter of 19 Aug. to GW and discussed with him on or before 26 Aug. the postponement of the first sale of city lots. On that date Jefferson invited James Madison to dinner and noted: "Since writing the above the President has been here, & left L'Enfant's plan, with a wish that you & I would examine it together immediately, as to certain matters, & let him know the result. As the plan is very large, will you walk up & examine it here?" (*Madison Papers,* 14:74). GW's memorandum may have been presented to Jefferson that day or as late as 29 Aug., when GW wrote to Jefferson about Jefferson's impending meeting with the commissioners for the federal district. GW's queries probably were drafted for Jefferson to pose to the commissioners, suggesting that they were written on 27 Aug., when GW conferred with Jefferson, Madison, and L'Enfant. On this day Tobias Lear wrote to L'Enfant that GW "wishes to see you about 5 O'clock—or from that to 6 as you can make it convenient—this afternoon" (DLC: Digges-L'Enfant-Morgan Papers). Jefferson and Madison may have been present at this meeting and may also have met with GW earlier this day to present their views on the matters committed to them on 26 August. Jefferson's letter of 28 Aug. to the commissioners mentions these meetings without revealing their chronology or participants: "Major Lenfant also having arrived here and laid his plan of the Federal city before the President, he was pleased to desire a conference of certain persons, in his presence, on these several subjects. It is the opinion of the President, in consequence thereof, that an immediate meeting of the Commissioners at George town is requisite, that certain measures may be decided on and put into a course of preparation for a commencement of sale on the 17th. of Octob. as advertised. As Mr. Madison and myself, who were present at the conferences, propose to pass through George town on our way to Virginia, the President supposes that our attendance at the meeting of the Commissioners might be of service to them, as we could communicate to them the sentiments developed at the conferences here and approved by the President, under whatever point of view they may have occasion to know them." Jefferson wrote that he and Madison would arrive 7–8 Sept. and proposed to confer with the commissioners on 8 Sept. (*Jefferson Papers*, 22:88–89). Jefferson reported on the conference to GW on 8 September.

1. For "Mr Peter's proposion," see GW to the Commissioners for the Federal District, 24 July and note 1.

2. This word was inserted by Jefferson.

From Henry Knox

War Department [Philadelphia] 27 August 1791. Informs GW that Lieutenant Sherman of the Rhode Island Company of the Second U.S. Regiment "has left his company on the march" and desires to resign his commission: "from received knowledge of his character, . . . his resignation will not injure the service."[1]

LS, DLC:GW; LB, DLC:GW.

1. Lt. Henry Sherman, Jr. (1759–1829), served as an officer of Rhode Island troops in the Continental army during the American Revolution from 1777 to 1783 and was recommissioned on 4 Mar. 1791. His resignation was accepted effective 27 August.

From Timothy Pickering

Sir,   Philadelphia August 27. 1791.

I did myself the honour to call at your house to-day, to speak with you: but you were engaged with Mr Jefferson. And the time not admitting another opportunity (as I wish to leave town on Monday morning) you will permit me to communicate what I had to say, in writing.

As you thought it expedient, I went to New York, to converse with Mr Osgood on the business of the post-office. The contracts for the carriage of the mail were made in the beginning of November last, but continue until the first day of January next. Those contracts were made after public advertisement for proposals for contracts: but Mr Osgood thinks it will be most eligible to contract with the present contractors; and not to advertise for new proposals. I concur with that opinion: because the present contractors have the business in train, & appear, generally speaking, to have conducted it with propriety and as much punctuality as circumstances would allow: because it would take some time for new contractors to get the business as well arranged, & understood by their agents: and because at the next session of congress a new law for regulating the post office may probably be enacted. Therefore, instead ⟨of⟩ calling for new cont⟨racts⟩, it seems to me adviseable, to propose to the present contractors, to continue to carry the mails, on the terms of their present contracts (with perhaps a few alterations easy to be made) until the regulations of the expected law shall be known, or rather, until they shall receive notice when the terms of the present contracts shall cease.

I have not reappointed any deputy postmasters: for it appeared to me expedient to give a little time for information concerning them; by which it might be better known whether any and what changes should be made.

Whilst at New-York, I waited on Governor Clinton. He had received Genl Knox's first letter; expressing, on the part of the United States, their disavowal of the public sanction given by me, at the late Indian treaty, to the assignment of land to the two Indian children of Ebenezer Allan, & to the lease made by the Cayuga Chiefs to John Richardson, of the tract of land called the Cayuga Reservation. He had also received a second letter from Genl Knox, inclosing a copy of my letter, in which I gave a more particular account of the *grounds* and *inducements* upon which that public sanction was given, than I had rendered in my report. A copy of that letter he told me he would lay before you; for I felt a solicitude that you should be informed of the facts therein detailed.[1]

Governor Clinton showed no symptoms of dissatisfaction with the steps I had taken relative to the Cayuga lease. I observed to him, that perhaps the terms I had used in my report & letter might have led to some misapprehension of the force, or effect, of the public sanctions given to the conveyances before mentioned: That they amounted to ⟨*illegible*⟩ more than this—Certificates by the Commissioner of the United States, that at a public treaty held Under their authority, those conveyances had been executed by the Chiefs of the Seneka & Cayuga nations, respectively: and that such certificates could neither add to nor diminish the validity of the *titles* purported to be conveyed by the deeds them⟨selves: like the⟩ acknowledgements of deeds, in ordinary cases, before certain magistrates, which are required by the statutes of several states, but which in no way affect the *title* of the lands expressed to be conveyed: to the justness of whi⟨ch⟩ ideas he readily assented. In the course of the co⟨n⟩versation, he said (what I had concluded to sugge⟨st⟩ to him as expedient) that he should not, *at p*⟨*mutilated*⟩ take any step in the affair, which should ha⟨*mutilated*⟩ the exciting of any uneasiness in the minds of ⟨*mutilated*⟩ Cayuga chiefs.

When I left home, I had no information that any public office was vacant; & I expected soon to return. My private affairs & those of my offices under Pennsylvania require my presence at Wilkesbarré, that I may make a suitable disposition of the former, & deliver over the latter to my successor. For those purposes I should wish to be at home three or four weeks, & to set out on Monday morning, if, sir, it should be agreeable to you.[2] I have the honour to be, Sir, most respectfully⟨,⟩ your obedient servant

Timothy Pickering

ALS, DNA: RG 59, Miscellaneous Letters; ADfS, MHi: Pickering Papers.

1. For the controversy over the sanction given by Timothy Pickering to certain land transactions at his council with the Six Nations, see Henry Knox to GW, 17 Aug. and notes 2 and 3.

2. Tobias Lear replied from Philadelphia on 29 Aug.: "The President . . . commands me to inform you, that he can have no objection to the wish which you expressed in your letter of yesterday to him, of your being absent from the seat of Government for three or four weeks; presuming that you are sufficiently acquainted with the nature of the Office in which you are now engaged, to enable you to form a proper judgement of the time when you should return. With respect to the contracts for carrying the mail the ensuing year, the President commands me to inform you, that he shall take the matter into consideration, and will let you know his determination upon it when you return to this

city, which, according to the usual time of making arrangements therefor, will be in due season. In the mean time, the President observes, that the general Post Office being considered as a branch of the revenue department, it is his wish that, in all matters of arrangement relative thereto, a communication may be had with the Secretary of the Treasury; and more especially in the present instance, as the President will probably be in Virginia at the time of your return to this City" (DLC:GW).

From John Bertles Shee

Honor'd & Esteemed Sir.　　　Philada August 27th 1791.

I hope that your Philanthropic Soul will pardon the Temerity that actuates the Person who now addresses you to write you I have Sir taken this unbounded Liberty on the Consideration of your being acquainted with my Father & Connections It will be necessary to inform you that thr'o Misconduct (& to my Shame & I confess it) that I incurred my Father's displeasure insomuch so that I was forced to abandon his presence & ever since that Time have been doomed to wander about the wide World, I hope you will not Honored Sir be offended when I inform you that I was bred to the Law but thro' Rashness wch is incident to youth have been brought thus low my father justly incensed against me will not permit me to appear in his presence I am now at this present a wretched Outcast, Pity Sir my unhappy & Deplorable situation, I am myself the bearer of these Lines to your Excellency my Cloaths are so bad that I am perfectly ashamed to come even to your Door I can Sir get a School in the Country but for want of a small Sum am hindered to buy a few decent Cloaths—I hope ever Honored Sir you will pardon this Temerity in my writing you & Oh! rescue an unhappy Mortal from this his Abyss of Miserey. I am with the greatest Respect your Excellency's most obdt & devoted servt

John Bertles Shee

ALS, DNA: RG 59, Miscellaneous Letters.

John Bertles Shee (1767–1799) was the son of John Shee (1740–1808), treasurer of the City of Philadelphia from 1790 to 1797, who served under GW in 1776 as colonel of the 3d Pennsylvania Regiment. The younger Shee was a private in the Pennsylvania militia in 1789, and Henry Knox suggested him to GW on 11 July for a vacant ensigncy.

To Charles Carroll (of Carrollton)

Dear Sir,   Philadelphia, August 28. 1791.

Your favor of the 11th instant came duly to hand—and I have also received the papers from Mount Vernon which, in my letter of the 31st of July, I informed you I had written for.

Enclosed you have an exact copy of the decree of the Court of Chancery in Virginia, under which I became the purchaser of Clifton's land. I likewise send you the opinion of the Attorney-General of the United States upon it, and other papers which have been laid before him relative to this business.[1]

By the decree it appears that the sums of £243.13/1 sterling and £67.4/7 Virginia currency were ordered to be paid to Messrs Carroll and Digges; but then the cost of suit viz. 4536 lbs. of tobacco at two pence p. lb. (so settled by the Commissioners) and 50/ were, by the Decree, to be deducted therefrom, and paid to the Plaintiff, Clifton, and this having been done the sum of £67.4/7 is reduced to £26.18/7 which together with the sterling sum of £243.13/1 I am willing and ready to pay the instant a proper conveyance is made to me and the bond is delivered up agreeably to the requisites of the Court—Nay, Sir, if payment at the time mentioned in your letter of the 16 of July is more convenient to you, it shall be made upon the passing of your bond to me, ensuring a compliance with the above requisites; or giving an indemnification if they are not; for I have no desire to withhold the money from you one moment.

By the laws of Virginia, to which this transaction is subject, all sterling debts are to be discharged at 33⅓ p. cent which makes the sum of £243.13/1 when turned into Virginia currency £324.17/5—and this added to £26.18/7. makes 1172⅔ dollars if my calculations are right. With great esteem and regard, I am dear Sir, Your most obedient and very humble Servant

G. Washington.

P.S. In procuring evidence to the Deed it would be well to recollect Characters who attend the Courts in Alexandria—for it is there the record of it must be.

LB, DLC:GW.

1. The enclosed decree and the opinion of Edmund Randolph have not been found.

Tobias Lear to Oliver Evans

Sir,   Philadelphia August 29th 1791

The President has been informed by his manager at Mount Vernon that the work of his mill is in such a stage as not to admit of any delay in erecting your improvements without stopping the whole progress of the work, which at this time would be a serious inconvenience. The mill-wright who has been employed in repairing the President's mill has been to view your improvements at the Ochoquan mills, and with the insight he has obtained from that view, aided by a plate of the improvements, he has no doubt of his being able to execute the work completely, and he has the character of being an excellent workman[1]—but, as the President is desirous of having it done in the most perfect manner without a hazard of its not answering the purpose fully, he wishes to know if you still hold your determination of going into that part of the Country as you mentioned your intention of doing so, and in case you should, and would go on *immediately*, he will give directions to the mill wright to wait your arrival before any thing is done to the improvements—But if you do not go *immediately* the President must give orders for the person now engaged to go on with the work himself, as the season will admit of no delay.[2]

Let me know whether you go to Virginia directly or not—that if you should a letter might be sent to you on Wednesday for mount Vernon.[3] I am Sir, &ca

Tobias Lear

LB, DLC:GW.

Millwright William Ball began repairing GW's mill in May. See George Augustine Washington's agreement of 16 April with Ball (DLC:GW). After observing Ball's progress GW apparently decided to install the machinery designed by Oliver Evans. Tobias Lear entered into correspondence with Evans when GW returned to Philadelphia, and Evans replied in a missing letter of 28 July in which he discussed millers' wages and other such matters (see Lear to Evans, 24 Feb. 1792 [DLC:GW]).

1. The plate was probably that published in the *Universal Asylum and Columbian Magazine* in January 1791.

2. Evans replied to Lear on 1 Sept. that either he or his brother Evan would go to Mount Vernon to oversee the work. GW sent Evans's letter to Anthony Whitting on 4 Sept. with a license to erect Evans's patented invention at the mill: "If Mr Evans or his brother, agreeably to the tenor of the enclosed letter,

is not there by the time Mr Ball has compleated the other parts of the work, let him go on without; but with those parts first, as are mentioned in the letter. . . . This license after Mr Ball has seen it must be lodged with the Major."

3. Lear wrote to Oliver Evans on 4 Sept.: "In reply to your letter of the 1st instant, which has been duly received, the President directs me to inform you that having procured of Mr Leslie a patent for erecting your improvements at his mills, he shall forward it this day to Mount Vernon with directions for the Mill Wright to proceed in the execution of the work—for it will admit of no further delay, the work of the mill being in that state as to make it necessary to erect the improvements now or lay them aside altogether. As the man who is now engaged in the President's mill seems fully confident of his being able to execute the whole of the work in a proper manner the President thinks it would not be necessary for your brother to attend to it, which must be a considerable encrease of the Expence. As you mentioned when you were here that you intended to be in that part of Virginia about the time that the improvements would be erecting, the President wished in that case that you might be present when the works at his mill were executing—But he does not think it would be necessary for you to quit your own business, which you say is at this time very pressing, for the *sole* purpose of directing the execution of this piece of work" (DLC:GW). Evans's response of 7 Sept. has not been found, but Lear wrote him on 9 Sept.: "In consequence of the representation made in your letter of the 7th instant, respecting the erecting of your improvements, the President wishes that your Brother may proceed to his mills in order to superintend those which are to be put up there, and he has this day sent directions to Mount Vernon for the mill wright who is now employed to govern his work accordingly—But if your brother was on his way to the President's mill at the time of your writing he will undoubtedly get there before the President's letter of to-day reaches Mount Vernon" (DLC:GW). When GW reached Mount Vernon on 20 Sept., he found Evan Evans at work at the mill (see GW to Lear, 23 September).

To Thomas Jefferson

Dear Sir   [Philadelphia] Monday Morning August 29th 1791

The enclosed for Mr Young, I pray you to put under cover to Mr Johnson—the other for Mr Vaughan may go in like manner, or otherwise, as you may think best; both however by the Packet.[1]

The letter for Mr Carroll I also return—besides which, were you to write a line or two to Mr Johnson, addressed to the care of the Postmaster in Baltimore, *it might be* a mean of giving him earlier notice of the intended meeting.[2] The Plan of Carrollsburgh sent me by D. Carroll it will be necessary for you to take along with you.[3] To settle something with respect to *that* place

and Hambg which will not interfere with the genl Plan is difficult, but essential. There are other Papers also which it may be
useful for you to have. Mode of improving, regulations—&ca
&ca will be subjects to occupy your thoughts upon. I am always
Yours

Go: Washington

ALS, DLC: Thomas Jefferson Papers.

1. The enclosures for Joshua Johnson, U.S. consul at London, were GW
to Arthur Young, 15 Aug. and its enclosures, and GW to Samuel Vaughan,
25 August.

2. The "letter for Mr Carroll," probably in response to Daniel Carroll's letters to GW of 5 and 15 Aug. concerning difficulty in obtaining title to the lots
in Carrollsburgh, has not been found.

3. Carroll had sent GW a plat of Carrollsburgh on 5 or 15 Aug., which is
probably the one now in DLC: Map Division. See fig. 1.

From Samuel Langdon

Sr   State of N. Hampre—Hamptonfalls Augt 29 1791
    The deep impressions of my obligations to you, induce me
now to present a Volume which I have just published.[1] I hope it
will recommend itself to your notice as an attempt to give an
easy, rational, & useful explication of a sacred book, heretofore
often abused by whimsical interpretations, & on that account too
much neglected & despised by many modern christians. If I
have proved from that divine prophecy that we live in the very
times precisely marked out for the beginning of surprizing Revolutions in the world, it may serve greatly to confirm the truth
of the holy Scriptures; & the honours which divine Providence
has conferred on you will afford double satisfaction. With highest Esteem I am, Sr, your most obedient humle Servt

Saml Langdon

ALS, DLC:GW.

1. The accompanying volume was probably Samuel Langdon's *Observations
on the Revelation of Jesus Christ to St. John. Which Comprehend the Most Approved
Sentiments of the Celebrated Mr. Mede, Mr. Lowman, Bishop Newton, and Other Noted
Writers on This Book; and Cast Much Additional Light on the More Obscure Prophesies;
Especially Those Which Point Out the Time of the Rise and Fall of Antichrist* ...
(Worcester, Mass., 1791), which was copyrighted in New Hampshire on 15
July.

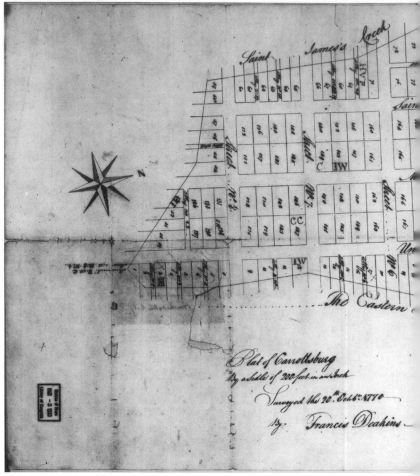

Fig. 1. Francis Deakins's plat of the projected town of Carrollsburgh, Maryland. (Courtesy of Library of Congress; see GW to Thomas Jefferson, 29 Aug. 1791 and note 3)

To Anthony Whitting

Mr Whiting,   Philadelphia August 29th 1791.
    In a letter which I wrote to you on friday last, I acknowledged the receipt of yours of the 22d, and informed you that I should again write as on this day, by the Post, who would also be the bearer of the materials for the Bolting Chest.[1]
    The latter is accordingly sent, directed to the care of the Post

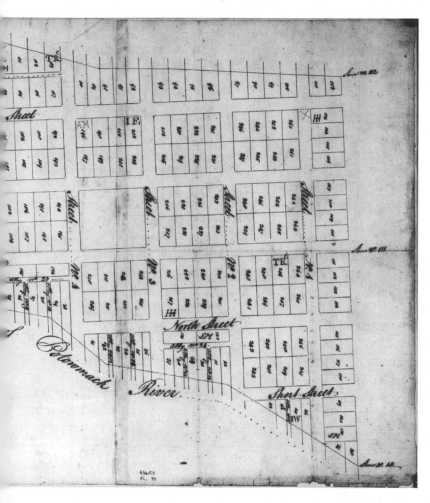

Master in Alexandria, and hope it will be in time for the Work of Mr Ball.

In my last, I informed you that I approv'd of the Carpenters going on with the house at Dogue run, agreeably to the first plan, as Richards house would do very well for an Overseers house at Muddy hole, where one was much wanting—this I repeat; but in my opinion, before they had got any new scantling for the first mentioned house, they ought to have pulled down the old one (called Wades) in No. 2 at that place; ascertained how much of those materials could, with propriety be worked into the new, and then, to have compleated what it would lack from the Woods. If this has not been done, that house as has been the fate of all the rest, under similar circumstances, will be lost; as my negros dismantle them as their occasions require, without leave, and without scruple.[2]

If Colo. Mason, or Mr Chichester, gives the person who has applied to be Overlooker of that place, a good character, it will be sufficient; as they are proper judges of the requisites, & will not, I dare say, advance things to serve him that are not warranted by facts. His getting a wife will be no objection, as it will induce him from inclination, to do what he ought to be obliged by articles, to agree to—that is—to be always at home.[3]

The reasons which you have assigned for treading out Wheat at the Ferry, are satisfactory, as they also are for Sowing the grass-seeds in the Mill meadow before the Corn is taken off; for I am clearly in sentiment with you, that it is high time that grass-seeds for Autumn sowing were in the ground. I am much pleased to hear that your Wheat seeding is so near completion; but the acct given of the grounds getting dry again, is much to be lamented, as it happens at a very critical time for most things—especially for Corn.

As Mrs Washington & myself expect to be at Mount Vernon by, or before the end of next month, I request that you would pay particular attention to the Meats, that I may have such as are fat, and proper for the Table while I am at home which will be till the middle of October; when I shall be under a necessity of returning to this City again. By fat meats—I mean Mutton, Lamb, Veal (if there are any calves young enough)—perhaps a small Beef also. I am—Sir Your friend & Servant

Go: Washington

ALS, PWacD.

1. GW's letter to Anthony Whitting of 26 Aug. has not been found. A chest requires cloth of a peculiar open weave to sift flour in a mill. GW probably was referring to this cloth.

2. For the plans to erect an overseer's house at Dogue Run, see GW to Whitting, 14 August.

3. For the agreement between George Augustine Washington and Henry Jones, the new overseer at Dogue Run, see GW to Whitting, 14 Aug., n.3. Jones

apparently had served as an overseer for either George Mason or Richard Chichester (c.1736–1796) of Fairfax County, whose daughter Sarah was married to Mason's son Thomas.

Letter not found: from Anthony Whitting, 29 Aug. 1791. GW informed Anthony Whitting on 4 Sept.: "Your letter of the 29th of last month came duly to hand, with the report of the preceeding week."

Tobias Lear to Thomas Jefferson

[Philadelphia] 30 August 1791. At the request of Attorney General Edmund Randolph, encloses for the office of the secretary of state fifteen patents signed by the president.[1]

ALS, DNA: RG 59, Miscellaneous Letters; LB, DLC:GW.

1. Thomas Jefferson docketed the receiver's copy: "The Secy of State 30th Augt 1792" and listed on it that the enclosed patents were for Englebert Cruse, James Rumsey, Nathan Read, John Stevens, Jr., John Fitch, James Macomb, and John Biddis & Thomas Bedwell for improvements in steam power, milling, distilling, and tanning (DNA: RG 59, Miscellaneous Letters).

From Giuseppe Chiappe

Excellence   Mogador le 31 Aout 1791

Extiment de mon devoir La continuation a Vôtre Excellence de Toutes Les Novelles de cet Royaume particullierement sur ce qu'il peut servir de gouvernement aux Venerables Etats, J'ai L'haute honneaur de Les umillier a V.E. & dans Le même temps de supliquer tres humblement vouloir m'honnorer de ⟨*illegible*⟩ ordres tres respectables ⟨*illegible*⟩ Toutes mes humbles precedentes pour me Tranquilliser de la doute que J'ai de si elles Soient parvennues a V.E.

S.M. Imperial est passê de Salè a Darelbeyda & chemin faisent â chatisées Les Revolteaux des Provinces de cette contê pansent de suivre jusque ici, St Croix & Maroc pour en exectuter du même avec Les deplus, Le suivent à propos un nombreuse camp, mais lui êtoient arrivè un Courrier de La part d'un de ces Comendents aux Frontieres de Ceuta d'Espagne qu'il lui portet La Novelle, d'être Sorti de cette Place un officier, un Intreprete & quelques Soldats, & que Le dit Officié avoit intimê, que

si S.M.I. êtoit en Paix avec L'Espagne devoit retirer Son Camp &
que si elle êtoit en Guerre Les Espagnols procureroit de La faire
retirer a forse; Confirmê cette Novelle pour des ministres de la
Secte S.M.I. s'animâ & dans Le moment prit Le chemin par ce
conté La, convoquent ces Troupes pour Le suivre, & passent de
Tanger on â comptées plus de 10 m. persones qu'il Le Suivoit,
en outre une plus grande Nombrè d'autres qu'il attendoient
dans Les Montagnes proches de Ceuta & Tetuan, & entre eux il
y avoit beaucoup de Princes vû que pour eux c'est une Guerre
de Religion & qu'ils doivent y être.

Est presque incompréensible une Tele determination puisque
Le Rois Ansali un des Capitains de Navir de S.M.I. est bien peu
de Temps q'il passá a La Cour de Madrid avec Les Preliminaires
de Paix deja Signées de S.M. Impl. & que en vertû des mêmes
La Court Susditte avoit ordonês a Cadiz de fournir au Rois Peres
tout ce qu'il Lui seroit de besoin per La garnison de quatre Freg-
ates, ce qu'il â ⟨choisir⟩ a son plaisir & même un gros Navire
Espagnol Les à apportées a Tanger.

Est aussi sur, que La Court d'Espagne avoit deja destinè La
Seconde Ambassade & que avec La même elle devoit envoier
700/m. Piastres dûes encore au Roy mort pour Le Droits de
Bleds & autres charges a Darelbeyda, & on croit que cette expedition â ête suspendue pour une Lettre que le Prince Mulei
Selema frer ⟨de⟩ S.M. â êcrit a la Court de Madrid, La prevenent
de ne remetre pas la susditte Somme aux mains de son Fraire a
raizon que elle appartenoit aux ⟨*illegible* Cre⟩ditaires seule-
ment, & particullierement jusqu'a voir. Informê S.M.I. de cette
prevention â repondû que Le tel argent apartenoit aux
⟨troupes & au⟩ Tresor Royal.

Depuis peu de temps ⟨retourne⟩ de la Court les Rois Ansali &
êtoient mal content de son recette, & pour avoir eûes quelques
disputes avec Le premier Ambassadeur Si ⟨Mulai⟩ Ben Ottomen
(au present encore a la Cour de Madrid) il a rapresentè Toute
Le mal possible contre La Cour & Le Susdit Ambassadeur, dis-
ent contre ce dernier qu'il êtoit plus Cretain des Cretains, Tout
ce que à aigrû de plus en plus S.M. pour aller contre Ceuta, &
nous Savons que cette Place est resollue a une defence jamais
vûe puisque dans Le premier affront elle en n'a pas fait cas, &
non ⟨obstent⟩ nous croyons que Les Choses Se arengeront.

J'ai l'haute honneaur ⟨de⟩ umillier a V.E. deux Notes des Presents faits par Les Ambassadeurs d'Englaterre & Dinamarque, mais la premiere il à âjoute Les monitions de Guerre qu'on attend ⟨de⟩ Londres en outre, les autres choses qu'ils ont êtêes consignêes Secretement depuis La même Ambassäd⟨e⟩.[1] Les deux Embassadeurs on êtês recûs avec Les honneaurs accotumés, & ils fur presentêes pour Le Tres Humble Serviteur de V.E. mon Frer Francois, q⟨ui⟩ à êtè ⟨ex⟩pediè de S.M. a Tanger pour recevoir L'Ambassadeur Suedois & le Comte Potoschi Po⟨lo⟩nois, note de Presents des queles je n'ai encore reçue.[2]

L'Ambassadeur Ollandois attend en Gibraltar Les Présants de ca République qu'ils y ont êtês expediês avec une Fregate Le 17 Juillet & les reç⟨oi⟩vent passerà a Tanger ò Tetuan pour Les presenter à S.M. Impl.

Le Consul de Françe en Salès Monsr du Roché L'attend aussi de Marseilles en û il fut apell⟨é p⟩our L'Enchargê de l'Ambassade avec Le Titre ⟨d'⟩Envoyê & il porte une bone Suite & des beaux presents.

On attend encore a chaque moment L'Ambas⟨sade⟩ de Venize.

Je Repete aux Venerables Etats & a V.E. Mes Tres humbles Serviçes & Toujour a ces ordres je l'ai L'haute honneaur d'être Tres profoundement de V. Exe Le Tres Humble & Tres Obbt Serviteur.[3]

Giuseppe Chiappe

LS, DNA: RG 59, Despatches from Consular Officers: Tangier; LS (duplicate), DNA:PCC, item 98. Tobias Lear docketed the cover of the source text: "From Guiseppe Chiappe 31st Augt 179⟨1⟩—(duplicate) The first sent to the Secy of State." The duplicate in DNA:PCC covers an enclosure, "L'Embassadeur Suedois."

For Chiappe's previous letters to GW, see Chiappe to GW, 18 July 1789, 13 May 1790, and 18 Jan., 10 April 1791.

1. The enclosed "Note des Presents de L'Ambassadeur Danois" and "Present de L'Ambassadeur Englois" are in DNA: RG 59, Despatches from Consular Officers: Tangier.

2. On 22 Mar. Francisco Chiappe sent to GW from Rabat lists of presents that the Danish and Swedish ambassadors had given to the emperor of Morocco. See James Simpson to GW, 13 April 1791, n.2.

3. Lear transmitted this letter to Thomas Jefferson on 3 April 1792 with GW's desire that if Jefferson found anything requiring GW's "particular attention" that "he would report it to him" (DNA: RG 59, Miscellaneous Letters).

From James Craik

Dear Sir   Alexandria [Va.] Aug 31st 1791

I am very Sorry to inform you that I was honoured with yours of the 14th Inst. only last night, not being in the habit of sending to the Post Office, The Post Master did not choose to give himself the trouble to send it, or to inform me such a letter was there, tho I might have expected such a favour from him—In answer to your request with regard to my very Worthy freind the Major. I am sorry to inform you, that I cannot help thinking his Case dangerous, And have been under considerable apprehensions for him for some time past. But his uncommon Anxiety to promote your Interest, and to give satisfaction carried his exertions beyond what his Constitution could bear, and notwithstanding every remonstrance I could make he would still persist untill he got so dibilitated that he found he could not hold out any longer. I with much difficulty at last perswaded him to leave of all business and travel for his health. Before he left home he had several attacks of Spitting of Blood, and I think matter at times, the Complaint in his Breast very troublesome, and many Symptoms of an Approaching Consumption. Indeed I think his Lungs a little touched, but would gladly hope from the Regemen I have laid down, and the manner of Conducting himself, that he may yet get better. However I cannot think that he will ever be able to undertake any kind of Active business, I mean such as will require much exertion—Since he went from home I am informed he is Something better, but the disorder is so flattiring and so apt to recur that I cannot say what may be the result. I must own I fear much—Your present Manager Mr Whiting tho to appearance a Stout able, well made mans I am affraid is not free from the same danger. altho he complains of no pain at present, yet he has had repeated discharges of Blood from his Lungs lately, which recur on any fit of Anger, or extraordinary exertions of the Lungs, which I am affraid may for[m] an ulcer at last. I have prescribed Rules for him to follow which I hope may have a good tendency to prevent bad Consequences and enable him to do his Duty—A Gentn who left the Sweet Springs last Wednesday brings Account of the death of Mrs W. Auge Washington in Twenty four hours after her Delivery the Child still alive.[1] Mr Lund Washington in pretty good health but quite Blind. Doctr Brown, it is said is much better, but I am affraid it is only Temporary[2]—Mrs Washington and the Children at Mount Vernon are well. My Daughter Nancy is there, by way of Amusement a while—She begins to be tiered of her Fathers house and I believe intends taking an old Batchelor Mr Hn for a play mate Shortly—What is wonderful to tell.[3] I had advised Miss Muir to Long Island to drink & Bath in the Sea Water for her health.[4] Mr Donaldson took the hint and pursued, and last Post writes back to Mr Hartshorn to rent out his house, as he beleives he shall bring back a wife with him.[5] Mrs Craik & family join me in Sincere prayers for the preservation of your health & happyness including that of Mrs Washington. And I am with Sincere Affe. your Devoted Sert

Jas Craik

ALS, DLC:GW.

1. William Augustine Washington, only son of GW's half brother Augustine, had married in 1777 Jane Washington (1759–1791), daughter of GW's brother John Augustine. The marriage produced five children who survived early childhood. This last child did not.

2. Dr. William Brown of Alexandria died in 1792.

3. Ann (Nancy) Craik, a friend of George Augustine's wife, Fanny Bassett Washington, married Alexandria merchant Richard Harrison in 1791.

4. "Miss Muir" was Elizabeth Muir, only sister of John Muir (c.1731–1791), an Alexandria merchant.

5. "Mr Donaldson" was Robert Donaldson, an Alexandria wheat and flour merchant and the business partner of William Hartshorne (died c.1802).

Tobias Lear to Henry Knox

United States [Philadelphia] September 1st 1791.

By the President's command T. Lear has the honor to transmit to the Secy of war a letter from Mr Andw Ellicott, to the President, proposing that Mr Joseph Ellicott should proceed immediately to Georgia to explore the head of the Oconee River preparatory to Mr Andw Ellicott's executing his business of running the line between the territory of the Creeks & the U.S.[1]

Should the Secretary of war conceive from Mr A. Ellicott's account of the man & the business, that it would be proper to accede to his proposal, the Secretary of War is requested to have the necessary credentials prepared & forwarded to Mr Ellicott by the post of tomorrow.[2]

Tobias Lear.
S. P. U. S.

ADfS, DLC:GW.

1. The letter from Andrew Ellicott recommending his brother Joseph to GW has not been found.

2. Henry Knox informed Tobias Lear this day that he wrote Andrew Ellicott on 31 Aug. "that if he had an assistant who was capable of the business in Georgia that he should repair immediately to this city to receive his instructions, and the necessary advance of money, and go from this place in a vessel which will sail from hence in a few days—This letter Mr Ellicott will receive on saturday—I submit therefore to the President—whether the business ought not to go on in its present train? I believe it will be the most expeditious, and I will again enforce it by another letter to morrow morning" (DLC:GW). Lear noted at the bottom of the letter: "The President thought with the Sey of War that the business had better go on in the present train." After GW approved Joseph Ellicott to run the boundary line agreed to by the Creek nation and the United States in the 1790 Treaty of New York, Knox instructed Ellicott on 8 Sept. to leave immediately for Rock Landing in Georgia and provided letters to be delivered to Gov. Edward Telfair, Alexander McGillivray, Maj. Richard Call, and the army contractors in Georgia. It was expected that Andrew Ellicott would finish his survey of the federal district and take over the Creek boundary survey before his brother carried the work past Currahee Mountain (*ASP, Indian Affairs*, 1:128–29).

Tobias Lear to Pierre-Charles L'Enfant

Dear Sir,   [Philadelphia] Septr 1st—7 O'clock A.M. [1791]
      The President wishes to have the map of the federal City to shew to some Gentlemen about nine o'clock this morning—and requests you to send it either by the bearer at this time, or if it should be more convenient for you, he shall call for it a little before nine.[1] I am Dear Sir with much esteem Your most Obedt Servt

Tobias Lear.

ALS, DLC: Digges-L'Enfant-Morgan Papers.

For background to this letter, see Pierre-Charles L'Enfant to GW, 19 August.

1. When he arrived in Philadelphia at the end of August, L'Enfant presented his plan for the Federal City to GW but retained his map in order to have it engraved before the initial sale of lots in October. While in Philadelphia

L'Enfant placed the map in the hands of a French engraver, M. Pigalle, who failed to complete his task before the sale (see Tobias Lear to GW, 6 Oct.; see also Thomas Jefferson to GW, 8 Sept., n.4).

Ratification of the Holland Loan

[Philadelphia, 1 September 1791]

Now Know ye, that the President of the United States of America having seen and considered the said contract, hath ratified and confirmed, & by these presents doth ratify & confirm the same and every article thereof.[1]

In testimony whereof he has caused the seal of the U.S. to be affixed to these presents, and signed the same with his hand. Done at the City of Philadelphia the first day of September in the year of our Lord one thousand seven hundred & ninety one, & of the independence of the U.S. of America the sixteenth.

G: Washington

LB, DLC:GW.

This ratification was for the two Holland loans, the unauthorized Holland loan of 1790 and the Holland loan of March 1791. For background to the 1790 loan, see Alexander Hamilton to GW, 26 Aug. 1790 (second letter) and notes. For the March 1791 loan, see Hamilton to GW, 10, 14 April 1791.

1. The contract for the 1790 loan, submitted for GW's approval reads: "To all whom it may concern—greeting. Where as the Legislature of the U.S. of America by their acts passed on the fourth and twelfth days of August, one thousand seven hundred and ninety, authorised the President of the U.S. to borrow on their behalf certain sums of money therein named, or any lesser sums, for the purposes therein stated, and to make contracts respecting the foreign Debt of the U.S.; and the President thereupon gave to Alexander Hamilton esquire, Secretary of the Treasury of the U.S., full powers by himself, or any person appointed by him, to carry the purposes of the said Acts into execution, and the said Alexander Hamilton in pursuance of the said powers, having authorised Messieurs William & John Willink, & Nicholas & Jacob Van Staphorst & Hubbard in that behalf, the said William and John Willink, and Nicholas and Jacob Van Staphorst & Hubbard have accordingly entered into Contract with certain persons for the Loan of three millions of Florins which contract was made known, & acknowledged by the said William Willink for William & John Willink, & by the said Nicholas Van Staphorst for Nicholas & Jacob Van Staphorst & Hubbard before Petrus Cornelius Nahuys Notary at Amsterdam in the U. Netherlands on the twelfth day of November in the year one thousand seven hundred and ninety, and is in the words following, to wit;

"On the twelfth day of November in the year seventeen hundred & ninety appeared before me Mr Petrus Cornelius Nahuys, Notary at Amsterdam admitted by the Court of Holland, Messrs William Willink, partner of the house of commerce, trading within this City, under the firm of William & John Willink; and Nicholas Van Staphorst partner of the house of commerce trading here under the firm of Nicholas & Jacob Van Staphorst & Hubbard, and likewise for & in the name of their aforesaid Houses of trade.

"The appearers dwelling within this City, makeing known, that the aforesaid houses of commerce of these appearers, have received from Mr Alexander Hamilton, Secretary of the Treasury of the United States of America, sundry Instruments passed by the congress of the United States of America, and His Excellency the President George Washington, whereby he, Mr Alexander Hamilton, is qualified and empowered for the purposes expressed in those acts to borrow at home, or in foreign parts, to the amount of twelve millions, and two millions of Dollars; provided that the interest from the monies so to be borrowed shall not exceed five in the hundred, and no engagement entered into, whereby the United States of America, should be precluded from reimbursing the monies borrowed, within fifteen years after the period, same shall have been borrowed: Authentic copies of all which deeds in the English language with translations thereof, have been delivered unto me Notary, to be annexed unto the minute of these presents.

"That the aforesaid Mr Alexander Hamilton, Secretary of the Treasury of the United States of America, in pursuance of the power vested in him, as aforesaid, by an act (authentic copy and translation of which, have likewise been delivered to me in manner aforesaid, and are annexed to the minute of thes presents) in name of the United States of America, has authorised & qualified them, Messrs William & John Willink, & Nicholas & Jacob Van Staphorst & Hubbard, or in case of the decease of any of them, the survivors thereof, to borrow on behalf of the United States of America, either by confirmation of the advertisement given out by the Houses of commerce of these appearers, or otherwise, as may be eligible, a Sum or Sums of money not exceeding three millions of Guilders, Subject to the conditions stipulated in the acts herein before mentioned; and further, to pass in the name & on behalf of the President of the United States of America, such contracts, Bonds or instruments as are requisite to that end, and customary in like cases, and to bind the good faith of the United States for the performance & fulfillment of all the aforesaid conditions: the said act accepting, approving, ratifying & confirming, in name and on behalf of the United States of America the Loan of three millions of guilders current money of Holland, dated the first of February of this present year, at the interest of five per cent per annum, the advertisement whereof has been given out by the houses of commerce of these appearers.

"And these appearers do, by virtue of the aforesaid authority, and the power therein delegated to them, acknowledge in the name and on behalf of the United States of America, to have received from sundry persons, or money Lenders, the Sum of three Millions of guilders current money of Holland; renouncing by these presents the exception of untold Monies, as likewise so far as is needful, the Beneficium divisionis, together with, de duobus vel pluribus reis debendi, signifying a division of the Debt, and that where there are two or more Debtors, each one may plead the payment of his share thereof as a full discharge from the remainder; these appearers promising in name as aforesaid, not to have recourse to those or any other evasions; as likewise that this Bond shall never be subject to any imposts or Taxes, already laid, or that shall hereafter be laid in the United States of America, even in case (which God forbid) any division hostility or War shall take place between the United States of America, & the States of these Countries; so that under no pretext or pretence whatever the payments of the interests, and of the reimbursements of the principal of this Bond, may be hindered or protracted.

"And these appearers further promise, in name of the aforementioned United States of America, to reimburse and pay in this City, the aforesaid principal sum of three millions of guilders current money of Holland, free from cost & charges unto the respective money lenders, within the period of Fourteen years, from the first of February of this current year seventeen hundred and ninety; which reimbursements shall take place on the first day of February in the years eighteen hundred, eighteen hundred & one, eighteen hundred and two, eighteen hundred and three, and eighteen hundred and four; one fifth part of six hundred thousand Guilders, in each of the said years; to which end, six hundred following numbers shall be drawn out of a Lottery, to take place before a Notary and Witnesses in the month of December preceding each of the aforegoing years, the result of which shall be published in the Gazettes; unless the United States of America shall prefer to reimburse the whole or a part of this negotiation sooner, which those appearers expressly reserve to the United States the faculty & power to do; the reimbursment in which last case, shall likewise take place by a drawing, and be advertised in the Gazettes.

"That in the mean time, the interest upon the whole of the principal sum, and successively upon the remaining or unredeemed part shall be paid untill the full discharge or reimbursment thereof, at the rate of five per cent per annum on the day it shall fall due, calculating same from the date of the recipesses of this & this Loan already delivered, & thus on the first day of February in each year, upon Coupons to be signed by or on behalf of these appearers.

"And there shall be made three thousand Bonds of participation in this act, under each of which shall be placed a receipt for one thousand Guilders; to be signed by the firms of the houses of commerce of these appearers, numbered from No. 1. to ⟨3⟩000 and countersigned by me, notary, & to be recorded and enregistered upon the minute of this Deed.

"For the performance and fulfilment of all which, these appearers, in name as aforesaid, do bind the good faith of the United States of America.

"Thus passed at Amsterdam in presence of Jacob Nicholas Michell, and Bernardus Jacobus Peronneau Van Leyden, witnesses

Petrus Cornelis Nahuys
Noty"

The contract for the loan dated 2 Mar. 1791 reads: "To all whom it may concern—greeting. Whereas the Legislature of the United States of America, by their acts passed on the fourth and twelfth days of August one thousand seven hundred and ninety, authorised the President of the United States to borrow on their behalf certain sums of money therein named, or any lesser sums, for the purposes therein stated, and to make contracts respecting the foreign debt of the U.S. and the President thereupon gave to Alexander Hamilton esquire, Secretary of the Treasury of the U.S. full powers by himself, or any person appointed by him, to carry the purposes of the said acts into execution, and the said Alex: Hamilton, in pursuance of the said powers, having authorised William Short Esquire, chargé des affaires of the United States of America at the Court of France, in that behalf, the said Wm Short hath accordingly entered into contract with certain persons therein named for the loan of two millions and a half of Florins, which contract was executed at Amsterdam in the United Netherlands on the second day of March in the year one thousand seven hundred and ninety one, and is in the words following to wit,

"On this 2d day of March in the year of our Lord 1791. appeared before me Nic: Obbes, Notary of Amsterdam, admitted by the honorable Court of Holland: William Short, chargé des affaires of the United States of America at the Court of France, in the capacity of being authorized by Alex: Hamilton, actual Secretary of the Treasury of the said United States of America, as empowered and qualified by virtue of a certain commission, power & authority, of the President of the United States, under two acts of Congress passed on the 4th & 12th of August 1790. to raise in any part of Europe for & in behalf of the sd United States a sum of money not exceeding that contained in these presents and on the premises to make or cause to be made such contract or contracts as shall be required, as more fully appears by the authentic copies & translations of the original commissions & power exhibited unto me the said Notary, and deposited in my Custody, in behalf of the joint Money-Lenders.

"And the appearer in his aforesaid quality, and thus in behalf of the above-mentioned States of America, acknowledged himself to be duly & lawfully indebted unto and in behalf of Sundry persons, or Money-Lenders, in all, a sum of two millions & five hundred thousand Guilders, Dutch current money, arising from, and on account of so much ready money received by him the appearer, in his capacity as aforesaid to his perfect satisfaction from the said money-lenders pursuant to the receipt hereafter mentioned to be signed by the appearer under the Bonds of participation, therefore expressly and formally disawowing the excuse of untold moneys.

"And the appearer, in the quality he in the premises does appear, did promise to reimburse and pay within this City unto the aforesaid Money-lenders or their assigns free from *charges* & *Damages*, the above expressed sum of two millions five hundred thousand Guilders at the expiration of fifteen years after the first day of March 1791. in the manner following; Vizt

"That the aforesaid Principal shall remain fixed during the space of eleven years and that at the expiration of the eleventh year, and thus on the first day of march 1802. a sum of five hundred thousand guilders shall be redeemed of the aforesaid principal of two millions and five hundred thousand guilders; and thus from year to year after the first day of March 1802. inclusive, in manner that the whole principal shall be redeemed & paid off, within the space of fifteen years as aforesaid, however it shall be lawful for the said United States to make a sooner discharge of the whole, or part of this Loan: And that meanwhile for the said principal, at first for the whole, and afterwards for the residue, at the expiration of every year, Interest shall be paid at the rate of five per Cent per annum, commencing with & on the first day of March 1791., and to continue until the whole is paid off & this on Coupons to be signed by or on the part of said Appearer in his capacity as aforesaid.

"That the said redeemings shall be performed by drawing of five hundred following numbers to be done in the presence of a Notary and Witnesses within this City, after the expiration of the first mentioned eleven years, & which said redeemings & Payments of Interest shall be made at the counting-houses of the gentlemen directors, as shall be advertised in the public papers.

"That the Directors of this Loan, shall be, Messrs Wilhem & Jan Willink and Nicholaas & Jacob Van Staphorst & Hubbard of this City merchants, who are by these presents hereunto named and appointed by the appearer in his said quality.

"The Appearer promising & engageing in the names of his Constituents, that the amount of the interests & of the redeemings to be made from time to time of the said principal, shall be remitted in due time unto the aforesaid gentlemen Directors, their heirs or Successors in good Bills of exchange, American produce, or in coin, without any abatement or Deduction whatsoever.

"That this Bond or obligation shall never be subject to any imposts or Taxes already laid, or in time to come to be laid in the said United States of America, or any of them, even in case (which God forbid) any war, hostilities or dissension should arise between the said United States, or any of them, on the one side, and the States of this Country on the other side, and that the payments of the principal or the interests of this Bond or obligation accordingly can in no wise, nor under any pretext whatsoever, be hinder'd or delayed.

"The appearer in his aforesaid quality, promising and engaging moreover on behalf of the said United States, that there shall never be made or entered into by them or their parts, or by any of them, in particular, at the making of Peace or otherwise, any convention or Treaty, public or private by which the validity & fulfilling of these presents might be prejudiced, or whereby anything contrary thereto might be stipulated, but that without any exception, the contents of these presents shall be kept & maintained in full force.

"The appearer in his said capacity, likewise promises, engages & binds himself by these presents, that this Engagement shall be ratified and approved as soon as possible by the President of the United States, & that authentic copy & translation of the said ratification together with its original, shall be deposited in the custody of me the said Notary, there to be kept with the said copy authentic translation of the commissions & Powers of him the said Appearer & the engrossed hereof for the security of the money-lenders, untill the above mentioned principal and the interests shall be redeemed & paid off and (as he the appearer in his aforesaid quality consents) there shall be made of this act, besides and above the aforesaid engrossed two thousand five hundred Bonds of participation which shall be of the same force & value, and have the same effect as the engrossed one, under every one of which said bonds of participation a receipt shall be placed of one thousand Guilders Dutch current Money, either on name or in Blank at the choice of the money-Lenders, to be signed by him the said appearer, and which receipts shall be, repectively numbered from No. 1. to 2500. inclusive and countersigned by the aforesaid Gentlemen Directors, & duly recorded by me the said Notary as a testimony that no more than two thousand five hundred Bonds are numbered by virtue of this act.

"All which Bonds of participation, with the receipts placed thereunder, shall at the redeeming of the principal be restored by the Bearers.

"For the fulfilling & performance of all the above written, he the said Appearer in his said quality, binds the *faith* of the United States of America in manner as is expressed by the acts of Congress, bearing date the 4th & 12th of August 1790.

"He the appearer renouncing in the names as aforesaid for that purpose expressly the Beneficium de duobus vel pluribus reis debendi, as likewise, (if need be) the beneficium ordinis, divisionis et excussionis, the sense of which are fully known unto him, he the said appearer promising in his aforesaid capacity never to have recourse to the said or any other evasions whatsoever.

"This being passed (after a translation was made hereof into English, which is likewise signed by the Appearer and deposited in the custody of me the said Notary) in the City of Amsterdam as aforesaid in the presence of Jan Trelich and Jan Augerman, witnesses.

W: Short."

GW's instrument of ratification, printed above, appears at the end of the letter-book copies of both contracts.

From John Clark

Sir,   Borough of York [Pa.] September 2d 1791.

A few Days since, when I had the pleasure of seeing you at McAlisters Town, on your return from the Southward; I did not expect that I should have occasion to write you so soon; but my Friend Colonel Hartley, having informed me that he believed the Office of Auditor was vacant, by the refusal of Mr Smith, whom I had understood was appointed; I beg leave to propose myself a Candidate for that Office.[1]

If my conduct as an Officer in the Military line, and while an Aid to the late Honbe Major General Greene, or as an Auditor of Accounts in the main Army, should have merited your esteem; I trust since my retirement, that my character in the line of my Profession, will add to it; and as to the former, I beg leave to refer you to a copy of a Letter you did me the honor (while lingering with a wound that I had received) to write the then

President of Congress;[2] and for the later, either the Honble Judge Wilson, or Chief Justice McKean if necessary, will give you the fullest information. Should you vouchsafe to honor me with this appointment, every thing within the compass of my power shall be exerted to execute the Office, so as to merit your, and the public esteem. If I should be unfortunate in this application, perhaps there may e'er long, be a vacancy, that you may think me deserving off; and I beg leave to assure you, it will be agreeable to me, to do every thing in my power, that may tend to support a Government you have rendered so respectable by presiding over it. With Compliments and best wishes for your future health and happiness as well as that of your amiable Lady, I have the honor to be Sir, Yr Most Obdt Hble Servt

Jno. Clark

ALS, DLC:GW.

Maj. John Clark (1751–1819) earned his commission in the 2d Regiment of the Pennsylvania flying camp troops in September 1776 for his bravery as a first lieutenant at the battle of Long Island and became an aide-de-camp to Maj. Gen. Nathanael Greene in January 1777 (Clark to Greene, 8 Nov. 1776, n.1, *Greene Papers*, 1:342; see also GW to John Hancock, 5 Oct. 1776, n.6). Clark impressed GW with his successful intelligence-gathering missions before injury to his right shoulder before the Battle of Brandywine incapacitated him. In February 1778 Clark accepted appointment as auditor to the army, serving until November 1779. After the war he was admitted to the state bar and unsuccessfully ran for Congress in 1819 (Spangler, "Memoir of Major John Clark," 77, 78, 85). GW appointed Clark a major in one of the new Legionary Corps formed in the spring of 1792 (see GW to the U.S. Senate, 9 April 1792; *Executive Journal*, 117, 119).

1. GW breakfasted on 2 July 1791 eighteen miles from York at Hanover, Pa., founded in 1763 by Col. Richard McAllister (*Diaries*, 6:168). William Smith did decline the appointment of U.S. auditor, and GW named Richard Harrison to the office in November 1791 (see Tobias Lear to GW, 19–20 June, n.8).

2. GW wrote a letter of introduction for Clark from Valley Forge to Henry Laurens on 2 Jan. 1778, describing him as "active, sensible, and enterprising." GW concluded: "It is somewhat uncertain, whether the State of the Major's Health will admit of his remaining in the military line, if it should, I may perhaps have occasion to recommend him in a more particular manner to the favor of Congress at a future time. At present I can assure you that if you should, while he remains in the neighbourhood of York, have any occasion for his Services, you will find him not only willing, but very capable of executing any of your Commands" (LS, DNA:PCC, item 152).

From George III

[London, 2 September 1791]

George the Third by the Grace of God, King of Great Britain, France and Ireland, Defender of the Faith, Duke of Brunswick and Lunenburgh, Arch-Treasurer, and Prince Elector of the Holy Roman Empire &ca To the United States of America sendeth Greeting. Our Good Friends. Having nothing more at Heart than to cultivate and improve the Friendship and good Understanding which happily subsist between Us; and having the fullest Confidence in the Fidelity, Prudence and other good Qualities of our Trusty and Welbeloved George Hammond Esqr. We have thought proper to appoint him Our Minister Plenipotentiary to reside with You, not doubting from the Experience We have had of His good Conduct on other Occasions, but that he will continue to merit Our Approbation, and at the same Time conciliate Your Friendship and good Will, by a strict Observance of the Instructions he has received from Us, to evince to You Our constant Friendship, and sincere Desire to cement and improve the Union and good Correspondence between Us.[1] We therefore desire that You will give a favourable Reception to our said Minister Plenipotentiary, and that You will give entire Credence to whatever he may represent to You, in Our Name, especially when, in Obedience to Our Orders, he assures You of Our Esteem and Regard, and of Our hearty Wishes for Your Prosperity: And so We recommend You to the Protection of the Almighty. Given at Our Court of St James's the Second Day of September 1791 in the 31st Year of Our Reign. Your very good Friend

George R.
Grenville

Copy, DNA: RG 59, Notes from Foreign Legations, Great Britain.

One of the matters that Gouverneur Morris, GW's special envoy to Britain, was instructed to discuss with the British administration was its failure to dispatch a minister to the United States (see GW to Morris, 13 Oct. 1789 [second letter]). British ministers attributed the lapse to the difficulty of finding a diplomat of suitable stature who would be willing to accept such a minor and distant assignment; several candidates had declined the appointment. The duke of Leeds, then British foreign secretary, told Morris in September 1790 that he "hoped soon to fix upon a Minister to America" (Morris to GW, 18 Sept. 1790). Only after the United States seemed intent on precipitating a crisis the following spring by passing legislation that would discriminate against British trade was George Hammond recalled from his diplomatic post at Madrid and named first minister plenipotentiary to the United States.

1. George Hammond (1763–1853) was secretary to British minister plenipotentiary David Hartley at Paris in 1783 during the peace negotiations with France and the United States and served as chargé d'affaires at Vienna from 1788 until September 1790, when he was sent to Copenhagen in the same capacity and then to Madrid. For news and rumors about the appointment of a minister to the United States, see Hamilton to GW, 11 April, Jefferson to GW, 17 April, William Stephens Smith to GW, 6 June, and Lear to GW, 19–20 June 1791, n.10. Hammond's instructions were debated and drafted that summer and finalized by new foreign secretary Lord Grenville on 2 September. Hammond's first priority was to secure American execution of the provisions of the Treaty of Paris of 1783 respecting the claims of British creditors and American Loyalists. He was also to counteract the discrimination movement in Congress, offer British mediation in the conflict between the United States and the western Indians, and discuss the basic principles of a commercial treaty, although he was not authorized to conclude a final settlement on the Northwest posts or commercial issues. His private instructions are printed in Mayo, *Instructions to British Ministers*, 2–5. Hammond arrived at the American capital on 20 Oct., two days before Thomas Jefferson returned from Virginia, and met with the secretary of state, with whom he had formed an acquaintance in Paris in 1783, on 26 Oct. (Jefferson to Hammond, Hammond to Jefferson, 26 Oct., *Jefferson Papers*, 22:234–35). However, he did not present this letter until later. William Loughton Smith reported to Edward Rutledge on 10 Nov.: "Mr. Hammond appears at present only in the character of Consul General having instructions not to assume the rank of Minister Plenipotentiary until the U. S. appoint a similar officer to reside in G. B." (Rogers, "Letters of William Loughton Smith," 228–31; see also Ternant to Montmorin, 13 Nov., in Turner, *Correspondence of the French Ministers*, 68–72). In 1793 Hammond married Margaret Allen, daughter of Loyalist Andrew Allen of Philadelphia, and the couple returned to London in 1795.

From Pierce Butler

[Philadelphia, 3 September 1791]. "I received the inclosed letter while I was at dinner—It is my duty to send it to You."[1]

ALS, DNA: RG 59, Miscellaneous Letters.

1. The letter of Isaac Motte, naval officer for the port of Charleston, S.C., to Senator Pierce Butler, dated Boston, 21 Aug. 1791, reads: "I have just heard of the death of my worthy and good friend, Mr Geo: Abbott Hall—There's a necessity for a successor to be appointed to the Office he held, as soon as possible, especially as I am absent, and as I may be thought of by some of my friends to be a proper person, I beg leave to inform you, that I wou'd not wish to hold the place, I wou'd rather keep the one I now have, for many reasons,

which I will give when I have the pleasure of seeing you. I think it woud be improper in me to write anything of the kind to the President, and as I know of your intimacy with him, request the favor of you, to let it be known, that it wou'd not be agreeable to me, to accept of the Appointment of Collr of the Port of Charleston, shod I be thought worthy. . . . I mean to set off for New Hampshire some time this week & then return to Rhode Island, from whence I wou'd immediately go to Charleston, was my health so established as to enable me to attend to the duties of Office, but as that is not the case, it wou'd be v⟨ery⟩ unwise in me to leave it 'till the cool weather sets in" (DNA: RG 59, Miscellaneous Letters). Tobias Lear this day transmitted to Alexander Hamilton Motte's letter by order of GW to "shew the necessity of making a change in the Commissions for the Port of Charleston, if they should not have been forwarded" (DLC:GW). GW had already decided to make Motte collector, and the commission apparently had been made out but not yet sent. Hamilton sent Lear two recalled commissions on 5 Sept. (DLC:GW), and the next day Lear sent Hamilton a new one temporarily appointing Isaac Holmes collector (DLC:GW). The permanent commission of Holmes, dated 7 Nov., was made out and sent to Hamilton for transmittal on 10 Nov. (State Department Memorandum Book, DNA:PCC, item 187, 118). For GW's appointments of the Charleston customs establishment, see Pierce Butler to GW, 3 Aug., n.1.

From Philip Schuyler

Dear Sir   Albany [N.Y.] September 3d 1791

I did not receive the letter you did me the honor to address of the 25th ult:, until it was too late, to acknowledge its receipt, by the return of the post who brought it.

On the Objects to be ascertained, so great a diversity of Opinion prevails, even amongst the best informed, that it seems requisite, the decision in every instance, should be the result, of what has really occured, or at present exists, I shall therefore extend all my Attention to the compleatest investigation of facts, I am capable of, and state the reasons that least to my conclusions.

Some important business will call me from home in a few days, and wholly engross my Attention for Eight or ten days more, but immediately thereafter, I shall devote myself, without intermission, to enable me to transmit answers to your interesting enquiries.[1] I have the honor to be with every sentiment of respect, Esteem and Affectionate regard, Dear Sir, Your most Obedient Servant

Ph: Schuyler

ALS, DLC:GW.

For background to this letter, see GW to Arthur Young, 15 Aug., n.2, and Circular on the State of American Agriculture, 25 August.

1. There is no evidence that former Senator Philip Schuyler ever returned answers to the agricultural queries of GW. GW did not forward them to Young with the other responses he sent on 5 Dec., and only the reports of Thomas Hartley, Thomas Johnson, and David Stuart appeared in Arthur Young's resulting publication, *Letters from His Excellency General Washington, to Arthur Young* . . . (London, 1801).

From Robert Ballard

Sir   Baltimore Septemr 4th 1791

I must once more take the liberty of trespassing on your time with a few lines, which respects the compensation to be allowed me for my services as Inspector of the Revenue.[1] The Supervisor in his Circular Letter to me, says that, "as it was supposed that the Office would add but little trouble to the Office of Surveyor, no particular compensation is allotted." I cannot find any part of the Law which warrants such an opinion—and I am sure that in exercising the duty, I find the entire service falls on me. Mr Gale performs not any duty other than that of furnishing me with blank Cerficates, and semiquarterly a Copy of my proceedings. I am, sir, to acknowledge the very great obligation I owe you for your goodness in bestowing this second kind favor on me; and permit me to assure your Excellency, that I shall observe the most watchful attention in the exercise of my duty— but sir, if Mr Gales Opinion prevails, that is to say, I do all the duty, and he receive all the pay, then I am more than ruined. My fees arising from my Surveyors Office is far short of maintenance, and nothing but the kind indulgence of my Creditors prevents me from Suits. The duty of an Inspector of the Revenue, is very arduous, and the office important & respectable— at present I keep only one Clerk who does nothing but write in the Office; to him I give £100 ℔ Year. In the Spring when the Crops of Spirit comes in, I must have an additional Clerk. It is a melancholy reflection where my whole time and service is yielded to the Public to know that the emoluments allowed, falls considerably short of Support: especially as I am growing old & have a large family to maintain and educate—and that is all I now look up to.

I have, may it please your Excellency, been thus particular, well knowing that when any case comes fairly before you that the strictest justice will be done, I must furthermore add that the Ex⟨*mutilated*⟩ business falls considerably heavy on my other duty, without any reward for it. The Gauger and Weigher are paid for their share of that duty, and nothing is allowed to the Surveyor.[2] I have the Honor to be with the greatest respect Your Excellency's most Obedt humble Servt

Robert Ballard

ALS, DNA: RG 59, Miscellaneous Letters.

1. On 3 April Robert Ballard, surveyor for the port of Baltimore, solicited from GW the post of excise inspector for the port. He apparently already assumed his duties under Maryland district supervisor George Gale, although his appointment, together with that of the other inspectors, was not confirmed until mid-March 1792 (*Executive Journal*, 111).

2. Tobias Lear informed Ballard on 7 Sept. that he first should have brought the matter to the attention of Secretary of the Treasury Alexander Hamilton: "As it is impossible for the President to attend to the minutiae of business which may be communicated by Individuals, he wishes always to receive such information as may be proper to come before him, relating to the several Departments, thro' the heads of the Departments to which the business properly belongs. Upon this view of the matter the President is persuaded, Sir, that you will not consider his declining to reply to the subject of your letter, at this time, as a singular case; for he observes the same conduct on all occasions of this nature" (DNA: RG 59, Miscellaneous Letters). Lear forwarded to Hamilton Ballard's letter along with a similar one Boston collector Benjamin Lincoln wrote Lear (Lear to Hamilton, 7 Sept. 1791, DLC:GW; see also GW to Lincoln, 14 Aug., n.3, and Hamilton to Ballard, 17 Oct. [letter-not-found entry], in Syrett, *Hamilton Papers*, 9:401).

Letter not found: to John Greenwood, 4 Sept. 1791. Greenwood wrote GW on 10 Sept. that "I Received yours dated the 4th by the hand of sr John Jays son."

To John Jay

My dear Sir, Philadelphia Septr 4th 1791.

The indisposition, and consequent absence from Mount Vernon of my Nephew, Majr Washington, to whom the care of my private business is entrusted, makes it indispensably necessary for me to go home before the meeting of Congress.[1]

My stay there will be longer or shorter according to circumstances—but it cannot exceed the middle of October, as I must be back before the meeting of that Body.[2]

Will you permit me, my dear Sir, to make a similar request to the one I did last year—and to pray that your ideas may not be confined to matters merely Judicial, but extended to all other topics which have, or may occur to you as fit subjects for general, or private Communications.[3] With sincere esteem and affectionate regard I am—My dear Sir Your Obedt & very Hble Servt

Go: Washington

ALS, NNC; Df, DLC:GW.

1. For the trip of George Augustine Washington to Berkeley Springs for his health, see his letter to GW, 1 Aug., n.8.

2. The first session of the Second Congress was scheduled to convene on the fourth Monday of October (1 *Stat.* 198). GW mistakenly assumed that day would fall on 31 instead of 24 Oct. (see Lear to GW, 9 Oct., and GW to Alexander Hamilton, 14 October).

3. GW had made his "similar request" to John Jay on 19 Nov. 1790. Jay docketed the receiver's copy of the above letter as received on 9 September. He replied to GW from New York on 10 Sept.: "My attention shall be immediately turned to the Subject alluded to, and I shall be mindful to avoid unseasonable Delays" (N.F. Saltykov-Shchedrin State Public Library: International Exchange Section, St. Petersburg, Russia; see also John Greenwood to GW, 10 Sept. 1791, n.1). Jay forwarded his suggestions to GW on 23 September.

To Anthony Whitting

Mr Whiting,   Philadelphia Septr 4th 1791.

Your letter of the 29th of last month came duly to hand, with the report of the preceeding week, and I am sorry to find by them that the weather had become dry again, but as we have had some fine rain here in the course of last week[1]—as it is now raining, and has been doing so near twelve hours—and has all the appearances of a general rain, I hope in your next to hear, that you have participated in them, and that your crops are benefitted thereby, & not very unpromising.

I am very sorry to hear that no more ground was sown in Buck-wheat for *a Crop* than the remains of No. 5 at Dogue run. The want of it may be a serious misfortune to me, as your Oats have, and Corn may, turn out very short. The weather about the time Buckwheat *ought* to have been sown, was as dry here as it could be with you, & the ground broke up as hard; nevertheless the Farmers persevered until they got in the seed & now nothing can be more promising than it is—the scanty crop of Corn therefore, to them will scarcely be felt in feeding their stock; & it was the apprehension of this that induced them, notwithstanding the difficulty in preparing of the ground, to encrease the quantity as a substitute; by doing which they will find their account in an ample provision for their Harvest.

Field No. 2 at Dogue run, is the next for Corn, & the one which, (if you find any advantage from the practice this year) you will list with furrows, thrown back to back on the unbroke earth, as was the case last Fall. I mean to adhere to my system *at that* Plantation, as the only one (in my opinion) that will ever restore my fields to any degree of fertility; for I see clearly that it is in vain to expect that they can be kept up by manure in the manner you speak of; and to crop them hard without, is like pushing a horse that has a long race to perform to his full speed at first; the result of which must be, that he will grow slower and slower every round he takes, until he is unable to move. I saw very little progress when I was last at home, in manuring by Cowpens; & none by Mud; & without these, it is impossible that the winter pens, & stables, can supply the dificiency. What then, besides vegitable manure and laying (in grass if possible) can keep the land in tolerable heart? or, if constantly in use, can save it from destruction? I speak from experience; for I used to get ten, twelve, and more bushels to the acre from Corn land laid down in wheat—and what do I get now—you can answer this! yet, I am willing that you should pursue your own course (except at Dogue Run) next year.

Among several sorts of Wheat which I sowed for experiments in the fall of 1788, there was a white wheat (not bearded) that I had conceived a very high opinion of, & intended to have gone largely into the growth of it; Can this be the white lammas which you condemn? that, and the yellow bearded, as it resists the Hessian fly, I meant to have propagated principally—I hope every precaution will be used to prevent the different kinds from mixing.[2]

What has been done to the Dogue Run meadow since I left Mount Vernon? by the reports I perceive a good deal of labour has been bestowed on it, and am much pleased therewith. It would be a most desirable thing if the wet parts of the meadow at the Mill, next to be prepared, could be well grubbed—cleansed—and broke up, as the lower part (now in Corn) was last Autumn, before the weather became too cold & wet to work in it. The same wish, as far as it is practicable to accomplish it, I would extend to the Swamp which is now ditching at French's. The Summer, and early part of the Fall, are the only proper seasons for that sort of work.

I am very glad to hear of the good performance of the Mill. If Mr Evans or his brother, agreeably to the tenor of the enclosed letter, is not there by the time Mr Ball has compleated the other parts of the work, let him go on without; but with those parts first, as are mentioned in the letter. I send the license for erecting this machine[.][3] It is taken for one pair of stones only, because no more are employed in the manufacture of wheat.

Have you heard of the missing horse yet? I am certainly the most unlucky person living in horse flesh, *on my Estate*—& almost as bad indeed in other species of Stock, as no report is made without deaths; although I am always culling the old ones to prevent them. I remain Your friend &ca

Go: Washington

ALS, ViMtV.

1. The letter of Anthony Whitting of 29 Aug. and its enclosed farm report, which probably noted a missing horse, have not been found.

2. For GW's experiments of 1788 with wheat, see George Morgan to GW, 31 July–5 Aug., GW to Morgan, 25 Aug., to John Beale Bordley, 17 Aug. 1788; *Diaries,* 5:390, 391.

3. At this point in the MS, GW inserted a symbol for the following note along the right margin: "This license after Mr Ball has seen it must be lodged with the Major." For the work of Oliver and Evan Evans and William Ball on GW's mill, see Tobias Lear to Oliver Evans, 29 August.

From "Adolescens"

May it please your Excellency ⟨Friday 5⟩th Septemr 1791.

Tho' an address, most respected Sir, to one in your exalted Station, to which a fictitious name is subscribed may seem altogether strange & uncommon, yet the Contents of this letter will I hope be a sufficient apology for its Author's temerity, and, I flatter myself that a Man whose heart is ever alive to the calls of Humanity, will not deem it an impertinent intrusion.

That I may not trespass for long on your goodness Sir, I will, with the utmost diffidence proceed to lay before you my distressed situation. The person who now has the honor to claim your Excellency's attention is the most wretched of Men. I am the son, Sir of a professional gentleman who was once very eminent & who is still I believe generally esteemed as a man of very superior abilities, but an unfortunate attachment to Company & an unhappy partiality for pleasurable pursuits has for some years past put it out of his power to pay that attention to Business which his Employers expected—in consequence of which his practice has considerably decreased & he is now barely enabled to maintain his family genteelly—Whatever may have been his foibles however, he has always been a tender & kind Father, and his anxiety for my future Welfare, is now the cause of all my woe. Some considerable time past I formed an attachment which as it was then disagreeable to my friends I endeavoured to stifle in its infancy, but having frequent opportunities of conversing with one of the most amiable of Women, I found the attempt utterly vain & impossible, & every exertion but confirmed me a slave to her perfections. She had as is natural to be supposed many other admirers, but always honored me with particular attention & in every Company for every occasion I was preferred—not considering the consequences I then courted her esteem & Oh most sacred Sir! words are wanting to express my transports, when with a candour that did honor to her own intrinsic worth, she confessed that I was entire Master of her affections, & that she lived but to make me happy—Then, Sir, oh then! I was at the summit of Bliss, my felicity was to exquisite to be of long duration for from that moment which made me the happiest of Men, from that Moment I date the completion of my misery. My own misfortunes I could bear with patience & a calm resignation to the divine will, but shall I for a moment cause an uneasy sensation in the breast of one who lives but to make me happy, oh my God! the thought distracts me, the Idea peirces my very Soul—but alas! where am I going Oh Sir! pardon my anguish, I will no Longer trouble you with my distress but continue my Narrative.

My parents I believe have no objection to my entering into the matrimonial State, but my age (being only 19) & my situation—it is not in their power at present to put me in any line of business by which I could obtain a subsistence for a family, and the dear object of my affections has not a fortune at her own disposal. Her father it is true is a man of some property, but he is determined not to let any part of his Estate go out of his own hands until his death, & indeed even then, he has Several other Children who have an equal right to his paternal bounty—Now Sir you have heard my Situation candidly laid open & oh let your sensibility be awakened—have Compassion on an unhappy Couple whose only misfortunes proceed from a virtuous attachment to each other & not having it in their power honorably to gratify their mutual affections. But perhaps your Excellency may doubt my veracity & look upon the Author of this address as a villainous imposture, & alas! what language can I use to convince you to the contrary—Oaths & protestations are now Sir so common that I cannot expect they will have much weight, but with permission I will pledge you my most sacred honor Sir that what I have here asserted is most strictly true & that my condition is just as I have related, I once thought a personal application the most proper to obviate this objection, but the mortification which my Connexions would have suffered had they known it, entirely deterred me & indeed my own resolution was ⟨scarcely⟩ adequate to the Task—however if your Excellency still suspects my sincerity, I will wait on you with pleasure at any hour you may be so condescending as to appoint and in the mean time permit me Sir Submissively to beg that I may receive a line of information on this head on Wednesday morning next when I will take the liberty to call for that purpose, and let me beseech you to pardon my presumption, & oh Sir let your Generosity be exerted in my favor, & may your liberality snatch a Wretch from the brink of despair & perhaps of Eternity whose whole happiness entirely depends on your Goodness, and whose constant prayers shall be for your eternal Welfare & felicity. I am With every Sentiment of the most profound Respect Your Excellencys most devoted & very humble Serv't

Adolescens

AL, DLC:GW.

There is no evidence that GW met with this pseudonymous supplicant before leaving Philadelphia on 15 Sept. or provided him any assistance.

To Armand

Dear Sir, Philadelphia, September 5th 1791.

I have had the pleasure to receive your letter of the 22nd of march last.[1]

Being indisposed on the day when Monsieur de Combourg called to deliver your letter I did not see him—and I understood that he set off for Niagara on the next day.[2]

The interesting state of affairs in France has excited the sympathy and engaged the good wishes of our citizens, who will learn with great pleasure that the public deliberations have eventuated in the permanent happiness of your Nation—and no one will more sincerely rejoice in that event than Dear Sir, Your most obedient servant

G. Washington

LB, DLC:GW.

1. The letter from Charles-Armand Tuffin, marquis de La Rouërie, of 22 Mar. 1791, reads: "Mr le chevalier de Combourg a noble man of the State of Britany & a neighbourg of mine, is going over to north america. the purpose of that Journey, I presume, is to inrich his mind by the active Contemplation of such a moving & happy country, and to satisfy his soul By seeing the extraordinary man & thoses respectable Citizens who, led By the hand of virtue through the most difficult contest, have made their chief Counsellor of her in establishing & enjoying their liberty—his relations, for whom I have a very great regard, desire me to recommand him to the notice of your Excellency; I do it with pleasure, Because that gentleman has allways appeared to me to have a good right to the Commendable reputation which he does enjoy—he is a man of wit, and much of his time has Been taken up By the Cultivation of that natural gift. our political af⟨f⟩airs in this part of the world, are in the most deplorable situation. loyalté, good sense, firmness, seems to be Banished from our unhappy & perhaps more guilty, country—the Compassion of god almighty is the only resource which remain to us; But I am sure he is Just, and of Course I fear his mercy will be only felt long after his severity. may france, By her present Condition, be now and in all future times a tremendous instance for all peoples on earth, of the great risk and destruction which threaten nations, when without any regard to their moral & physical circumstances, instead of wisely & slowly reforming abuses and repairing breachs made to their constitution; they confide the over setting of the whole into the hands & at the discretion, of ambition, avarice, ignorance, caprices, and of all the private interest which follow of Course—may your dear Général follow, while this world will last, the impulsion given her by your great heart your incomparable wisdom, & By that Candour which so well characterize the present génération of north america—I have been honöred in January last with

your letter of the 13th of October 1789—Mr du moustier is not the speedyest nor the most faithfull messenger in europe—but at this time, it appears ⟨essential⟩ to thoses men to Counterpoise with all their hability, the conveniency and inconveniency of all their steps; even that of delivering up a letter directed from a free Country to a lover of that Country who reside in our—I Beg leave to offer here to lady Washington the best homages of my respect" (DLC:GW). GW's letter to Armand of 13 Oct. 1789 has not been found. Eléanor-François-Elie, comte de Moustier, the former French minister to the United States, left America in October 1789.

2. For GW's illness of July 1791, see A. Hammond to GW, 8 July, n.3. French author François-Auguste-René, chevalier and later vicomte de Chateaubriand (1768–1848), who after the Bourbon Restoration served as French minister to Great Britain and minister of foreign affairs, was born at the castle of Combourg and served as a sublieutenant in the French army before the French Revolution. The excesses of the Parisian mobs convinced him in January 1791 to leave France and pursue an earlier plan to search for the Northwest Passage in North America. After visiting Armand he embarked from Saint-Malo, Normandy, on 8 April and landed at Baltimore on 10 July. He took a carriage to Philadelphia and claimed to have visited GW at home: "When I went to carry my letter of recommendation to him, I found once more the simplicity of the ancient Roman. . . . After a few minutes, the general entered the room: tall in stature, of a calm and cold rather than noble bearing, he resembled his engraved portraits. I handed him my letter in silence; he opened it and glanced at the signature which he read aloud. . . . We sat down. I explained to him as best I could the object of my journey. He replied in monosyllables in English and French, and listened to me with a sort of astonishment. I remarked this and said to him, with some little animation: 'But it is less difficult to discover the North-West Passage than to create a people, as you have done.' 'Well, well, young man!' he exclaimed, giving me his hand. He invited me to dinner for the next day, and we parted. I took care to keep the appointment. We were only five or six guests at the table. The conversation turned upon the French Revolution. The general showed us a key from the Bastille. . . . I left my host at ten o'clock in the evening, and never saw him again" (*Memoirs of Chateaubriand*, 1:136, 158, 161–62, 179–83, 207, 210–11). Chateaubriand may have misremembered the period of his visit with GW, but no mention of it is made by GW in his surviving diaries. For the key to the Bastille that Lafayette had sent GW, see Lafayette to GW, 17 Mar. 1790, n.3. Chateaubriand received no encouragement in Philadelphia for his explorations and traveled to New York, Boston, and Albany before setting out west. He broke his arm at Niagara Falls and spent twelve days recuperating with the Indians before accompanying a party of traders to Pittsburgh and into the interior. Chateaubriand abandoned his romantic trip when he read in a newspaper of the flight of Louis XVI and his arrest at Varennes, and he returned to Philadelphia and embarked for Le Havre on 10 Dec. to join the counterrevolutionary armies (*Memoirs of Chateaubriand*, 1:216–30, 236–37, 246–47, 259).

From Henry Knox

[Philadelphia] 5 September 1791. Encloses the resignation of Thomas Seayres, "who was appointed an Ensign on the 30th of April 1790, and a Lieutenant on the 4th of March last—But he never joined the troops, and therefore his resignation is not to be regretted."[1]

LS, DLC:GW.

1. Thomas Seayres (Thomson, Thompson Sayres), son of Col. John Seayres (d. 1777), was commissioned an ensign in February 1781 in the 5th Virginia Regiment of the Continental army. He was promoted to lieutenant the following May and retired from the service in January 1783. GW appointed Seayres an ensign in the additional U.S. Infantry Battalion created by an act of 30 April 1790 and promoted him when John Steele declined a lieutenancy (GW to the U.S. Senate, 2 June 1790, and 3 Mar. 1791, enclosure; *DHFC*, 2:73, 554, 5:1274–1301). Seayres resigned his commission on 2 September.

To Moustier

Dear Sir,   Philadelphia September 5. 1791.
    I have had the pleasure to receive the letter which you were so good as to write to me from Berlin on the 26 of April.[1]
    The favorable sentiments which you express of our country and its councils are very agreeable to me—The kind interest which you take in my personal happiness excites a grateful sensibility.
    You will learn with pleasure that events have realised the most sanguine hopes of our national prosperity—The influence of the general government has extended to every relation of political improvement, and to the promotion of our social happiness.
    The interesting state of affairs in France excites the sympathy, and engages the good wishes of our citizens, who will rejoice to hear that the public deliberations have resulted in the permanent dignity and happiness of your nation. In the joy, which that event will diffuse, no one will participate more sincerely than he who is, with great regard, Dear Sir, Your most obedient Servant
                                                                G. Washington

LB, DLC:GW.

1. The translation in Tobias Lear's hand of the letter of 26 April of French minister at Berlin Eléanor-François-Elie, comte de Moustier, to GW reads: "I received but yesterday the letter with which you honored me on the 6th of November last. Its date recalled to my mind the place where I had the satisfac-

tion of paying my first homage to you. That interesting period of my life will always be recollected with the same sensibility. The Country life, which you know, Sir, how to render as useful to your Citizens by your examples, as agreeable to yourself, is well worthy of engaging as much of your time as you can give it. I have learnt with very great satisfaction the influence which it has had on your health. It is there that the relaxation of the mind & the exercise of the Body dispell those evils which are occasioned by the restraint of living in a City, and which is peculiarly unfavorable to those who are constantly occupied in the painful cares of Government. The success which attends your cares, Sir, in the administration of the United States, is a flattering recompence for those labours which you have so long devoted to your Country. So well am I convinced of the wisdom & virtue of the American Congress that I never fail to present it as a model for my fellow-Citizens. If you have ever read the preface, placed at the beginning of a translation which I solicited, of the American Laws digested by order of Congress in 1789, you would there have seen my opinion. I am the Author of these reflections which I have developed on more than one occasion. The Wits who rase themselves to extremes in my country are not yet disposed to receive them. Instead of the energy which results from a public force well organized, we see that violence reign which results from a force plac'd without its centre. The end has been missed, I however, love to flatter myself that it will return. They have exaggerated the evils which they suffered & have employed, in consequence thereof, remedies excessively violent and in no manner suited to the disorder which they had to handle. I hope those who are firm have a desir⟨e⟩ to return upon their own steps, which requires more courage & talents than to go straight forward. Any sacrifice, even that of self love, ought not to be accounted as any thing by a good Citizen, and if they pretend that Kings make an avowal of their errors—why should simple Citizens pretend to persevere in theirs? I did not attach myself to any party during my stay in France, I flattered no idol of the moment because I had never flattered any heretofore. I love my Country with Ardor. For a long time I have devoted myself to her. I lamented the abuse of the former Government—I lament that they have not made the one which follows it better. I wait until they renounce those Chimeras, & descend from the regions of perfection which do not belong to human space. I confine myself to filling in my sphere the duties which are alotted me. Our nation deserves to be happy. The crime of leading her from happiness is great in proportion as it is easy to conduct her to it. The tissue of a false glory—the enthusiasm of the perfection of Government—Cupidity—vengence & hatred are not good ingredients for forming the chief of a Revolution. It was good perhaps to demolish—but it is rare that a demolition is suitable when the passions dispell the Judgement. I have seen you, Sir, grieve as a *Henry*. How many Henrys have we in France? In whatever situation I may be I shall not cease to prove the lively Interest which I take in the prosperity of the United States, and I shall always regard it as a mark of good fortune to have been in a situation to admire you & to give testimonies of the veneration which is due to your virtues & to your eminent qualities" (DLC:GW). The original receiver's copy (in French, DLC:GW) appears in CD-ROM:GW.

To Edward Newenham

Dear Sir,   Philadelphia, September 5th 1791.

I have the pleasure to acknowledge the receipt of your letters of the 31st of January, and 10 of March last, and to express my obligations to your flattering and friendly assurances of regard.

The interest which you are so good as to take in the welfare of the United States makes the communication of their prosperity to you, a most agreeable duty. You will learn with pleasure that events have justified the most sanguine expectations entertained of the influence of the general government on the political and social happiness of America.

Public credit established—Justice promptly and impartially administered—Industry encouraged and protected—Science progressing—Liberty, civil and religious, secured on the liberal basis of reason and virtue, are the rich rewards of the past exertions of our citizens, and the strong incentives to future patriotism.

The manufacture of maple sugar is in a very promising train, and, as the tree grows in several of the States, there is every reason to conclude that its cultivation will be prosecuted with success. Colonel Jeremiah Wadsworth is of Connecticut, and, at present, one of the Representatives of that State in Congress.[1]

The multiplied cares of my public station do not permit me minutely to indulge the pleasures of private correspondence, and they oblige me to resort to the candor of my friends to excuse a brevity, which might appear abrupt, or a seeming inattention that nothing else could justify.

I shall realise with the most sensible satisfaction your purposed visit to our country, as it will afford me an opportunity personally to assure you of the great regard and esteem, with which I am, Dear Sir, Your most obedient Servant

G. Washington.

LB, DLC:GW.

1. Sir Edward Newenham had inquired of GW on 31 Jan. "whether Colonel Wadsworth of New Hampshire be alive, as I have often wrote to him, & never receivd an Answer—I am not Sure whether he is of Connecticut or New Hampshire." Newenham wrote to GW on 10 Mar. that Janet Livingston Montgomery had sent him a sample of American maple sugar: "if your states should make Sugar to Supply themselves, it will be a real fund of Wealth." For maple sugar production in New York, see Thomas Jefferson to GW, 1 May 1791, n.4.

From William Loughton Smith

New York, 5 September 1791. Encloses for GW's perusal a letter from Arnoldus Vanderhorst, the intendant of Charleston, recommending his uncle Elias Vanderhorst as consul for the port of Bristol—"I beleive the Intendant would not recommend any person unworthy of the Station"—and calls "attention to Col. Motte, as Successor to Mr Hall, & to Mr Bounetheau for the place of Naval Officer: From my own knowledge & inquiry I beleive the latter gentleman eminently qualified for it."[1]

ALS, DLC:GW.

1. GW appointed Elias Vanderhorst consul at Bristol the following spring (GW to the U.S. Senate, 3 May 1792 [first letter]). For the death of the collector of Charleston, George Abbott Hall, and the promotion of naval officer for the port, Isaac Motte, see Pierce Butler to GW, 3 Aug. 1791, n.1. Tobias Lear informed William Loughton Smith on 9 Sept. at GW's command that GW had appointed Isaac Holmes collector at Charleston before receiving Smith's letter, as Motte had expressed a wish to be continued as naval officer (DNA: RG 59, Miscellaneous Letters). Smith had previously recommended Peter Bounetheau to GW as federal loans commissioner or revenue inspector (Smith to GW, 17 July 1790).

Letter not found: from Charles Carroll, 6 Sept. 1791. GW wrote to Carroll on 11 Sept.: "I have been duly favored with your letter of the 6th instant."

From Aulay Macaulay

Claybrook near Lutterworth, Leicestershire

Sir   6th Septr 1791

I beg leave to appeal to your humanity on behalf of a poor old man in this neighbourhood whose name is Thomas Franklin—and who stands in the relation of first cousin to the late Dr Benjamin Franklin—His Father and Dr F.'s Father were Brothers—He is now in indigent circumstances—and sinking under the pressure of age and infirmities—Dr Franklin once took some notice of him tho' he made no mention of him in his will—At the time that the Doctor first heard of his having so near a relation in Leicestershire—the poor man happened to be imprisoned for debt—but Dr F. released him[1]—and besides other marks of kindness and generosity he took his kinsman's daughter under his protection—and gave her a good education—This young Lady was married by Dr Franklin's consent to a Mr Pearce, who went to America in 1783 (his wife having died a year before) and left his Son—who was then about four years old under the care of his Grandfather Thomas Franklin—He has never heard from the Boy's Father, but once since he left England—The letter was dated Annapolis in Maryland—July 1784—The Boy is still with his Grandfather—He has no other relation or protector in this part of the world—and when the old man dies—he will be in a very pitiable situation.[2]

Be assured Sir such is my veneration for the memory of Benjamin Franklin—that were I in circumstances to afford effectual relief to the Old man—and to provide for the Boy—I Should not have troubled you with a representation of their case—but I have nothing more than the very limited income of a country curacy and therefore I can contribute little besides my sympathy and good wishes—I flatter myself that the American Congress would not be averse to take under their protection those poor distressed relations of their great Benefactor—and I am persuaded that an appeal to their generosity through you Sir—cannot fail of success.[3]

I am happy Sir to embrace this opportunity of expressing my veneration for your character—and the high sense which I entertain of your distinguished services to mankind—and with best wishes for your happiness—private & public—temporal & eternal I remain Sir your most humble Servt

A. Macaulay

ALS, DLC:GW.

Aulay Macaulay (1758–1819), eldest child of minister John Macaulay of Lismore, Scotland, and uncle of historian Thomas Babington Macaulay, received the M.A. from Glasgow University in 1778. He took holy orders in 1781, became curate at Claybrook the following year, and was rector at nearby Frolesworth from about 1792 to 1796, when he obtained the more lucrative living of Rothley, Leicestershire, which he held until his death. Macaulay made two tours of the Continent and published several volumes, including a history of Claybrook, as well as travel accounts in the *Gentleman's Magazine*.

1. Thomas Franklin, Sr. (1683–c.1752), was actually the only son of John Franklin, brother of Benjamin Franklin's father Josiah. Benjamin Franklin wrote from London to his sister Jane Franklin Mecom on 17 July 1771 that "our Father's Brother John . . . was a Dyer at Banbury in Oxfordshire, where our Father learnt that Trade of him, and where our Grandfather Thomas lies buried" and referred to Thomas Franklin, Jr. (born c.1715), who was "now

living at Lutterworth in Leicestershire, where he follows the same Business, his Father too being bred a Dyer, as was our Uncle Benjamin. He is a Widower, and Sally his only Child. These two are the only Descendants of our Grandfather Thomas now remaining in England that retain that Name of *Franklin*" (*Franklin Papers*, 18:184–87; see also 1:li, lxviii–lxix).

2. Thomas Franklin brought his daughter Sarah (Sally; c.1756–1781) to London in 1766, probably after the death of his wife, and left her with Benjamin Franklin, later hoping she would be taken to America (Benjamin Franklin to Deborah Read Franklin, 11 Oct. 1766, 22 June, 5 Aug. 1767, ibid., 13:444–66, 14:192–95, 224–26). Instead, after gaining Franklin's trust and affection by her loyal and effective service in his household, she married in April 1773 James Pearce, "a substantial young Farmer at Ewell, about 13 Miles from London; a very sober industrious Man" (Benjamin Franklin to Samuel Franklin, 7 July 1773, ibid., 20:276–77; see also Benjamin Franklin to Deborah Read Franklin, 1 Dec. 1772, 6 April 1773, ibid., 19:395–96, 20:144–45). According to Benjamin Franklin Sally Pearce apparently was pregnant with her first child by September 1773, and the family included three daughters and a son at the time of her death (Mary Hewson to Benjamin Franklin, 30 May 1779, ibid., 29:579; see also 1:lii). Dorothy Blunt in 1776 loaned Pearce £50, with which he was able to furnish a house and lease it out for lodgings, and three years later Elizabeth Wilkes offered him free of charge "a detached apartment sufficient for Pearce's family & business" (Hewson to Benjamin Franklin, 8 Sept. 1776, 30 May 1779, ibid, 22:594–96, 29:579).

3. Tobias Lear replied to this letter on 14 Nov.: "In obedience to the President's commands, I have the honor to inform you that the President brings no business before Congress but what is of a public nature, and such as his official character renders it necessary for him to communicate to that Body. His departure therefore in this case from his uniform practice could not be warranted. The President moreover directs me to inform you that Dr Franklin has left several near relations with handsome property in this city, to whom, or through whom it seems most proper that application should be made, and that there is most probably a Grandson of Dr Franklin's in London at this time (he having gone over there last Fall). The President has a proper sense of your good wishes, which you so warmly express for his happiness" (DLC:GW). For the trip to London of William Temple Franklin, see GW to William T. Franklin, 25 Oct. 1790.

To John Cannon

Sir, Philadelphia, September 7th 1791.

I have received your letter of the 10. of August[1]—and am very sorry to find that so far as it relates to my property under your care, I have no further satisfaction than the assurance which you have given in all the letters received from you, that *I shall have* a statement of my interest committed to your care—But Sir, I surely had a right to expect something more than the *promise* of a statement before this time, as it is now better than four years since my lands were committed to your care—As the rents were to be paid in wheat it was certainly proper that time should be allowed for converting it into cash before I could receive any thing from you—But as yet I have received *only fifty pounds*—and, considering the length of time that you have had an agency in this business, and the great demands for wheat and flour, particularly last year, when, it is a fact known to every one that it not only commanded a higher price in that part of the country than perhaps had ever been before known there, but ready money also, I am persuaded you will yourself allow that I have just cause to complain.

I hope, Sir, you will, therefore, for your own sake, take such steps in the business as will put it upon a footing satisfactory to me as well as to yourself—and as you see the unfavorable impression which the thing, in its present state, makes upon my mind, I trust it will not be long before you endeavor to remove this impression by putting the business in the situation where it ought to be.

As I intend to leave this place next week for Mount Vernon and shall not return until the latter part of October, I shall not probably see you here unless you should be in this place the last of that month—but this will make no difference as the business can be equally well done with Mr Lear.

In reply to your request that I would mention your name to the Governor of this State as one of the County-Judges, I must inform you that I make it a point never to interfere, on any occasion, in any State appointments. I am Sir, your humble Servant
G. Washington

LB, DLC:GW.

1. John Cannon's letter of 10 Aug. to GW has not been found. Not having received a reply to this letter, GW wrote him again on 19 April 1792: "After the letter which I wrote in September last, I did not expect to have waited 'till this time for a reply. I therein stated, in as strong terms as decency would permit, the impression that your conduct, with respect to my business in your hands, had made upon me; and had no doubt but it would have drawn you to a settlement of your accounts with me, or at least produced some explanation from you: Neither of which have, however, been effected by it. It is unnecessary for me to make any comment on your conduct in this business—You must yourself be forcibly struck with the impropriety of it. I shall, therefore, only

observe, that however painful it may be to my feelings, and opposite to my wishes, yet I shall be obliged, in justice to myself, to pursue another mode of application, if this should be found ineffectual" (LB, DLC:GW).

From George Clinton

Sir   Greenwich [N.Y.] 7th September 1791

I do myself the Honor to transmit to your Excellency Copies of certain Dispatches, which I this Day received from Lieutenant Colonel Woolsey, commanding Officer of the Militia of Clinton County in the Northern Part of this State; with an Extract of his Letter to me in which they were inclosed.[1] The repeated Insults which our Citizens have experienced from the British; both before, and since my last Communications to your Excellency on this Subject have been extreamly mortifying, and I have reason to conclude have in a very considerable Degree obstructed the Growth of the Settlements in that Quarter.[2] Until the Receit of the inclosed Information I was induced to ascribe this Conduct to the unauthorized Insolence of Inferior Officers at their advanced Posts and flattered myself that it would soon have ceased; But the recent Proceeding of Colonel Tomlinson as stated in Mr Moore's Letter appears to be too formal and unequivocal to admit of a Doubt that the present meditated Incroachment is sanctioned by the Orders of the British Government.

On this Occasion I presume I should stand justified in issuing Orders to the Militia to repel the Invasion; but as this might be attended with Consequences which would probably terminate in an Interruption of the Peace of the Union; I have thought it most adviseable to submit the Matter to your Excellency's Consideration previous to my giving any Directions on the Subject.

Permit me Sir to observe that this State has already abundant Reason to complain of the Conduct of the British Government for the Retention of different Military Posts within it's acknowledged Limits contrary to the Articles of Peace; and should they now be permitted to establish new Ones it will not fail to encrease the already prevailing disatisfaction.[3] I have the Honor to be with the highest Respect Your Excellency's Most Obedient Servant

Geo: Clinton

ALS, DNA: RG 59, Miscellaneous Letters.

For background to British occupation of the posts on northern Lake Champlain, see Thomas Jefferson to GW, 5 June, n.2. For the administration's policy "to repel force by force" in order to bring the matter forcibly to the attention of the British government and compel "propositions to an amicable settlement," see Jefferson to GW, 27 Mar., GW to Jefferson, 1 April 1791. Dissatisfied with the boundaries drawn by the Treaty of Paris of 1783, the British desired to limit American settlement along the Canadian border in order to pursue future opportunities to redraw the line, especially in the Old Northwest, where they hoped to establish an Indian buffer state. In northeastern New York and northern Vermont their policy was to warn off potential American settlers from disputed areas. In February 1791 the governor of Quebec complained to the British commander at Point au Fer on Lake Champlain that the Canadian border had been "destroyed" in 1775 and 1776, and that "there is no frontier. When a frontier treaty shall be formed, all foreign improvements on the Canadian side will be lost. Those who complied with the warning will be satisfied; those who stealthily made a pitch, as they call it, will probably be punished more than could be wished by the loss of their time, labour, and expense. This is to be repeated to them from time to time with civility and good humour" (Lord Dorchester to Lieutenant Colonel Buckeridge, 14 Feb. 1791, calendared in Brymner, *Report on Canadian Archives, 1890*, Q. 50–1, pp. 283–84). In writing to other post commanders, Dorchester's military secretary stressed "that the people shall always be treated by the troops in a gentle, friendly manner" and "to be told civilly to remove and warned of the loss they will sustain if they refuse to obey the warning" (Francis Le Maistre to British commanders, 14 Feb., 8 April 1791, ibid., 284, 286). Reacting to Lord Dorchester's dispatches of June 1791, Lord Grenville instructed George Hammond on 2 Sept.: "You will represent, that it is absolutely necessary both in point of Justice and from the regard which is due in return for the friendly line of conduct now adopted by His Majesty that no steps should be taken by the American Governments to alter the relative situation of the two Countries, such as it now exists de facto, pending the Negotiation to which your Mission will give rise. And therefore, that every degree of discouragement should be given [by] those Governments as well as [by] His Majesty's officers to any Americans who may under these circumstances attempt to settle themselves within the limits of the Country now occupied by the British. Some recent Circumstances of this nature which have occurred make it particularly necessary that you should urge this point, and I am persuaded that if the American Governments are really desirous to promote a good understanding, it will not be difficult for you to convince them how repugnant it is to such an object to suffer points of so much magnitude to be brought into discussion by the Enterprises of Individuals, instead of being made the Subject of temperate and friendly negotiation between the two Governments" (Mayo, *Instructions to British Ministers*, 13–17).

1. The documents are printed below as an enclosure and notes.

2. The "last Communications" from George Clinton to GW on the subject were probably his letter and enclosures of 21 May 1790.

3. GW replied on 14 September.

Enclosure
Extract of Melancthon Lloyd Woolsey to George Clinton

Sir   Burlington (Vermont) 17th August 1791

"The enclosed Papers will show your Excellency the Nature and necessity of my Business here any farther explanation of my Motives will also I conceive be unnecessary, how far the Measures I have pursued will be consistant with your Ideas of the Nature and Tendency of this Business I am at a loss to determine; The peculiar Delicacy of my Situation, and consequent embarrassment I presume may be easily immagined; to escape Censure from the Government, or reproach from the People. To draw the True Line between Rashness and Timidity, and to avoid Hostility and be obedient to the Laws of my Country appears to me exceedingly difficult—Either a Depopulation of the Northern Part of the County of Clinton or hostile Opposition cannot much longer be avoided.[1]

"Your Excellency's last Letter to me contained Instructions but they were too general for my satisfaction at the present Juncture.

"That the Mode I have pursued already in seeking Advice here will be approved of I can hardly doubt; that Measure was consistent with Judge Tredwells Ideas & something that might be a Justification of my Conduct, appeared to me of Consequence—Governor Chittendon seemed pleased with the Attention—assured me of every support in Case of extremity and kindly offered at any Time to furnish me with the Means of communicating Dispatches if necessity required it. Our unprovided situation for Defence is much to be regretted, The Want of Arms & Ammunition is general on both Sides the Lake & the impossibillity of making the Provision unequivocal.

"I hope to have your Excellency's Directions as speedily as possible peremptory for every possible Emergency. I am &ca"

Mel. Ld Woolsey

Copy (in Clinton's hand), DNA: RG 59, Miscellaneous Letters.

Melancthon Lloyd Woolsey (1758–1819) was the only son of Col. Melancthon Taylor Woolsey of Long Island, New York. He served as an officer in the Continental army from 1776 until his retirement in April 1779 and was afterwards a major of the New York levies on the frontier and an aide to Governor Clinton. In March 1779 Woolsey married Alida Livingston (1758–1843), daughter of Henry and Susan Conklin Livingston, at Poughkeepsie, N.Y., where he established himself in business after his father's death (Woolsey, *Memoir*, 5, 8, 10, 11). Impoverished by wartime inflation, Woolsey began a fresh start in 1785 on a hundred acres on Cumberland Head on Lake Champlain. When Clinton County was established in 1788, Woolsey became head of its militia and first clerk of the county court (Woolsey, *Memoir*, 12–14, 18–19, 23). GW appointed him collector of the newly created customs district of Champlain in March 1793, upon the recommendation of Congressman James Hillhouse, husband of Woolsey's cousin Sarah Lloyd (ibid., 27; Hillhouse to Alexander Hamilton, n.d., and 2 Mar. 1793, both DLC:GW; *Executive Journal*, 138; 1 *Stat.* 336–38; *JPP*, 81, 83, 169–70).

1. The enclosures were two letters and a memorandum, copies of which Clinton forwarded to GW. The first letter was written by Pliny Moore to his friend Colonel Woolsey. Moore was appointed justice of the Court of Common Pleas and a justice of the peace of Clinton County upon its establishment. Ever since his arrival to the area in 1785, he "was visited, on the first of each month, by a corporal and file of men, sent from Point au Fer to notify him that his claim of title from the state of New York would not be recognized. No attention was paid to these repeated warnings" (Peter S. Palmer, *History of Lake Champlain, from the First Exploration by the French in 1609, to the Close of the Year 1814* [Albany, 1866], 175). Moore's letter to Woolsey, dated Champlain Town, N.Y., 13 Aug., reads: "Two Days ago seven British Officers were at my House among whom I was informed was a Colonel Tomlingson who commands in the District of Montreal or in that Department a Captain Adams who acts as Engineer, Capt. Steel &ca. The Colo. desired Capt. Adams to communicate their Business to me, which he did by shewing me a paper on which he said was a Draft of a Redoubt to be thrown upon the Ground where my House stands—Told me the Ground was in Canada in the British Dominion, and the Colonel was come up to view the best Ground on the River with Orders to establish a Post here. That they should commence the Business within two Days or four or five at farthest—The Engineer informed the Colo. in my hearing that about four hundred Men and four Pieces of Ordinance the Post would require—They asked me many questions, To which I made such Answers as my Duty suggested, tho' I presume a little Time for reflection might have arranged them to more Advantage—They strongly recommended it to me to remove my Familly and Effects—I told them when they carried me a prisoner I supposed I should be obliged to go Not till then would I remove a Shillings worth of my Effects: if a Part must become a Sacrifice the whole might—I intimated a wish that they might dare to carry their Threats into Execution, for that I was Tired of repeated Insults—They expressed much of an insulting sorrow and insulting Pity that so good a Situation, Buildings and Improvements must be so altered and distroyed; but concluded that the Service required it, That tho' they were sorry to be the Agent must do their Duty &ca—Thus much for Information of the Fact" (DNA: RG 59, Miscellaneous Letters). The second letter, from Moore and Justice of the Peace William Beaumont to Woolsey with the same dateline as the first, reads: "Should the British attempt an Invasion according to their Threats to Mr Moore we shall proceed against them as Rioters as far as we can—which should they come with force probably will be no

farther than to command them to dispurse We shall then give you the earliest Information. In the Mean Time our Confidence in you as Commander of the Militia—leaves us no Room to doubt but you will take the most proper Measures to give us speedy Relief—Our Opinion is should they make the Attempt as they expect no Opposition they will not come prepared for any Resistance" (DNA: RG 59, Miscellaneous Letters). The third enclosure was a memorandum written by Thomas Chittenden and Ira Allen at Williston, Vt., on 17 Aug.: "Whereas Colo. Melancton L. Woolsey of the County of Clinton and State of New York has represented to us that Col. Tomlinson Commander of the British Force stationed at St Johns &ca with a Number of British Officers did on the Eighth Day of August Instant come to the House of Pliny Moore Esqr. of Champlain in said County and that said Colo. Tomlinson did then and there publickly declare that the Place where Mr Moore's House stood was the Place he had pitched upon to build a Redoubt and proposed to bring on a Force of four hundred Men to erect and defend said Redoubt & requested in a hostile and threatning Manner Mr Moore to remove his Effects from said Place—Whereupon Colo. Woolsey requests our Advice. On a short Consideration of the Matter we are fully of Opinion that it is Colo. Woolsey's duty to transmit the Information he has received on said Subject to Governor Clinton and in the Mean Time to direct Pliny Moore Esquire &ca in said County of Clinton that in Case the British Troops attempt to take Possession of any Improvements, Buildings or Property of any of the Inhabitants of said County that they personally make every Opposition in their Power except that of Military Force, and that Colo. Woolsey suspend that ⟨un⟩till he has received Orders from his Superiors" (DNA: RG 59, Miscellaneous Letters).

To d'Estaing

Sir,   Philadelphia 7th September 1791.

I have had the honor to receive your letter of the 30th of May by the hands of Monsieur de Ternant.[1] and I beg you will be assured that I have a proper sense of the very polite and obliging manner in which you are pleased to express your personal regard for me.

The manner in which you speak of M. de Ternant is highly honorable to him—and, from his talents, discretion, and proper views, united with the extensive information which he possesses, there is but little doubt of his rendering good services to both Countries.

Such is the state of your political affairs by our last accounts that further information must be received to enable us to form an opinion respecting them. But, in any event, the welfare of the french Nation cannot but be dear to this country; and that its happiness may in the end be established on the most permanent and liberal foundation is the ardent wish of every true American, and of none more sincerely than of him who has the honor to be, with due consideration, Sir, Your most obedient Servant

G. Washington

LB, DLC:GW.

1. Jean-Baptiste, chevalier de Ternant, most likely delivered to GW the letter of Charles-Hector, comte d'Estaing, on 10 Aug. (see Louis XVI to GW, 28 May, n.1).

From Thomas Jefferson

Sir   George town [Md.] Sep. 8. 1791.

We were detained on the road by the rains so that we did not arrive here till yesterday about two oclock. as soon as horses could be got ready, we set out & rode till dark, examining chiefly the grounds newly laid open, which we found much superior to what we had imagined. we have passed this day in consultation with the Commissioners, who having deliberated on every article contained in our paper, & preadmonished that it was your desire that they should decide freely on their own view of things, concurred unanimously in, I believe, every point with what had been thought best in Philadelphia. they decided also the following additional matters.[1]

Quere 2. lots to be sold in four places, viz., on the Eastern branch, near the Capitol, near the President's house, & in the angle between the river & Rock creek.[2]

3. The ready money payment at the sale to be increased to one fourth, & so advertized immediately. they will send advertisements to some printer in every state.

7. the houses in the avenues to be *exactly* 35 feet high, that is to say their walls. none to be higher in any other part of the town, but may be lower.

11. the compromise stated to you by mister Johnson has put this matter out of all dispute.[3]

13. the map to be engraved on account of the Commissioners, & the sales of them for the public benefit.[4]

19. they have named the City & the territory, the latter after Columbus.[5]

Tomorrow they meet to take measures for carrying into execution all the several matters contained in the paper which I have the honor to return to you, as I believe you have no copy of it.[6] Mr Madison & myself propose to pursue our journey in the morning. four days more will bring me to my own house. we were told in Baltimore that that place was becoming better humored towards this, and found it better that the government should be here than in Philadelphia. I have the honor to be with sentiments of the highest respect & attachment Sir Your most obedt & most humble sert

Th: Jefferson

ALS, DLC:GW.

For background to this document, see Memorandum for Thomas Jefferson, c.27 August.

1. On 31 Aug. Jefferson invited Pierre-Charles L'Enfant to dine with him and James Madison the next day "to converse with him before their departure on several matters relative to George town" (*Jefferson Papers*, 22:112). Whether L'Enfant accepted is uncertain. Jefferson and Madison left Philadelphia on 2 Sept. and arrived at Georgetown on 7 Sept., spending that afternoon examining the ground selected for the Federal City, where workmen under the direction of L'Enfant and Andrew Ellicott were busy opening paths through the woods for streets. On 8 Sept. Jefferson and Madison met with the three commissioners for the federal district.

2. The decision to sell lots at four widely separated places in the Federal City was undoubtedly intended to appeal to the interests of all of the proprietors. As indicated by Jefferson's notes on GW's second query in the enclosure below, the commissioners postponed designating the specific location of the lots to be sold. On 9 Sept. Ellicott suggested to the commissioners selling lots near the Eastern Branch and Georgetown, since these could be readily developed for commercial purposes, but he urged them to delay selling lots around the federal buildings, shrewdly noting that these would rise considerably in value once the buildings were constructed. Instead, he suggested selling lots on the edges of the city that might be appropriate for gardens or pasturage. The commissioners considered Ellicott's recommendations but did not instruct him specifically which lots should be surveyed before the October sale. Ellicott also sent to L'Enfant a report on the commissioners' meeting, expressing surprise that they had not rendered a decision about the lots to be sold (Arnebeck, *Through a Fiery Trial*, 61).

3. Jefferson is alluding to the problem of acquiring the lots in Hamburgh and Carrollsburgh from dozens of owners. Earlier efforts at outright purchase had been unsuccessful (see William Deakins, Jr., and Benjamin Stoddert to GW, 9 Dec. 1790, and GW to Deakins and Stoddert, 17 Feb. 1791). Thomas Johnson apparently had suggested to GW exchanging each lot in the undeveloped towns for one lot in the Federal City (see Jefferson's note to query 11

in the enclosure below). This was the solution adopted by the commissioners in 1793–94.

4. This decision resolved an issue raised in Jefferson's letter of 19 Aug. 1791 to L'Enfant: "A person applied to me the other day on the subject of engraving a Map of the Federal territory. I observed to him that if yourself or Mr. Ellicot chose to have this done, you would have the best right to it." The commissioners did not agree with Jefferson that L'Enfant or Ellicott possessed the right to publish a map of surveys performed while employed by the federal government, and Jefferson's opinion might have contributed to L'Enfant's belief that he was independent of the authority of the commissioners (*Jefferson Papers*, 22:47–48).

5. The commissioners had agreed to name the Federal City "Washington" in honor of the president, as Jefferson informed GW in a note at the bottom of the enclosed memorandum. The idea of naming the Federal City in honor of GW had been proposed publicly as early as August 1789 (Bowling, *Creation of Washington, D.C.*, 225). William Loughton Smith had suggested to L'Enfant in April 1791 "calling this new Seat of Empire, Washingtonople" (Matthews, *Journal of William L. Smith*, 62).

6. On 9 Sept. the commissioners drafted a memorial to the state of Maryland seeking legislative sanction for the proposal to exchange lots in Hamburgh and Carrollsburgh for lots in the Federal City and requesting authority to license the sale of liquor and the building of wharves in the district, as well as to regulate the disposal of earth displaced for cellars, wells, and foundations, to establish a registry of deeds for the district, and to give a bill of sale from the commissioners the same legal force as a deed. They also asked that the Maryland legislature pass a law permitting foreigners to purchase land in the District of Columbia. On 9 Sept. the commissioners officially informed L'Enfant of the names of the Federal City and the district as well as the alphabetical and numerical system for naming streets. They also instructed him to have 10,000 engraved copies of his plan prepared in advance of the October sale (Arnebeck, *Through a Fiery Trial*, 61–62).

Enclosure
Memorandum for Thomas Jefferson with Jefferson's Answers and Notes

[Philadelphia, c.27 Aug.–8 Sept. 1791]

Will circumstances render a postponement of the Sale of Lots in the Federal City advisable? If not   not adviseable?

[2.] Where ought they to be made   left to be considered ultimately on the spot, the general opinion being only that the leading interests be accomodated.

[3.] Will it in that case, or even without it, be necessary or prudent to attempt to borrow money to carry on the difft works in the City?

doubtful if a loan can be proposed without previous legislative authority, or filled till a sale shall have settled something like the value of the lots which are to secure repaiment. the ready money paiment increased to one fourth. Must wait for money. the property of reclaimed lands to be considered of.

Whether ought the building of a bridge over the Eastern branch to be attempted—the Canal set about—and Mr Peter's proposion with respect to wharves gone into *now*—or postponed until our funds are better ascertained & become productive?

At what time can the several Proprietors claim, with propriety, payment for the public squares wch is marked upon their respective tracts?

Whenever the money shall have been raised by the sale of their own lands.

Ought there to be any wood houses in the town?

No.

[7.] What sort of Brick or Stone [Houses] should be built—& of wht height—especially on the principal Streets or Avenues?

liberty as to advancing or withdrawing the front, but some limits as to height would be desireable.[1] no house wall higher than 35 feet in any part of the town; none lower than that on any of the avenues.[2]

When ought the public buildings to be begun, & in what manner had the materials best be provided?

the digging earth for bricks this fall is indispensable. provisions of other materials to depend on the funds.

How ought they to be promulgated, so as to draw plans from skilful Architects? and what would be the best mode of carrying on the Work?

by advertisement of a medal or other reward for the best plan. see a sketch or specimen of advertisemt.

Ought not Stoups & projections of every sort & kind into

no incroachments to be permitted.

the Streets to be prohibited *ab-solutely?*

[11.] What compromise can be made with the Lot holders in Hamburgh & Carrollsburgh by which the plan of the Federal City may be preserved?

a liberal compromise will be better than discontents, or disputed titles.

Ought not the several Land holders to be called upon to ascertain their respective bounderies previous to the Sale of Lots?

certainly they ought.

[13.] Would it not be advisable to have the Federal district as laid out, (comprehending the plan of the Town) engraved in one piece?

it would.

to be done; but whether by the Commissioners or Artists, to be considered of.[3]

[14.] Names of streets, alphabetically one way & numerically the other. the former divided into North & South letters, the latter East & West numbers from the Capitol.

[15.] lots with springs on them to be appropriated to the public, if practicable without much discontent, & the springs not to be sold again.

[16.] The public squares to be left blank, except that for the Capitol, & the other for the Executive department which are to be considered as appropriated at present. all other particular appropriations of squares to remain till they are respectively wanted.

[17.] Soundings of Eastern branch to be taken in time for the engraving.

[18.] Post road through the city, will see to it immediately.

19 Name of city and territory, City of Washington & territory of Columbia.

[20.] Meeting of President & Commis on **after**noon of Oct. 16.

AD, DLC:GW. The queries on the left are in **GW's** hand, and the replies were written later by Thomas Jefferson, who also **num**bered some of the queries, inserted the word in square brackets in **query** 7, and wrote the notes at the bottom of the second page before returning the document to GW.

Jefferson seems to have written most of his answers to GW's queries before meeting with the commissioners on 8 Sept. and might have written them as early as late August when he discussed the memorandum with GW. That GW and Jefferson, and probably also James Madison, conferred in August about GW's questions is indicated by Jefferson's comment in the covering letter that the commissioners had "concurred unanimously in . . . every point with what had been thought best in Philadelphia." Notes fourteen through twenty were added by Jefferson on 8 September.

1. This part of the answer to query 7 seems to reflect a general principle agreed to in Philadelphia before Jefferson's departure.

2. This part seems to reflect a decision made by the commissioners on 8 September.

3. This response suggests that Jefferson wrote most of the answers to GW's queries before the specific decision made by the commissioners on this point at the meeting of 8 Sept. and described by Jefferson in the covering letter (see also n.4 to that letter).

To Henry Knox

My dear Sir.   Philadelphia September 8. 1791.

I have heard of the death of your promising Son with great concern, and sincerely condole with you and Mrs Knox on the melancholy occasion.[1]

Parental feelings are too much alive in the moment of these misfortunes to admit the consolations of religion or philosophy; but I am persuaded reason will call one or both of them to your aid as soon as the keenness of your anguish is abated.

He that gave you know has a right to take away—his ways are wise—they are inscrutable, and irresistible.[2] I am ever Your sincere and affectionate friend

G. Washington

LB, DLC:GW.

1. Henry and Lucy Flucker Knox commissioned Joseph Wright to paint a portrait of Marcus Camillus Knox (1783–1791), their second son to have survived infancy, after the boy's death on 8 September. His funeral procession to St. Peter's Church the next day was attended by "the Professors and Preceptors of the College and Academy" of Philadelphia "and a numerous train of mourning friends," including his schoolmates at the academy (*Gazette of the United States* [Philadelphia], 10 Sept.; Monroe H. Fabian, *Joseph Wright: American Artist, 1756–1793* [Washington, D.C., 1985], 71, 132).

2. Knox replied this day to GW: "The arrow with which we are stricken is indeed barbed with the Keenest anguish. In this moment neither reason Philosophy or religion have their proper effect. Perhaps the lenient hand of time, may reconcile us to this strong handed event, which we alass could not

controul. Wounded and shorn to the quick as we are, we feel most sensibly the Kindness of your sympathy" (DLC:GW).

Letter not found: to Frances Ramadge, 9 Sept. 1791. The receiver's copy of Ramadge's letter of 22 Aug. to GW was docketed: "Ansd 9 Sept."

Tobias Lear to John Churchman

Sir,   Philadelphia Septr 10th 1791
I received your letter with its enclosure last evening, and agreeably to your request submitted them to the inspection of the President of the United States.[1]

There has ⟨been⟩ no other letter for you passed through the Presidents hands, except the one which you mention to have received.[2]

The manuscripts, pamphlets & Charts which accompany this, were received by the President some weeks ago, by a vessel from Hamburg—and as they treat of the subject of your Variation Chart &ca—I send them to you by the Presidents order[3]—and wishing you such success in your pursuit as may render it useful to Mankind & beneficial to yourself—I am, with due respect Yr most Obedt Servt

Tobias Lear.

ADfS, DNA: RG 59, Miscellaneous Letters; LB, DLC:GW.
For background to the navigational work of John Churchman, see Thomas Ruston to GW, 20 Mar. 1789, and Churchman to GW, 7 May 1789, 9 Aug. 1790. For Rodolph Vall-travers and his association with Churchman, see Vall-travers to GW, 20 Mar., 21 July 1791.
1. The letter of John Churchman to Tobias Lear, dated "South second Street No. 183 [Philadelphia] September 8th 1791," reads: "Having taken the Liberty of addressing to the President of the United States, a Variation Chart &ca of the Northern Hemisphere, I am thankful for his favourable acceptance expressed in a letter by his direction, which I received in due time, dated the 28th of August 1790. Nor can I well help expressing myself under many obligations to the President & his Secretary, for their care in forwarding to me a Letter from Baron Vall-Travers of Hamburg, which came to my hand through the Channel of the Post office. As the Baron makes mention of the President in this Letter, together with the motives for sending it to his care, I make bold to enclose a Copy; be assurd that it was with difficulty that I prevailed upon myself to be the cause of this additional trouble, Bu⟨t⟩ in the Beginning of the Barons Letter, he gives me to understand that he wrote to me another of an earlier date which I have not received, & after making diligent

enquiry at every other place which I could think likely, I was at a loss to know whether Baron Vall-travers might not have sent his former one likewise to the care of the President; as I expected a little Book with his first Letter both of which may be very useful to me, I hope to be pardoned for this freedom of enquiry. As I have heretofore had a hope that the Legislature would view this question of so much national consequence, as to forward a thorough investigation of the principles of the Variation Chart, & considering the President of the United States a branch of the Legislature, whose Character is universally established as the patron of useful Arts & Sciences, I was encouraged to hope it would not be disagreeable to him to know how this publication has been received in Europe, hence I make bold to Copy also a Letter from the Princess of Daschkaw, President of the Imperial Academy of Sciences at St Petersburg, & one from the Royal Academy at Lisbon. Notwithstanding my application to Congress was negatived in the House of Representatives last session, I have understood ('tho not officially) that the British had or were about to fit out two Ships to Baffins Bay last Spring, to prove the truth of this Scheme, altho a Letter of thanks which I received from the Royal Society of London, acknowledging the receipt of the Chart Book &c., makes no mention of this expedition. After requesting the favour that this Letter & the other Copies may be presented to the president for his perusal. I beg leave to make an humble offering of my service & esteem" (DNA: RG 59, Miscellaneous Letters). The texts of the enclosed letters of Ekaterina Romanovna Dashkova, née Vorontsova, to Churchman, 27 Feb., and Joseph Corrèa de Serra, secretary to the Royal Academy of Sciences at Lisbon, to Churchman, 19 May 1791 (both in DNA: RG 59, Miscellaneous Letters), appear in CD-ROM:GW.

2. The enclosed copy of Vall-travers's letter of 2 April to Churchman reads: "Since my last, having applied to my Friend The Kings principal Astronomer, Mr Bernoully [Johann Bernoulli] at Berlin, for a more exact Note of the Memoirs of the Swedish royal Academy at Stockholm, relative to your object; particularly those of Mr *Wilke*: I received the inclosed Answer; by which means, I soon got sight of them. They are many, very instructive, & peculiarly interesting, for *establishing* your Theory; being the Result of many thousand Observations, carefully made by several Members & Sea Captains, both in regard to the Magnetic Needles Declinations, as Inclinations, at various times and places, both regular & irregular; accounting, very minutely, for the Effects of Electricity, Thunder, Lightning, Tempests & Hurricans; & still more for those of the frequent Aurora borealis, visible & invisible, happening in the Day-Time, as well as at night, & much stronger towards the Poles, than towards the Equator, to a far greater Extent. To collect all these, and to translate them into English with the necessary Maps & Figures, would take up at least six months close Application; but would furnish you with a rich supply of new & very useful materials for your work in Hand—The magnetic Almanac. The german Edition made by Professor Kastner [Abraham Gotthelf Kästner] at Leipzig, containing the Philosophical Transactions of the Swedish Academy of Sciences, with many Copper Plates, and two copious alphabetical Indexes, consists of about 50 Vols. octavio & costs at Leipzig, a Dollar each volume in Sheets. Perhaps your philosophical Society is already furnished with a complete

copy? & understanding, either the Swedish original, or the german learned Translation of Mr Kastner, with his remarks, stands in no need of English Extracts from the same. But should it be otherwise, & my further Assistance, on this and other Occasions, prove acceptable to the Congress, or to any of the confederated States, or their learned & patriotic Societies, or to your self Friends & Patrons in particular: You may freely command, & dispose of my time & Labour, whilst living and unengaged; for whatever Compensation of unavoidable expences and Trouble, that shall be thought adequate & equitable; It being still (tho far advanced in age, born in 1723.) my utmost Ambition, as it was that of my deceased Friends Dr B. Franklin, Thos Hollis, Gen. H. Laurens of Charles town &c. to promote even in my (narrow) Sphere every philanthropic Pursuit; agreeable to the duties of our various Powers & Destinations in Life. These were the motives, which prompted me, to direct the whole of my present Communication to your great Protector Genl Washington: with an Intimation of my readiness of chearfully obeying any commands of his excellency: and of doing you also, what further Services, you may wish for within the reach of Sir Yr obedt hble Servant" (DNA: RG 59, Miscellaneous Letters).

3. The enclosures have not been found. Vall-travers wrote of them to GW from Rotterdam on 6 June 1792: "The Packet, with instructive Materials, collected from the Academies of Berlin, Leipzig, Petersburg and Hamburg, in Aid of Mr John Churchman's, your ingenious Countryman's, Labors, towards an experimental very interesting Theory of magnetical Motions and their Variations, transmitted to Your Excellency, by Captn Bell, from Hamburg, in March 1791 hav[e] been kindly received & forwarded to that worthy Gentleman, by Tobias Lear, Esqr. your Exccy's Secretary, the 10th of Septembr following, to his very great Joÿ" (DLC:GW).

From John Greenwood

Sr   New York Septr 10—1791

I Received yours dated the 4th by the hand of sr John Jays son, this moment saturday 12 Oclock, in Which you seame to think I have neglected you, or the article Miscaried,[1] I Received them safe, but Whas out of stuff that is I had none Good enuf for the purpose, and so did not procede till I Could Get it, of Which I procured Whith Dificulty, on tuesday And have began it, Which you Will Get next Week, the reason I did not rite and answer to Yours I Expect'd to Get the stuff and have them done suner, I shall Observe all the defitiences you mention and try to remedy them.

P.S. Sr your directions how to remedy or make the next is as plane to Mee As if present, and I Will Observe them to a title,

nevertheless it is dificult to do these things Whithout being on
the spot, Which I shall take a trip to philadelphia in November,
God be Willing and I have my helth, then I Can Alter them.
from your Obedient and Humble servant

John Greenwood

ALS, DLC:GW.

1. GW's letter of 4 Sept. to his dentist John Greenwood of New York City
has not been found but was apparently sent under cover to John Jay. Jay informed GW this day that he received upon his return to New York the previous evening GW's letter of 4 Sept., noting: "This morning my Son [Peter Augustus Jay] delivered your Letter to Mr Greenwood, and was informed by him
that your prior ones had not come to Hand" (N. E. Saltykov-Shchedrin State
Public Library: International Exchange Section, St. Petersburg, Russia). The
"article" safely received by Greenwood was a set of dentures that GW had sent
for adjustments on 16 February.

To Lafayette

Philadelphia September 10. 1791

The lively interest which I take in your welfare, my dear Sir,
keeps my mind in constant anxiety for your personal safety
amidst the scenes in which you are perpetually engaged. Your
letter of the 6th of June by Monsieur de Ternant gave me that
pleasure which I receive from all your letters, which tell me that
you are well—But from the account you there gave it did not
appear that you would be soon relieved from your arduous
labours—and from the information we have received of an important event which has taken place since that time it does not
appear likely that the clouds which have long obscured your political horizon will be soon dispersed. As yet we are in suspense
as to what may have been the consequences of this event—and
feeling, as we do in this country, a sincere regard for the french
Nation, we are not a little anxious about them—Opinions we
are not able to form here, therefore none can be given on the
subject—But at any rate you may be assured, my dear Sir, that
we do not view with indifference the happiness of so many millions.[1]

I am glad of M. de Ternant's appointment to this country; for
I have a good opinion of his abilities, discretion, and proper
views; and, as you observe, as he seems to belong to both Coun-

tries, there is no doubt but this joined to the good information which he possesses of the relative and particular interests of both, will enable him to render as much service and be as acceptable to each as any man can be.[2]

I shall next week set off for Mount Vernon with Mrs Washington and the Children, where I shall, if possible, enjoy a few weeks of retirement before the meeting of Congress in the last of October. Indeed my presence there (as it will not at this time interfere with my public duties) is necessary for my interest, as George, your old Aid, has for some time past been too much indisposed to pay attention to my concerns, and is now over the mountains for his health—the last account from him was favorable—he had received benefit from his journey[3]—I sincerely wish, my dear Sir, that the affairs of your country were in such a train as would permit you to relax a little from the excessive fatigues to which you have of late been exposed—and I cannot help looking forward with an anxious wish, and a lively hope to the time when peace and tranquillity will reign in your borders, under the sanction of a respectable government founded on the broad basis of liberality and the rights of man—It must be so— the great Ruler of events will not permit the happiness of so many millions to be destroyed—and to his keeping I resign you, my dear Sir, with all that friendship, and affectionate attachment with which you know me to be yours &ca

G. Washington.[4]

LB, DLC:GW; copy, Lafayette Papers, La Grange, France, microfilm on deposit at DLC; translation, Lafayette, *Mémoires*, 3:185–87.

1. The "important event" to which GW referred was most likely the attempted flight from the Tuileries of the French royal family and their recapture at Varennes on 20–21 June. William Short's dispatches to Thomas Jefferson of 22, 29 June describing the event and its immediate political consequences were received on 23 Aug. (*Jefferson Papers*, 20:561–63, 584–88).

2. For the appointment of Jean-Baptiste, chevalier de Ternant, and his arrival at Philadelphia on 10 Aug., when he probably delivered to GW Lafayette's letter of 6 June, see Louis XVI to GW, 28 May, n.1.

3. For the trip of George Augustine Washington to Berkeley Springs, see George A. Washington to GW, 1 Aug., n.8. His wife wrote to Martha Washington on 25 Aug. that "the Major was getting better," but no direct report from him to GW of appropriate date has been found (Martha Washington to Frances Bassett Washington, 29 Aug., in Fields, *Papers of Martha Washington*, 233).

4. The printed translation of this letter has a 21 Sept. 1791 Philadelphia

postscript that is actually the final paragraph of GW's letter to Lafayette of 22 November.

To La Luzerne

Sir,   Philadelphia, September 10th 1791

In acknowledging the receipt of your letter of the 15 of May, which reached me but a few days ago, I cannot forbear to express the sensibility with which I receive those warm effusions of personal attachment and respectful remembrance which are contained in it. and at the same time I beg you will be assured that I reciprocate them with truth and sincerity.

As the happiness of the french Nation cannot be indifferent to the people of this country when we remember the aid which we received therefrom in an hour of distress, you will readily believe that we view with no small anxiety the troubles which, for some time past have agitated that kingdom—and the suspense in which we are held as to what may be the consequence of a late important event which has taken place there, deprives us, in some measure, of the full enjoyment of those feelings, which would naturally result from a reflection on the prosperous situation of the United States—But, however gloomy the face of things may at this time appear in France, yet we will not despair of seeing tranquillity again restored—and we cannot help looking forward with a lively wish to the period when order shall be established by a government respectfully energetic, and founded on the broad basis of liberality, and the rights of man, which will make millions happy, and place your nation in the rank which she ought to hold.

In a tour which I made last spring through the southern States I confirmed by observation the accounts which we had all along received of the happy effects of the general government upon our agriculture, commerce, and industry—The same effects pervade the middle and eastern States with the addition of vast progress in the most useful manufactures—The complete restoration of our public credit holds us up in a high light abroad—Thus it appears that the United States are making great progress towards national happiness, and if it is not attained here in as high a degree as human nature will admit of its going—I think we may then conclude that political happiness is unattainable—But at the same time we wish it not to be confined to this Country alone—and, as it expands through the world, our enjoyments will expand with it—and that you may find it in your nation, and realize it yourself is the sincere prayer of Sir, Your most obedient, humble Servant[1]

G. Washington.

LB, DLC:GW.

1. Anne-César, marquis de La Luzerne, the French minister to Great Britain, died in London on 14 September.

Letter not found: to Edmund Randolph, 10 Sept. 1791. Randolph wrote to GW on Monday, 12 Sept., of "your communication to me on saturday last."

From Tubeuf

Sir,   Richmond [Va.] 10th September 1791.

One of the advantages which I expected from a letter which M. the Marqs de la Fayette has remitted to me, in which he has recommended me to you, was to present it with my own hands, and to lay before you the plan of an enterprize which I am just about to undertake on the bordes of Clinch. A passage of 85 days from Havre de Grace to this place, longer by half than what I had calculated upon, does not leave me a moment to dispose of, and presses me to hasten to my distination, which is distant from hence more than 300 miles, in order that I may arrive there in season, to prepare a shelter against the severity of winter for 35 persons, whom I have engaged to proceed with me to form the establishment. With this view, I have purchased, upon the borders of Clinch, in the County of Russell 55,000 Acres of land, at the rate of nine livres Tournois per Acre, of which I am at this moment going to settle 5000 Acres, by eight families of my relations & friends, consisting of 13 masters & 22 domesticks & workmen. If my first establishment succeeds, in proportion to the facility & encouragement which the government of Virginia gives us, the honor which we shall gain will induce many other french Emigrants, more considerable than those here, to follow, who propose to join us in the ensuing spring, and I am just now going to dispose them to it. Deign, I beseech you, Sir, to favor my enterprize, guide me with your lights, and aid me with your Councils, by which I may render it useful & agreeable to the State. We carry with us all the means necessary to form our settlement.

I beg permission, Sir, to come myself to render you an account of it, and to put into your hands the letter of M. the Marqs de la Fayette, as soon as it is possible for me to leave, for a few days, my little Colony without inquietude & without inconvenience.[1] I am, with the most profound Respect Sir, Your very humble & Obed. Serv.

de Tubeuf.

At Colo. Tatham's-near the Capitol in Richmond

Translation, DLC:GW; ALS, in French, DLC:GW. The text is taken from a translation in the hand of Tobias Lear; the receiver's copy, in French, appears in CD-ROM:GW.

François-Pierre, le sieur de Tubeuf (Tuboeuf, Thubeuf; d. 1795), purchased in 1790 from Richard Smith, a British speculator, a large tract of land on the Clinch River in southwestern Virginia with the intention of establishing a French settlement. The following year he made indentures with tradesmen and farmers and their families, who agreed to live on the land for four years to pay off their passage, and Tubeuf left his wife in Normandy and sailed from Le Havre on *La Petite Nanette*, Captain Pitalugo, on 30 May 1791 with his eldest son, Alexander (born c.1774), a niece, and four servants. They arrived in Richmond about 22 Aug., and Tubeuf apparently spent some time there lobbying the state for assistance before he departed for the frontier with his people. On 20 Dec. the legislature ordered a road to be constructed from the courthouse of Russell County to the French settlement, later called Sainte Marie, and granted the French settlers a loan of £600 (13 Hening 317). Tubeuf, Louisa Duchesne, Charles de Speda, Cesare Lefebre, Eusebe Delaplanche, and Simon Perchet signed a bond in Russell County on 31 Jan. 1792 promising repayment of the loan by 1 Jan. 1799 (*Calendar of Virginia State Papers*, 5:432–33, 435, 452, 453–54). The only other child of Tubeuf, Peter Francis (born c.1779), joined the settlement in early 1793 and acted as interpreter for his father, but both sons left Russell County for Petersburg and Norfolk, Va., after the murder of their father and returned to France after 1803. The bond of Tubeuf was forfeited, his settlement abandoned, and the "French Lands," later discovered to contain rich coal deposits, were subjected to numerous lawsuits (ibid., 8:364–65; Elihu Jasper Sutherland, *Some Sandy Basin Characters* [Clintwood, Va., 1962], 186–224).

1. No letter of Lafayette's recommending Tubeuf to GW has been found. Tubeuf also wrote to Thomas Jefferson this day and mentioned another letter of introduction from Lafayette (*Jefferson Papers*, 22:141–42). The one for GW

had not been forwarded in mid-1793, when Tubeuf indicated he would deliver it by his son Alexander, who was personally to solicit a military commission from GW that September (Tubeuf to GW, 26 June 1793).

To Charles Carroll (of Carrollton)

Dear Sir, Philadelphia September 11. 1791.

I have been duly favored with your letter of the 6th instant.[1]

The indisposition and consequent (unexpected) absence of my Nephew from Mount Vernon, to whom my concerns there are entrusted, will oblige me to visit that estate before the meeting of Congress.[2]

Thursday I propose to leave this city, and on sunday afternoon expect to arrive in Baltimore—I shall come provided with 1172 ⅔ dollars for your use—but must again take the liberty of calling your attention to the Decree of the High Court of Chancery in Virginia—copy of which I transmitted to you in my last—By this decree you will perceive that the surrendry of Clifton's bonds among which is one to Ignatius Digges "in the penalty of £1268.10.8 sterling, conditioned for the payment of £634.5/4 sterling and interest together with such counter-bonds as the Pláintiff entered into" &ca &ca is made a condition of the payments.

I do not know that Clifton's bond to Mr Digges is of *much* consequence to any of the Parties—but, without the surrendry of these bonds, the Commissioners would not at the time—nor could not legally have paid the several sums they did, agreeably to the decree under which they acted—consequently, as I am now acting in the double capacity of Commissr and purchaser of the land, it behoves me to call in Clifton's bond to Mr Digges, as was the case with the others, or to require an indemnification against it.

For the general purpose of security against any claim from the Representatives of Mr Carroll and Mr Digges, it was that I meant to ask your indemnification, if there should by any difficulty in obtaining a releasement of the mortgage, or surrendry of the papers, as required by the decree.

If you could make it convenient to be in Baltimore on sunday afternoon, I am persuaded every thing could then, or early on monday morning, be settled without difficulty, and to our mutual satisfaction, being well convinced that both of us mean to do what is right—I have mentioned *sunday* afternoon because I shall leave Town *early* next morning. I do not intend to give Mrs Lee any trouble in this business.[3] With very great regard and esteem, I am dear Sir, your most obedient, and affectionate, humble servant

G. Washington

LB, DLC:GW.

For background to GW's acquisition of the lands of William Clifton on Clifton's Neck and his recent correspondence concerning clearing the title, see GW to Benjamin Waller, 2 April 1760, n.1, GW to Charles Carroll, 31 July, 28 Aug., and Carroll to GW, 11 Aug. 1791.

1. Letter not found.

2. For the trip of George Augustine Washington to Berkley Springs, see George A. Washington to GW, 1 Aug., n.8.

3. GW sent this letter to Richard Lawson & Co. the same day for delivery to Carroll (ALS, OClWHi). GW and Carroll apparently met in Baltimore according to plan, and on 19 Sept. Carroll signed a document, witnessed by Bartholomew Dandridge, acknowledging receipt of $1,172.67 from GW, as surviving commissioner and purchaser of the lands of William Clifton, as full compensation for the claim of Carroll and Ignatius Digges against Clifton and the sum of Clifton's bond to Digges with interest (CSfU).

To Gouverneur Morris

Dear Sir, Philadelphia September 12th 1791.

Your letter of the 27th of may with its enclosures came duly to hand.

During my absence on my late southern tour the proposals of Messrs Schweizer and Jeannerett, made their appearance here, as well through Mr Otto, Chargé des Affaires of France, to the Secretary of State, as through Mr Short, to the Secretary of the Treasury—In pursuance of certain arrangements, made previous to my departure, an answer was given—which answer was in substance that it did not appear to be for the interest of the United States to accept those proposals.

The reasons which have been assigned to me as having dictated this answer are as follow.

First, That the rate of interest to be stipulated in the new contract, as well upon the part of the debt which had not fallen due, as upon that which had fallen due was 5 ⅌ cent. It was a question whether a contract stipulating such a rate of interest with regard to the first mentioned part of the debt was fairly within the meaning of that clause of the law which requires that the payment of it should be made upon "terms *advantageous* to the United States",[1] and while there was no reason to apprehend that it would be necessary to allow a higher interest than 5 ⅌ cent on any loans, which might be made to discharge the *arrears* of principal and interest, it did not appear expedient to forego the chance of a *lower rate*.

2nd The commission or premium of 5 ⅌ ct demanded in the proposals is one ⅌ ct more than is given upon the loans going on in Holland—This would amount to a loss of one ⅌ ct on the part, which the United States were bound immediately to pay; and in respect to that, which had not become due, would be an unnecessary sacrifice of 5 ⅌ cent.

3rd The immediate proposers are understood to be a House not of primary consequence themselves, and though they alledged, they did not prove, that they were supported by others who could be deemed Capitalists equal to the undertaking. From the difference of exchange between Holland and Paris they could afford sacrifices in the sale of the bonds of the United States; and if there was not great force of capital among those engaged in the undertaking, such sacrifices were to be expected—A great quantity of bonds, thrown suddenly onto the market, by persons, who were pressed to raise money from them could not but have effects the most injurious to the credit of the U.S.

4th Paris being the stipulated place of payment, if, from the state of exchange payments could be made *there* in *gold* and *silver* with a saving to the United States, there could be no good objection to profiting by the circumstance—but this advantage, and more, even to the full extent of the depreciation of the Assignats, would be transferred by the proposed bargain to the undertakers.

5th The single advantage which the proposals held out, of a prolonged period of reimbursement would be obtained of course by loans in the ordinary way—and as to the effect of the measure upon loans for the redemption of the domestic debt, this would be good or bad according as the undertakers might or not have occasion to bring the bonds of the United States to market.

The foregoing reasons appeared to me to have so much weight that I saw no ground for directing any alteration in what was done.

It appears in their letter to you that the Gentlemen in question are willing to wave the claim of premium or commisssion on the part of the debt not yet due; but this obviates only one of the objections which have been stated.

You observe also that they had given you proofs that persons of the first fortune were connected with them in the business— They were deficient in not having given the like proof to Mr Short, whose enquiries had been directed to this object.

The observations you make concerning the views, which ought to govern the United States in their reimbursements to France are founded in propriety—You may conclude that no unequitable advantage will be taken; and it is hoped that the measures now in execution will be more conducive to the real interests of that country than would have been an acceptance of the proposals of Messrs S. & J., who, it is presumable, founded their speculation chiefly upon the idea of availing themselves of the full benefit resulting from the depreciation of the Assignats.

Thanking you for the communication you have made me on the subject, I assure you that I do justice to the motives which dictated it.

Your other letter of the 27. of May by Mr Ternant and that of the 8th of June from London, have both been received—I am much pleased that you drew the balance *only* from Welch and Son—The deficiency was paid to Wm Constable & Co. as soon as this circumstance was made known to Dear Sir, Your much obliged and most affecte hble Servt

G. Washington.

LB, DLC:GW.

For background to this document, see Alexander Hamilton to GW, 26 Aug. 1790 and notes; Gouverneur Morris to GW, 27 May 1791 (first letter) and notes.

1. See section 2 of "An Act making provision for the [payment of the] Debt of the United States," 1 *Stat.* 139.

From Edmund Randolph

Sir   Philadelphia September 12. 1791.

If the Fœderal laws were ever so precise in censuring the conduct, to which you alluded in your communication to me on saturday last, I should doubt, whether the source of your information is not too delicate to become the groundwork of a public act.[1] Courts would be very reluctant in extracting testimony from the mouth of an associate, and perhaps the character of government demands, that while it will not suffer any violator of law, how distinguished soever in rank, to escape with impunity, it should not too suddenly seize, what in an unguarded moment may have been dropped.

But the law itself is, I fear defective.[2] The two first attempts, having been abortive, cannot be treated as consummated offences; and even the third has not yet been matured into a strictly legal crime. In what shape the last may finally appear, is still a secret; and for this reason only, if no other existed, the executive would probably forbear to act at present. Its issue is so uncertain, that I should find it difficult now to give an opinion, were it required, adjusted to the various combinations of possible events.

I beg leave, however, to lay before you the copy of a paper, which I prepared for the secretary of state, upon a subject, somewhat analogous to your inquiry. I have not thrown it into more form; because you expressed a wish, that the matter should not at this time be considered officially.[3] When the secretary returned the paper to me, he said, that he was convinced, that nothing could be done, as the law now stands.

Copy.

The question is, whether any punishment can be inflicted on persons, treating with the Indian tribes, within the limits of the United States, for lands, lying within those limits; the preemption of which is vested in the United States?

The constitution is the basis of fœderal power.

This power, so far as the subject of Indians is concerned, relates

1. To the regulation of commerce with the Indian tribes.
2. To the exclusive right of making treaties.
3. To the right of preemption in lands.

1. Even if the act, supposed in the question, were really an infraction of the right to regulate commerce, there could be no penalty, unless the law prescribed it.

Accordingly a law of the second session enters into such a case, but only forfeits the merchandize carried into the Indian country. No other law affects it.

2. Without an existing law, no treaty, or compact made by an individual of our nation with the sovereign of another, and not partaking of a treasonable quality, is punishable.

It seems indeed to be an assumption of the sovereignty of the United States in this respect.

But the compact being in the name of an individual does virtually disclaim any assumption of public authority. If it be void, the United States cannot be deprived of their rights.

It may be indecent and impertinent for a citizen thus to behave. But where no law is, no crime is.

3. As to the right of preemption.

No man has a right to purchase my land from my tenant.

But if he does purchase, I cannot sue him on the supposition of damages, arising from the mere act of purchase.

Nor could the United States sue the purchaser of the right of preemption, since the purchase itself is void, and their interest cannot be prejudiced by any purchase, which an individual can make.

Far less would the purchaser be indictable.

But it undoubtedly is in the power of congress, to regulate commerce with the Indians in any manner to guard the right of making treaties, by forbidding the citizens to meddle under a penalty, and to provide a security to their preemption by passing adequate laws.

Until this shall be done, I conceive that this commerce is protected by no law, but the act abovementioned; that an interference in the article of treaties has no penalty, denounced against it; and that the fœderal property, like that of individuals, must depend upon existing laws.

It may perhaps be proper, if the testimony be strong, to warn all persons by proclamation, that the rights of government will be inforced; and possibly a monitory message to the Indians might have a good effect.

(signed) Edm: Randolph

I have the honor, sir to be, with due respect yr mo. ob. serv.

Edm: Randolph

ALS, DLC:GW.

1. No written "communication" from GW to Edmund Randolph of 10 Sept. has been found. The conduct to which GW had alluded in it might have related to the activities of the Yazoo land companies that GW apparently discussed with his department heads after his return from the Southern Tour (see Thomas Jefferson to Henry Knox, 10 Aug., to William Blount, 12 Aug., *Jefferson Papers*, 22:27–28, 29–30). GW had talked about the Yazoo companies with his nephew and Gov. Alexander Martin of North Carolina and had earlier expressed concern about their settlements on Indian lands (see *Diaries*, 6:155, 158–59, Jefferson and Randolph to GW, 14 Feb., Proclamation, 19 Mar., GW to Tobias Lear, 11 June, n.4). GW consulted with Randolph the previous summer about Indian trade and the Treaty of Hopewell (see GW to Randolph, 12 Aug., and Proclamation, 26 Aug. 1790) and had apparently only recently learned of the attempts of Zachariah Cox of the Tennessee Company to establish a settlement at Muscle Shoals in early 1791 on land that the federal government guaranteed to the Indians at the Treaty of Holston, concluded with the Cherokees by William Blount on 2 July (see Knox to GW, 6 Aug., Jefferson to Blount, 12 Aug. 1791, *Jefferson Papers*, 22:29–30).

2. Randolph is probably referring to "An Act to regulate trade and intercourse with the Indian tribes," which GW signed on 22 July 1790 (1 *Stat.* 137–38).

3. GW did not request Randolph to report on federal laws for securing Indian land titles until 10 October.

To Anthony Wayne

Dear Sir,   Philadelphia, September 12th 1791

Your letter of yesterday was presented to me this day—but at a time when I was in conversation with a Gentleman on business.[1]

I embrace the first moment of leisure to acknowledge the receipt of it, and to add assurances of my belief that the account given by Mr Sheuber of his leaving the british service, and bringing letters to me whilst my quarters were at Rocky Hill is true.[2]

I have *some* recollection of the circumstance, but not enough to give a formal certificate to the fact.

The variety of occurrences, which, in those days, almost overwhelmed me—The time which has elapsed since—and an unwillingness to certify things that I am not positively sure of are my reasons for not complying with Mr Sheuber's request in a formal way; but if the sentiments, herein expressed, can be of service to him, I have no objection to his making use of them as coming from Dear Sir, Your most obedient humble Servant

G. Washington

LB, DLC:GW.

1. Anthony Wayne sent GW from Philadelphia on 11 Sept. two letters that Justus Hartman Scheuber (b. 1751/2) of Savannah had written Wayne, mentioning "certain facts relative to his quiting the British service at Newyork in the year 1783 after having resigned his Commission as an Officer in one of the German Regements—& that he brought a letter of introduction from Colo. Wm S. Smith, when Head Quarters was at Rocky Hill. The object that Mr Sheuber has in view is to be recognized by your Excellency, as having come out from Newyork under the Character of a Gentleman—which Character he supported whilst he remained in this City, as you will Observe by the inclosed letter from the Honble Fredreck A. Muhlenberg. shou'd these circumstances be such as to bring him to your recollection—the acknowledgment will be greatful to the feelings of a man of Worth & honor . . . I have to ask a thousand pardons for troubling you so often upon this Occasion—but as I shall sail on *Thursday next* for Charleston—I wished to have it in my power to Oblige Mr Sheuber—shou'd you have any Commands to that Quarter, I will do myself the honor to call for them on Wednesday—I expect to return here again in the Course of four Weeks" (DLC:GW). The enclosed letter from Muhlenberg has not been found.

2. William Stephens Smith wrote to GW on 5 Sept. 1783 that "By the Bearer Ensn Shyber late of the German Troops, I send the Caps for the Boy's, should they prove too large—smal cushons within the Crown will make them fit & sett easier than without. The aforemention'd Gentleman was A. D. Camp to Lt Genl De Knoblock has obtain'd a very honourable dissmission and intends settling in this Country" (DLC:GW). GW acknowledged the letter from Smith on 10 Oct. 1783. Ensign Scheuber served under Maj. Gen. Hans von Knoblauch from 1781 to 1783.

To George Clinton

Sir [Philadelphia] Sepr 14th [1791]

Your letter of the 7th instant, with its inclosure, did not reach me 'till yesterday.

The intelligence, it communicates, is of a nature both serious and important. Indeed, the step it announces, as about to be taken by the British, would be one so extraordinary in every view, as to justify a question, whether the indications, which are alleged to have been given, have not rather proceeded from some indiscreet levity on the part of the officers alluded to, than from any real design of doing what appears to have been threatened. A little time however will explain the true state of the matter.

Your Excellency need not I am persuaded be assured that, in connection with the more general considerations which are involved in the circumstance, I feel a due concern for any injury, inconvenience or dissatisfaction which may have arisen or may arise, in respect to the state of New York, or any part of its Inhabitants, in consequence of the detention of the posts, or the interferences, which may have grown out of it. Nor has the matter failed to receive from me the degree of attention to which it is intitled. Yet in a point of such vast magnitude as that of the preservation of the peace of the Union—particularly in this still *very early* stage of our affairs, and at a period so little remote from a most exhausting and affecting, though successful war, the public welfare and safety evidently enjoin a conduct of circumspection, moderation and forbearance. And it is relied upon that the known good sense of the community ensures its approbation of such a conduct.

There are however bounds to the spirit of forbearance which ought not to be exceeded. Events may occur which may demand a departure from it. But if extremities are at any time to ensue, it is of the utmost consequence that they should be the result of a deliberate plan—not of an accidental or hasty collision; and that they should appear both at home and abroad to have flowed either from a necessity which left no alternative, or from a combination of advantageous circumstances which left no doubt of the expediency of hazarding them.

Under the impression of this opinion, and supposing that the event which is apprehended should be realised, it is my desire, that no hostile measure be in the first instance attempted.

With a view nevertheless to such ultimate proceedings as the nature of the case may require, and that upon the ground of well authenticated facts, I have concluded to send a Gentleman to the spot—who will be charged to ascertain and report to me whatever may take place; *and with as much precision* together with the general situation of the part of the Country immediately affected by the vicinity of the British Posts.[1] An additional motive to this measure is the desire of obtaining information in reference to the establishment of the Custom House in the State of

Vermont; which is also connected with the position of those posts &c.[2] I have the honor to be with due consideration & respt Your Excellys most Obedt Sert

G.W.

Df, DNA: RG 59, Miscellaneous Letters; LB, DLC:GW; copy, NHi: Henry O'Reilly Collection.

1. Gov. George Clinton's letter of 7 Sept. arrived at the capital as GW prepared to leave for a month's vacation at Mount Vernon. As Thomas Jefferson had already left Philadelphia for Monticello eleven days earlier, GW immediately consulted with Henry Knox, and perhaps Alexander Hamilton, about measures to be taken in the face of the latest British encroachments on the Champlain frontier. On 13 or 14 Sept. Knox provided GW with a draft of instructions for a private gentleman secretly to make observations of the disputed area, and the two apparently decided, before GW left Philadelphia in the afternoon of 15 Sept., to send Maj. John Doughty on the mission. Tobias Lear drafted a letter to Knox that day, transmitting a copy of Clinton's letter and its enclosures and returning "the draft of Instructions relative thereto, wh[ich] have been submitted to the Presidt & meet his approbation" (DLC: GW). The letter-book copy of those instructions reads: "You having been appointed by the President of the United States, to ascertain the existing circumstances relative to the Posts or places which are occupied by the troops of his Britanic Majesty on Lake Champlain within the limits of the United States, are immediately to proceed on that business. You will observe, by the Copy of the annexed letter from his Excellency Governor Clinton, dated the 7th day of the present month, and the copies of the papers transmitted to him by Colonel Woolsey, that it would appear, the british Officer commanding on Lake Champlain, or in its vicinity, has had it in contemplation to establish a new military Post, further advanced within the territory of the United States, than the Posts which have been occupied by british garrisons since the conclusion of the late war, namely at point Au fer, and at Dutchman's Point. It is of high moment to ascertain whether the intentions of establishing such posts as expressed according to the above papers on the 11th day of the last Month to Pliny Moore Esquire, have been actually carried into execution. If you should find this to be the case, you will ascertain the relative distance and situation of such post, with the other posts hitherto occupied by the british troops since the late war. You will also ascertain the nature of such post, and the strength of its garrison, and, as far as possible, the reasons which have induced the measure. You will also inquire whether any of the Citizens of the United States have been injured in their persons or habitations by the establishment of such post. You will also endeavour to ascertain the times, causes and effects of the former insults stated by his Excellency Governor Clinton. In this part of your duty the prevailing tempers and dispositions of the british garrisons, and the neighbouring inhabitants or Citizens of the United States will be other objects of your inquiry, and also the distance of such Citizens or Inhabitants from the usual garrisons—and You will ascertain the distance of Point Au fer and Dutchman's Point from the 45° of Latitude. It has been stated that the law of

the United States has been obstructed in respect to the establishment of a Post at Allburgh, the Nothern part of the lake Champlain, it being alledged that the said place is within a district occupied by a british Garrison. You will investigate this matter, and finding it to be as stated, you will also ascertain upon full information such other place on the east side of the Lake, within the State of Vermont, as would be proper, all circumstances considered, to be substituted in lieu of said Allburgh, or until the United States shall come into possession thereof. Your business will be simply to ascertain facts with all possible precision. You will therefore conduct your inquiries with perfect temper and moderation, avoiding every appearance of menacing or threatening to the british troops. Having fully executed this trust, with which you are commissioned, you will return to this city and make in writing to me an ample and accurate report of your mission, in order that it may be submitted to the President of the United States" (DLC:GW). The matter apparently continued to press on GW's mind, as he asked Bartholomew Dandridge, who accompanied him to Virginia, to write Lear from Chester, Pa., requesting immediate transmittal of the relevant papers to Knox (see Dandridge to Lear, 15 Sept., in Lear to GW, 18–19 Sept., n.1). Knox informed GW on 19 Sept. that Doughty arrived at the capital after having been sent for by express and would leave for Lake Champlain immediately.

John Doughty (1754–1826) of Morristown, N.J., declined his promotion from major of the Artillery Battalion to lieutenant colonel commandant of the 2d Regiment, raised in March 1791 for Arthur St. Clair's campaign against the Indians of the Northwest (GW to the U.S. Senate, 3 Mar., enclosure; Knox to Doughty, 4 Mar., NNGL: Knox Papers; *DHFC*, 2:518), and instead retired from the service to care for his aged parents and sister. After the expiration on 1 June of the furlough he had enjoyed since the conclusion in late 1790 of the Wabash expedition of Josiah Harmar, Doughty apparently visited Knox at the capital and settled his accounts with the federal government (Doughty to Knox, 8 Mar., Knox to Doughty, 27 Mar., both in NNGL: Knox Papers). Doughty was probably considered for the Champlain mission not just for his availability, however. GW and Knox were well aware that he had the eye of an engineer, as demonstrated by his construction of forts Harmar and Washington on the Ohio River in 1788 and 1790 (see Knox to GW, 27 Nov. 1789, n.1), and they trusted his judgment and discretion, as shown by their selecting him for the delicate peace mission to the Cherokee and Choctaw in March 1790. Only Doughty's heroism saved the remnant of his command when renegade Indians ambushed that mission, and his coolness under fire on the Wabash expedition was also well noted (see GW to the Chiefs of the Choctaw Nation, 17 Dec. 1789, source note; *Diaries*, 6:83–85). Doughty's private letter to Knox upon the conclusion of the Champlain mission, dated Morristown, 26 Oct. 1791, reads: "I reached my distressed Cottage Yesterday & found it the seat of affliction, what with the Trouble of my family & the fateague of my Journey, (not a Day of which have I rested & the whole boisterous & disagreeable Weather). I find myself so unwell, as to make it impossible for me to leave Home immediately. My Mind disturbed & my Body scorched with a fever all last night, I have as well as I am able digested my notes upon my late Mission &

have sent them to you, I hope they will be satisfactory—I have endeavoured to gain the best Information upon every Point that you wished—I beg you to dispense with my personal Attendance at Philada for the present, as soon as I am able I will wait upon you, if it is necessary immediately, every Consideration shall give Way to that of Duty—let me know by the first Post, direct to me at New Ark to the Care of Abrhm Ogden Esqr. You mentioned to me that you wished my Mission to be kept perfectly secret, this Injunction has been sacredly observed by me, but how could it be expected the Buisiness should be secret? Govr Clinton had written to Coll Woolsey that a Gentleman would be appointed to this Duty, & wrote by ⟨me⟩ that I was the person—Govr Chittenden gave Hints of the Buisiness to several Gentlemen after having read my Instructions—I did not see Coll Woolsey, nor did I forward his Letter till on my Return—my Informations of Course was obtained informal & without any Person on the spott knowing that I acted in a public Capacity. I have sent you a short Journal of my Tour, it will convince you that I have not been idle—I never saw such boisterous disagreeable Weather as the whole of the Time I was on the Lakes—it was impossible several Days to go out of Port—on the 13th it snowed hard & was good slaying at St John's. The enclosed map is sent by Coll Keys to Coll Hamilton, you will observed I have marked the Places mentioned in my official letter—please to give the Map to Coll Hamilton. I beg you to make my best Respects to Mrs & Miss Knox & to beleive me your affecte friend & servt" (NNGL: Knox Papers). Neither the map nor his notes and journal has been found. Only fragments remain of the copy of Doughty's report of 26 Oct. to Knox (N: George Clinton Papers) that burned in the New York Capitol fire of 1911. The editors wish to thank Theodore J. Crackel and Kathryn M. Willis of the Papers of the War Department, 1784–1800, East Stroudsburg University, East Stroudsburg, Pa., for their assistance in locating that report.

2. For the disturbances over the new customhouse at Alburg, Vt., see Jefferson to GW, 5 June, n.2.

To James Seagrove

Sir,   Philadelphia September 14th 1791.

Three letters of yours—two bearing the 16th and the other the 25. of August are just come to hand—Your former letters in July have also been received.[1]

The Secretary of war will write to you on the subject of Indian affairs—and the Secretary of State will do the same on the business which respects the Negroes, when he returns from the visit he is now making to his family in Virginia.[2]

It falls to my province to thank you for your communications of a private nature, which are very interesting and satisfactorily detailed—At all times it will afford me pleasure to receive information with respect to the situation of matters in that quarter, not only as they regard ourselves, but neighbours also—Spaniards and Indians. I am Sir, your most obedient, humble servant

G. Washington.

LB, DLC:GW.

1. None of these letters from James Seagrove to GW has been found. For Seagrove's mission to St. Augustine, see GW to Seagrove, 20 May.

2. For the agreements on fugitive slaves that Seagrove negotiated on 2 and 6 Aug. with Spanish governor Juan Nepomuceno de Quesada of Florida, see *Jefferson Papers,* 22:407–8.

To Alexander Hamilton

Dr Sir,   Head of Elk [Md.] 16th Septr 1791.

Whilst I was in Wilmington waiting breakfast to day, I made the best enquiry time & circumstances would permit, for some fit character to fill the office lately held by Doctr Latimer. Several persons were mentioned, but the weight of information was in favor of one Andrew Barratt. He was spoken of by Mr Vining as a man of respectable character, of decision and temper. He now is, or lately has been high Sheriff of the county of Kent; & no man, it is said, could have discharged the duties of that Office better. Mr Bedford, though he had another person in view, (Majr Jacquet), accords in this opinion of Barratt. Doctor Latimer, whom I afterwards called upon, at New Port, for the purpose of enquiry, also speaks well of Barratt. He did indeed, before I mentioned the name of Barratt to him, say that he thought Majr Patten of Dover the best person that readily occurred to him for this office, but yielded a ready assent to the qualifications of Barratt. None knows whether he would, or would not accept the appointment. Among other things, urged in his favor by Mr Vining, are his living near the centre of the State—amidst the Stills, and where the most discontent is said to be. To Mr Chew of Philada Mr Vining particularly appeals for the character of Mr Barratt.[1]

If his testimony is in favor of this character, I think it will be an eligible appointment. A blank Commission, signed, has been left with Mr Lear for the Supervisor of the Delaware District.[2]

With much esteem & regard I am Dear Sir, Your mo: obt Servant

G: Washington

LB, DLC:GW.

1. For the appointment and resignation of Dr. Henry Latimer as supervisor and inspector of the revenue for the District of Delaware, see GW to the U.S. Senate, 4 Mar. (third letter), and Executive Order, 15 Mar. 1791. Understanding that the vacancy had not yet been filled, Latimer's nephew Dr. James McCallmont (1755–1824) wrote GW on 8 Oct. from Christiana Bridge, Del., soliciting the office and naming George Read, Gunning Bedford, Jr., and John Vining as references (DLC:GW). On 15 Sept. Tobias Lear sent Latimer's returned commission, along with those of John Cogdell and Andrew Pickens, to Henry Remsen, Jr., at the State Department (DNA: RG 59, Miscellaneous Letters).

2. Alexander Hamilton replied to GW on 6 Oct. that, as Benjamin Chew had "confirmed the character received by you, of Mr [Andrew] Barratt, I have written to Mr Vining requesting him to ascertain whether the appointment will be acceptable to him." After Barratt proved amenable GW nominated him supervisor on 31 Oct., and the Senate confirmed the appointment on 7 Nov. (GW to the U.S. Senate, 31 Oct. [first letter]; *Executive Journal*, 87, 88). See also GW to Hamilton, 10 Oct., Hamilton to GW, 16 October.

From Alexander Hamilton

Sir,   Philada 16th Septr 1791.

I have the honor to enclose the copy of a letter from Mr Brown of Kentucke, to Genl Irvine, giving an account of some interesting particulars in the Western Country.[1] Part of the letter, I have understood, has been forwarded to you, but not the whole.[2] Genl Irvine is of opinion that the waters will be still so far practicable as to permit the progress of the Troops under Genl Butler; by the expedient of dragging the Boats in the shallowest places. With perfect respect &a &a

A: Hamilton

LB, DLC:GW.

In his instructions of 21 Mar., Henry Knox authorized Arthur St. Clair to undertake desultory expeditions of mounted Kentucky militia against the Indians in order to discourage incursions against frontier settlements (*ASP, Indian Affairs*, 1:171–74; see also Knox to GW, 22 Feb., n.9). After the success of Brig. Gen. Charles Scott's expedition against the Ouiatanon (Wea) towns on the Wabash River of early June (see Knox to GW, 6, 8, 27 June, 6 Aug., n.2),

St. Clair directed the Kentucky board of war on 24 June to prepare another foray, and it selected James Wilkinson, a Kentucky militia lieutenant colonel who was second in command of Scott's expedition, to lead 500 Kentucky cavalry troops against the villages at the junction of the L'Anguile or Eel River and the Wabash, near present-day Logansport, Indiana. St. Clair's instructions to Wilkinson of 31 July noted: "It is the positive orders of the President of the United States, that all such captives be treated with kindness, and that they be carried and delivered to the commanding officers of some post of the United States upon the Ohio" and concluded: "To you, sir, I know I have no occasion to recommend clemency, but am under the express command of the President of the United States. The luster that is shed upon success by generosity, and the reputation that accrues to a country from a temperate use of victory, is clearly understood and appreciated by you, to whom nothing could be more contrary to your own natural disposition than an act bordering upon inhumanity. I beg you, sir, to oblige the people under your command to refrain from scalping the dead. It is an act which, though it does no injury to the dead carcass, debases the persons who commit it. Should they be disposed to it, you have a powerful argument to adduce from the example set in the former expedition, and the very general approbation it has met with" (Smith, *St. Clair Papers*, 2:222–23, 227–29). Wilkinson left Fort Washington on 1 Aug. and reported to St. Clair on 24 Aug. from Frankfort, Ky., at the conclusion of his mission (*ASP, Indian Affairs*, 133–35). See Knox to GW, 22 Sept. (second letter).

1. The enclosed copy of the letter of 22 Aug. from John Brown at Danville, District of Kentucky, to William Irvine, reads: "An Express from Gen: Wilkinson has this moment reached this place informing of his success. He has destroyed a large Indian Town situated at the banks of the Wabash; also a Kichapoo town containing about 30 houses, & has killed & taken 42 of the enemy. His loss two men killed & one wounded. I have not as yet heard where the Express left him, but expect he has repassed the Ohio before this time. Genl St. Clair is now here endeavouring to procure aid from the Kentucke militia. His regular force, as yet, does not exceed 500 or 600 men & the river is too low to admit of Boats descending from Fort Pitt. I fear he will meet with great difficulty in obtaining assistance from this Country as the Militia are extremely averse to a co-operation with the regulars, & I am doubtful whether they can be compelled by the Laws of this State, especially as the Executive of Virginia has given no orders upon the subject to the Lieutenants of this District" (DLC:GW).

2. The extract that Henry Knox sent to GW on this day consisted of only the first four sentences of the letter.

From Henry Knox

Sir   War office [Philadelphia] Septr 16 1791
General Irwin has received a letter from Mr Brown of Kentuckey, via Richmond which renders General Wilkinsons success

and return indisputable. The following is the extract "Danville 22d Augt 1791. An express from Genl Wilkinson has this moment reached this place informing of his success. He has destroyed a large indian Town, situated on the forks of the Wabash, also a kickapoo Town containing about 30 houses, and has killed and taken 42 of the enemy. His loss 2 men killed and one wounded. I have not as yet heard where the express left him, but expect he has recrossed the Ohio before this time."[1]

As it may be proper on receiving the official information to tender your thanks to Genl Wilkinson, and Corps, in the same manner as to Genl Scott, I shall take the liberty of doing it, unless you should please to direct otherwise.[2]

Yesterday afternoon I received a letter from Genl St Clair of the 8th of August referring to one of the 3d of the same month by Capt. Mills which I have not yet received.[3]

He complains that neither Genl Butler or the quarter Master had joined him, although it would seem that a Great part of his forces had.

He also complains that the contractors Agent had not at that period authority to procure the horses to transport the provisions, and that he had directed a former order of his own for the purchase of 800 horses to be carried into execution.

He mentions that upon reconsideration he shall take tents; That he shall not be able to move forward with the whole army until 1st Sept. but that he should move with the troops he had, the next day about 6 miles in advance, and there wait for Genl Butler. I have the honor to be with perfect respect Your Most Obedient Servant

H. Knox

ALS, DLC:GW; LB, DLC:GW.

1. For a complete copy of John Brown's letter of 22 Aug. to William Irvine, see Alexander Hamilton to GW, 16 Sept., n.1.

2. Henry Knox sent to Arthur St. Clair on 29 Sept. the following undated extract from Knox's letter to James Wilkinson: "I have, by this post, instructed Major General St. Clair to thank you, if he had not already performed that pleasing duty, in the name of the President of the United States, for the zeal, perseverance, and good conduct, manifested by you in the command of the expedition, and for the humanity observed towards the prisoners whom you captured; and also to thank the officers and privates of the volunteers, for their activity and bravery while under your command; and to express his hope, that you and they may enjoy, in future, entire peace, as a reward for your services"

(*ASP, Indian Affairs,* 1:182). For Wilkinson's official report on his mission, see Knox to GW, 22 Sept. (second letter).

3. Knox acknowledged receipt of St. Clair's letter of 8 Aug. on 22 Sept. and of its duplicate on 29 Sept. (ibid.).

From Samuel Wall

Sir   Newport [R.I.] 16 Sept. 1791

I have this Inst. learn'd the Unwelcome & Melancholy tidings from the Cape where I have liv'd near nine Years. My Acquaintance is general & intimate with not only the Citizens of that Town but throughout the Island therefore I need but say, to be believed that I feel the most sensible distress for their Shocking Situation—I am told an Express has arriv'd to you, praying your Assistance[1]—which none ever ask'd in Vain. As the people of that Island possess my Affections, I am willing to share in Common with them their danger & offer my Services in any Capacity you may be pleas'd to place me without a wish of any pecuniary reward—I have serv'd this, my Country, both by Land & Sea in respectable Stations—I am personally Known to Mr Lear your Secretary who has been at my House in the Cape[2] I am perfectly Acquainted with all the landing places about the Cape, the People their Manners & Language which leads me to believe I cou'd be of Service—should you be Convinced of this, I beg Sir you'l Command me by a Line direct'd to me at York to Care Henry Bowers Esqr. or to Providence to myself, & say, how I shall proceed be pleas'd to pardon the incorrectness of this Scrawl as 'twas wrote in a hurry the Packet being on the Point of sailing.[3] I am respectfully Sir Your Most Obt & Very Humble Servant[4]

S. Wall

ALS, DNA: RG 59, Miscellaneous Letters.

According to Nathaniel Cutting, who recommended him to Thomas Jefferson on 8 July 1790 (DLC:GW), Maj. Samuel Wall (1738–1813) served in the Revolution, was captured at the fall of Charleston, S.C., and later toured France to acquire the language (see also *D.A.R. Patriot Index,* 3:3083). Wall wrote GW from Philadelphia on 14 Dec. applying for the post of U.S. consul for Hispaniola after having heard of the resignation of Sylvanus Bourne: "I enterd early in the Service of my Country in the late War & Continued untill its close, when I visited the Island of Hispaniola, where I have form'd an Establishment & resided seven Years, having Acquired a knowledge of the People, their manners & Language I flatter myself that invested with The Authority I solicit I should be serviceable to my Country. Numberless Impositions are practised upon the Americans—the Public Bureaux exact much higher Port-Charges than they have a right to demand & the Law directs—having lived long at the Cape & done Business as a Merchant—I think that as I am more perfectly Acquainted with that Island & the Abuses which the Americans are Subject to there, I cou'd do them away with more facility & more effectually than a person who should go a perfect Stranger. If you think the Circumstances of my having served my Country during the late War & being Acquainted with the Island, where I wish still to Continue in its service, can give me pretensions to the appointment I ask, I shall ever retain a grateful & respectful remembrance of the Honour done me. Permit me to add that I am well known to Mr Lear, who has been at my House at the Cape also to many Gentlemen members of both Houses of Congress from whom I can bring Letters of Recommendation if necessary" (DLC:GW). Wall also sent a similar application to Jefferson on 15 Dec. (DLC:GW).

1. Late on 22 Aug. a general uprising, which had been coordinated weeks in advance by slaves Boukman Dutty, Jeannot Bullet, Jean-François, and Georges Biassou, was announced by the burning of several plantations in the Acul district on the North Plain in Saint Domingue and the murder of planter families. The next day almost two thousand slaves marched west into Limbé district, as those on plantations in Petite-Anse parish also rose up and destroyed that village by the night of 24 August. Upon meeting armed resistance on 25 Aug. at Plaisance, the insurgents in the western part of the plain fell back into Limbé, set up military outposts, and fortified their troops, while other rebels marched on Quartier-Morin, Limonade, Plaine du Nord, and Morne-Rouge. The rebels were to converge on the capital and burn Cap Français with the assistance of rebellious slaves and mulattoes in the city, but only desultory attempts were made on 30–31 Aug. against the upper part of the city of 50,000 people. On 24 Aug. Governor Blanchelande dispatched deputies to solicit provisions and military supplies from Cuba, Jamaica, and the United States (Fick, *Making of Haiti*, 91–103; *Independent Chronicle: and Universal Advertiser* [Boston], 22 September). See also Charles Pinckney to GW, 20 Sept., Sylvanus Bourne to Thomas Jefferson, 8 Sept., *Jefferson Papers*, 22:133–34, and *General Advertiser and Political, Commercial and Literary Journal* (Philadelphia), 10, 11 October.

2. Little is known of Lear's early years, and no other evidence has come to light proving that he traveled to Saint Domingue before he was named U.S. consul there by President Thomas Jefferson in 1801. Wall possibly might have mistaken Lear for his father, Tobias Lear of Portsmouth, N.H. (1737–1781), a West Indies sea captain and trader, or Lear actually might have sailed to the Caribbean on one of his father's vessels sometime before leaving Governor Dummer Academy in Byfield, Mass., in 1779 (Brighton, *Checkered Career of Lear,* 18–20).

3. Merchant Henry Bowers lived at 63 King Street in the North Ward of New York City (*New York City Directory*, 1790, 16; *Heads of Families* [New York], 124).

4. No evidence suggests that Lear opened and forwarded this letter to GW

at Mount Vernon, and thus GW probably did not read it until after his return to Philadelphia on 21 October. GW's first notice of the uprising in Saint Domingue was probably that sent by express by Henry Knox on 22 Sept. (first letter; see also Lear to GW, 21 Sept. [second letter]). GW received Lear's first letter of 21 Sept., mentioning rumors of the slave revolt, sometime after 23 Sept. (see GW to Lear, 26 Sept.), and received before 2 Oct. Ternant's letter of 24 Sept. detailing its outbreak (see GW to Ternant, 2 October).

From Tobias Lear

Sir,   Philadelphia September 18[–19]th 1791.

The Instructions, and other papers relating thereto, I returned to General Knox on Thursday forenoon. And immediately on my return home, after accompanying you out of town, I secured your room in a manner agreeable to your wishes, and took the key into my possession; so that before I had the pleasure of receiving Mr Dandridge's letter from Chester, the directions contained in it had been executed.[1]

Colo. Hamilton called upon me on friday morning and shewed me letters from the Honle Edd Rutledge & General Pinckney on the subject of an Inspector for Survey No. 2 in So. Carolina, in place of John Cogdell who had resigned. These letters mention, that a Mr Benjn Cudworth had been employed in that Survey, by the Supervisor, since Mr Cogdell's resignation, and that he had given him hopes of obtaining the place. Under these circumstances these Gentlemen thought it would be best to appoint Cudworth to the office; tho' they acknowledged, that if he had not been employed & received assurances, they should not have brought him forward; but they thought it would be proper to employ him now, as otherwise, (being considered as rather a factious character) he might throw obsticles in the way of executing the law. Holding the office he wou'd feel himself interested in the support of the system which gave it him, and would undoubtedly exercise his influence (which is said to be considerable in that quarter) to good effect. A Commission was accordingly filled with his name and delivered to Colo. Hamilton. Colo. Hamilton, at the same time, observed, that a Mr Brown had been mentioned to him as a proper person to succeed Mr Cogdell in the Collectorship of George Town; but he wished to get further information of his Character from some gentlemen belonging to Carolina before the appointment is made.[2]

The Commission for the person who may be appointed Attorney for the Virginia District, has been delivered to the Attorney General agreeable to your direction.[3]

There have been no arrivals from Europe since you left the City; but it is said there are several vessels in the River, among which is one or more from Europe. If so, they will probably be up in the course of the day, and in case they bring any later intelligence than we have received I will obtain it, if possible, before the mail closes in the morning, and transmit it with this letter.

We are much pleased that the weather has been so remarkably fine since you left us, and are in hopes that you will have had an agreeable Journey. Major Jackson is getting better and desires to be presented in terms of respect. The rest of the family are well. Mrs Lear unites with me in a respectful & affectionate remembrance to Mrs Washington & yourself—love to the Children & best wishes to all friends. I have the honor to be, with the greatest respect & attachment Sir, Your obliged & obedt Servt

Tobias Lear.

Monday Morng Sept. 19th The Vessels which were said to be in the River have not got up.

ALS, DLC:GW.

1. GW, Martha Washington, and their traveling party, including Bartholomew Dandridge, left Philadelphia in the afternoon of 15 Sept. and reached Chester, Pa., later that day (*Dunlap's American Daily Advertiser* [Philadelphia], 19 Sept.), where Dandridge wrote to Tobias Lear that GW "directs me to request of you to have the windows of his room securely barred, and to take the key into your possession—he also desires that the instructions and other papers for General Knox (if not sent to him already) may be immediately forwarded" (DLC:GW). For the papers for Henry Knox, see GW to George Clinton, 14 Sept., n.2.

2. For the resignations of John Cogdell, see GW to Alexander Hamilton, 8 May, n.1. Lear transmitted to Thomas Jefferson on 5 Sept. the returned commissions of Cogdell, as well as those of William Nelson, Jr., and "Sundry papers . . . which have been submitted to the President . . . from the Consul of the U.S. in London to the Secretary of State" (DNA: RG 59, Miscellaneous Letters). Lear forwarded to Hamilton on 16 Sept. a new commission for Benjamin Cudworth (c.1753–1814), a native of Massachusetts who removed to South Carolina before the Revolutionary War and served under William Moultrie at Savannah and Charleston (DLC:GW).

3. Early on 15 Sept. Lear wrote to Henry Remsen, Jr., at the State Department: "The President directs a commission to be made out for the Supervisor of Delaware—and one for the Attorney of the Virginia District—both to be left blank as to the names & dates—It will be necessary to have these commissions sent for the Presidents signature before twelve O'clock—as he will set off for Virga at that hour if the weather shd be fair" (DNA: RG 59, Miscellaneous Letters). Lear transmitted the Virginia district attorney commission to Edmund Randolph on 16 Sept. (DNA: RG 59, Miscellaneous Letters), and Randolph informed GW on 1 Oct. that he had forwarded the commission to Alexander Campbell (see GW to Randolph, 10 October). Campbell wrote to GW on 7 Oct. from Fredericksburg, Va., accepting the office of Virginia district attorney (DLC:GW), and GW nominated him on 31 Oct. (GW to the U.S. Senate, 31 October). The appointment of Campbell was confirmed on 7 Nov., and a permanent commission sent him on 10 Nov. (*Executive Journal*, 87, 88; State Department Memorandum Book, DNA:PCC, item 187, 118). He resigned the office before his death in 1796 (see Campbell to GW, 20 Mar. 1796, DNA: RG 59, Miscellaneous Letters).

From Henry Knox

Sir　　　　　　　　　　War office [Philadelphia] 19th Septr 1791

I have the honor to transmit a copy of a letter from Major Genl St Clair dated at Danville in Kentucky on the 23d ultimo, which is confirmative of Genl Wilkinsons success.[1]

I have not yet received Genl St Clairs prior letters of the 8th of August and the one from Lexington. I should presume his business at Kentucky was to make up what he might have deemed a deficiency of numbers.[2]

Major Doughty was sent for by express, and he has arrived here, and will immediately set off for Lake Champlain.[3] I have the honor to be sir with perfect respect Your humble Servant

H. Knox

ALS, DLC:GW; LB, DLC:GW.

1. The enclosed extract from Arthur St. Clair to Henry Knox, dated Danville, Ky., 23 Aug., noted that Brig. Gen. James Wilkinson had just informed Brig. Gen. Charles Scott that "He has been compleatly successful at L'Anguille suprized it, and has killed and taken forty two. Particulars are not mentioned, saving only that circumstances, prevented his prosecuting the enterprize against the Kickapoo Town in the Prairie, but that he had destroyed one of their villages of 30 houses, and had but two men Killed, and one wounded. I left Fort Washington on the 18th, and shall set out on my return tomorrow" (DLC:GW). Knox informed St. Clair on 22 Sept. that he had received his letter from Danville, dated 24 Aug. (*ASP, Indian Affairs*, 1:182).

2. In his letter of 23 Aug., St. Clair informed Knox that "I gave you a particular account from Lexington" of his consultation with John Brown and Harry Innes. That letter, dated 4 Aug., arrived at the War Department on 30 Sept. (see Knox to GW, 1 Oct. 1791). Knox wrote to St. Clair on 29 Sept., acknowledging receipt of duplicates of St. Clair's letters of 6 July and 3, 8 Aug., and originals of 17 and 29 Aug. (*ASP, Indian Affairs,* 1:182).

3. For the mission of Maj. John Doughty to the Lake Champlain frontier, see GW to George Clinton, 14 Sept. 1791, n.2.

From Louis XVI

[Paris, 19 September 1791]
Translation of the King of France's letter of Sep. 19. 1791 to the President.

Very dear, great friends & allies. We make it our duty to inform you that we have accepted the Constitution which has been presented to us in the name of the nation, & according to which France will be henceforth governed.[1] We do not doubt that you take an interest in an event so important to our kingdom & to us; & it is with real pleasure we take this occasion to renew to you assurances of the sincere friendship we bear you. Whereupon we pray god to have you, very dear, great friends & allies in his just & holy keeping. Written at Paris the 19th of September 1791. Your good friend & ally

Louis
Montmorin.

Translation (AD in the hand of Thomas Jefferson), *Forbes Magazine* Collection, New York; LB, DLC:GW; LB, DNA: RG 46, Second Congress, 1791–93, Records of Legislative Proceedings, President's Messages; DS (in French), DNA: RG 59, Communications from Heads of Foreign States (Ceremonial Letters). The original French version appears in CD-ROM:GW.

The cover of the receiver's copy is docketed "Recd March 2, 1792." For its receipt and presentation to Congress, see GW to the U.S. Senate and House of Representatives, 5 Mar. 1792.

1. After their final debate on the new French constitution on 3 Sept., the deputies of the National Constituent Assembly immediately submitted the document for ratification to the king, whose legislative power under it would be limited to a three-year suspensive veto of decrees of the National Legislative Assembly. Louis XVI solemnly swore allegiance to the new constitution on 14 September. The National Constituent Assembly held its last session on 30 Sept., and the new members of the new Legislative Assembly first met on 1 October.

Letter not found: from William Blount, 20 Sept. 1791. Henry Knox reported to GW on 28 Oct. (first letter) on "a letter from governor Blount of the 20th of September last" that GW had referred to him on 10 October.[1]

1. The letter was offered for sale in the *Collector,* 55, no. 3 (Jan. 1941), item 631. The original apparently covered the memorial that the officers of the Mero District wrote to GW from the Southwest Territory on 1 August.

From Charles Pinckney

Dear Sir   September 20: 179⟨1⟩ In Charleston [S.C.]
    I had the honour to write you lately by the Delaware since which an occasion makes it necessary for me to address you again, on the subject of the inclosed application to me from the general Assembly of St Domingo[1]—By these inclosures you will percieve the wretched & distressed situation in which these unhappy people are & I am afraid if not checked in time it is a flame which will extend to all the neighbouring islands, & may eventually prove not a very pleasing or agreeable example to the Southern States—I have considered it in some measure my duty to transmit this application with my answer, which was the only one my situation would permit[2]—I believe it has been in the power of M: Polony to procure some shipments of Grain here, & every assistance which can be afforded by individuals no doubt will chearfully be given—taking it for granted you have been particularly informed of their situation it is unnecessary for me to repeat it. The detail of the almost indiscriminate Slaughter of all the whites who had fallen into their hands—The conflagration of the largest & most valuable Sugar Estates on the Island—The general destruction of property, & a probable famine are particularly unpleasant to us who live in Countries where Slaves abound. No doubt some application has been made to you[3]—but unless it may be in the articles of arms & provisions I do not see what assistance can be given them by Congress—besides, there is a difficulty arises in my mind which I will take the liberty of stating & which even if we had the means & authority in this State would make me very cautious how I acted—it is this, that there is at present not an Union of Sentiment in the french Empire & although we all *wish well* to the efforts of the patriotic

party & hope that their exertions will terminate in the establishment of a free & *judicious system,* yet it is impossible to say at present what may be the consequence, or whether they may be obliged before it is settled to proceed to hostilities—In any event, it must be the policy of this country to appear to favour no particular party or opinion—Our connection is with France, under whatever Government they may establish nor would we wish to risque offending them unnecessarily, for I have always been of opinion that our connection with her has never yet been throughly understood or improved to those useful purposes it might—in this situation I am therefor⟨e⟩ rather pleased than otherwise, that I have been officially obliged to give the kind of answer, which if I had possessed a competent authority to have interfered, I should certainly have been inclined to[4]—I shall ever be pleased to hear of Your welfare & to assure you that I am with the highest Esteem & Respect Dear Sir Yours Truly

Charles Pinckney

LS, DNA: RG 59, Miscellaneous Letters; LS (duplicate), DNA: RG 59, Miscellaneous Dispatches.

For the slave uprising that broke out on 22–23 Aug. in northern Saint Domingue, see Samuel Wall to GW, 16 Sept., n.1.

1. Charles Pinckney is probably referring to his letter to GW of 18 August. The enclosed undated application for assistance from the general assembly of Saint Domingue to the governor of South Carolina reads: "The miseries of St Domingue are at their highest pitch—this superb country will soon be nothing more than a heap of ashes—the planters have already bathed with their Blood the Ground that their hard Labour had rendered fertile—fire is in this moment consuming those productions which made the splendour of the french Empire—Principles destructive of our properties, have brought flames into our Cities and armed our very Slaves against us—Philosophy in general the comfort of men brings to us despair. In this hour of Desolation we have cast our thoughts around and have found some consolation in recollecting the intercourse which has long since subsisted between the State of South Carolina and ourselves—and then relying on your attachment the General Assembly of the french at St Domingo have thought it most proper to send a deputation to you to intreat you to give to this unfortunate Country some speedy help consisting of troops ammunition and provision—for famine will soon be over the Country and we should have only saved our inhabitants from the sword to see them fall by famine. The General Assembly has chosen to present you this request Mr Polony one of its members—He will deliver this Credential with the resolve in which he is named and the Proclamation made to solicit help from all our neighbouring powers—He will also deliver to you an Act of our Constitution which constitutes our Legal character as representative⟨s⟩ of the french at St Domingue" (DNA: RG 59, Miscellaneous Letters).

The accompanying extract of the minutes of assembly held at Léogane on 9 Aug. reads: "The General Assembly simply and purely constituted after having in the Sessions of the 5th, 6th, & 8th, of this Month discussed its constitutional points—has resolved and doth resolve on the majority of Sixty seven votes against forty six that it acts legally in virtue of the powers of its superiors the General Assembly of the french of St Domingue. The Assembly thus constituted wishing to leave no doubt of the purity of its intentions and principles till it has been able more formally to make them manifest—being taken up with the constitution of St Domingo—Declares that St Domingo being a portion of the french Empire acknowledges that to the national Assembly alone belongs the power irrevocably to pronounce on the political and commercial concerns that unite St Domingo to france agreeably to the plans that shall be presented by the General Assembly. Declares besides that to its protection and the loyalty of the Citizens are intrusted the interests of the merchants of france and of this Island—that it will maintain the strict observation of the Laws— and to this effect it will dispose in its [favor] the whole influence of public strength and opinion. It invites all the Citizens in recollecting the Oath of Union they are to make to beware of all unfavorable impressions and not to beleive any thing but the acts which flow from the Assembly and are Officially certified by it. And this is directed to the Lieutt General Government—to all the provincial assembly's parishes municipalities committee's and all Bodies of Justice and Police" (DNA: RG 59, Miscellaneous Letters). The accompanying "Extract of the Register's of Deliberations" of the 24 Aug. session of the General Assembly reads: "The french of St Domingo find themselves in the most imminent danger—the Slaves have risen, the houses are on fire—the whites who had the government of them are murdered—those who have escaped the sword of the assassins are obliged to retreat into their towns and abandon their properties. In this critical situation the General Assembly of the french of St Domingo in union with their Governor—Considering that the assembling together of the Negroes increases every day and that soon the inhabitants will find it imposible to defend themselves even within their towns and Considering that the scourge which is now laying waste the most valuable french possessions in America threatens all the neighbouring Colonies if they do not unite to destroy the source of it—Resolve that all the neighbouring powers shall be instantly invited in the name of humanity & their respective interests to give to the french of St Domingo now in imminent Danger a speedy and fraternal releif and to send with the greatest Celerity troops, ammunition and provisions, that they may be enabled to put a stop to the progress of an evil which would terminate in the final annihilation of the American Islands—Resolved besides that the Governor shall be requested to join to the present a particular request to the same neighbouring powers to solicit their services" (DNA: RG 59, Miscellaneous Letters). Also enclosed was a copy of the minutes for 26 Aug.: "The Assembly in the Session of the 24 of this month having resolved to send one of its members in quality of Commissary to his Excellency the Governor of South Carolina to request from him the speedy help that the french of St Domingo stand so much in want of—wishing to secure to themselves the success of this deputation which is rendered more and more important by succeeding circumstances. Resolve that there shall be chosen from among its members a Commissary to present the above mentioned petition and request the same help the first commissioned member did. In consequence whereof Choice has been made of Mr Polony who has accepted and given Oath faithfully to fulfill the commission delegated to him—and for this reason has received all the powers relative thereto. Mr Provost having offered himself as interpreter the Assembly has accepted his offer and he has given Oath faithfully to fulfil the duties of his charge" (DNA: RG 59, Miscellaneous Letters).

2. The enclosed copy of Governor Pinckney's answer reads: "I have received from Mr Polony the Letter which the Assembly of St Domingo have done me the honour to address to me, and have taken the earliest opportunity of transmitting the only answer which my situation and the circumstances of our Government will permit. By the constitution of the United States all national powers are transferred to the General Government who alone have the power to direct the national force or enter into agreements or compacts with foreign powers, their citizens or Subjects, or to afford them any assistance or support in seasons of danger and calamity—the individual States are expressly restrained from any interference without the consent of Congress. Thus situated the Assembly must at once perceive that as by our constitution the General Government are the only power competent to afford support—that to them all applications must be made for that purpose and as it appears that Mr Polony is furnished with dispatches to the supreme Executive I hope little or no inconvenience will arise from the delay that has been occasioned by the application to me. Permit me while I lament that for these reasons it is not in my power to afford the assistance you request to assure you that I feel sincerely for the deplorable & unexampled sufferings of the people of St Domingo—it is our duty gratefully to recollect that in the time of our most imm[in]ent distress the arms and treasure of france were generously devoted to our releif—not only in common therefore with the other citizens of the American Union must we lament the excesses which have laid waste one of the richest and most valuable possessions of the french empire—but when we recollect how nearly similar the situation of the southern States and St Domingo are in the possession of Slaves—that a day may arrive when they may be exposed to the same insurrections, we cannot but sensibly feel for your situation and have a particular interest in hoping that such support will be afforded by your friends as will enable you effectually to crush so daring and unprovoked a rebellion—that your decided success will prove the general detestation in which such attempts are held & will always be opposed & that your situation & the fate of the insurgents will have a happy effect in operating as an example to prevent similar commotions in other countries" (DNA: RG 59, Miscellaneous Letters; this copy is dated 12 Sept.; a duplicate in DNA: RG 59, Miscellaneous Dispatches, is dated 20 September). After they convened Pinckney presented the application to both houses of the legislature of South Carolina on 5 and 6 Dec. and on 12 Dec. presented another letter of M. Polony, dated Charleston, 25 November. On 16 Dec. the legislature unanimously resolved to furnish up to £3,000 worth of provisions and stores to Polony ("Journal of the S.C. Senate," 15, 55, 83, 101; "Journal of the S.C. House of Representatives," 13, 99, 121).

3. For the request for assistance made to the national government, see Ternant to GW, 22 September.

4. The following lines of the complimentary close are in Pinckney's hand. GW received this letter in late October after he returned to Philadelphia and was preoccupied with preparing his annual address to Congress. He requested Thomas Jefferson to write a reply, which was drafted on 6 Nov., and GW acknowledged this letter two days later (see Jefferson to GW, 6 Nov., GW to Pinckney, 8 Nov. [first letter]).

From Thomas Lee Shippen

Sir,   Philadelphia September 20. 1791.

This will be presented to you by Mr Jorre a gentleman of France who comes last from Ireland. He brought me some very warm letters of recommendation from Ireland, and particularly from the celebrated Mr Grattan, who requests it of me as a very particular favor that I would introduce him to you. Your absence from Philadelphia leaves me no other way but this, of complying with Mr Grattan's wishes, and I am sure you will forgive me for taking the liberty of introducing to you a French man who has made sacrifices in the cause of Liberty, and who comes to this Country so powerfully recommended. My correspondents speak of Mr Jorre as a gentleman of approved talents, integrity, and character, and extremely well acquainted with several of the modern languages and pledge themselves for his faithful performance of whatever he undertakes.[1]

I mention this to you Sir, as matter of information, in case he should make any application to you which might lead you to make enquiries about him.

I pray you Sir to remember me very affectionately and Mrs Shippen likewise to Mrs Washington and to believe me when I in truth assure you, that no one respects you more highly, or is more truly sensible of his obligations to you, than Sir, your most devoted and obedient servant

Thos Lee Shippen

ALS, DNA: RG 59, Miscellaneous Letters.

1. For the arrival of the adventurer Jorre in Philadelphia and his reception by GW in early November, see Jorre to GW, 29 July 1789, n.3. James McHenry also recommended Jorre to GW, writing from Baltimore on 25 Sept.: "Mr Stephen Willson an eminent and much respected Merchant of Baltimore has requested me to introduce to you Mr Jorre, who comes recommended to him as

a man of various talents and strict integrity, by persons of the first consideration in their own country, in whom he places the utmost confidence. Mr Jorre has spent a day with me, and appears to be a man of taste, learned, modest and intellegent, qualities which you know will naturally prepossess and interest independent of other recommendations" (DLC:GW).

From Tobias Lear

Sir.   Philadelphia September 21st 1791

I had the honor of writing to you on the 18th; since which nothing has transpired among us worth relating. The arrival of a Vessel from Liverpool brings European Accounts down to the 28th of July. I have not learnt that she has brought any other intelligence than what is contained in the enclosed papers. An insurrection of the Negroes in Hispaniola seems to have put the inhabitants and property of that Island in a most alarming & distressed situation. Report says 4000 whites have been killed there; but as no such account appears in the papers with the general statement of the situation of things, I presume it must be only a report.[1]

In looking over the debates of the Senate of this State on Monday, on the subject of erecting a House for the President &ca I observed Mr Smilie asserted that Mr Morris received a rent of 700£ per Annum for this house[2]—and no contradiction was made to the assertion, altho he was answered by Mr Powel who must have known that the rent was fixed at 500£—In order to place this matter upon indubitable ground, as well as to ascertain the day when the rent becomes due, and to whom it must be paid, I wrote a letter to Mr Fisher, a copy of which I have now the honor to enclose.[3] I did not think it best to notice, in this letter, the observation respecting 700£, lest it should afford ground to Mr Fisher to beleive that I had misunderstood him respecting the rent, or that I had forgotten the sum which he had mentioned to me.

Yesterday about noon Mr Powel called upon me, accompanied by the Mayor of the City; and after requesting that he & Mr Barclay might have some private conversation with me, he told me in a very formal manner, that he had several interrogatories to put to me, which he requested I would answer[4]—After assuring him that I would if they were such as I could answer with propriety—he observed, that a Gentleman of the house of Representatives of this State had informed him that I had, in a conversation with another member of that house, mentioned "that you was well satisfied with the accommodations of your present residence, and that you was very sorry to find the matter of building a house for the President of the United States, seemed to have been taken up on the ground of your not being satisfied with the house which you now occupy—and further, that if a house was built you should not think of removing into it"—and wished to know if I had communicated things of this nature to any person. I informed him I had—and, more over, that I was very glad of the present opportunity of repeating the same to him; which I did, in the same or nearly the same words of the enclosed copy of a letter to him.[5] Mr Powel turned to the Mayor, & observed that this was precisely the same which they had heard as coming from one of the members of the Assembly; to which the Mayor assented. Then addressing himself to me, said he had no doubt of Mr Gallatin's veracity in relating the conversation; but as it had passed through others before it reached him (Mr P.) he was apprehensive there might have been some mistake in the matter, & had therefore called upon me to be satisfied, which he now was, that I had communicated these sentiments to Mr Gallatin.[6] Altho Mr P. would not venture to say that these were not your sentiments; yet he seemed to intimate that I might have mistaken your meaning—as I might have heard it in a transient way—or something to that effect—I was then under the necessity of saying, that you had made the observations to me, and in so direct a manner that I could not mistake them. He took his leave with the Mayor; but did not appear well pleased. Reflecting on the subject, & the manner in which Mr Powel appeared to receive the information, I thought it would be best (in order to prevent any mis-apprehension or mis-construction of what I had related to him) to communicate the same in writing⟨;⟩ which I did in the afternoon, by a letter, a copy of which I do myself the honor to enclose.

I have not yet received an Answer from Mr Fisher on the points mentioned in the letter to him. He sent a verbal reply, that the corporation would meet in a few days when the matter should be brought before them.[7]

Mrs Lear unites with me in sentiments of the highest respect for yourself & Mrs Washington—love to the children—and best wishes to all the family. I have the honor to be, with the greatest respect & most sincere Attachment Sir, Your obliged & obedt Servt

Tobias Lear.

ALS, DLC:GW.

1. For the slave uprising that broke out on 22–23 Aug. in northern Saint Domingue, see Samuel Wall to GW, 16 Sept., n.1.

2. John Smilie (1741–1812), a native of Ireland, immigrated to America in 1760 and settled in western Pennsylvania. He was a member of the state assembly from 1784 to 1786 and of the state senate from 1790 to 1793. Smilie was elected to the U.S. House of Representatives in 1793 and served again in Congress from 1799 until his death.

3. The enclosed copy of Tobias Lear's letter of 20 Sept. to Miers Fisher reads: "As one year has nearly elapsed since the President of the United States first occupied Mr Morris' house in High Street, I shall be much obliged to you to inform me of the day when the Rent commenced—the annual amount of the Rent—and to whom it must be paid; in order that a settlement for the first year may take place when that year expires. I have taken the liberty, Sir, of requesting this information from you; because all my communications on this subject have hitherto been with you. . . . P.S. You informed me in the spring that the Rent would be five hundred pounds currency; and I only mention it now to be clearly ascertaind with the other points" (DLC:GW).

4. John Barclay (d. 1816), a native of Ireland, immigrated to Pennsylvania before 1779 and established himself in Philadelphia as a merchant. He served as president of the Bank of Pennsylvania, as alderman, and as mayor of Philadelphia in 1791–92.

5. The enclosed copy of Lear's letter of 20 Sept. to Samuel Powel reads: "In order to prevent any misapprehension of the purport of the conversation which I had the honor to hold with you today, I beg leave to communicate, in this way, the observations of the President which I before conveyed verbally. Upon reading in the papers the debates of the Legislature of Pennsylvania, upon the bill for granting a sum of money to defray the expenses of building a House for the President of the United States &ca—The President observed to me, that he was sorry to find some of the Gentlemen had taken up an idea that he was not accommodated to his satisfaction in the house which he now occupies; and seemed *on this ground* to urge the necessity of having a house erected for the President. But he wished the Gentlemen to be informed that this was not the case; for he felt himself perfectly satisfied with the house in which he resides. The President further observed, that if the house in question was even now finished he should not go into it; for he had, at a very considerable expense, accommodated his furniture to his present residence, and it was not probable that it coud be made to suit another house so well; and as the time for which he was elected to his present station would expire within two years, his getting new furniture answerable to a house which might be built,

was out of the question—And again repeated that he was perfectly satisfied with his present accommodations, and should not remove into any other house (if he was permitted to occupy this) during the term of his Presidency. These sentiments the President wished might be known, by some indirect communication, to the Legislature. But at the same time wished them to be conveyed as sentiments relating to himself *personally;* for he was apprehensive, from the idea held up in the House of Representatives, that measures might be taken to build a house for the President, at this moment, with a view to accommodate *him,* when, otherwise, it might be thought best to delay or defer it. The President likewise wished it to be impressed, that he could not have the most distant intention of interfering in anything which the legislature of Pennsylvania thought proper to do on the subject, by conveying these sentiments; but finding the matter had been taken up on the ground of his not being well accommodated, he thought it necessary to give this explanation in order to do away that opinion. In a conversation with Mr Gallatin, I communicated these things to him. He informed me that the bill had passed the House of Representatives and was then before the Senate; and wished to know if he might be at liberty to relate the substance of our Conversation. I told him he might; and find that he has done it accordingly. I will take this opportunity to mention, that some time before my conversation with Mr Gallatin, I had, by the President's order, conveyed the same sentiments to Miers Fisher Esquire, in answer to some inquiries he had made respecting the President's accommodations—building a house &ca. The trouble of this letter needs some apology to you, Sir, which I hope will be found in my wish to give a clear explanation of the subject of it" (DLC:GW).

6. Albert Gallatin (1761–1849), a native of Switzerland, immigrated to the United States in 1780 and settled in western Pennsylvania in 1784. He was a member of the Antifederalist Harrisburg convention in 1788 and of the Pennsylvania constitutional convention of 1789–90. Gallatin served in the Pennsylvania house of representatives from 1790 to 1792. He was elected to the U.S. Senate in 1793 but was deprived of his seat in 1794 on the grounds that he had not been a citizen of the United States for nine years prior to his election. He was elected to the U.S. House of Representatives in 1794 and served in that body until his appointment by Thomas Jefferson as secretary of the treasury in 1801.

7. The efforts of the Pennsylvania legislature to secure the permanent residence of the federal government in Philadelphia by erecting federal buildings there would defeat the intention of the Residence Act, which called for the removal of the federal government to the Potomac after ten years. GW earlier met this challenge to the establishment of the Federal City on the Potomac with deliberate aloofness, maintaining that his term would end before he could be called upon to occupy the proposed presidential mansion in Philadelphia (see GW to Jefferson, 1 April 1791). For further correspondence on this matter, see Lear to GW, 25, 30 Sept., and GW to Lear, 26 Sept. 1791.

From Tobias Lear

Sir,   [Philadelphia] Wednesday Evening Sept. 21st 1791.

Since I had the honor of writing to you this morning, I have been making inquiries respecting Blankets, and find that Messrs Sitgreaves have the largest quanty—the best assortment—and the lowest prices that are to be found. I enclose a list of their prices & qualities in order that you may, if you think proper, point out the kind most suitable for your purpose—and likewise have the prices compared with the Alexandria prices, in order to determine whether it would be better to get them at this place or there.[1]

General Knox having just informed me that he was about to dispatch an express to you, I embrace the opportunity of sending this, as it will reach you sooner than a letter by the next post—and thereby afford me an earlier answer, which may be advantageous in this matter as these goods are going off very fast.[2] I have the honor to be, with every sentiment of respect & attachment Your obliged & Obedt Servt

Tobias Lear.

ALS, DLC:GW.

1. George Augustine Washington reported to GW on 7 Dec. 1790 that the price of "Dutch Blankets" in Alexandria was high and advised that more than one hundred and fifty blankets would be needed to supply the slaves at Mount Vernon, but no purchase was made that winter (see also George A. Washington to GW, 14 Dec. 1790). GW informed Tobias Lear on 19 June 1791 from Virginia that "near two hundred" blankets would be needed at Mount Vernon in the fall and instructed him to "make a pretty diligent enquiry after them before I arrive." The enclosed undated list of prices that Lear obtained from W. & J. Sitgreaves, the Philadelphia firm of William Sitgreaves (d. 1800) and John Sitgreaves (d. 1798) at 48 South Front Street, reads:

Striped Duffells 115/ to 180/ per piece of 15 blankets—

2 point twilled blankets		16/6 pair
2½ point "	do	23/6 —
6/4 Rose		15/ per pair
7/4 "		23/ —
8/4 "		30/ —
9/4 "		42/6 —
10/4 "		56/3 —
Diaper rugs		10/ to 13/6 piece.

Lear noted at the bottom of the list that the 2- and 2½-point twilled blankets were "Indian Blankets" (DLC:GW). The correspondence between GW and Lear about the purchase of the blankets continued until 16 October. GW instructed Lear to purchase blankets of sufficient quality and size to avoid distress among his "people" (see GW to Lear, 26 Sept., 2, 7 Oct. 1791, and Lear to GW, 30 Sept., 11, 14, 16 October).

2. See Henry Knox to GW, 22 September.

From Thomas Mifflin

Philadelphia, 21 September 1791. Transmits an exemplified copy of an act of the General Assembly of the Commonwealth of Pennsylvania entitled "An Act ratifying, on behalf of the State of Pennsylvania, the first amendment proposed by Congress to the Constitution of the United States."[1]

Copy, DNA: RG 46, Second Congress, 1791–1793, Records of Legislative Proceedings, President's Messages.

1. On 2 Oct. 1789 GW submitted to the governors of the states the amendments to the Constitution proposed by Congress. Gov. Thomas Mifflin enclosed the act of the Pennsylvania legislature ratifying the first of these twelve proposed amendments, which limited the size of the U.S. House of Representatives. For the background to this proposed amendment, see GW to the U.S. Senate and House of Representatives, 8 March 1790, n.2. The Pennsylvania act of ratification was signed by William Bingham, speaker of the Pennsylvania house of representatives, and Richard Peters, speaker of the Pennsylvania senate (DNA: RG 46, Second Congress, 1791–1793, Records of Legislative Proceedings, President's Messages). GW presented it to Congress with its cover letter on 26 October.

From Alexander Hamilton

Sir,   Philadelphia 22d Septr 1791.

I have received a letter from the Minister of France, of which the inclosed is a copy.[1] Having full authority from you in relation to payments to France, & there being funds out of which that which will constitute the succour: requested may with propriety be made; and being fully persuaded that in so urgent & calamitous a case, you will be pleased with a ready acquiescence in what is desired. I have not hesitated to answer the Minister that the sum he asks is at his command.[2] With the most perfect respect and truest attachment, I have the honor to be Sir, Your Most Obedient & Most Hble Servant[3]

                                                    A: Hamilton

LB, DLC:GW; copy, RG 233, Third Congress, 1793–1795, Records of Legislative Proceedings, Committee Reports and Papers.

Jean-Baptiste, chevalier de Ternant, reported to the French minister of foreign affairs on 28 Sept.–2 Oct. that M. Roustan, the agent sent by the colonists of Saint Domingue to solicit assistance from the federal government, had arrived at New London, Conn., on 20 Sept. and had been persuaded by the French vice-consul general at New York to confer with Ternant about his mission. Persuading Roustan that the French minister to the United States was the proper intermediary between the colonial assembly and the federal government, Ternant assumed control of the negotiations and approached Alexander Hamilton. Judging it essential to obtain funds in addition to those at his direct command, the French minister explained to the comte de Montmorin that he thought it would be more economical and dignified to request the necessary amount from the loan repayments due from the federal government than having to deal with private businessmen. Such an official request might also serve to test America's good intentions toward France and would secure an immediate source of emergency funding in case of future disturbances on Saint Domingue (see Turner, *Correspondence of the French Ministers*, 45–51, especially 48).

1. The enclosure was a translation of Ternant's letter to Alexander Hamilton, dated Philadelphia, 21 Sept.: "The distressed & very alarming situation in which the French Colony of Hispaniola is now reduced by an insurrection of the Negroes which threatens the most fatal consequences, puts me under the necessity of causing large supplies of provisions to be speedily forwarded to that Island. The means I can command, at present, being insufficient for the purpose, I have to request you will enable me, if possible, to draw on your fœderal Treasury, to an amount not exceeding forty thousand Dollars, to be accounted for in any future reimbursement of the United States to France. I hope the extreme urgency of the case, & the interest I am convinced you take in the welfare of my Nation, will induce you to grant this request, which I am going to lay immediately before the President of the United States" (DLC:GW).

2. Hamilton expressed regret to Ternant on 21 Sept. over "the calamitous event announced in your letter of this day" and reported that "the sum you desire is at your command to operate as a payment, on account of the debt due to France," adding that it would be most convenient if the advance Ternant requested could be paid in three installments over sixty days, but that the French minister was "at liberty to draw for the whole or any part of it as fast as you may find it necessary" (Syrett, *Hamilton Papers*, 9:220). Ternant informed Montmorin on 7 Oct. that he had yet to make use of the money put at his disposal and that Hamilton assured him that the funds would be available for as long as Ternant judged convenient (see Turner, *Correspondence of the French Ministers*, 56).

3. GW replied to Hamilton from Mount Vernon on 24 Sept.: "I have received your letter of the 22d inst: enclosing a copy of one from the French Minister; & have to inform you, that your proceedings with respect to the

request of the Minister of France, meet my entire approbation" (LB, DLC:GW).

From Henry Knox

Sir,   War Department [Philadelphia] 22d September 1791.

The Minister of France has written me a Letter of which the enclosed is a copy[1]—As this crisis of affairs is of the highest importance to the essential interests of France; and as it appears a singular opportunity for the United States, to manifest their zeal to repay in some degree the assistance afforded us during the perilous struggles of the late war, I have assured him of every aid in my department, which shall be authorized by you—Accordingly I have instantly dispatched an Express, to receive your orders on the occasion.

The articles which are requested are in readiness, and may be spared from the Arsenal of West-Point, without any detriment to the public service—excepting the Cartridge-boxes which are much damaged, but which however might answer in this exigency.

In order therefore to save time, I have also dispatched a person to West Point to have the Arms and stores prepared for sea transportation, and forwarded to New York—but to wait your orders for the final delivery.[2]

As the aid requested is for the exigent service of a nation, with which the United States are in close alliance, and from which they received the most eminent support during the late war, and being for the purpose of quelling an internal rebellion, no foreign nation can take umbrage at the measure; as it can be afforded without impediment or injury to the public service, and as all the stores in the Arsenals are under your direction as President of the United States and Commander in Chief, I feel but little hesitation in submitting as my opinion, that the circumstances of the case render it highly proper to afford the supples requested, and that your authority is competent to the occasion.[3] I am Sir, With the highest respect Your most Obedient huml. servant

H. Knox
secy of War

LS, DLC:GW; LB, DLC:GW.

For Jean-Baptiste, chevalier de Ternant's report of 28 Sept.–2 Oct. to the French minister of foreign affairs on the arrangements he made with the federal government to obtain aid for the colonists of Saint Domingue, see Alexander Hamilton to GW, 22 Sept., source note. Ternant informed the comte de Montmorin that the most economical source of quality arms and military supplies was the federal arsenal at West Point, which alone could provide the island the requisite materials in a timely manner. In explaining his motivations in officially approaching the U.S. government, Ternant claimed that the heads of the federal departments had assured him that his demands would not be without success (see Turner, *Correspondence of the French Ministers*, 45–51, especially 48).

1. The enclosed copy of Ternant's letter to Henry Knox, dated Philadelphia, 21 Sept., reads: "The distressed and very alarming situation, in which I learn the french settlements of Hispaniola have just been reduced, by an insurrection of negroes, that threatens the most fatal consequences, obliges me to forward immediately to that island, a supply of musquets, cartridges, and powder, which the government appears to be in the most pressing want of—As those objects can be better and more speedily obtained, from the federal arsenal of West Point, I have to request as a signal service, that you will give immediate orders for sending to New York, and delivering to Mr [Antoine-René-Charles Mathurin] de la forest: 1000 Musquets complete. 1000 Cartridge boxes 50,000 Cartridges to suit the musquets, and about 20 thousand weight of musquet powder—Those objects may either be returned in nature or accounted for in a future settlement of accounts between our natives, as the President of the United States may choose to determine. I hope the extreme urgency of the case, and the interest I am convinced you take in the welfare of my nation, will induce you to gran⟨t⟩ my request, which I am going to lay immediately before the President of the United States" (DLC:GW).

2. Knox dispatched Capt. Constant Freeman on 21 Sept. with orders to the keeper of the public stores at West Point to deliver to Freeman 1,000 muskets and bayonets; 110,000 cartridges; 10 barrels of the best musket powder, as well as musket balls, cartridge paper, and thread to make up cartridges; 5,000 musket flints; 5,000 gun screws; 1,000 bayonet scabbards and belts; 1,000 brushes and priming wires; and 1,000 "of the best cartridge boxes and belts at the post, to be picked out of the whole number. and every other article to render the equipment perfect" (Knox to George Fleming, 21 Sept., DLC:GW).

3. GW replied to Knox from Mount Vernon on 24 Sept.: "I have recd your letter of the 22d Inst. enclosing a copy of one from the French Minister, and I do empower you to comply fully with the request of the Minister of France for certain supplies mentioned in his letter" (LB, DLC:GW).

From Henry Knox

Sir   War Department [Philadelphia] 22d September 1791.

I have the honor to submit a Copy of a Letter from General Wilkinson to General St Clair, containing the particulars of the expedition against L'Anguille[1]—The result being thirty prisoners—the destruction of the villages, and the consternation arising, from the demonstration of their being within our reach, must all tend to the great object the establishment of peace.

I have also the honor to enclose the copy of a private letter shewing the desire of General Wilkinson, to enter into the military service of the United States—and also the Letter of the Board in Kentucky.[2]

I have received a Letter from General Butler, dated on the 5th at Muskingum, in which he says, "that the water having risen three feet, will ensure them a passage to Fort Washington, by the 10th or 12⟨th⟩ at furthest, and that all the troops precede him." I have the honor to be Sir, With the highest Respect, Your most Obedt hume servant

H. Knox

LS, DLC:GW; LB, DLC:GW.

1. For the background to the expedition of Lt. Col. James Wilkinson, see Alexander Hamilton to GW, 16 Sept., source note. The enclosed copy of Wilkinson's report to Arthur St. Clair, dated "Frankfort on Kentucky," 24 Aug., is in DLC:GW. It was later presented to Congress (see GW to the U.S. Senate and House of Representatives, 27 Oct. [first letter]) and is printed in *ASP, Indian Affairs*, 1:133–35.

2. Wilkinson's letter of 26 Aug. to Henry Knox reads: "I flatter myself an acquaintance contracted in arms, at an early period of the American Revolution, and continued thro' the most trying vicisitudes of that revolution, will justify this intrusion and excuse me for trespassing a few minutes on your time. By the same hand which delivers this letter, I flatter myself you will receive from the military board of the district, a copy of my report to Governor St Clair, comprehending a detail of the operations of the late volunteer corps at the Ouiattanans; if the issue answers the expectations of government, and meets your approbation, I am content—By the next conveyance I will forward you an accurate draft of my route, as well as that of General Scott with critical remarks, on the soil, water, timber, and local advantages of the whole country which fell under my observation—should this information prove in the smallest degree useful to government, and satisfactory to yourself my objects will be accomplished. In the organization of the several volunteer corps to act against the savages of the Wabash from this district, no provision was made for field or regimental staff: But I must flatter myself when you reflect how

impossible it is, for a commanding officer in person, to support the load of duty arising from the necessary attention to a body of five hundred horsemen marching thro' an hostile, unexplored, swampy, close country, and who when in the best order practicable would cover more ground than 2000 infantry, that you will make a reasonable allowance to my aid de Camp, brigade major, and quarter master, all men of merit, whose services entitle them to consideration. During a residence of more than seven years in these woods, I have spared no pains, nor no expence to make myself acquainted, with the extensive regions watered by the Mississippi, and its tributary streams, from the Baliza to the lakes—I have personally explored much of this extensive tract, have acquired an exact knowledge of a great part and a general knowledge of the whole—It is my wish to be employed in some station in which I may be able to employ and apply my information, and my small abilities to the public advantage, and my own honor. In short, permit me to say, with a frankness becoming a soldier, that I feel a strong desire to enter once more upon the stage of military life, and that if you can favor me with some appointment, consistent with my former rank, I will not disappoint your expectations, or injure the service; but will ever cherish the warmest sense of gratitude for your attention" (DLC:GW). GW appointed Wilkinson lieutenant colonel in command of the 2d Infantry Regiment of the U.S. Army on 22 Oct. in place of John Doughty, who declined the commission (see Knox to GW, 31 Oct., GW to the U.S. Senate, 31 Oct. [first letter]), and the Senate confirmed the appointment on 7 Nov. (*Executive Journal,* 1:86–87, 88).

The enclosed copy of the letter of Charles Scott, Harry Innes, and John Brown to Knox, dated Danville, Kentucky District, 30 Aug., reads: "In our last letter of the 24th June, we had the honor to inform you that genl St Clair had Authorized the second detachment of mounted Volunteers to be embodied, in consequence of which the board proceeded to make the necessary arrangements for carrying the measure into effect, and appointed general Wilkinson to the command, who commenced his march on the 26th July to Fort Washington, where the detachment crossed the Ohio. It is with singular pleasure we inform you that this enterprize has also proved successful and for a detail of particulars we refer you to the enclosed reports of Genl Wilkinson to the Board and a copy of that he made to General St Clair. which we hope will prove satisfactory to Government. We also transmit to you the muster Rolls of the late detachment by Mr James Parker of Lexington, under an expectation that they will reach the war-Office before Mr [John] Belli the paymaster leaves Philadelphia, but if it should happen otherwise, we take the liberty of requesting that you would direct the payment of the amount of the expedition to be made to Mr Parker who has been so obliging as to undertake the transporting of the money and delivering it to the paymaster, should you not embrace this oppertunity, we fear another may not offer before the spring, which delay would prove to be very injurious to the Volunteers. General Wilkinson, anxious for the success of the enterprize, thought it advisable to employ a few pack-horses for the purpose of transporting Medecine, ammunition and tools, and for two of the guides who could not provide themselves with horses; the amount of this expenditure is inconsiderable when compared with the great object in contemplation, and the benefits, which we trust government will derive from the success of the enterprize: We refer you to the enclosed account on this subject, relying that you will be so fully convinced of the propriety of the measure as to direct a payment of it, Otherwise Genl Wilkinson who had no other motive than that of promoting his Country's Cause, will become answerable therefor; he having pledged himself to the individuals for payment in case government rejects the account" (DLC:GW).

From Hugh O'Connor

Please your Excellency,   Philadelphia Septr 22nd 1791

I hope youll Excuse the liberty I take in addressing you. I am a Native of Ireland and a Bror of mine Councellor John oConnor wrote to me last year a most flattering letter to come to America with my family. at the same time he Inclosed me a Contract he made with Coll Wm Deakeins Junr for 40000 Acres of his Lands Situate from 15 to 25 Miles from the head Navigation of the Patowmack River in Consequence of this Contract a friend of mine mr Charles oConnor and I: got upwards of thirty Gentlemen of Fortune some of which are the first Merchants in Dublin and the Cashier of the Bank of Waterford who all agreed for the purchase of the above tract of Lands provided they answered the Description set forth by mr Deakeins in his Contract, they Commissioned a mr Charles mcDermott and me to come out to regulate all preliminaries relative to this purchase. but my being obliged to waite to Dispose of my Lands in Ireland and having along family Consisting of a wife and seven Children wee could not be together. but on my Arrival here I was Informed that mr mcDermott Waited on mr Deakeins and his Answer was that he had no ground this Side of the Alleagany mountains. on which mr mcDermott went to Ireland before I arrived here without purchaseing any ground. however I have as much power as he had. if I could get a tract of land in any of the three States this Maryland or Virginia in a good Country Convenient to A Navigable River and Commercial Town I would purchase it and go to Ireland and leave my family here and I would bring out this Collony. I have been the principle Sufferer by mr Deakeins not abiding by his Contract, for my Voyage Cost me upwards of £200. and I was so provoked at the Disopointmt that I would return, but some friends of mine prevailed on me to

Waite some time and Endeavour to make out a Clear plantation for myself. but I am quite at a loss for any friend that would find me Such a tract as I want. but from your great and Humane Character I take this liberty of Informing you of my Situation and hope you will honor me with an Answer directed for me to mr Cary the printer here[1]—I am with great respect your Excellency's most obedt Humble Servant

> Hugh OConnor

ALS, DLC:GW.

Hugh O'Connor apparently belonged to the conservative Catholic mercantile family of O'Connor prominent in Dublin in the late eighteenth and early nineteenth centuries (L. M. Cullen, *Princes and Pirates: The Dublin Chamber of Commerce, 1783–1983* [Dublin, 1983], 56).

1. O'Connor was probably acquainted with the well-to-do Christopher and Mary Sherridan Carey of Dublin and their six children, one of whom, Mathew, immigrated to America in 1784 and became a printer in Philadelphia (see Carey to GW, 27 Oct. 1788, source note; Campbell, *Friendly Sons of St. Patrick and the Hibernian Society*, 368–70). Bartholomew Dandridge replied to O'Connor from Mount Vernon on 3 Oct.: "By desire of the President of the United States I have to inform you that your letter to him of the 22 ult. has been received—The President directs me also to let you know that with respect to the contract, which you say was made with Mr Deakins for land, it is his opinion that there must have been some considerable misunderstanding in the matter, as no land situated in the part of the country you mention, can be bought for any thing like the price of half a dollar per acre, which is the price the President understands you were to have the lands for—The President not having been concerned in buying or selling land for some considerable length of time, cannot give you any information, with certainty, where or at what price you can suit yourself in land, nor is it in his power (from the multiplicity of business to which he is obliged to attend) to make any enquiries of that kind in your behalf; but being willing to afford you every assistance he can he directs me to transmit to you the Virginia Gazette and Alexandria advertiser, wherein you will find advertised for sale by Messrs [Robert T.] Hooe and [Charles] Little of Alexandria, sundry parcels of land, among the rest *one* called the Catoctan tract, on the Patomac river, which he thinks would answer your purpose as it will be sold in a body, or divided into small tracts as may suit the Purchaser, and from what knowledge he has of that part of the country, he believes the land to be pretty good—The price of the land and title which can be made to it the President must leave to your further enquiries—he has reason however to believe that the price will be from two to three pounds per acre" (DLC:GW). For the ad to which GW referred, see *Virginia Gazette and Alexandria Advertiser*, 15 September.

From Ternant

sir   Philadelphia septr the 22d 1791

A most alarming insurrection of the negroes broke out on the 23d of last month in our Settlements of hispaniola: many devastations and massacres have already taken place, and more distressing ones are Still likely to follow, if the colony does not receive an immediate assistance[1]—a speedy supply of arms, ammunition and comestibles, being what it Stands most urgently in need of, and the means I can command at present, being unsufficient for the purchase of those objects, I found myself under the necessity of requesting the secretary of the threasury to put funds in my disposal to the amount of forty thousand dollars, to be accounted for in any future reimbursement of the United States to france[2]— I have al⟨so⟩ requested the secretary at war to let m⟨e⟩ have 1000 Stands, 50 thousand cartridg⟨es⟩ and 20 thousand weight of powder, ⟨to⟩ be either returned in nature, or account⟨ed⟩ for in the same manner with the funds advanced me from the feder⟨al⟩ threasury, as you may chose to determin⟨e⟩.[3]

I hope the extreme urgency of the case will excuse any irregular⟨ity⟩ in my applications, and that the President of the United States wi⟨ll⟩ not disapprove a measure which may rescue from imminent da⟨nger⟩, and perhaps from a total ruin, a⟨n⟩ important posession of their first and most attached ally.[4] I am with great respect sir your most obedient very humble servant

                                                                Ternant

as soon as I have been able to collect the details of this unfortunate event I shall have the honor of forwarding them to the President.[5] no arrival from france, and no news from the Packet.

Translation, DNA: RG 59, Notes from Foreign Missions in the United States; LB, Arch. Aff. Etr. The text of the French copy appears in CD-ROM:GW.

Jean-Baptiste, chevalier de Ternant, sent copies of his relevant correspondence with the administration to his superior, the comte de Montmorin, on 28 Sept.–2 Oct. and reported that he first addressed himself to the secretaries of war and treasury because the president and secretary of state were both in Virginia. Ternant wrote that Henry Knox and Alexander Hamilton responded in a most satisfactory manner, proceeding to meet his needs with zeal and eagerness: Knox immediately dispatched a courier with orders to transfer the necessary arms and munitions from West Point to New York, and Hamilton put at France's disposal the sum of $40,000. Ternant notified Montmorin that he also informed GW by letter of his proceedings with the department heads and that the president's response consisted of all he had hoped (see Turner, *Correspondence of the French Ministers,* 45–51, especially 48–49).

1. For the slave uprising that broke out on 22–23 Aug. in northern Saint Domingue, see Samuel Wall to GW, 16 Sept., n.1.

2. For the request of Ternant to the secretary of the treasury, see Alexander Hamilton to GW, 22 Sept., n.1.

3. For the request of Ternant to the secretary of war, see Henry Knox to GW, 22 Sept. (first letter), n.1.

4. GW replied to Ternant on 24 September.

5. Ternant sent details of the uprising to GW on 24 September.

Index